Philosophical Issues in Religious Thought

Geddes MacGregor

Originally Published by
Houghton Mifflin Company · Boston
Atlanta   Dallas   Geneva, Ill.   Hopewell, N.J.   Palo Alto

Copyright © 1979 by

University Press of America, Inc.™

4710 Auth Place, S.E., Washington D.C. 20023

ISBN: 0-8191-0677-1

Library of Congress Catalog Card Number: 78-65851

TO MY STUDENTS
graduate and undergraduate
who share with me the joy of looking critically at life

Books by Geddes MacGregor

So Help Me God
A Literary History of the Bible
The Sense of Absence
God Beyond Doubt
The Hemlock and the Cross
The Coming Reformation
Introduction to Religious Philosophy
The Bible in the Making
Corpus Christi
The Thundering Scot
The Vatican Revolution
The Tichborne Impostor
From a Christian Ghetto
Les Frontières de la morale et de la religion
Christian Doubt
Aesthetic Experience in Religion

PREFACE

This book is intended to have a dual function. It is designed for use as a university text in providing, principally in Part One ("Problems in the Philosophy of Religion") an account of the basic contemporary issues in religious thought presented with a view to stimulating reflection on and discussion about them. It also offers in Part Two ("God as Kenotic Being") an original proposal for what I consider a central question in the philosophy of religion.

The two functions should be mutually supportive. My hope is that the second function of the book, by giving the student a specific position that he can criticize and with which he can disagree (or perhaps even, in some cases, agree), will diminish the inevitable limitations of the first. The judicial character of the student's agreement or disagreement, apart from which his critique would be worthless, should be assured by his having conscientiously worked through the problems in Part One before he is expected to cope with Part Two.

In addition to the two functions mentioned, there are several ways in which the book may be used. Students with little previous knowledge of the subject ought to attend closely to the methodological considerations presented in the introductory material, "The Nature and Interpretation of Religion," before proceeding to the more exacting demands of Part One. Some students already well prepared by introductory courses may be able to go straight into Part One. Again, the use of the book will vary according to the time available. An average student might be expected to handle in one semester all the material in the Introduction and Part One. With that aim in view, one chapter a week could be covered with the work of each week divided between lecture or guidance by the instructor and discussion by the class. Given such limitations of time, the average student's responsibility might be confined to the Introduction and Part One, while more industrious or experienced students might tackle Part Two on their own. In some situations they might do so on an extra-credit basis. Where sufficient time is available to spread the work over the whole academic year, all three parts would be included as a normal goal for everyone.

Bibliographical suggestions are provided as much for the convenience of the instructor as for the information of the student. They consist of a general bibliography at the end of the Introduction, followed by fourteen special bibliographies, i.e., one for each chapter in Parts One and Two. A glance will show that these bibliographies go far beyond what even the most avid student could possibly cover in any course. They should be regarded as source lists for work on specific topics. When students develop a special interest in one of the topics considered, they will have at hand a convenient list of materials for further study, and their instructor may guide them according to his own interests and preferences. Some of the bibliographical items are annotated.

In a book on so difficult a subject as religious thought, technical terms cannot be entirely avoided without detriment to the quality of the student's enterprise. A glossary is provided, therefore, so that the student may conveniently look up any unfamiliar term or refresh his memory later about one whose meaning or function remains obscure. He will bear in mind that the usage of a particular author may deviate from the commonly accepted norm. The title of Part Two, for instance ("God as Kenotic Being"), will send many readers to the glossary for the meaning of the word *kenosis,* which will give at least a clue to what I have in mind as the central motif of Part Two.

The student who wishes to work entirely alone has been by no means forgotten. I hope very much that such students, often older persons whose interest in or opportunity for study has developed later in life, will find what they need in my treatment of the subject. They, no less than others, should bear in mind the admirable advice of that great French critic, Emile Faguet, who, in his *L'Art de lire,* wisely enjoins the reader to read slowly.

I wish to express my thanks to Professor F. J. Streng for checking the transliteration of some Sanskrit terms, to Dr. E. K. Dawson for leading me to the contemporary medical literature on autism, and to the editors at Houghton Mifflin who saw the book through the press. My grateful acknowledgement goes also to four secretaries who in turn transformed the labyrinth of my manuscript into copy for the press: Gayla Blasdell, Katia Argyropoulos, Olga Loos, and Sharon Priest. Above all, my thanks go to the innumerable students, graduate and undergraduate, who in various ways are continually showing me new guises in which old problems reappear.

Geddes MacGregor

CONTENTS

Existentialism and Process Thought / The Emergence of the
Existentialist Mood / Involvement, Commitment, and
Concern / Is Faith a Kind of Knowledge? / What Kind of
Cognition Could There Be in Faith? / "Believing in" and
"Believing that" / Knowing and Believing / The Role of
Doubt in Faith / Conditions of Faith / A Skeptical
Objection to the Faith-Existence Model

THE NATURE
AND INTERPRETATION
OF RELIGION

Religion has nothing more to fear than not being
sufficiently understood.
> *Stanislas Leszczynski, King of Poland (1677–*
> *1766), Maxims*

Religion is life, philosophy is thought.... We need both
thought and life, and we need that the two shall be
in harmony.
> *James Freeman Clarke (1810–1888), Ten Great*
> *Religions*

Before we ask where we should begin the philosophical study of religion,
we may well ask, why begin at all?

To ask that question is not necessarily to express lack of interest in the
subject. By asking it we may mean, rather, that religion is of two kinds,
one of which is unworthy of our examination and the other too good for
it. That is, we may be assuming that one kind of religion is too fine, too
personal, and too enduring to be subjected to intellectual scrutiny, while
the other is too spurious, too disgusting, or too moribund to deserve it.
We are all aware of the cheap, shameless racketeering that can and does
go on under cover of a religious label, but we are also aware that what
are by any reckoning the noblest acts and the most sincere engagements
among human beings have been undertaken under strong and definite
religious motivation.

Yet though the distinction between good and bad religion is indeed a
real one, the sheep and the goats are by no means so easily separated. No
religion is either entirely pure and holy or completely vile and rotten. As
there is some taint in even our noblest deeds, and some redeeming feature
in even the worst of them, so religion is never so wholly good or so totally
evil as would suit our tidy minds and passionate hearts. Not only was there
one Judas among the twelve disciples, but the Gospels, in telling us how
Peter denied his Master in the hour of trial, suggest there was a little Judas
even in him whom they depict as the most passionately loyal of all the

disciples. The truth is, of course, that there is at least a little Judas in us all. There is also some good in the worst of us. One reason for studying religion with the intellectual tools at our disposal is that such study can help us to sift the good from the bad. It may also enable us to find a basis for making intelligent judgments as to what to praise and what to condemn, for one of the advantages of the philosophical study of religion is that it helps us to be more discriminating. There are many other reasons for the fact that the philosophical examination of religion is not only rewarding but an indispensable part of the education of every mature person. These will become apparent as we go on. For the present we need ask no further reason than the one already given.

Some may feel, nevertheless, that while they can see the importance of philosophizing about contemporary religion, they can see little use in referring to its historical aspects. Many people today are untrained to appreciate what history can teach us about what is going on now. The reasons for including historical considerations in our approach will also manifest themselves as we proceed, but for the present, those who feel they need to justify troubling about historical background will do well to bear in mind that almost all reflections on religion that people untrained in such matters take to be contemporary, or novel, or even their own original discovery, have been well known and thrashed out in innumerable forms for centuries. Some, indeed, were current two or three thousand years ago in India or China or Greece. The inclusion of some historical knowledge in our philosophical study of religion spares us from imagining that we are the first people in the world to notice what we do notice. Of course, some of us may indeed have an occasional novel idea. In order to find out, however, whether we have or not, we had better first do some digging.

Method

Every novice in every field naturally starts with the questions he is in fact already asking. The questions of a beginner may not be entirely useless, but they are unlikely to be as useful as those he will ask a few years later when experience and reflection have taught him to formulate his questions with greater economy of intellectual energy. In philosophy, asking "good" questions is more important than getting "right" answers.

"Does God exist?" seemed to our great-grandfathers a simple enough question, demanding a plain yes or no. The difficulty lay rather, it seemed, in justifying one's answer, and an enormous amount of energy was therefore expended in trying to provide supporting demonstrations. To say the least, these demonstration-supported answers now seem much less satisfactory than they once did. The failure does not lie in the old answers, which exhibited great intellectual ingenuity and power, so much as in the question, the formulation of which is far too ingenuous. There are hidden ambiguities in it that the beginner does not readily see.

There may also be more fundamental questions that he has overlooked. Many questions that inexperienced inquirers ask are badly formulated because the inquirer "jumps the gun," as would an inexperienced hostess who asked, "How do you like your mushrooms?" instead of, "Do you like mushrooms?" A guest allergic to mushrooms might be compelled to reply that he liked them with as little existence as possible.

Yet one can imagine a case where there is an even more basic question. The guest may not know what mushrooms are, in which case "Do you like mushrooms?" can lead nowhere. Nor is it then even enough to ask, "Have you ever tasted mushrooms?" for the guest might truthfully reply, "Well, I did think I tasted them once, but somebody afterwards told me that what I had been eating was asparagus, so I am not sure." The hostess might then have to lead the guest into the kitchen and point to the mushrooms, saying, "*There* they are—do you feel like taking the risk?"

The greatest difficulty, however, does not lie so much with defects in the questions others put to me as with faults in the questions I put to myself. A teacher is not doing enough when he begins "where the student is." A good teacher, though he will take his student's situation into account, will also try to lead the student to formulate the questions more usefully than even the most thoughtful and perspicacious beginner could do unaided.

Special Difficulties   In our proposed field of inquiry, which involves asking intellectual questions about the affirmations of faith, the ordinary difficulties are aggravated by special circumstances. Most people lack either the logic and acumen to pose the questions or the religious insight and experience to know what the questions should be. Many lack both. Even the comparatively few individuals who both possess philosophical training and enjoy genuine religious insight are often unable to apply their critical faculties to the subject. Not only may an emotional block impede their invasion of the field; it may more subtly divert their attention from the best use of their own critical equipment, so that they end by playing intellectual games with themselves instead of making useful discoveries.

He who embarks upon a philosophical examination of religion must not only be equipped with the current tools of a philosopher; he must have the extreme openness of mind that is proper to the authentic philosopher of every age and that by no means all professional philosophers have attained. Yet no less must he be capable of appreciating the nature and the value of religious disclosures when they cross his path.

The medieval methodology of Thomas Aquinas, for instance, served its purpose well in the thirteenth century. It does not serve ours today. St. Thomas himself, great mind that he was, would not be a Thomist today. Modern thinkers who are interested in religion might well wish for a single methodology of one sort or another that would deal with religion philosophically without destroying its vitality. In the present philosophical climate, however, it is difficult to see what methodology would satisfy everyone concerned. It would seem that, as Henry Duméry has observed, the philosopher of religion, being "too religious for the unbeliever and not religious enough for the believer, has few friends." [1] Philosophers, however, are always lonely to the extent that they pursue their philosophical inquiries in fields that people generally prefer left untouched. A philosopher who studies art from a philosophical standpoint is likely to displease most people, for his readers are likely to be either (a) uninterested in art (whether they happen to be philosophers or not), in which case they will not be interested in his philosophizing about it, or else (b) interested in art, in which case, unless they happen also to be philosophers, they will want to contemplate art and to "do" art, and will resent those who try to analyze it intellectually. Philosophers of religion have a similar problem, aggravated by the fact that religion so affects every aspect of life that both those who hate it and those who love it above all else tend to suspect the genuineness of every attempt at a philosophical approach to it.

The greatest difficulty the authentic philosopher of religion must face (so great in fact that he is sometimes psychologically incapable of facing it) is the difficulty of grasping the profound nature of the overwhelming conviction of the believer and of truly doing justice to the immensity of the believer's truth-claim, while at the same time honestly inspecting that religious truth-claim, and all religious problems, on ground other than the one the believer stands on. In short, the philosopher of religion, far from being the over-timid skeptic and the emasculated believer of Duméry's epigram, ought to be in fact *at least* as religious as the believer and *at the same time* as incisively critical as the most hostile skeptic. Only such a philosopher of religion can hope to step beyond both the believer's profound and special insight and the unbelieving critic's penetrating yet sometimes barren thought. To put the matter another way, he must excel the skeptic in skepticism and outdo the believer in openness to belief.

Methodological Reflections Though the methodology to be adopted in the present work will not exclude, of course, the analytical procedures to which professional philosophers are accustomed today, it will be, especially in this Introduction, phenomenological rather than analytical. That is, without using the technical language of phenomenologists such as Husserl, we shall always seek to discover above all else what *is* the phenomenon in which the problems emerge that call for attention. To say there is no use our talking about something unless we know what we are talking about may seem too obvious to need stating; yet the reminder is not needless, for perhaps there is no other field in which so many clever people write with so much skill and so little understanding of that to which their skill is devoted. We need a method whose procedures and techniques will enable us, as far as possible,

[1] Henry Duméry, *Foi et institution,* in *La foi n'est pas un cri,* suivi de *Foi et institution* (Paris: Editions du Seuil, 1959), p. 394.

to see what we are examining as it really "gives itself" to us. This means stripping away everything that impedes such understanding. In order to understand a tradition other than my own, I must learn to set aside as far as possible my own presuppositions, and before I can undertake that enterprise I must first discover what they are. I say "as far as possible" because we must begin somewhere, so of course we shall always be starting with some presuppositions. To recognize this is not, however, to admit that we might as well start with one as with another. To say that one presupposition is as good as any other is to say that in an inquiry entitled "Who am I?" I might as well begin by supposing that I am Napoleon or Old Mother Hubbard.

Our choice of presuppositions ought to be governed by experience and learning. Experience is the best teacher, but before it can teach me I must interpret it. Not only must I interpret my own experience; even more obviously I must interpret the experience that others have claimed. What Moses claimed is in many ways strange to me, for his whole life-situation was very different from mine. To help me interpret what Moses believed was revealed or disclosed to him, I need first to understand as far as I can what his situation was, and that requires extensive learning.

But why should I bother with what Moses or Plato said? Why should I read Shankara or St. Paul? All these men died many centuries ago. Much has been learned since their time. Why not attend more carefully to what I actually experience instead of poring over what has been written by or about the prophets and sages of antiquity? Why take second-hand experiences when I can get my experience first hand? This question must be taken seriously, not least because the answer to it will exhibit the way in which my own experience grows and is enriched. I do not study Moses and Plato merely in order to clarify my mind about what they were saying; I read them so that my experience may be enriched by an understanding of theirs. My knowledge of history would be of little value if all it did was to tell me how people thought and lived in the past *in contrast to* how I think and live. Its value lies, rather, in the immense enrichment of my own experience, which experience, so enriched, enables me better to understand history, which better understanding of history once again enriches my personal experience, and so on. There is a two-way street: by listening carefully to others I do not diminish the force of my own experience; I augment it. My sensitivity is not weakened but refined.

A routine yet good piece of advice to travelers is to read about a place before *and* after visiting it. If we read between every visit, every visit will be a richer experience than the one before. Our appropriation of what is there to be discovered grows when our observation and our learning are nicely polarized. Historical learning can never supplant personal experience; but it can develop an experience that would otherwise be minimal, not to say moribund. And the more sensitive a person is when he is still ignorant, the richer his experience and the more intense his delight after he becomes informed. Even a person with little musical sense will profit from learning something about music, but he will not profit so much as one who, knowing nothing about it, is entranced by it from the first. The application of all this to our subject must be too obvious to need specification.

The enrichment of our experience would seem to give rise to the need for a more careful and therefore special language to express it. There is a temptation to invent new jargon. The temptation is short-lived, however, in all but the most dreary among us, for we soon discover that technical jargon stultifies rather than promotes our development and tends to obscure rather than to clarify our communication of it to others. Nevertheless, an occasional neologism may be very helpful (every term was a neologism at one time or another), and the use of traditional as well as contemporary language is necessary to express what has to be expressed. Indeed, he who hopes to express and communicate religious ideas, not least the extremely subtle and complex ideas of Christian thought, must learn to use several languages at the same time. By this I do not mean, of course, that he is to use them indiscriminately so as to produce a Babel of religious confusion. I am saying, rather, that he must hold them together in balance and use them as a clever juggler handles the instruments of his prowess.

Care in the use of language is much emphasized by contemporary thinkers, and rightly so, for sloppy, ambiguous language not only obscures communication with others; it hurts our own appropriation of the disclosure that would be otherwise available. Yet I think it is possible to exaggerate the mischief that linguistic ambiguities can cause. Great as it is, it is much less than the havoc wrought by our violent prejudices and destructive monomanias. When people are wholly obsessed by extreme political prejudices, for example, not even the most judicious choice of language can stop the rot in their minds.

Yet when that is said, we must also note that in the interpretation of religious experience we learn sooner or later that certain symbols are not only more apposite than others for what we want to do; they are also more economical. That is to say, they are the best kind of shorthand for our purpose. Whether one system of shorthand must always remain the best is not beyond question; nevertheless, we should be very reluctant to discard traditional symbols till we have found others that do at least all that has been done by the older forms. Some of the biblical symbols are now difficult for most people to grasp, and for purposes of communication no doubt we need to find alternatives to the shepherd/sheep sort of figure that came naturally to an agricultural community and is odd or unintelligible to a highly industrialized one. We should be cautious, however, about throwing such traditional imagery away, for it is usually part of a wider spectrum, a larger system of imagery, the parts of which are interdependent. In the history of Christian thought, the Trinity, for example, is formulated in a way that requires for its understanding a great deal of highly specialized learning that most people cannot hope to acquire. An alternative may be helpful for this or that expository purpose, but to throw out the language of the ancient Councils of the Church because it is antique and inseparable from an older mode of conceptualization would be to deprive the most sensitive and eager among future students of a means of enriching their experience. For an understanding of religion we must set against the melody of contemporary thought the counterpoint of ancient theological symbols.

Scholarship in religious studies is nowadays highly specialized, so that even among theological scholars few can do more than try to keep abreast of their own special field. The detachment of many professional philosophers from the humanist tradition in which philosophers have played a central role has meant that comparatively few of them have the training to understand the demands and the importance of the methodologies of the distinct disciplines—linguistic, literary, historical, and scientific—that lie behind and minister to scholarly work in religious studies today. He who can bring some humanistic scholarship to his study of our field is at an immense advantage in approaching it.

Why Not a Common Denominator? The objection to talking of "religion" rather than of "religions" has weight, for it calls attention to one of the most deep-seated built-in obstacles to even the most rudimentary understanding of the nature of religion. I shall have more to say about this later. For the present I wish to consider a methodological question that the objection raises.

Paul Weiss, an American philosopher of Jewish background and an outstanding metaphysician of our time, has a perspicacious observation on what I have in mind:

> He who isolates a least common denominator, the common truth of all, is bound to find that others see him as only one among many, holding a particular doctrine which itself must yield some truth common to itself and all others. Also, a common element is rather jejune. A thin schema, it leaves out the juice of living religion and, in fact, rejects this as irrelevant or perverse. Its very stress on some common truth to be found in all, involves a dismissal of the distinctive affirmations of each. Actual religions are given up, then, for a philosophic category, an idle universal. To be sure, there is a nucleal core to be found in all religions. But this is no category or universal. It is a particular religion purged of its bias and thus, though concrete and vital, purer than that religion or the religion's competitors. To get to it one must return to the ultra-natural and to religious experience, and use them to guide a recovery of the essence of the dedicated community and a life of faith.[2]

Belonging to a religion, like belonging to a tribe, does seem to be such an immediate experience, conferring such an intimate sense of "belongingness" that no one "outside" could possibly understand what being "inside"

[2] Paul Weiss, *The God We Seek* (Carbondale, Ill.: Southern Illinois University Press, 1964), p. 150.

means. Though I am not a Jew, I might conceivably become a rabbinic scholar so erudite that even the greatest Hebraist in Jewry would revere my learning; yet how could I, for all that learning, ever hope to know what it means to feel Jewishness as a Jew feels it? Does not religious observance put one immediately into the life stream of a religion in a way that no intellectual exercise can ever do? Does not the Muslim who observes the fast of Ramadan and the other observances of Islam know more of what being Muslim means than could any non-Muslim Arabist?

Because religion is from one standpoint a question of life and blood rather than intellect and logic, the answer to all these questions is, from that standpoint, an unqualified yes. You who are outside "our" religion can no more understand it than you who are outside "our" family can presume to understand "us."

What has been called in Jesuit piety "having the Mind of the Church" is really "having the Heart of the Church," and indeed Ignatius Loyola spoke of *sentir con la iglesia;* that is, "to feel with the Church." Only individuals can have intellects. A society may be said to have a heart; it cannot so well be said to have a mind. It has a common feeling, a common goal, a common purpose, and a corporate life. This community of spirit and purpose would seem to be appropriately expressed in a common ritual rather than in an accepted theological formula or agreed system of metaphysics.

Anglicans have long noticed that their manner of understanding their common bond has been different from those *traditionally* handed down, at least since the sixteenth century, by Rome on the one hand and by Geneva on the other. These other traditions have stressed doctrinal agreement, insisting that ritual forms are mere expressions of the Church's teaching and are subject to variation, as is attested by the diversity of rites within those Eastern Churches that own their submission to the Pope. What binds Anglicans together, as many Anglican divines have shown, is, on the contrary, a common liturgical standard enshrined in the Book of Common Prayer, together with a common notion of the ordering of the Church's ministry, which, reflecting the historic creeds and formularies, provide a locus of theological dialectic.[3] In this respect the Anglican tradition resembles that of Eastern Orthodoxy and is alien to the greater doctrinal formalism that fits the legalistic genius of Rome.

Should Christians Avoid Focusing on Christianity?   Textbooks on the history of religions generally distinguish what are commonly called the "major" religions of the world or, more popularly, "world" religions. Among these are listed Hinduism, Buddhism, Christianity, Judaism, and Islam. They are so classified not only because of the number of their adherents but also

[3] See *Doctrine in the Church of England* (Report of Commission on Christian Doctrine appointed by the Archbishops of Canterbury and York in 1922) (London: S.P.C.K., 1938), pp. 27–39. Cf. my own *Corpus Christi* (London: Macmillan & Co., 1959), pp. 10–13.

and more importantly because of their influence in the history of mankind. Then is not a focus on Christianity insular and narrow-minded?

The question has an additional thrust because some writers take the view that Christianity is not intended to be a religion at all, but a means of liberation from all religion. In any case, however, even if Christianity is to be accounted one of the religions of the world, people will differ in their estimate of its place among them. Some will rate its importance very high; others will put it lower. Among Christians themselves are many views of the relation of Christianity to other religions. Some acclaim it the only true religion; others account it only the best of all religions; still others account it, rather, the means for abolishing religion in any sense that anthropologists and sociologists could recognize. There are even persons who claim to be Christian yet think Christianity possesses no more than a portion of the truth that is in all religions. In face of such a conflict of views, should not we avoid as detrimental to our study the temptation to use Christianity as our fulcrum and the pivot of our discussions?

The answer is simple. Christianity is so extraordinarily variegated and rich that, *even apart from all truth-claims,* it serves as the best focus for what we are to do. Whether it is to be accounted merely one of many religions, or the best among all, or the only true religion, or the best means of liberation from all religion, it provides the best vantage point for us, because in it is to be found, in microcosm, all the religious ideas we need for a philosophical study of all religion.

Whatever view one takes of the relation in which religions stand one to the other and however we approach the question of possible methodologies for comparing different modes of symbolizing deity and other conceptualizations in the various "world religions," the position of Christianity is peculiar, not least because all the tendencies and divergencies we see in the history of religions (cosmic and acosmic pantheism, theism, deism, panentheism, and so forth), as also the tendencies toward and against so-called otherworldliness and the urge to "de-religionize" from time to time, all appear within Christianity itself. That is what Adolf von Harnack saw clearly when he made a now celebrated utterance at a rectorial address in Berlin in 1907. In obvious allusion to a remark by Max Müller,[4] "He who knows one religion knows no religion" (*Wer eine Religion kennt, kennt keine*), Harnack observed, "He who knows *this* religion [Christianity] knows all religion" (*Wer diese Religion kennt, kennt alle*).

Harnack's observation, which inexperienced inquirers in the field might take as mere parochialism, was in fact very profound: Christianity is indeed a microcosm of all religion. This fact has no bearing, of course, on the

[4] Max Müller (1823–1900) was a renowned Anglo-German orientalist and philologist. His approach to the comparative study of religion accorded with that of the influential History of Religion School (*Religionsgeschichtlicheschule*), which flourished in between 1880 and 1920 and engaged in such enterprises as the discovery of Egyptian, Babylonian, and other parallels to Jewish and Christian ideas.

truth or falsity of the claims of either Christianity or any other religion. Nor does it have any bearing on any of the numerous stances that might be taken up about religions in general. Such is this richness of Christianity that it is difficult for historians to find anywhere any important variety of religious feeling or thought that is not already contained somewhere within the history of the Christian Church. To say this is not to denigrate the importance of studying other religions ("What should they know of England who only England know?"),[5] but it is to assert that in the Christian heritage and consciousness there is all a philosopher needs for his investigation of religion.

By this I do not mean that there are no distinctive ideas in other religions. That would be an absurd claim. Probably nothing corresponds *precisely* to what yoga-aspirants in India call *ahiṁsā* and which the Occident, taught by Albert Schweitzer, roundly translates as "reverence for life." No doubt we westerners too glibly explain the *bodhi* or enlightenment that is said to have come to Gautama after his serene meditation under the Bo-tree, for our western modes of thought are so different that injury to the original intention is inevitable. We tend to identify the Evil One who tempted Gautama with the Satan of Jewish and Christian lore when a strict translation of such archetypal ideas from one culture to another is impossible. I am far from intending, then, that all ideas that occur in the history of religions are to be found in Christianity any more than all categories of books in the Dewey decimal system are to be found in the Library of Congress Catalog; such an analogy would not hold at all. What I am saying is, rather, that the most important classic problems in the philosophy of religion and the great religious controversies that are of philosophical interest in the history of religions may be adequately studied in the form in which they appear in Christianity.

For instance, "God" and "Nature" are both ambiguous terms; nevertheless, the problem of the relation of God and Nature, as presented in the history of Christian thought, and the controversies surrounding it, furnish us with what we need for a philosophical study of a problem that occurs in almost all religious traditions. Is God Nature? Or is God a product of Nature? Is God coeternal with Nature, acting upon it as does the divine artist in Plato's *Timaeus?* Is Nature a part of God, providing God with an internal "given" not of his own making? Or is Nature the creation of God as are, according to some, Space and Time?

Again, the endless disputes about grace and freedom for which Christianity is notorious might provide as useful a starting point as any for the examination of a philosophical problem that appears in many religions and under many guises. It is a problem that involves the general question of determinism and indeterminism; yet it is not simply that problem as it

[5] Rudyard Kipling, *The English Flag.*

appears in the history of philosophy, for there is a special dimension in it (including, for instance, the presumptive action of divine Being) that does not and should not enter into the discussions that engage the attention of philosophers when religious assertions or hypotheses are not being entertained.

The bitter controversies that have characterized the history of Christian thought are not precisely the same as those that have affected the development of other religions; nor is it our concern whether they are or not. What matters to us is that the controversies do encompass the central problems that a philosopher of religion needs to face. He could examine them in Hinduism or Buddhism, too; but generally speaking, he need not do so. The point is, in short, similar to the point that may be made in answer to a question some students ask about the history of philosophy itself: why study the Greeks and Kant? Why not the Vedas and Confucius? The answer that they are our intellectual progenitors is apposite but inadequate. The further reason is that they also give us a heritage of controversies that are central and important enough. for our needs, for our enterprise in the philosophy of religion Christianity is in a similar case. Of course, we may occasionally find that the concepts and ideas of other religions conveniently serve our purpose. We shall even find that for understanding the range of the phenomena of mystical experience and other special purposes, we shall have to take into our discussion the concepts of many religions. In general, however, the phenomena of the Christian heritage will provide almost all the pabulum we need. The student, therefore, need have no misgivings about the preponderance of Christian references in our treatment.

What Is Religion?

The term "religion" is not only ambiguous; it shelters several different kinds of ambiguity that must be cleared up before a definition may be proposed.

In the first place, since the term "religion" has been generally connected with the Latin verb *religare,* "to bind," Reinach's contemptuous definition ("an assembly of scruples impeding the free exercise of our faculties") would seem to have at least some etymological support. Moreover, people who are generally accounted religious do find themselves bound by various precepts, rules, and obligations imposed upon them by the laws or observances of the religion to which they adhere. Religion seems to foster a tendency to loyalism. Yet the adherents of Buddhism and other religions all claim, in one way or another, some sort of release, some kind of liberation, which seems to contradict that known characteristic of every religion to impose binding duties and required observances on its adherents. Jesus promised his followers that they should know the truth and that the truth should make them free. How can a religion be a constricting force and a liberating power at the same time?

In the second place, religion, as a social dynamic, is notoriously conservative. For many centuries the religion of the Indus Valley, which we call Hinduism, provided sanctions that preserved the great caste system in India. Buddhism, originally an offshoot from Hinduism, was in part intended to provide a way of liberation from the morally debilitating effects of a rigid system of social caste. Christianity has been charged, not without reason, with having at various points blocked social development and change. To Christianity has also been attributed, and no less plausibly, the provocation of the most important social revolts in the western world—for example, the abolition of slavery in the United States over a hundred years ago and, in our own time, the civil rights movement. How can religion be the reactionary enemy of social change, so antagonizing political revolutionaries, and be at the same time the provocative agent of social change, so distressing political conservatives?

In the third place, religion seems to be internally subject not only to development and change but to maturation and death. On the one hand, what was accounted religion yesterday is condemned as superstition today, suggesting that the religion of today may be the superstition of tomorrow. On the other hand, religions have a history. They seem to go through stages of development and decay. After a period of spring freshness, originality, authenticity, and power, a religion may blossom, then wane, and finally petrify. Then an archaeologist comes along, disinters the fossil, and places it in a glass case in a history-of-religions museum. Nevertheless, in looking at religion after it has lost its pristine vitality, we may well wish to temper our distaste with our admiration for what it once was—a living force that moved the hearts, vivified the minds, and commanded the wills of men and women no less vigorous, intelligent, or full-blooded than we. Conventional religion, however irritating, is not wholly despicable unless we allow ourselves to forget that it is, as Bergson observed, "a derivative perversion of a once-living reality."

In the fourth place, religion sometimes appears in the guise of a highly intellectualistic enterprise, involving not only metaphysical presuppositions, hidden or affirmed, but a whole array of dogmatic utterances that raise complicated questions calling for a great deal of logical map-work. In this guise religion appears as a cold betrayal of the warm, deeply human thing that religious people privately experience. The Upanishads, for instance, constitute a classic document of Hinduism, and in terms of their age they were as much intellectual as emotional in content and style. Bhakti, on the other hand, is a type of Hindu piety that is unashamedly ablaze with personal warmth and emotion. In Latin Catholicism there is a similar range of interest and attitude that extends from the closely argued responses in the *Summa* of Thomas Aquinas to the affective language used in devotions to the Sacred Heart. Among the heirs of the Reformation we find expressions that range from the dreary tomes of old Dutch divinity to the cheerful bugle notes and clanging cymbals of the Salvation Army.

Religion is by any reckoning an odd phenomenon. The more we examine it, the more contrary, if not contradictory, its attributes seem to be. Now we hear the complaint that it is too detached and intellectual, now that it is too emotional and subjective. It is at once the chief bar to social change and the principal cause of social revolt. Under the banner of religion the loftiest moral struggles have been conducted along with the perpetration of the cheapest sorts of vice. In some societies religion is conspicuously associated with prostitution. It has been called an opiate for the people, a device of crafty priests to subjugate people to their power, and a haven for neurotics. It has been likened to "a giant gymnasium where we develop our spirituality by our own exercise." [6] Institutional religion provides, indeed, a sort of gymnasium whose equipment is used by some while others spectate, but it also functions as a school, a hospital, and much else besides. We know how to define a gymnasium, a school, and a hospital, but how shall we define a social institution that is appositely called all these things and much else, and that comprehends as well a vast range of noninstitutional, even anti-institutional elements?

Religion or Religions To clear the ground for the definition of religion we ought to notice at this point the common objection that since religion is an abstraction that cannot be empirically inspected we ought to turn instead to what *can* be empirically examined, namely, religions. For we can go into a Jewish synagogue or a Hindu temple or a Muslim mosque and watch the behavior of the worshippers; we can study the classical documents of Buddhism and Christianity, applying to them the tools of literary criticism, and studying the history of the religions for which they are normative. Although in such ways we could learn much about the religions of the world as social and historical phenomena, we should nevertheless be as far as ever from understanding the nature of the interior forces that brought these phenomena into being and continue to sustain them.

That religion cannot be understood simply by the methods of observation is an important point for the kind of work we are to be doing. If it could be reduced to what can be so observed, it would be reducible to what sociologists and psychologists by their special methods can exhaust. That it might be so reducible is, of course, a possible stance, but it is by no means one that any philosopher of religion can take without further ado. For a vast body of literature persistently attests that the essential character of religion, whatever it may be, is not observable as are flora and fauna. Even art and architecture, even political institutions, cannot be fully understood without reference to the motivations behind them, which are not observable as are buildings and dramatic performances. You cannot understand America by looking at monuments like the Capitol, attending sessions of Congress, or scrutinizing the Declaration of Independence or the Constitution; for behind the whole complex system of government, institutions, culture

[6] Sterling W. Sill, *Leadership* (Salt Lake City: Bookcraft, 1958).

and life, lies a vast array of ideas that are not directly observable. So it is with religion. Religion entails not simply modes of behavior but ideas and interpretations of life.

The Unreflective Element in Religion The notion that there is also an important and irreducible *un*reflective element in religion is one that should be taken seriously, not least in an age in which, Marshall McLuhan has reminded us, tribalism is again coming into its own. It is coming in on an unprecedented scale made possible by television and other mass media that are binding together into tribal unity not, as in primitive societies, a group of two hundred or two thousand people but a group of two hundred million people and eventually a world state of our worst nightmares. Such a gargantuan tribe is likely to be as unreflective about religion as it is about all else. Bound by a spirit or ethos, it is increasingly uninterested in rational reflection. When televised communication is absorbed to the point of extinguishing the literary heritage without which genuinely critical analysis and rational reflection are atrophied in all but an intellectual elite, a ritual dance inevitably seems a more fundamental and appropriate expression of the tribal religion than does any theological essay or philosophical critique. Denigrating the gods of the Enlightenment and beating the drums in praise of the tribal deities of blood and fertility (which are appropriately honored by the heart, not the intellect) become fashionable developments once again.

The danger of political demagoguery and fascism that all reflective people see frighteningly near in such developments brings to mind, of course, the classic twentieth-century example of Hitler's Germany, in which, on an already colossal scale, a new tribal religion was developed with all the characteristic trappings of a religion: processions, fanfares, banners, sacred anthems, worship of the national *Geist,* and other ritual acts, observances, and paraphernalia. I have in my possession a photograph of Hitler I took while a student at Heidelberg in 1938. It is slightly fuzzy because I could not keep my camera from moving with the immense crowd, which was swaying in ecstasy at the sight of him whom they acclaimed as virtually their deified saviour. The crowd was heaving like a vast wind-troubled sea, as thousands upon thousands of the worshippers raised their right hands in the ritual gesture of salutation borrowed from ancient imperial Rome. Cries of *Sieg Heil,* like so many shots from a vast human cannon, filled the air with savage roars of primitive devotion to the *Führer.* The very earth seemed to tremble beneath us as soldiers marched to the haunting beat of the *Horst Wessel* anthem. Blood and soil! These were the stuff of which the religion was made.

For that, too, is religion. Nevertheless, Naziism lacked one of the ingredients that make a religion honest and morally desirable: there was no openly admitted self-critical element in it at all. That self-critical element, bringing truth-claims under intellectually honest scrutiny, is, however, completely indispensable to any religion that is to be acceptable to a morally alert and intellectually honest human being.

Irreducibility Religion is not necessarily either good or bad, moral or immoral, reflective or unreflective. Religion, whatever it is, cannot be reduced to any single element. Rudolf Otto's attempt in *Das Heilige* to reduce the religious mode of experience to what he called the numinous element (the sense of the holy or the eerie, an unanalyzable *mysterium tremendum*) was ingenious; but all such reductionism is bound to fail because religion, like life itself, not only has many facets but cannot be reduced to any of them, or to any single element at all. By its very nature it spreads itself out in innumerable ways and holds itself in innumerable tensions. Polarity and tension are, indeed, essential to its nature. This fact about the nature of religion is reflected in the attempts of various religious thinkers to call attention to its paradoxes. Zen teachers, for instance, urge their students to meditate on logical absurdities, such as the sound of one hand clapping, by way of trying to lead their disciples into a dimension of existence and thought that transcends the commonplace dimension in which most people spend most of their lives. Kierkegaard speaks frequently, in a notoriously tantalizing phrase, of a "leap of faith." Martin Buber, in *The Eclipse of God,* distinguishes between the philosopher who makes assertions about God and the religious man who enters into relation with God. Yet entering into a personal relation with the *kind* of deity that Judaism and Christianity proclaim *entails* reflection, to say nothing of what is entailed by entering into relationship with the less transcendental deities that are objectified in some other religions.

Buber, in insisting that the specifically religious attitude consists in what he calls an I–Thou relationship, provides a salutary antidote for those who tend to think that, on the contrary, the essence of religion is something else, such as contemplation or togetherness. Nevertheless, he does not fully exhaust the nature of religion. Perhaps an even more attractive attempt at putting the essence of religion into a capsule definition is Whitehead's celebrated epigram "Religion is what the individual does with his solitariness." Such a definition plainly excludes, however, everything that people do corporately, for example, in Christian-motivated enterprises for social reform, and in the liturgy of the Church. It *might be* that what the individual does with his solitariness is the essence of religion, while the corporate endeavors are derivative; but in a working definition we should not determine such questions in advance. We must avoid excluding any manifestation, whether it may eventually turn out to be at the core of religion or at its periphery. Nor must we make judgments in advance either lauding religion as always indisputably good or denigrating it as always unequivocally bad. We have already seen indications that religions may be very bad and even if we are not already favorably disposed to any religion, we have no reason to deny that they may be indeed good.

When we come to examine religion comprehensively, in its institutional, mystical, ascetic, doctrinal, relational, contemplative, cognitive, and conative modes, and in every other mode we can discover, and when we look at its practical manifestations as conventionally classified (e.g., Islam, Vedanta, Taoism, Reform Judaism, Unitarianism, Greek Orthodoxy, and Quakerism), the more observant and reflective we are, the more we shall be tempted to despair of finding any common element that might furnish the basis for a definition. While some religions stress the uniqueness of the individual, others seem to belittle it; while some are life-affirming, others seem to be life-denying; while most talk in one way or another of a deity, some, though appearing to have the cultic and attitudinal characteristics of a religion, lack and may even specifically repudiate the concept of God. Even within the same religion are to be found many widely differing traditions, and within each of these many different attitudes and interpretations. Indeed, even the same individual, the same *homo religiosus,* houses many widely differing religious moods and expresses them under many guises. Some students of religion, noticing how peculiarly personal and special are the most lively and influential of religious discernments and disclosures, have preferred to deny altogether the possibility of defining religion.

Are There Distinctive Religious Attitudes?   The jejune reduction of religion to, say, inhibited sex or neurotic aggression makes some chary of defining religion at all. Religion has pathological, psychological, sexual, sociological, institutional, corporate, individual, ethical, rational, cognitive, conative, emotional, and many other aspects. To reduce it to any of its aspects is to abandon the task of defining its fundamental nature. The vast multiplicity of its aspects is, indeed, a common occasion for despair at definition. How shall we include all aspects of religion yet specify a characteristic that will distinguish religion from everything else? Are there, in short, attitudes that distinguish religious phenomena from, say, moral or aesthetic or political or commercial phenomena?

We need not expect to find religious attitudes always conspicuously present in all aspects of religion. What characterizes commerce and trade is plainly a profit-making motive; yet that motive is not observable at every single turn of trade. A business corporation and a large charitable or educational trust both have a great complex of activities, including perhaps the use of computers for fact-finding and for bookkeeping, so that a casual observer might take them to be the same sort of organization. The business corporation, however, is in business to make money, while the charitable trust is in business to give it away. Business corporations do not always succeed in making money, and charitable trusts sometimes fail to give away as much money as is required of them. Nevertheless, the distinguishing characteristic of the business enterprise, the characteristic that sets it apart from charitable trusts and all other organizations, is that it owes its existence to a profit-making motive. This profit-making motive is not present throughout the organization in exactly the same degree. Among salaried file clerks, for instance, it is likely to be minimal; salesmen, on the other hand, will be very conscious of it, while among the owners or promoters of the business it is likely to be a consuming passion. Are there, then, some counterpart motives or attitudes which, though not equally distributed throughout all religious acts and institutions, distinguish religion from all else?

Though there are educational and healing aspects to religion, religion is neither simply a school nor simply a hospital. Even the intuitional or mystical element, which has often been accounted the essence of religion in its maturity, is not a defining characteristic of it and is indeed, on the contrary, a frequent source of misunderstanding of the nature of the religious attitude. Baron von Hügel tells us the Jesuit Père Léonce de Grandmaison had gently chided him for seeming to assume that the mystical sense was universal or at least a common endowment of mankind.[7] Not only is the mystical a highly special aspect of religion; it may well be the one that above all others spawns the cheap imitations that engender suspicion of all religious attitudes and activities.

While we must reject all such possible candidates for what we seek, finding them, in Aristotelian language, properties rather than essences (like the bookkeeping in our business analogue), we fare better when we consider that religion seems to be nothing apart from its valuational attitude. Even if my value-judgments are to be accounted distorted or false, there is a religious quality in them. So a man may be said "to make a religion of golf" or "to be religiously careful about his dress." To subscribe to the dictum that "cleanliness is next to godliness" is to take a religious attitude toward physical hygiene, placing it very high in the hierarchy of one's values. So when St. Paul deplores those "whose god is their belly," [8] he is not merely reproaching them for a weakness for good food, which would be venial in even the holiest of men. He is saying that they have a false religion: they have enthroned the enjoyment of eating as if it were the highest good in the universe. Whatever a man really esteems above all else, and therefore reverences and may be said to worship, may properly be called his god, for it is the supreme focus of his valuation. To call attention to the danger of idolatry is to make a fundamental value-judgment: the good is the enemy of the best, so that those who claim x as the central focus of value must beware how they treat other foci of value in their hierarchy (even important ones such as peace or courage or enterprise) lest these supplant the x that is central. We are saying something like this when we say that a person

---

[7] Friedrich von Hügel, *The Mystical Element in Religion*, 2nd ed. (London: J. M. Dent & Sons, 1927), vol. 1, pp. xi f.
[8] Philippians 3:19.

"has the wrong values" or that he "has his values all mixed up." We mean that he is not putting his various foci of value in the perspective that we account correct; he does not know the "right" scale of importance. To say this is really to challenge his religious outlook. A person who is ready to die for his collection of Meissen china is not irreligious; he seems, however, to have a false religion. To say, as we did, that Hitlerian religion is "bad" is to say it is idolatrous.

At the same time we must note that in religion there is always more than a contemplative attitude in a calculus of values. The religious person can never be content to acknowledge and admire the central focus of his valuing, which he generally calls God. He wishes also in some way to appropriate it or to attain it. His preoccupation with this subjective desire for salvation from a personal loss of the valued central focus may be so strong as to diminish his concern for the reality of the focus itself. In such a case he may be said to have fallen into a kind of idolatry—perhaps the worst kind, a religious self-love. Calvin's well-known emphasis on acknowledging the sovereignty and majesty of God was designed as a safeguard against that, which he accounted the most fatal departure from "true worship." As William Temple once wittily remarked, "A false mental image of God may be more idolatrous than a false metal image."

It would seem, then, that any satisfactory definition of religion would have to take into account the notion that religion, while always entailing some degree of personal commitment to a more or less explicitly delineated system of valuation, is fundamentally an acknowledgment of the hierarchy of values that the system sets forth. Moreover, among the elements religion contains, the intellectual one can be alienated from it only at the price of removing intellectual assurance of the rightness of the value system, making any acknowledgment of it intellectually dishonest and therefore worthless, and of destroying the sincerity apart from which no profession of personal commitment has any force. A self-critical element is indispensable to protect religion from degeneration into mumbo jumbo and, worse, into a depraved self-deceit that can function as a very good instrument for every sort of moral turpitude.

An obvious objection is that simple people do not seem to exhibit any intellectual element in their religious outlook. Unlike the religion of educated and thoughtful people, theirs seems to be exclusively intuitive, not to say emotive. To argue thus, however, is to misunderstand the functioning of the primitive mind, which is capable of very genuine thought and therefore of self-criticism, though it cannot express itself in a way philosophers would commend. Scholars have often distinguished between "higher" and "lower" religions, asserting that the former are self-critical and the latter are not. No religion, however, could be at the same time honest yet entirely non-self-critical, for otherwise it would not be intelligible to its own adherents. There are gradations in the exercise of self-criticism, and many of us tend to underestimate the extent to which even the crudest forms of religion, whether within Christianity or elsewhere, have a self-critical element in them. If they entirely lacked it there would be no religious controversies, and every historian of religions knows that these are inseparable from the history of religions at almost every level.

Some Objections to Defining Religion The more you know of the history of religions and especially of the contemporary debate about its interpretation, the more diffidently will you embark upon the task of proposing a definition of religion. According to some contemporary theologians, of whom Thomas Altizer is a fairly representative American example, the uniqueness of Christianity consists in its *not* being a religion. What has more than anything obscured understanding of its nature is, in this view, the persistent tendency to treat it as a religion, whether as one religion among many or as the best of all religions.

Again, the question "What is *a* religion?" is similar in scope and difficulty to philosophical questions such as "What is a thing?" and "What is a fact?" For what we label a religion is a mixture of historical events, codifications of law, traditional ideas, metaphysical presuppositions, sociological structures, and much else. For instance, though the phenomena we call Hinduism are very ancient, the word "Hinduism" dates only from 1834. The people whom we call Hindus do not use the term "Hinduism" at all unless they are consciously engaged in dialogue with Christians or other persons alien to their tradition. They do talk a great deal about "philosophy" and "philosophies," terms they use for the metaphysical systems that are the intellectual expression of the numerous facets some scholars have called, quite simply, the traditional way of life of the Indus Valley. Christian usage at first never referred to Christianity as a religion but as "the Way." The fact, however, that I never refer to my liver does not affect my having one. There are certain ranges of phenomena that cannot by any reductionism be classed as *simply* economic or utilitarian or social or moral or even mystical, and these ranges of phenomena are conveniently designated religious.

A Tentative Definition The ground is now sufficiently clear to permit us to consider a tentative definition of religion. We may need to exclude the possibility of a definition that would include every kind of religion. A definition that would apply to Hitler's religion as well as to Hosea's, to St. Benedict's as well as to Aimée Semple McPherson's may be impossible. Perhaps no definition could cover all religion, good or bad, lively or dead.

Nevertheless, all religion does seem to entail a system of value-judgments and some sort of interpretation of life in terms of that system, which usually has a focal point, such as is designated in monotheistic religions by the term "God." The commitment it presupposes excludes its being reducible to ethical convention or aesthetic contemplation.

With this in mind let us consider the following:

Religion is characterized by
(1) interest in,
(2) concern for,
(3) encounter with,
(4) sense of absence from,
(5) sacrificial love of,
(6) commitment to, and
(7) joy over,

that which is judged to be more important than anything else in one's experience and which, so conceptualized, is taken to be a symbol of that which lies at the heart of all possible experience.[9]

The clarity of the judgment will depend, of course, on the individual making it. A primitive savage, in his religious engagement, will not exercise the quality of intellectual judgment that would be expected of, say, a learned historian or perspicacious philosopher who happens to be a religious man. Nevertheless, the savage, in making his religious engagement, whatever it be, is in some way judging his ritual act or tribal custom to be an expression of that which is more important than anything else in his life. If you doubt this, try inhibiting him from the exercise of his ritual or preventing him from the observance of his custom. The savage, in his own way, has made the judgment that will entail his engagement in the ritual act and his observance of the tribal custom, and sometimes he will defend them, if necessary, even to the death.

The very tentative definition I have proposed clearly excludes the kind of ethical or aesthetic reductionism that has been already held to be excluded by the kind of commitment the religious attitude entails. The obvious objection that it is too lofty in tone to apply to all the crude forms of religion that most particularly interest anthropologists and other students of primitive societies has been met in the preceding paragraph and elsewhere, at least to the extent of showing that a savage, though he fails to make our "civilized" intellectual distinctions, can think well enough in his own way so that his judgments can be as genuine in their way as those of a Kant. A still more fundamental objection, however, must be considered here. If, as has been contended, religion is not necessarily as good as Abraham's or Gautama's or Albert Schweitzer's but may be as bad as Hitler's, how can the proposed definition apply to it? How can we predicate of a religion that is by any reckoning wicked, inhumane, and a positive evil for mankind, the high-sounding characteristics that have been set forth in our definition?

National Socialism in Germany, with its brutal tyranny, its monstrous system of internal espionage, its ruthless liquidation of all forces of opposition

---

[9] The term "God" functions as such a verbal symbol, as do corresponding terms in other religions, e.g., Brahmā, Allah, and the Tao, though in nonmonotheistic religions the focal point may not be so specifiable.

and dissent, and above all its barbarous extermination of six million Jews and persecution of many non-Jews, did produce a recognizable phenomenon—a genuine commitment that had all the characteristics envisaged in our definition. Let us look at them in some detail. Germans, especially the teenagers who had been educated under the Nazi system during their intellectually most impressionable years, did make very definite judgments—for example, that the triumph of the Aryan race as masters of the earth was more important than anything else in the history of mankind and a symbol of the victory of the strong over the weak that is at the heart of the human struggle for what was celebrated in many popular anthems as "freedom."

The interest in all that this judgment entailed was not at all like, say, the interest of many Americans in the education of minorities, or like anybody's interest in music or painting, or like even the most fanatical fan's interest in football. It was like a devout Catholic's interest in his Church or a faithful Muslim's interest in his Qur'ān. The unfortunate victim of Hitler's educational system was also concerned, not as I am concerned for the welfare of my neighborhood or even for the welfare of my wife and family, but as a man is concerned for his salvation, even as he is concerned for the truth he believes he finds in his religion. The German of that day believed also that, both as an individual and as a member of the "master race," he encountered something that was at the heart of everything—a principle of evolution at the core of all values. Though he may have felt at times, perhaps in the excitement and fanfare of a big Nazi celebration, that he was in a state of mystical union with the principle he was tacitly worshiping, he much more often found himself "distanced" from his ideal. His sacrificial love for that to which he was committed can hardly need exposition: not only was the courage of the Nazi soldier attested by his military opponents, but the ordinary German civilian was more passionate in his love and more willing to sacrifice his life, if need be, than are many Christians and Buddhists toward their respective foci of value.

When in a small Bavarian town in 1938 a stolid old farmer told me he would die for the *Führer,* I thought at first he must be pretending, but as I looked into his earnest blue eyes, welling with tears as he had spoken, I could find no room to doubt the deep sincerity of his commitment. Least of all was there any doubt of the joy these people took in what can only be called their religion. The popular "Strength through Joy" (*Kraft durch Freude*) movement, nominally connected with work, travel, and sport, represented a much deeper principle: the fulfillment of the aims to which one's deepest religious commitment is directed must always, in the long run, bring superlative joy. The joy of seeing the triumph of Aryan supremacy and the abject enslavement of all non-Aryans was one of which Nazis always spoke with an emotional sense of anticipation that was plainly to be deemed the counterpart of the Christian's hope for the Kingdom of God and the joy that it will bring, the incomparable "peace that passeth understanding."

About the same time I also had a conversation with a fairly intelligent and certainly very earnest German clergyman of the State Church, about the traditionally important New Testament passage[10] on the *Kenosis* or "humiliation" or "emptying" of God in Christ. The *Pfarrer* offered the following interpretation. The humiliation, he affirmed, was poetically perfect, since God humbled himself to the lowest nadir of being: he became a Jew. Millions of Germans at the time would have applauded his exegesis. I cite this remark in support of my contention that (a) the object of a religious commitment may be true or false, and religious aims good or evil, and (b) the tentative definition we have before us can fit what many will call a monstrous perversion of religion as well as it fits the religion of Amos or Shankara. My liver would be no less a liver even if I had cirrhosis, nor your psyche less a psyche even if you were psychotic. The defining characteristics of a healthy liver or a healthy mind have no reference to disease, which would introduce, of course, distortion; but even the diseased entity is still definable in terms of the condition in which it is found when healthy.

We must now examine more carefully the forms of the definition.

Interest   By "interest" I mean a volitional act, a focusing of the mind on the religious object. For reasons already suggested, interest will not be uniformly present in all thoughts, words, acts, and observances associated with religion. People often unthinkingly mumble their prayers in church, for instance, exhibiting boredom rather than interest or attention. Interest in that which is judged to be more important than anything else in one's total experience nevertheless underlies everything that can be called religious. It is correlative to the special kind of value attributed to the religious "object." How the interest is initiated or aroused is a separate question. The religious man may point to what he accounts a revelation or disclosure from what he may take to be a supernatural source. The truth or falsity of the claim is not for the moment relevant. What I have in mind is, rather, the indefatigable pursuit of an object, everything connected with which has, for the devotee, an irresistible magnetism and fascination. The nearest analogy in other human affairs is that of deep love between husband and wife or between parent and child.

As nothing pertaining to humanity can be alien to the mind of a man deeply conscious of his being a man,[11] so to the Christian *societas* the discovery of even a fragment of a hitherto undiscovered manuscript of an early letter about Jesus is sure to cause widespread interest and excitement. To a learned and observant Jew the remotest echo of a Talmudic phrase or the hint of a biblical idea is enough to attract his attention, even in the midst of a conversation geared to very different matters. From the abundance of

[10] Philippians 2:7 f.
[11] Cf. Terence: "I am a man: nothing human is alien to me." (*Homo sum: nil humani a me alienum puto.*)

possible objects of our attention we all select what for one reason or another interests us most. To meet one about whom your whole life revolves and who has "captured your heart" entails a concentration of your whole being upon the object of your attention. Such is the kind of interest religion commands, an interest that is not casual but fundamental, springing from a fundamental commitment to one's conception of the structure of Being itself.

Concern   To the extent that any thought, word, or deed is religious, it is colored by a special concern. Paul Tillich has called it "ultimate concern." The phrase "ultimate concern" sounds to many people more subjectivist than Tillich ever intended.[12] Tillich's "ultimate concern" is not, strictly speaking, a concern *for*. I am using my expression "concern for" independently of Tillich's use and as part of my general schema, aside from which the mere notion of "concern for" an object would do little toward a definition of religion. Still, in communities that have their origin in and owe their existence to such an "ultimate concern," there may be a great deal of unconcern. Not only is there at least some wickedness in every religious institution and community; there is also a vast lack of concern, an immense "couldn't-care-less"-ness, which is a far greater impediment to the attainment of the religious community's purpose than ever turpitude could be. For while the religious community, through its concern, can in the long run turn even wickedness to a good purpose ("evil also serves"), unconcern is a deadly stranglehold upon it. In any case, as we have seen, religion is not necessarily good, and even a religion whose purpose is wicked, and whose life is a neurotic parody of a healthy religion, is enfeebled by its adherents' unconcern. Unconcern saps the strength of the religious community at its roots. Nevertheless, a community is properly called religious when a concern of the kind Tillich called "ultimate" is the principal reason for its existence.

Encounter   The relation in which the individual or the community stands to that which commands the interest and evokes the concern is not constant. A devout person whose life is deeply consecrated to a religious aim is not in *conscious* relation *all the time* with that which commands his interest and evokes his concern, any more than a man who loves his wife deeply can truly claim that he thinks about her all the time. Nor, of course, would any intelligent woman expect him to do so. The love of a man who thought of nothing but his wife would not be worth having since he would not really be a man at all. The obvious truth of this trite reflection does not diminish in any way the honesty of his claim to constancy and fidelity. On the contrary, it exhibits the meaning and the force of that claim.

Nevertheless, the whole meaning of the relationship depends upon the

---

[12] The reason is that many overlook the fact that it translates the German *das was mich unbedingt angeht,* where *angehen* refers to activity on the part of *das was,* which is independent of the speaker.

reality of an encounter with that to which one is related. An awareness of the nature of this encounter is precisely that which enables one to claim to distinguish the reality of the encounter from one's own narcissistic experiences that seem to mimic or (it may be) foreshadow the inimitable experience of encounter with that which Rudolf Otto has called the "Other." Martin Buber has taken the relationship of encounter to be the essence of religion and that which distinguishes it from what he accounts philosophy. I have already rejected that view as too exclusive and therefore misleading, while acknowledging nevertheless that it does call attention to an indispensable characteristic in religion.

Sense of Absence Encounter entails, of course, presence, and a sense of divine presence is a familiar notion in most religions, whether they characteristically conceptualize deity in a transcendental mode (e.g., Judaism and Islam) or see deity more typically (as is the case with many Oriental forms of religion) in a pantheistic guise. Nevertheless, the sense of presence is not by any means constant even in those pantheistic forms of religion that readily conceptualize God as an air we breathe or an ocean in which we swim rather than as a Being who stands apart from us and who, while he reveals, also hides his face, that is, his presence.

The sense of the absence of God is precisely that which makes faith such a profound concept and important category in biblical thought. The *locus classicus* of the sense of the absence of God is the cry of Jesus on the cross, quoting the Hebrew psalmist: *Eli, Eli, lama sabachthani?* ("My God, my God, why hast thou forsaken me?") Faith becomes the important category it is in the whole biblical tradition just because the presence of God is not sensed immediately but indirectly and obliquely, according to Kierkegaard, whose genius as an interpreter and critic of Christian thought makes his observation on this subject noteworthy. Hence the significance of the notion that God may be better known through his absence than through his presence. Such a sense of the absence of God is incompatible with total atheism, since one cannot have a sense of the absence of something one knows nothing about.[13]

Sacrificial Love That love is at the heart of the religious attitude and typical of the religious mood is universally recognized. The implications of the notion are not always, however, clearly seen. Even human love is, as Dante observed, "of terrible aspect." The love of that which is judged to be more important than anything else and to which, the Gospel warns us, must be subordinated, if need be, even the love of our parents, the love of our children, a man's love for his wife, and a woman's for her husband, is more terrible still. Not only may it entail sacrifices too horrible to

[13] I have dealt with this theme in *The Sense of Absence* (Philadelphia: J. B. Lippincott Co., 1968).

contemplate (such as the torture and martyrdom that many have felt compelled to endure rather than renounce their faith); when corrupted, it turns into a hate more diabolical than any ordinary human hate can be. While it brooks no rival, accounting every rival an idol, its severest conflict must always be with the idols it regards most highly, for those it sees as the most dangerous. There is little danger of an educated twentieth-century American's slipping into the worship of a primitive man's stone image, but there is a real danger of his succumbing to an idolatrous attitude toward his pet political or social theory. As we say, he "makes a fetish" of it. The sacrificial love which religion entails makes unconditional demands.

Commitment What we properly look for, above all, in every religious situation, is commitment. Yet though commitment is characteristic of religion, neither institutions nor individuals are always strikingly committed to that which commands their interest and evokes their concern. In many cases the commitment seems to be minimal. One can "believe in" a religion without "living" it, just as one can "believe in" racial equality and yet be horrified by the idea of actually having a neighbor of a race other than one's own. A man who flies into a rage and punches you in the nose may nevertheless honestly believe as well as profess that, as the Hebrew proverb says, a soft answer turns away wrath. If, however, there were *no* commitment in the life of an individual or community, there would be no religion. Religion always entails commitment to that which commands interest and evokes concern.

Joy The crowning characteristic of the religious attitude, in whatever guise its life is embodied, is an interior joy in the reality of that upon which it focuses attention. Teilhard de Chardin wrote: "As far as I can go back, in my childhood, nothing seems to me more characteristic or familiar in my inner disposition than the taste or irresistible need for some 'one and only sufficing and necessary' thing: in order to be fully at ease, to be completely happy, the knowledge that 'some essential thing' does really exist, to which everything else is no more than an accessory or, maybe, an embellishment. To know that, and unceasingly to rejoice in the consciousness of its existence. . . ." [14] The joy of which the classical Christian mystics write is a joy inseparable from a cognitive claim such as is implicit in the definition of religion I have proposed. All religion, however, that is not dead or moribund has that kind of joy as its crowning characteristic, though the forms in which the joy is expressed are as manifold as the religions and, indeed, the religious attitudes themselves.

We are not to expect, of course, that joy will be manifest at all times

[14] Pierre Teilhard de Chardin, *Le coeur de la matière*, as quoted in *Teilhard de Chardin Album*, ed. Jeanne Mortier and Marie-Louise Aboux (New York: Harper & Row, 1966), p. 12.

in the outlook or demeanor of religious people, any more than we should expect never to catch them with their interest flagging or their commitment at a low ebb. In recognizing joy as an essential characteristic of the religious attitude, I am affirming that all religion, however strongly it may insist on the need for painful sacrifice and what might be called the long-faced virtues, always has within it an essential element of hope. It may even be called hedonistic in the very large sense that it always claims to be directed to human happiness in the long run, and it often promises this happiness even in the short run. The deep sense of gratitude for the opportunities life affords, and indeed for life itself, that is characteristic of the religious response to the human situation entails a sense of joy.

Religious people commonly attest that the destruction of radical self-centeredness (a characteristic religious aim) brings with it an interior joy that makes the former "unregenerate" life seem in retrospect a hell on earth. To feel "snatched as a brand from the burning" or "delivered out of the jaws of hell," to use the language typical of much Protestant piety, *means* to possess a special quality of joy. The Buddhist who feels he is making some progress in emptying himself of the desire he believes to be at the root of all human misery cannot but mean, in affirming his sense of losing human desire, that he is experiencing the inward joy that his loss of what he takes to be the cause of human misery entails. An analogy might be the joy an athlete feels when his rigorous and painful training seems to be paying off in greater quickness of eye or fleetness of foot.

Some Reflections on the Definition   The definition of religion I have proposed is, I think, at least a useful working definition. That is not to say that it is by any means irreformable. It is certain, indeed, to be in the long run inadequate, but that need not inhibit its use till a better one replaces it.

There are, of course, many attempts at a simpler definition, including an earlier one of my own.[15] Professor John Hutchison of the Claremont Graduate School has offered two short, separate definitions: "Religion is a system of holy forms," and "Religion is a belief which to change is to change myself substantially." Such attractive but over-neat definitions always stress far too much one or another aspect of the total religious phenomenon. Religion, in my view, does entail belief, as it entails much else; but the category of belief is too restrictive. It attends to only one aspect of religion. Much more philosophical reflection is needed to achieve a working definition of religion, even of the most tentative sort.

As already indicated, monotheistic religions, at least, are God-centered; that is to say, the term "God" or an equivalent term is used to designate the conceptualization of "that which is judged to be more important than anything else in one's experience and . . . lies at the heart of all experience."

[15] Geddes MacGregor, *Introduction to Religious Philosophy* (Boston: Houghton Mifflin Co., 1959), p. 2.

The omission of fear as a defining characteristic of religion will seem odd to many. A much-quoted remark by an ancient Roman poet affirms that it was fear that first created gods in the world.[16] That religion is due primarily, if not exclusively, to fear of the unknown is an old contention of its detractors, representing a form of reductionism that is far too simplistic to do justice to the complexity of religious phenomena; nevertheless the objection has some force, not least when one thinks of the extreme importance of the motivation of fear in the outlook of primitive peoples who set forth daily in terror of the "evil eye" and spend their whole lives in fear of the powers of darkness. Moreover, out of a very different and monotheistic tradition comes the assertion of the Hebrew psalmist that the fear of the Lord is the beginning of wisdom.[17]

Fear might well be included in a definition of religion, but I prefer to exclude it because it relates to a primitive emotion that all religions, to the extent that they recognize the supremacy of love, are bent on overcoming.[18] The liberation that religions promise often includes liberation from the fears that plague primitive people. Of course, even the man who feels confident of divine aid or protection is not likely to suppose he has nothing whatsoever to fear. He may continue to fear his own weakness, his own lack of trust in God, or (if he so believes) the power and cunning of Satan. Though a healthy man does not go about in terror of disease, he nevertheless has a "healthy respect" for it and does not needlessly expose himself to it. In the same way, fear is not to be wholly excluded from the attitude of a religious man. Still, it is in my view a negative concomitant rather than an essential characteristic of that attitude.

Concern for holiness, though it finds different forms of expression, is typical of all religious commitments, but for the purposes of a definition its very universality may be argued against it. That is, it may be so general a term as to contribute, in a definition, nothing but circularity. If, as Otto holds, the religious sense *is* the sense of the holy, we naturally must ask what it is. We are then told it is *unentwickelbar*, unanalyzable, which is to say it is undefinable, since in the absence of the means of analogy its structure cannot be exhibited. In such a view there are no similarities with anything else in experience, so one will not try to define religion except to those who already claim to know what it is, who therefore need no definition. To say that a religious man is characterized by a sense of the holy is tautological, like saying that a playwright or an actor is characterized by his sense of the dramatic, which does nothing to tell us what drama is.

Existentialists and others in the Kierkegaardian tradition might complain likewise that there is no mention of *Angst*, the peculiar anguish of the religious man. If, however, that notion of *Angst* is as difficult as the existentialists

---

[16] "Primus in orbe deos fecit timor": Statius, *Thebais*, bk. 3, line 664. Also attributed to Petronius.

[17] Psalms 111:10.

[18] Cf. the New Testament dictum that "perfect love banishes fear" (1 John 4:18 [N.E.B.]).

insist, and at the same time as comprehensive as they say, it would not be helpful for the kind of definition we need to work with. For similar reasons the term "faith," which many would account (as I would myself) a fundamental category of religion, is not specifically mentioned in the tentative definition. We shall be considering these concepts later.

What Is Philosophy of Religion?

The term "philosophy of religion," as the name of a formal academic discipline and separate sphere of scholarly investigation, is historically associated with the last glow of the German Enlightenment.[19] The term does not occur before that period, and probably not before the last decade of the eighteenth century, when books bearing titles such as *Philosophie der Religion* and *Religionsphilosophie* made their appearance.[20] It soon came to be specially connected with the name of Hegel, and its fortunes fluctuated with those of that great thinker. In the nineteenth century, when his influence was in the ascendant, it was highly esteemed. When in the twentieth century he fell out of fashion, it was denigrated.

Its disrepute in the twentieth century was independently fostered, however, in various very different intellectual circles. It was fostered, for example, among the so-called Neo-Orthodox Protestant theologians such as Karl Barth, who claimed that since Christianity was not "a religion" but "the revelation of God to man," the whole notion of philosophizing about it in the old Hegelian manner was as useless from a believer's standpoint as it was futile from a philosopher's. The early twentieth-century logical positivists, who accounted all God-language meaningless because unverifiable and unfalsifiable by the particular sort of empiricist criteria they insisted upon, disliked philosophy of religion not only because they accounted it a typical product of Hegelian modes of thought but for various other, more technical reasons. Even apart from objections from such special standpoints, however, philosophy of religion, as a formal academic discipline taught at universities and other institutions of higher learning, has suffered from the narrow and confining circumstances of its birth in the twilight of German rationalism.

What, then, were the ancient Vedic and Upanishadic writers doing when they wrote reflectively upon the religion of the Indus Valley many centuries before the Christian era? What was Plato doing when he critically inspected the religious heritage of his day in ancient Athens? What were Maimonides and Thomas Aquinas doing in the Middle Ages when they explored their own heritages, Jewish and Christian respectively, with the intellectual tools of their day? What was the function of those later writers who wrote on what they called "natural theology," distinguishing their approach from

---

[19] See *Die Religion in Geschichte und Gegenwart*, vol. 5 (Tübingen: J. C. B. Mohr, 1961), pp. 1010 ff.

[20] It was used in the title of a book by J. C. G. Schaumann, *Philosophie der Religion* (1793) and of one by J. Berger, *Geschichte der Religionsphilosophie* (1800).

the dogmatic theology that was part of a narrow ecclesiastical training and consisted primarily in ways of systematizing doctrine? Were not they also, along with Plato and Maimonides, "philosophers of religion"? If not, how did they differ? No doubt they would not have recognized themselves under that name, and perhaps they might even have had some difficulty in understanding precisely what it was intended to mean. Before 1750, when Baumgarten first used the term *Aesthetik* to designate the philosophical critique of art and analysis of beauty, no one would have understood what "aesthetician" meant in the sense in which that unbeautiful word is used today; yet everybody from the dawn of history onwards who ever gave a moment's thought to the nature of art and beauty has been an aesthetician.

We are fully entitled, then, to call any thought about religion in some sense philosophy of religion, and we may with propriety call Plato, Duns Scotus, and Sir Thomas Browne philosophers of religion, though none of them would have used or even have readily understood the designation. We may even use the term of the most obscurantist seventeenth-century dogmatic theologian, though we would probably add that he was a bad philosopher of religion.

The Relation of Philosophy to Religion   The relation in which philosophy and religion stand to each other is an exceptionally difficult question, not least since any answer to it must depend on one's view of two highly controversial questions: the nature of philosophy on the one hand, and, on the other, the nature of religion. We have already seen the difficulties we encounter in specifying with any degree of precision what religion is. The question "What is philosophy?" is also very difficult and controversial. The nature of philosophy has been differently understood, for example, by the Sophists in Socrates' time, the Neo-Platonic school that took possession of the Third Academy, the thirteenth-century schoolmen, the seventeenth-century continental rationalists, the British empiricists, the nineteenth-century idealists, and the twentieth-century linguistic analysts, Neo-Thomists, Marxists, phenomenologists, and existentialists. Philosophy has included what are now called the physical and biological sciences, which in some traditionalist places of learning have been officially called "natural philosophy" even in the present century. Philosophy has sometimes been understood in such a large sense as to include almost everything suggested by its etymology (from the Greek, "the love of wisdom") and sometimes, especially in our own day in the English-speaking world, in a sense so narrow as to be almost reducible to logic.

There are, however, some things that would be generally agreed about the nature of philosophy. For instance, it is essentially an intellectual pursuit. Whether almost identified with mathematics or carefully distinguished from it, philosophy resembles mathematics in being purely an activity of the mind. Even those who, like the existentialists and the vitalists, wish to draw attention to the importance of nonintellectual elements do so by means of an intellectual exercise and a presentation that is intended to appeal to the intellect, not to, say, the poetic or artistic sense, and certainly not to the emotions or instincts.

All philosophers, a Bergson no less than a Plato, a Hegel as well as a Hume, even a Kierkegaard and a Marcel as well as an Aristotle and a Spinoza, are trying in their own way to convince by means of an appeal to their readers' *minds*. Though philosophy has a speculative element without which it lacks creativity and destroys itself, even this speculative element is essentially an activity of the intellect. Philosophy is also always at every point critical. The critical spirit *is* a philosophical spirit, even though we might wish to insist that it does not encompass the whole of the philosophical spirit. Philosophers, like other men, have their own predispositions and even presuppositions, but they are not good philosophers unless, at any rate in their working hours, they do their best to discard them. All this is to say that philosophy, whatever it is, is essentially intellectual. Whether, historically, a philosopher be classed as a rationalist or an empiricist, he always proceeds by "rational" intellectual techniques.

Religion, by contrast, though it has intellectual aspects, is not at all characteristically an affair of the mind. That is not to say it is essentially emotive. It might be, for instance, like art, a different mode of spiritual activity. Or it might be, as some would tend to say, volitional rather than emotional or intellectual. Whatever it is, it is distinguishable from philosophy at this point: unlike philosophy, it is not purely intellectual. It may include or even entail an intellectual element, but that is not the basic stuff of which it is made.

Philosophy, whether speculative or critical, is by its nature abstract. Even existentialist philosophies, which are highly sensitive to this fact, and whose fundamental aim is to take account of the involvement and subjectivity of human relations, cannot escape the fact that even when a philosophy recognizes its own limitations it is still subject to them. Philosophy has a tendency, therefore, to kill religion. Yet religion, whose essence is life and whose law is love, cannot escape philosophical self-criticism. It has to take stock of itself, to value itself. "Difficult as it is, therefore, we cannot avoid the valuation of religions, either explicit or implicit. For if all ideas about anything, including religions, are equally good, valuable, and true, either we are talking about nothing, or else all such ideas are equally false, worthless, and evil." [21]

Religious literature is, indeed, largely an expression of this self-valuation. This is true even of mystical literature, supposedly the most anti-intellectual kind of religious literature. The fifteenth-century Indian mystic poet Kabir sought throughout his life to bridge the seemingly impassable gulf between Hindu and Muslim. A Muslim by birth, he was technically classed with

[21] Winston C. King, *Introduction to Religion* (New York: Harper & Brothers, 1954), p. 13.

the Sufis, to whom much theological latitude was allowed, so that though he was persecuted his life was spared, and eventually, when he died in 1518, the Muslim and Hindu authorities fought for possession of his body, which the latter wanted to burn and the former to bury. The synthesis Kabir achieved in his writings was, of course, a poetic synthesis. Nevertheless, in his cry that Brahmā (the great fact compared with which "the distinction of the Conditioned and the Unconditioned is but a word") is both more fully the Absolute than any philosophical abstraction and also more fully personal than the most personal aspect of an individual human being, Kabir detected one of the most baffling problems in the philosophy of religion. A pure monism, which in effect identifies the self with God, finding expression in the Vedantist formula "Thou art thou," destroys the very heart of all religions, namely, the loving relationship that lies between man and God, giving life to every religious *motif.* Kabir does not attack the underlying problem in the manner of a philosopher of religion; he approaches it as a fifteenth-century Indian mystic. In the very recognition of it, however, and in the poetic attempt to overcome it, he has already engaged, in his own way, in an exercise in the philosophy of religion. Yet he is at the same time exhibiting, however unwittingly, the difference between "doing" philosophy and "doing" religion. His advantage is that, having two religious backgrounds, he can be philosophically critical of both from within both.

The difference between the philosophical and the religious mind may be seen in the way their respective outlooks issue in almost any discussion of ethical questions. Henry Fielding, in *Tom Jones,* provides an amusing if mischievously overdrawn example through two contrasted characters, Mr. Thwackum, a clergyman, and Mr. Square, who symbolizes philosophy. Both were educated men, but they "scarce ever met without a disputation." An incident in the story evokes this indignant question from Mr. Thwackum: "Can honor teach anyone to tell a lie, or can any honor exist independent of religion?" Mr. Square, the philosopher, characteristically observes at this point that it is "impossible to discourse philosophically concerning words till their meaning" is "first established," and that "honor" and "religion" are notable examples of words that enshrine a splendid array of ambiguities. Thwackum no less characteristically retorts, in a textbook example of *ad hominem,* that Square is motivated by "the usual malice of all the enemies of the true Church." The terms "religion" and "honor" hold no ambiguities for this eighteenth-century divine; he knows exactly what he means by them: "When I mention religion, I mean the Christian religion; and not only the Christian, but the Protestant religion; and not only the Protestant religion, but the Church of England." And, "When I mention honor, I mean that mode of Divine grace which is not only consistent with, but dependent upon, this religion, and is consistent with and dependent upon no other." His point of view, that is, depends not only on an interpretation of the meaning and purpose of life (an interpretation so deep-seated that he has ceased to question it radically, if he ever did) but also on a moral determination to fulfill his role, as he sees it, in the structure of the universe and the destiny of man. Square, on the contrary, though equally dogmatic in his own way (he "held human nature to be the perfection of all virtues, and that vice was a deviation from our nature, in the same manner as deformity of body is"), is interested in discussing ideas and their meaning rather than in defending a "stance" and evangelically promoting a "way of life."

Historically, there have been several views of the relation in which philosophy and religion should stand. Some have accounted the two so closely connected that almost no distinction is to be made at all. This view may seem natural to those whose principal focus of philosophic interest happens to be a religious one. It fails, however, to do justice either to philosophy or to religion: to philosophy, because it lacks the detached purity of abstract speculation and logical reasoning; to religion, because it inevitably strangles the life of religion in the attempt to weave it into the philosopher's web.

These dangers are clearly enough seen by those who have asserted, on the contrary, that philosophy and religion, having nothing to do with each other, must be kept completely separate. This view will not meet the case unless religion is to be accounted, arbitrarily and without further ado, exclusively an expression of emotions to which philosophical inquiry is as irrelevant as it is to certain modern art forms, having no meaning, providing no mode of knowledge, and leading to no kind of truth.

The medieval schoolmen recognized, in their own way, that neither of these attitudes was adequate to the case. St. Thomas developed a synthesis of what could still be called, in medieval fashion, "reason and faith." Through reason, the schoolmen taught, one could attain truth in a certain way and up to a certain point; for the rest, faith was needed. The truths revealed by faith could not be discovered by reason alone, and so theology, which treats of such divine revelation, was even grander than philosophy. Theology, on this medieval view, is Queen of the Sciences, that is, Queen of Knowledge, while philosophy is her *ancilla,* or handmaid. This did not mean, as superficially it might appear to mean, that philosophy is merely theology's slave or tool. It meant, rather, that each had its own domain. The mistress has no more right in the kitchen than has the kitchenmaid in the parlor. Theology operates in one dimension, philosophy in another. Truth is one, but there are different ways of approaching it. In modern terms a Thomist might say: the truths of algebra do not conflict with the truths of geometry; they are different appropriations of truth, which is one.

How Does the Philosopher Differ from the Religious Man? Sometimes, we have seen, religion and philosophy are close to each other; sometimes they seem far apart. To clarify what is at issue, let us consider some instances.

Hegel and Kierkegaard, though they happen to be as opposed as much as they could be in their general approach to philosophy and religion, and though many modern philosophers do not like either of them, both show how closely philosophy and religion can be allied. Both were above all else interested in religion.

Hegel, in his early days, was a theological student, and as he developed his thought he came to the view that religion is a sort of baby philosophy, a picture-thinking kind of philosophy, suitable for people who are not very good at abstract thinking.[22] Philosophy, in Hegel's view, is a superior form of the same activity in which the religious man engages. It is, so to speak, religion "grown up." What Hegel never doubts is that the subject matter of religion and philosophy is really the same, whether it be called, in the religious man's style, God, or, in the manner of the philosopher, Absolute *Geist.* Ironically, Hegel went out of fashion among both philosophers and religious men, and despite a recent revival in some circles he is still suspect by many religious people because they think that in looking patronizingly on religion as a kind of immature philosophy he misses the fundamental meaning of the religious act.

Kierkegaard, who reacted vehemently against Hegel, must be reckoned by any account a deeply religious man, for though he is a bitter critic of conventional religion and especially of churchmen, he hardly ever talks about anything other than topics directly or indirectly bearing on a man's faith in his Creator. Though many professional philosophers today would say either that Kierkegaard was a bad philosopher or that he was not a philosopher at all, he always thought of himself as a philosopher answering Hegel not in the latter's own language but in an idiom of his own, invented for the express purpose of showing how wrong Hegel was. What he never doubted, any more than Hegel ever doubted, was that philosophy, whatever it may be, is *about* God.

In contrast to these, one might look at the Italian Neo-Idealists, Croce and Gentile, on the one hand, and, on the other, twentieth-century logicians such as Tarski and Carnap. These two groups of philosophers differ greatly in their conception of what philosophy is; but both seem sure that the subject matter of philosophy, whatever it is, is not God. Then one might look at two religious figures such as, say, William Booth, the founder of the Salvation Army, and Bernadette Soubirous, who believed that the Blessed Virgin Mary appeared to her and gave her certain explicit directions, and with whom is associated Lourdes as a place of pilgrimage and healing. They are in many ways very dissimilar human beings; yet they are both unmistakably religious in interest and outlook, and neither of them could possibly

---

[22] In fairness to Hegel, we should recognize his claim that the truth is actually in the content present to thought (*Gedanke*); that is, the immediacy of the form is inadequate, but what it contains is not.

be called, by their most fervent admirers or their most vigorous detractors, a philosopher. Both are much too concerned with what they believe they have grasped by direct revelation and too sensitive to the urgency of their mission to have much time for intellectual reflection about it.

In the view we have taken, they could not have been totally unreflective. They must have engaged in some sort of self-criticism, as indeed they did; but it was minimal, and compared with the intellectual agonizing about religion that we find in Pascal and Kierkegaard it hardly seems worth mentioning at all. By the same token, perhaps the most "secular" of philosophers may occasionally indicate some interest in a subject that religious people would account important; but if they did, it would be too fleeting a reference to justify being called, by any stretch of language, religious.

In a previous section we have discussed the relation between philosophy and religion. We have seen that they are never to be identified, and we have found some basis for distinguishing the one from the other. It is one thing, however, to have a theoretical basis, another to distinguish in practice when a man is functioning as a philosopher and when as a religious man. In some cases, of course, there could be no possible doubt. There is no difficulty when philosophers choose to avoid discussion of the problems that interest religious people. Plainly, a philosopher writing on mathematical logic is not "doing religion." Even when religious people might well be interested in a certain kind of philosophical problem, such as the nature of belief, there may be no doubt that a particular discussion of that problem is purely philosophical.[23] One might not be so confident that Spinoza, though his work is certainly philosophical, may not be "doing religion," at least according to some understandings of "religion." His talk is "God-talk" and indeed a thoroughly convinced follower of Spinoza's philosophy might almost be called a devout Spinozist. How are we to decide, then, when a man is functioning as a philosopher and when as a religious man?

Let us consider one possible view of the matter from an impressive twentieth-century Jewish thinker. Martin Buber, in *The Eclipse of God*, contrasts the figures of Epicurus and Gautama Buddha. The former, he says, is a philosopher and the latter a religious man. Epicurus, though he utters dogmas and engages in cultic practices, has no religious sense. The Buddha, though he smilingly nods to the popular gods, neither proclaims them nor worships them, being the Awakened One who points beyond them to a religious reality about which he declines to make assertions, and so is essentially a religious man rather than a philosopher.[24] Buber is able to make this clear-cut distinction because what is for him decisive for the authenticity of religion is the relating of oneself to Being who is standing "over against." What Aeschylus makes the chorus in the *Agamemnon* say to Zeus and what Euripides makes the old queen say to Zeus in the *Trojan*

---

[23] E.g., A. Phillips Griffiths, ed., *Knowledge and Belief* (London: Oxford University Press, 1967).

[24] Martin Buber, *The Eclipse of God* (New York: Harper, 1952), pp. 39 f.

Women appear alike; but they are separated by the chasm that lies between authentic religion and philosophical speculation, the "God of Jacob" and the "God of the philosophers." In the *Agamemnon* the chorus invokes Zeus,

> whoever he is,
> If it pleases him so to be called,
> With this name I invoke him.

In the *Trojan Women*, Zeus is invoked,

> O Foundation of the earth and above it throned,
> Whoever thou art, beyond our mind's poor grasp,
> Whether Zeus or Fate or spirit of men,
> I implore thee.

Aeschylus, though he speaks of God in the third person, is genuinely addressing him; Euripides, though he says "Thou," cannot have an authentic I–Thou encounter, since by the implied "total immanence" in his allusion to "the spirit of men" as a possible identification of Zeus, "the religious situation is abolished." [25]

While the criterion Buber proposes here is very plausible indeed, it depends, at least in some measure, on the particularly sharp distinction he makes between the I–Thou relationship of subject-to-subject encounter and the I–It relation of detached study. From such a standpoint what matters is whether God is, in effect, being addressed or just talked about. If the former, the talk is that of a religious man; if the latter, then it is philosophy, though not necessarily good philosophy. In this view, St. Augustine, in using a special literary form for his *Confessions,* the whole of which he addresses to God as in a great Ode, is clearly talking as a religious man, while in, say, the *Enchiridion,* he is philosophizing. For even though the *Enchiridion* is all about such topics as God, Christ, grace, and sin, and indeed even though in the course of it he raises, in his own fourth-century way, the very point Buber is making, it is a book in which he addresses himself intellectually to the entailments of faith. Such a discussion is philosophical—philosophical theology, if you like, but philosophical—not the talk of a man functioning in a religious capacity. Even God-talk is not religious unless it conforms to the requirements Buber specifies.

The manner in which Buber makes his distinction and his presentation of his criterion is adequate, I think, for our present purposes. Though I happen to take the view that it is too cut and dried to be wholly satisfactory in the long run (some of my reasons will become apparent later), I submit Buber's criterion as a useful and practical one for general purposes.[26]

[25] Ibid., pp. 41 f.
[26] I think Buber's position is partly influenced (as indeed, in principle, he personally admitted to me at his house in Jerusalem the year before he died) by the Hegelian mould of what he understands by "philosophy," which "begins with abstractions from the concrete" and "sees the absolute in universals." I have discussed my own critique of Buber's position in an article, "Is There an Intellectual Element in Christian Faith?" in *Anglican Theological Review*, vol. 52, no. 1 (Jan. 1970), from which I have freely drawn in describing here what Buber says.

When a Francis of Assisi sets forth with zeal on a program of social and religious reform, we have no problem in identifying him as a "man of God," not a philosopher, even though what he says may contain some critical reflections of interest to a philosopher. His speech, whether it be about God or what people would commonly call "mundane" affairs, turns readily into prayer. On the other hand, even the prayer of a very "secular" philosopher like Hume would be in danger of turning into critical questioning or logical analysis. The problem arises when a person happens to be both devoutly religious and a critical thinker. According to Buber he cannot be both at the same time. By any reckoning, a distinction must be made, and we have seen one way of drawing it.

Before leaving this question we may note another distinction that is germane to what is before us. Philosophy and religion differ in the manner of their transmission. Philosophical ideas, occurring in the minds of a small number of people who happen to be inclined to intellectualization, travel slowly and, so to speak, from desk to desk. In the long run they may influence behavior; but usually they do not have a notable effect on the general outlook or social conduct of people for a very long time, and they may never affect it at all. Religion, on the contrary, as soon as it takes hold of even a comparatively small community of people, moves swiftly. In the face of it, philosophical ideas tend to remain known only to an intellectual aristocracy, unless they can find a means of expression in a religious cult, which may bring them within the ambit of the masses. Historically, there was a point at which Neo-Platonism was such an influential school of thought that it looked as though it might outstrip Christianity, whose fortunes did not at the time look particularly promising. In fact, however, Neo-Platonism declined in the sense that it soon became no longer a live option. It could not possibly have rivaled Christianity, still less threaten it as, later on, Islam was to do. The enormous influence of Neo-Platonic ideas on patristic and medieval thought, on the other hand, especially in the mystical tradition, can hardly be overestimated. Religion is not readily promulgated (if at all) through philosophy; but certain kinds of philosophical ideas can find in religion the means they need for their transmission into the popular outlook, and through religion they can profoundly affect the life of everyman.

Philosophy of Religion and Dogmatic Theology From the standpoint of the philosopher, the work of the dogmatic theologian is at best a hybrid. For though the dogmatic theologian, as the spokesman of the religious man, does engage in some kind of critical, philosophical activity, he is bound by theological rules that philosophers find methodologically alien to philosophy. The dogmatic theologian starts out with what his religion claims God has disclosed to men by what he calls technically "divine revelation." This disclosure or revelation may be regarded as consisting of or at least entailing a set of metaphysical axioms which by the theological rules are excluded from further inquiry. Propositions such as "God is the Creator of the world," and "Christ is the Redeemer of the world," are instances.

By the theological rules, this set or network of propositions is beyond dispute. Nevertheless, the propositions raise many questions that are not held to be indisputable, and these questions—for example, "How does Christ stand to God?" and "Why does the world need redemption?"—call for philosophical acumen and enterprise. The theologian may then go on, functioning at this point very much as a philosopher, to ask questions about meaning such as "What is meant by redemption?" and even "What, given the network of 'indisputable' propositions, is the meaning of 'God'?" The degree of philosophical critique in the theologian's work may be minimal or considerable. What vitiates it from the standpoint of the philosopher of religion is that even the most philosophical theologian does not permit himself to raise the very questions that philosophers in general would take to be the most obvious ones, such as "Do we need the God hypothesis at all?" The philosopher is not content to assume that the situation must be set up the way the dogmatic theologian is obliged by his rules to specify. He wishes to look at the situation in every way it is possible for the human mind to look at it. The theologian seems to be simply extrapolating from what he chooses to take as given, not really inspecting the situation at all. The philosopher of religion notes, moreover, that the theologian's categories seem to have been all arranged in advance, and that even when the theologian asks about meanings, he asks about them within a context he has already invested with a nexus of meaning in such a way as to determine all questions of meaning in advance.

The philosopher of religion, while pursuing his own work in his own way, should nevertheless be mindful of the reasons for the theologian's different attitude, which springs from a peculiarity in religion itself. Though religion has a revolutionary aspect and religious motivation has been behind some of the most radical and effective social revolutions in human history, religion is also by its nature essentially conservative. Its conservatism is of a special kind: all religion emerges in one way or another from some form of survival. If, however, the peculiar values it seeks to conserve and evolve are authentic ones, they can never be injured by intellectual scrutiny that is honest, thorough, and sincere.

The attitude of the philosopher of religion will be different, then, from that of the theologian who is simply undertaking to explicate a traditional creed or to expound systematically and dogmatically the faith of the Church or other religious community in which he functions. By the same token, the language of the philosopher of religion will differ from that of a systematic theologian. He will not presuppose, as does the theologian, that the starting points commonly accepted in the religion or the modes of thought employed in expounding it are necessarily adequate or even correct. He will not commend himself to the faithful, therefore, as a lively expositor of the faith they hold, for his is a very different métier from the theologian's. Nevertheless, he must try above all else to understand what religious people are saying. Here their spokesman, the theologian, is of key importance to him. The philosopher of religion must be able to learn from theologians whether his understanding of religion is adequate for his purpose; for if he fails to understand religion, he is philosophizing about nothing, and his results, whether sympathetic or antipathetic to religion, will be irrelevant.

Though the theologian is also—in some measure, at least—a philosopher, and must therefore in some degree communicate a spirit of philosophical inquiry and critique, his commitment and function are such that he cannot really be a philosopher of religion *at the same time* that he is a systematic, dogmatic theologian. If he tries to be both simultaneously he will succeed in neither. The same person can conceivably be both, however, as a philologist may also be a pianist, a mathematician or a beekeeper, though not at the same time.[27]

The Truth-Claims of Religion   The philosophy of religion, whether dressed in Thomist, Kantian, Hegelian, or modern fashion, and whether appearing as a type of modern analytical philosophy, or of existentialist enterprise, or of old-fashioned "natural theology," or in some still earlier guise, takes whatever importance it has from the cognitive claims of religion.

Where religion is reduced to psychological, sociological, anthropological, and cultural phenomena, there is no place for a genuine philosophy of religion, though there may be some opportunity for negative, critical work destined to show that philosophy of religion is philosophically useless; for since in such a case there are no meanings to ascertain, there are therefore no predications to be called true or false. Philosophy of religion emerges, however, only because the truth-claims of the religious consciousness are taken to have meaning. To show that religion is not really making truth-claims at all but only uttering what the unwary take to be such claims would be to show that when the philosopher has shown this he can have nothing else to do with religion.

Philosophy and religion stand opposed to each other because religion must make truth-claims, which the believer accepts and the unbeliever rejects. However self-critical the religion may be, it cannot in the last resort effectively examine these truth-claims, because to do so *is* to stand out of the religious ground upon which the truth-claims are uttered. The philosopher, however, when he tries to deal with religion, has a problem that seems at first sight insurmountable: how can he (as he must) stand outside the ground on which the religion stands and yet do justice to the truth-claims of the religion he is examining?

---

[27] For a detailed discussion of the relation between theology and the philosophy of religion from the standpoint of a distinguished contemporary Roman Catholic thinker, see Karl Rahner, *Hearers of the Word,* trans. M. Richards (New York: Herder & Herder, 1969), especially pp. 167–180.

For the truth-claims of religion are not general truths, like the truths of mathematics, that can be made from any ground; nor yet are they like the truths of physics or biology which can be seen by anyone who shares the common ground of being in the human situation. The truth-claims of religion are made from a particular standpoint. They are presented as revelations, unfoldings, or disclosures of truths that are commonly unnoticed or hidden. In this they are *in one respect* like the truth-claims of art. The artist says, in effect: "You have passed this way every day for twenty years, and among much else you never noticed, and which now I have shown you through my painting, is that there are at least three shades of pink and one of blue-green in the old clock-tower you took to be brown. See! I have disclosed to you something that you had overlooked." The religious prophet says, in effect: "You have looked at all human life and history for twenty years in a conventional way and till I proclaimed the Word of the Lord as it came to me, you never saw in human life and history the hand of God, as now you can see it if you will. You interpreted all human life and history in various conventional ways till suddenly through the message I am presenting to you, you can now see it in a new and richer way, so that your whole attitude to life and history will be changed. Behold the truth that I proclaim, and so appropriate the new dimension of life it opens up to you."

The believer, in responding affirmatively to that which is presented to him, is conscious of grasping a supremely important truth that radically affects his whole life and outlook. The revelation or disclosure, by its very nature, comes to him in a distinct and particular way; he does not learn it as he learns the multiplication table, or the number of chemical elements, or how to distinguish oaks from elms—all of which he could learn in a classroom or on a study tour. The religious disclosure, if it comes at all, can come only in an extremely intimate and personal way, and to come in this way it must come on special ground. The Christian doctrine of the Incarnation of God in Christ exhibits this characteristic of all religious revelation. It may entail for the Christian believer a great deal of deeply authentic philosophical criticism; yet there is a point beyond which no philosophical criticism, conducted from the believer's ground, can possibly take him. The believer, *qua* believer, cannot go beyond his own ground, where he feels himself to have been, as religious people sometimes say, "convicted" or "seized" by God.

Nevertheless, even the most convinced believer may recognize that, inviolable as is the authenticity of the truth revealed to him in the particular way that has meant so much to him, there may be other revelations too that are not entirely subsumed under the one to which he points. For instance, some orthodox and traditionalist Catholic Christians, while insisting that in the person of Christ lies the "full and final" revelation of God to man, would feel free to admit that, at least on other planets or in other galaxies, there might be other and very different forms of divine revelation.

The truth-claims the religious man makes are generally made in terms of a *credo*. For example, he says, "I believe that Jesus is my Saviour" or he might even say, "I believe that space and time, having been created by God, will end in the year 2084." He does not usually say, "I know"; he says, "I believe." The same believer, however, will say, "I know 2 and 2 are 4," and if he has what is generally accounted adequate evidence he will not hesitate to say, "I know my Aunt Mary has a glass eye." If he is a genuine believer he may well be willing to suffer torture and death for his belief that Jesus is his Saviour, but he is very unlikely to be willing to forgo even his breakfast for the sake of upholding the knowledge he claims about his aunt's glass eye. If belief, in such a context, were merely a weak form of knowledge, one might well expect the reverse to be the case.

By "belief" we often do intend, however, nothing more than a weak form of knowledge. I may say, "I do not *know* Jones stole my wallet; but I *believe* he did." That would be to say something like, "The evidence I have is insufficient to make me feel justified in publicly claiming that I know Jones to be a thief, but I do have enough evidence to make me suspect him in my own mind, and I am willing to share my suspicions with my trusted friends." The religious believer, whatever he is saying, is not saying anything of that kind. What he does mean by "I believe" is a very difficult question, which will be considered later. For the moment let us simply recognize that religious belief purports to be in some sense cognitive; that is, it makes truth-claims.

What Difference Does a "Religious Truth-Claim" Make? First, let us make one point clear: we are *not* to be talking about a claim that this or that theological position might be true or false. We are not considering the claim that one theologian might make in discussion with another that the doctrine of the Virgin Birth of Christ is "true" while that of the Immaculate Conception of Mary is "false." We are to be talking about a much more fundamental matter—whether *any* theological proposition may be called true or false. The question is: what difference does it make to say that any such truth-claim is, at least theoretically, explorable by some kind of technique that might be properly called logical, intellectual, rational? Religious truth-claims also raise, of course, basic philosophical questions about truth-claims in general. These, however, at least at the present stage, need not concern us.

First let us consider some alternative ways of looking at religious utterances, ways based on a denial of the possibility of taking seriously the philosophical explorability of religious truth-claims. We may begin with what some would call religious psychologism. While nobody would deny that all religion has within it a very important psychological element, there are those who would reduce all religious phenomena to a species of psychological phenomena, maintaining therefore that there is no element in them that cannot be shown to consist in a psychological impulse, tendency, or drive. Such a theory need not be a Freudian one, but it well might be.

In such a view, religion may be accounted a neurotic manifestation; yet it may be a desirable neurotic manifestation, by providing a safety valve against a worse one. It is held to be good that a neurotic young man should go to church daily to sing the Madonna's praises, if it keeps him from raping the girl next door. It is bad if, on the contrary, it inclines him to a manic condition that results in suicide or, much worse, a paranoiac one that results in murder. In such cases, however, "good" means psychologically successful in directing the patient toward what is deemed mental health, and "bad" means what has the opposite effect. So long as adherence to religious doctrines or the performance of religious duties issues in behavior that seems to be good for the mental health of the neurotic patient, they may be encouraged—much as a physician might encourage a cardiac patient to take certain pills to help his circulation, since he is happy to do this and unlikely to take the walking exercise that would be better for him. Religious sublimation is always to be encouraged where it is believed to have such therapeutic effects. Nevertheless, it is still, in the view in question, a neurotic manifestation and may sometimes be an exceedingly bad thing, as, for example, when it leads to psychosis. The philosopher who contends that all religion is psychologically reducible in such a way has nothing further to do, once he believes he has established that point.

Religion has also been identified with art. Santayana, in effect, has made such an identification. Religion, from this standpoint, may be regarded as a special kind of art, perhaps a more comprehensive kind than any other, but nevertheless having its essential nature in the artistic mode of experience. According to the particular aesthetic theory that is embraced, religion may then be regarded as a vast game or great act of artistic expression. If it were regarded as somehow the most fundamentally and comprehensively recreational of games, perhaps it might be accounted the healthiest of all, and if it were considered the grandest or best form of artistic expression, it might well be deemed man's noblest work of art. More often it is regarded, within this general view, as a very special and possibly not very desirable game, or else as a distorted and "sick" kind of artistic expression. In any case, there is nothing for the philosopher to do, once he has shown all this, except to subsume philosophy of religion under the general head of aesthetics. If religion be deemed a highly special or distorted form of art, then of course its place will be secondary or peripheral even in that very specialized kind of philosophical enterprise.

Again, no one who knows anything about religion would seek to deny that there are aesthetic elements in it, even that they may be very important constituents of it. If, however, religion be *entirely* reducible to art, it is likely (at least in most modern understandings of the nature of art) to be very bad art indeed, since didacticism and many other factors always tend to impede freedom of artistic expression.

Some groups calling themselves religious identify religion with ethics. In this view, the meaning of theological propositions and religious language in general is considered to lie exclusively in their moral implications. Modern situationists, rejecting the notion of an absolutist ethic, would say that the moral truths that religious propositions "mean" are truths relative to the moral aspect of some human situation, not truths independent of that situation. Since there are ways of expressing moral propositions much more clearly and without the useless extra "baggage" that religion introduces, religion, on such a view, can be at best no more than a "baby" moral philosophy, as it was to Hegel a baby metaphysic. It does nothing but express clumsily what ethics expresses with greater clarity and neatness. If moral approbations and disapprobations are themselves then shown, in Humean fashion, to be mere affirmations of feeling ("you ought not to steal" $\equiv$ "I dislike thieves" and "girls must be chaste" $\equiv$ "I like chaste girls"), then, of course, the futility of religious propositions, being only moral ones in disguise and poorly constructed, is easy to see.

From the standpoint taken in this book, the result of a philosophical inquiry in religion might be to reduce religion in one of the ways I have been describing, but in that case the philosophy of religion would have accomplished its task once and for all. This may be, indeed, its proper aim. Some contemporary philosophers have claimed that it is. It would also be (though strictly speaking, it is none of our business here), the death knell of religion even considered as, for example, art. For if the Gospel according to John differs from *Mary Poppins* only in scope and tone, then, as I have elsewhere suggested,[28] two results follow: (a) it could be much improved by anybody with a little theological learning and some dramatic skill, and (b) it could never possibly be good enough art, even then, to warrant its being declaimed to the same audience every week from the lips of even Sir Laurence Olivier, let alone from those of an ungainly assistant curate, even if the editing of the script were under the joint directorship of Alfred Hitchcock and the Archbishop of Canterbury.

As soon as religious language is taken to be stating or implying proposals containing truth-claims, there is a possibility of philosophical investigation, including logical exploration, of these proposals. For if religious people are saying something intelligible the fact that they are saying it in an odd or special or even awkward way does not matter. The business of the philosopher of religion is to understand what they are saying, to clarify it if need be, to point out what is implied, and to call attention, if necessary, to the blunders that religious people, like others, do make and which, if they are at all sincere, they are willing to inspect. It is also his business, however, to draw

[28] *God Beyond Doubt* (Philadelphia: J. B. Lippincott Co., 1966), pp. 163 f.

attention to alternative ontological, metaphysical, or other positions, and to demand why the alleged "revelation" the believer claims to possess is to be accounted a more adequate interpretation of human experience, even when this experience is supposedly illuminated by special "disclosures."

In other words, the philosopher of religion, without admitting the believer's claim, may take it seriously and nevertheless question whether the believer is really doing justice to his own beliefs and is not, on the contrary, traducing them by failing to examine and evaluate them. Needless to say, he will be exposing himself to the believer's displeasure at this point, more especially if the believer, in holding his beliefs, feels that kind of insecurity that often issues in obstinate refusal to examine them. The philosopher of religion may feel, of course, that he needs to go further, having shown the believer to be holding something that is untenable or even unintelligible.

By showing the believer's particular belief to be false or unintelligible he does not necessarily exhibit the falsity or unintelligibility of *all* religious belief. Moreover, to the extent that he is a genuine philosopher who, as such, cannot without ado admit the believer's spectrum of "revelation" or "disclosures," any more than he can accept without question any set of metaphysical presuppositions, he will be encouraged to examine further his own position in hope of finding hidden metaphysical presuppositions in it that might vitiate the authenticity of his philosophical skepticism. For if he were to fail in this self-criticism, he would be making himself liable to the same condemnation which he has rightly made of the believer and would merit the latter's *tu quoque*.

BIBLIOGRAPHICAL SUGGESTIONS

Abernethy, George L., and Langford, Thomas A. *Philosophy of Religion*. 2nd ed. New York: Macmillan Co., 1968 (first published in 1962). A very good selection of readings.

Allport, Gordon. *The Individual and His Religion*. New York: Macmillan Co., 1950. Useful and readable study of personality and religion.

Bergson, Henri. *The Two Sources of Morality and Religion*. Translated by R. A. Audra and C. Brereton. New York: Doubleday, Anchor Books, n.d. (first published in French in 1932). An important and influential work showing how the forms of religion are highly susceptible to growth.

Bertocci, Peter A. *Introduction to the Philosophy of Religion*. Englewood Cliffs, N.J.: Prentice-Hall, 1951. Written from the standpoint of theistic personalism.

Burr, N. R. *A Critical Bibliography of Religion in America*. 2 vols. Princeton, N.J.: Princeton University Press, 1961. A valuable scholarly tool.

Chan, Wing-tsit; Isma'īl Rāgī al Fārūqī; Kitagawa, J. M.; and Raju, P. T. *The*

Great Asian Religions. New York: Macmillan Co., 1969. An annotated anthology of key passages from the classical texts of the great Asian religions. Useful tool for beginners.

Clark, Gordon H. *Selections from Hellenistic Philosophy.* New York: Appleton-Century-Crofts, 1949. An anthology, useful for providing students with source materials for Hellenistic thought in the period between Aristotle and Augustine.

Collins, James. *The Emergence of Philosophy of Religion.* New Haven, Conn.: Yale University Press, 1967. A full-scale history of the development of philosophy of religion, with accounts of Kant and Hegel.

Ducasse, C. J. *A Philosophical Scrutiny of Religion.* New York: Ronald Press, 1953. Unsympathetic to theism.

Durkheim, Emile. *The Elementary Forms of the Religious Life.* Translated by J. W. Swain. New York: Collier Books, 1961. An anthropological classic.

Dye, J. W., and Forthman, W. H. *Religions of the World.* New York: Appleton-Century-Crofts, 1967. A collection of readings from classical texts of the great religions of the world.

Ferré, Frederick. *Basic Modern Philosophy of Religion.* New York: Charles Scribner's Sons, 1967.

Feuerbach, L. *Lectures on the Essence of Religion.* Translated by R. Manheim. New York: Harper & Row, 1967. Major work by an author who greatly influenced Marx and Freud. It is thoroughly reductionist: the gods are the wish-beings men create.

Frazer, J. G. *The Golden Bough.* New York: Macmillan Co., 1922. An abridgement of a very extensive and celebrated study of magic and religion in primitive societies.

Fromm, Erich. *Psychoanalysis and Religion.* New Haven, Conn.: Yale University Press, 1950.

Hartshorne, Charles. *The Logic of Perfection and Other Essays in Neoclassical Metaphysics.* La Salle, Ill.: Open Court Publishing Co., 1962. Not easy. Important modern defense of the ontological argument.

Hartshorne, Charles, and Reese, William L. *Philosophers Speak of God.* Chicago: University of Chicago Press, 1953. An anthology of key passages in the philosophy of religion.

Heschel, Abraham J. *God in Search of Man.* New York: Farrar, Strauss & Giroux, 1955. An attempt at a philosophy of Judaism.

Hick, John. *Philosophy of Religion.* Englewood Cliffs, N. J.: Prentice-Hall, 1963. Slender, but treats major issues succinctly.

Hume, David. *Dialogues Concerning Natural Religion.* Edited by N. K. Smith. Indianapolis: Bobbs-Merrill Co., 1963. Important classic.

Hutchison, J. A. *Paths of Faith.* New York: McGraw-Hill, 1969. A survey of the religions of the world.

James, E. D. *Prehistoric Religion.* New York: Barnes & Noble, 1957. An archaeological study.

Kant, Immanuel. *Religion Within the Limits of Reason.* Translated by T. M. Greene and H. H. Hudson. New York: Harper Torchbooks, 1960. Important classic.

Kaufmann, Walter. *Critique of Religion and Philosophy.* New York: Doubleday, Anchor Books, 1961. A lively critique of religious ideas.

Lewis, H. D. *Our Experience of God.* New York: Macmillan Co., 1959.

Lewis, H. D. *Philosophy and Religion.* New York: Barnes & Noble, 1965.

MacGregor, Geddes. *Introduction to Religious Philosophy.* Boston: Houghton Mifflin Co., 1959.

Macquarrie, John. *Twentieth-Century Religious Thought.* New York: Harper & Row, 1963. Useful survey of contemporary thinkers.

Magee, John B. *Religion and Modern Man.* New York: Harper & Row, 1967.

Mascall, E. L. *He Who Is.* New York: Longmans, Green & Co., 1943.

McPherson, Thomas. *The Philosophy of Religion.* Princeton, N.J.: Van Nostrand, 1965.

Nock, A. D. *Conversion.* New York: Oxford University Press, 1961 (first published in 1933). A study by a distinguished Harvard scholar of the impact of new religious ideas on the Mediterranean world from Alexander the Great to St. Augustine.

Norbeck, E. *Religion In Primitive Society.* New York: Harper & Brothers, 1961. An anthropological study.

Noss, John B. *Man's Religions.* 4th ed. New York: Macmillan Co., 1969. An excellent survey of the great religions of the world.

Onians, R. B. *The Origins of European Thought.* Cambridge: At the University Press, 1951. Very valuable study of key terms.

Otto, Rudolf. *The Idea of the Holy.* Translated by J. W. Harvey. 2nd ed. New York: Oxford University Press, 1950. A widely influential work which all students should read.

Phillips, D. Z. *Faith and Philosophical Enquiry.* New York: Schocken Books, 1971.

Popkin, Richard. *The History of Skepticism from Erasmus to Descartes.* New York: Humanities Press, 1960.

Porteous, A. J. D., Maclennan, R. D., and Davie, G. E., eds. *The Credibility of Divine Existence.* New York: St. Martin's Press, 1967. See especially pp. 375–397.

Rahner, Karl. *Hearers of the Word.* Translated by M. Richards. New York: Herder & Herder, 1969 (original German edition, 1963). Especially provocative on the question of the relation of theology to the philosophy of religion.

Schleiermacher, Friedrich. *On Religion.* Translated by J. Oman. New York: Harper & Row, 1958 (first published in 1799). A celebrated work and very influential on nineteenth-century Protestant theology.

Smart, Ninian, ed. *Historical Selections in the Philosophy of Religion.* New York: Harper & Row, 1962.

Smart, Ninian. *The Religious Experience of Mankind.* New York: Charles Scribner's Sons, 1969. A perceptive survey by a well-known scholar.

Smith, R. G. *Secular Christianity.* New York: Harper & Row, 1966. The best treatment in English on the theology and background of the "Death of God" movement that was influential in some circles in the sixties.

Taylor, E. B. *Religion in Primitive Culture.* New York: Harper Torchbooks, 1958 (first published in 1871). A standard work by a pioneer in anthropology.

Thomas, G. F. *Philosophy and Religious Belief.* New York: Charles Scribner's Sons, 1970.

Thomas, G. F. *Religious Philosophies of the West.* New York: Charles Scribner's Sons, 1965.

van Leeuwen, Arend Th. *Christianity in World History: The Meeting of the Faiths of East and West.* Translated by H. H. Hoskins. New York: Charles Scribner's Sons, 1964. A profound work by an erudite Dutch scholar who is both thoroughly accustomed to modern cybernetics and a master of Oriental languages as well as a penetrating theologian.

Wach, Joachim. *Types of Religious Experience.* London: Routledge & Kegan Paul, 1951.

Whitehead, Alfred North. *Religion in the Making.* New York: Macmillan Co., 1926. Not easy, but an important work by a great twentieth-century process philosopher.

Zuurdeeg, Willem F. *An Analytical Philosophy of Religion.* Nashville, Tenn.: Abingdon Press, 1971.

PROBLEMS IN THE
PHILOSOPHY OF RELIGION

I

PARADOX IN RELIGIOUS LANGUAGE

That is not good language that all understand not.

> *George Herbert (1593–1633),*
> *Jacula prudentum*

Human understanding has vulgarly occupied itself with
nothing but understanding, but if it would only take
the trouble to understand itself at the same time it would
simply have to posit the paradox . . . .

> *Søren Kierkegaard (1813–1855),*
> *Journal*

Religious Language

Twentieth-century philosophers have been more interested in linguistic
problems than were their precursors. Techniques have been developed for
the philosophical analysis of language, which entails special preoccupation
with questions of meaning. Contemporary philosophy of religion not only
reflects that general trend and conspicuously recognizes the importance of
such questions but is much concerned about them. The reason is simple.
The terms characteristically used in religious discourse are highly ambiguous.
True, many terms used in nonreligious subject matter are ambiguous, too:
even in the eighteenth century Berkeley was already alluding to that
ambiguity in his reply to the "minute philosophers" to whom he pointed
out that the terms physicists were using, such as "matter" and "force," were
just as ambiguous in their way as are theological terms like "grace" and
"faith." Theological language does present special problems, however, as
was seen long ago by religious philosophers like Thomas Aquinas and even
indeed by Plato.

Behind the whole literary history of mankind lay a long period of oral
tradition in which religion played a very important part. The key terms
used in attempts to express foci of religious interest were no doubt ambiguous

from the first and in the course of conceptual development became more and more so. The term "God" is a particularly outstanding example. To the ancient Greeks, the word *theos,* which it translates, could mean any wonder or unusual person or occurrence, such as a tornado or a man of sufficiently striking personality to cause a stir. We have a remnant of that primitive attitude in our acclamation of football "stars" and in our allusions to hurricanes as "Hilda" or "Bertha." The Hebrews, like other primitive peoples, had a particular tribal deity, Yahweh; and when, under the influence of their prophets, they came to acknowledge in monotheistic fashion one universal Lord of all things, they continued to use the same terminology they had applied to their local god. After Christianity had spread to the Gentile world and had assimilated its modes of conceptualization, philosophical subtleties in the term *theos* developed, for instance, in the highly specialized and intricate Trinitarian controversies. The ambiguity of the central term of religious discourse in the West was now great enough to be capable of spawning innumerable misunderstandings.

Much nearer our own time when, within the last century or two, Western scholars first tried to talk seriously about Eastern religious ideas, they naturally enough but with intellectually unfortunate consequences used the same term "God," in its various European translations, to represent both the extremely transcendental Allah of the Muslims and the many different sorts of pantheistic deities of the Orient. The term "God," though it functioned fairly well in practice within Christian society for hundreds of years, the ambiguities notwithstanding, has ceased to function at all well in today's highly pluralistic society, even as a practical device for those who are less careful in their use of terms than philosophers must be.

Anyone capable of even the slightest degree of abstract thinking can see that "God," even within the general framework of our Western tradition, is a very peculiar term and behaves, therefore, in a peculiar way. There is a temptation, on the one hand, to try to "pin it down" by "clothing" it with attributes: "God is a Mind or Spirit, just, loving, all-powerful," and so forth, till we end with an entity that is not so much incredible as unintelligible. On the other hand, we are tempted so to denude the term that it becomes, like "Nature," one that is applicable to every state of affairs. Then whatever is, is right because "God wills it," so that "God" becomes an omnibus name for "the way things are" or "the manner in which things behave." Once this despecification is established, anything you try to predicate of God yields only vacuousness. For instance, "I shall go to Cairo tomorrow, God willing": if "God" means simply the way things are or behave, then to say that is to say, "I shall go to Cairo tomorrow if my going to Cairo is what will in fact happen tomorrow," which is a glaring tautology. Worse, it might be a tautology used with deliberate intent to dress my selfish motives in the habiliments of religious piety, as when a Muslim promises to act if Allah so wills, meaning that he has no intention of ever taking action. He will not act "till the cows come home"; that is, he never will.

Analogical Method

The medieval scholastic way of treating the problem of attributing qualities to God may be summarized briefly as follows. When we apply qualities to God (e.g., "good" or "strong" or "loving") we are not applying them *univocally,* i.e., exactly as I might apply them to you or your dog; we are applying them in a special sense. Then the objection arises: if they are to be applied in a sense totally different from all others (i.e., in scholastic language, *equivocally*), we cannot possibly attach any meaning to it, since we have no way of comparing it to anything. In such circumstances, to say "God is strong and loving" is like saying "God is plik and plok." I can learn what a temperature of −40°F. is, though I may never have experienced a subzero temperature; but I cannot learn the meaning of a quality which, being allegedly *sui generis,* provides me with no clue to its nature. The schoolmen said, however, that there *is* a clue: our knowledge of God is, in their language, neither univocal nor equivocal; it is analogical. God's strength, though far grander than any human or even animal strength could ever be, is nevertheless not totally unlike it. In our attempt at conceptualizing God we are dealing with what is so far beyond us that we must not expect the divine attributes to be like anybody else's. If they were, we should *know* we were not talking of God, and we might well be justified in suspecting there was no God to talk about. Yet through the analogical method we are able to talk meaningfully of God.

This analogical method is attractive to the religious mind. It sits well with the experience of religious people. They admit they cannot pinpoint God as they could plot the latitude and longitude of Manhattan, or describe God as they might well feel able to describe an odd-shaped teapot or an unusual breed of horse; yet they feel they are aware of a Being who is far beyond them and beyond all else they know. There are no entities with which that Being may be properly compared; nevertheless, they find that he acts in a way that does have analogies. The baby mouse that encounters me and runs in terror no doubt finds me both awe-inspiring and unlike anything it has ever encountered before; yet no doubt also it instinctively recognizes in its own way that my awful presence and odd behavior are not totally different from its own. There is, as the schoolmen would have said, some *connaturality.* In the same view, we, being God's creatures, have some connaturality even with God, since he is our Creator.

As we shall soon see, analogy is closely related to paradox, to which we must now give our attention.

Paradox, Nonsense, and *Koan*

Tertullian, in the second century, wrote: "The Son of God died; it is by all means to be believed because it is absurd (*ineptum*). And he was buried and he rose again; the fact is certain, because it is impossible (*impossibile*)." [1] At first sight this utterance sounds parallel to one such as: "Camels are canaries: you are to believe me because you know, as I do, that camels cannot be canaries. Moreover, camels, which, as I have just said, are canaries, were systematically exterminated, became an extinct zoological species, and were then discovered to be roaming the earth in great abundance. This is, of course, impossible: that's why it is certainly true."

Some writers do, in fact, take the function of utterances like Tertullian's to be paradoxical in the sense in which the paradoxes used in Zen are paradoxical. Zen uses paradoxes to jolt people out of their ordinary ways of thinking and bring about a state of mind that is accounted by Zen teachers a desirable one. The process of so leading disciples into that mystical state is called *satori*. The subject of their meditation is called a *koan*. For instance, the teacher asks the student to meditate on the following *koan*: "the sound of one hand clapping." The act of clapping hands, as in applause, entails two hands; for without two hands it is physically impossible to do a hand-clap. In asking you to meditate on the sound of one hand clapping, the Zen teacher is obviously trying to perplex or shock. The *koan* "an armless man carrying a book under his arm," would also be suitable for the purpose, or, for that matter, "a virile mother." Such utterances used for therapeutic purposes are not, however, genuine paradoxes, and if Tertullian were doing no more than presenting a *koan*, he would not be uttering a genuine paradox at all. He would be doing, rather, something more like what an old history teacher of mine used to do when he thought the attention of his class was wandering: continuing in a rather soporific voice, he would say something like "Queen Victoria was so distressed at the news that she immediately called Disraeli on the telephone." Such an utterance, so used, is not intended to convey any kind of truth at all. It is intended to shock people, by its absurdity, out of inattention or out of their habitual grooves of thought. It is not a statement at all; it is more like an oblique version or special case of the utterances that John Austin called "performative," such as "shush" and "hurry up." That is to say, it is a way of mentally shaking up an audience.

Religious speakers sometimes resort to such methods, and to the extent that they do they are not doing anything fundamentally different from what a resourceful evangelist would be doing if, despairing of attracting his audience's attention by any other means, he rode a motorbike up the nave of the church. Paradox as used in religious language such as Tertullian's

[1] Tertullian, *De Carne Christi,* chap. 5.

may contain such an element, and with this in mind we shall reconsider Tertullian's paradox later; but at least some religious language is intended to do much more.

Paradox and Logic

"Paradox" comes from the Greek *paradoxon*, which suggests the notion of an unexpected meaning, a meaning somehow beyond (*para*) what is ordinarily to be expected in the discourse, beyond "received opinion." Logicians discuss various sorts of paradox, such as the famous "liar's paradox" associated with the ancient Cretan philosopher Epimenides, which arises when someone says, "I am lying," which is true if false and false if true. The paradoxes used in religious language are unlike this one. All paradoxes, however, relate to language and the questions they raise are logical questions. "Let us mobilize for peace" is more like the kind of language theologians use: while the verb "mobilize" is generally used of a nation's recruitment of soldiers for war, it is here used of a pacifist campaign. More like religious paradox still is the assertion that the more terrible the prospect of thermonuclear war the more improbable its actual occurrence. This is at first sight absurd. Then I suddenly see the point: "Oh, you mean because everybody would at last see what it would really be like and so take fright?"

Explorability of Paradox

Paradox as used in religious discourse is not as a rule logically inaccessible, to use the Bishop of Durham's phrase. It is logically explorable.[2] That is to say, it is not nonsense, such as "Tuesday is twins." It is not, however, straightforward statement, such as "sugar is sweet." People who are accustomed to thinking only in sugar-is-sweet ways inevitably find religious language strange, and some of them are inclined to suspect it must be nonsense. Of course some religious language can be nonsense just as can other sorts of language. Neither religious nor nonreligious language carries a guarantee of sense. In the absence of evidence to the contrary, I would take "the Incarnation is an onion" to be just as nonsensical and therefore as logically inaccessible as "Tuesday is twins."

Paradoxical pronouncements, as Ninian Smart has noticed in a passage cited by the Bishop of Durham,[3] "fulfil such a number of functions that by understanding the gist of them one can penetrate to the heart of the philosophy of religion."[4] Some religious writers, such as Tertullian and

---

[2] I. T. Ramsey, "Paradox in Religion," in *New Essays on Religious Language,* ed. Dallas M. High (New York: Oxford University Press, 1969), pp. 138 ff. The present discussion owes much to Ramsey.
[3] Ibid., p. 138.
[4] Ninian Smart, *Reasons and Faiths* (New York: Humanities Press, 1959), p. 20.

Kierkegaard, use very striking paradoxes; but all language, in so far as it may be called religious language, is basically paradoxical. When we say, as in the ancient collect, that "to serve God is to reign," [5] the first reaction might well be, "That's nonsense, for reigning is the opposite of servitude; no servitude, however enlightened its conditions, can be equated with reigning, because to reign is to be able to act as freely as one can possibly act, and to serve implies at least some measure of lack of that freedom." To this the Christian theologian in the wings will rejoin: "Yes, indeed; but you are missing the point. The point is that this particular act of serving is different from all other acts of serving because not only is it the only service I really want to perform; I so enjoy performing it that in the performance of it I feel, as we say, 'as happy as a king' and 'as free as a bird.' " If, however, one had to explain everything at this length one would never get past Sunday School level.

The classic Christian doctrine of the Virgin Birth is an especially interesting example of the use of paradox. It will also serve to introduce a consideration of Tertullian's paradox. When the antagonist of the doctrine of the Virgin Birth says, as he is naturally inclined to say, "This is biologically impossible," the naïve protagonist may fall into the trap by asking, "But how do you know it is impossible? Parthenogenesis in nonhuman species is not unknown to biologists. What if there should be incontestable evidence of a case of it in a contemporary human female? Or two cases? Or three? How many cases would you need?" Of course the situation is the opposite of what such a protagonist supposes. Anyone who provided even a single case of such human parthenogenesis would be destroying the whole point of the theological assertion about the Virgin Birth, which is intended to call attention to the extraordinary character of the event with which it is alleged to be connected.

When you affirm to an Orthodox Jew that the Son of God died, as is affirmed in Tertullian's paradox, you shock him deeply, for to him the gulf between God and man is so great that the idea of God's becoming man and of his being born and eventually dying sounds blasphemous, as blasphemous as if one were to say that God urinates. The Gentile world, however, which the writers of the Gospels had to keep in mind, was accustomed to pagan theological notions that allowed a much easier transition from deity to humanity and from humanity to deity. As in India, where avatars of deity are almost commonplace, so in the Hellenic world the notion of de-divinization and re-divinization was, as part of the folklore, a foolish old wives' tale rather than a horrific blasphemy. In communicating to Gentiles the nature of the Christian assertion, you had to spell out the character of the assertion. Before you could explore the logic of the paradox,

---

[5] *"Deus . . . cui servire, regnare est."* H. A. Wilson, ed., *The Gelasian Sacramentary* (Oxford: Clarendon Press, 1894), p. 272. Cf. St. Augustine, *Meditations,* chap. 32. The Anglican Book of Common Prayer has: "God . . . whose service is perfect freedom."

you had first to show that it was indeed a paradox and not, as the Greeks tended to think, a triviality. You had to explain that this was not another of the common stories about gods walking the earth. Because the event was *par excellence* extraordinary, it must be attended by extraordinary circumstances. If the biblical God became man, the event would be attended by extraordinary circumstances. If virgin births were merely rare, the occurrence of one would not be appropriate for a unique event. It would be appropriate only if it were (as we generally account it to be) wholly unknown in the human race. You are calling attention to the extreme oddity of your assertion, which is unlike any other assertion anybody could ever make about anything. You are not merely saying that the event had a few very unusual features; you are saying it is unparalleled.

The person who thinks that a few instances of human parthenogenesis would help to make the story more credible misses the whole point, which is that only when you appreciate the absurdity of the assertion are you in a position to believe or to disbelieve. Only then is the assertion *credible*, that is, *capable* of being believed. The first step is to grasp the absurdity of the assertion. There is nothing absurd about the notion of water floating in oil till you are aware of the scientific reason why it cannot happen. When you make the central assertion that God, the biblical God, has taken flesh and become man, you are saying something absurd precisely because, while other deities are expected to do that sort of thing, it is the one thing that the biblical God is not expected to do. The story of the Virgin Birth, as a satellite assertion, provides a pointer to the character of the central assertion.

So far, there is indubitably a large element of *satori*, of jolting the audience into seeing that the central assertion is not trivial, as you might suppose, but unique. It also appears to be absurd. Then the question may be put, "Now that you understand the character of the central assertion, do you believe or disbelieve?"

In point of history, Tertullian was arguing against a special view, that of the Marcionites, who held that the Incarnation did not actually occur. They held that it only appeared to occur, that is, that what people had actually seen was an appearance (*dokēma*): it *seemed* to them that Christ walked among them, was crucified, died, and rose from the dead. Not only, the Marcionites taught, was the resurrection of Christ a mere appearance; so also was the whole drama of the life and death of Christ. The Marcionites' interpretation of the central assertion of Christian orthodoxy made it seem more plausible to an influential school of thought of the day. Tertullian, in the very act of repudiating the Marcionite view and affirming that God did not merely present himself in appearance but actually took human flesh, is calling upon his audience to recognize the nature of the paradox. He has in fact begun its logical exploration, which later writers continued in their development of the doctrine of the Trinity, which is a highly elaborate exploration of the paradox.

The development of Trinitarian doctrine is so complex that an exposition of it within the space at our disposal is out of the question. It would need volumes. The modes of thought and language the patristic authors used are now outdated. Some of their thinking may have been muddled even in terms of their own modes of conceptualizing. Their undertaking was, however, an attempt to take very seriously the central assertion and to explore the logical structure of the paradox it involves, that "God [the biblical God] was in Christ, reconciling the world to himself." [6]

Religious discourse, then, is neither more nor less free of susceptibility to logical error than is any other kind of language. In religious discourse one can fall into the mistake of mixing up types or levels of language just as readily as one can when talking about zoology or town planning. Moreover, since most people are less accustomed to the use of religious language than they are to the use of other kinds, they are more likely to fall into logical errors in "God-talk" than in talk about other subjects. A person might be so inexperienced and untrained in the handling of religious language as to see no logical impropriety in asking for a photograph of the Holy Ghost, though it would never occur to him to ask for a photograph of energy. Most religious assertions are couched in such an extremely cursive shorthand that their deceptive simplicity may trap even the wary. For instance, consider the statement "God is love." This is logically akin to "War is hell." Both call for much more explication, and in the course of the explication, paradoxes will be unfolded. Their unfolding will demand logical exploration, as do utterances such as "happiness is a bluebird" and "this job is the Devil."

Falsifiability

Some modern philosophers have accounted religious discourse meaningless because they claim that it abuses language in such a way as to void it of meaning. Those who defend the meaningfulness of religious discourse argue that, on the contrary, religious discourse, far from so impoverishing the meanings of words, enriches words by investing them with new meanings. The occasion for the dispute lies in the characteristic use of paradox in religious discourse.

Let us consider a case cited by Professor Alasdair MacIntyre to bring out the point at issue.[7] By saying "I have seen red grass," I attract the interest of a botanist who asks me to point to what I have in mind. "But that is green," he says. To which I reply, "Well, I call it red." When it turns out that I am calling mailboxes red too—that is, making no distinction between red and green and calling them both red—the botanist is no longer interested in my assertion. It is plain to him that I am abusing language.

[6] 2 Corinthians 5:19.
[7] Alasdair C. MacIntyre, *Difficulties in Christian Belief* (New York: Philosophical Library, 1960), pp. 29 ff.

Perhaps the reason is that I am colorblind and therefore unable to make the fine discrimination in the length of light waves that people with normal color vision can make. Perhaps I am just playing a practical joke on my botanist friend. No matter. The point is that through my abuse of language I have obliterated the contrast between "red" and "green." There is no longer any use in asking me whether anything is red or green, because I do not make the distinction. You might as well ask a person tone deaf and wholly ignorant of music whether the orchestra had been playing Beethoven or Chopin. He could not tell, for he would call both noise.

The Christian believers, MacIntyre reminds us, are charged with abusing language precisely in that way. Christian believers assert, "God is good; God loves us." "To say that we are cared for by an all-good, all-powerful being would ordinarily lead us to expect immunity from ills; if this is said in such a sense that we are not entitled to expect this then language is being distorted and misused." [8] Since the utterance could not be falsified it does not really say anything; therefore, it is not an assertion at all. It is in the same case with the "red grass" utterance, which after all turns out to be no assertion either; for in order to make an assertion that *x* is red I must be able to call things blue, green, yellow, and so forth, and when I call everything red, the word is meaningless.

The "God loves us" case is said by some to be similar because "it is of the essence of assertions that they declare one state of affairs to hold at the expense of others," and believers talk in such a way that it would seem that no conceivable events could shake their confidence that God loves them. If God blesses their lives with every sort of joy, they say he is showing his goodness by sparing them from affliction; if God sends them more plagues than Job knew, they say he is showing his goodness by chastising them, to mark his having singled them out for special favor. Whatever God ordains is not only right but an expression of his love, whether he surrounds them with bounty or sends them cruel disasters. The objection, then, is that "God is good; God loves us" becomes meaningless: it does not "declare one state of affairs to hold at the expense of others," for there are no others.

MacIntyre points out that the objection does not really stand. The believer "holds to his faith *in spite of*" the disasters that befall him. The believer does recognize a contradiction between his afflictions and his belief that "God is good; God loves us." "He could not see even an apparent contradiction of this kind if he treated his assertions as unfalsifiable." [9]

I think an even more important objection is that the believer may also acknowledge the possibility of a very different state of affairs. The universe might be godless, in which case both the "blessings" and the "disasters" would be entirely fortuitous. They would attest nothing at all other than

[8] Ibid., p. 31.
[9] Ibid., p. 32.

themselves. The belief that "God is good; God loves us" (upon whatever evidence it is grounded) does make an assertion and is therefore meaningful, for there is another possible state of affairs that it very sharply excludes.

Paradox in Symbolizing God

There remains a situation that is properly called paradoxical. The belief in God's goodness and love for his creatures is not based on the number or even the quality of the blessings the believer thinks he is getting. The believer has already determined his belief on other grounds. So he can say (and here of course is the paradox) that God is guiding him through life at all times. God has not promised a smooth passage. As the fourteenth-century English mystic Mother Julian of Norwich put it, "God has not told me I shall not be tempested, or travailed or afflicted; he has promised only that I shall not be overcome."

To say this does not, of course, dispose of the problem of evil,[10] which is one of the thorniest in our field and will be considered in a later chapter. In the typical believer's answer that Mother Julian provides is to be found, however, a clue to the resolution of the paradox we have been considering. When I trustfully put myself into the hands of a skipper, I do not expect him to provide me with a calm sea all the way. What I expect is that, in rough seas or calm, he will see me safely to my haven. Whatever the grounds of my trust that justifies my putting myself in his hands, I expect of him only that he can handle any situation. Every morning when I wake up, I rejoice that he is at the helm. My gratitude for and joy in having him to take care of me, far from waning in a rough sea, is more likely in that circumstance to be augmented and intensified.

The objector will now say something like this: "Religious people, in saying as they do that we are to think of God as a super-skipper, are attempting to describe his function, in relation to us, as they do in other similar figures such as that of the Good Shepherd. But they are cheating. For at other times the same people call him "Father Almighty," saying that he creates everything and can create everything any way he chooses. Why, then, since he is said to be not only almighty but also good and loving *par excellence,* doesn't he create everything in such a way as to preclude suffering?" What this question seems to disclose is: while the skipper explanation attends to the paradox as set forth, there is another, separate paradox, *apart from* other paradoxes that may arise in regard to the problem of evil. Where God, in his relation to us, is said to function with almightiness, the figure of a trustworthy skipper or loving shepherd ceases to be appropriate, for the skipper's skill and the shepherd's tender care are necessary only because

---

[10] Mother Julian has in fact a special view of the problem of evil, arising from her Neo-Platonist tendencies. The correctness or otherwise of her view on that subject is irrelevant to the point with which we are now concerned.

every skipper, however skillful and trustworthy, like every shepherd, however loving and careful, is facing forces that resist him, while it would seem that God, being creator, almighty, all-powerful, faces no such forces but, rather, *creates the forces he also controls*. What skipper creates the ocean he sails, to say nothing of the boat and its passengers? What shepherd creates the sheep under his hand and the very ground on which they graze? It would seem that where God is called "almighty" we cannot properly say that he functions in such ways, with the specific limitations that such functioning implies.

This separate paradox may be stated as follows. Since God, being all-benevolent and all-competent, faces no limiting forces that he has not created, the use of figures that imply that he does face such limiting forces is singularly inappropriate; yet religious people habitually depict him by figures that imply such limiting forces, and they consider the use of them singularly appropriate.

We should notice carefully here that, as the foregoing presentation of the paradox suggests, religious people may be simply making a mistake in logic. That is, it may be that to acclaim figures like "skipper" and "shepherd" as appropriate qualifiers for God while at the same time using the qualifier provided in the traditional Creeds, "Father Almighty" (which *ex hypothesi* excludes as inappropriate the use of such figures), is due to a logical oversight. It may be, then, furthermore, that this oversight should cause religious people to say, "Oops, didn't notice—must choose one alternative and reject the other, so demolishing the paradox." In fact, however, religious people are by no means willing to let the matter be disposed of in that way. On the contrary, they are usually inclined to say, rather: "No, the paradox says something special about God. It's not an either-or; it's a both–and." But how can it be?

In the particular case in point the paradox might be approached in the following way. In symbolizing the concept of God two separate and distinct models are being used as if they were not separate and distinct, with inevitable confusion. On the one hand God is conceptualized as the Creator of all things, including of course both man and nature; on the other hand God is conceptualized as the divine artist, in the manner of Plato's *Timaeus*. In the latter case the skipper/shepherd type of figure is appropriate; in the former case it is not. We must therefore either choose the one and exclude the other, or else find a way of exhibiting the structure of the symbol so as to make all the qualifiers (e.g., skipper and Almighty Father) fit the restructured model. For instance, God, though he creates nature and exposes his creatures to it in the course of giving them the opportunity to accomplish their spiritual evolution through struggle with it, might assume also the skipper/shepherd type of function to aid them in the struggle. Such a restructuring would not solve the whole of the problem of evil, of course; but it would exhibit the character of the model with which we are confronted and that gives rise to the paradox we have just been considering. As one writer puts it, the type of meaning a symbol has may be "a function of the degree of specificity of its definition." [11]

We might acquiesce in principle in Bochenski's view that probably "the great majority of believers, as they are now, do not have any real experience of God at all"; and that the term "God," as used by them, must be functioning, therefore, as a description learned from their creeds, not as a name for the subject of an actual encounter.[12] Nevertheless, as that author admits, though they have no knowledge of God beyond what the creeds have described to them, they do add to this description a subjective factor, out of their own personal state of mind. The result of all this is that when they are presented with a paradox in what they are saying, they have no referent to look to that would enable them to explore it and therefore readily account it, to use Ramsey's term, logically inaccessible. Such "believers," not claiming "experience of God" or "encounter with God," would talk of "mystery"; but by "mystery" they would intend only the subjective puzzlement and perplexity that a logically inaccessible paradox evokes. Or else, in other cases, they might mean that they were confronted with an interesting possibility such as the existence of a monster in Loch Ness.

What Is Mystery?

Much confusion arises over the use of the term "mystery." To believers who, rightly or wrongly, are convinced that their belief has an ontological ground, religious language is not mysterious in the sense that its meaning is inaccessible or that it deals with an interesting possibility. It is mysterious in the sense that it calls for exploration. Such a believer's reaction is not entirely unlike that of a scientist who is confronted by a phenomenon that does not fit what he knows of "nature" but which he knows must fit and therefore is the occasion for exploration. Gerard Manley Hopkins once wrote to Robert Bridges: "You do not mean by mystery what a Catholic does. You mean an interesting uncertainty. . . . But a Catholic means by mystery an incomprehensible[13] certainty . . . the clearer the formulation, the greater the interest." [14]

Where "mystery" means an interesting uncertainty, there is no need for paradox because one is dealing with a mere possibility. The Loch Ness monster is mysterious in the sense that, though on the one hand there may

---

[11] Frank B. Dilley, *Metaphysics and Religious Language* (New York: Columbia University Press, 1964), p. 113.
[12] Joseph M. Bochenski, O.P., "The Structure of Religious Discourse," in *Religious Language and the Problem of Religious Knowledge*, ed. Ronald E. Santoni (Bloomington: Indiana University Press, 1968), pp. 125 ff.
[13] That is, "presently incomprehensible" *not* "incapable of being comprehended."
[14] *The Letters of Gerard Manley Hopkins* (Oxford: Oxford University Press, 1935), pp. 187 f.

be no such creature in the lake, on the other hand such a creature may after all be there, which is an interesting subject for reflection and further investigation. This is not at all what is meant by, say, the mystery of the Trinity. Here we are saying: God is Three; yet, as the Jewish Shema proclaims, God is One. The utterance purports to be a truth-claim, and the claim is that the paradoxical utterance is not comprehensible in the sense in which "there are three buttons on my jacket" is comprehensible. Nevertheless, though not comprehensible in that manner, it may be logically explorable, and that is what is normally to be expected of religious utterances. This does not mean that the exploration will turn out to yield satisfying results in every case, for some of the utterances may have been ill-conceived in the first place. As we have seen, religious language is not at all immune from the logical errors that enter into other kinds of language.

Open-mindedness

In order to explore a paradox, one must be sufficiently open-minded to inquire into the situational context. The statement "I was in an earthquake and didn't know it" would sound paradoxical to many Londoners and New Yorkers, who tend to think of an earthquake as the sort of disaster that devastated San Francisco in 1906. When I first went to live in California I occasionally received anxious letters from kind friends who, having read of an earthquake in California, feared I might have been swallowed up and besought me for reassurance of my escape. I had to explain that seismographs often record tremors that are reported as earthquakes but are so slight that most people scarcely notice them.

Again, suppose I were to tell a villager on one of the Greek islands that the English are notoriously fond of animals yet will not allow donkeys on their best roads. He might well think it very paradoxical: if you really liked donkeys, what could possibly make you keep them off your roads, especially your best roads?

One man's paradox is another's truism: to anyone living in Los Angeles or New York the assertion that you can be lonelier in a large city than anywhere else in the world is a truism; but to a person who had always lived in a rural community the notion that you could be lonely with millions of people around you might seem so paradoxical as to evoke incredulous laughter. At a more sophisticated level the notion might still seem paradoxical: the city, the great civilizer of men, makes them feel more alienated from one another than country folk in sparsely populated areas commonly feel among themselves. When to this we exclaim, "How so?" we mean we should expect the opposite, *at any rate at first sight*. We call the statement paradoxical because something that seems necessary to its logical structure is missing. To this crucial point we shall return at the conclusion of this chapter.

Analogy and Paradox

In early forms of reasoning, for example in ancient Chinese thought, simple forms of analogy constitute a standard method of exhibiting logical connection. There is always paradox. The sea is like a raging monster; a girl is like a flower; the earth is like a mother. All these assertions are obviously open to objection. The sea is in many respects as unlike a raging monster as anything could be; girls, unlike flowers, can be intelligent or stupid, cowardly or brave; and no geophysicist would ever use motherhood as a key idea for dealing with his subject matter. Nevertheless, there are respects in which the assertions are all true. If, for instance, we call the earth a mother, we are drawing attention to those respects in which she does function in one way or another as a mother functions, and we are dimming out as irrelevant to our particular interest those other respects (no doubt far more numerous) in which she is no more like a mother than is a potato or the Rock of Gibraltar. As better instruments are devised for exhibiting logical structure, loose analogical methods give place to more precise forms such as the syllogism. These more accurate logical forms are sharper and therefore for many purposes also better instruments; but for other purposes they are not so well adapted and so do not work. Their unworkability is especially noticeable when we come to deal with relations between religious concepts, especially when the conceptualization of God is directly involved.

In the thirteenth century, the medieval schoolmen of western Europe developed and made use of the analogical method we have already considered, in their attempts to exhibit what they took to be the relation in which God as Creator stands to his creatures, that is, to all that is not God. The greatest of these medieval thinkers, Thomas Aquinas, taught that while God is fundamentally beyond human knowledge (his being the Creator *means* his being beyond the grasp of his creatures), he is *not in all respects* intellectually inaccessible to us. While the logically puzzling, disorienting quality in paradoxical statements is often blatant, it may be less so when it is hidden or veiled under an analogy. The notion that there is a paradoxical element in analogy requires some examination. For this purpose we may look at the analogical method that is classic in medieval discussion of God.

The medieval method of analogy has been much reexamined by contemporary thinkers.[15] The most familiar form of analogical method used in theological discussion suggests that though God and man are infinitely separated, so that man cannot really be said to know God, man's ignorance is nevertheless not total. This is not to say that God and man are in the least like each other. It does mean, however, that as between the relation in which God stands to his being and the relation in which man stands to his being, some likeness may be affirmed.

---

[15] E.g., Eric Mascall, *Existence and Analogy* (London: Longmans, Green & Co., 1949).

All such analogies are based on presuppositions. For instance, a quantitative analogy such as $\dfrac{5:25}{16:80}$ presupposes that numbers behave in a certain way. Analogies do not provide logical proofs, deductive or inductive. On the contrary, they exhibit paradox. For example, God and man are so disparate that nothing can be predicated of the one that can be predicated of the other; yet there is some connection that gives us a clue, so that we cannot be said to be totally without knowledge.

How does the classic analogical method work? An analogy has four terms. The number 5 has no resemblance at all to the number 16; but the relation in which 5 stands to 25 is analogous to the relation in which 16 stands to 80. When Keats, in his "Ode to a Nightingale," dreams that

> haply the Queen-Moon is on her throne,
> Cluster'd around by all her starry Fays,

he does not assert that there is any likeness between any queen and the moon; nor does he suggest that the court ladies really resemble stars. What he does say is that the *relation* between the moon and the stars that surround it on a clear night has something in common with the *relation* between a queen seated on her throne and the ladies of the court who attend her. We can, if we please, call the moon a queen and the stars her ladies-in-waiting; but if we forget the analogy of relationship we shall have lost the clue to the resemblance. Even if we remember the clue we must remember also that in the clue is but the affirmation of a paradox.

Professor Macquarrie, in reminding us that analogical language (and all symbolic language) is paradoxical, writes: "Simply to affirm an analogue or symbol is to fall into that over-literalness which, if we are applying the image to God, leads into an attitude of idolatry. Whatever symbol or analogue is affirmed must be at the same time denied; or, better still, whenever one symbol is affirmed, others that will modify it and correct it must be affirmed at the same time." When Christ is called a door, we must remember that he is also called The Way; he is called Shepherd, but also Lord; Son of man, but also Logos. In a perceptive passage, Macquarrie also draws attention to what happened when Bishop Robinson's much publicized rebellion against the use of high, "up-there" imagery led him to shift the stress to symbols of depth; the last state was even worse than the first. Neither symbol in isolation will do well; but "if these two symbols were held in tension, a big advance would be made toward a more adequate thought of God." [16]

Not the least value of the analogical method is that it exhibits polarities in such a way as to advance thought about God. The paradoxical language it uses is a protection against that literalistic one-sidedness that leads to idolatry. Pascal's hint that God is to be likened to a point moving at infinite speed is enlightening only when it is seen as part of the paradox that God

---

[16] John Macquarrie, *God-Talk* (New York: Harper & Row, 1967), p. 228.

is also to be conceived as the ground of all being—and much else besides. The logic of paradoxical language about God can never be seen in the easy, cut-and-dried manner in which we see the Law of Contradiction. We might as well hope to explain biological phenomena by physics. Logicians have developed some very finely honed modern instruments, but the finest of chisels or screwdrivers is no better than the crudest when what you need are forceps. By the same token, when you need forceps, even a pair of pliers possibly might do—but a screwdriver, never.

What Makes Paradox Logically Explorable?

We have seen that some paradoxes, such as the *koan*, are intended to be logically unexplorable. Trying to explore the logical structure of such a paradox would be as misguided as trying to explore logically what is being predicated in an exclamation like "whee" or "whoosh." We have also seen, however, that a statement may be called paradoxical when something necessary to its logical structure appears to be missing, resulting in what looks like a contradictory or otherwise unintelligible utterance. As a commonplace example from nonreligious discourse we might consider, "Sour cream is not sour." If I happened to be unfamiliar with the condiment that is so called, I might well protest: "Stop, you are contradicting yourself. If the cream is sour, as you call it, it cannot be nonsour, as you say it is." You would then easily enough explain the reason for my misunderstanding, and we should agree that the paradox had been resolved.

The resolution is not always so easy, however. To say we all begin to die as soon as we are born (as has often been said) is readily intelligible to any biologist; yet you would not account me entirely stupid if I objected, "No, no, you mean we begin to *live* then, as separate beings." You might have to say quite a lot about the nature of growth and decay before I was willing to say I was satisfied. If you could have said to anyone last century that space is curved, he might well have thought it as silly as saying "time is wavy," or even, "Tuesday is triangular." Yet every educated person today would understand your meaning. If you were to say, as Christians characteristically say, "I didn't know what freedom was till I became Christ's slave (*doulos*)," then a hearer unfamiliar with the nature of Christian experience might very well never admit that the paradox was logically explorable at all. To any Christian, however, the experience is so familiar that he has to remind himself that it can seem paradoxical, much as a biologist has to remind himself that not everybody can be expected to see at once that everything begins to die as soon as it begins to live.

What makes a paradox logically explorable is (1) that it is intended to make sense, and (2) that it is at least theoretically possible for an unprejudiced person to inquire whether it does or not. Let us see more precisely what this means, especially in regard to religious discourse.

Donald Baillie, after noting that for Christians the Incarnation is "the supreme paradox," goes on to say that there is an "all-round paradox" and that the Incarnation is, rather, "the point at which the constant and ubiquitous paradox reaches its peak." Noting that Kierkegaard's thought has been called "the theology of paradox," he observes that there are many historical sources for the paradoxical tendencies of all theological thought. He suggests, indeed (rightly, I think), that religious discourse is by its very nature paradoxical.[17] "The reason why the element of paradox comes into all religious thought and statement is because God cannot be comprehended in any human words or in any of the categories of our finite thought.[18] God can be known only in a direct personal relationship, an 'I-and-Thou' intercourse, in which He addresses us and we respond to Him. As it has sometimes been put, God cannot legitimately be 'objectified.' " This "logic of encounter" as Frederick Ferré calls it,[19] is open to the obvious objection that what is taken to be colloquy is in fact soliloquy. Though Baillie deals in advance, in his own way, with that objection, the objection is in some ways more serious than he recognizes. Yet on examination we find that it is not a logical objection. A typical presentation of it would include drawing attention to the admitted possibility of error. A religious person may, and a deeply religious person often will, admit that what he took to be a genuine encounter with God has since been shown, in his own experience, to be no more than a probing of his own psyche, in contrast to another experience that he still holds to be "the real thing." But how can we know that this latter experience will not turn out to be yet another soliloquy dressed up as colloquy? How indeed? But that is a metaphysical question. Important though it be in its own right, it does not necessarily affect the explorability of the theologian's paradoxical language.

Even a lunatic's language may be logically explorable. He claims to be Napoleon. You say, "Don't be silly: Napoleon died more than a century ago." He *may* retort by throwing the table at you, showing that he is unwilling to explore the paradox with you; but he might reply (as well-educated and intelligent psychotics often will, for they can often be extremely rigorous in their logic, once you grant their major premise) that the supposed evidence of Napoleon's death is unreliable, that in fact he was deep-frozen, has just recently come out of it, as in the science-fiction stories, and is in good health. Restraining your smile you say, "How then, Excellency, do you speak English with such a definitely American accent?" "I studied it in my last months at St. Helena under an American teacher." And so forth. You would be very far from convinced by his claim, of course; yet even in such an extreme

---

[17] D. M. Baillie, *God Was in Christ* (New York: Charles Scribner's Sons, 1948), pp. 106 ff.
[18] Cf. Tersteegen's much quoted observation, "a God comprehended is no God."
[19] Frederick Ferré, *Language, Logic and God* (New York: Harper & Row, 1961), Chap. 8, pp. 94 ff.

case it would have become less easy to assert that what he was claiming was unintelligible, for in his own way he would have already attended in advance of the interview to the various logical entailments.

So much for the most extreme case, that of the lunatic. Consider now, briefly, that of an innocent man accused of murder and caught in a web of circumstances that all point to his guilt. The prosecution is even able to produce photographs first showing him taking the deceased woman into his arms on the edge of the cliff and then showing her hurtling through the air to her death on the rocks below. In defense he asserts that he was in fact tenderly embracing her on the cliff when someone hidden in a fissure of the rock below threw up an "invisible" nylon rope, lassoed her ankle, and jerked her out of his arms, precipitating her to her death. In face of the evidence, the accused's claim might well seem to be not only false but so absurd as to be meaningless. The counsel for the prosecution would be quick to tell the jury that since the accused's story did not even make sense he would not even have to trouble them with an attempt at rebuttal. He would assert that there could be no rebuttal, since the story, being not even a cleverly constructed falsehood, was without meaning and therefore could not be either intelligibly asserted or refuted. If, however, evidence came out years afterwards proving that the accused's story was after all a substantially correct account of what had happened, people might then say, in effect: "Since it turned out to be not meaningless after all, the Court ought to have taken it seriously and examined it." In other words, it had been logically explorable all the time.

Donald Baillie is right in pointing out that religious discourse, which is characteristically paradoxical through and through, refers to oddities in the experience of the individual who utters the paradoxes and is logically explorable only in terms of that experience. No one can fail to see the obvious objection to Baillie's standpoint, namely, that all religious discourse may refer to a purely subjective state of mind. Indeed, Baillie makes himself peculiarly vulnerable to that objection by shifting the ground, as he does, from the Incarnation, as the central paradox of Christian faith, to the paradox of grace, which he calls a "far greater and deeper paradox" still.[20]

Ronald Hepburn, a vigorous critic of religious truth-claims, points out that where the "vital analogy . . . is that between meeting people and meeting God," as in the case of "encounter" arguments like Baillie's, the "earthly" analogue is not strong enough to bear the weight of the "heavenly" one.[21] In other words, statements about God turn out to be really statements about human experience, and all orthodox Christians would reject that understanding of the meaning of their faith. This objection, however, though it holds good as a critique of the tendency to try to "prove" the existence of "God" from an explication of the meaningfulness of certain items of

[20] D. M. Baillie, *God Was in Christ,* p. 114.
[21] Ronald Hepburn, *Christianity and Paradox* (London: Watts & Co., 1958), p. 30.

theological discourse such as "grace" and "freedom," does not injure the explorability of the paradoxes. To explore them is, indeed, what all theology is trying to do. The paradox will reveal an oddity within human experience, such as that when I most feel like crying I laugh or that when I am at my wits' end the solution suddenly "comes to me"; but if that is all a paradox of religious discourse reveals, it must not be used as a pretense for proving the existence of a Being independent of us human beings who is our Creator. Questions about the existence and nature of such a Creator are questions about truth, while questions about paradox are questions about meaning. In arguing that paradox is logically explorable our concern has been only with questions about meaning. In a later chapter we shall turn to questions about the evidence for and proof of truth-claims.

QUESTIONS ON CHAPTER I

1 Why are modern philosophers, including philosophers of religion, so concerned about problems of meaning?

2 What does the analogical method claim to do?

3 What is the difference between a paradox and a *koan*?

4 "Men die as do cats and dogs; yet for men death is the gate of fuller life." Explain the paradox.

5 What would proved instances of human parthenogenesis do for the orthodox Christian doctrine of the Virgin Birth? Explain.

6 Critically consider Bochenski's view that lack of firsthand religious experience deprives the majority of believers of a referent that might enable them to explore religious paradox.

7 Consider ambiguities in the term "mystery."

8 What makes one paradox logically explorable and another logically inaccessible?

BIBLIOGRAPHICAL SUGGESTIONS
See also under Chapters II and III.

Bendall, Kent, and Ferré, Frederick. *Exploring the Logic of Faith.* New York: Association Press, 1962.

Bochenski, Joseph. *The Logic of Religion.* New York: New York University Press, 1965.

Burnaby, John. *Christian Words and Christian Meanings.* New York: Harper & Row, 1955.

Evans, Donald. *The Logic of Self-Involvement.* London: Student Christian Movement Press, 1963. An attempt at understanding theological language as performative.

Ferré, Frederick. *Language, Logic, and God.* New York: Harper & Row, 1961.

Flew, A., and MacIntyre, A., eds. *New Essays in Philosophical Theology.* London: Student Christian Movement Press, 1955. A widely quoted collection of essays, most of which are hostile to theism.

Hepburn, Ronald. *Christianity and Paradox.* New York: Humanities Press, 1958. Very critical of some contemporary theologians.

High, Dallas M., ed. *New Essays on Religious Language.* New York: Oxford University Press, 1969.

Hutchison, J. A. *Language and Faith.* Philadelphia: Westminster Press, 1963.

Macquarrie, John. *God-Talk.* New York: Harper & Row, 1967.

Mascall, E. L. *Words and Images.* New York: Ronald Press, 1957.

Mitchell, Basil, ed. *Faith and Logic.* London: Allen & Unwin, 1957.

Moreau, J. L. *Language and Religious Language.* Philadelphia: Westminster Press, 1961.

Ramsey, Ian. *Christian Discourse: Some Logical Explorations.* London: Oxford University Press, 1965.

Ramsey, Ian. *Models and Mystery.* London: Oxford University Press, 1964.

Ramsey, Ian. *Religious Language.* New York: Macmillan Co., 1957.

Ramsey, Ian, ed. *Words About God.* New York: Harper & Row, 1971. Very useful collection by authors of widely divergent opinions.

Santoni, R. E., ed. *Religious Language and the Problem of Religious Knowledge.* Bloomington, Ind.: Indiana University Press, 1968.

Savage, C. W. "The Paradox of the Stone." *The Philosophical Review* 76 (1967): 74–79.

Srzednicki, T. "On Metaphor." *The Philosophical Quarterly* 10 (July 1960): 228–237. Religious language is not specifically discussed.

Wilson, John. *Language and Christian Belief.* New York: St. Martin's Press, 1958.

Wisdom, John. *Paradox and Discovery.* Oxford: Basil Blackwell, 1965.

II

SYMBOL AND REALITY

There is no more welcome gift to men than a new symbol.

Ralph Waldo Emerson (1803–1882),
Letters and Social Aims

...no one "invents" the picturesque slang spoken in America; it just springs up in inexhaustible abundance from the fertile soil of colloquial speech. Religious rites and their stock of symbols must have developed in much the same way from beginnings now lost to us.... They have grown spontaneously out of the basic conditions of human nature, which are never invented but are everywhere the same.

C. G. Jung (1875–1961), Psychology of
Religion: West and East

What Is a Symbol?

Among the ancient Greeks two *symbola*, or tallies, were used by the parties to an agreement. They were made by breaking a bone or coin, one half of which was kept by one party and the other half by the other. The term *symbolon* was also applied to treaties or covenants between two states. Though it has several senses and is associated with a nexus of ideas, the dominant idea is that of the coming together of two parts that fit, the one somehow attesting the other. A symbol is nowadays commonly defined as a visible thing that stands for or suggests something invisible. We must try to see what this means.

Symbols are indispensable in religion. If there were any way of conveying God without symbols, there would be no need for religion at all, since one could possess the reality that the symbol purports to represent. Religious concerns cannot be expressed without symbols, as we shall abundantly see. The basic terms of religion are symbols, and so must also be every expression of it, verbal or nonverbal. The Chinese Tao Tê Ching begins as follows:

> The Tao that can be told of
> Is not the Absolute Tao;
> The names that can be given
> Are not Absolute names.[1]

We should first of all observe, however, that although symbols play a special part in religious communication and although religious thought needs a special symbolic structure, symbols are by no means peculiar to religion. We could not get through even the most commonplace day of our lives without the use of symbols.

Prose, Poetry, and Symbol

A statement such as "the cat ate the goldfish" uses symbols, for words are symbols. It is, however, a statement in pure prose, in contrast to

> Time, you old gypsy man,
> Will you not stay,
> Put up your caravan
> Just for one day?[2]

which is pure poetry. Prose is not, as some suppose, nearer reality than poetry; indeed, it is more remote. Austin Farrer, a born poet as well as a trained philosopher and highly original theologian, expressed this truth vividly: "There is a current and exceedingly stupid doctrine that symbol evokes emotion and exact prose states reality. Nothing could be further from the truth: exact prose abstracts from reality, symbol represents it. And for that very reason, symbols have some of the many-sidedness of wild nature." [3] Here is one of the most profound insights into the nature of symbols. We shall return to it later.

Symbol and Sign

Paul Tillich distinguished symbols from signs, noting, however, that they do have something in common.[4] Symbols "point beyond themselves to something else." A sign, such as the red light at a street intersection, points beyond itself to something else, namely, the command to stop traffic. It is, however, no more than a conventional device. The "stop" sign might as well be purple and the "go" sign pink. Red has no connection with stopping except by an entirely formal convention. We talk of algebraic signs,

---

[1] Lin Yutang, ed., *The Wisdom of China and India* (New York: Random House, Modern Library Edition, 1955), p. 583.
[2] Ralph Hodgson, "Time, You Old Gypsy Man," in *Poems of To-day* (London: Sidgwick & Jackson, 1918), p. 7.
[3] Austin Farrer, *A Rebirth of Images* (Boston: Beacon Press, 1963), p. 21.
[4] Paul Tillich, *Dynamics of Faith* (New York: Harper & Row, 1957), p. 41. ·

such as those for "plus" and "minus," which are likewise simply conventions. We might just as well signify "plus" by means of an acute accent and "minus" by a grave one. Language is at least partly in the same position.

Tillich wished to distinguish sharply such conventional signs from symbols, which in his view "participate" in that to which they point, as signs do not. The distinction may seem forced. For instance, he cites the example of the flag, which "cannot be replaced except after an historic catastrophe that changes the character of the nation which it symbolizes. An attack on the flag is . . . considered blasphemy." One might object, however, that the flag is also, like all heraldry, highly conventional. There are well-known heraldic conventions—for example, stars, crowns, lozenges, and cadency marks—which could very well be changed; indeed a nation does sometimes change its flag, as it sometimes changes its anthem or totem, without a radical change in the nation's character. Though there are usually strong historic attachments to the flag in use, there is no connection so strong that people cannot change such things if they wish. If there were an overwhelming popular demand to replace the American eagle by a hawk, a dove, or a zebra, there is no reason why the change could not be made. Nor need the change always imply a radical change of meaning.

One might prefer to deny, then, that symbols and signs need be so sharply contrasted and to say, rather, that some symbols are highly conventional (like + and −) while others have a special character (the one to which Farrer alludes in suggesting their affinity with the wildness of nature) that remains to be considered. At any rate, if we are to distinguish sign and symbol in the way Tillich does, at least we must notice that a symbol may also *function* as a conventional sign; for example, the cross, an ancient symbol of the Christian faith, can also function as prosily as a traffic sign, such as when it is used simply to signify to people the bare fact that the building over which it stands is a Christian, not a Jewish or Buddhist one.

When Tillich goes on to say that a symbol opens up both new dimensions of reality for us that would otherwise remain inaccessible and also depths of our being that would otherwise remain hidden, he comes near the nub of the problem we have still to consider: how does a symbol function? Finally, borrowing a concept of Jung's, Tillich says that religious symbols are created, or at least accepted, by the collective unconscious of the group in which they appear. We have not the power either to invent symbols or to destroy them, for, not being conventions but "living things," they grow when the situation is ripe for them and die when the situation has changed.

God: Symbol and Taboo

Since that which we take to be our ultimate concern (to use Tillich's language) always transcends the realm of finite reality, there is no conceivable finite expression of it. Central in religion is the name of God. God so transcends finite expression that symbols (for example, the word "God") easily degenerate into "bad" language, being used trivially as vulgar oaths. Hence the ancient Hebrew prohibition of the verbal use of the Tetragrammaton, the name of God, and its replacement in speech by a conventional "stand-in" term, so that the sacrosanct one will not be "defiled" by profane utterance of it. Another not unconnected reason was the superstitious confusion of the symbol with the reality, a confusion typical of primitive societies: because the symbol is readily taken to be the thing it symbolizes, one must be careful not to expose it where the profane might desecrate it.

A similar rationale lies behind the prohibition of pictures ("graven images") that is characteristic of both the Jewish and Muslim traditions. The reason for the prohibition is partly the danger that people will confuse the symbol with the reality and, not noticing the difference, idolatrously worship the symbol. In primitive times people were ready to accept the taboo because of their superstitious fear that the reality might spill out, so to speak, through the symbol, and be lost or, worse, be destroyed through the aggressive onslaughts of the profane. In primitive societies people are by no means altogether unaware of the difference between symbol and reality; but because they lack adequate means of specifying that difference to themselves, they fear that the relationship may be such that if an enemy injures an image of their deity, the deity itself will suffer harm and in an extreme case perhaps even be killed. The best safeguard in such circumstances is to try to avoid, so far as it is possible, any risk of exposing the divine power to profane forces.

In our highly intellectualized climate, the situation is almost the opposite. We are reluctant to see how, if the reality transcends the symbol, the symbol can convey it. If it does convey it, what is the process? So we come back to the fundamental question: how does a symbol function? First, however, let us look at the different forms symbols may take. A glance at these will give us at least a general notion of what symbols are intended to do. Then we may hope to investigate how they do it.

Symbolic Forms

Making symbols is so characteristic of man that Cassirer goes so far as to define man as *animal symbolificum,* the symbol-making animal.[5] What differentiates us from the lower animals, according to Cassirer, is not speech (parrots "talk" and monkeys "chatter") or intelligence (dogs and cats exhibit much ingenuity); nor is it the ability to signify our needs (donkeys bray),

[5] See Ernst Cassirer, *Language and Myth* (New York: Harper, 1946), and *The Philosophy of Symbolic Forms,* trans. Manheim, 2 vols. (New Haven: Yale University Press, 1953–55); also Cassirer's disciple Suzanne Langer, *Philosophy in a New Key* (Cambridge: Harvard University Press, 1942).

but the ability to conceptualize and hold the concepts in a storehouse of symbols. That is what thinking is, and its close association with speech is clear. To think and speak *is* to symbolize; we think and speak in, with, and through symbols.

Since all thought and language are symbolic in character, there is plainly no question of compiling a complete list of the symbolic forms of religion. We shall look, rather, at what seem to be some instructive examples of characteristic types of symbols in order to see whether religious symbolism in general has any specific character.

To us the most familiar of all symbols, then, is the word. It "holds" an idea or ideas, which can be stored in it, brought out for use when required, and replaced again, somewhat as we deposit ten dollars into a bank account, then withdraw the money and later redeposit it into the account. Religion, however, is certainly much older than writing. We are apt to forget that, in the perspective of the paleontological and other evidence of the great antiquity of man on our planet, the art of writing is a comparatively recent development. Moreover, though writing may have been invented some seven thousand years ago, the ability to read and write was a very rare accomplishment throughout the great ancient civilizations. In the Middle Ages even princes were often illiterate; indeed illiteracy was still very common in Europe and America only a hundred years ago, and in other parts of the world much more recently than that.

Religion, in a primitive mode, may antedate even the spoken word. A still more ancient symbolic form than words is the visual image. Since the dawn of history, the vast majority of people have had to rely exclusively on images of one sort or another. Their imaginations were highly developed, for through them alone they had to try to understand both the world around them and their own place and destiny. In comparison with the imaginations of even our fairly recent ancestors, ours, like our memories, seem almost atrophied for lack of use. Nevertheless, so strong are many archetypal images in the psychic history of mankind that they continue in our own day to function vigorously, and not least as religious symbols.

These archetypal visual symbols relate to fundamental and universal human experience and do service for many ideas, so that we need not be astonished to find the same image performing, say, a sexual, political, social and religious function. Woman, for example, is an obvious case of such a multifunctional symbolic image. As virgin she symbolizes ritual purity; as mother she is the bearer of life. She is at once the untouchable mystery and the object of desire; she is both the very stuff of sensuousness who drags humanity down and the divine goddess who lifts mankind to heaven. Since all polarities seem to be enshrined within her, she is easily identified with everything good and bad, but especially with the stream of life, the fertility of the earth, the beginning of all things, and the sustenance of man.

Earth, sky, fountains, blood, fire, rivers and, not least, water are among the basic images that have played a large role in man's archetypal life. As religious ideas develop, the images become innumerable. Every flower, for instance, acquires a special symbolic meaning and often, indeed, a variety of meanings.[6] Visual imagery takes on symbolic meaning in curiously arbitrary ways. For instance, one may almost trace the course of the plague in Europe from the churches dedicated jointly to St. Sebastian and St. Roch. These two saints had nothing to do with each other: St. Roch, after devoting himself to the service of victims of the plague, contracted the disease in Piacenza and withdrew to the woods to die, accompanied by his dog. St. Sebastian, who is supposed to have lived about a thousand years earlier than St. Roch, had nothing at all to do with the plague, being generally represented in art as shot with arrows, to which punishment he had been condemned by Diocletian. In ancient times, however, the plague was believed to have been brought by Apollo's arrows, so by an irrational process of association medieval piety conjoined the two saints and their functions, aided no doubt by other irrational identifications: St. Sebastian's arrows with the pain of the victims of the plague, for example, or the appearance of the nodule caused by the disease with the bite of a dog, like the faithful companion of St. Roch. In the imagery of religion one can, in a way, read the whole religious story, but in order to do so one must first accustom oneself to such "wild" processes of association.[7]

Verbal Symbols

Now we may turn to words. In the oral tradition, which long antedates the literary one,[8] stories are developed that both use and foster such symbolic imagery. In this process the use of metaphor is fundamental. Metaphor gives depth to language. As in visual imagery, a skull stands for death and acquires macabre appositeness by accidentally suggesting a mocking grin. Thus, when Dante opens his epic with a reference to the road (*cammino*) of life, our whole conception of life is immediately deepened: it is seen no longer as a period of time between birth and death, but as a journey. Through the constant and developed use of metaphor, the language itself is deepened so that in its function it does more than it did when a road was nothing but so many yards of mud or stones.

Myth as a Symbolic Form

We have already considered paradox and analogy in another chapter. They, too, are part of the same general process of language-deepening. Let us

[6] Cf. R. B. Onians, *The Origins of European Thought* (Cambridge: At the University Press, 1954); also Mircea Eliade, *Myths, Dreams and Mysteries* (New York: Harper & Row, 1960).
[7] For examples of Christian symbolism, see George Ferguson, *Signs and Symbols in Christian Art* (New York: Oxford University Press, 1961).
[8] See Eric A. Havelock, *Preface to Plato* (Cambridge: Harvard University Press, 1963).

now look briefly at myth. Myth (*mythos*) is a basic symbolic form that shapes itself in the human psyche. The meaning it conveys cannot be conveyed in nonmythical ways. That is to say, it cannot be translated into nonmythical language. Plato's myth of the Cave in the *Republic* is a brilliant example of the use of myth to demonstrate philosophical or religious truth.

The great myths of antiquity seem to be timeless. The Orphic myth, for instance, which represents us humans as the offspring of gods and devils, still speaks to us to the extent that we still find ourselves today to be both the *sales cochons,* the dirty swine, that Sartre calls us and the fine heroes we can sometimes rise to be. Nature still seems the kind mother Byron called her, our biological studies notwithstanding. Myths do not give the whole truth about anything. Whatever their function is, it is not that. The penalty we pay, however, for failing to appreciate the indispensability of metaphor and myth and for trying even to dispense with them in favor of constructing a mythless language that we hope may be more "scientific" because more "literal" is that we fall into adopting myths without even recognizing that that is what we are doing. The nineteenth-century myth of progress is an obvious example. It was accepted so completely and uncritically that at the zenith of optimism about the future of humanity, which unconscious acceptance of the myth engendered, people were incapable of seeing any other possibility.

All the great myths spring from and convey a vision of the fundamental nature of things. The karmic myth, prevalent in Indian thought, is an example. Myths, despite their timeless qualities, do have to be updated, however. The common remark among contemporary theologians that Rudolf Bultmann's celebrated program of "demythologizing" is really a program of "remythologizing" demonstrates the point in question. Myths are like ancient buildings: they have to be repaired, and sometimes there seems to be little of the original stone left; nevertheless, for all the repair work that has been done on Canterbury Cathedral, it still has the same general form that it had hundreds of years ago. So old myths are refurbished but continue to convey the basic truths they have always conveyed.

Not all myths, however, survive, and this fact is of great importance for us. For while some myths convey timeless insights, others have much more limited reference-points. The quality of timelessness has nothing to do with the dress of the myth; the dress can be changed. The myth of St. George and the dragon is couched in a dress so ancient that we are apt to laugh at it before we take the trouble to grasp its meaning. The truth it conveys, however, is by no means alien to our modern condition.

Sacrament as Symbol in Action

In religion, the truth-conveying myth, together with a whole hierarchy of symbolic forms, is gathered up in the supreme symbolic form of sacrament. "A symbol," writes Evelyn Underhill, "is a significant image . . . . A sacrament is a significant deed, a particular use of temporal things, which gives them the value of eternal things and thus incorporates and conveys spiritual reality. Hence sacraments involve an incarnational philosophy. . . ."[9] In the sacraments, the symbolic principle works *par excellence.* The worshipper takes with the fullest seriousness what the symbolic form can do and seeks to appropriate the reality it conveys in and through the symbols under which the reality is veiled. Therefore, if we can understand how a sacrament functions, we shall know how symbols in general function.

In the sacrament, the religious man sees the action of God taking effect through the symbols. Spiritual power is conveyed in, with, and through a natural process. The power of Christ is given and received in the Eucharist. Something happens such that a spiritual presence and communion are created that were not there before. While most religions have special sacramental foci, the whole of religion is in some way sacramental, so that people are always finding the inward in the outward.

The Swiss Reformer Zwingli likened the Sacrament of Communion to a woman's wedding ring, which is a token of her marriage and a reminder of its character. The vigorous opposition of Catholic thought and sentiment to this Zwinglian conception of the sacrament sheds much light on the nature of sacramental symbolism. In the Catholic view the bread and wine, the "materials" or "elements" of the sacrament, are indeed a token; but they are much more. As words are coinage, so sacraments are tokens; but as words have a function beyond that of coins or tokens, so too do sacraments.

Religious people have always recognized that there is a mysterious quality in words and sacraments that transcends their function as simple signs or tokens. Lovers know the mysterious power of words. That is why they are not content with a mere comprehensive assurance of love: they want to hear the words over and over again, for the words, though mere coinage, are fraught with power far beyond their face value. Men and women have been healed by words and have even been brought back from the edge of death by a smile. The sacrament exhibits in a special way a mysterious quality that is present in all symbolic forms: what it holds always exceeds our actual appropriation of it. More is available than we can ever take. It is an inexhaustible mine. Words, too, have such a mysterious quality. The dictionary lists a primary meaning and perhaps a dozen other meanings, but in many cases the list can never be exhaustive. In religion, words have a sacramental character, so that preachers are often astonished to find that while their "best" sermons go over like cold mutton their worst are sometimes the means of bringing home to one person a religious disclosure of such startling power that it changes his whole life. The sacrament encompasses both the visual and the verbal mysteries of symbolism. In the Christian tradition, one of the greatest insights into its nature is that upon which

[9] Evelyn Underhill, *Worship* (London: Nisbet & Co., 1936), p. 42.

both St. Augustine and the Reformers so much insisted, that both the Word and the Element (that is, the material water or bread or oil) must be present for the sacrament to function.

Moreover, the sacrament provides a notable exemplification of the danger to which all symbolic forms, as we have seen, are subject: namely, the taking of the symbol for the reality. Doing that is akin to what the miser does when, mistaking the gold coinage for the goods it can buy, he finds his joy in caressing his money bags and letting the coins run through his fingers.

Confused Thinking or a Forgotten Language?

What we have explored in the previous sections suggests that either religious symbolism is a haphazard way of communication based on confused thought or else our general attitudes toward language are wrong, calling for a new theory of language. In fact, symbolism as used in religion does often reflect some intellectual confusion, as we have seen; yet it also points to the need for a theory of the nature and function of language very different from that which our general attitudes to language presuppose.

Many people in contemporary society, including some old-fashioned logicians, are inclined to look on language as primarily literal, in the sense that words are cashed in and out for concepts to which they directly refer and correspond. This view does not preclude, of course, an appreciation of secondary, figurative referents, as when "weaving," though its original referent is the process of interlacing threads to make cloth, also has secondary, figurative meanings connected with traffic, boxing, and story-telling. Nor does this view ignore special forms of emotive speech such as squeals and screams ("ouch," "oops," "wow"), or John Austin's "performative utterances" (noted in passing in Chapter I), which are not intended to communicate concepts at all and are therefore not symbolic in Cassirer's sense, but whose function is, rather, to move people to action, such as "gettup" and "whoa." Adherents of this view may even be willing to recognize the explorability of utterances that do not at first sight appear to be explorable. Nevertheless, the general view of language that this view promotes is one in which a primary, literal usage is accounted the basic, most reliable, and most manageable type of language upon which all others depend, as a family budget for luxuries depends on its budget for necessities.

The language situation is in fact quite different. All symbolic forms, including verbal language, emerged from man's communion with life about him. From the first, they reflected the richness and complexity of that communion, and as the richness and complexity have been immeasurably enhanced by our highly developed literary and religious heritage, language has become the repository of a wealth of meaning far beyond the power of any analytical tools, however finely honed. That is not to say that language is unanalyzable. On the contrary, linguistic analysis is an indispensable procedure. Living language, however, remains largely beyond the scope of any analytical method. Symbols, including words, not only bear meanings as musical vibrations bear overtones, not only act as repositories of the history of human life; but, as Cassirer and others have seen, they actually create special new experiences by their conjunction with special human situations. That is one reason why, when poetry is read correctly but woodenly, it both nauseates us and makes us long for "ordinary" or "scientific" language; yet when it is read expressively in a well-modulated voice by a reader sensitive to its vast potential of meanings, it can not only "move our hearts" but (which should be more interesting to philosophers) disclose to us meanings that prose simply does not have to give. For while prose intentionally restricts our choice of meanings in highly conventional ways, poetry puts us on notice to look out for vast spectra of meanings; to grasp these is to be carried beyond our present range of experience to one that transcends it, providing us with a new dimension of life.

The consequences of such a view of symbolism and language are plainly far-reaching. This view leaves room, moreover, for a wide variety of interpretations. Where symbols are regarded as the products of a psychically wild, nonrational life, as in dreams, we are not to look for any rational pattern of cohesion. Dreams are notoriously irrational, so that I ought not to be astonished should I find myself waking to remember that I dreamt I was driving a Mercedes through the streets of Athens, where I talked to Cicero in French over a glass of California wine. Such dream symbolism might tell a psychoanalyst something about me, but it would not be a medium for the communication of concepts that could be arranged in any rational manner. There could be no "grammar" of such symbols as there is a "grammar" of music or of, say, the symbolism in a medieval church. From the fact that some religious symbolism may originate in such dream-life experience we cannot, however, deduce anything about the general functioning of symbols.

No student of religion can fail to see that religious symbolism is sometimes an attempt to clarify the nature of deity in an intelligible, philosophical manner. Jung, borrowing a Tantric notion of the lotus as the symbol of the eternal birthplace of the gods, speaks of *mandalas*. The *mandala* is a quaternity, such as a globe with four quarters, a four-leaf clover, or a four-block city. He takes the four evangelists, who are often depicted in conjunction with four pillars supporting a cupola, and the rose window in which the Christus Victor sits, to be examples of the *mandala* in Christian tradition.[10] He also recognizes that modern *mandalas* may have no deity in them, but have as their reference point, rather, the wholeness of man.[11]

[10] C. G. Jung, "Psychology and Religion," (Terry Lectures, Yale, 1937), in *Psychology and Religion: West and East* (London: Routledge and Kegan Paul, 1958), p. 72.
[11] Ibid., p. 82.

Jung's colossal structure of psychological theory, in which he deals engagingly and convincingly with "hidden" symbolic meanings, is based on two views, both radical, of the whole of human knowledge.

In the first place, Jung is anything but a materialist. Having noted that "it is exceedingly difficult to believe that the psyche is nothing, or that an imaginary fact is unreal," he goes on to say: "It is an almost absurd prejudice to suppose that existence can only be physical. As a matter of fact, the only form of existence of which we have immediate knowledge is psychic." [12]

In the second place, however, he is also strongly relativistic and therefore metaphysically agnostic. His metaphysical agnosticism makes it impossible for him to take seriously the notion of a revelation or disclosure of a reality wholly transcending man. As a practicing medical man Jung felt he had to use whatever lay at hand, and if one dogma could be used clinically with success while another failed, then, of course, he used the one that "worked" better for his clinical purpose. Where one worked as well as the other, it was as good as the other. Beyond that, his elaborate theory of symbolism could not possibly take him. In short, he was interested in and deeply impressed by the reality of the human psyche as he found it, but not by any metaphysical theory about a meaning the symbols might bear beyond the total human situation in which they occur.

The religious man, however, considers the symbolic function differently. While recognizing the superabundance of meaning that is discoverable in symbols without our needing to go beyond the human condition for explanation, he claims that symbols do in fact function in a still more fundamental way: they bear meanings that relate to truths that are not, in the last analysis, relative only to the human condition. In discussing at last the functioning of symbols, we must take into account this characteristic and all-important religious claim.

How Do Symbols Function?

The typical religious symbol is, as we have seen, more than a token to be cashed in or exchanged for a concept to which it is held to be equivalent. It is more like a coupon which one may use to choose from a varied stock of goods carried in a store; it cannot buy whatever happens to come into the purchaser's head, but it can be used to select from a sometimes magnificent array of goods.

It is easy to see on what principle one makes the choice: one chooses what suits one's needs at the time. It is much more difficult to understand on what basis the store stocks its shelves: why, for instance, is p always available, q usually, r sometimes, s seldom, and t never? The more one knows,

[12] Ibid., p. 12.

however, of the history of the store, the clearer become its stock-keeping principles, and perhaps if one knew everything about its history there would no longer be room for puzzlement. In any case, the stock-keeping is never such that I might wonder whether to get, say, a dozen bananas or a frying pan. There is always some sort of connection, though it is not the kind of connection that could ever be the outcome of a neat, logical classification. It is, rather, the sort of connection one finds in wild nature. It seems to have its own laws, its own ways of working; but one certainly cannot get at them by any *a priori* rules or principles. One has to learn these laws through a laborious process, as one acquires empirical knowledge. How one goes on to *interpret* one's knowledge is another question, to be treated later.

So far we have considered only what an individual does with the coupon he takes to the store and what he gets for it. Religious symbols also have such a function, as when a worshipper gazes at an ikon and sees something more than or different from what he saw there yesterday. While a whole congregation may view the same religious scene, book, or picture, each individual will take away something different, according to his own needs, like the shopper in a store. There would be, we may suppose, a common element of some sort; that is, all the goods in the store would definitely be related to each other in some way. Yet everybody would go home hugging what he had obtained for his own individual requirements. What, then, of the communicative function of symbols? How can symbols be used communicatively without a hopeless tangle of ambiguities?

In the first place, the difficulty is not so great in practice as it might appear in theory to those unaccustomed to the life of religious community. Though meanings do change as the symbols pass hands, they still have much in common, so that the difference in meaning is in its angle or perspective, rather than its content. The situation is not unlike that of "ordinary" day-to-day life in any society. Every society has certain conventional ways of looking at things, which it either accepts or unconsciously adopts for working purposes. We have a common or "family" understanding of our situation, whether the "family" be a trade union, a student body, a professional club, a national society like the French or the American people, or just one's own little household. We can talk with each other as we cannot and do not talk to "the people next door." We can use a kind of conversational shorthand, sometimes a special slang, that other groups can never really understand—not because they do not know the words, which any person with a linguistic flair could quickly learn, but because they do not really see things exactly the way we do.

A religion which, as we remember, binds people together, always has a special way of looking at everything, so that when people within it go to the "store" with their "coupons" they pick out the "purchases" that function in their group according to certain accepted patterns and styles; that is, they exchange their "coupons" for goods they can use within their special family context. So while they have some degree of choice (and in the more highly organized and developed religions a very high degree of choice), they are nevertheless shopping in the same general areas. This consideration explains, by the way, why the ritual, dogmas, and forms, which are much despised by those who look at religion superficially, have such an extraordinary importance and why, therefore, religious people cling so tenaciously to them. They are the keys to the symbolic structure. Without them there would be no real communication and no real life, and the religion would consequently wither and die.

Two Theories of the Functioning of Symbols

Two main and opposing theories of the "grammar" of religious symbolism may be distinguished. Jung has vividly described his interest in one of them, which his disciples have popularized. It is, as was Hegel's in its own way, a Neo-Gnostic theory. By that is meant that it has marked affinities with presuppositions, some hidden, some expressed, that resemble those of the ancient Gnostics. Gnosticism, which took many forms in the ancient world and flourished in a quasi-Christian form (especially in the second century), is a difficult movement to define because it was more a climate than a particular philosophical school, more a general outlook than a definite metaphysical position. Nevertheless, one element common to all its forms was a belief that the spiritual world had its own nature and its own workings—as we might say, its own chemistry—which could be taught by a competent teacher and studied much as one studies physics or chemistry today. Within such a context, symbols are highly systematic. They set up an edifice that is an answer to man's "search for the divine," conducted on the basis of certain mythological presuppositions. Though the symbols cannot be understood apart from the system, they can be used with some precision once the system is understood. Every meaning they bear, however, echoes the whole mythology of the system, which may be and usually is a highly elaborate one. If one knew the system thoroughly and understood its metaphysical presuppositions, one could go far toward grasping all that the symbols could purport to carry. One might never be able to do so in practice; but it is theoretically possible.

Jung recognizes that "psychological truth by no means excludes metaphysical truth, though psychology, as a science, has to hold aloof from all metaphysical assertions . . . . Though we do not possess a physics of the soul . . .the soul is the only experient of life and existence . . . .The symbols it creates are always grounded in the unconscious archetype, but their manifest forms are moulded by the ideas acquired by the conscious mind." [13] A physics of the soul is, however, precisely what Jung would have liked to have had. It is the ideal to which he seeks an approximation. He states his whole theory of symbolism succinctly as follows: "Considered from the

[13] C. G. Jung, *Symbols of Transformation*, vol. 1 (New York: Harper Torchbooks, 1956), p. 231.

standpoint of realism, the symbol is not of course an external truth, but it is psychologically true, for it was and is the bridge to all that is best in humanity." [14] In this theory of symbolism, the symbols, metaphysical or psychological, are inseparable from the system they express.

The other theory of religious symbolism is different in one radically important respect. Here the symbols purport to represent God, considered as "wholly Other" (Otto), the eternal "Thou" (Buber), "Being-itself" (Heidegger), transcending not only the human situation but even Nature itself. This second theory, plainly committed to a much more ambitious enterprise than is the first, is beset with difficulties. The "Other" whose meaning the symbol purports to convey is hidden, unknown; yet through the symbol it is disclosed, being somehow adapted to fit man's finite intellectual need. Man does not grasp God, which is impossible; yet he does know God through the symbol: he knows what he needs to know of God. But then, what other kind of knowledge can I have of anything? Is not that the only kind of knowledge I have of New York City, for example? If, as is surely true, nobody in the world knows New York City better than that, there is nothing remarkable in this limitation on our knowledge of God. What remains remarkable is the claim that in the case of God we can have any such knowledge at all.

Both the nature of the claim to knowledge of God and the philosophical puzzles attending it, on this second theory of the functioning of religious symbols, are well brought out in a medieval controversy in the Greek Orthodox Church. According to the Hesychasts, a group of mystics among the monks of Mount Athos in the fourteenth century, man could attain a vision of the Godhead through the practice of certain ascetic exercises, including some with an affinity to the yogic exercises developed in India. To have claimed to uncover the hiddenness and unknowability of God would have appeared blasphemous in light of the strongly agnostic element that Christian teaching derives from its Hebrew, biblical heritage. The Hesychasts preferred to say, therefore, that while they did not attain to a vision of the essence (*ousia*) of God, they did attain to a vision of his action (*energeia*). This view, though it eventually found a champion in Gregory Palamas, stirred opposition, especially on the part of Barlaam, a monk influenced by western thought, on the ground that the unity of God precluded such a distinction between the divine essence and the divine action. The Hesychast controversy unfortunately developed into a partisan fight between Eastern Orthodoxy and Rome; but the point at issue, however expressed, is crucially important for any theory of religious symbolism that takes seriously the notion of symbolizing what purports to be a divine disclosure to man.

Man must be "open" to the symbol, but he must first have the symbol to which to be open. Without the symbol he has no means of access to the disclosure at all, for the symbol is, so to speak, God's card of invitation

[14] Ibid.

to understanding. The recipient, when he receives it, understands the meaning of that which he is invited to understand. So through a simple parable like that of, say, the prodigal son, is disclosed to us an affirmation about God, an understanding of whose meaning no philosophizing could ever have revealed to us, because it is not anything that we could possibly deduce about God from any logical inquiry or rationalist metaphysical system. It is as novel as new empirical knowledge.

There are nevertheless obvious philosophical questions, and perhaps the most obvious of all is: how could there be any guarantee that the symbol points to any truth? Hume long ago suggested that many of even the verbal symbols used in everyday language have no referent in any reality beyond the minds in which they are conceived. Kant, in trying to salvage some of them, rooted them in the nature of mental processes, leaving us with the *phenomenon* (the table as it appears to me) and forcing us to maintain a radical agnosticism about the *noumenon* (the table as it is in itself), the *Ding-an-Sich*. If the symbol we use to convey the notion of a table can carry us no farther than "the table as it appears to me," how can anyone possibly claim that a symbolic representation of God could carry us farther than our own minds? Moreover, as Kant has decisively shown, the human mind brings an important contribution to the cognitive act, so that no claim to knowledge of the thing-in-itself (*Ding-an-Sich*) is trustworthy. Yet the difficulty about symbols that purport to convey meaning and disclose truth about God who lies beyond human experience is much more than that. The difficulty is not, as in the case of the external world, that we can be shown to contribute something to the epistemological situation; the difficulty lies in showing that we do not contribute all.

In order to see how religious symbols function interpretatively let us consider a general question about the genesis and development of symbol-making.

The Genesis and Development of Symbol-Making

We are so mesmerized by the use of symbols that we are often in danger of forgetting how we came by them in the first place. We cannot think except in symbols; yet there is an experience that antedates them. The human mind would never begin to symbolize at all, were it not first confronted by realities beyond it which invite understanding. We first use symbols in response to such confrontations.

Cassirer cites two cases to illustrate and contrast the nature of the genesis and the nature of the development of symbol-making.[15] Mrs. Sullivan, whose spectacular success in educating Helen Keller, a blind deaf-mute child, is well known, relates how Helen took "the second great step in her education."

[15] Ernst Cassirer, *An Essay on Man* (New Haven: Yale University Press, 1944), pp. 33 ff.

That step consisted in the discovery that everything has a name. "This morning, while she was washing, she wanted to know the name for 'water.' When she wants to know the name of anything she points to it and pats my hand." Later on, when Helen held her mug out in one hand, Mrs. Sullivan spelled "w-a-t-e-r" in deaf-mute language in Helen's other hand. Helen "dropped the mug and stood as one transfixed. A new light came into her face. She spelled 'water' several times. Then she dropped on the ground and asked for its name and pointed to the pump and the trellis and suddenly turning round she asked for my name." In a few hours Helen had added thirty words to her vocabulary. She gave up her former attempts at signifying reality by mime because now she had acquired a much better instrument, the use of verbal symbols. "And we notice," Mrs. Sullivan records, "that her face grows more expressive each day." [16] Miss Drew, the teacher of Laura Bridgman, another blind deaf-mute, recounts a similar experience.[17]

The feature of these stories that we should note first of all is that both Helen and Laura knew the objects before they could name them. True, they could not do much with the kind of knowledge that they had. Nor could it make their faces light up. Yet it was sufficient to provide them with referents so that when they did have words, they could attach them to what was already in some way known. Mrs. Sullivan's stupendous educational feat was in making the breakthrough with the water symbol, which triggered the discovery that, *per analogiam,* everything can be symbolized and that by structuring symbols we can create a model of how everything is related to everything else. As soon as Helen had even a small vocabulary, however, she was already interpreting one symbol in terms of its relation to another; she was constructing a symbolic world. This is what Laura did, too. It is what we all do, and the more intelligent and responsive we are, the more deftly we can use the symbols as their connection with the objects to which they refer recedes. The world we so create is, however, our view of the world; it is the world "as we see it."

Once we grasp the importance of this architectonic principle in the functioning of symbols, we can begin to see all our language activity as interpretative. As Dorothy Emmett says, "The mind is not a mirror, but a selective and interpretive activity which builds up symbolic constructions." [18] Perceptual experience may then be seen, not as "direct apprehension nor of likeness, but as a highly simplified and abstract projection which nevertheless bears some relation of systematic concomitant variation to the things projected." [19]

[16] "Supplementary Account of Helen Keller's Life and Education," in Helen Keller, *The Story of My Life* (New York: Doubleday, Page & Co., 1902, 1903), pp. 315 ff.
[17] Mary Swift Lamson, *Life and Education of Laura Dewey Bridgman, the Deaf, Dumb, and Blind Girl* (Boston: Houghton Mifflin, 1881), pp. 7 f.
[18] D. Emmet, *The Nature of Metaphysical Thinking* (London: Macmillan & Co., 1953), p. 95.
[19] Ibid., p. 62.

Interpretative Selecting and Grouping

Language does not create what we take to be facts, but it contributes to the formation of what we call facts. Facts, then, might be better called, as one writer has proposed, "interprefacts." [20] The process by which we get our "interprefacts" is one of selection and grouping through an interpretative activity that always accompanies symbol-making.

Michael Polanyi has called attention to a special aspect of the interpretative activity that emerges with *Gestalten,* being "the outcome of an active shaping of experience performed in the pursuit of knowledge. This shaping or integrating I hold to be the great and indispensable tacit power by which all knowledge is discovered and, once discovered, is held to be true. The structure of Gestalt is then recast into a logic of tacit thought, and this changes the range and perspective of the whole subject." [21] Polanyi goes on to account the art of the expert diagnostician "a somewhat impoverished form of discovery" and, after suggesting a sort of calculus of impoverishment, ends by proposing that "Perception, on which Gestalt psychology centered its attention, now appears as the most impoverished form of tacit knowing." Perception, in this view, becomes, indeed, a mere "bridge between the higher creative powers of man and the bodily processes which are prominent in the operations of perception." [22]

Not only do we start such a process of selecting, grouping, and interpretative perceiving and knowing at the most rudimentary level; we fall easily into certain ways of selecting, grouping, and interpretative shaping that come naturally to us because of environmental conditioning and inherited tendency. Pretending to be immune to presuppositions is therefore almost as unconvincing as would be pretending to be immune from the effect of genes. Careful study, however, can help us discern our presuppositions, and although in this enterprise we may never be entirely successful, we can divest ourselves of many of the presuppositions that prove a hindrance to the clarity of our thinking and to the attainment of our human stature. By examining the perspectives that our presuppositions have led us to adopt, we can reach perspectives that seem more "adequate" than were our earlier ones. The obvious question, "adequate for what?" brings us to the center of the problem of symbol and reality, which we shall now consider.

[20] Olford, "History, Theology, and Faith," *Theology Today* 14 (April 1957): 20.

[21] Michael Polanyi, *The Tacit Dimension* (New York: Doubleday, Anchor Books, 1967), pp. 6 f.

[22] Polanyi is a scientist-turned-philosopher; but in the very different context of the Italian neo-idealism of the late Benedetto Croce, "ordinary" perception (contradistinguished from intuition in Croce's technical sense) falls similarly into epistemological degradation. For though the aesthetic or intuitional mode of experience in Croce's system is theoretically below and therefore independent of all other modes of experience, it is in fact to be reached only by the arduous task of shedding the special distortions peculiar to ordinary perception and shifting to a "purer" and therefore more basic and comprehensive mode.

Symbol-Making and Perspectival Thinking

Perspectival thinking is characteristic of all metaphysical inquiry. By attempting to view the whole of reality, as it confronts us in our experience, in this or that perspective, we have already taken a metaphysical stance and made a metaphysical judgment, whether we have become aware of it or no. The religious man, in making his response to what he takes to be a divine disclosure, takes a metaphysical stance, too, but his stance is not given him either from his inherited way of looking at things or by his own rationalistic inquiry. Rather, he finds it in the disclosure or revelation he claims to have received. It comes, so to say, with the invitation.

That distinction between two kinds of perspectival thinking, both of which are metaphysical but one of which is something more, should not be underestimated. The religious stance, though perspectival, is determined by what is taken to be divine disclosure or revelation, so that, being unadjustable, the metaphysical stance it entails is not radically alterable. If the religious man happens also to be a philosopher, he may be able to think of many ways in which the perspective could be improved from a metaphysical viewpoint; but he has to take what is given, for his stance is not that of a system-builder but the response of one who has been captivated by what he is convinced he has been shown.

When a philosopher embarks upon metaphysical inquiry, he uses root-symbols which depend, in turn, upon judgments, examined or unexamined, that form the ground of the metaphysical theory. The religious man who "finds salvation" likewise uses root-symbols to express his theological affirmations, and these root-symbols refer to the new perspectival view he has received of the hierarchy of Being. In the language of piety, he "has seen the Lord," who "has spoken to his condition."

Metaphysical assertions are, as is often remarked, compatible with any state of affairs, for that is the nature of perspectival thinking. To the extent that religious assertions are metaphysical they share in that peculiarity. Metaphysical *relations* can be pabulum for mathematical logic or any deductive procedure; metaphysical *assertions* cannot, yet these are not synthetic, as are statements of the order "this dog is black," so that neither could any inductive method, as induction is commonly understood, be appropriate. As Kierkegaard, however, saw very clearly in his polemic against Hegelianism, religious assertions are not *only* statements of metaphysical perspective; they are not a created system of relations based on a perspectival judgment. They have more affinity with synthetic than with analytical utterances. The religious man does not invent the symbols he uses; he claims that he responds to the disclosure that is given to him through them. In this respect he differs radically from the metaphysician. Nevertheless, he shares with the latter a perspectival preoccupation that is not amenable to treatment by any kind of logical atomism. So both the religious man and the metaphysician are

SYMBOL AND REALITY *87*

fascinated by the perspective they uphold, preferring it to the "flatness" of the view such logical atomism engenders. What they claim is better focus.

Metaphysical enterprise is often called speculation, a word that means etymologically, "a looking into, through, and out of," from *speculum,* a mirror. If we concur in Dorothy Emmet's view that the mind is not a mirror but a selective and interpretative activity, we cannot find "speculation" an apposite term unless construed in the larger, Aristotelian sense of contemplative activity. To my mind, "focusing" is a better term, for where there was vagueness, fragmentation, and flatness, now there is clarity, wholeness, and depth.

To the question "adequate for what?" we may now answer, "adequate for a grasp of the whole." With my camera lens, the picture I can get of the tower of a great palace may be inadequate for providing a grasp of the whole. As I say, I cannot "get it all in." With a wide-angle or other special lens I might do better. Yet whatever lens I use, I must always expect, from those more expert in such matters than I am, remarks such as: "Oh, but that doesn't really catch your subject. That's not 'the real' Windsor Castle; it's only what you get on any postcard." In other words, "it's a stylized, conventional, dull distortion." The true philosopher prefers any distortion to that one, for while that is a *familiar* distortion, a different, *unfamiliar* distortion might trigger in our minds a better way of piercing through to the spirit of the castle.

An objection may be stated thus: "I can understand that throughout the ages philosophers have built systems by which they hoped to explain the structure of the universe. By this means they expected to understand man's place in it and even individual human destiny. Each of the rival systems they concocted is plausible in its way. They are all the fruits of imaginative genius, testaments to man's creative capacity. But they are, after all, no more than grand-scale guesses, and the fatal indictment of them all is that one guess is as good as another. They are like the rival snapshots. Now I admit that from the standpoint of a thoroughgoing philosophical skepticism the explanations of modern science are not insusceptible to this same objection. Nevertheless, they are based on such an overwhelming weight of evidence that the perspective they give us is sufficient for all our practical purposes. If we are to talk of 'an adequate grasp of the whole' of experience, this perspective provides it. Any attempt at going beyond it is mere guesswork and, however imaginative, only a very grandiose sort of daydreaming."

Such a position, which would have many adherents, overlooks or considerably underestimates the nature as well as the extent of what the sciences cannot explain. The perspective afforded by the natural sciences (physical and biological) is indeed adequate for a particular *range* of human experience. It would do nothing, however, to help us discern what is characteristic of the humanities, nor would it even answer any of the most obvious questions that everyone asks about human behavior.

The social sciences (such as sociology and experimental psychology), which follow the methodologies of the natural sciences with some modifications and adaptations, are adequate for explaining a certain range of human experience, so long as questions about human behavior do not go beyond that range of experience.

Sociologists can tell us a great deal about the way people behave in respect to certain "public" activities and conventional classifications. For instance, if I want to know how many Baptists go to football games in comparison with the number of Methodists who do so, a sociologist is the person to ask. He may even be able to predict, within a small margin of error, how many Muslims will be among the spectators on a particular Saturday. Conversely, he may very well be able to tell us, if we want to know, what percentage of convicted shoplifters are Roman Catholics and what percentage are Presbyterians. Naturally, he can also make more intricate and useful discoveries, but being relevant only to the same range of experience, they will never tell us, for example, anything about what it means to be an Anglican or a Jew, or help me to determine in my own conscience whether I should become a Buddhist or cease being a Quaker.

Of course, if I am not interested in such questions or choose to think them unimportant or even meaningless, then the sociological answers will not only seem to me adequate; they will *be* adequate for my needs. The perspective they give will be sufficient. By the same token, if I find myself entirely conformable to the psychological pattern provided for in a Watsonian behaviorism, I shall find the answers of such a behavioristic psychology acceptable and their determinism will not trouble me. My dissatisfaction will arise only to the extent that I find that such methodologies do not cover the whole realm of my experience. If anything is left out I shall be in that measure dissatisfied. If what is left out is what I find the most interesting aspect or dimension of my experience, I shall be thoroughly dissatisfied.

Rules for the Interpretation of Symbols

The rules to be adopted for the interpretation of symbols will reflect and depend on the metaphysical stance. Having already considered two radically different stances, we may begin with these.

In the view that symbols are part of a closed system, whether psychological or metaphysical, the basic rule of interpretation must be coherence with the system. This requirement is not as restrictive as it may sound. It allows for a rich variety of symbol-making. Each symbol, though it must conform to the system, may conform to it by modifying other symbols or by acquiring a special modifying feature of its own. Symbols can be so multifunctional that, for instance, trees may be taken as phallic symbols, as mother symbols, and as symbols of life, and one could go on extending the list; nevertheless, a tree could not be made to perform the function of a bird or a lion. A tree can, however, by attachment to another nexus of symbols, become a symbol of knowledge. Where the whole system of symbolism either exhibits the contents of the psyche, conscious or unconscious, or expresses a metaphysical structure, the symbols can be rearranged so long as they do not interfere with the systematic whole. The reason is simple: because the symbols do not purport to mean anything except the structural whole, they have no *individual* meaning beyond that structural whole. The rule for the interpretation of their appropriateness will always be, therefore, a coherence rule.

When symbols purport to do more, a different set of rules is required. For instance, the primary symbols of a Christian theology that purports to express revealed truth about God who transcends his creation require different rules of interpretation. We should note in passing, however, that such a theology may also contain a system of secondary symbols that it subsumes within its structure, and these will have coherence rules such as we have been discussing. Hagiography, for instance, is such a dependent satellite system within the framework of Christian theology, which has adopted it and has conferred a special meaning upon it. Such a system of secondary symbols, deriving its meaning from the primary disclosure symbols of the theology to which it is subordinated, functions similarly to any other system of the sort envisaged in the preceding paragraph and is subject, therefore, to coherence rules of interpretation.

A system for arranging the primary symbols of a theology that purports to express revealed truths requires, on the contrary, rules that envisage, as the principal danger, not incoherence but idolatry. This is not to minimize the importance of coherence. It is to say, however, that when we are constructing a disclosure-theology, our first concern will be to avoid idolatry. Once this has been provided for, the coherence tests can be applied to any satellite systems that are incorporated into the theology. Let us consider the application of this principle.

When we take seriously the notion that a symbol for God (for instance, fatherhood) disclosed in a revelatory literature such as the Bible, might in some way be appropriate for deity, there are three formal possibilities. First, one might take the extreme view in which the symbol is held to function *only* in a purely negative way, the *via negativa* familiar to all students of the mystical tradition. In this view, God and his creatures are so completely different that there is no way at all in which one could find any point of resemblance, so that any symbol for God would always mean something entirely different from what it could ever mean in any other context. Therefore, if we call God compassionate we do not refer in any way to any kind of compassion that could ever be predicated of even, say, Albert Schweitzer or Francis of Assisi. This view breaks down, of course, when one goes on to ask: then why use the symbol "compassionate" at all, since one might just as well use "equine" or "leonine" or even "cruel." And indeed, when mystical writers do talk extravagantly about the negativity of religious symbols, all they are usually doing is to emphasize by hyperbole how slight is the thread of meaning between, say, human generosity and the generosity of God.

Second, one might maintain that through the whole structure of reality, including Nature, man, and God, run certain unitary characteristics. As materialists would call matter such a unitary characteristic, idealists would so account mind. Where God and Nature are held to have an element common to both, the symbol-making task is to abstract the common element and so symbolize it that the abstraction functions much as light functions in any physics text to denòte both the light from my desk lamp and the light from Sirius or the moon. From an idealist's point of view, I am not at all like God in respect of my body, but in respect of my mind I might perhaps be as like him as the light of the candle is like the light of the sun.

The third way is analogical, and to this our concluding section will be devoted.

Interpretation Rules for Analogical Symbols

The analogical understanding of the nature of religious symbols fits any system that envisages a hierarchical structure in being; that is, qualitatively different degrees, levels, or orders of being. It fits, for example, an evolutionary as well as a Platonic system. In evolutionary development there are curious "leaps" from one type of life to another that is somehow of an indisputably higher order. For instance, as we have already seen, man does not merely talk or think better than monkeys or parrots; by his "leap" to the use of symbols he is able to think and talk as no other animal can do. Yet not only does he not cease being an animal; other animals may look as though they are on their way to being human. I can say that my dog, when he barks or wags his tail, is talking "after a fashion" or "in a sort of a way," that is, analogically. My dog is not really talking, of course; but what he is doing is to him as talking is to me. I could not properly suggest, therefore, that he was eating or sitting or biting when he barked or wagged his tail, for there would be no analogy. Contrariwise to say that when he wagged his tail he was doing *exactly* what I do when I thank my hostess for coffee would also break the interpretation rule.

Or again, anyone who wishes to ridicule an extremist's "reverence for life" doctrine can raise a laugh easily by satirically proposing that we should not take penicillin for pneumonia since by doing so we are committing murder on our cousin the pneumococcus. The difference between bacteriological life and human life, the killing of which could result in a murder trial, is so great that to identify them seems laughable; yet it would not even be laughable were there no connection at all. The mode of life of a bacillus is ludicrously different from mine; yet a bacillus is indubitably alive as a typewriter is not, so that in respect of life I am more like a bacillus than a typewriter. Is "God the Father" a futile anthropomorphism? Not necessarily. To call an amoeba a father sounds mildly silly; but amoebas do "father" by fission. God "fathers" by creation. In both cases the fathering is by analogy with the male procreative activity in human coitus. Once again, instinct and intelligence are by no means the same; nevertheless, one might well say there is a connection such that the instinct of a fly is to the fly what intelligence is to me.

In poetry and folklore, analogical symbols are easily accepted. In telling stories to children we sometimes, for example, invest animals with human characteristics; Mrs. Bear not only dresses in a coat and skirt but scolds her children in plain English. Children enjoy such literary figures because they can appreciate the point of the analogies. They know that animals do not dress or talk, but they know also that animals do things which to them are in some respects as dressing and talking are to us. Few small children would readily understand Shakespeare's more sophisticated allusion:

> the morn, in russet mantle clad,
> Walks o'er the dew of yon high eastern hill;[23]

because here the dress analogy is carried further than most small children could go. With education and training, however, the step can be taken, because the analogical connection is there. From the notion that a courting peacock dresses in his finest clothes one may gradually go on to invest morning with personality so that to her also may be figuratively assigned a wardrobe. Again, however, there must be an analogical connection. By no stretch of symbolizing could a poet dare ask us to accept anything like

> the morn, with joyous shout,
> Leaps to strip bare the purple of the hill.

True, the morning no more walks than leaps and no more dresses than shouts, so why, one might ask, can the poet get away with one set of empirical absurdities but not the other? The answer is once again that with literary training we can be shown that there is a relation between what happens in the morning and what happens when a woman dons a russet dress, and if we go on to personalize "morning" we may see an analogy between what "morning" then "does" and what a woman does when she walks. The shouting-and-leaping alternative is inapposite and therefore bad poetry, but it would have been even worse God-talk, had Shakespeare been trying to symbolize a disclosure of divine Being.

The case of God-talk is unique only because of the truth-claim. We are not concerned at present with whether any such claim be true. (That is to be considered in the next chapter.) We are concerned, rather, with whether

[23] *Hamlet,* act 1, sc. 1, line 166 f.

God-symbols could tell us anything about God, and what kind of knowledge they could possibly convey in practice, if any knowledge of God were theoretically available.

Analogical methods provide a safeguard against arbitrary symbolizing. If, as in Thomism, the ground of the whole method is an analogy of Being (*analogia entis*), then the symbolizing must be done within very strict confines indeed, for in the last resort all that can ever be predicated of God can be predicated only in the sense that the predication stands to divine Being as it would stand to my Being. It is therefore not the same predication, though it is not a totally different one. Symbols so used of God, though they purport to suggest to us the divine nature, cannot describe it as I might describe to you what sort of boy my nephew is.

Such a use of analogical procedure by no means precludes commonplace figures. I might still suggest to a small child that God rolls out the sky and twirls the stars into place. Not only might God be said to twirl a star as I am said to grasp an idea; what would also be claimed is that saying God twirls stars into place is infinitely less misleading than saying they just happened to roll into their places. To say that my heart pumps the blood through my arteries and back again into my veins may mislead me if I am so stupid as to suppose that my heart stands inside me, hard at work with a pump like the village pump. But even if I literally believed that, it would not mislead me so much as would what people commonly believed before Harvey's treatises on the heart and the circulation of the blood,[24] namely, that blood does not circulate at all. All that is being said is that the action of my heart in relation to my blood stands in a relation that is like that in which the action of the village pump stands in relation to the water it pumps. A physiologist has better, less childish terminology, of course, but no terminology could escape the limitations of the analogical method unless there were an ostensive referent. In the case of God that condition is plainly always ruled out.

The Wildness of Religious Symbols

We should now be better able to see the force of Austin Farrer's observation that "symbols have some of the many-sidedness of wild nature." What one sees in the wildness of symbols is a function of metaphysical stance and also, in part, of training. In verbal language, even grammatical structure, though not a symbol, has what Langer aptly calls a "symbolific mission." It unites symbols structurally "to make one complex term, whose meaning is a special constellation of all the connotations involved." [25] Religious symbols however, are "wild" in a special sense.

[24] William Harvey, *De Motu Cordis,* 1628, and *De Circulatione Sanguinis,* 1649.
[25] Suzanne Langer, *Philosophy in a New Key* (New York: Mentor Books, 1948), p. 55.

When we inspect the second of the two theories that we have distinguished for the functioning of religious symbols, we find that it presents us with a unique situation. In contrast to the terms of a system of analytical psychology such as Jung's, and in contrast also to metaphysical terms, which explain each other in terms of an artificially constructed system, the terms in a systematic theology do not and never could fully explain each other at all, for the whole system describes, in its own way, the disclosure that is alleged to take place in the utterances to which the theological system relates. The purpose of the theological system is, indeed, to exhibit how the term "God," for instance, functions within what is said to be disclosed in the symbolic structure. No theology, however, can do more than conceptualize and critically arrange what is claimed to be disclosed in the symbolic structures. The theological system, purporting to be to the disclosure only what a botanical system is to wild flowers, can never replace the revelatory symbols, the symbols of disclosure, by the symbols of a metaphysical system. One can invent a system of symbols as one invents an artificial language like Esperanto, and make it (as is Esperanto) both less difficult and less irrational than the "wild," living system, but such a system will die. All it seems to lack is what makes possible its survival. The symbolic structures of a living religion are modified, as are living tissues, but they live on.

The study of theology could never in itself bring about a religious conversion. The *condition* of such a conversion is exposure to the revelatory symbols "in the wild." Since there is no guarantee, however, that such exposure will cause anything to be disclosed in any particular case, a serious philosophical problem remains. For though the alleged disclosure does indeed entail interpretative activity, there can be no question of that kind of criterion of interpretation that one would seek in judging between two rival metaphysical systems. The religious person claims to have been to the scene of the disclosure itself and to have found not merely a metaphysical key but, through the symbolic structure, the living *action* to which that structure refers. In his excitement he may be subject to confusion about detail, but he enjoys an inner assurance of having been confronted by the reality of Being itself. Having that, he sees no reason to care whether he has the trappings exactly right. His very sense of certainty, however, gives rise to misgivings even on the part of the least skeptical philosopher. Whether there could be any way of adducing evidence to prove his religious truth-claims will be considered in the next chapter.

QUESTIONS ON CHAPTER II

1   What difference do you see between the literal and the symbolic?

2   Discuss Polanyi's view of the process of selecting and grouping.

3   What does Austin Farrer mean by calling religious symbols "wild"?

4   What relation do you see, if any, between analogy and paradox?

5   "The Creation stories in Genesis are *merely* symbolic." What misunderstandings do you think that statement might spawn, and what objections, as a philosopher of religion, would you raise against it?

6   John Hick remarks that, according to Paul Tillich, a symbol "participates in the reality to which it points. But, unfortunately, Tillich does not define or clarify this central notion of participation." Tillich says that a flag participates in the power and dignity of a nation, but he neither explains precisely what this means nor in what respect a religious symbol is supposed to operate similarly. "Again, according to Tillich, everything that exists participates in Being-itself; what then is the difference between the way in which symbols participate in Being-itself and the way in which other things participate in it?" (John Hick, *Philosophy of Religion* [New York: Prentice-Hall, 1963], p. 83.)

Discuss the issue and consider possible ways of dealing with it.

7   Macquarrie, remarking that the once immense power of some ancient symbols has declined, suggests that the symbol of light, for example, might be revivified by the use of the word "openness."

Discuss the principles involved in this proposal and consider whether, for the symbol "shepherd," plainly long outmoded in urban societies, might be substituted, say, the word "foreman." If not, why not?

8   "In a way every sentence is metaphorical, conveying to the single word a meaning beyond its dictionary sense." (Martin Foss, *Symbol and Metaphor in Human Experience* [Princeton, N.J.: Princeton University Press, 1949], p. 59.)

Consider possible effects of such a view on a theory of religious symbolism.

BIBLIOGRAPHICAL SUGGESTIONS
See also the bibliographical suggestions following Chapters I and III.

Aquinas, Thomas. "De Divinis Nominibus." In *Summa Theologiae*, I, 12, 1–12. The classic passage on analogy in St. Thomas.

Aulén, Gustav. *The Drama and the Symbols.* Translated by S. Linton. Philadelphia: Fortress Press, 1970.

Bevan, E. *Symbolism and Belief.* London: Allen & Unwin, 1938.

Cajetan, Tommaso de Vio. *The Analogy of Names.* Translated by E. A. Bushinski and H. J. Koren. Pittsburgh: Duquesne University Press, 1953. A classic study of analogy as understood in scholastic philosophy.

Cassirer, Ernst. *Language and Myth.* Translated by Suzanne Langer. New York: Harper & Row, 1946. A good introduction to Cassirer's thought.

Cassirer, Ernst. *The Philosophy of Symbolic Forms.* 3 vols. New Haven, Conn.: Yale University Press, 1953–57.

Cell, Edward. *Language, Existence and God.* Nashville, Tenn.: Abingdon Press, 1971. An introduction to analytical philosophy in relation to philosophy of religion. He discusses Wittgenstein, Wisdom and Tillich, and he concludes with an analytically oriented defense of existentialist theology.

Eliade, Mircea. *Myths, Dreams, and Mysteries.* Translated by P. Mairet. New York: Harper Torchbooks, 1967. First published in French, 1957.

Farrer, Austin. *The Glass of Vision.* London: Dacre Press, 1948.

Farrer, Austin. *A Rebirth of Images.* London: Dacre Press, 1949.

Jung, C. G. *Symbols of Transformation.* Translated by R. F. C. Hull. 2 vols. New York: Harper Torchbooks, 1962 (first published 1956). An examination of religious symbols from Jung's psychoanalytical standpoint.

Kitagawa, J. M., and Long, C. H., eds. *Myths and Symbols.* Chicago: University of Chicago Press, 1969. Studies in honor of Mircea Eliade.

Langer, Suzanne. *Philosophy in a New Key.* Cambridge, Mass.: Harvard University Press, 1942.

Mascall, E. L. *Existence and Analogy.* London: Longmans, 1949.

Shibles, Warren A. *Metaphor.* Whitewater, Wis.: Language Press, 1971. An annotated bibliography, philosophical, literary, and linguistic.

Tillich, Paul. "Symbols of Faith." In *Dynamics of Faith.* New York: Harper & Brothers, 1957.

Whitehead, Alfred North. *Symbolism, Its Meaning and Effect.* Cambridge: At the University Press, 1928.

III

RELIGIOUS TRUTH-CLAIMS: EVIDENCE AND PROOF

when one's proofs are aptly chosen
Four are as valid as four dozen.
Matthew Prior (1664–1721),
Alma

Truth, Sir, is a cow, which will yield skeptics no more
milk; so they have gone to milk the bull.
Samuel Johnson (1709–1784), as quoted in
Boswell's Life of Samuel Johnson

The Difficulty of Disengaging Religious Truth-Claims

We observed at a much earlier stage that while artistic people as such do
not make any particular claim to knowledge, the believer does. When he
says he believes in the Ascension he need not mean, on the one hand, that
Christ rose vertically from the earth and, having disappeared from view,
eventually reached his destination, a place situated above the inverted blue
bowl sitting over the earth. He could not possibly mean this unless he
happened to subscribe to a very primitive and antiquated cosmology. On
the other hand, he certainly does *not* mean that the story of the Ascension
is a story like *The Sound of Music.* No matter how he interprets the doctrine
of the Ascension, he recognizes, at least implicitly, that it contains a
truth-claim and he is admitting that claim.

If we look at typical religious utterance, however, we find that on the
whole there is usually no precise truth-claim that we can directly examine.
The reason is simple. Religious people are not as a rule consciously
preoccupied with making intellectual claims; but from their way of talking
one may see that implicitly they are making such claims, which must then
be disengaged from or distilled out of their discourse. We may even affirm
that religious utterance never *begins* with a truth-claim. Like the language
of lovers, it begins typically in expressions of joy, resolutions of sacrifice,

and aspirations and hopes that the relationship may never end. From the language religious people use, we discover, nevertheless, beyond the attitudes of love, implied truth-claims. For instance, when a man says, "I shall see you next year, God willing," he has made no direct truth-claim; yet no atheist would talk like that, and everybody who knows anything about religious utterance knows that in the attitudinal stance of the speaker we may see a nexus of truth-claims, for example: "There exists a Being who is able to control human destiny," and "That Being in fact exercises his power in the lives of men." Indeed religious truth-claims that are explicitly made often turn out to be of only comparatively trivial religious interest, such as "Jesus was crucified in a suburb of Jerusalem," which in itself is of no religious interest apart from the affirmations of religious faith that identify the subject as "the divine Redeemer of men."

When religious people do utter statements in which truth-claims seem to be affirmed more directly, they are commonly difficult to examine in the form in which they are presented. Christians say, "Jesus Christ is God." Jews declare, in the Shema, "The Lord our God is one God." These affirmations, however, apart from their doctrinal contexts, cannot usefully be treated as proposals about which evidence can be adduced. *Prima facie,* the first seems nonsensical and the second an outstandingly ridiculous tautology. What else should God be but one? Here, of course, is precisely the point: the Shema *contends against* those earlier polytheistic ancestors of the Jews who persistently thought of gods in the plural and attributed limited power to each of them, as indeed do all polytheists.[1] "Jesus Christ is God" looks as though it had the same logical form as "Napoleon is God" and "Jesus Christ is bearded," but in fact it has no such logical form, being, on the contrary, a shorthand phrase for a vast network of truth-claims involving beliefs about the history of God's alleged dealings with Israel and metaphysical beliefs about the nature of divine Being, together with many truth-claims about the meaning of human experience. None of these truth-claims is of such a kind that any evidence could conceivably tell for it, or against it, *when it stands alone.* The truth-claims, however, that might be eventually disengaged or distilled from an influential portion of religious literature, Christian or Jewish, could conceivably be investigated by an open-minded philosopher.

The believer, then, seldom makes his most important truth-claims explicit. Indeed, unless he happens to be particularly interested in metaphysical questions, which is very rarely the case, he is unlikely ever to put his truth-claims into a form in which philosophers would wish to have them if they were asked to try to see precisely about what there might or might not be evidence. On the contrary, religious discourse tends to obscure the underlying truth-claims in several ways. First, it has a very odd frame of

[1] This "protesting" element in religious dogma was much stressed in one of my earliest books, *Christian Doubt* (London: Longmans, Green & Co., 1951).

reference, a very special "map" to whose rules one must first be introduced before one can possibly make head or tail, even in the most general way, of what is being said. In the *Bhagavata Purāṇa* we read: "Raising the syllable Om to the heart by means of Prāṇāyāma, one should add to it the vowel. The Om is like the continuous peal of a bell, and extending in a thin line like a thread in a lotus stalk. . . . Within the body there is the lotus of the heart, with its stalk above and point below, and with eight petals and a pericarp." [2] No one could even begin to discover the meaning of such a passage without some familiarity with Hindu lore; even then there would be no way of stating a truth-claim without relating it to a whole *Gestalt* of truth-claims that hang together so that each must eke out the meaning of the rest. The same is true of a doctrinal statement like that of Pius IX, which may be paraphrased as follows: "Though the Blessed Virgin was conceived without sin, she was nevertheless redeemed by Christ like the rest of the human race, but in a more sublime manner." Here is a truth-claim that is unintelligible without a considerable knowledge of medieval Latin theology. It would require, therefore, much explication.

Basic Truth-Claims

Even if we do take the trouble to understand the theological context, see the pattern of the *Gestalt,* and disengage or distill the doctrinal truth-claims from it, we have not finished the preliminary groundwork, the result of which a philosopher would wish to have before him to enable him to attempt an examination of evidence. For under truth-claims of the kind we have been considering lie more basic, metaphysical claims. These are the truth-claims that are most rarely specified in religious discourse. They are, rather, hidden, subsumed, unconsciously presupposed.

Professor William Christian of Yale calls the first sort of truth-claim (e.g., "The external operations of the Trinity are undivided") a doctrinal proposal and the second (e.g., "Nature, being a creature of God, is wholly dependent upon him") a basic proposal.

Conditions for Susceptibility to Evidence

What conditions are needed to make disagreement possible and evidence therefore adducible? Professor Christian asks whether a Taoist and a Christian could agree or disagree on whether the Holy Ghost proceeds from the Father *to* the Son (as the Greek Church says) or from the Father *and* the Son (as the Latins and others in the West say), and he denies that they could. His reason is similar to those that have already been suggested here: "No common

---

[2] *Bhagavata Purāṇa*, Book 11, trans. Swami Madhavananda, as quoted in J. W. Dye and W. H. Forthman, *Religions of the World* (New York: Appleton-Century-Crofts, 1967), p. 83.

rules of relevance, much less common rules of judgment, can be formulated." Dr. Christian cannot rest with such a position, however, for it would suggest that adherents of religion *A* could never properly discuss the tenets of religion *B* at all, and he is unwilling to go so far as that. But we may be able to find a common reference.

Suppose the Apostle Paul and his rabbinic teacher Gamaliel were arguing over the proposal "Jesus is the Messiah." The Roman philosopher Seneca is listening in. At first there would be great confusion, because by "Messiah" the rabbi would mean "a nondivine being who will restore Israel as an earthly community and usher in the consummation of history." Paul might explain, however, his belief: "Jesus is the one [whom] God promised to send to redeem Israel." To this Gamaliel could say a definite "no" to Paul's insistent "yes," but Seneca would still be puzzled. A Stoic, sharing neither Paul's nor Gamaliel's presuppositions about the nature of divine Being, he would object that God does not "promise" things in such a way and does not "send" people in such a way, so both Paul and Gamaliel are talking nonsense—somewhat as if they were saying that the law of gravity had decided to appoint an ambassador. Seneca would be implicitly denying a presupposition contained in the "Jesus is the one [whom] God ..." proposal. If we expressed this hidden presupposition in terms such as "The being who rules the world acts in history," Paul and Gamaliel would agree and Seneca would now have something on which he could, and doubtless would, disagree. In such ways the range of possibility of significant religious disagreement could be much extended. The value of achieving that goal lies in the extension of the range of truth-claims.[3]

We have now seen that, because of the nature of religious discourse, the truth-claims of the believer must be disentangled before they can be susceptible to evidence. There is no evidence that could conceivably be brought in for or against "I take refuge in the *dharma*" or "O that we might reign for ever in the Lord's Kingdom" or even "The Lord is a lamp unto my feet" until first we have somehow distilled from such characteristically religious utterances a proposal or proposals for which evidence can be adduced for or against. Let us consider, by way of approaching the heart of our problem, the four requirements that Dr. Christian lays down:[4]

(1) The proposal must be capable of self-consistent formulation.

(2) It must be liable to significant disagreement.

(3) It must permit a reference to its logical subject.

(4) It must permit some support for the assignment of its predicate to its subject.

[3] For Dr. Christian's discussion of the point at issue, see W. A. Christian, "Truth-claims in Religion," *Journal of Religion* 42 (1962): 52–62.
[4] Ibid.

By (1) is meant that there must be something that may be judged to be true or false. Because of the paradoxical character of much religious language, the unravelling of the utterance so as to provide a proposal for examination may sometimes be very difficult. Suppose the speaker, having offered one utterance after another, is at length forced into saying something like, "Well, I can't do any better. Surely you can see what I mean?" I may well reply, "Indeed, I think I do see that there is something in what you say." That is as far as I could go. I could not say the utterance was true; nor could I say it was false.

As required by (2), the proposal must also be susceptible to disagreement. It is not enough that it should have logical entailments. If I say that God exists and that by "God" I mean precisely that which scientists call "nature," you could find no ground for disagreement, so there would be nothing to produce evidence about. A statement like Tillich's "God is the ground of being" could be construed as such a tautology. The Buddhist "Nirvana is the supreme goal of life" could also be so construed, since *nirvana* can mean here whatever you want it to mean. Nothing could count for it or against, which is to say there could be no evidence.

Nevertheless, religious utterances that look tautological often turn out not to be tautological after all. Suppose I say to you: "I am a firm believer in God. I believe that God is whatever is the noblest and grandest ideal I set before me. Whenever I strive as hard as I can, crying to myself, 'Excelsior,' I am invoking God. God is the pinnacle of human ideals." You might reply. "No, no. God is not that at all. God is the ground of all being." Then we should be coming closer to the formulation of a truth-claim. That is why it is generally very difficult to see that the historic creeds of the Church are saying anything significant till you learn enough of the historic background to appreciate what it was that they were repudiating. For example, "We repudiate the notion that God is the mind-principle, contradistinguished from the matter-principle, and we affirm, on the contrary, that God is 'the Father Almighty, Maker of heaven and earth and of all things visible and invisible.' " Once we specify what is being repudiated we are usually better able to see the meaning of what is being affirmed. The fulfillment of this condition alone, however, is not enough.

The third condition is that reference to the logical subject of the proposal must be possible; that is, the disputants must mean the same thing when they use the subject. We have already seen, in the Paul-Gamaliel-Seneca example, an instance of the effect of the absence of this condition and suggestions for remedying the confusion. Take, however, a still plainer case: If I asserted that JHWH is the Lord of Life, you might very properly object that you could not agree or disagree since you did not understand the reference point. It would do no good for me to say "JHWH is holy" or "JHWH is powerful"; you would remain perplexed. I might be able to adduce an alleged fact, however, as a starting point, such as "the one whom the Hebrews believed to have led them out of Egypt as recorded in the Book of Exodus." If you then said, "Oh, you mean that old tribal deity the Hebrews used to carry around in a box?" I might reply that Hebrew literature attests a belief in JHWH that implies a more definite ontological claim, such as that he is the one who creates all that is not JHWH. By such methods we could move toward a logical subject that could function appropriately in our discussion.

The fourth and last condition of making a truth-claim is that it must be possible to bring in some kind of evidence for or against it. This brings us to the heart of our problem. At the present stage we are not concerned with the judgment upon the evidence, which might satisfy one judge but not another. We are concerned, rather, with the kind of evidence that is admissible because it is appropriate. Let us suppose that we have two subjects, *x* and *y,* both of which fulfill the requirements set forth in (3)—for example, the sun and Lourdes water. I say that *x* is holier than *y.* You ask me what the predicate means, and I explain that I am proposing to use it in the same manner in which Otto uses it in *Das Heilige.* To ascertain what manner this is you might find that you had to read the book if you were not satisfied by my attempted account of it; but in the end you would have to say, "Now I am in a position to hear evidence. Bring it in." For in Otto's category of "the holy" are certain qualities or elements or characteristics; for example, the holy is both (a) numinous and (b) susceptible to rational schematization. A singer endowed with what is popularly called "charisma" might seem to qualify under (a) better than would, say, the peninsula in the Aegean Sea that has been the home of the Athonite monks for more than a millenium and is much revered in Eastern Orthodoxy. At least the singer is alive, not a geographical location. In terms of (b), however, Mount Athos would win every time, as also would even "Old Man River," the Mississippi. Though we cannot by such means say we have a complete set of rules of evidence, at least we have pointers in the required direction. We can now begin to muster evidence with some hope of sifting it and reaching a judgment.

What Kind of Evidence Is Relevant?

So far we have been principally concerned with two questions: (1) the difficulty of disengaging from religious discourse the truth-claims it contains, especially the ones that are most important for the believer himself, and (2) the conditions under which a truth-claim in religion could be susceptible to proof. Now suppose that at last we have before us an assortment of truth-claims that are sufficiently clear to be examined. We need evidence. What *kind* of evidence is relevant and therefore admissible in our court of judgment?

As soon as we begin examining the truth-claims, we find that in the case of some of them the kind of evidence required is straightforward. So long as the truth-claim relates to a fairly primitive and unreflective type of religion or else to a matter that is of only peripheral importance from any religious standpoint, there is no great difficulty. For instance, consider the statement "Devotion to St. Anthony of Padua is effective in recovering lost property." Any sociologist could undertake the necessary survey and collate the evidence from suitable samplings of two segments of the population, one of which was given to such devotions and the other not. Suppose he found that out of 1,000 Irishmen who prayed to St. Anthony, 231 had recovered lost property within forty-eight hours of their prayers; while among 1,000 Irishmen who did not invoke St. Anthony's aid only 183 found their lost belongings, attributing their recovery to accident or good fortune. Most people would probably be inclined to take that as evidence that there is no particular efficacy to be expected from St. Anthony. Some, however, would be impressed, contending that even a slightly higher record of recovering the property of the devout is enough to show that there might be something to the claim. Others would demand further tests, even if the successes neared 100 percent among the devout and only 25 percent among the others. Then if the devout consistently had a clear edge over the rest of the population, even the most skeptical would concede there was sufficient evidence to prove at least some connection between devotion to St. Anthony and the recovery of lost property. In short, the methods used would be those familiar to sociologists in determining, for instance, incidences of poverty and literacy by applying standards of evidence approximating as closely as possible those used by chemists and physicists and those admissible in courts of law.

Now suppose that an enlightened Roman Catholic were to say: "Though I do not share the superstitious attitude of simple-minded people who think of St. Anthony as a magic umbrella-returner, I do believe that God's saints and angels help to watch over people and that there are even circumstances in which, by the power of God's love mediated through his saints, a person might recover a valued object such as a missal or even an umbrella. If so, however, there could never possibly be any means of establishing a correlation such as you have been trying to find. I would no more believe in St. Anthony's efficacy because of a 99 percent rate of success than I would disbelieve in it because of a 99 percent rate of failure." That expresses an attitude most religious people would applaud. What kind of evidence would then be accounted relevant? What would count for or against belief?

Whatever kind of evidence might be needed, it would have to do with *Gestalten* and their interpretation. No proposal about devotion to the saints, especially to anything so peripheral as the recovery of lost property through the mediation of one of them, could be susceptible to proof in itself. No evidence about it could be relevant to the fundamental religious claim. The principle in question applies not only to religion (though there it is very conspicuous) but to other matters such as a general political or economic theory. No convinced Marxist would ever be affected by a demonstration of this or that failure of Marxism, as no free-enterprise man would consider the rightness of his views in danger by reason of the failure of the system here or there, even over a wide range of time or circumstance. Nor, far more importantly, does anyone ever really come to favor either Marxism or a free-enterprise system through adding up the advantages and disadvantages, successes and failures of the respective systems, for all that people sometimes think they do. When Mr. Krushchev had the misfortune to encounter a nonworking elevator during his visit to the United States and jokingly remarked something to the effect that it illustrated the failure of the capitalistic system, everybody took the aside good-naturedly because, of course, even a widespread failure of elevators in New York could no more count against capitalism than such a breakdown in Moscow could count against the Soviet economic system. If any kind of evidence could change people's views on such matters, it would have to be of a very different sort.

If I were to say, "My life shows the hand of divine Providence," what evidence could I adduce for such a claim? I could point to a hundred incidents in support of it, but you would be perfectly in order in pointing out a hundred other incidents in my life that seemed to indicate lack of any such providential agency. Yes, there was the time I was almost drowned, when suddenly a man appeared on the scene who, having rescued me, then told me that he had had no intention of going to the beach that day but while at prayer suddenly felt a inner directive to do so and had even mentioned it to several people before he set out. But then there was also the time I prayed as never before for the safety of my baby son who shortly afterwards was run over by the only vehicle that had entered our village in three days. Had I forgotten the latter occurrence and many others in my zeal in collecting the "evidence for"? So, though the evidence produced might seem to be the kind that both sides would expect, there could be no proof. How could there be? Even if the opposition could muster very few cases illustrating my personal misfortunes, and these trivial cases, while I could cite a multitude of startling instances in support of my claim, such evidence could never really suffice. Believers would be deeply impressed, of course; but then they would need no evidence, nor, *ex hypothesi,* would I. The evidence could be expected to serve the interests only of the unbelievers, and these would properly say: "True, you have brought the only kind of evidence there could be. You have brought much of it. You have proved nothing."

John Wisdom on Interpretation

John Wisdom, in a much-quoted paper, cites a passage in John P. Marquand's novel *H. M. Pulham, Esquire* to illustrate how it is "possible to have all the items of a pattern and still to miss the pattern." A man, talking to a friend about his own marriage, observes that "Kay and I are pretty happy. We've always been happy." Since his friend seems skeptical, the man offers the explanation that, though he and Kay have had some quarrels, the sum total of their lives "adds up" to happiness.[5] Of course, it is not at all a question of addition, as though one were setting liabilities and assets against each other on a balance sheet and finding the corporation solvent after all. It is a question, rather, of the interpretation of the pattern of the marriage.

Wisdom also suggests an example of his own that makes, in effect, just that point. Two people are discussing two characters in a story both have read. One says, "Really, she hated him." The other disagrees, "She didn't; she loved him." There is no incident in the book that either has overlooked, but perhaps one notices something in the pattern that the other has not noticed. The remedy seems simple: the one points out to the other the element in the pattern that he thinks the other has not noticed. Yet to make such evidence stick is notoriously difficult, and often the discussion is like a discussion about whether waves stick up in the air like mountains or whether the air between them presses down making valleys in the water below. Who can tell whether a man's life is happy or not? People have seen him suffer many misfortunes and have listened to his lamentations for years; yet perhaps he says he is happy. There is no way in which, if his estimate of his life as a whole is favorable, we can prove him wrong. Nor could he prove himself right if he were so minded. That is why, in a court of law, the facts may be beyond dispute, yet no one can conclusively prove whether the defendant was sufficiently careful or showed negligence, for this is a question of interpretation of the facts, and here evidence is not available in the same way.

Wisdom also mentions another element in connection with his parable of the dispute about the two characters. Though the one disputant may have noticed something that the other has not, in real life there may be no such superior literary discernment. There may be no expressible reason to offer in support of the one view over the other, because the judgments depend on two different understandings of life, two different metaphysical stances.

Basic Proposals and *Gestalten*

Now our problem comes into focus. While relevant evidence about peripheral truth-claims in religion is easy to specify, evidence about basic religious truth-claims seems unspecifiable. The reason is that religious truth-claims relate to interpretations at the most fundamental level of the whole pattern of existence. Suppose we can disengage the most basic of all religious proposals

[5] John Wisdom, "Gods," *Proceedings of the Aristotelian Society* Vol. XLV (1944–1945), pp. 185 ff. Also see Wisdom's *Philosophy and Psycho-Analysis* (Oxford: Basil Blackwell, 1953), pp. 149–159.

and set them forth with some precision. We may find them logically explorable in the sense that they may be demonstrably intelligible and that their satellite truth-claims may all cohere perfectly. There is still no conceivable way in which we could prove them in the sense of compelling the assent of everybody, even every literate and intelligent adult.

The lineaments of a metaphysical view might be clearly exhibited. You might even say: "Now that I see as a whole what it is you are saying, I am willing to admit it is not so nonsensical as at first I had thought. I will go further: it now seems to me to be not at all irrational but, on the contrary, quite plausible. I am not a step nearer concluding, however, that there is evidence that your view, plausible enough though I now see it to be, corresponds to the actual state of affairs." You would be granting that I had followed good procedure. For instance, I had made no category mistakes by confusing the descriptive or scientific or ethical with the religious elements in the assertions, and I had not argued as if there were *a priori* norms when there were none. In short, you might well be congratulating me on my logical acumen while denying my interpretation of the state of affairs.

That the situation is inevitably so springs partly from the circumstance that, as we have already seen, the basic proposals on which all others depend are metaphysical proposals, and that the whole nexus of these proposals is an interpretation of the total pattern of experience. I offer you a *Gestalt* that you agree is an acceptable one; yet since other *Gestalten* are possible there is no reason that you should be convinced that you must accept this particular one. When I claim there is a cat in the next room and adduce "the evidence of your own eyes" to prove it to you, the reason you can no longer contest my claim is that you have already implicitly agreed to certain ground rules regarding the admissibility of evidence. That is not the case, however, with propositions about, say, general political theory. As we have seen, if you are a convinced Marxist, I shall never be able to produce evidence to convince you that my very different political view is right and yours wrong. If I demonstrate to you that a certain proposition you have been using in your argument is false, so affecting your total presentation, you will not say, "Oh, now I see and am ready for political conversion." You will say, rather, "You're right about that proposition. But never fear, I can work out the whole thing all over again in another way and I'll have the result ready for you next Tuesday." For while such basic proposals may be in a sense technically arguable, the conclusion need not compel assent. The principle here applies pre-eminently to religion.

Two Traditional Arguments for the Existence of God

The inadequacy of the traditional arguments for the existence of God has frequently been shown by modern critical thinkers. We may now briefly consider the "cosmological argument" and the "teleological argument" together and then take up the "ontological argument" separately.

Critique of the cosmological argument (everything must have a first cause, and contingent and changing beings *entail* an underlying necessary and changeless Being) shows what is fundamentally wrong with all such arguments: they assume what they set out to prove. Once you see a vision of the universe as necessarily depending on something outside of itself, then of course you are delighted by, and find logically irrefutable, the formal argument that there must be a God to start the universe and sustain it. You now see argued out the reason that he must also be greater than the universe of which he is the "first cause," and so forth. You find the argument logically irrefutable because it *is* logically irrefutable, once the hidden major premise is granted. Once you undermine that major premise, however, the argument falls.

Many have found, as did Kant, that the teleological argument (the universe exhibits a design and purpose such as points to a purposeful creator) is less unsatisfactory than the cosmological one. The very reason for this nod of respect to the second argument, however, shows us, from an opposite direction, what is wrong with all the traditional methodology in devising proofs for the existence of God. The interest of the teleological argument lies precisely in the fact that if you look at the universe in one way it does seem purposeful and therefore supports belief in the existence of a purposeful God, but if you look at it in another way it looks dysteleological and therefore supports, rather, an atheistic position. In each case your judgment depends, not upon the facts, but upon your interpretation of them, that is, upon the *Gestalt* or pattern that you see predominating.

Thomas Aquinas, who advanced five forms of argument, must have seen that no such methods of proving God's existence could constitute a logical proof, for if there ever could have been such a logical proof, one form of it would have sufficed, and others could have added nothing to it. In fact he called the five forms he advanced "ways" (*viae*), not strictly arguments but, rather, demonstrations—ways—of showing forth a truth. That one way should be needed to eke out the other demonstrates precisely the point that is being made here. No proof along the lines of either the cosmological argument or the teleological argument could possibly be conclusive in itself because, in order to be convinced, one must not only go beyond logical argumentation but one must decide the issue either by virtue of an interpretation, for which there can be no such evidence and therefore no logical proof as we generally understand logical proof, or else by reference to a basic metaphysical presupposition, which is similarly beyond the scope of such standard methods of proof.

In view of the tendency among some philosophers to assess each argument for the existence of God in total independence of all the others, we should note that, except for the ontological argument, which is to be considered separately as a special case, such an expectation must be ruled out. Nor should we fail to observe that if a similar requirement were to be made in science, the result would be that most, perhaps all, of our accepted scientific theories would have to be set aside. More will be said on that in Chapter XII in reference to the development of the quantum theory that has revolutionized modern physics.

The Teleological Argument

Kant's nod of respect to this argument, which we have already noted, would not in itself justify our dallying longer over it; but its perennial popularity is such as to warrant our more carefully examining what may be said for and against it.

In the eighteenth century, William Paley asked his readers to consider what they would think if, never having seen a watch, they found one on the sands. The close adaptation of the mechanical parts of the watch to one another would cause the finder of the watch, even if he could not tell for what purpose it had been designed, to infer that it had indeed been designed for a purpose. In its construction he would detect the hand of an intelligent being. He went on to argue that such was the case with the universe around us, the orderly design of which, he said, shows the unmistakable mark of having been created by such a being. "The heavens are telling the glory of God," sings the psalmist, "and the firmament proclaims his handiwork." [6] Joseph Addison put that thought that the psalmist had lyrically expressed into the more flowery language of the eighteenth century, calling attention to the new force that a mechanistic view of the universe seemed to have bestowed upon the poetry of a bygone age: "the spacious firmament" and "the spangled heavens" proclaim "their great Original," and the sun "publishes . . . the work of an Almighty hand." [7]

The eighteenth-century proponents and opponents of the argument under consideration had a mechanistic view of the universe that, of course, finds no support in twentieth-century science. They could see justification for likening the universe to a watch, but scientists today, however they may regard the universe, cannot possibly see it like that at all. Quantum theory and the concept of space-time do not destroy the teleological argument. What is to be said for and against that argument, in the light of our contemporary scientific understanding of the universe, is, rather, simply accentuated.

We have learned that the fit survive, but we must notice the mysterious fact that they arrive. For every success in the evolutionary process, there seem to be innumerable failures; yet the successes can hardly be said to be accidental, and that reflection suggests purpose, which in turn may suggest the existence of God. When we ask, however, what kind of God it does

[6] Psalms 19:1.
[7] Hymn, "The Spacious Firmament on High."

suggest, the proponent of the argument must speak less confidently. Indeed, Kant's chief objection to the argument as it was presented in his day was that even if it were held to prove the existence of a divine Being, it could not be held to prove the existence of the kind of God it purported to prove. For instance, we have just talked of "failures" and "successes"; but what constitutes failure and success? What do these terms mean? If we say that cosmic success means that which ministers to a cosmic purpose, we beg the question: what purpose? Moreover, even if we accept the view that purpose is clearly present in the universe, we must go on to ask, what *sort* of purpose?

To that question the answer might be, "One cannot say precisely, perhaps; but it is plainly a *good* purpose." The terms "good" and "evil" are, however, what John Austin used to call "trouser words." That is to say, we need to know, when we hear one of them, what the contradictory would exclude. If I say, "This table is mahogany," my meaning is clear without my explaining that the table is not oak, not walnut, and so forth; but when I say, "This is a very good table," you are entitled to ask me, "Do you mean it is a very valuable table, perhaps a rare Sheraton that should be in the Metropolitan Museum, or do you mean that it is a very good table for chopping vegetables on?" To see good purpose in the universe might mean that one sees operative in it a principle whereby it achieves a goal; but how can we tell what the goal is? If we could tell, the purpose would be known to us more precisely than even the most vehement proponent of the teleological argument would claim. If, as seems the case, we cannot tell what the goal is, there is nothing we can predicate of the divine Being who is said to have the purpose. In any case, that divine Being might be simply the universe itself or "the-way-things-are."

Since such arguments for the existence of God hinge upon interpretation and the invocation of arguments of probability, there is a further difficulty. Interpretation of the universe cannot proceed as can interpretation of phenomena within it. When we have access to a large number of facts or entities and can inspect them one by one, we may hope to tell what may be expected of *A,* what of *B,* and so on, because we have bases for comparison. When we are interpreting phenomena within the universe, we may make very good use of probability arguments. The proponents of the teleological argument have generally stated that argument also in terms of probability. They have suggested that, though there are dysteleological elements as well as teleological ones in the universe, the latter either manifest themselves in more frequent occurrences or else are for one reason or another to be accounted weightier. Hence, they have argued, we may say that the universe is at least "in all probability" demonstrably the work of a divine Being who is guiding it. We cannot properly apply such probability arguments to the universe, however, because (if by "universe" we mean "the totality of all that is") there can be nothing with which to compare it. There is no means, therefore, of comparing my *Weltanschauung* with yours in hope of showing that one conforms better than the other to what ought to be expected. The one cannot be said to be more rational than the other, for rationality is predicated of that which we take to conform to the orderly understanding of a connected and intelligible whole. To say that, in an inspection of the universe as a whole, we find certain tendencies that conform better than do other tendencies to what we are entitled to expect, or to what ought to be, or to what is God's "way of doing things," either makes no sense at all or else is no more than a clumsy way of saying something from which we can conclude only that in the universe no coherent pattern of purpose or design can be detected.

Of course, if we could say that we found such a pattern of purpose or design running all the way through the universe, we might decide to give the name of God to whatever principle might be held to lie behind that pattern. The objection to the teleological argument as traditionally presented, however, is that it is advanced as an argument in favor of the existence of either the biblical God or the God of classical theism, and in the face of the acknowledged fact that there are present in the universe at least some elements that seem to be, to say the least, very difficult to square with either of these understandings of the nature of divine Being. On that, much more will have to be said in a later chapter specially devoted to the very important problem that seemingly dysteleological elements in the universe present for classical theism.

The Ontological Argument

The ontological argument has a special interest. Its two most celebrated exponents in the past were St. Anselm in the late eleventh century and Descartes in the seventeenth century.[8] The philosophers who are most noted for having repudiated it are also separated from each other by about five centuries: the thirteenth-century Thomas Aquinas and the eighteenth-century Kant.

Let us look briefly at the classic exposition of the argument, as Anselm presents it in the *Proslogion*. It is tantalizingly neat. In the Bible, the psalmist mentions a fool (*insipiens*) who says in his heart that there is no God.[9] Anselm affirms that that same fool, when he hears the words "that than which nothing greater can be conceived" understands what he hears and what he understands is in his understanding, even if he does not understand it to exist. Anselm fully recognizes even at this stage the obvious objection that something can exist in the mind though it does not exist in reality,

[8] Bonaventure, Leibniz, and Hegel, each in his own way, also accepted in principle the ontological argument.
[9] Psalms 14:1 and 53:1.

that is, independently of the mind.[10] He argues, however, that if the x that is in man's mind be such that we cannot conceive of something greater, it does not exist solely in the mind of man, for if it were there only, one could go on to compare it in one's mind with an x^1 that exists in reality, and that x^1 would then be seen at once to be greater than the x and would therefore become the x. If the x were in the mind alone, it would both be and not be something than which nothing greater can be conceived, and that, he thinks, will not do. He concludes that the x exists both in the mind and in reality independent of the mind. So necessarily does such an x exist that "it cannot be thought of as not existing."

In the fourth chapter of the *Proslogion* Anselm raises a point that is often overlooked. If, as Anselm thinks he has shown, God's existence is, as we should say, self-evident, how is it possible for the fool to deny "in his heart" what he could not but think in his mind? In one sense, Anselm says, we think of an x when we think of the word that signifies that x, and in another sense we think of it when we think of the thing itself. Anselm argues that though it is possible in the first sense to think of God as not existing, it is not possible in the second sense.

When Gaunilo, a French monk, raised the objection (an obvious one to any modern reader of Anselm) that if one is asked to think of an island of greater beauty and riches than any other place on earth, indeed the most perfect island imaginable, one could very well do so, but it would by no means follow that such an idyllic island existed. Gaunilo also objected that we have no distinct notion of God from which to infer his existence.

To these objections Anselm replies that Gaunilo is right, of course, in the case of the island; but the case of God, says Anselm, is not the same. It is unique. Here we are dealing not with *a* being or *a* perfection, but with the greatest being, Being itself, the supreme perfection, Perfection *in se*. The force of Anselm's argument, whatever we may think of it, springs from his view of the nature of Being, of what is unique in the notion of Being, considered as absolute. Anselm thinks of God as Being *par excellence*. God is the essential Being on which all other beings depend. Nothing non-God is Being, in that plenary sense. Once that is understood and granted, the ontological argument, far from being refutable, becomes a sort of elaborate truism. That is not to say it becomes wholly pointless; truisms can be useful. If we grant the Anselmic way of thinking, which was part of the Platonic and Neo-Platonic heritage he shared with the early medieval world generally, then to say that there are beings (as we all admit) but that they have no source, no essential Being, is like saying there are rivers that come from nowhere. As a river is by definition a body of water flowing from a source, so beings by definition have their source in essential Being, and what that Source is, is what we mean by the word "God." The "greater," the *majus*

10 *Proslogion*, Chapter 2.

in Anselm's argument, is really a *melius,* a "better"; that is to say, it is not a mere quantitative "greater" but a qualitative "greater." It is also qualitatively distinct, as the spring is from the river that flows from it and could not exist without it.

Till comparatively recent years, the ontological argument was accounted perhaps the deadest of all the traditional arguments, and the reason for the noteworthy revival of philosophical discussion of it[11] is of some importance.

Contributors to the discussion have reached many varying conclusions. Professor J. N. Findlay claimed to provide an ontological argument for the *dis*proof of the existence of God. Through a consideration of the conception of God as presented by Anselm in the ontological argument, Findlay concludes that either the existence of God is impossible or the concept is meaningless. Professor William P. Alston, contending that the traditional critiques are unsatisfactory, has offered a new refutation of the argument. The late Karl Barth, champion of modern Protestant Neo-Orthodoxy and accounted by many the greatest theologian of his day within the Reformation heritage, devoted a whole book[12] to showing that the Anselmic argument is not a philosophical argument at all but a theological exposition of the manner in which God illuminated the mind of Anselm by the gift of faith: "God gave himself to him to know and he was able to know God." [13] Taking it to be a philosophical proof was, in Barth's view, a fundamental misunderstanding. The Anselmic argument was never intended to be a philosophical proof and should be considered, rather, a description of the revelation or unfolding of God to the mind of Anselm. Both Paul Tillich and Charles Hartshorne have interested themselves in the argument. The latter, in an extensive study of it,[14] has tried to show that there are two separate lines of argument in Anselm and that only one of them is vulnerable. His conclusion is that what the argument really says is that *if* "God" stands for something conceivable, it stands for something actual and this should be formulated: "If the phrase 'necessary being' has a meaning, then what it means exists necessarily, and if it exists necessarily, then a fortiori, it exists." In other words, we may say: "The necessary being, if it is not nothing, and therefore the object of no possible positive idea, is actual."

One of the most interesting of all contemporary contributions to the discussion is that of Professor Norman Malcolm who, like Hartshorne, distinguishes two lines of thought in Anselm. Malcolm takes the first of these to be similar to the one presented later on by Descartes, and the second to be a very different one. While Malcolm rejects the first as inconclusive,

[11] See Alvin Plantinga, ed., *The Ontological Argument* (New York: Doubleday, Anchor Books, 1965).

[12] Karl Barth, *Anselm: Fides Quaerens Intellectum,* trans. Ian Robertson (Richmond, Va.: John Knox Press, 1960).

[13] Ibid., p. 170.

[14] C. Hartshorne, *Man's Vision of God* (New York: Harper & Row, 1941).

he defends the second. He is willing to go along with Kant in principle in accounting the first of Anselm's arguments "fallacious because it rests on the false doctrine that existence is a perfection (and therefore that 'existence' is a real predicate)." He argues that the second line of argument, however, is not subject to the same criticism and has something important to say, namely, that, if God exists, his existence is necessary. "Thus God's existence is either impossible or necessary. It can be the former only if the concept of such a being is self-contradictory or in some way logically absurd. Assuming that this is not so, it follows that He necessarily exists." Professor Alvin Plantinga has contended, however, that Malcolm's version of the argument is inadequate. Plantinga thinks Malcolm has failed to show that the proposition "There is a being who neither comes into nor goes out of existence and who depends upon nothing" is a necessary proposition.[15]

Logical Validity Need Not Compel Assent

We need not particularly concern ourselves here with upholding or refuting Malcolm's argument. What we should note is that having raised the question of the relation of the argument to religious belief, he goes on to say: "I can imagine an atheist going through the argument, becoming convinced of its validity, strongly defending it against objections, yet remaining an atheist. The only effect it could have on the fool of the Psalm would be that he stopped saying in his heart, 'There is no God,' because he would now realize that this is something he cannot meaningfully say or think. It is hardly to be expected that a demonstrative argument should, in addition, produce in him a living faith." [16]

In this perceptive observation we approach the root of the whole question of attempted proofs, not only of the existence of God, but of any basic proposal in religion. Even though the proposal may be shown to be logically unobjectionable (that is, that there is no way of showing it to be inconceivable or incoherent), there is still no way of compelling the assent of anyone who chooses to withhold that assent. You might not be able to offer any argument that made Plato's doctrine of ideas as found in the *Republic* radically unacceptable; yet I could not on that account tell you, "Then if you are an intellectually honest person you must accept it, and I shall rightly despise you if you don't." You might admit that though there may be centaurs on another planet (since centaurs are not inconceivable, as is a pregnant stallion) you are very far indeed from being persuaded that there are any centaurs anywhere. Moreover, not only would you see no reason for accepting the proposal I offered you and to which you could find no radical objection;

[15] See A. Plantinga, *God and Other Minds* (Ithaca, N. Y.: Cornell University Press, 1967), pp. 82–94.

[16] Norman Malcolm in *The Ontological Argument,* ed. A. Plantinga (New York: Doubleday, Anchor Books, 1965), p. 159.

you would have an alternative proposal which you *preferred*. If we were to ask why you preferred it, the answer might be that it fitted in better with your *Gestalt;* but why should you prefer your *Gestalt* to mine? Is there any criterion for any such preference?

Can Religious Experience Serve as Evidence?

One way of dealing with the question just posed is to answer that the preference can be determined only in terms of "religious feeling." If by this answer is meant the dismissal of proof on the ground that religion is a matter of feeling a personal relationship rather than pursuing an intellectual inquiry, it is open to the objection that from feeling nothing can be inferred but feeling. Furthermore, as Hume demonstrated, a causal relationship can be significantly asserted only where both terms of the relationship are observable states of affairs. Where my experience is asserted as the sole ground of my truth-claims in religion, all I can hope to establish is that I have the experience and can conduct some kind of introspection into it. I can tell you that you are spiritually blind, that you suffer from a moral defect comparable to the physical defect of colorblindness, and that that is why you cannot enjoy the experience I enjoy. You may concede that all that may indeed be so; but you might add that even if you were as morally perceptive as I seemed to claim to be, how could you achieve more than the knowledge that you had an experience of feeling, an intensely interesting experience, no doubt, yet one which, for all the uniqueness it presumably would have in your life-pattern, would still be no more than your experience of feeling, as mine is no more than my experience of feeling?

Or again, I claim I feel both a sense of alienation from God and also God's guiding hand in my daily life. You reply that you do not feel either of these, but you do often feel insecurity and anxiety, and also frequently have an instinctive sense of what to do in perplexing situations, though you never connect it with anything beyond yourself—your ancestral heritage, physical and psychological, or your social environment, for example. Since we are referring everything simply to feeling, there can be no standard of judgment for preferring one feeling to another.

The hypothetical position just proposed is in fact close to, though a caricature of, that of Friedrich Schleiermacher (1768–1834). It is thoroughly unsatisfactory both to the philosopher of religion and to the religious believer. First, it is unsatisfactory to the philosopher of religion because it simply dismisses all possibility of relating the truth-claims of religion to any evidence at all. Such a facile reduction to feeling is unwarranted by the religious phenomena themselves. Second, it is unsatisfactory to the believer because, though of course nobody would deny that intense feeling may be a concomitant of religious activity or faith, the believer is not interested in a calculus of feeling that would give his religious experience a place on a scale, in competition with other candidates such as alcohol or marijuana. He is not claiming simply an interior illumination, an inner light. Whether rightly or wrongly, he is implicitly making truth-claims that have an ultimate reference beyond himself in a Being other than himself, and at least in the classic Jewish and Christian traditions, other than the whole created universe.

One might argue that the experience is self-authenticating and that religious people can never have any difficulty, therefore, in distinguishing it from other experiences such as the feelings associated with sexual activity, hallucinatory drugs, or even musical joys. When we ask, however, precisely what the self-authentication can be, we find it could be only the authentication of the feeling as, say, the richest or finest or most unusual in one's experience. If it authenticated a truth-claim, how could believers sometimes be mistaken and be ready to admit they had been mistaken in their claims to have had a religious experience when the experience turned out to have been indisputably induced through a hallucination or a hoax? Moreover, proponents of the "self-authenticating feeling" view often hold, as Schleiermacher and his numerous modern counterparts insist, that everybody has the capacity and aptitude for religious feeling in some degree. Yet how can this be, since some people say they cannot even attach any meaning to the notion?

Besides such difficulties, which are posed by all appeals to feeling as the sole criterion of religious truth-claims, there is another objection that should be stated before we leave this topic, namely, that for me to say something is true because I feel it, leads me into being willing to claim anything I choose to claim. By any reckoning, then, the appeal to interior feeling alone can do nothing to illumine our understanding of religious truth-claims. That is not to say, however, that the believer will or ought to refrain from any allusion to his feeling. The feeling need not be in dispute, but in the last resort, it can have no more relevance to the truth-claim than a chemist's feeling of joy and triumph in discovering a new element has to do with the evidence for the discovery.

Scientific Hypotheses and Religious Faith

The foregoing considerations establish that whatever the evidence for religious truth-claims might be, it could not possibly be either solely logical demonstration or simply intensity of feeling. That is not by any means to say that neither logical activity nor feeling can play any part in religious conviction. Indeed both do. We are still left with the question, however, of the relation of the evidence to the truth-claim.

The category that rightly predominates in popular discussions of religion is that of faith. That it should often be contrasted with knowledge is unfortunate. Neither need we make the complete disjunction that such a contrast usually implies, nor need we say that faith is a kind of feeble species of the genus knowledge, as modern epistemologists would generally say of belief. Religious faith, whatever it be, certainly looks as though it were more to be associated with the inductive methods of the scientist than with the deductive arguments of the mathematical logician. There are, of course, obvious differences, especially in procedures of verification; yet we may note that in a scientific experiment one begins, not with any kind of knowledge relating directly to what is to be found out, but with an hypothesis. The scientist, since he is dealing with empirical situations, has no logical principle to guide him into making the right hypothesis and so arriving at the discovery "first shot." If he had, he would not have needed to make the hypothesis at all; he would already have made the discovery. Instead, he often makes many hypotheses before hitting on the one that turns out to be right. He uses, of course, certain approved methods of verification. For the moment we are not concerned with these. Let us ask instead: how does scientist p come to hit on the right hypothesis while scientist q does not, though q may be (and p may very well admit that q is) a more learned and experienced scientist than p?

The ability for hitting on the right hypothesis, like the diagnostic ability that some medical men possess, does not seem to be *directly* related in any way to professional knowledge or experience. Some will talk of it quite freely as a "flair," or a "nose," or even as a "gift," as religious people talk of faith as a "gift." In both cases, that is, there is no clearly known explanation. One might suggest that a medical scientist, for instance, has his "knack," though he is no more learned or experienced than his colleagues in the field, because he is more "attuned to Nature," or to that aspect of it on which they are all working (for example, osteogenic sarcoma), than they are. That would be indeed very vague. The scientist who believes he has the right hypothesis, or is at any rate approaching it, is not, however, entirely indistinguishable from his colleagues. Characteristic of him is his determination to work at the verification, his perseverance in doing so, and his confidence that he is on the right track; also, he often gives others the impression of being a little crazy. Beyond that, however, he is intellectually indistinguishable from other workers in his field. Furthermore, he may turn out to have been wrong after all and so have to try another hypothesis; but even if he turns out to have failed and to have been wrong, he may nevertheless feel—indeed, characteristically does feel—that he was on the right track and still is, having only been temporarily misled by a "red herring trailed across the path of truth."

The obvious objection to this parallel with religious faith is that there is surely a great difference: the scientist has certain well-recognized methods for verifying his hypothesis which the religious man seems to lack. To this the latter might reply that he is constantly verifying his faith by a very rigorous method indeed, and that though his methods of verification differ from those of the scientist, they are nevertheless appropriate to his case. He might claim that they issue, moreover, from what more and more compels his assent as surely as the scientist's assent is compelled by his verificational procedures.

In the first place, the religious man claims to be confronted by what he calls a revelation, which is the unfolding, presentation, or disclosure of Being, inviting him to take certain stances about such concerns as the meaning of human existence, the destiny of man, and the nature of that which is revealed or disclosed as Being. His response to this invitation (as he takes it to be) is affirmative, constituting what religious people call faith. It is an attitude of trust and confidence. It says, in effect, "I have got the hang of things at last. I don't know all the details yet, all the workings-out; but I have the blueprint, which is the key to everything else that matters." This is his claim. What evidence does he produce to justify his adherence to it in face of all rivals, of which there may plainly be many?

Beyond *Bliks*

So far, all we have is what R. M. Hare has pleasantly immortalized as a *blik*.[17] As Hare points out, Antony Flew's error in attacking the religious believer's position is that he takes the *blik* for some sort of *explanation*. That it is not and cannot be this is surely now clear. But how then can one *blik* be proved right and another wrong, or even one better and another worse? If there is and can be neither logical explanation nor scientific verification, how do we know that a believer's faith is any different from a lunatic's *blik*? Hare himself *suggests* an answer: "As Hume saw, without *blik* there can be no explanation; for it is by our *bliks* that we decide what is and what is not an explanation." [18]

Evidence and Proof

Once he has accepted the *blik*, the man of faith feels, but is not content *only* to feel, what Chesterton characteristically described as the convert's joy:

> The sages have a hundred maps to give
> That trace their crawling cosmos like a tree
> . . . . .
> And all these things are less than dust to me
> Because my name is Lazarus and I live.[19]

The joy is accompanied, however, by certain moral and other expectations. For example, the convert does not feel content simply to luxuriate in his

[17] R. M. Hare, "Theology and Falsification," in *New Essays in Philosophical Theology*, eds. A. G. N. Flew and A. MacIntyre (New York: Macmillan Co., 1955), pp. 100–102.
[18] Ibid., pp. 101 f.
[19] G. K. Chesterton, "The Convert," in *T. P.'s Weekly*, July 20, 1929. Quoted by kind permission of Miss D. E. Collins and Dodd, Mead & Co. of New York, publishers of *The Collected Poems of G. K. Chesterton*.

feeling of joy, as though his conversion *consisted in* the *blik.* He is eager to begin working at his faith; that is to say, he is eager to test his expectations. The fulfilment of these expectations is part of his verificational procedure. The *blik* is expressed in his credo, in what he says he believes; but though that belief, far from being a mere weak form of knowledge, has become a key principle in his thinking, he is not usually preoccupied with it in the way a metaphysician might expect. Indeed, unless the convert is philosophically and theologically minded, he is unlikely to have more than a minimal preoccupation with the details of the *blik* itself; as a rule, he will be far more interested in the practical results. Not only, let us suppose, has he a greater peace and serenity of mind, favorably affecting even, it may be, his bodily health, but he finds he is better able to help other people. Not only does he find his whole outlook more constructive; he sees happy, practical results from his new constructiveness.

Most strikingly, he is less self-centered in his attitude to life in general. He can feel the results of this change in his orientation, and he may be able to find means of expressing his feeling to others who are on a similar track of spiritual development, but there is obviously no direct way in which he can explain what the loss of self-centeredness means to someone who is still bound by its shackles. To be able to do so would be like being able to give a vivacious sense of humor to a person who conspicuously lacked one. The person who is still self-centered is likely to say such things as, "But how could I function as a self if I lost myself as you seem to be enjoining me to do?" To which the convert might reply, "You don't *really* lose yourself: you get a 'better' self." This would probably evoke something like, "Then why lose yourself at all? Why not just improve the self you have? I can see no possible advantage to losing any part of myself, though I can see an advantage in extending or enriching the self I have or am." The convert may have said much the same himself only yesterday. Today his dominant reflection is likely to be that now he sees, as he could not see before, how narrow and constrained his former state was.

Let us suppose that the convert also finds that while his moral expectations are fulfilled, the moral fruits are of an even better quality than he could have conceived before his conversion. What he formerly accounted the most noble of actions that he could conceive were beyond his capacity to perform; now he finds himself performing actions that he sees are even finer than those he had ever thought of. By the standards of the biblical observation that thorns do not bear grapes nor thistles figs,[20] and the promise that "by their fruits ye shall know them," [21] the convert has verified *in his own experience,* which extends over his intellectual, moral, and emotional life, the rightness of the *blik* from which he started. He now sees intellectually *why* it gave him such joy when he first made the decision to accept it or, to use Kierkegaard's language, took the "leap of faith." Not only can he now

[20] Matthew 7:16.
[21] Matthew 7:20.

formulate (if he happens to be inclined to such intellectual exercises) the formal, metaphysical truth-claims implicit in his *blik*; he has the evidence in his own life to substantiate them, and this is as much proof as he can ever need, be he the most discriminating and critical philosopher in human history.

All this is not to say he proves his case every day of his life and at all hours. Like the scientist who finds the verification of his hypothesis no straightforward, continuous succession of triumphant practical demonstrations, but often, on the contrary, an extremely arduous and almost lifelong task conducted despite much ridicule, the religious man is likely to go through great periods of temptation and will often find himself woefully failing to "produce the evidence" even to his own satisfaction. Nevertheless, unless the faith was spurious and the *blik* false, he gradually unfolds the evidence of its rightness to himself with such certitude that he can say in honesty that what his *blik* implicitly affirms has been so fully demonstrated that he would rather doubt anything else, even his own name. That is not to say, of course, that he may feel the slightest reason to doubt his name: it is only a way of exhibiting the cognitive status his truth-claim has achieved in his calculus of concerns.

Falsification and Proof

We have elsewhere noted the much stressed notion that verification is by no means the whole, and perhaps not even the fundamental requirement. Perhaps even more important is falsification. Is there anything that would count *against* our hypothetical convert's belief? Here we should note an often overlooked point that John Hick makes. Critics of the possibility of obtaining any evidence appropriate to the truth-claims of religion are inclined to assume that verification and falsification are, as he puts it, "symmetrically related." Indeed, of course, they often are, as in the case of a proposition such as "there is a man in the next room." Verification and falsification do not necessarily stand in relation to each other in such a neat, symmetrical arrangement, however; they are not like two sides of a coin. Sometimes "one can fail to verify without this failure constituting falsification." Hick cites the proposition that there are three successive sevens in the decimal determination of π. So far as the value of π has been worked out, it does not contain a series of three sevens; nevertheless, such a series might occur at a point not yet reached in anybody's calculations. That is to say, the proposition, if true, may one day be verified; yet, if false, it can never be falsified.[22]

The negative application of these considerations to the question should not be overlooked. It may well be that in the nature of the case, our hypothetical convert's *blik*, if false, can never be formally falsified. Mistaken

[22] John Hick, *Faith and Knowledge*, 2nd ed. (Ithaca, N. Y.: Cornell University Press, 1966), pp. 174 f.

from the start, or driven by a libidinal compulsion to arrange his psychological archetypes in a certain way, he may have succeeded not only in
rationalizing everything in his life to fit in with his *blik* but in producing
moral results such that he was able to make himself find satisfaction in
them over a long period, even till the end of his life. There would be no
way in which he could actually prove himself wrong and certainly no way
in which he could be proved wrong by someone else. In short, the *blik,*
though not falsifiable, is nevertheless also still unverifiable.

The religious man, in response to such an observation, would agree; yet
he would also smile, assured that the case envisaged, though formally possible,
involves too much coincidence to be seriously entertained. To the man of
faith, it would be like saying that if you discovered a child whose capacity
for composing music suggested that he was a musical prodigy, a person
skeptical of the claim might very well go on objecting that the child might
be getting promptings from some musical relative and so, though gifted
with a good musical memory and a flair for showing off, was not the budding
Mozart you thought. The child might go on until he was writing symphonies
at the age of ten. The whole pattern of the unfolding of a musical prodigy's
early life might be manifesting itself more and more to you every day;
yet there might really be, *in the circumstances,* no completely watertight
way of proving the rightness of your claim about the child. *You* would not
doubt its authenticity; the child could not possibly doubt it. Yet formally
it would be possible for an obdurate skeptic to do so, at any rate for a
very long time, and if the child died before he got to the point of writing
symphonies and operas, the skeptic would never need to feel compelled to
admit your claim. By the same token, it is formally possible to deceive
yourself in thinking you have the kind of religious development that
establishes in your own mind the conviction that you are right with God
and are reaping the appropriate fruits thereof. No one who has had any
religious experience such as we have been considering would be willing to
pay much attention to the notion, because the known difficulties and hazards
of the way of faith would seem to such a person to preclude taking that
notion seriously.

Has Faith a Special Logic?

In a later chapter we shall consider the notion of faith at much greater
length and with reference to what modern existentialist writers have to say
about it. We shall then have an opportunity to examine certain special
questions relating to its cognitive and conative aspects. We shall postpone
till then the discussion of certain technical questions about the nature of
the cognitive element and of how the relation of belief to knowledge is
to be understood. For the present it is convenient, however, to raise an
obvious question about the nature of faith and then to attend to some
general considerations about the nature of evidence.

Faith may be presented as having a cognitive and a conative element. On the conative side it may be considered akin to courage. Some might call it a special form of courage; others would insist that on that side it must be *sui generis*. Whatever it is, it is a way of coping with the world as we find it. It is grounded, however, in a cognitive element, and on this side it is plainly interpretative. It is a way of looking at and understanding the world. Is there any basis for preferring one interpretation, one *blik*, to another?

The man of faith is not the only one to experience the world as multidimensional; but among those who do, he alone finds it the locus of encounter with a Being who transcends the world yet breaks in upon it. Unlike the mystic who, as we shall see much later on, feels able to talk of the vision of God and even of converse and union with God, the man of faith, as such, is always distanced from the one to whom his faith is directed. The mystic, to the extent that he claims a vision of God, a sense of the divine presence, has no need of faith. The man of faith experiences absence at least as much as, and often much more than, presence. In Newman's words: "The night is dark"; he is "far from home" and does "not ask to see the distant scene," but only one step. Yet he does see something: a light shining as far ahead as that one step in the darkness. His assurance springs partly from another knowledge: the remembrance of having learned how such a light had guided him in the past, so that it will now serve his purpose till he reaches his haven and what he has "lost awhile." [23]

If we ask how, precisely, Newman's interpretation would have differed from that of a hypothetical atheist fellow-passenger, we ought to note that both share much common information about, for example, their latitude and longitude, their port of embarkation, and their intended destination. They share common ignorance, too: neither can tell how long the voyage may take, nor can they be sure what will become of them on the way. The difference lies in the interpretation of their total situation. Is there any way of judging between their respective interpretations, or must we simply take them as two of a number of *bliks* for which no reason can ever be given for preferring one to the other, since they are simply ways of taking us *to* the world without really telling us anything *about* the world?

The Nature of Evidence

In view of the nature of faith, the question of evidence assumes new force. On the one hand, some would say there is no conceivable kind of evidence that could be produced in support of preferring one *blik* to another. They

[23] Newman (1801–1890) composed the hymn "Lead, Kindly Light," from which these words are taken, in an orange-boat, the only transportation he could get to Marseilles after a three-week wait at Palermo. The orange-boat was then becalmed for a whole week in the Straits of Bonifacio, and it was then, or just before, that he wrote the hymn.

would look upon religion, as does J. H. Randall, Jr., as a human activity whose function is to nourish and strengthen man's commitment to ethical values and to cultivate often neglected dimensions of human life. As art calls attention to certain dimensions, so religion calls attention to others and thereby enriches those who use it. Beyond that there can be no cognitive element in religion such as would make possible the production of evidence about it.

When we examine *any* kind of evidence, however, we see that it is always sufficient only for a particular purpose and that its admissibility depends upon the nature of that purpose. For instance, when a person accused of murder is arraigned in court, there are rigorous rules concerning the admissibility of evidence. If evidence is offered that does not conform to these rules, the judge will direct the jury to exclude it from their consideration. For a jury to convict a man, all the evidence they take into account must conform to these rules, and even then the jury will sometimes spend a very long time discussing interpretations of the evidence the court has allowed them to take into consideration. Before the person can even have been accused, however, the police must arrest him. In order to do so, they do not need the kind of evidence the jury will eventually require, but they cannot arrest him simply because they do not like the look in his eyes or the expression on his face. They, too, need evidence to justify their making an arrest at all. Likewise, even before a private citizen may properly report his suspicions to the police, he would certainly require some evidence; at the very least, he would have to declare, for example, that he had seen the person about whom he made the report behave in a manner that would arouse suspicion in a reasonable person. At the other end of the spectrum, even the strongest evidence of guilt might in the long run, years afterwards, turn out to have been insufficient. That consideration is used, indeed, in one of the stock arguments of those who oppose capital punishment. One can *never* be absolutely sure, even after all the precautions that the wit of those responsible for the administration of justice can devise, that the evidence shall have been sufficient.

QUESTIONS ON CHAPTER III

1 In a truth-claim about religion, what conditions are needed to make disagreement possible and evidence therefore adducible?

2 What value, if any, do you see in the traditional arguments for the existence of God, and what are the basic objections to them?

3 What kind of evidence might there be for preferring one *blik* over another?

4 What procedures might be used for verifying faith-statements, contradistinguished from scientific statements?

5   The question of the relation of evidence to truth-claims would seem important both to philosophers as such and to religious men as such, yet in different ways. What would be the difference?

6   "To say 'He knows' is a correct way of giving a judgment only when it is about the validity of the claim. Thus we say that people in the fifteenth century did not know and could not have known that the earth was flat, because it is not flat, even when we allow that they might have been justified in saying that they knew. Whether the claim is justifiably made or not is irrelevant to whether we are to say 'He knows.' " (Alan R. White, "On Claiming to Know," in A. Phillips Griffiths, ed., *Knowledge and Belief* [London: Oxford University Press, 1967], p. 108.)

Critically consider.

7   "I know it is raining" is a stronger claim than "I believe it is raining." The claims of the religious believer, then, would seem to be a weaker form of truth-claim than "I know it is raining."

Critically consider.

8   (a)   If you were about to commit suicide, what kind of proof would convince you of the meaningfulness of life?

    (b)   What kind of proof would convince you of the necessity to commit suicide if you were convinced of the meaninglessness of life?

    (c)   What conclusions, if any, can you draw from your answers to (a) and (b) that might throw light on the question of proving religious truth-claims?

BIBLIOGRAPHICAL SUGGESTIONS

See also under Chapters I, II, and VII.

Ammerman, R. A., and Singer, M. G., eds. *Belief, Knowledge and Truth: Readings in the Theory of Knowledge.* New York: Charles Scribner's Sons, 1970. A book of readings. Very useful for the student.

Ayer, A. J. *Language, Truth and Logic.* 2nd ed. London: Victor Gollanz, 1946. A well-known book, the first edition of which appeared in 1936, in the early days of logical positivism.

Blackstone, W. T. *The Problem of Religious Language.* Englewood Cliffs, N.J.: Prentice-Hall, 1963. Treats the question of whether religious language is cognitive.

Chisholm, J. M. *Theory of Knowledge.* Englewood Cliffs, N.J.: Prentice-Hall, 1966.

Christian, William. *Meaning and Truth in Religion.* Princeton, N.J.: Princeton University Press, 1964.

D'Arcy, M. C. *The Nature of Belief.* New York: Sheed & Ward, 1945.

Dilley, F. B. *Metaphysics and Religious Language.* New York: Columbia University Press, 1964.

Flint, A. *Agnosticism.* Edinburgh: Blackwood & Sons, 1903. Though very outmoded, still a useful treatment of nineteenth-century questions.

Griffiths, A. Phillips, ed. *Knowledge and Belief.* New York: Oxford University Press, 1967. A useful collection of modern philosophical papers.

Hartland-Swann, J. *An Analysis of Knowing.* London: Allen & Unwin, 1958.

Hick, John. *Faith and Knowledge.* 2nd ed. Ithaca, N.Y.: Cornell University Press, 1966 (first published 1957). Very readable and a most useful book.

Hintikka, J. *Knowledge and Belief.* Ithaca, N.Y.: Cornell University Press, 1962.

Hurlbutt, R. H., III. *Hume, Newton, and the Design Argument.* Lincoln, Neb.: University of Nebraska Press, 1965.

Lecomte de Noüy, Pierre. *Human Destiny.* New York: Longmans, Green & Co., 1947. A probability argument for the existence of God. For a critique of this argument, see W. I. Matson, *The Existence of God.* Ithaca, N.Y.: Cornell University Press, 1965, pp. 102–111.

Martin, C. B. *Religious Belief.* Ithaca, N.Y.: Cornell University Press, 1959. Considers the cognitive value of religious experience.

Matson, Wallace. *The Existence of God.* Ithaca, N.Y.: Cornell University Press, 1965.

Mavrodes, George. *Belief in God: A Study in the Epistemology of Religion.* New York: Random House, 1970.

McKinnon, Alastair. *Falsification and Belief.* The Hague: Mouton, 1970.

Miles, T. R. *Religion and the Scientific Outlook.* London: Allen & Unwin, 1959.

Mitchell, Basil, ed. *Faith and Logic.* London: Allen & Unwin, 1957.

Newman, J. H. *An Essay in Aid of a Grammar of Assent.* New York: Doubleday, Image Books, 1955 (first published 1870). Cardinal Newman's study of the nature of inference, with special reference to religious persuasion, including his treatment of the illative sense. Though naturally outdated, still valuable and provocative.

Price, H. H. "Some Considerations about Belief." *Proceedings of the Aristotelian Society,* 35 (1934–1935): 229–252.

Schmidt, Paul F. *Religious Knowledge.* Glencoe, Ill.: Free Press, 1961. A short critique of religious knowledge as claimed by the major religions of the world, concluding with the view that all religions are outmoded expressions of basic life-attitudes.

Smith, Norman Kemp. *The Credibility of Divine Existence.* New York: St. Martin's Press, 1967. Also includes a collection of other papers by the same philosopher.

Wisdom, John. *Philosophy and Psycho-Analysis.* Oxford: Basil Blackwell, 1953. Contains the well-known section, "Gods."

Wittgenstein, Ludwig. *Philosophical Investigations.* Oxford: Basil Blackwell, 1953.

Woozley, A. D. *Theory of Knowledge.* London: Hutchinson, 1949.

IV

GOD AND NATURE

The perfections of Nature show that she is the image
of God; her defects show that she is only his image.
Blaise Pascal (1623–1662),
Pensées

Are God and Nature then at strife,
    That Nature lends such evil dreams?
    So careful of the type she seems,
So careless of the single life.
Alfred Lord Tennyson (1809–1892),
In Memoriam

The Term "Nature"

The term "Nature" comes from the Latin *natura*, derived from the verb
nasci, "to be born." The early Greeks had used the term *physis* for everything
that is or ever has come into being. They made no radical distinction between
matter on the one hand and life and consciousness on the other. After
Democritus, the special interest in man that the Sophists developed led to
a contrast between the "natural" (that which anything is from the beginning)
and the "conventional" (that which is the result of human intervention):
law, custom, and language, for instance, belonged to the latter category.
Later, under the influence of Plato and Aristotle, the sharp distinction made
between "mind" and "matter" brought about an identification of Nature
with the "material" part of the universe, including the human body as the
"physical" part of man. Because Christian thought was cross-fertilized at
a very early stage with Platonic and Neo-Platonic influences, the dichotomy
between matter and mind that tended to range Nature (*physis*) with the
former, pervaded much of medieval thinking, notwithstanding some counteracting influences. Despite the various humanistic movements in the later
Middle Ages and the sixteenth century that is commonly accounted the
Renaissance period, which all provided an ambience more sympathetic
toward the "material" world, and the eventual revival of the older Greek

conception of Nature, the identification of Nature with the material world persists in popular thought to the present day. The confusion has affected even scholarly writers, who have sometimes equated "naturalism" with "materialism."

The term "Nature" has a wide variety of meanings in the history of thought. Aristotle used it to describe what he took to be the internal principle that accounted for the structure of any individual thing and its development. He also used it, however, for the totality of all such things. When modern scientists use the term "Nature" they intend it to signify the general order they find in the universe, the aggregate of entities that are or can be observed. These entities include man, so far as man is susceptible to scientific investigation. The interest of the modern scientist lies in the order, regularity, and predictability of the universe. It is the "cosmos," which term comes from the Greek *kosmos,* meaning "order." By any reckoning, then, Nature, whatever it may be taken to be, is *kosmios,* orderly. That is not to say that we are to take scientific "laws" to be, as some scientists in the past tended to suppose them to be, the ultimate realities of the universe. We cannot so account them, for the modern scientist finds in the universe not only the orderliness scientists have always found but also a no less noteworthy randomness. In quantum theory, and in biology (e.g., mutation of the genes and the operation of natural selection) the random element is conspicuous. The "laws" *are* to be taken, nevertheless, as descriptions of the invariancies the scientist has been able to abstract from Nature.

Classical Christian theology, both before and after the Reformation, complicated the understanding of the term "Nature" by recognizing a "natural" and a "supernatural" order. Theologians traditionally used to recognize two sharply separated orders: (a) the order of "Nature," the realm of the physical universe, mechanistically conceived, which is the proper study of the "natural" sciences, the *Naturwissenschaften,* as the Germans came to say, and (b) the "supernatural" order, the realm of the spirit, which is the proper study of theology and of those allied disciplines that the Germans came to call *Geisteswissenschaften,* the spiritual or mental sciences, such as metaphysics and ethics. Though the natural order functioned according to its own principles, God could intervene, overriding the functioning of the natural order by the application of the supernatural one. Miracles came to be accounted typical examples of such intervention, though there is nothing at all written into the original New Testament Greek term *sēmeion* to require such a special understanding.

This cleavage between a "natural" and a "supernatural" order is now widely discarded by modern theologians. When these wish to express the multidimensionality of Being, they prefer to use a supposedly less weighted term, such as "supranatural" or "ultranatural," which is not so irretrievably connected with a now outmoded dichotomy. Theologians no longer think in terms of a universe that is like a clock made by a divine clockmaker who makes occasional adjustments to his handiwork. The God–Nature antinomy remains, however, a basic problem. We must try to specify its meaning and express various possible ways of understanding it.

The Pantheistic Solution

In the history of modern western philosophy, the most celebrated exponent of a pantheistic solution of the God–Nature antinomy is the heterodox Jewish philosopher Spinoza. Hegel, the thinker most associated with the development of the term "philosophy of religion" as the name for a separate philosophical pursuit, was a diligent student, in his youth, along with Hölderlin, Schelling, and other classmates of Spinoza.[1] According to H. A. Wolfson, one of Spinoza's most reliable present-day interpreters, the originality of Spinoza consists chiefly in his accepting the consequences of the unity of God and Nature, which Wolfson takes to be already implicitly discoverable in earlier Jewish thought.[2] For Spinoza, .God and Nature are so closely connected that by *natura naturans* (Nature as active) is to be understood "that which is in itself and is conceived through itself," which is to say God *in se,* God "in his essence," and by *natura naturata* (Nature as passive) is intended "all that follows from the necessity of God's nature . . . that is, all the modes of the attributes of God." [3]

On such a view, God and Nature are virtually identified. Yet he accords Nature a multidimensionality that was alien to the thought of the seventeenth century in which Spinoza lived.[4] He cannot well be accused of reducing God to Nature as understood in terms of his day. To say he argues that Nature exhibits the qualities traditionally attributed to God might perhaps be less misleading. On the Spinozistic view, the God–Nature antinomy evaporates into an all but indiscernible distinction; hence his celebrated phrase *Deus sive natura,* God *or* Nature.

The term "pantheism," which is used to signify the belief or theory that God and Nature are identical, is a modern one, unknown to Spinoza himself. It was invented by John Toland, who coined it in 1705. His opponents took it up and it soon became a generally accepted term in philosophical

---

[1] For accounts of the development of Hegel's thought, see J. N. Findlay, *Hegel: A Re-Examination* (New York: Macmillan Co., 1958), pp. 131–143, 341–344; W. Kaufman, *Hegel* (New York: Doubleday & Co., 1965), pp. 41–69, 95–100, 273–278; and G. R. Mure, *The Philosophy of Hegel* (London: Oxford University Press, 1965), pp. 43–51, 102–109, 194–199.

[2] H. A. Wolfson, *The Philosophy of Spinoza* (New York: Meridian Books, 1960), pp. 331 ff.

[3] Spinoza, *Ethics,* I, 29 schol.

[4] Spinoza is of special interest to philosophers of religion as a philosopher who was also a precursor of modern methods of biblical exegesis. On this see H. G. Hubbeling, *Spinoza's Methodology* (Assen, Holland: Van Gorcum & Co., 1964), pp. 58 ff., 63 f.

and theological discussions. It refers to an identification of God and Nature that is to be found in the thought of the ancient world, especially in India, where it is still characteristic of much of Hindu thought. It stands in sharp opposition, however, to the view that is characteristic of the orthodox teaching of several of the great religions of the world—Judaism, Christianity and Islam.

Panentheism

Modified forms of pantheism, such as are to be found in Schelling and Hegel, and their English disciples Bradley and Bosanquet, do not identify God and Nature; but typical of their teaching is the view that, though God includes and permeates all of Nature, so that all Nature exists in God, nevertheless God's Being is more than, and is not exhausted by Nature. Views of this kind (which might include that of Malebranche) are called by modern scholars panentheistic. The term was coined by K. C. F. Krause (1781–1832) to designate his own system.

By the time of Hegel the influence of Hume and Kant had made impossible the acceptance of what Hegel called the "old rationalism" (*Altrationalismus*). So he rejected all attempts to move directly from the perception of order in Nature to God, as the old rationalists had tried to do; for he saw that, as James Collins puts it, all such attempts "are vitiated by the assumption that Nature and the natural condition of man are simply there, as the starting points for a process of reasoning that leads to God." [5] Such a procedure, Hegel thought, ends either in the kind of identification between God and Nature that we have seen in Spinoza, or in an impossible leap from the natural to a God who transcends it. Yet Hegel's theory of finitude, through which he hoped to overcome the particular difficulty in question, enabled him to make the transition from finite to infinite Being only within a highly rarefied intellectual construction.

Panentheistic explanations of the God–Nature antinomy not only fail to satisfy the religious consciousness of Christians and others who are committed to the view of God as Creator and Lord of Nature; they also raise special philosophical difficulties of their own. If God and Nature are to be even as closely identified as they are in panentheist forms of thought, one naturally questions why they should be separated at all. Is not this to multiply entities without necessity, in flagrant disregard of the principle of Occam's razor? If God so permeates Nature that all Nature is "in" God, speaking of God and Nature looks a somewhat artificial proceeding. Why not talk, rather, like Spinoza, of *Deus sive natura* and then, as the case arises, allude to one

---

[5] James Collins, *The Emergence of Philosophy of Religion* (New Haven: Yale University Press, 1967), p. 294.

of the modes, attributes, or dimensions, according to the philosophical model adopted, when there seems need to talk of what is popularly called God and what is popularly called Nature?

When Christians, under the influence of Greek philosophy, developed the very complex doctrine of the Trinity with its *hypostases* or *personae* to express, *inter alia,* the notion of God as the ground and source of Being on the one hand and, on the other, the God who, as the incarnate Logos, goes forth into the world, they were able to refer to these *hypostases* or "persons" without abandoning the comprehensive term "God," which dominated all their thinking on the subject. This term seemed to them, notably to St. Augustine, to safeguard the all-important doctrine of the divine unity against vulgar tendencies towards tritheism. Why then, should not panentheists do similarly, making Nature and God part of a greater and all-important reality in their system? After all, Hegel, in developing his triadic system, had borrowed from his early days as a theological student at Tübingen the model of the Trinity. In principle, a panentheist system would seem to distinguish Nature from God no more than the Christian Fathers distinguished the divine Logos from the Triune God. To speak of the divine Son or Logos was to speak of God; yet it was not to exhaust God, who is also, for instance, the immovable and impassible Source, Ground, and Creator of all things. In short, panentheism often comes so close to pantheism that the problem of the relation of God and Nature, though it exists, is not really very serious. The terms are defined in such a way as almost to provide an explanation in the very act of defining them. It is simply to say that God–Nature is multidimensional in such and such a way. We shall return to this point later. Meanwhile two other conceptions of the relationship must be considered. Both take seriously the notion of the transcendence of God over Nature, and in one of them belief in the transcendence is accompanied by belief in God's complete independence from Nature.

Nature and the Divine-Artist God

In the *Timaeus* Plato presents God as the divine artist working like a painter or sculptor on material that stands apart from himself and to which he gives form. The notion that there is a stuff or inchoate mass upon which God is eternally imposing form was congenial to the Greek mind, which hated the unlimited or infinite (*to apeiron*), and admired form (*hē morphē*). Aristotle also believed matter to be coeternal with God, and in the Middle Ages this view was generally taken to be the "scientific" one. It was held by Averroes and others. Yet it was in conflict with the doctrine of the Latin Church, which interpreted the Bible as teaching unequivocally that matter, as God's creation, is not coeternal with him. This point is not in fact so clear in the Hebrew Bible as medieval scholars supposed. The first chapter of Genesis, for instance, being comparatively late and exhibiting much Greek influence, is not, to say the least, incompatible with a divine-artist interpretation. Moreover, such is the structure of the Hebrew verb that there is no tense to convey the explicit past definite or perfect tense of the family of languages to which we are accustomed, so that "created" can mean "was creating" or "is creating." In any case, whatever the Hebrews thought, the Gentile world was certainly well accustomed and favorable to the notion that matter is a "given" that God is eternally working upon. Nevertheless, such a view savors too much of a God–Nature dualism to have satisfied Christian thinkers such as Augustine, Thomas Aquinas, or Calvin, who, each in his own way, insisted upon the absolute sovereignty of God as Creator of "all things visible and invisible."

The divine-artist theory of God is one that Brightman and others have revived and adapted to modern thought patterns. According to this view there is a "given" in the realm of fact, and God, as the focus of the realm of value, eternally faces it and is eternally bringing it under control. In such a view God is not *omnipotens* (omnipotent) in the sense understood by Thomas Aquinas—that is, able to do anything except what would be contrary to his own nature, such as making a lie true or constructing a triangle with four sides. Yet God might be called *pantokrator* (all-powerful, in control of all things), which is the word in the Greek Bible that the Latin *omnipotens* translates, since he is able to subdue the recalcitrant stuff that eternally faces him. To be always subduing it is, indeed, his nature. Despite the contention of modern exponents of this view that it is not technically a dualism, it is difficult for us to ignore its dualistic tendencies. It certainly deprives God of the sovereignty and independence traditionally attributed to him.

Nevertheless, if it be a dualism, it is a one-sided dualism. Therein, indeed, lies much of the philosophical difficulty that attends it, for it seems to be pre-weighted on one side. The stuff, chaos, or out-of-which that is coeternal with God, though it is recalcitrant, is not only always malleable and ductile; resistant to God though it be, its susceptibility to God is always assured beforehand. In the eternal battle between God and the chaos, the latter is always, so to speak, pre-beaten by the former. It cannot hold out for ever against God, who is eternally victorious over it. God, eternally imposing form, which is to be accounted value, on the formlessness that is to be judged non-value, is assured of victory over that which eternally co-exists with him.

When we come to ask about "Nature" in this schema, a further and still graver difficulty confronts us. For the proponents of this divine-artist view, when they talk of the stuff or inchoate matter out of which God evolves all things, are not talking about Nature as commonly understood either among the ancients or among modern scientists. Nature, whatever it is, has always been accounted *kosmios,* orderly. That is why we talk of a uni-verse or cosmos. It is, indeed, so orderly that scientifically-minded people often see no need to recognize any other order: everything, they feel satisfied, is accounted for in the study of Nature, the study of whatever it is that physicists, biologists, and others are trying to understand. What is called "Nature" may then be deemed cruel or kind, lovely or odious, as it happens to strike us. These are human judgments; they are like those of the mother who, to console her child who has hit his head against the piano, says, "Bad piano!" Nature is neither good nor bad.

It is also, however, for all the random element we have already noted, anything other than disorderly or inchoate. Whatever is evolved is evolved according to the way Nature behaves. This does not mean that Nature cannot exhibit "wild" qualities, tendencies that have not so far been developed. It does so, for instance, in the development first of life, then of consciousness. The principles on which it so develops, however, are all built-in principles. Our fathers, borrowing from the conventional human concept of law, traditionally spoke of "the laws of Nature" to express the built-in principles that make possible the scientific enterprise. The "stuff" in the divine-artist schema could never be the subject of scientific inquiry. A scientific mind might conceivably be willing to posit the metaphysical theory of its existence as the out-of-which of the universe, but if so, the "stuff" still could have no scientific interest, since it would be *ex hypothesi* as inexplorable as were atoms accounted in the past when they were believed to be unsplittable. The out-of-which would be a barrier to further investigation, as the atoms were once supposed to be. The scientist might say, indeed, that he was studying everything else other than the out-of-which, a study of which would be futile because impossible.

In saying all this, then, the scientist would also be saying, in effect, that the traditional distinction between God and Nature is otiose. What scientists find susceptible to study may be called God or Nature, as you will. The theological position that would most nearly fit such an outlook would be, of course, the pantheistic one: *Deus sive natura* would be the object of the physicists' and biologists' investigations. There could be no question of anything that might transcend the universe that was being studied, for that universe would be, of course, the totality of all existence. The inchoate out-of-which would be excepted only because it is scientifically nothing and therefore could be dismissed much as Sartre can dismiss as *le néant* (nothingness) that which alone can be said to lie beyond and so be called (though only as a sort of joke) "the father" of existence.

The divine-artist schema, in one or other of its updated versions, is popular among those modern philosophers who happen to be both (a) sympathetic to the compassionate and humanitarian aspects of traditional Christian ethical teaching and (b) impressed (perhaps over-impressed) by the now traditional enmity between science and religion. Newtonian science in its day posed a threat to religion and continued to pose it through the great science-and-religion controversies of the nineteenth century. Modern thinkers, when they happen to be religious, are often curiously tied, even though they may know much better, to outmoded mechanistic conceptions of science. Recognizing, like the eighteenth-century Kant, two realms, "the starry heavens above" on the one hand, which is the proper study of the sciences, and on the other "the moral law within," which, as the realm of spiritual values, requires some other kind of treatment, they seek a way of attending to two different kinds of truth.

In the Middle Ages the Averroists had also tried to support a double-truth theory. That truth must be one was the mainspring of the Thomistic teaching that repudiated it. In the divine-artist view, God does indeed encompass two elements: he is both (1) what is traditionally called "Nature" and (2) what theologians seem to be most concerned to specify as the peculiar realm of "the divine," namely, the realm of the spirit where (as Plato has it) *nous* is king and (as is the testimony of sages and at least the hope of all "good men" in every generation) moral values finally prevail. So then the God–Nature antinomy is to be preserved: the "Nature" dimension to be studied by the scientists and the "God" dimension by the others. The two dimensions in the divine Being spring from the nature of his eternal work on the inchoate "stuff." He has to come to terms with it, for, as every sculptor and indeed every artist knows, the stuff is to be conquered only by yielding in some measure to its force, as the boughs bend under the weight of snow, according to the Zen principle of *wu-wei*.

"Nature," as traditionally conceived, may be regarded, then, as God in the act of coping with the chaos. God faces conditions not of his own making. These conditions are written into the toil and sweat that attend his eternal labor in subduing the resistant chaos. So emerge the conditions we all find in "the way things are." They are neither pleasant nor unpleasant, neither good nor bad, except as they happen to affect our interest, and God himself is engaged in the same struggle with them at the most radical level. As Kepler is alleged to have said as he looked through a telescope at the stars, "O my God, I am thinking thy thoughts after thee," so the modern exponent of the "divine-artist" metaphysical theory might wish us to say, "O my God, through your inevitable success in the war you are waging, I am enabled to participate in it as your humble aide-de-camp, facing the heat of the battle with you and ever sustained by your supremely effective leadership."

The presuppositions in this view are patently sympathetic to a religious stance: the right, together with all the moral virtues that attend devotion to it, will in the end prevail. The process through which they are doing it is an evolutionary one. One aspect of that process is the evolution of the universe that confronts us and is the object of scientific study; another aspect is the evolution, through conflict within the process, of spiritual beings who will in the end join in the divine victory over the sub-moral process that is the biological dimension of the universe. One might expect God to be evolving with the process itself; but though some forms of evolutionary naturalism so envisage the emergence of God, the weightier body of modern thought along the "divine-artist" line tends to presuppose that God and the stuff, as coeternal, are beyond the evolutionary process.

That presupposition reflects, of course, the monotheistic background and interest of the proponents, as it also indicates their concern to do justice to the scientists' account of the process. The weakness of the resultant view is that it may end by doing justice to neither the facts that the sciences exhibit nor the truths that religious men proclaim. Nevertheless, however inadequate it may seem, from one point of view or another, it is a stance that must be taken into account in any discussion of the God–Nature problem. Its strongest appeal seems to occur at those times in human history when religion and science appear to be most strikingly in conflict, as in the thirteenth century when the recovery of Aristotle had forced men into coming to terms with the scientific thought of the day, and in our own time in which the cleavage between science and religion has been acutely felt for several centuries.

When all that is said, however, we must recognize the attractiveness to many of the view we have been considering. Not only has it weighty advocates such as Hartshorne and Whitehead; it does ease many of the thorny problems that attend a theistic interpretation. In *Man's Vision of God,* Hartshorne envisaged a sort of halfway house between traditional theism and traditional atheism, in which God has an unchanging essence but completes himself in a developing experience. Such a view relieves its proponents of having to talk so much of mystery and hiddenness in God, which is embarrassing to philosophers, whose métier is to clarify. We should also notice that champions of this view of the God–Nature antinomy do attempt to provide for an element of the transcendence that classic theism demands. Whitehead, for instance, finds a place for a primordial as well as a consequent Nature in God. Moreover, as we have already observed, the notion of a God who has a "given" to contend with and who in some way fulfills himself by contending with it may not be as unbiblical as has been traditionally supposed. The God of the Bible is anything other than static. Whether the dynamic qualities of the biblical God demand the metaphysical underpinning of a God who wholly transcends his creation, including its spatiotemporality, is another question, and, it may be, the most profound question of all.

Nature as God's Creation

According to the classical theistic view, which represents the mainstream of theological orthodoxy in Judaism and Islam as well as in Christianity, everything that constitutes the universe (including space-time, which some take to be the ultimate matrix of Nature) has its source and ground in the divine Being who, as its Creator, *fons et origo,* transcends it. We are not particularly concerned here with the philosophical plausibility of such a way of conceptualizing deity, but only with the manner of setting up the antinomy between Nature and God, as so conceived. In approaching the God–Nature antinomy as it is presented to us in Christian orthodoxy we are, of course, already specifying both "Nature" and "God" as understood by those who make the antinomy within the context of a traditional theological model.

Traditionally, Christian orthodoxy has stressed the notion that God creates "out of nothing" (*ex nihilo*). The phrase has been severely attacked by recent critics. The intention behind its use was to repudiate explicitly the notion that God uses a "stuff," an inchoate mass of an indeterminate *je-ne-sais-quoi* material, as in the divine-artist theory. When someone asks, in effect, "Well, if you deny that God creates out of something, out of what does he create?" The question is a leading question. It presupposes that everything must be made out of something, which is precisely what the proponents of what is now traditional Christian orthodoxy, when they came to the specification of God's activity, rightly or wrong wished to deny. They ought perhaps to have parried the question with "God does not create 'out of' anything"; but in fact they not unnaturally got into the habit of saying, in effect, "If you insist on putting the question that way, the answer is 'nothing.' You and I make bread out of flour and water and wine out of grapes; but God, who creates all things, creates 'out of' nothing." Such an "exasperation answer" is akin to the one that would be given to someone who inquired as to the whereabouts of happiness. If you answered him with a "nowhere," pointing out that happiness cannot be "in" any place, he might well retort with gleeful naiveté, "Yes, and of course I knew all the time that happiness does not exist." You would then say, "Oh, but it does; it's 'in' human hearts," hoping, perhaps in vain, that his ingenuousness would not lead him so far as to ask a surgeon to investigate the truth of your claim by cardiac dissection.

In the theological model before us, then, God stands over against Nature, neither in opposition to it nor in cooperation with it, but in bestowing existence upon it and, with existence, the freedom to develop and to bring forth the novelty required for each evolutionary "leap" to a new dimension of being. Nature (*physis*) has indeed built into it that emergence of which process philosophers like Whitehead and Teilhard de Chardin, no less than evolutionary naturalists like Samuel Alexander, have made so much; but it has it by virtue of its being itself the process of emerging. Nature cannot but be hierarchical because it is emergent, but the hierarchical character of Nature arises from its having the freedom to develop what is not yet actually there though it is already potentially there.

Suppose, now, that we say, "All right, Nature has the characteristics you specify, but why go beyond it for an explanation of them? Why not simply state that that is the way things are, always emerging, and leave it at that, instead of seeking an explanation by positing an *x*, to be called 'God,' as the Source of Nature? Why God?" To this the theistic proponent of the view of God–Nature that is under discussion will reply in terms such as: "Your observation might be very weighty indeed if the natural process were inevitably always successful, that is, progressive or, in other words, not in danger of the possibility of accident. In fact, however, Nature is not so self-assured, and the testimony to this fact is to be found in the very objections that are made to people who hold my opinion, namely, that the story of Nature, far from being one of a succession of triumphs, records many failures such as the dinosaur and the dodo. What you are ignoring, by the terms of your question, is the element of risk that permeates Nature. This element of risk springs from the act of divine creation, the nature of which you cannot understand till you have first understood that the presence of the risk is due to the freedom that is conferred by the divine act, the outpouring of God's love in the creation of Nature."

There is an obvious objection, of course, that such an answer does no more than assert that the proponent's explanation of the character of Nature is necessary to an understanding of the way Nature manifests itself. The critic might well express his objection by saying: "But while *you* feel you need an explanation, *I* do not. I am as well aware of the characteristics of Nature as you are; yet I am content to go no further. The proceeding in which you engage when you demand an explanation of why Nature emerges leads you to the God-postulate; but that in turn leads to one's having to ask for an explanation of God. As many a child asks when he hears that God has made everything, 'Who made God?' All such speculation is idle. Better rest content with no explanation instead of asking these absurd questions such as 'Why a universe?' and 'Why Nature?' Nature is all the 'God' we need."

We have seen that that is in fact the thoroughgoing pantheist's theological position. It is important to understand why the classical theist is dissatisfied with it, for that will show us more clearly what *kind* of antinomy he is asserting between Nature and God, which will clear the way for an analysis of the antinomy.

Newton saw space and time (duration) as a divine sensorium,[6] a sort of nervous system for God. Though this antiquated seventeenth-century model may perhaps point in the believer's general direction, somewhat as does the vague metaphor of St. Teresa of Ávila, a Spanish mystic of the preceding century, who speaks of the members of the Church as the hands and feet of Christ, the classical theist is really saying much more. He notices that from the very fact that mind emerges from Nature—so that from an empirical standpoint Nature seems to be "creating" mind—we are

[6] Isaac Newton, *Mathematical Principles of Natural Philosophy*, in *Great Books of the Western World* (Chicago: Encyclopaedia Britannica, 1952), vol. 34, p. 258.

led to the real explanation: mind is active throughout the whole process.[7] This is, of course, an observation that a panentheist might make. Hocking, who held a panentheistic view, remarks that it is indeed in Nature's "ultimate opposition to me and my wishes, of high superiority to any doings or thinkings of mine, that Nature begins to assume for me the unthinkable aspect of Other Mind." [8]

The champion of classical theism is certainly no less impressed by such considerations. For him, however, there is a problem that he must account deeper. Like the panentheist and unlike the positivist, he finds that Nature suggests an element that transcends it. He can therefore applaud what panentheists say on this subject; but while the panentheist sees Nature as "in" God and inseparable from God—being that out of which, by evolutionary process, he eventually draws forth life and mind—the classical theistic position is that Nature with all its entailments, such as the evolutionary process, *is* created. This point is of enormous importance in specifying the relationship between Nature and God. It also makes an immense difference to the way in which God is conceptualized and therefore in our attitude to him.

In both the "divine-artist" and the panentheistic view, we may account ourselves coworkers with God, but in the view of classical theism we are to account ourselves, rather, fellow creatures with Nature. Nature, then, is indeed our mother, as the ancient mythologies depict her, who brings us forth in travail; but as part of her, issuing from her womb, we stand with her in sharp contrast to God, who has no need to bring Nature into being in the first place and does so only because, being the God he is (with a freedom beyond our largest concept of freedom and a generosity beyond our fullest notion of self-giving) he chooses so to do. When we come to ask why he chooses to bring both Nature and us into being (a question that raises the problem of evil in the special form it takes within classical theism), we may say, in the first instance, that there is no reason why he should not do as he pleases, since that is his divine prerogative, but then we have to take into account the no less central claim of classical theism that God is nothing if not righteous and good. This is the God who both puts Nature at our disposal and makes us subject to her. If we develop this model in terms of the familiar biblical metaphor of "Father," we seem to have an image of a God as a father who sends his child to boarding school under the care of a housemother who turns out to have no interest in children, neither liking nor disliking them but nevertheless sometimes providing them with very delectable goodies and sometimes letting them fall through trap doors without so much as a tear of regret.

To this objection, the classical theist may reply that in contrast to the model as so developed, the real situation is, rather, that this "father" never loses sight of what is going on. He is in constant communication with the

[7] Cf. William Temple, *Nature, Man and God* (London: Macmillan & Co., 1951).
[8] W. E. Hocking, *The Meaning of God in Human Experience* (New Haven: Yale University Press, 1944), p. 265.

child and is using the housemother only by way of providing the child with a means of growth and maturation. (The child will never grow up properly unless he is trained to be on the lookout for trap doors.) It is important to notice that such an explanation (a) may be quite plausible in respect of the children who graduate either without ever falling through trap doors or who, when they do fall through them, suffer only reparable injuries, and (b) seems very implausible in respect of those children who fall through one of the housemother's trap doors to be dashed to pieces in the stone cellar below, perhaps even on his first day at school. Here, however, we are confronted with the problem of evil that is treated in a separate chapter.

We must notice particularly that because Nature is, in the view in question, a creature, God has dominion over Nature as he has over us. There is nothing in this view of God, however, to suggest that God has any special purpose for Nature in herself. That is to say, God does not have a purpose for Nature that might differ from the one he has for us in such a way that our ends and Nature's might be in competition. There is no scheme envisaged in which we might find ourselves rivals with Nature. On the contrary, Nature is always to be seen as something to which we belong, as a child to his mother, and so also as something whose apron strings we must eventually cut, as a child must eventually cut himself loose from his mother's. Unwise indeed, however, is the child who tries the apron string cutting while he is still only toddling, and since our experience teaches us that we are still very much toddlers in respect to Nature, we had better not be so foolish as to try asserting an independence of her for a long time to come.

Why a God–Nature Antinomy?

Is the last picture at all a realistic one of the way we find things? Can we think of Nature as a fulcrum—partly a severe housemother and partly a kindly one, partly an educational toy to enable us to develop our powers of imagination and thought and partly a baffling puzzle? Can we then think of God as inviting us to obey yet use Nature, our fellow creature, as a springboard for reaching out to the destiny to which God is calling us, which somehow transcends Nature? To such questions the believer will have as little hesitation in answering "yes" as the unbeliever will have in answering "no." Each will answer in terms of his own experience. It is difficult to see how there could be any way of finding logically assent-compelling evidence on one side or the other.

We may well ask, rather, why set up such a model at all? Is not the sharp division it entails between Nature and the *x* that is alleged to be distinct from and in some way independent of Nature a needless and also a misleading one? On this I think we might reach a more definite conclusion. The model according to which Nature is not deified but is so arranged as to leave room for an *altera natura,* another dimension of Being, opens the way to several possible explanations, any one of which would be more satisfactory than the special position that identifies *Natura* and *Deus* either under a pantheistic or under a scientistic guise. Unless we start out with an intractable prejudice in favor of a radically monistic view of experience, we are forced to admit that all our experience seems to suggest that we are living in a multidimensional world and that more particularly we are confronted by at least two contrasting *kosmoi*—the first an amoral *kosmos* to which we directly owe our biological existence as we owe our life to our parents, and the second a moral *kosmos* that somehow seems to interpenetrate yet is quite distinct from the first. When we then ask whether they are mutually independent and, if not, which is subordinate to which, our answer will depend upon our interpretation of what we see in the workings of our own lives, but at least the model will have provided us with a way of reaching that answer in terms of what actually confronts us in life. I do not think we can escape the finding that we do live in a world in which there are at least two orders that *prima facie* do conflict and that cannot—except by too facile, too neat, and too glib a procedure—be metaphysically distilled into one. Which of them has the primacy cannot be a matter of interpretation. To deny that there are two worlds confronting us in the totality of our experience is to take up in advance and very patently a particular presupposition that does not really accord with the experience of anyone. If it did, Kant's distinction between the starry heavens above and the moral law within would have been unintelligible to most people, while in fact no one with even a rudimentary acquaintance with the history of thought has ever found it so.

From our study of the God–Nature antinomy we find ourselves no nearer a theistic than an atheistic conclusion. Nevertheless, we should be satisfied, I think, that making the distinction between God and Nature that theists make is not only philosophically defensible but the best way of drawing the map.

God as Self-Limiting

Before we leave the present chapter we should consider a notion, the importance of which will become obvious as soon as we broach the problem of evil that will be the subject of our next chapter.

As we have seen, once we make the distinction that theists make between God and Nature, the question of their relation to each other becomes central. One possibility, already discussed, is that God and Nature eternally confront each other. That possibility is ruled out, of course, by those who uphold the classical view that God creates Nature and therefore has it wholly within his control. Much misunderstanding arises, however, in respect to the kind of control that God, on the classical theistic view, is supposed to exercise. Many, not least among them the opponents of theism, are inclined to

assume that God *ought* to control Nature in such a way that he is
to be seen as always commanding Nature at every point, with a rein so
short and tight that it is hardly a rein at all. On such an understanding
of the classical theist's concept of the relation between God and Nature,
Nature becomes little more than a set of tools in the divine hand. When
the tools do not seem to produce what is said to be the will of God, one
is inclined to say, using the same model, "But either God deceitfully purports
to be benevolent towards his creatures or else he is a bad workman who
can't handle his tools." There is, however, another possible interpretation
of the classical theistic view.

That alternative interpretation has been neatly put by Simone Weil, a
young Frenchwoman of such an extraordinary combination of intellectual
genius and devotion to humanity that a few words about her may illumine
what she says even if they cannot strengthen its force. Simone earned her
bachot (the French university entrance examination) at the astonishing age
of fifteen and, having beaten Simone de Beauvoir in the entrance examination
for the Ecole Normale Supérieure, left that institution at twenty-one as
a qualified teacher of philosophy. Jewish by birth, she practiced Catholicism
with an extraordinarily deep piety yet without ever consenting to be baptized.
She despised what she found stultifying both in her ancestral Jewish tradition
and in the Roman Church that so deeply attracted her. She was unusually
plain and awkward in appearance, a chain-smoker with big spectacles, a
forward lean, and a staccato and monotonous voice. She also suffered from
poor health. Plunging herself into proletarian causes, she shared the hardships
of the workers and refugees she tried to serve. Her confident belief that
a resolute simpleton can attain truth as well as can the ablest mind exemplifies
her humility and sincerity. She gave away so much of her salary as a
schoolteacher that she had to exist for a whole winter without heat. Having
gone to work in London in November 1942, in the midst of aerial bombard-
ment, she refused the extra food the doctors ordered and insisted on restricting
herself to the rations to which her compatriots in occupied France were
then limited. There is little doubt that her self-denying austerities hastened
her death, which overtook her at a sanitorium in England in August of
the following year, when she was thirty-four.

In a paper written to her spiritual director, the Dominican Father Perrin,
just as she was leaving France in May 1942, she wrote that "it happens,
although extremely rarely, that a man will forebear out of pure generosity
to command where he has the power to do so." She goes on to observe,
"That which is possible for man is possible also for God." Then, formulating
the problem of evil in her own way ("either God is not almighty or he
is not absolutely good, or else he does not command everywhere where he
has the power to do so"), she prefers the last of the three possibilities, adding
the paradox, "Thus the existence of evil here below, far from disproving
the reality of God, is the very thing which reveals him in his truth." The

explanation comes only by seeing that, as she puts it, "On God's part creation is not an act of self-expansion but of restraint and renunciation. God and all his creatures are less than God alone. God accepted this diminution. . . . God permitted the existence of things distinct from himself and worth infinitely less than himself. By this creative act he denied himself, as Christ has told us to deny ourselves. God denied himself for our sakes in order to give us the possibility of denying ourselves for him. This response, this echo, which it is in our power to refuse, is the only possible justification" for the divine folly of creation.

To drive home her point, she even goes so far as to assert that those religions that represent God as commanding wherever he has the power to command are false, and that even though they be monotheistic religions they are to be accounted idolatrous. Only those religions are true that have a conception of the divine renunciation.[9] That renunciation is the ground, moreover, of the antinomy of absence and presence in our experience of God that will be treated in a later part of this book ("God as Kenotic Being"). "God causes this universe to exist, but he consents not to command it, although he has the power to do so. Instead he leaves two other forces to rule in his place. On the one hand there is the blind necessity attaching to matter, including the psychic matter of the soul, and on the other the autonomy essential to thinking persons." [10]

The concept of the Creator God as *pantokrator* yet renouncing his governing power over Nature is a subtle one that accords well with biblical tradition, Jewish and Christian. Though not without philosophical difficulties, it merits serious consideration. It expresses in a peculiarly dramatic form the intense insistence on human freedom that is characteristic both of the biblical tradition and of the existentialist mood that Simone Weil, however "unofficially," represents. God is seen neither as a skipper with his hand ever at the binnacle of his ship nor as an authoritarian parent depriving his children of the opportunity to make any decisions at all, but as the One who, having given his creatures the priceless gift of human life, leaves them to battle with "the blind necessity" that is also his creation. True he does not leave them utterly alone; yet without leaving them utterly alone he nevertheless leaves them perfectly free, so that they may work out their own salvation.

Such a laissez-faire God, in refusing to make puppets of his creatures, bestows upon them a unique kind of freedom that reflects in the world of human finitude something of the splendor of his own infinite freedom. The freedom he bestows, however, makes the pilgrimage of his creatures very perilous. Such a God is to be symbolized, not as an overprotective parent, but as one who, letting his children go free with his blessing and in the knowledge of his love, risks the ever-present danger that they may fall victim to the accidentality that is inseparable from all process and from

[9] Simone Weil, *Waiting on God* (London: Collins, Fontana Books, 1959), pp. 101 f. (Original French edition, *Attente de Dieu*, 1950.)
[10] Ibid., p. 114.

all growth. It is inseparable because to grow *is* to survive ecological dangers. The danger increases at every new level and with every new dimension of growth. In the view propounded by Simone Weil and shared by many in the classical theistic tradition, the bestowal of freedom with all its attendant perils is a condition of spiritual growth. Only because the snowdrop might have failed to pierce the snow does it exhibit to us its unique beauty as the herald of spring. Nothing in our experience is precious except to the extent that it has faced extinction and survived. In the view Weil expounds, Nature is the indispensable agent of that growth, with all its attendant dangers.[11]

The same theme is expressed in the Lucifer myth; at the angelic—that is, the highest—level, the danger is more acute than it could be for lesser beings. The loftier the undertaking, the greater the risk. So the mightiest of the angels is susceptible to a more terrible accident than any other being. Milton's Satan perceived that there had been "hazard in the glorious enterprise." [12] Milton makes God say of him:

> I made him just and right
> Sufficient to have stood, though free to fall.
> Such I created all the Ethereal Powers
> And Spirits, both them who stood and them who failed;
> Freely they stood who stood, and fell who fell.[13]

These evil spirits could have no just complaint,

> As if Predestination overruled
> Their will, disposed by absolute decree
> Or high foreknowledge. They themselves decreed
> Their own revolt, not I. If I foreknew,
> Foreknowledge had no influence on their fault,
> Which had no less proved certain unforeknown.[14]

In other words, the freedom the Creator gives to his creatures—which they enjoy in proportion to their attainment of it, as a healthy man is able to enjoy health to the extent to which he maintains and develops his body in health—is always susceptible to abuse. Nor could it be otherwise, so long as the freedom were genuine, for the divine bestowal of the freedom *is* the self-limiting of the God of Love. That is why the decision of the Satanic hosts was completely their own and would have been taken irrespective of whether God foresaw it or did not foresee it. On this question there is, as is well known, a whole tradition of argument in classical Christian theology.

---

[11] A parallel notion, though in a very different context, occurs in the later Heidegger. See, for example, his *Poetry, Language, Thought* (New York: Harper & Row, 1971), pp. 101 ff. More will be said later on Heidegger's notion, which is also associated with the poet Rilke, in our last chapter.

[12] *Paradise Lost,* Book 1, line 89.

[13] Ibid., Book 3, lines 98 ff.

[14] Ibid., Book 3, lines 114 ff.

Such theological disputes need not concern us here. What we should note is the concept that the Creator God creates both Nature and finite agents, making Nature a blind fulcrum and finite agents as free as their finitude permits. God's relation to Nature is, then, one aspect of his self-limitation; the freedom he permits to the finite agents is another aspect of his self-limitation. Freedom is what God celebrates in so restricting the exercise of his own power. So God, who is the source of all beings, lets the beings be free. The Nature that is his creation is indeed an indispensable condition for the structure of that finite freedom. The questions raised by such a view will reappear in the next chapter as we consider the mystery of evil in relation to classical theism.

QUESTIONS ON CHAPTER IV

1 Consider ambiguities in the term "Nature."

2 When Nature and God are distinguished, as in all forms of theism, what do you take to be the most important issue for the philosopher of religion, and why?

3 To what extent and in what way, if any, might a post-Einsteinian understanding of the universe, contradistinguished from a Newtonian one, affect the God–Nature question?

4 How would a stance on the God–Nature question affect our understanding of miracle?

5 Simone Weil asserts that creation is not on God's part an act of self-expansion but of restraint and renunciation. (*Waiting on God* [London: Collins, Fontana, 1959], p. 102.) What consequences does such a view suggest to you?

6 "The views of Nature offered by science and by providence are not inimical. They might be compared with the two ways of looking at man: body and mind. As a man has personal depth which cannot be discerned by scientific methods, so the processes of nature and history have a divine personal depth which science and historical positivism do not grasp.... In a three-dimensional space, such as that in which we live, a creature whose sensible capacities limit him to two of the three dimensions and who lives in what Abbott has called 'Flatland' will know the regularities, invariancies and scientific probabilities in a two-dimensional form and explain them in that way. He will be oblivious to the dimensional depth in which there are forces operative, guiding his two-dimensional structures and observing the laws which apply to

the latter." (Eric Rust, *Science and Faith* [New York: Oxford University Press, 1967], pp. 286 f.)

Critically consider, with reference to the God-Nature distinction.

7 "The universe is a process: it is born. Yet we impose upon it the category of substance. The naturalistic evolutionists, unconscious of the philosophic pattern of their thoughts, think it to be scientific to consider the universe as self-sufficient, as able to evolve itself. But this is comparable to saying that the seed left alone can germinate itself, and bear fruit; and in effect it is to say that the seed is its own ground, the foetus its own womb, the egg its own hen. And yet this absurdity is preferred to admitting that the universe needs a 'Ground,' and this 'Ground' directs it, brings out its potentialities and leads it to fulness. The universe does not contain its process like some monad or self-enclosed seed, for such a view would be a metaphysical contradiction." (E. R. Baltazar, "Teilhard de Chardin: A Philosophy of Procession," in *Continuum,* Spring 1964, as quoted in Jerry H. Gill, ed., *Philosophy of Religion* [Minneapolis: Burgess Publishing Co., 1968], p. 318.)

Why should the view Baltazar attacks be a metaphysical contradiction, and how far does his own argument, as here presented, go toward support of a theistic claim?

8 "Naturalism is not committed to any theory concerning which categorial *terms* are irreducible or basic in explanation. . . . What all naturalists agree on is 'the irreducibility' of a certain method by which new knowledge is achieved and tested." (Sidney Hook, "Naturalism and First Principles," in Sidney Hook, ed., *American Philosophers at Work,* as quoted in Steven M. Cahn, ed., *Philosophy of Religion* [New York: Harper & Row, 1970], p. 356.)

What do you see as the issue here? Is the identification of God and Nature identical with naturalism as Hook specifies it?

BIBLIOGRAPHICAL SUGGESTIONS

Baltazar, E. R. "Teilhard de Chardin: A Philosophy of Procession." In *Philosophy of Religion,* edited by J. H. Gill. Minneapolis: Burgess Publishing Co., 1968.

Barbour, Ian G. *Issues in Science and Religion.* Englewood Cliffs, N.J.: Prentice-Hall, 1966. A good survey of the issues.

Barbour, Ian G. *Science and Secularity: The Essence of Technology.* New York: Harper & Row, 1970.

Barbour, Ian G., ed. *Science and Religion.* New York: Harper & Row, 1968.

Chung-yuan, Chang. *Creativity and Taoism.* New York: Julian Press, 1963.

Collingwood, R. G. *The Idea of Nature.* New York: Oxford University Press, Galaxy Book, 1960. A very useful introduction to the history of the term "Nature."

Einstein, Albert. *Out of My Later Years.* New York: Philosophical Library, 1950. An enlightening collection of Einstein's essays, letters, addresses and papers, some of which are highly illuminating for the science-religion issues.

Einstein, Albert, and Infeld, L. *The Evolution of Physics.* New York: Simon & Schuster, 1938. A readable account of the story of the decline of the mechanical view in face of the relativity and quanta theories. Very useful for students unfamiliar with this background.

Farmer, H. H. *The World and God.* London: Nisbet & Co., 1935. Though in some respects dated, still a classic study of the problem as it affects the Christian theologian.

Forsyth, T. M. *God and the World.* London: Allen & Unwin, 1952. Succinct treatment of recurrent problems.

Gilkey, Langdon. *Religion and the Scientific Future.* New York: Harper & Row, 1970.

Hare, Michael M. *The Multiple Universe: On the Nature of Spiritual Reality.* New York: Julian Press, 1968.

Heim, Karl. *The Transformation of the Scientific World View.* London: Student Christian Movement Press, 1969.

Keller, Ernst, and Keller, Marie-Luise. *Miracles in Dispute.* Edited by C. W. Hendel. London: Student Christian Movement Press, 1969.

Kuhn, Thomas. *The Structure of Scientific Revolutions.* Chicago: University of Chicago Press, 1962.

Lewis, C. S. *Miracles.* London: Geoffrey Bles, 1947.

Lonergan, B. J. F. *Insight.* London: Longmans, 1964.

Lucretius. *On Nature.* Translated by R. M. Geer. Indianapolis: Bobbs-Merrill Co., 1965. Exposition of the atomic theory of nature by a pre-Christian Roman writer.

Margenau, H. *The Nature of Physical Reality.* New York: McGraw-Hill, 1950.

Margenau, H. *Open Vistas.* New Haven, Conn.: Yale University Press, 1961.

Moule, C. F. D., ed. *Miracles.* London: Mowbray, 1965.

Murray, Michael, H. *The Thought of Teilhard de Chardin.* New York: Seabury Press, 1966.

Nagel, E. *The Structure of Science.* New York: Harcourt, Brace & World, 1961.

Planck, Max. *Scientific Autobiography.* Translated by F. Gaynor. New York: Philosophical Library, 1949. A particularly important classic for an understanding of the science-and-religion issues.

Polanyi, Michael. *Personal Knowledge.* London: Routledge & Kegan Paul, 1958.

Polanyi, Michael. *Science, Faith and Society.* Chicago: University of Chicago Press, 1964 (originally published by Oxford University Press, 1946).

Polanyi, Michael. *The Tacit Dimension.* New York: Doubleday & Co., 1966.

Pollard, W. G. *Chance and Providence.* New York: Charles Scribner's Sons, 1958.

Popper, K. *The Logic of Scientific Discovery.* London: Hutchinson, 1959.

Rahner, Karl. *Spirit in the World.* Translated by W. Dych. New York: Herder & Herder, 1968.

Ramsey, Ian. *Religion and Science.* London: S.P.C.K., 1964.

Russell, Bertrand. *Religion and Science.* New York: Oxford University Press, 1935. Extremely hostile to religion.

Rust, Eric. *Science and Faith.* New York: Oxford University Press, 1967. A clear, readable presentation of the development of science-and-religion issues.

Scheffler, Israel. *Science and Subjectivity.* Indianapolis: Bobbs-Merrill Co., 1967.

Schilling, H. K. *Science and Religion.* New York: Charles Scribner's Sons, 1962. Argues that science and religion complement each other.

Teilhard de Chardin, Pierre. *The Divine Milieu.* Translated by Bernard Wall. New York: Harper & Row, 1960.

Teilhard de Chardin, Pierre. *The Phenomenon of Man.* Translated by Bernard Wall. New York: Harper & Row, 1959.

Teilhard de Chardin, Pierre. *The Vision of the Past.* Translated by J. M. Cohen. New York: Harper & Row, 1966.

Temple, W. *Nature, Man and God.* London: Macmillan & Co., 1934. A classic in its time, representing a transitional stage between idealism and process philosophy.

Torrance, T. F. *God and Rationality.* New York: Oxford University Press, 1971.

Torrance, T. F. *Space, Time and Incarnation.* New York: Oxford University Press, 1969.

Toulmin, Stephen. *Foresight and Understanding.* New York: Harper Torchbooks, 1961.

Toulmin, Stephen. *The Philosophy of Science.* New York: Harper Torchbooks, 1960. A useful introduction.

von Baltazar, Hans Urs. *Science, Religion and Christianity.* Westminster, Md.: Newman Press, 1959.

Waismann, F. *How I See Philosophy.* London: Macmillan & Co., 1968. Especially good on the implications of the quantum theory for classical thought-patterns.

Weiss, Paul. *Modes of Being.* Carbondale, Ill.: Southern Illinois University Press, 1958.

Weiss, Paul. *The God We Seek.* Carbondale, Ill.: Southern Illinois University Press, 1964.

Westfall, R. S. *Science and Religion in Seventeenth-Century England.* New Haven, Conn.: Yale University Press, 1958.

Whitehead, Alfred North. *The Concept of Nature.* Cambridge: At the University Press, 1920.

Whitehead, Alfred North. *Modes of Thought.* New York: Macmillan Co., 1956.

Whitehead, Alfred North. *Science and the Modern World.* New York: Macmillan Co., 1925.

V

EVIL IN CLASSICAL THEISM

"Did you say the stars were worlds, Tess?"
"Yes."
"All like ours?"
"I don't know; but I think so. They sometimes seem
to be like the apples on our stubbard-tree. Most of them
splendid and sound—a few blighted."
"Which do we live on—a splendid one or a blighted
one?"
"A blighted one."
> *Thomas Hardy (1840–1928),*
> *Tess of the d'Urbervilles*

And thus, my brothers, at last it is revealed to you,
the divine compassion which has ordained good and
evil in everything; wrath and pity; the plague and your
salvation. This same pestilence which is slaying you
works for your good and points your path.
> *Albert Camus (1913–1960), La Peste*

Why Evil Is a Special Problem in Monotheism

Within a monotheistic framework the presence of evil in the universe is
a grave difficulty. Even the most unquestioning minds are not unpuzzled
by it, and to the rest of us it constitutes by any reckoning a special problem.
Some would account it the greatest obstacle to belief.

The presence of evil in the universe has puzzled monotheists because God
is understood to be above all not only *fons bonitatis,* the source of all that
is called good, but the creator of all finite being while also unlimited in
power. To some monotheistic believers it has seemed not only an intellectual
problem but a cosmic moral affront. Where, as in the Hebrew Bible, God
is depicted as justice personified, one might expect to find the righteous
rewarded with health, prosperity, and that longevity that the Hebrews were

inclined to account a mark of divine favor, and to find the wicked plagued by pestilence, crushed by poverty, and punished by early death. Job was much troubled by reflection on the fact that, on the contrary, the righteous are often tried with sufferings almost beyond endurance, while the wicked, enjoying all the commonly coveted blessings, live on to mock them. "Why do the wicked live, reach old age, and grow mighty in power?" [1] The emphasis on justice and other ethical notions that was characteristic of the late period in Hebrew literature to which Job belongs made the flagrant injustice he discerned in human affairs look like a reproach to God. The question then seemed to be: which is defective, God's goodness or God's power? To say either sounded blasphemous.

Within the historic framework of Christian faith, which had deep Hebrew roots as well as other—acquired—ideological connections, the perplexity became even more acute. For not only did Christians inherit the Deuteronomic strain in Jewish teaching, emphasizing the ethical supremacy of love, in which Paul saw the greatest of what have come to be known in Catholic theology as "the three theological virtues"—faith, hope, and love;[2] they read in the New Testament the specific declaration: "God is love." [3] Whatever that means, the kind of evil we find in the world seems inconsistent with any all-powerful deity of whom love could be predicated in such a way that human love would provide even some sort of analogy for it. True, even human love is by no means always gentle or sweet. Since the greatest human love is—as Dante knew—"of terrible aspect," the divine love might be expected to have correspondingly terrible features. The objection is not to the "terrible swift sword" of God ("as a man disciplines his son . . . God disciplines you") [4] but to what seems to be a fundamental lack of relation between Nature and God, between what goes on in the world and what Christians say of God's love for it.

A Solution Restricting God's Control of Nature

Among those twentieth-century philosophers who, though critical of traditional expressions of Christian orthodoxy, are sympathetic to some Christian ideas and inclined to a philosophy that would express these ideas in current terms while discarding what they take to be outworn and untenable dogmas, a widely favored solution to the problem of evil is the one already considered in the previous chapter: God, though indeed as benevolent as the devout say, eternally faces conditions not of his own making. As in the *Timaeus,* God is the divine artist ever working on a recalcitrant and eternal stuff. Upon this inchoate stuff he is imposing order. The stuff is "evil" in the

[1] Job 21:7 (R.S.V.).
[2] 1 Corinthians 13:13. They are contradistinguished from "the four cardinal virtues," i.e., prudence, temperance, fortitude, and justice, a list taken over from Plato and Aristotle.
[3] 1 John 4:8.
[4] Deuteronomy 8:5.

sense that it is an obstacle that the divine goodness has to overcome and subdue. All the chance and arbitrariness commonly associated with a naturalistic view of the universe are in it. It is *physis* (Nature). To say Nature is cruel is to read into it a human interpretation. Nature is simply indifferent; but that seems to us cruel—as when sailors talk of "the cruel sea," which, of course, is cruel only in the sense in which a brick wall seems cruel to me when I run into it. In this view even God finds Nature like that, and so in our struggle with Nature we find ourselves coworkers with God. The scope of his struggle is presumably far greater than ours and his power and skill far beyond ours in coping with Nature, but the task is essentially the same.

This view, a favorite with the "Personalist" school that flourished in Boston and Los Angeles earlier in the present century, was perhaps most explicitly enunciated by Edgar Sheffield Brightman.[5] It represents, however, a mode of conceptualizing God that is to be found in Whitehead and other highly influential modern thinkers. Even Einstein, in so far as he was interested in religious ideas, seems to have been better disposed toward such an interpretation of God-and-the-world than toward the one which, in the West, at any rate, has been normative for both Jews and Christians.[6] Because Brightman and other exponents of the view have wished to exhibit it as compatible with traditional Christian belief, they have tried to minimize its dualistic aspects. The dualism, however, is undeniable: on the one side God and an eternal realm of mind, will, and values such as we apprehend in moral and aesthetic experience; on the other side an eternally "opposite," recalcitrant realm of "brute fact." This view may be made plausible as metaphysical theory, and for those who accept it, the classic problem of evil is much mitigated, if not eliminated. The problem appears to diminish as soon as such a metaphysical dualism is introduced. The Judaeo-Christian monotheistic tradition is generally inhospitable, however, to that dualism, which envisages a chaos eternally resistant to God, a dysteleological surd, to use the term that Brightman, borrowing a mathematical notion, popularized in promulgating his view.

The Demonic

The Jewish Lucifer myth that Christianity inherited could not help us here. According to it Satan directs his own evil realm in defiance of God and is manifestly very successful in doing so. Satan, however, though a morally corrupt agent, is operating within the structure of the God-created and God-controlled universe by divine permission. There are, indeed, philosophical problems connected with the Satanic myth also, but they are not

[5] *A Philosophy of Religion* (Englewood Cliffs, N.J.: Prentice-Hall, 1940), especially chaps. 8–10.
[6] E.g., Albert Einstein, *Out of My Later Years* (New York: Philosophical Library, 1950), pp. 26 ff.

the special problem of evil with which we are concerned here. Suppose we assume the Satanic realm within the divine order; then if God faces conditions not of his own making, so also does Satan and, in terms of the model, Satan would be even more likely than God to be thwarted by them. The mythos of a Satanic agency that tempts humans, luring them away from duty and from God, plausibly symbolizes—within the Christian framework— that irrational wickedness in the social dynamic that Paul Tillich and Reinhold Niebuhr liked to call "demonic," but it does not help us with our special problem. In human relations there is indeed much that seems best described as diabolical. The heart of our problem, however, does not lie in moral waywardness or the depravity that is at war with God's purposes; it lies, rather, in the meaninglessness and arbitrariness that the atheist takes to be at the heart of the universe, hints of which make even the theist wonder whether there may not be a meaningless constituent in the divinely ordered universe in which he believes.

The Augustinian View

The Judaeo-Christian view that received classic expression for Christians in the West is that of Augustine, whose theological authority has been acknowledged in various Christian theological traditions—Roman, Anglican, Lutheran, and Reformed alike. Augustine, before his conversion to Christianity, had subscribed to the philosophy of Mani, an ancient and typical form of mind–matter dualism. He had then renounced that Manichaean philosophy in favor of Neo-Platonism. After his conversion he retained many Neo-Platonic notions which through him influenced Christianity in the West as they had already, through other channels, influenced Christianity in the East; but he completely repudiated his Manichaeism, supporting instead what he took to be the biblical view that God, though self-sufficient, created the universe—which, being his creation, is intrinsically good, like himself. Everything God has created must be good, therefore, in its own way, though there are degrees of goodness as there are degrees of importance in any structure: my thumbs are important to me, but not to the same degree as are my kidneys. What we call evil, in this view, is good gone wrong, spoiled good. No evil comes from God. It emerges through the distortion by finite creatures of what is inherently good but, like all good, is susceptible to distortion or decay. Evil is not the illusion (*maya*) that some oriental religions account it. It is indisputably real, as the decay in a tooth is real, together with the pain it may entail for me; but its reality arises from something that has happened to the good after it has, so to speak, left God's hands.

This Augustinian view seemed for long plausible in respect of moral evil, though not wholly unobjectionable even there, but nonmoral evil presented much thornier and more fundamental difficulties. The plausibility of the

Augustinian view may be exhibited as follows: God creates finite beings such as ourselves with a benevolent purpose: in his superabundant love he wants to create beings who can enjoy him. One cannot enjoy God to order, however, any more than one can fall in love to order. One must be free to fall in love or not as one may choose. Even God, therefore, cannot create finite beings and compel them to love him; he must make them free agents who can choose to love or not to love. Parents may endow their children with healthy minds and bodies, but they cannot guarantee what the children will do with them, for the children are free to abuse their minds and bodies to the point of eventually inducing incurable disease. There could be no possible guarantee against that. As we shall see later, the reason is important for our whole argument: health is not something you can preserve in a container as you preserve fish, for a time, in the refrigerator; it is something you have to maintain, as an athlete has to maintain muscle tone and coordination, which are things that, once he has them, he cannot store away like furs in a mothproof cedar chest. As degeneration takes place in the athlete's leg the day he stops exercising it, so freedom to hate God and act against his will is logically inseparable from capacity to love God and responsibility to act according to his will.

A Standard Modern Objection

A standard modern objection to this aspect of Augustinian teaching may now be considered together with its conventional rebuttal. The objection has been put by J. L. Mackie in a well-known article: "If there is no logical impossibility in a man's freely choosing the good on one, or on several occasions, there cannot be a logical impossibility in his freely choosing the good on every occasion. God was not, then, faced with the choice of making innocent automata and making beings who, in acting freely, would sometimes go wrong as the classic Augustinian tradition presents the case for the inevitability of moral evil: there was open to him the obviously better possibility of making beings who would act freely but always go right." So, Mackie argues, God cannot be both omnipotent and wholly good.[7] Antony Flew has argued similarly.[8]

Conventional Rebuttal

We shall have to return to this objection later in the present chapter to develop our philosophical discussion. Meanwhile let us consider a conventional theological rebuttal that calls attention to an ambiguity in the term "freedom." The objector is calling men free whose freedom turns out to

[7] J. L. Mackie, "Evil and Omnipotence," *Mind* 64 (April 1955): 209.
[8] A. Flew, "Divine Omnipotence and Human Freedom," in *New Essays in Philosophical Theology,* ed. A. Flew and A. MacIntyre (New York: Macmillan Co., 1955).

be an appearance of freedom only. So long as I cannot freely choose to defy God I cannot choose to love him with that freedom of choice that Christians have always considered to be essential for genuine decision. In such circumstances my "freedom" would be like the "freedom" that I have to avoid being a kangaroo. As I am "free" to avoid being a kangaroo because I cannot by any means be one, so I should be free "to love" God because I cannot help it any more than I can help breathing. What Augustine is saying, however, is that the kind of joy God wishes to make possible is a good that is impossible without genuine freedom to choose to do the right thing or the wrong. He is saying, in effect: true, you can create certain kinds of good though you are compelled to choose that good, but then it would not and could not be the kind of moral good I am talking about, the kind that is required by the nature of the joy God wants to make possible for his creatures.

We might find an analogy in the type of man who seems so well endowed by fortune that everything he has makes him tend towards business success. Besides inheriting a considerable fortune from his parents, he happens to be by nature industrious, prudent, thrifty, tactful, energetic, enterprising, and persevering. He has no notable vices, such as a tendency toward alcoholism or a weakness for women that might put in jeopardy the almost certain success that any discerning person would predict for him. The virtually inevitable success he achieved would be indeed success, not failure; but he could never know in it the delight another would feel whose success was against seemingly impossible odds and in face of seemingly insurmountable obstacles. The "no cross, no crown" adage needs extrapolation: without effort you may get an honorary degree, and you may even get some pleasure out of it, but the pleasure that it gives can never be the same as the satisfaction you have in the degree you have laboriously earned. I have always been able to walk and I try to be thankful for it, but the polio victim who has had to learn to walk through years of patient effort knows the joy of a victory that cannot be mine. He has learned to walk in a sense in which I have not, since my walking came almost instinctively. The joy God wants to make possible to his creatures is the joy of having learned through struggle.

The writer of the Apocalypse, when he asked the angel to identify the white-robed multitude he saw in his vision with palms of victory in their hands, was told they were those who had "come out of the great tribulation. . . . Therefore are they before the throne of God, and serve him day and night in his temple." [9] They have learned that "to serve God is perfect freedom" is true, and their acquisition of that knowledge has required as its condition the exercise of their own freedom in "coming out of the great tribulation." As we saw in an earlier chapter, the assertion that any kind of service is perfect freedom is a paradox that any normal and intelligent person would take to be sheer nonsense unless he had experienced what it is to acquire that knowledge through the exercise of freedom.

[9] Revelations 7:14–15.

To put the whole situation another way: Augustine is saying, in effect, that there is no room in the divine economy for anybody who is free only to love and serve God and not free to hate and defy him. Such a view is close to the genius of Christian teaching as expressed, for instance, in the parable of the Great Supper. In this parable the spiritual leaders of Israel, the "birthright" heirs of God's promises, answer the invitation with the conventional excuses that Jerusalem protocol demanded as a preliminary to an eventual acceptance. The host, recognizing after a while that they are too smug or too proud to accept the banquet he has prepared, fills their places with the outcasts of society, who are able to enjoy the feast as none of the originally invited aristocracy of Jerusalem could have enjoyed it, for the latter are of such a rank that their presence on great occasions is always taken for granted; they are not really free to stay away. Only the outcasts—those who, weighed down in life's struggle, can feel they have nothing to lose—are free to make a genuine choice.[10]

Suffering Disproportionate

Though most philosophers find rebuttals of this kind unsatisfactory, to say the least, many theologians use them and some even feel they take care of the objections popularly expressed in questions such as "Why does God permit war?" "Why does he allow poverty?" and the like. For within the context we have set, war, poverty, and other social diseases are the result of human turning away from God, and we, as members of the human race, suffer the consequences. The consequences are not, however, by any means necessarily in the proportion in which we have contributed to the ills. Moreover, since the rich may have contributed most amply to the economic ills that cause the poverty of others, while the poor, though they may have shared in the common sin of mankind, have contributed to it very little by comparison, the hardships and misery the latter endure are ridiculously disproportionate.

Even granting Augustine's point about individual freedom, could not an almighty deity so order human conditions that the individual sinner suffered for his own sins rather than those of others? To say that all men sin so all should suffer sounds somewhat like saying to a class of children, "Since all children are naughty from time to time, I'm punishing all of you now, for if you don't all deserve it today you will tomorrow." The force of the

---

[10] Professor Joachim Jeremias of the University of Göttingen has argued persuasively from rabbinic sources and other evidence that the host (at any rate in the form the parable takes in Luke and the Gospel of Thomas) is to be understood as a rich, parvenu tax-collector who, having sought entrée into Jerusalem society, is snubbed by his aristocratic guests who, one by one, decline his invitation with flimsy excuses. Such an exegesis underscores the point made here: the grandees could neither accept nor decline freely; they had to make specious excuses. The beggars needed only a word of encouragement to overcome their genuine shyness in accepting an invitation they so much welcomed. See J. Jeremias, *The Parables of Jesus* (New York: Charles Scribner's Sons, 1963) pp. 176 ff.

objection is augmented when we consider that in the climate of biblical thought, in which our theological traditions were forged, the importance of the group was well known but the notion of individuality was only emerging, so that the importance of the individual was not recognized in the way it is today. Today we should be inclined to say, "True, I have some responsibility for my brother, but it seems unfair that I should suffer abject misery because I have been a little greedy while my brother, after cruelly exploiting millions of people, flaunts his champagne dinners in my malnourished face!"

Surd Evil

The problem of evil that we are considering is seen in a different and perhaps even more radical form when we look not at poverty, war, and the like, but at nonmoral evil, including not only the stupendous pain and suffering that abound in nature (big fish eating little fish) but also the nonpainful forms of the seeming absurdity of the universe. Planets whirl in orbit around their sun for millions of years, then there is a stellar explosion, producing a collision, a cosmic (or, rather, an acosmic) accident. Even if we are willing to see purpose in the orderly whirling, how can we see any in the disorderly accident? The dinosaur, after taking millions of years of evolution to develop into what he is, becomes extinct. Some writers call this aspect of evil "surd evil," because it seems to be irreducible in terms of the standard theological devices for explaining the presence of evil in the universe.

That creation should entail evolution rather than a divine wand-waving fiat need not astonish anyone; nor is it incomprehensible that such a process should entail waste. On the contrary, once we perceive that the attainment of anything worthwhile demands struggle and entails sacrifice, it is easy to appreciate that there must always be a painful element in all processes of growth. We see it in human adolescence, for instance. As we watch an adolescent in the throes of his growing-up pains, we may sigh a little at the awkwardnesses that are embarrassing him, but we are never roused to anything like moral indignation at a deity who can permit such anguish, for we can see it as part of what we acclaim a familiar and splendid process of coming of age. The difficulty is that when we look at the universe it seems to be behaving quite differently. There are backwaters in it, like our own planet, with areas in which some human beings like to believe there is great purpose behind what happens, diseases and accidents notwithstanding; but when we look at the universe less parochially, there at least we must surely feel the absurdity of which the nihilistic existentialists complain.

Of course, there is no reason why the universe should please us or minister to our pleasure. Nor have we any right to demand that it should be a challenge exactly suited to our needs, as though it were a vast school specially designed for training us to develop our potentialities. What troubles the serious inquirer is that he can find no evidence, perhaps not even the slightest plausible suggestion, from all that the sciences, physical or biological, can tell him, of any process that could have a purpose for any person, except what that person cares to invest it with. Even if there are other inhabited planets, with possibly far more intelligent beings on them than we, there are also enormous emptinesses and a wildness into which not even the most reverent and theologically-minded observer can honestly discern the slightest hint of meaning or purpose. As the Pythagoreans imagined the planets made celestial music as they whirled, so by projection of romantic human longings that would seek to read purpose into the most seemingly dysteleological blankness, we may be able to "live with" the universe we know, but our rationalizations may be all poetic, anthropocentric solace and no more than a highly civilized way of whistling in the dark.

The Leibnizian Solution

Leibniz (1646–1716) provided a solution of the problem of evil that is perhaps at once the most celebrated and the most criticized and ridiculed, notably in Voltaire's satirical *Candide.* Leibniz's treatise on the subject, *Essais de Théodicée sur la bonté de Dieu, la liberté de l'homme et l'origine de mal,* published in 1710, was the only work of this great rationalist philosopher to appear during his lifetime. In it he showed much familiarity with the extensive philosophical literature on the subject that had already appeared. The problem, as he saw it, is the one now classically formulated: if God is all-powerful yet does not choose to remove evil from the world, he is not all-good; if he is all-good yet cannot remove it, he is not all-powerful. Leibniz accepted the creation *ex nihilo* doctrine in which, we have already seen, the problem presents itself in the most acute form.

Pierre Bayle, Leibniz's French contemporary and an influential skeptical writer, had already proposed a solution that Leibniz found intolerable, and his *Theodicy* may be regarded as an answer to Bayle, who had argued that evil in the world cannot be reconciled to the alleged goodness-and-almightiness of God. Bayle offered a dualistic solution: the world is affected by two opposing ultimate principles, good and evil. He saw, indeed, that this solution was not philosophically satisfactory from a rationalist standpoint, but not being a rationalist, as was Leibniz, he had no difficulty in freely admitting its unsatisfactoriness from such a standpoint. He contended, in empiricist fashion, that the scope of reason is limited and that no rationalist answer to such a question can be expected. You deal with the problem either by not believing in such a view, or you believe in such a view and acknowledge that there is a mystery of faith that is beyond human reason. Leibniz disliked Bayle's answer not only because he thought such problems must be amenable to rational treatment but also because he felt that Bayle's treatment would lead to philosophical skepticism of the kind that ends in sterility of the intellect and its inevitable concomitant, loss of zest for the search after truth.[11]

Leibniz, no less than the medieval schoolmen, was in his own way convinced that, since truth is one, there can be no radical conflict between what is true, whether it be a truth demonstrated by reason or an article of faith that is in fact true. He points out that all that can be opposed to the goodness and justice of God is nothing but appearances which, though they could well function as evidence against a human being, carry no weight in light of the proofs of the infinite perfection of the attributes of God.[12] Though few modern philosophers would take a purely rationalist standpoint, much less share Leibniz's confidence in the traditional theistic "proofs," Leibniz makes a claim that merits the scrutiny of anyone dealing with the problem of evil in classical theism. The problem, he argues, is in the last resort a problem of *metaphysical* evil. Because God is an absolute, perfect Being, there is no need, Leibniz thinks, to argue for each particular kind of perfection, such as goodness. Since God is metaphysically perfect, *all* his acts must be good. One can indeed imagine possible worlds without sin and without unhappiness. That is to say, they are *conceivable*. These worlds would not be so good as ours, however; ours is the best of all possible worlds.[13] He thinks he can demonstrate this to be the case.

If one has in mind only human beings and their happiness, then plainly one can very easily conceive a better world. God's purposes, however, extend beyond human beings. Man is only part of a vast cosmos. Man's limited viewpoint is the reason for his seeing his own sufferings writ so large in the scheme of things. Man is only a part of God's immense concerns. Not only has God the whole universe to consider, but he must "fill" the universe perfectly. As Leibniz puts it, he must get in the maximum number of "compossibles," as one gets in the maximum number of tiles in a given area that is to be covered.[14] There can be no such plenitude without variety: King Midas turned out to be poorer when he had nothing but gold. So the greatest number of compossibles had to be actualized, and some of these inevitably entailed evil and even opened the door to vice, for otherwise there would have been some vacant metaphysical "spaces." There is in every creature an original and inherent imperfection. This circumstance follows from the very nature of creatureliness; in other words, creatureliness entails

[11] Bertrand Russell notes a further reason for the importance of the problem in Leibniz: "the emphasis which he laid on final causes." (Bertrand Russell, *A Critical Exposition of the Philosophy of Leibniz* [London: Allen & Unwin, 1937], p. 191.)

[12] G. W. Leibniz, *Theodicy*, trans. E. M. Huggard (New Haven: Yale University Press, 1952), p. 98.

[13] Ibid., p. 129.

[14] G. W. Leibniz, "The Monadology," in *The Monadology and Other Philosophical Writings*, trans. Robert Latta (London: Oxford University Press, 1965), pp. 340 ff.

imperfection. Therein lies the ultimate source of evil. Because that source is found in metaphysical imperfection, evil is to be regarded as having no efficient cause at all. Rocks being what they are cannot but have in them the possibility of evil for a man or a horse who runs his head against one. Tigers being what they are may eat men, and men being what they are may shoot tigers. God does not "cause" these evils. If he is to be said nevertheless to "permit" them, we must point out that the permission is simply the concomitant of his choosing to actualize the best possible world.

To meet the objection that such divine permission means his positively willing the evil, Leibniz distinguishes between God's antecedent will and his consequent will. Antecedently, God wills the good for all things considered individually. Consequently, he wills the best of all possible worlds, permitting the evils that such a world necessarily entails. Leibniz also argues that, though evil is in his view fundamentally privative, it can minister to the good of the whole. It can be instrumentally good, serving the total purpose of God, which is intrinsically good.

Leibniz's argument on this subject has evoked both idle ridicule and serious philosophical critique. An appreciation of his position is important, no matter how unsympathetic we may feel toward it, if only because Leibniz shows us how far the rationalist case may be pressed and what happens to it when it is so pressed.

His argument that man is only a small part of God's creation and that much of the difficulty we see in the problem of evil arises from our failure to appreciate the force of this circumstance, is weightier than some critics have wished to allow. That we, human beings that we are, should have humanistic concerns, is natural, but these concerns are only a sort of patriotism, after all, geared to humanity at large rather than to America or France; however, they are, from a metaphysical standpoint, no less selfishly parochial. If we are to be authentic philosophers we must see beyond these human concerns, which in looking at the cosmos as a whole are as parochial as would be a village council's in relation to world affairs. Who are we that we should think the whole universe should be for the benefit of us humans in this backwater of the universe called Earth? Russell's considerable critical interest in Leibniz may not have been unconnected, indeed, with his own ambiguous position as an exponent of naturalism who was nevertheless passionately devoted to the interests of humanity. If, like Leibniz, we are to try to look at the universe as a whole, we must not allow our very understandable human squeamishness to interfere with our quest for truth.

The situation is different, however, when we examine, even sympathetically, his argument that God has to fill the universe with all the compossibles, each of which has the imperfections that are inseparable from its own nature. This argument is impressive as a metaphysical explanation only till one asks precisely why a better world, though conceivable, is not possible. Leibniz admits that the reason is as yet unknown to man. In the long run, therefore, the argument that purports to explain the presence of evil without injury to the traditional attributes of God has to fall back on an admission of ignorance: Leibniz admits he cannot say why the principle of compossibility is as he says it is. He is not able to tell us why God cannot better arrange the principle itself. Here, indeed, is the very nub of one of the most fundamental aspects of the whole question before us in this chapter: If there is a principle such as Leibniz's compossibility, how can God be said to create *ex nihilo*? Is he not creating, rather, out of something which is already given to or determined for him? If he were really free, he would create a "better" set of principles—including a "better" principle of compossibility. So far as Leibniz can show in his rationalistic way, either God chose to have this principle or he was forced to use it.

Even this objection is by no means necessarily fatal. Leibniz is willing to say that we can conceive of a better world, but perhaps his error is in admitting so much as that. Perhaps we think we can conceive of a better world, but can we? Would not it turn out to be a world in which it might be that when you had gone upstairs you had not? In other words, is not Leibniz fundamentally making the same point that Thomas Aquinas had made several centuries earlier (Leibniz's philosophical advance on St. Thomas and the consequent difference in their conceptualization and language notwithstanding), namely, that God cannot do anything contrary to his own nature, which is "rational" in the sense that it has its own built-in laws? His almightiness, then, would be subject to these laws of his own nature, the same laws that make it impossible for him to behave as though he were pure will, which is how some caricatures of Muslim doctrine make Allah seem to be.

Against such a possible defense of the Leibnizian position, however, we must note that theists (contradistinguished from the eighteenth-century deists[15] who repudiated the notion of God's "interfering" with his creation) have always insisted that God, who providentially cares for every sparrow, does enter into human situations in very special ways—for example, to guide Israel and save his chosen people and, according to Christian doctrine, by entering incarnationally into the human condition in order to make the salvation of men possible. Such an act, though humanly inconceivable in principle, is said to be revealed, thereby showing the unlimited power of God. One might then ask a Christian how it could be that God, who could do the supposedly undoable (the Incarnation), could be unable to "do"

---

[15] The term "deism" came to be used in opposition to "theism" to denote a special view, developed in the late seventeenth and early eighteenth century, which attributed the creation of the universe to God but denied that he ever intervened thereafter in its working. In France, Voltaire, Rousseau and the Encyclopaedists all expounded a deistic position, which in Germany also influenced Kant. The classic exposition of it is in John Toland, *Christianity not Mysterious* (1696).

a better principle of the compossible. In such objections we see, to say the least, weaknesses in the Leibnizian argument, and many would account them fatal.

Accidentality

Now that we have looked at some of the difficulties traditionally subsumed under the problem of evil, we may try to explore the root of the problem in a more special way. The late Austin Farrer, a brilliant champion of Christian orthodoxy, provides a suitable cue. After suggesting that God creates a whole physical world into which he puts us his creatures, so attaching us to it that we are initially turned to it, finding in it our natural concern, Farrer then proposes that nevertheless, because of our origin in God's creative act, we are, despite the native physicality of our strong animal minds, also capable of and inclined to a knowledge of our Creator.[16] When we then go on to ask why God should put us in this particular kind of universe where, because of "the mutual interference of physical systems," there are many flaws, the answer proposed is that while any single adverse accident could have been prevented if circumstances had been altered, the alteration of the circumstances would have "made other accidents," for "accidentality is inseparable from the character of our universe."

Here is an interesting proposal, whatever we may think of the presuppositions. We are created by God as finite spirits capable of growth, and for this growth we need an environment that entails accidentality as part of its fundamental nature. It is not a disorderly universe; still less is it hostile to us or to our purposes; but it is one in which accidents *must* happen, so that we are not to expect the assured correlation between our efforts and our environment that a potter expects between the clay he uses and the work he puts into it. We are subject, rather, to pure chance in a world that is nevertheless by no means "all chance." So while your industry proves fruitless because of a ridiculous accident that spoils years of diligent toil, the cards happen to turn out in my favor so that my feeble efforts reap for me a tremendous reward. If it could be argued that you have a bigger hurdle to surmount than I, so as to provide you with larger opportunity for accomplishment, there would be no problem—you would be somewhat like a golfer with an agreed-upon handicap—but the cosmos is not the arena of a game with rational rules but, rather, a wilderness. Without coming to terms with its nature you can never hope to conquer it, and you will surely fail unless you learn the principles of its behavior; but even if you knew as much about it as all the scientists in the world, and behaved more shrewdly and wisely toward it than all the earth's sages, your efforts would be no less subject to ruin through a perhaps absurdly trivial adverse chance.

[16] Austin Farrer, *Love Almighty and Ills Unlimited* (London: William Collins Sons and Co., Fontana Library, 1966), p. 71.

Why should such an odd universe be supposed to suit so perfectly the development of us creatures whose Creator presumably could have provided us with any universe he pleased? Why does he present us with a curious mixture of rational cosmos and acosmic chance? If the universe were obviously hostile to us we might "put our tongue out" at it, like Sartre, or else fight it all along the line—like a St. George fighting his dragon. Such reactions are inappropriate, for not only is the universe indifferent to us, but we must face it both as seemingly regular and predictable in its behavior and also as the scene of hideously macabre accidents that no degree of skill or knowledge or daring can prevent. The unbeliever's thesis seems at this point more plausible than the believer's. How, then, could such an orthodox Christian as Farrer reconcile the accidentality of the universe, as well as the vast suffering of the animal world, with the overarching providence of a divine Creator in whom he deeply believed, great personal sorrow in his own life notwithstanding?

Two Concepts Kaleidoscoped

A clue to the solution of the puzzle might possibly lie in the fact that in such a Christian orthodoxy we are dealing with two distinct understandings of "goodness" which are often kaleidoscoped with intellectually disastrous consequences. First, there is the goodness of God, which is never conceived as attained or won but always as eternally there as a source. God's is the only kind of goodness that can come unearned, unattained. It can so inhere in God because the order of the divine Being is radically different from that of anybody or anything in creation. In this orthodox view, to try to make God's and man's goodness resemble each other would be blasphemous. So then, second, there is another kind of goodness, one that depends upon God's for the very possibility of its development but which nevertheless must be developed, attained, won. For its optimum development special circumstances are needed, and *ex hypothesi* the universe that is our environment provides these. This universe, though not by any means necessarily "the best of all possible worlds," is supposedly as good as any possible environment for the development of the moral potentialities with which we have been endowed.

Such a statement of the relation between the human situation and the cosmic condition is not nonsensical. This state of affairs *could* be so, but the view that it *is* so does represent a very special understanding of the way things are. We should be very clear what that special understanding is.

Let us look at what it expects of us. We are called upon to refuse praise to any so-called goodness that is not hard-earned, for it cannot be genuine goodness unless it *is* hard-earned. Within the tradition of Christian orthodoxy people are taught from early childhood that the apparent courage of a strong and mighty man who hardly knows the meaning of fear is scarcely courage at all, while the courage of a miserable little waif who, though terrified, stands up to his bullying adversaries, is much to be commended. Yet the case of God turns out to be exceptional in a very odd way: God, though he is "beyond" all struggle, all suffering, all development, is always and *par excellence* to be praised. To praise God is, indeed, the first duty of man; yet whatever we do when we praise God, we are not praising him as we praise an alcoholic or a drug addict who, after a Herculean effort, has "kicked his habit." In praising God we are rejoicing that at the fountain of all things there is a God such as the Bible suggests to us. We are praising the reformed addict for his heroism in overcoming temptation. In his own small way the addict, through his heroism, his victory over a morally debilitating habit, has created a new value. His creation of it, being entirely dependent on God's creative activity, which has provided the conditions that make it possible, is radically different from that divine activity. ·

So therefore the nature of our praise is different. We do not say, "Praise John Smith in x degree and praise God in x^n degree," for there can be no correlation, no question of a ratio in the praise to be allotted. It is more like "praise the snowdrop for having pierced to hard earth in response to the dimly shining sun above it, and praise the blazing sun without whose presence over 90,000,000 miles away there would be no vegetation at all." The believer praises God because without God we should not exist; he may then also but very separately praise me for what I do or fail to do with the existence that is mine.

If the goodness of man were to be calculated simply in terms of the grandeur of his moral effort or (to talk more theologically), his response to the divine invitation or call, the whole matter might be allowed to stand there as an open question upon which philosophers could have nothing more to say, being simply a question of individual interpretation of the meaning of human existence in the light of the way one finds things. We cannot, however, so easily dispose of the matter. Mackie's question, already quoted, must be seriously considered. If God can create, by his simple fiat, without a stuff to work with (that is, *ex nihilo,* as the theologians traditionally say), why cannot he simply produce creatures whose wills are so geared to his goodness that they will always by their own free choice do the right? If, as is reported in the first chapter of Genesis, he can say, "Let there be light," so that light then appears ready-made and forever after always illumines, why cannot he produce finite creatures who always freely choose the good? In other words, why does not God create beings who can never go wrong, as he creates light that never goes out?

Mackie's article was followed by considerable discussion in subsequent papers in philosophical journals. Ninian Smart pointed to the nub of the problem, however, by his suggestion that the concept of "goodness," as used in ethical discussions, *means* resisting temptation, overcoming evil.[17] For though the splendid creatures Mackie envisions might actually exist, we could not even engage in meaningful ethical discussions about them. To call them brave or kind would not be what it means to call me brave or kind. If you call me brave, you mean that I have overcome in some degree my natural fears, my tendency to the cowardice that comes naturally to us humans and is·the very stuff of our nature. If you call me kind, you mean that instead of being the wild and selfish boor I well might be, I have tamed my tendencies and have succeeded in some measure in being thoughtful and considerate to others. If I happen to be healthy or handsome, you do not praise me for it as for a moral achievement; on the contrary, you are more likely to remind me how fortunate I am to have such unearned qualities. Because of them, indeed, more effort is expected of me—*noblesse oblige.* That is exactly, indeed, what we might be tempted to say to one of Mackie's "instant supermen" if he descended upon us.

Further Theological Complications

Theological orthodoxy is saddled with yet another doctrine that further complicates the problem. For before the Fall of Lucifer (however this theological notion is to be understood) the situation is supposed to have looked very much as Mackie thinks it ought to look now, if an omnipotent deity reigns. According to the traditional Judaeo-Christian myth, time was when there was no question of sin; Lucifer and his angelic consorts must have seemed impeccable. Moreover, we are surely to suppose that if we could call on Adam and Eve in the Garden of Eden ahead of the serpent, we should find them morally admirable creatures—admirable because, having been created "good" and being still untainted by the sin that now affects all humanity, they would be everything we in our loftiest moments want to be, and so do everything the way we yearn to do it. They would presumably put us to shame by the splendor of their every action. While we with a mighty effort might succeed in being courageous or kind, they would behave effortlessly, and as a matter of course, the way we should wish to behave all the time.

Entertaining Adam and Eve at that period of their career would be in some ways like entertaining a mathematical genius who, lacking all mental blocks and gifted with an extreme degree of abstract reasoning, could work out naturally and quickly—without any training in algebra, let alone calculus—what even highly trained professional mathematicians might have to labor over for hours. We could not say to him, "Well done—how we admire your mastery of the subject! How you must have wrestled and toiled

[17] Ninian Smart, "Omnipotence, Evil and Supermen," *Philosophy* 36 (April/July 1961): 188–195.

to achieve such skill!" for the prodigy would probably reply, "Not at all, it's as easy as falling off a log." The reply might irritate us; nevertheless, we could not help admiring, not to say envying, the prodigy's gift: he would be behaving as we should very much want to be able to behave. For all that, there would be a difference between us and the mathematical genius: whatever skill would be ours would have been won by our own sweat. The less our natural endowment, the greater the praise we should merit. If with a subnormal aptitude you succeeded at last in learning to do quadratic equations, your friends would rightly applaud you more loudly than they would the prodigy who could do differential calculus while brushing his teeth.

As has already been noted, much of the difficulty that confronts us in these matters is that the traditional theological account has kaleidoscoped two very different concepts of goodness. One is the goodness of God, unearned, unattained, but simply there, from which the goodness of created spirits derives and effortlessly follows. There would seem to be after all no reason, as Flew and Mackie have contended, why God could not have ordered affairs so that the finite beings he created should have been protected against the Fall.

The Mythological Context

Returning the whole question to its original mythological context, we might say God could have so ordered cosmic affairs as to exclude from the Garden of Eden the troublesome serpent, so preserving the spotless purity and moral power of Adam and Eve. Such divine protectiveness could no more injure the moral health they are reported to have enjoyed than the precautions my parents took against my catching smallpox have made me a less healthy man. A wise mother does not coddle her child by protecting him from every possible danger, but only a cruel or crazy mother would fail to protect her child as far as was in her power from fatal poisons. One would expect no less of God. But then we meet the other concept of goodness, no less biblical: goodness is not something to be maintained, like the good health inherited from a sturdy stock, but something to be earned, more like a medal or a college degree. Smart is right to point out that this is the kind of goodness we are talking about when we talk ethics. Moreover, the theologian may go on to say that in our fallen human condition goodness can only mean the overcoming of evil, much as to a sick man in hospital health can only mean conquering the disease that has brought him there.

A bedlam of intellectual confusion has developed out of the weaving of both concepts into one complex myth. Skillful theologians can indeed sort out the ambiguities by relating the two concepts to the orthodox doctrine of the Fall, but the question remains: why should God have permitted the Fall? Eve blamed her waywardness on Lucifer (the serpent, the devil), but

Lucifer, if taken to task on the matter, might contend that he would never have fallen headlong from heaven as he did if only God had used just a little more care in the cosmic arrangement so as to safeguard him from the great temptation that was his undoing.

Myth and Science

We may now bring the problem into focus by asking, why any temptation at all? The source of it is said to have lain in Lucifer's own heart; in his pride he wanted to be equal with God. The seed of that wrong notion must have been present, however, in creation, for how else could it have assailed the mind and poisoned the heart of Lucifer, first among the angels of heaven? As John Hick has observed in his attempt to present a Christian theodicy for today, "The story of the fall of man is part of a more comprehensive cosmic story" which is "the official Christian myth," but "myths are not adapted to the solving of problems." They do have useful functions, but they must be expected to contain incoherences and other illogicalities. They also grow out of date, losing their practical usefulness. For instance, "we know today that the conditions that were to cause human disease and mortality and the necessity for man to undertake the perils of hunting, and the labours of agriculture and building, were already part of the natural order prior to the emergence of man and prior therefore to any first human sin, as were also the conditions causing such further 'evils' as earthquake, storm, flood, drought, and pest." [18]

Nothing we know about the universe excludes the possibility of a divine Creator, but everything we know about it suggests that what we call evil is an integral part of a cosmic process. The physical and biological sciences see evil as an integral part of the development of matter and life, while the social sciences see as an integral part of human nature those psychological tendencies in man that make his whole psychic life a struggle, perhaps hopeless, against their overwhelming force.

Is Nonaccidentality Conceivable?

The question associated with Leibniz—whether the world we know is the best of all possible worlds—was much discussed in the past. A more fundamental question for our present concern is whether a world without accidentality is conceivable as a universe in which we could be. A universe in which accidents could not occur is a rationalist philosopher's dream, imagined after the pattern of a clock having mechanistic perfection, in which there is no element of chance and therefore no probabilities but only certainties. Such a universe, if indeed it is conceivable at all, would have to be one in which no growth or development ever took place, for growth

[18] John Hick, *Evil and the God of Love* (New York: Harper & Row, 1966), pp. 283–285.

without the possibility of accident is inconceivable. Growth *entails* accidentality. If the tender young shoot were to grow in safety from all hazards, it would not be growing at all in the sense that we understand growth. It would be simply following a strictly planned and perfectly regulated course, as does the pendulum of a clock. No universe in which the development of plants, animals, and beings like ourselves could occur is conceivable without the thwarting, irritating element of "accidentality" that we have seen to be so much at the heart of what we call the problem of evil. So if we are to believe in its creation by God we must find some special way out of the difficulty.

To affirm that God, the source of all existence, creates a universe full of accidentality with which we are called upon to cope and which is somehow supposed to provide us with good material for the whetting of our spiritual tusks, is a standard attempt at such a way out. The conventional objection to it is that it does nothing to mitigate the odd combination of arbitrariness and injustice inseparable from such a universe. Nor does the accidentality seem to be tempered by any observable factor in nature. On the contrary, the noblest of men tends to be slain and the basest spared. The compassionate and courageous man who rushes to rescue a child from a burning building is likely to perish, while a more selfish and cowardly one slinks away in triumphant survival. It may be that in the lower stages of evolutionary development the fittest species survive, but that is only to say that those species most capable of surviving have in fact inevitably survived. If we account the survivors the best just because they are the survivors, we are proposing a moral calculus that has no provision for the moral qualities that humanity generally recognizes and esteems.

These qualities do not seem to fare well in the tooth-and-claw competitiveness of nature. For centuries strong men and nations have been attacking and wiping out weak ones. It might be argued that in course of time, man will become sufficiently law-abiding to counteract and overcome that destructive aspect of nature, and so tend to discourage the wicked and encourage the good. Such an argument, however, leads nowhere. Even if we grant its suppressed premise and concede its validity, we have no guarantee that a major accident such as the extermination of the human race by a few well-placed nuclear bombs will not take place before the expected moral development of mankind can be achieved. Moreover, even if that particular "accident" does not occur, nothing can diminish the moral outrage we feel at the triumphant success of the wicked over the good that has already taken place and that nothing can now alter. To say the least, Nero and Hitler had good innings. To suggest that the wicked are tormented by their conscience is futile, for the more wicked they are, the less sensitive is their conscience. Indeed, the noblest of men and women are far more likely to be troubled by conscience over mere peccadilloes than are the foulest over their most monstrous sins.

A psychological factor should now be noted that not only aggravates but builds a new dimension into our tragic theme. Modern psychologists recognize the profound truth of the notion that Oscar Wilde expressed in his well-known line, "All men kill the things they love," and that Shaw similarly perceived in pointing out that if you want to learn the deeds done for love you should look at the murder page of the newspaper. We do tend to destroy what we most cherish. Nowhere is this more dramatically obvious than in suicide, where the self-centered man kills the self he too exclusively loves. Yet even the most altruistic virtues that society enthrones bring about similar results. In the Middle Ages the two virtues most admired were holiness of life, represented by the monks who pursued it in the cloister, and chivalry, represented by the knights who in their campaigns found scope for the bravery and daring proper to their vocation. The monks, sworn to celibacy, were forbidden to perpetuate their species, while in the nature of the case the knights were killed off in war. The very virtues a society most prizes are the ones it tends to destroy. The family with the strongest sense of solidarity is the one that most often destroys itself either by inbreeding or by infighting.

Not a School but a Jungle

Even apart from these psychological aspects of our problem, a terrible fact remains. Though I were the finest humanitarian that ever lived and had been extraordinarily fortunate in successfully overcoming all obstacles to the most splendid of programs in which I was engaged for the welfare of my fellow men, one little "accident" might ruin all at the crucial moment when my noble aim seemed just within grasp. Because the accidentality of the universe precludes its being a school for our moral training, we have to face the alternative: it is a jungle. A jungle explorer may develop all sorts of virtues in the course of his safari—for example, courage, patience, and endurance. He may also develop qualities less generally admired—cruelty, ruthlessness, and cunning. Only by an abuse of language, however, could we on that account call the jungle either a school of virtue or a den of vice. It is simply a jungle where a tiger may eat him up just as he is emerging with priceless new scientific information about the pathology of cancer.

If nonaccidentality is inconceivable in a universe in which there is to be growth as we know it, we may feel we can go on to say that even God cannot arrange matters otherwise, so that whether he creates *ex nihilo* or out of a "stuff," he cannot avoid the stupendous waste the process entails. Such a position might be compatible with an optimistic view about the future of the human race, such as is expounded by Teilhard de Chardin, but it affords no basis at all for reconciling with the traditional concept of deity the values of the individual to which Christian faith and also some strains in classical Jewish teaching attach so much importance. Christian devotional literature is full of testimony about individuals "snatched as brands from the burning," but what is to be said of those individuals who through the accidentality inherent in the process of evolution and growth might be said to have "fallen into the fire"?

In short, the universe we know does not seem to be reconcilable with the traditional Judaeo-Christian concept except by some very special type of belief, the evidence for which, if it existed, would have to lie in a special interpretation of and judgment on an individual's personal experience, not in any examination of the universe itself, even through the eyes of an observer sympathetic to Christian belief. The values of the universe, "earned" against the odds of accidentality, do not fit at any point that which is conceptualized in the traditional concept of God as Creator, unmoved mover, changeless and impassible. Early Christian thinkers perceived in their own way the difficulties we have considered in the present chapter, and they developed their own techniques for dealing with them through highly theological doctrines such as the Trinity, the Incarnation, predestination, and election. Such theological doctrines might indeed affect our treatment of the question before us, as it is typically posed in the traditional ways: "How can an all-powerful God permit suffering?" "How is a universe like ours compatible with belief in a divine Creator?" We must modify either what we know of Nature, or our concept of God, or our understanding of their relation to each other. We cannot with intellectual honesty modify what we claim to know of Nature, so the solution must lie in one of the two other alternatives.

Evil and the Self-Limiting God

The problem of evil, however it be presented, always presupposes a specification, hidden or patent, of the nature of the goodness as well as of the almightiness of God. The presumption is usually explicit that God, being by theological definition the creator of Nature ("all things visible and invisible"), must not only be able to control her but must will to control her at every point, with an infinitesimally short rein. Also included, however, and not always so explicit, is a built-in presumption of an "ought": God *ought* to behave in a certain way in order to qualify as "good" or "loving."

The modern philosophers who try their hand at restating the old objections with which the problem of evil confronts theism, use as their model what theologians aver about the nature of God and his relation to Nature. They do so properly, of course, since the problem with which they purport to deal arises only in a theological context. It would be pointless apart from that context. They do not usually take into account, however, the whole theological context, preferring to confine themselves, rather, to certain doctrinal propositions that may be accounted the most easily manageable for logical treatment. In the case of the forms of the argument put forward by Mackie and by Flew, the neglect of the rest of the theological picture to which the propositions belong is so conspicuous as to make theologians wonder how they could rest content with a model that is a distorted diminishment, a caricature that ludicrously traduces the theological situation in which the problem arises.

The classical theologians all insist that God does not need to create anything at all. As we saw toward the end of our last chapter, divine creation, in Simone Weil's words, "is not an act of self-expansion but of restraint and renunciation." God, in creating, does not seek "to get something out of it," as we so often do in our human enterprises. The divine enterprise is not only wholly generous; it entails self-restraint, even self-renunciation. This entailment has sometimes been obscured by our inheritance of the Greek emphasis on the "impassibility" of God: God, being "pure act," cannot be acted upon and so cannot suffer from the act of any agent upon him. The entailment has been obscured by those who neglect to notice that God, though he cannot suffer in the sense of being acted upon by another agent, could (and, according to all orthodox Christian theology, does) suffer in the sense of enduring the consequences of his own self-renunciation and self-sacrifice. This theme is fundamental in all classical theology about the Incarnation and Passion and Death of Christ. It has been interestingly reemphasized and restated in modern terms by a Japanese theologian, Dr. Kitamori, who goes so far as to affirm that pain belongs to the essence of God.[19] The nature of God, he contends, can be comprehended only from the nature of Calvary.[20] He invokes Luther as a proponent of the position he wishes to reemphasize, that in the sacrifice of Christ is an absolute principle grounded in God himself. "The gospel," writes Luther, "was proclaimed even before the foundation of the world, as far as God is concerned." [21] Dr. Kitamori quotes the dramatic assertion of one of his compatriots: "It is impossible for us to understand the logic of Paul completely unless the death of Christ means the death of God himself." [22]

In the hyperbole of that striking dramatization we can grasp the characteristic classic Christian insistence that the self-sacrifice of Christ on the Cross is not to be understood as something that God undertook to do as a last resort to surmount a special situation that had arisen in the world as a result of the Fall. It is to be understood, rather, as belonging to and exhibiting his nature. We properly say God is love, not because of a remedial action he generously took to give human beings the opportunity of getting out

---

[19] Kazoh Kitamori, *Theology of the Pain of God* (Richmond, Va: John Knox Press, 1958), pp. 44 ff.
[20] Ibid., p. 47.
[21] Kazoh Kitamori, quoting Martin Luther, *Sämtliche Werke* (Weimar: Böhlau Weimarer Ausgabe, 1883), vol. 45, p. 415.
[22] Kazoh Kitamori, quoting Masahisa Uemura, *Uemura Zenshu* ("Complete Works of Uemura") (Tokyo: Kankokai, 1932), vol. 3, p. 403.

of their predicament, but because even if there had been no Fall and no Calvary, God would have manifested his self-renouncing, self-sacrificial love, in creating non-God.

Because of our built-in metaphysical models for divine being, this concept of self-sacrifice in the divine love is difficult to grasp. Why should creation entail God's self-limiting? We ask that because we have already in our own minds limited the nature of divine being to that of a deity who commands wherever he can, and in the course of doing so, he decides to create. The Cross is then seen as an exceptional instance of divine heroism, if one may so speak, but as for creation, is not that God's very métier, a function that for some unfathomable reason he assumes? The answer of all classical Christian theology to that question is negative. It is usually expressed in the insistence that God depends in no way on anything beyond himself, yet he creates. In creating, he renounces himself, and his self-renunciation is not imposed upon him; it is wholly his free act, and it is what we are to understand by our saying he is love. He loves us, indeed, by his creation as well as by his redemption of us, and as the Gospel has it he loves us that we might "have eternal life." [23] The opportunity afforded us is, in the nature of the case, an opportunity to attain that eternal life, whatever it be, through our own self-renunciation. This self-renunciation on our part does not mean self-annihilation, but it does mean the pain of self-restraint, self-limitation, self-sacrifice. We have to do, in our mode, what God does in his. Only through such participation in God's way of being and acting can we so be and act as to "enter into eternal life."

God, then, creates Nature and with it he creates us. He *could* command Nature and he *could* command us, but that is not his way. To express what "not his way" means, Augustinian theology says that God "wants to make us free." Freedom, however, in such a context, may be interpreted and understood in various ways. Even as automata in the hands of a benevolent commander we could be defined, in some sense, as free. We can best avoid the confusions attendant on the ambiguities that are obviously built into the concept of freedom by noticing the datum of Christian theology that God is not a commander. That God sits on a throne ordering the appearance of light and commanding the storm like a Byzantine emperor ordering his breakfast is a primitive conception. To conceive of God as a heavenly king or super-skipper or grand-architect merely transposes the primitive conceptualization to a more sophisticated-sounding key.

From the standpoint of classical Christian theology all such ways of understanding God are as primitive as any savage's because God is then conceived as a benevolent tyrant, able to do anything and therefore looking about, so to speak, to see how much he can do, and they ignore the costliness that the creation of any value entails. God, though not limited by having to face conditions not of his own making, engages in his own self-limitation

[23] John 3:16.

as the necessary ground for his creatures' growth, not merely as an exemplar for their self-development. Only by free self-discipline, self-restraint, self-sacrifice, does any creature come to be sufficiently like God to participate in that which makes possible the attainment of "eternal life." This view introduces a situation such as the one in the *Timaeus* discussed in the last chapter, *except that the limitation is self-imposed*. The objections raised by Mackie and Flew are objections to the presence of evil in the creation of an omnipotent and omnibenevolent sultan, rather than in that of the Christian God.

That is not to say, of course, that no mysteries remain for the committed Christian believer. They do. For instance, is not the creative process highly extravagant? We may still ask also whether the accidentality is not very arbitrary—like a battlefield or jungle rather than a school. Nevertheless, the situation has become very different from the way in which it is commonly presented by contemporary objectors.

There is also another theological doctrine—special providence. Though it is not a doctrine that we as philosophers of religion would ordinarily expect to be called upon to treat, it, too, is part of the general situation that we must take into account if we are to understand what the problem of evil is that we are expected to study. According to biblical teaching, God, though he creates Nature as a blind fulcrum for us to work in and creates us as free as our finitude permits, does not leave all humanity to sink or swim. He "provides" for and "watches over" his creatures in special ways. This doctrine of "special providence," whatever the philosopher of religion may think of it, further modifies the situation that he has to consider when he attacks the problem of evil in classical theism.

The presence of apparently "surd" evil, poignant though it is, does not really present Christian theology with the kind of problem to which the objections of typical hostile critics are generally confined. The Christian Gospel is, indeed, a special expression of a way of resolving the problem of evil, the problem that was extremely familiar to all thoughtful people such as Job before the time of Christ. At least partly for this reason was it acclaimed "the Evangel," or "Good News." To the extent that the historic problem of evil is resolved by the Christian proclamation, it does raise, however, a deeper problem still—the nature of the God of whom love is predicated. That problem will be suggested in later chapters, including the next one, and there will be some consideration of it when we come to discuss, in the last chapter of the book, the nature of love.

QUESTIONS ON CHAPTER V

1 Is accidentality inseparable from the character of our universe? Give reasons.

2 The view that evil is to be understood as the absence of the good is of ancient and reputable lineage. What objections do you see to it?

3 Wherein lies the plausibility of the theodicy of Leibniz, and what objections tell most against it?

4 Consider the notion of surd evil.

5 "Natural" evil has generally been distinguished from "moral" evil. Is the distinction to be upheld? What are the consequences, respectively, of (a) upholding it and (b) repudiating it?

6 "Theologians ... ask, which is better—men with free will striving to work out their own destinies, or automata-machinelike creatures, who never make mistakes because they never make decisions?" (H. J. McCloskey, "God and Evil," *The Philosophical Quarterly*, 10 [1960].) Is the question fairly put? If not, why not?

7 "If God wills that Jones stab Smith and God's will is effective or sufficient (as it is), then Jones stabs Smith. This is an essential part of the Christian doctrine that whatever God wills to be the case, *is* the case *ipso facto*, and that nothing contingent can be the case that God has not willed to be so." James F. Ross, after noting this, in *Philosophical Theology* (New York: Bobbs-Merrill, 1969, pp. 262 f.), goes on to say: "It should be obvious that 'God wills that Jones stab Smith' does not entail 'God approves of Jones' conduct in his act of stabbing Smith.' "

Discuss.

8 "As St. Athanasius understands the matter, evil is rather 'lapsing into nothing' or 'ceasing to be' which is a standing threat to all created beings. These beings have been created out of nothing, and it is possible for them to slip back into nothing or to advance into the potentialities for being which belong to them. Evil is this slipping back toward nothing, a reversal and defeat of the creative process." (John Macquarrie, *Principles of Christian Theology* [New York: Charles Scribner's Sons, 1966], p. 234.)

Consider this statement with reference to the notions that creation involves risk and that only by risk-taking can God be a God of love, since love must be both self-giving and letting-be.

BIBLIOGRAPHICAL SUGGESTIONS

Augustine, St. *The City of God,* Book 14, 13–14, in *Basic Writings of Saint Augustine*, vol. 2, New York: Random House, 1948.

Farrer, Austin. *Love Almighty and Ills Unlimited.* New York: Doubleday & Co., 1961.

Ferré, Nels F. S. *Evil and the Christian Faith.* New York: Harper & Row, 1947.

Flew, A. "Divine Omnipotence and Human Freedom." In *New Essays in Philosophical Theology,* edited by A. Flew and A. MacIntyre. New York: Macmillan Co. 1955. A contemporary statement of a standard objection to theism.

Floyd, W. E. G. *Clement of Alexandria's Treatment of the Problem of Evil.* London: Oxford University Press, 1971. A specialized study; useful for understanding the way in which the problem presented itself in the patristic period, more especially in the Alexandrian school.

Hick, John. *Evil and the God of Love.* New York: Harper & Row, 1966. A careful exposition and analysis of the problem, with accounts of traditional theodicies including a presentation of his own which in principle follows that of the early Christian apologist Irenaeus.

James, John. *Why Evil?* London: Penguin Books, 1960.

Laird, John. *Mind and Deity.* New York: Philosophical Library, 1941. See especially chapter 6.

Lewis, C. S. *The Problem of Pain.* New York: Macmillan Co., 1950. A discussion at a fairly popular level by a celebrated Anglican exponent.

Lewis, Edwin. *The Creator and the Adversary.* New York: Abingdon, 1948. An exposition from the standpoint of belief in a deity limited by conditions not of his own making.

Mackie, J. L. "Evil and Omnipotence." *Mind* 64 (1955): 200–212. A contemporary statement of a standard objection to theism.

Madden, E. H. and Hare, P. H. *Evil and the Concept of God.* Springfield, Ill.: Charles C Thomas, 1968.

Mavrodes, G. J. "Some Puzzles Concerning Omnipotence." *Philosophical Review* 72 (1963): 221–223.

McCloskey, "God and Evil." *Philosophical Quarterly* 10 (April 1960): 97–114.

Mill, John Stuart. *Three Essays on Religion.* New York: Holt, Rinehart & Winston, 1884. A classic exposition of the solution of the problem by limiting the divine power.

Penelhum, T. "Divine Goodness and the Problem of Evil." *Religious Studies* 2 (1966): 95–107.

Pike, Nelson, ed. *God and Evil.* Englewood Cliffs, N.J.: Prentice-Hall, 1964.

―――. "Hume on Evil." *The Philosophical Review* 72 (April 1963): 180–197.

Raab, F. V. "Free Will and the Ambiguity of 'Could.' " *Philosophical Review* 64 (1955): 60–77. A discussion of the freedom of the will in relation to the problem of evil.

Rashdall, Hastings. *The Theory of Good and Evil.* Vol. 2. London: Oxford University Press, 1924. A study of the problem from the standpoint of the philosophical position known as personal idealism.

Savage, C. W. "The Paradox of the Stone." *Philosophical Review* 76 (1967): 74–79.

Smart, Ninian. "Omnipotence, Evil and Supermen." *Philosophy* 36 (1961): 188–195. A reply to Mackie and Flew.

Tennant, F. R. *Philosophical Theology*. 2 vols. Cambridge: At the University Press, 1928 and 1930. See especially vol. 2, chap. 7. Tennant's view has been called "empirical theism," since he held that conformity to the world gives a reasonable basis for explanation in terms of theistic belief as most consonant with the facts.

Tsanoff, Radoslav A. *The Nature of Evil*. New York: Macmillan Co., 1931.

Weiss, Paul. "Good and Evil." *Review of Metaphysics* 3 (Sept. 1949): 81–94. Evil considered as conflict between opposing goods.

VI

THE NATURE OF MAN

Man is the genuine offspring of revolt.
William Cowper (1731–1800),
Hope

Man is something that shall be surpassed.
Friedrich Wilhelm Nietzsche (1844–1900),
Thus Spake Zarathustra

The Importance of the Question

What is man? The question is so far-reaching that one contemporary writer calls it "not a question, but a whole universe of questions." [1] It is also an old question, at least as old as the Upanishads. It is familiar to us in the ancient Hebrew psalm, "Ah, what is man that you should spare a thought for him, the son of man that you should care for him?" [2] The ancient Greeks began their philosophical questioning by asking about the structure of the universe or, as a later age might have said, "the nature of ultimate reality." When they tired of these investigations, they turned to questions about man. Why? Because, they felt, that is where we, being men, can be on sure ground. It is therefore the proper place for us to begin our search for further knowledge. The question seemed natural, partly because of an ancient injunction that Socrates much approved: *Gnōthi s'auton,* "Know yourself!" The right place to begin *any* inquiry seemed therefore to be with a question such as "What is man?" In this respect the ancient Greeks evoke a sympathetic response from many of us today who share their mood: instead of talking of God or trying to unravel the mysteries of the universe might not we do better to try first to understand ourselves? Pope's well-known couplet expresses the sentiment many have felt throughout the ages:

> Know then thyself, presume not God to scan;
> The proper study of mankind is Man. [3]

[1] José Ferrater Mora, "The Idea of Man," (Linley Lecture, University of Kansas, 1961), p. 1.
[2] Psalms 8:4 (Jerusalem Bible).
[3] Alexander Pope, *Essay on Man,* epistle 2, line 1 f.

Deviations and Human Essence

There was also, however, another reason for the focus on man. For centuries there was a point of dispute: what is it that constitutes the *essence* of man? That man *has* an essence from which individual human beings depart seemed generally axiomatic. The physically or mentally crippled, though indubitably human, lack something of the full human essence, and one might argue (as many have) what precisely that "essential nature" of man is. Monsters, such as are exhibited at circuses, might have seemed marginal cases, perhaps even, as we might say, "barely human," yet on reflection there could be no doubt that they were accounted monsters precisely because they deviated from a standard or norm that everybody believed to be somehow available to human understanding, if not tacitly understood, no matter what arguments there might be about the correct way of stating it.

Even as recently as two hundred years ago, Hume—for all his skepticism about the self—could still write of man with much of the traditional confidence in the general acceptance of a known "human nature" as his starting point: "The science of man is the only solid foundation for the other sciences." [4]

Hume did suggest, indeed, an insight that was important in its way and was taken up long after by Dewey: "Human nature is at least a contributing factor to the *form* which even natural science takes, although it may not give the key to its *content* in the degree which Hume supposed." [5] Yet even Dewey, writing in the twentieth century and accounted in his day a very advanced thinker, still talked, like Hume, of "our common nature." [6] Cultural "habitude and trend" diversify "the forms assumed by human nature," but "there are always intrinsic forces of a common human nature at work." [7]

Slavery

Slavery provides an interesting special case because the ancients, for all their confidence in an "essential" human nature, generally took for granted one or another form of slavery, and this institution imposed certain limitations on "human rights" so great as to put the "human nature" theory in jeopardy. Only freemen were entitled to those theoretically inalienable rights that were accounted by many to be proper to the dignity of man. Such rights as slaves possessed were derived only through attachment to their masters. These rights might be recognized by law, but slaves could not have such

[4] David Hume, *A Treatise of Human Nature*, in *Hume Selections*, ed. Charles W. Hendel, Jr. (New York: Charles Scribner's Sons, 1927), p. 4 (Introduction).
[5] John Dewey, *Human Nature and Conduct* (New York: Henry Holt & Co., 1922). Foreword by John Dewey to the Modern Library Edition (New York: Random House, Modern Library, 1930), pp. vi–viii.
[6] Ibid., p. vii.
[7] Ibid., p. viii.

rights except derivatively, as granted by their masters or by society. The reason was that their humanity was accounted somehow ambiguous. Though they were human they did not enjoy the "essential nature" of man as independently as did free men. They were at best like perpetual infants. No doubt sensitive and thoughtful people were perplexed about slavery. Yet even Aristotle could defend that then seemingly indispensable institution, arguing, for example, that the slave is in essence "an instrument for the conduct of [human] life"; that is, he is "a living possession." [8] A man is a slave by nature if he is capable of becoming the property of another.[9]

The objections that men of lofty mind in the ancient world frequently raised against slavery were generally objections only to its arbitrariness. For this reason the enslavement of peoples conquered in war could easily be shown to be odious. Yet no one questioned the wide disparity that exists among human beings in respect of intellectual capacity and moral reliability. In India the Buddhist protest against the rigorous caste system of Brahmanism was a protest against its institutionalistic basis, not against caste as a spiritual reality.

Moral Aristocracies

The great moral reformers in the history of mankind, far from questioning the aristocratic principle, have sought, rather, to call attention to the legalistic and institutionalistic abuse of that principle. In all the long tradition in which a moral elite was widely recognized—from the *chün-tzu* the Confucians revered to the chivalric ideal admired in medieval Europe, from the holy poverty of the Hindu *sunnyasi* to the talmudic learning of the Jewish rabbi, from the patrician virtues admired in ancient Rome to the gentlemanly ideal accepted in English society—there was embedded a presupposition that if these were indeed the moral aristocracies they purported to be, they were so because they eminently manifested the "essential nature" of man. They were what a man ought to be but seldom is. One liked to hope a man might be so, somewhat as we tend to hope that a lecture will be interesting and exciting, since we know that is what a lecture ought to be, though we may be usually disappointed.

Essence or Process?

During the last hundred years or more, the traditional view that man has an "essential" nature has come into question, if indeed it has not broken down completely. As modern scientific methodologies have been developed for the conduct of anthropological studies extending from prehistoric to modern times, great evolutionary changes have been detected. When we

[8] Aristotle, *Politics,* 1254 a.
[9] Ibid., 1254 b.

consider the course of the evolutionary development leading to what we now call "man," the notion of a human "essence" or even of a standard or norm becomes very difficult to maintain. Can we apply to man as we find him now and as we reconstruct him as he was in the mists of prehistory any common standard that could serve even as a guide in determining a straightforward answer to the question, "What is man?" We can talk of an intellectually average American college senior, taking the middle quintile of the graduating class or some other standard of reckoning from which poor students and bright ones deviate a little and morons and geniuses a lot; but could we possibly find any such standard for man? Even without going beyond primitive peoples, in the same epoch we find customs and values so diverse that the diversity may be more noticeable than common features such as upright gait and the symbol-making capacity that so much impressed Cassirer and his disciples. As we look, however, at a long slice of the story of mankind we find that the notion of any common human standard becomes increasingly untenable. The difference between a particularly low specimen of Neanderthal man on the one hand and an Einstein or a Schweitzer on the other is so great that we feel, when our minds are asked to move from one to the other, that we are not so much inspecting a widely varying species as witnessing part of a great evolutionary process.

Our puzzlements and misgivings about man spring by no means only from such archaeological and anthropological studies. Contemporary work in the biological sciences brings into question in several radical ways conventional notions of the nature of man. Dr. Philip Hefner dramatizes as follows the effects of biotechnology on our thinking: "What does it mean to be a man, when the heights and depths of human emotion (the emotional range worthy of an Oedipus Rex or a Lear) can be manipulated by chemicals or by electrical charges? What does it mean to be a man when asexual reproduction of life is foreseeable? What do life and death mean in an age when resuscitation of the heart, transplanting of organs and employment of certain drugs make it possible to maintain heart and lung activity indefinitely? For centuries the 'mirror test' (holding a mirror to a man's mouth in order to detect breath of life) served as a legal definition of death; today, physicians speak in terms of the state of a man's brain (revealed by various tests) as the definition—since certain kinds of brain damage render life nothing more than 'vegetable existence' regardless of the state of heart and lung activity. What does this do to theological concepts of life and death? What do human development and achievement become if it proves feasible to manipulate intelligence through genetic engineering, or if memory can be improved through injections?" [10]

[10] Philip Hefner, "The Churches and Evolution," *Changing Man: The Threat and the Promise,* ed. Kyle Haselden and Philip Hefner (New York: Doubleday, Anchor Books, 1969), pp. 113 f.

The formulation of these questions will suggest to some either a nihilism such as that of Sartre when he calls man "a useless passion" (*une passion inutile*) or else at least the notion that man is an epiphenomenon, not to say an offscouring, of nature. In both cases humanity would then seem to be nothing but a bubbling in the fetid river of existence on its way from nowhere to nowhere. Sartre's emphasis on freedom, with the consequent absence of that determinism that has characterized some expositions of the behavioral sciences, would do nothing to enhance the assessment of man's nature, for though Sartre recognizes as man's distinctive glory his capacity freely to thumb his nose at his own existence, that existence itself provides nothing to justify man's hopes for betterment here or hereafter. If, relishing bad jokes, you cared to file a paternity suit against existence itself you would find the putative father to be *le Néant*, Nothing.

The questions Dr. Hefner poses need not issue, however, in such answers. His own answers, indeed, are very different, and we shall have occasion later to turn again to matters that he raises—for instance, the nature and meaning of human death. All his questions, however, suggest answers that do clearly diminish any residual confidence we might have in the notion of an "essential" human nature. They point to an interpretation of man in terms, rather, of process. Such an interpretation need not exclude convenient practical definitions of man such as Cassirer's *animal symbolificum*, already considered in an earlier chapter; nor do they exclude a recognition of the truth expressed in the old Orphic myth (man is both god and devil, angel and beast), in the Christian doctrine of sin and redemption, and in Pascal's much quoted phrase, *la grandeur et la misère de l'homme*, "the greatness and the wretchedness of man." This theme of Pascal's is echoed by many, including Newman, who, calling man a "strange composite of heaven and earth," addresses him thus:

> Who never art so near to crime and shame
> As when thou hast achieved some deed of name.[11]

What a "process" interpretation of man does seem to put in jeopardy, if not entirely to exclude, is any definition purporting to specify what belongs "intrinsically" to the human race as wetness belongs intrinsically to water. Even to call man a process of life is too restrictive a definition, since he might well be depicted as having one foot in the biological process and one leaping out beyond it. Even a century ago Emerson was already prophetically observing, "Man is not order of nature, sack and sack, belly and members, link in a chain, nor any ignominious baggage, but a stupendous antagonism, a dragging together of the poles of the Universe." [12] Indeed, everything we know about man suggests movement on a nicely poised tightrope rather than the kind of definition that came so easily to the ancients

---

[11] John Henry (Cardinal) Newman, *The Dream of Gerontius*, line 291.
[12] Emerson, "Fate," in Conduct of Life.

who were still close enough to the now outmoded primitive ontology that enabled Epictetus to say simply, *psycharion ei bastazon nekron,* "Man is a little soul carrying around a corpse." [13] We should not forget, however, that such a notion did perform a very important and useful function in its day, expressing in an ancient idiom a truth about man that we must now state in other ways.

Even the strong late nineteenth-century awareness of the evolutionary principle at work in man did not automatically assure a complete emancipation from the traditional understanding of man as a definite species. Indeed, even when T. H. Huxley, accepting with some reservations Darwin's evidence about the origin of man, sought to uphold the old conclusion of Linnaeus ("the great lawgiver of systematic zoology" as Huxley calls him) "that man is a member of the same order (for which the Linnaean term *Primates* ought to be retained) as the Apes and Lemurs," [14] we are still only on the threshold of a new vision of man as process. Huxley was impressed by the "entire absence of any transitional form or connecting link" between the anthropini or man family and the immediately following family, the catarhini or old world apes, as between, say, the catarhini and their next lower family, the platyrhini or new world apes. Moreover, the families of primates were found to range all the way from the anthropini down to the lemurs, which come close to bats and rodents and simulate insectivora. "It is as if nature herself had foreseen the arrogance of man . . . admonishing the conqueror that he is but dust." [15] The question of man's nature still tended to harbor something of the old assumption that there *ought* to be a specific, scientific conception of a human nature, different though it might be from the classical one.

The implications of an evolutionary understanding of Nature gradually came to be seen, however, and today in Teilhard de Chardin we have a striking example of a system that combines metaphysical speculation grounded in theological doctrine with a careful scientific exposition of evolutionary history. "Teilhard points out that just as there was no absolute line of demarcation between the mega-molecule, the virus, and the living cell, so there is no absolute discontinuity between the animal's nervous system, the material support of its consciousness, and that of man." Nevertheless, man is not at the end of a process. He is "at the growing tip of evolution." "There is no evidence that man has advanced morphologically" for at least thirty thousand years, and evolution "on the somatic and cerebral level appears to have reached its structural limit as far as the individual is concerned," so we should not be looking forward to a "megacephalic superman." [16] According to Teilhard, evolution is proceeding along other lines.

[13] Epictetus, *Fragments,* 26. Also quoted by Marcus Aurelius, *Meditations,* 4, 41.
[14] T. H. Huxley, *Man's Place in Nature* (New York: Appleton & Co., 1898), p. 145.
[15] Ibid., p. 146.
[16] Michael M. Murray, *The Thought of Teilhard de Chardin* (New York: Seabury Press, 1966), p. 18.

Whatever we may think of Teilhard's very distinctive combination of speculative boldness and scientific discrimination, the formulation of such a system in our time, and the interest it has created in the minds of many, show how radically our thinking about the place of man in Nature has moved away from classical models. More and more we can see the force of Pascal's cry: "What a chimera, then, is man! What a novelty! What a monster, what a chaos, what a contradiction, what a prodigy! Judge of all things, imbecile worm of the earth; depositary of truth, a sink of uncertainty and error; the pride and refuse of the universe! Who will unravel this tangle? Nature confutes the skeptics, and reason confutes the dogmatists." [17] We can no longer even speak, as Nietzsche could make his Zarathustra say, that man is a thing to be surmounted," [18] for we may be compelled to say, rather, that man is the name for the surmounting process as we presently know it. Paradoxically, an early eighteenth-century English poet's insight better expresses, perhaps, the view of man to which contemporary knowledge of man and Nature seems to drive us: "Nature revolves, but man advances." [19] Man seems to be a special dimension of the process of Nature, a dimension in Nature yet somehow transcending all else in Nature that we know.

Religious and Nonreligious Interpretations

The understanding of man as process rather than essence need not issue in either a religious or an antireligious mode of thought. Nor is it even necessarily nonreligious. The notion of man-as-process is susceptible to many sorts of interpretation. For though we may be able to see man as emergent and can know a great deal about his past, we can only conjecture about his future. Moreover, any specificity in such conjecture would seem to be foolish, since what we do know of his history shows that at no point in the evolutionary process could anybody participating in it have guessed how the process might have turned out. A hypothetical spectator from another planet could not have foretold, for instance, the particular leap that was taken in the evolution of man. How, then, could we pretend to be able to tell at this point what the next movement in the process might be?

The most daring among us could hazard a guess only in terms of an underlying metaphysical presupposition or belief. The religious person would be likely to say something to the effect that whatever leap man takes will be guided by God and that man will take it under the attraction of the magnetic power of the divine love. A deeply religious man is usually very unwilling to go much beyond that into details. True, a religious person

[17] Blaise Pascal, *Pensées,* 434. In *Pascal's Pensées* (with introduction by T. S. Eliot) (New York: Dutton Paperbacks, E. P. Dutton & Co., 1958), p. 121.
[18] F. Nietzsche, *Thus Spake Zarathustra,* Introductory Discourse, section 3. Nietzsche uses the German verb *überwinden.*
[19] Edward Young, *Night Thoughts,* "Night 6," line 691.

wishing to give mythological expression to his faith, might talk language that the nonreligious man would find very strange. For instance, he might recall the number of the redeemed mentioned in the Apocalypse as having been finally victorious in their growth toward God and as now standing, all 144,000 of them, with the palms of victory in their hands. If, however, such a religious person did so, he would do it by way of symbolically expressing the notion that, though there is a law of entropy in the sphere of the spirit (perhaps a spiritual counterpart to the second law of thermodynamics in the physical order), there is happily a way of overcoming and conquering it, and perhaps comparatively few attain that victory. No intelligent religious person would pretend to know more than something of that sort about the cosmic process in which we, as human beings, are engaged.

Nonreligious people have, of course, no beliefs of that particular kind. They may nevertheless have other beliefs. Some, for instance, may feel sure that man is somehow moving toward greater control of the universe around him and may be expected to master it completely in the long run. Other nonreligious people may feel no less inclined to expect that man is rushing headlong to his own destruction and that there may come a time when consciousness—which is, after all, a comparative latecomer to the scene—will be extinguished, though Nature will go on, as presumably it did before consciousness emerged. Others again may be persuaded that the whole universe is "running down" like a clock, or dying like the embers in a waning fire, and that man will be extinguished with it. If, as many nonreligious people believe, man is a product of mere chance, he may be extinguished as accidentally as he emerged, and there is then no reason to believe he would emerge again. Indeed, that would presumably be very improbable.

To religious people views such as these will seem unacceptable, and to nonreligious people the alternative interpretations will seem at the best far-fetched. Yet there is no way in which either side can definitely prove the other wrong since we have no means of predicting the future of a cosmic process. I cannot even predict what may happen to me next week, though after what is to happen *has* happened, it may sometimes seem perfectly natural, if not even inevitable.

If man is, as we have seen him to be, a puzzle to human thought in general, he is certainly a problem for religious thought in particular. However we interpret religious awareness, we find it expressed only at the human level. However our attention may be focused on God, it is always we human beings who do the focusing. To the extent that religion ignores man it is simply metaphysical speculation. As soon as there is authentic religious concern, the spotlight inevitably falls on man, in the sense that religion is *about* the way in which man conceives himself as standing in relation to God, or, as some would prefer to say, it is about God's dealings with, or revelation to, man. In short, for the religious as well as the nonreligious person, man seems to be the proper starting point.

Man Is the Measure

Sound as may be the methodology that requires us to take man as the starting point in the discussion of religious as of all other important questions, it means, among much else, that the religious person is at once confronted with a very telling type of objection to his claims. As early as the fifth century before Christ, Protagoras, who was an older contemporary of Socrates, noticed that "man is the measure"; that is, all our judgments about everything depend on each man's individual conditions. For instance, if you have just come out of an overheated room into the street you may find the weather chilly, while I, having emerged at the same time from an ice-house will find it strikingly warm. Of two students taking the same college course, one may find it too difficult, while the other complains that it is not sufficiently demanding. How each feels about it depends on his ability and previous training. We all share a common human condition, however, in the sense that an elephant looks enormous even to the largest of men and a cat small even to a midget. When we reflect on that general principle (*homo mensura*, as is the traditional phrase), its implications for our religious attitudes become obvious. We can see the point of Heine's taunt that if God made man in his own image, man made haste to return the compliment.

Anthropomorphism comes in various guises. We may smile tolerantly at the crude images of children and simple people who actually imagine God as a huge man, perhaps with the beard and other accoutrements of primitive iconography. Even the most cultivated among us tends, however, to echo such anthropomorphism in the symbols we use in conceptualizing God, for example, those of shepherd and father. We see God as a great shepherd or father; but, of course, God could not but be greater than the greatest of fathers and better than the best of shepherds. Christians, opposing those who think of God as an impersonal force, have often vigorously insisted that God is personal; but, of course, while impersonality is far too restrictive an attribute for God, so also is personality: God must be somehow suprapersonal. Christians might even find they had to say, as some forms of Hinduism say of Brahma, that God is beyond both Being and non-Being. Yet it is always *we* who are saying these things, and however elegantly, thoughtfully, or subtly we say them, we cannot say them otherwise than from *our* standpoint. What we are looking at, then, as we saw in an earlier chapter on symbols, is mostly God as God stands in relation to us rather than God as God is apart from all else.

Does Man Make or Meet What He Worships?

The religious man who feels fully secure in his faith will readily admit all that, but his adversary may call his attention to an alternative that plainly will be unacceptable to him, namely, that man is not only the measure but the creator of his own concepts of divinity. In this alternative view, not only does man cut everything to his own measure, but he manufactures religious ideas according to his own needs. If he needs a father-image, the concept of God provides him with one. If his need is for a mother, he worships Mother Earth or, if the intellectuals in his culture have excluded that form of worship as improper or the legislators have forbidden it as illegal, he finds a way of meeting his psychological requirements; for example, in Catholic tradition he exalts Mary, hailing her as Queen of Heaven.[20] If, again, his need is for a feeling of personal security, he will concoct doctrines such as the immortality of the soul and the assurance of divine election. Since in primitive forms of religion, where the savage actually hews his idol out of stone or carves it out of wood, the "making of the god" is obvious, there is plausibility in the view that religious institutions are god factories.

The view that the roots of religion lie solely in human emotional needs is one that was proposed long ago and was familiar to thoughtful people in the ancient world. Demosthenes, in the middle of the fourth century before Christ, had already made an observation that might sound to us straight out of Freud: "What a man wishes he generally believes to be true." [21] The Epicurean school of philosophy attributed most if not all human ills to religion, and from before the time of Christ representatives of that school—for example, Lucretius—were already explaining the origin of the gods by human fear.[22] The Roman poet Statius, a younger contemporary of St. Paul, was to proclaim that by then already well-known view in his now celebrated line, *primus in orbe deos fecit timor;* it was fear that first made gods in the world.[23] In the nineteenth century, Ludwig Feuerbach, whose "materialistic" interpretation of Hegelianism exerted much influence on the thought of Karl Marx, accounted all objects of religious worship simply the creations of man's subjective longings. They are the *personifizierte Wünsche,* the "wish-beings," of autistic, that is, wishful, unrealistic thinking. After insisting that he is not calling religion nothing, but is saying, rather, that it "takes the apparent and superficial in Nature and humanity for the essential, and hence conceives their true essence as a separate, special existence," he makes his well-known pronouncement "Religion is the dream of the human mind." The dreamer does not deal with nothing, but he sees real things "in the entrancing splendour of imagination and caprice,

---

[20] Though Catholic theologians make a radical distinction between *latria* (worship), to be given to God alone, and *hyperdoulia* (a specially high form of the *doulia* (homage) that may be given to the saints), the distinction has been often obscured in practice.
[21] Demosthenes, *Third Olynthiac.*
[22] Lucretius, *De rerum natura,* Book 5, in Lucretius, *On Nature,* trans. R. M. Geer (New York: Bobbs-Merrill Co., Library of Liberal Arts, 1965), pp. 94–197.
[23] Statius, *Thebaid,* Book 3, line 664. Petronius, an older contemporary, makes the same observation.

instead of in the simple daylight of reality and necessity." The religious man changes the object of his dreams "as it is in the imagination into the object as it is in reality." [24]

What, then, is Feuerbach's concept of man? He is what he eats. He is also, however, the hidden object of his own religious adoration. "Man has his highest being, his God, in himself; not in himself as an individual, but in his essential nature, his species." [25] Marx's view of man, like Feuerbach's, was thoroughly tainted with this outmoded concept of man as having an "essential nature." Again, "In religion man has in view himself alone, or in regarding himself as the object of God, as the end of the divine activity, he is an object to himself, his own end and aim." [26] Finally, "Man is the God of Christianity, Anthropology the mystery of Christian Theology." [27] Feuerbach's understanding of the nature of man lies behind his interpretation of man's religious proclivities, which is a nineteenth-century expression of a very ancient critique of religion, especially where religion has claimed to enable man to encounter a reality that transcends both himself and the world around him.

Nearer still to our own time, Freudian psychoanalysis has immensely influenced contemporary understanding of the nature of man. Both Marx and Freud expound a deterministic view of man, but in Freud, a psychoanalyst, the determinism expresses itself more in the form of a clinical confirmation of the psychological relativism we have just seen in Feuerbach. Freud's more fanatical devotees have often and in many ways traduced his thought; and in particular, when they have developed his concept of the nature of man and of man's religious aspirations, they have frequently gone far beyond what he says. What he does say on the subject of man's religious concerns is nevertheless plain enough: they are the neurotic projection of our unrealizable wishes. Religion is therefore fundamentally unhealthy. "I believe," Freud says, "that a large portion of the mythological conception of the world which reaches far into the most modern religions is nothing but psychology projected into the outer world. The dim perception (the endopsychic perception, as it were) of psychic factors and relations of the unconscious was taken as a model in the construction of a transcendental reality, which is destined to be changed again by science into psychology of the unconscious." [28] He goes on to suggest that religion is really a form

[24] L. Feuerbach, *Das Wesen des Christentums*, preface to the second edition. In L. Feuerbach, *The Essence of Christianity*, trans. G. Eliot (New York: Harper Torchbooks, 1957), pp. xxxviii f.
[25] Ibid. (Appendix), p. 281.
[26] Ibid., p. 289.
[27] Ibid., p. 336.
[28] Though scientists in both the physical and biological fields would question the claims of psychoanalysis to be scientific in its methodology, Freud not only makes the claim repeatedly but often asserts it with a curious awe that is uncharacteristic of the authentic scientific temper.

of paranoia: "The gap between the paranoiac's displacement and that of superstition is narrower than appears at first sight." [29]

Jung, though generally accounted more favorable to religion, is so only in the sense that, in contrast to Freud, he sees it as often a beneficent rather than an unhealthy force. He attaches great importance to the archetypal ideas of religion. Like Freud, however, he sees in religious discourse no more than a description of what is going on in the human psyche.

That there are elements of truth in the contention that many religious preoccupations do serve psychological needs is, of course, beyond dispute. Moreover, that some do no more than serve such needs is so highly probable that few will boggle at the assertion. Nor would many intelligent people deny that much religion often exhibits the neurotic traits that Freud imputes to it. That is unremarkable. After all, as every medical man knows, much illness is hypochondriacal. Much medicine is nothing but a sop for the victim of the hypochondria. As such illness has its origin neither in the action of the external world upon the human body (as in a fractured femur sustained in a fall) nor in a physiological disorder (as in a hernia or tumor), but in the imagination only, the cause must be sought at the point of origin, which is the psyche. There may even be some hypochondriacal element in all illness. One might well admit all that as a matter of course without going on to say that *no* illness has any reality except in the psyche, which would be a very different contention indeed. In that event, the surgeon might as well exorcize a suppurating appendix as excise it. The issue raised by writers like Freud and Feuerbach is not whether religion may conform to their account of it but whether what they say about religion accounts for everything there is in it.

Those who are most thoroughly familiar with the inner structure of the religious consciousness are ready to see man's religious concerns both as conformable to what such psychological relativism has to say of them and as going far beyond such a narcissistic interpretation into one recognizing the possibility of genuine encounter with a reality beyond the human psyche. What that reality may be is another matter: it might be a pantheistic Nature-God or "the God of Abraham and Isaac." There is, however, an enormous difference between seeing religion simply as psychological illusion and seeing it as even occasionally and in a minimal degree as encounter with The Other.

That *homo religiosus,* to say the least, is not solely concerned with what he wants to believe, is as demonstrable as anything can be in enunciating any assertion about man. If religion were nothing more than a neurotic projection of our unrealizable wishes, men might concoct a vision of a happy afterlife nearer to God, but why should they fear, as do many, the possibility of exclusion from that joy? Moreover, though some forms of religion have little ethical content, many do. Some of them impose heavy burdens on

[29] S. Freud, *The Psychopathology of Everyday Life* (New York: Macmillan Co. n.d.), pp. 309 f.

their adherents. Why should an observant Jew, for instance, observe dietary laws which are as unpleasing to most contemporary palates as they are pointless to all contemporary minds? Why should so many Christians fight for social reforms that would be personally disadvantageous to them and take stands that make them unpopular with those whom they love, if they were simply believing what they wanted to believe? Furthermore, though in such a view one can understand why there should be pity toward, and regret and perhaps even distaste for, the religious-minded, why should religion evoke, as it certainly does, such extreme, bitter, and often unreasoning hatred? Perhaps Pascal more plausibly accounts for the facts and more suggestively raises the most important and searching psychological questions about religion viewed simply as a human phenomenon, when he says, "Men disdain religion; they hate it, fearing it may be true." [30]

Human Values—Individual and Social

Both individual and social values have generally been recognized in what the major religions of the world have had to say about the nature of man. The emphasis, however, has varied greatly. The tension between the two sets of values has also given rise to much perplexity and a great deal of confusion. In primitive societies the concept of man is, as we might expect, predominantly tribal. Man belongs to his family and his tribe. The fetishes he uses and the gods he worships are the fetishes and gods of the tribe.

Even at this stage, however, other values may be already emerging. Anthropologists have much disputed what determines the transition in primitive cultures from animism—in which all nature is haunted, as it were, by spirits—to a religion in which definite objects, gods, or spirits are worshipped. The first form in which religion generally appears seems to be the worship of animals, the totems, in the wake of which seem to follow the moral codes, the taboos. Freud once worked out an interesting suggestion that the transition is to be traced back to an upheaval in family relationships.[31] Now, if Freud is right that an upheaval in family relationships was in any way at the root of the change that introduced ethical concerns in even as primitive a form as the taboo, perhaps we may detect even at that very early stage an incipient concern for individual as well as social values. Still, at the primitive level the values of the community very much predominate over those of the individual.

Even long after the ethical rights, duties, and obligations of the individual have begun to be recognized, emphasis on man's social values persists. Almost all modern students of political history have been astonished when they discovered for the first time how totalitarian had been the concepts of the ancient world in respect to the State. They are often shocked to find that

[30] Blaise Pascal, *Pensées*, 187.
[31] S. Freud, *Totem and Taboo*, trans. J. Strachey (New York: W. W. Norton & Co., 1950).

even so great a thinker as Plato, for example, shared that commonly accepted view of the relation of man to his society. Though in one breath Plato speaks of the individual human soul as not only important but even immortal, in the next he takes for granted that in the ideal republic the individual, whatever his rank, is expected as a matter of course to sacrifice himself unquestioningly to the good of the State. Though the structure of the individual soul represents in microcosm the macrocosm that is the State and though, of course, the State has as its *raison d'être* the good of the whole society, the individual member of that society must always consider the communal values before even the highest values of his own as an individual human being. Indeed, the higher his position in the State the more self-effacing he must be, since nowhere more than in Plato's *Republic* does *noblesse oblige.* That is why, for example, the top-ranking members of society, those men and women who constitute the philosopher-guardians, are not allowed the personal choice of sexual partner that is permitted to members of the lowest class: the philosopher-guardians must breed according to the needs of the State, so as to reproduce (such is Plato's genetic theory) the best offspring in the interest of society rather than to indulge their own sexual whims in either permanent or casual unions. Neither are parents to know their children, nor are children to know their parents.

In the Byzantine empire and down to recent times in Japan and the Oriental world generally, the supremacy of the State over the individual was presupposed almost without question. The Church–State polarity in the medieval Latin West, for which St. Augustine's *De Civitate Dei* provided a model and intellectual justification, introduced a circumstance that turned out to be extraordinarily fortunate for the development of the individual. For while the individual, as a member of two societies, each in its own way under a divine sanction, had in respect of his duties and obligations a dual responsibility to Church and State respectively, he could by the same token play the one off against the other so as to assert in some measure his rights over both. Limits began to be seen in the claims of society over the individual. Princely power, unlike that of its despotic counterpart in the East, was not absolute, for always—at least in theory and sometimes also in practice—a people could rise up against a prince whose rule was flagrantly unjust. According to medieval political theory, the people could even lawfully kill such a prince. Their act in taking such an extreme step would not constitute, therefore, unlawful rebellion. The perpetrators of the act might properly be considered valiant knights rather than criminals or traitors. It was this liberating, though heady, medieval political doctrine that was to be eventually the remote ancestor of that of Locke, whose influence on the revolutionary ideas of the Founding Fathers of the United States of America is well known.

Meanwhile the sixteenth-century Renaissance and its twin movement, the Reformation, brought into focus an emphasis on individualism that had been for long slowly developing in the Western European concept of man.

The biblical renaissance that accompanied the Reformation contributed to the emphasis on the individual in a peculiar way whose importance can hardly be exaggerated; from the Bible, men's eyes were opened in a new way to the concept of man's rights and duties as an individual.[32]

Men are generally, however, more easily infatuated with their rights than convinced of their duties. In the various revolutionary movements Europe was to see in the course of later centuries, there were at best no strongly religious motivations. More often there was only a ruthless self-seeking. The language, however, was always, high-sounding and the ideals were sometimes great. The French Revolution, with all the bloodshed, cruelty, horror, and injustice it brought in its train before it spawned Napoleon, took for the first word of its battle cry the watchword of the new dream—*liberté*. It proclaimed a program for the liberation of humanity from the chains with which a too narrowly socialized and stratified political concept of man had bound him.

The new concept of man in the nineteenth century suggested a political ideal in which, so far as expedient, individual rights would be protected against society. The community would be for the individual, not the individual for the community. The result was splendid for those individuals who knew how to use the new concept to their own advantage, but what of the obverse side—the duties of the individual to society, in light of the new concept? Though many individuals in all classes of society displayed an extraordinary sense of responsibility in the face of the liberties they had won, there was often, as one might expect, less success in performing duties than in appropriating rights. By the end of the century men were turning once again to the other, communal aspect of man, leading to such characteristic twentieth-century socialist movements as the Bolshevik Revolution of 1917 in Russia and the National Socialist movement in Germany, which, under Hitler, precipitated World War II and is still, in other forms, a very real danger wherever the vision of the freedom of the individual, with the duties and rights attending it, is unappreciated or forgotten. Few societies know how to find a path between totalitarianism and anarchy, and rare indeed even in such fortunate societies are the individuals who have the strength of character to pursue that path with firm resolve.

Aggregation and Individuation in the Evolutionary Process

What, then, is the truth about man and whither is he bound? Is the polarity we have been considering an integral part of his nature, or is one or the other of the antinomies, the social or the individual, destined to overcome its partner? To ask such questions is to presuppose the very premise we

---

[32] The humanistic background of the development of individualistic human values is treated in a book of mine, *The Hemlock and the Cross* (Philadelphia: J. B. Lippincott Co., 1963); in *A Literary History of the Bible* (Nashville, Tenn.: Abingdon Press, 1968) I have exhibited the contribution of the biblical renaissance.

have seen to be widely rejected in contemporary thought, namely, that man has an "essence." If man is in process, he can presumably move more and more in one direction or the other, either becoming more antlike in the socialist fashion or else more individualistic in his style and aims.

Then can we see any general tendency in one direction or the other? Scientifically, the notion of the individuality of organisms is perplexing. For both philosophers and scientists, speaking of an organism as an individual presents at least as many difficulties as does speaking, as we commonly do, of an inorganic object as a "thing." In plants there is often no definitely shaped body but only a sort of tangle of filaments, as in most fungi and some algae. Branches of the banyan tree drop aerial roots that turn into new trunks. Where is the individual? In lower forms of animal life definition is hardly any easier. A termite might be accounted an obligatory partnership between an insect and certain protozoan inhabitants of its intestine that eat and digest wood as their function in the partnership. Such symbiosis takes many forms. When lower forms of life form colonies, temporary or permanent, these may have within them units that are compound, consisting of many cells, or single, like the protozoon. As we ascend the evolutionary ladder we find organisms still taking their origin from a piece of living substance that is detached from its parent or parents.

In the stream of life, then, it is as difficult to isolate the individual as it is to see a still in a motion picture. One may do so in the abstract, artificially for purposes of biological exposition, but in nature there is no such delimitation. At some stages such violent metamorphoses occur that different names are given, for instance, to tadpole and frog. Changes take place in higher organisms too, but they are less abrupt. In the higher animals, from each fertilized egg normally issues a single organism. Even in humans, however, there is occasionally division in the early stages, resulting in so-called identical twins, and in various forms of partial doubling, as in Siamese twins. Nevertheless, these are freakish instances. The evolutionary process does seem to move toward something more intelligibly describable as an individual than is found in the lowest forms of life.

When we examine such an individual man or woman more closely however, we encounter fresh difficulties. I am not at all like the little boy I once was, though there are important points of resemblance and connecting links that enable me to say confidently as I look at a picture of myself, "That's 'me' when I was three years old. See the likeness?" If, however, I were to show you a picture of myself at three *months,* I could hardly expect you to see any resemblance at all; indeed I probably could not recognize any myself. If the photograph is well attested, however, I may look at it with some interest as depicting "me" before I can remember "myself" and before I had developed the kind of self-awareness I was to acquire even at the age of three years. Can I then continue back in history and think of myself as an embryo or say, with the Psalmist, that my mother conceived "me"?[33]

---

[33] Psalms 51:5.

Can I really say that I, the grey-haired man I see in the mirror, am the same individual as the newly fertilized ovum in my mother's body? It is difficult to answer anything but "yes" to that question, and in that affirmation lies the source of much argument about many contemporary ethical questions such as abortion. Yet if I say "yes," what is the principle of identity?

Whatever the individual may be, he cannot be a static entity. He is, rather, a history. Trematoda or liver flukes, which are parasitic on sheep and more rarely on human beings, undergo so many metamorphoses during their life cycle that parasitologists generally distinguish separate individuals within the life cycle. Between tadpole and frog, as we have just noted, a very sharp change indeed occurs. In the history of what we call a human individual occur neither numerous metamorphoses as in the trematoda nor violent changes as between tadpole and frog. Nevertheless, there is continuous growth. The most traumatic occurrence in my history as a human individual was no doubt my birth. Of all the growing pains to which I have been subjected it was presumably the sharpest and most sudden. Nothing I can experience in the course of my biological history, even puberty, compares with it in suddenness or violence except, one may well suppose, the moment before my death, an inevitable future event. Yet even my birth does not seem to injure the individuality of the stream of history I call "mine." It is only a prominent punctuation mark. Of death we need say nothing here. In a later chapter we shall consider some aspects of it.

What we see at work in the biological process are two *tendencies*. We may call them aggregation and individuation. At first sight they seem to be working in contrary directions; that is to say, the first is a tendency to squeeze together a number of individuals into one aggregate unit, while the second is the tendency of a given unit towards separation and distinction from other units in such a way as to proclaim its individuality. Though the respective actions of aggregation and individuation seem at first sight contrary and do stand in tension, they also seem to work together in harmony, so to speak, within the evolutionary process. That is to say, after individuation may ensue aggregation, which, going into reverse, so to speak, may once again turn into a process of individuation.

Aggregation and Individuation in Man

Among instances of the life process, man is an exceptional case. He has somehow made an evolutionary leap, so that there is both continuity and discontinuity between him and the biological process that is his ancestry. He has been transformed in such a way that the transformation issues, for instance, in the novel symbolific capacity we considered in an earlier chapter, which enables him to organize his whole mental life into a continuing unity. Contemporary novelists and playwrights have celebrated in a new way the power of man not only to transcend his circumstances by the exercise of his symbolific power but to live a whole life beyond the spatial and temporal limitations of his physical and biological existence. Striking examples are provided by Proust and by Joyce, whose *Ulysses* takes longer to read than to happen. Man is as unlike his biological antecedents as he is like them. In him individuation takes on new meaning, for interwoven with his physical individuation is a mental individuality that varies in intensity but has no clear parallel in lower forms of life.

All that is known about evolution points to a progressive individuation as the life process unfolds. As we look back from our human vantage point, that life process seems to culminate in man, in whom the greatest individuation is achieved. As soon as we then turn again to man, however, we find that the old polarity seems to emerge in a new way. Man, the most highly organized of all the biological forms, in whom from a biological standpoint individuation seems to have reached its climax, further develops his individuality (his distinctive personality, as we may now say) by a new kind of aggregation. The individual man achieves his individuality by appropriating and organizing within himself a larger and larger number of facts and ideas, which he gets through encounter with his fellows.

Especially important in the achievement of the fullness of his individuality is the quality of man's human relationships. There are men who may be called "moral morons," who seem to be not only acutely self-centered and self-seeking but also incapable of loyalty of any kind and may even be entirely lacking in the most elementary kind of considerateness of other people. Not only are such people properly accounted more dangerous than the merely mentally defective, but they are less individual. The mentally defective may exhibit, in their own way, that tender affection and (within their capacity) thoughtful kindness that give them a distinctive personality. That personality, for all their mental limitations, can make them recognizably human beings. A merely weak-minded man or woman may make a real contribution to the life of the community despite crippling misfortune and disadvantage. The morally defective is not merely distasteful or unacceptable to society; his personality as a human being is underdeveloped in a radical way. He is not merely amoral like a cat, nor is he properly called subhuman; he is a monster, that is, an anthropological freak. If, as by no means is impossible, he happened to have a good intellect and to be, for instance, an excellent mathematician, his intellectual prowess would accentuate his freakishness rather than mitigate his monstrosity.

The reason is easy to see. The individual, if he is to grow, must get out of the cocoon of his own ego. In order to develop his personality, he must put himself into relation with an organized community. Only by somehow "losing" himself in the love and service of others can his personality grow. Therein lies at least one aspect of the meaning of the paradox enunciated in the Gospel: "He that findeth his life shall lose it; and he that loseth his life shall find it." [34]

[34] Matthew 10:39.

Aggregation, Individuation, and God

Even Robinson Crusoe (Defoe's fictionalized Alexander Selkirk) could not have prospered so well as he did in his solitude but for the strong moral and religious preparation that Defoe attributes to him before setting him on his uninhabited island. The life of a hermit may occasionally fit developmental needs arising out of the special circumstances of a particular individual during a limited portion of his life, as was presumably the case with the early Christian hermits in Egypt, the medieval anchorites, and the recluse Athonites of the Greek Church. There are also, in the West, semi-eremitical religious orders, such as the Carthusians and the Camaldoli, but these are atypical of Western monasticism. Generally speaking, both the development of human personality and the attainment of the spirituality that religious people seek require that the individual sharpen his spirit on the whetstone of the community. Great was the perspicacity of St. Benedict, who through his monastic rule required each monk to find his solitude with God in the closely knit community of his brethren.

The Hebrew people provide a classic example of how the individual–community polarity arises in the context of a religious attitude. Like other primitive peoples, the Hebrews had from the first a strong tribal sense, which was intensified by their circumstances both as slaves and as exiles. Their religion inevitably developed at first along community lines. Their leaders and prophets taught them that Yahweh, the God of their tribe, had entered into a covenant with them. Gradually they learned that they must not take that covenant for granted. It was binding on both parties only if both parties adhered to its conditions. The leaders assured the people that Yahweh would abide by his side of the bargain, for he was infinitely dependable. The onus lay, therefore, on the people. Their fidelity would determine whether Yahweh would account himself bound by the covenant or not. The prophets explained that Yahweh was a righteous God who would not continue to favor his people if they behaved badly. Thus in a typically tribal context did the Hebrew people first develop their deep sense of justice, of ethics, and of the universality of the moral law.

As time went on, however, the question of the status, value, and importance of the individual in the community became inescapable, affecting the Jews' understanding of the Kingdom of God that was the focus of their messianic hopes. By the time of Christ, they had moved far from their early covenanting type of religious attitude. Yet in their understanding of man an ambivalence had emerged. Though persecution had further welded them together, intensifying their national consciousness, they had already had to face the question of the individual. Plainly there were good men and bad even within the people of Israel; if God treated with Israel, surely he also treated with individuals.

Though some fanatical Jews expected the future Messiah to bring in an earthly Kingdom, their vision was nevertheless of individuals, each reigning by participation, so to speak, on his own throne in a victorious, theocratic Israel. Other groups, such as the Essenes and the Qumran community, were more pacific. Hating political revolution, they interpreted the coming of the Kingdom more spiritually, and with that transformation of the cruder form of Jewish apocalyptic expectation went the development of a hope of resurrection. The fulfillment of the faith of all good men would be found in that resurrection. This notion, alien to earlier forms of Judaism, is believed by some scholars to have been borrowed from Zoroastrianism, which had influenced the Jews during the Persian exile.[35] Such hopes, in christianized forms, indubitably played a great part in the early days of the Christian Church. They appeared in various chiliastic or millenarian teachings and were a familiar feature in the writings of the Christian Fathers. Although Origen (c.185–254) repudiated the notion of a Second Coming of Jesus, which seemed too crude for his speculative mind and allegorizing tastes, the notion persisted among Christian writers down to about the end of the fourth century.

The Superman in Early Christian Thought

The notion that the redeemed participate in the New Being, the Body of Christ, the Church, is familiar New Testament teaching, but another view was soon to develop. The interpretation of Christian salvation as the emergence of a race of individual supermen occurs clearly for the first time in Montanism, a Christian apocalyptic movement that flourished in the second half of the second century and which, though denounced as heretical, was extremely influential, deeply affecting, for example, even so great an early Christian thinker as Tertullian (c.160–220). Its leader, Montanus, claiming to be the mouthpiece of the Holy Spirit, is quoted by Epiphanius (c.315–403) as saying, "Why do you call a man who has been saved a superman?[36] The Holy Spirit says the just will shine a hundred times stronger than the sun, and the little ones among you who have been saved will shine a hundred times stronger than the moon."[37] The importance of that notion lies in the fact that, in contrast to the prevailing notion of Christian salvation as a restoration of the purity man had lost in Eden, it presents the exhilarating idea that man is being advanced from one state or level to a new one. Montanus is saying that the man who has received the charismatic gifts of the Holy Spirit will not merely be saved from whatever fate would otherwise have overtaken him; he is being raised to a new order or, as we might say, is entering upon a new dimension of being. He is

[35] This was held, for example, by Rudolf Otto. Other scholars, however, repudiate the view that the notion of resurrection in later Judaism had a Zoroastrian ancestry.

[36] The Greek text is: *ci legeis con hyper anthrōpon sōzomenon?* The term *hyperanthrōpos* also occurs in Lucian (c.A.D. 120–180). Nietzsche, as Walter Kaufmann suggests, probably drew the term *Übermensch* from such a classical pagan source.

[37] Epiphanius, *Panarion,* XLVIII, 10; in Migne, *P. G.,* Vol. 41, col. 869.

no longer mere man; he is not even merely man restored to his pristine glory, man as man "ought to be"; he is superman. With this conception we have the model for much religious thought and attitude nearer our own time.

It is a model that was alien to the mainstream both of medieval Latin Catholic and of Reformation thought. St. Thomas provided for a hierarchy of beings in which angels are superior to men, but though he held that in the future state of glory (that is, "in heaven") men would be "equal to the angels," "the distinction of natures will always remain." [38] Calvin, though he characteristically forbade "empty speculations" (*mataiōmata*) on the angels,[39] would not have had any particular quarrel with Thomism at this point, for he shared with St. Thomas the notion of an "essential" human nature. The question is interesting to us today because it shows that penetrating thinkers like St. Thomas did have difficulty in reconciling scriptural promise with the Aristotelian doctrine that man has his own "essence" as does every other order of being.[40]

The Superman in Late Nineteenth-Century Thought

The notion of the superman appears in several forms toward the end of the nineteenth century and the dawn of our own. No doubt Darwin's influential book, *The Origin of Species,* which had appeared in 1859, was prominent among the factors that had stimulated interest in the idea. In the light of what we have seen of the aggregation–individuation polarity, it raises interesting and very difficult questions. That man is a sort of gigantic bridge between the biological process and a further development beyond is an attractive and plausible theory; but we must go on to ask, what are the conditions for the birth of the superman? What will he be like? Presumably he will be freer than man, but how can we give enough content to the notion of such a freedom to enable us even to speculate on it, let alone to have the faintest inkling how to go about attaining it? Shall I trample down my weaker fellows, especially those who are clinging to conventional moral codes instead of making decisions for themselves in terms of what we should nowadays call a situational ethic?

Many people of the period who had been fascinated by the idea of the superman were inclined to such a mood. In Ibsen (1828–1906) we find a vehement exaltation of individual character and personality. When we ask, however, how that individuality is to be achieved, we find as many answers

38 St. Thomas Aquinas, *Summa Theologiae,* I, 108, 8 *ad resp.*
39 J. Calvin, *Institutes,* I, 14, 4.
40 Cf. Matthew 22:30; Luke 20:36. Cf. also St. Augustine, *De Civitate Dei,* XII, 9. St. Thomas resorts to the argument that, though man could never attain to the angelic order by nature, he can by grace, which is "supernatural," depending, as he puts it (loc. cit.) "on the liberality of God and not on the order of nature."

as there are advocates of the view. Ibsen, like Blake, was a sort of lone half-Christian mystic. His fascination with the problem of the clash between society and the individual is vividly reflected in the plays of the best known Ibsenite in the English-speaking world, George Bernard Shaw.

The notion of the superman belonged, then, to the age. From Nietzsche we might expect a clue to a better understanding of its nature. He has many affinities with process thought. Though historians of philosophy, for good, technical reasons, generally ask us to see him as a precursor of the twentieth-century existentialist movement, he wholly lacks the despairing, sadness-and-vomit mood of the modern French existentialists. He is very distinctly a man of his own age. When we come to examine what he says of the superman and of his "transvaluation of values," we do not find much precision. Nietzsche is vehemently antireligious, and his superman transcends the religious as well as the ethical ideas that might be expected to claim our allegiance; nevertheless he does not make his meaning entirely clear. That he has been absurdly caricatured (as providing, for example, the intellectual basis for the militarism of Germany in the first half of the twentieth century) is widely recognized, but careful scholars still find plenty of scope for controversy over his meaning.

The same kind of difficulty attends some other forms of the notion. In the evolutionary naturalism of Samuel Alexander, a British philosopher, and Henry Nelson Wieman, an American one, we find an unknown (because unknowable) God ever emerging and ever beyond the present stage of consciousness. Bertrand Russell clearly exhibited a basic difficulty in such thought by pointing out that Alexander, in order to avoid determinism, is forced to make the next stage of evolution impossible to specify and yet is willing to provide us with the assurance that, whatever it is, it is deity; but that says nothing more than that it is beyond man.

The Superman in Late Nineteenth-Century Religious Faith

Where the notion of the emergence of an evolutionary stage beyond man is set in a religious framework and linked to a metaphysical or theological structure having its focus in a God to whom some attributes are assigned, the concept of God might provide a clue to the nature of the process. That is to say, it might suggest the direction in which the process might be expected to move, but that is all. Teilhard, for instance, can speak of a movement from what he calls the biosphere to what he calls the noösphere, but what the next stage will be cannot, of course, be clearly specified.

The religious framework need not, of course, be a Christian one, but a condition for the workability of such a notion is that history be taken seriously. Alien to it, therefore, would seem to be the mainstream of Hindu thought, in which time and with it the whole idea of progress must be accounted illusion (*maya*) and so of no ultimate importance. The Hindu tradition is, however, multifaceted. Towards the end of the nineteenth century Aurobindo, a young Hindu, having completed a fashionable education at Cambridge, returned to India as an ardent nationalist more than fifty years before the end of British rule. He engaged in violent revolutionary activities and finally underwent a religious conversion that led to the development of his interpretation of man. His interpretation was novel in the tradition of Hindu thought. He was convinced that the intellectual and politico-economic upheavals he already saw engulfing the modern world were symptoms of a new stage in the evolution of man. Man is pressing on to a new level of higher perception. Human reason is a stage in the evolutionary process, but it is by no means the last word. A "supramental" consciousness must be established in humanity as a bridge or ladder making possible the realization of the next stage. The affinities with Nietzsche seem obvious, but Aurobindo found Nietzsche's hostility to Christian ideas distasteful. He knew Nietzsche at least in English translation and greatly admired him, but he thought Nietzsche showed the superman in too fierce and arrogant a guise. Aurobindo saw the true nature of that future level of consciousness as one in which a spiritually vivacious man might hope to triumph joyfully and securely, no more feeling need to trample on his inferiors in the evolutionary process than a mature and sensitive man would feel the need to crush a cat or a monkey. In typical Hindu fashion, Aurobindo accounted Jesus simply an exemplar of a spiritualizing trend in humanity rather than, as in orthodox Christian thought, when it exhibits process tendencies, the focus and ground of the process. Moreover, also in typical Hindu fashion, Aurobindo was still tied to a belief, characteristic of the Gnostics who flourished in the Mediterranean world in New Testament times, that somehow or other "flesh" stands in opposition to "spirit."

The optimism that all process thought tends to generate came naturally to the nineteenth-century American mind, but there were strong conservative forces operating against it in traditionalist religious circles. When Darwin first made an impact on the American scene, there was, as was natural and as is well known, a violently reactionary movement on the part of conservative churchmen. There were also, however, other voices, calling for the betrothal of religion and science. One of the most interesting among these was Minot Judson Savage (1841–1918) who started out as a conservative Congregationalist. He preached missionary sermons during the California gold rush. Later, becoming tired of the ferociously anti-Darwin polemic that was characteristic of the popular American pulpit of the day, he turned to the Unitarians, in the greatest of whose pulpits he preached the then unpopular doctrine that Darwin's theory of evolution pointed both to a more significant universe and to a greater God than men had hitherto been able to conceive. Darwin had been a service to the Christian faith, bringing out depths in it that man had not been previously able to probe. As Teilhard was to proclaim long afterwards, God who is working in evolution is both its alpha and its omega, its origin and its end.

So vast is the spectrum of human life that the difference between a man and a monkey is not so great as that between the highest and the lowest form of man. "The gulf that separates the highest animals from the lowest men is as nothing compared with the wider differences that lie between those lowest men and the Dantes, the Shakespeares, and the Newtons of the race." [41] Much more recently, Emily Hahn, writing in *The New Yorker*, relates that at Tange, in the Ituri forest of what was the Belgian Congo when she lived there for nine years, she had personally heard the Africans talk of pygmies as nonmen. One villager had asked, "Is he a pygmy or a man?" Yet when they spoke of chimpanzees they talked of them as of people. When she asked who had done some mischief, she received the reply, "No other person than Chimpo," referring to a chimpanzee she had adopted. She even suggests that Herodotus, who, after a trip to Egypt in the fifth century B.C., told of adult men no bigger than children, might have mistaken anthropoids for men.[42] Be that as it may, the line of demarcation between humans and nonhumans is not so easy to draw as many have supposed. Yet the difference between a Teilhard or a Schweitzer, on the one hand, and the village idiot, on the other, is startling.

Two Scottish-born theologians, James McCosh (1811–1894) and Henry Drummond (1851–1897) were also in the vanguard of the new evolutionary understanding of the Christian faith. In a passage that sounds almost like a translation of Teilhard, though McCosh wrote it while Teilhard was still a child, we read: "Life seized the mineral mass, and formed the plant; sensation imparted to the plant made the animal; instinct has preserved the life and elevated it; intelligence has turned the animal into man; morality has raised the intelligence to love and law. The work of the spirit is not an anomaly. It is one of a series; the last and the highest. It is the grandest of all the powers. It is an inward power . . . preparing the soul for a heavenly rest, where . . . rest consists in holy and blessed service." [43]

Drummond's vocabulary prefigures perhaps even more strikingly that of Teilhard. As a theological professor in Scotland he exerted considerable influence in his own country and beyond, and on his own and later generations. He attached the evolutionary principle to the theological doctrine of election. The "whole system of Nature" is moving "towards quality." In the course of evolution "Quantity decreases as quality increases." [44] He was invited to Boston to give the Lowell Lectures in 1893,

[41] M. J. Savage, *The Religion of Evolution* (Boston: Lockwood, Brooks & Co., 1876), p. 51.

[42] Emily Hahn, "A Reporter at Large," *The New Yorker*, April 17, 1971, p. 46.

[43] James McCosh, *The Religious Aspect of Evolution* (New York: Charles Scribner's Sons, 1890), p. 113.

[44] Henry Drummond, *Natural Law in the Spiritual World* (New York: James Pott & Co., 1904), p. 389.

which were published as *The Ascent of Man*. In this influential work Drummond described man as the end of previous evolutionary development and the beginning of further evolution. He wrote characteristically, "Man was always told that his place was high; the reason for it he never knew till now; he never knew that his title deeds were the very laws of Nature, that he alone was the very Alpha and Omega of Creation, the beginning and the end of Matter, the final goal of Life." [45]

John Fiske (1842–1901) had called evolution "God's way of doing things." Lyman Abbott (1835–1922), citing that remark, went on to say that "Theology also may be described as an attempt to explain God's way of doing things." He then proceeded to argue that "God has but one way of doing things" [46] and that "His way may be described in one word as the way of growth, or development, or evolution ... that there are no laws of nature which are not the laws of God's own being." Having reaffirmed his belief in a "personal God," he went so far as to say: "In so far as the theologian and evolutionist differ in their interpretation of the history of life ... I agree with the evolutionist." [47]

There are many others of that epoch[48] whose thought on the religious aspects of the notion of man-as-process anticipates the surge of contemporary writing of this kind. The whole of this literature, from Savage to more recent writers like Teilhard, not only would have religious men eagerly welcome and embrace all that the sciences can offer, but would also encourage them in a lively optimism about the future of all who are prepared to participate in the next stage of the omnipresent evolutionary process, which Teilhard has called "ultra-hominization."

Difficulties in the Concept of the Future Evolution of Man

The concept of the future evolution of man, though in principle a corollary of what has for long been known of the biological process of man's ancestry, raises many difficulties. Those who expound such a notion from a nonreligious standpoint must face the sort of objection that Russell raised against

45 Henry Drummond, *The Ascent of Man* (New York: James Pott & Co., 1894), pp. 115 f. The title was, of course, an allusion to Darwin's work *The Descent of Man* which had been published in 1871.
46 Cf. the medieval schoolmen's opposition to the Averroistic doctrine of "double truth." Abbott was making a point which had almost exactly the same function in the late nineteenth-century science–religion debate about the nature of man as St. Thomas's doctrine of the unity of truth had performed in the thirteenth-century science–religion debate.
47 Lyman Abbott, *The Theology of an Evolutionist* (Boston: Houghton Mifflin Co., 1897), pp. 3 f., 9 f.
48 E.g., among American writers, George Frederick Wright (1838–1921) and Henry Ward Beecher (1813–1887), whose sister Harriet Beecher Stowe wrote *Uncle Tom's Cabin*, a novel that helped to bring about the abolition of the slave-trade in America. A good description of the perplexities the scientific revolution produced in the minds of religious-minded people in the nineteenth century is provided in Basil Willey, *Nineteenth Century Studies* (London: Chatto & Windus, 1950), chaps. 8–10.

Alexander's theory. Modern exponents of an anthropocentric view of future evolution, such as George Gaylord Simpson and Theodosius Dobzhansky, write confidently of man's so controlling the future course of evolution as to rule out for the future all dependence on cosmic determinism. Evolution "may conceivably be controlled by man, in accordance with his wisdom and his values." [49] But even if we can conceive such a deification of man, how are we to conceive what his "wisdom" and his "values" then would be? How, indeed, are we to assign any content at all to the notion of such a superhumanity in the future unless we have some clue to the lines on which man will develop? A thorough-going anthropocentric account of the future of evolution excludes such knowledge, and so Russell's objection would still seem to apply to it.

The Future of Man: Evolution and Faith

The religious man may quite properly say that what he claims to know about the future process is no more than a corollary of what he "knows in faith" about the nature of God. For the man of faith to say he can look forward with serene confidence to whatever the future may bring, though he knows nothing of the details, is only to enunciate an entailment of his faith and trust in God. To have faith that at the heart of all things, at the source of all being, is an all-mighty and an all-forgiving One who cares infinitely for me *is* to be freed from all worries about the future, on this or on the other side of death. The man of faith needs to know no more. He can always go forth, like Abraham, not knowing whither he goes,[50] *because* he has faith that everything is fundamentally always well with him. "Yea, though I walk through the valley of the shadow of death, I will fear no evil: for thou art with me." [51] His responsibility, moreover, is simply to trust in God and to do the will of God so far as it is revealed to him. Such a Christian need ask no questions. He is simply an obedient soldier of Christ.

As soon as he claims any knowledge of the nature of the process, however, he assumes a different kind of responsibility. No longer can he say, simply, "Lead me, Lord"; he must make specific choices as a man who is no mere obedient soldier but, rather, a skilled craftsman who understands the principles of what is required of him and what he undertakes to do. A special sort of difficulty confronts the religious person when he claims to be "walking in faith" yet at the same time to see the future of man in terms of an evolutionary process that is fundamentally one with the evolutionary process to which he can look back. He knows too much to be able simply "to put his hand out into the darkness and into the hand

[49] T. Dobzhansky, *Mankind Evolving* (New Haven: Yale University Press, 1962), p. 347.
[50] Hebrews 11:8.
[51] Psalms 23:4.

of God," yet he claims too little to be able to exercise the responsibility that the knowledge he does claim seems to impose upon him. Assuredly he does have such a responsibility, for he is now a coworker with God. He knows that the next dimension in the evolutionary process will flow from the one he sees at work in natural and human history, yet he cannot tell what it will be. How is he called upon to behave so as to fulfill his responsibility in helping to bring it about?

All the difficulties inherent in the Christian ethic seem to be aggravated. For example, is he to cultivate the individualist or the collectivist virtues? Both, of course; but in what measure in this or that particular choice? Teilhard gives some general guidelines,[52] but if we accept his doctrine of the process of man, the application of these guidelines to individual circumstances is likely to provoke in an extreme form that existential anguish that will be the subject of our next chapter.

The rich man in the Gospel story asked Jesus, in the idiom of his day, how he could "inherit eternal life," and he received specific answers, including (because Jesus, "beholding him, loved him") the counsel to give away to the poor all that he possessed. He "went away grieved: for he had great possessions." [53] He was grieved because, presumably, he lacked the courage to obey the precept. Had he been able to claim as much knowledge as do some Christian process philosophers today, he might have been not so much grieved as puzzled, for he would know that in his circumstances there is usually much to be said both on the side of giving away riches and of keeping them in order to be able to exercise the power for good which, in a free society, they bestow. Indeed, Jesus himself, after the rich man had gone, had more to say. While admitting that it is difficult for the rich "to enter into the kingdom of God," he affirmed that it is not impossible.[54] If we could look forward with confident joy to a new being that is to emerge in a free society, we might well argue for keeping the riches to help to promote new values.

When, as in bygone ages, Christians held an "essence" theory of man, they had difficulty in reconciling the injunction to turn the other cheek[55] with the action of Jesus himself in driving away the money-changers in the temple with a whip he had apparently made expressly for the purpose.[56] The answer Paul and Silas gave to the jailer's question, "What must I do to be saved?" [57] was easier to follow: if he would simply believe in Jesus Christ he need not worry about his salvation, for it would follow as night the day. If, however, we know that an evolutionary process lies ahead, and

---

[52] E.g., in *The Phenomenon of Man* (New York: Harper Torchbooks, 1961), Book 4 ("Survival"), pp. 237 ff.
[53] Mark 10:17–21.
[54] Mark 10:24–27.
[55] Matthew 5:39.
[56] John 2:15.
[57] Acts 16:30.

that it is fundamentally part of the same process that lies behind us, all leaps and discontinuities notwithstanding, then our perplexity will not be merely over a question of biblical exegesis; it will be perplexity of a more radical and agonizing kind. It might be expressed in a cry such as this: "I know I ought to do something, but having no principles to guide me I cannot know for certain what it is." Whatever I do entails risk. Not only may my decision lead me to "diminishment" as Teilhard calls sin; if, as seems inevitable, there is in the spiritual world something like a counterpart of entropy (annihilation or hell), my very survival may rest upon a solitary decision, for the making of which I have some, but insufficient, knowledge.

To suggest that is, indeed, to caricature Teilhard's fascinating system. The objections offered here do not necessarily apply to it with the force here given them. Yet the objections do apply in general to all attempts to know the nature of our destiny beyond what follows from what we may claim to know of the fundamental character of God, which is quite different from claiming to know his ways. As we shall see in the next chapter, as soon as we abandon the agnosticism about God that plays so important a role in the most profound thought of all the great religions of the world (for instance in Hinayana Buddhism, but conspicuously in Christian tradi- tion, not least as expressed in the teaching of St. Thomas, who derived it from Maimonides) serious difficulties emerge. We are no longer "walking in faith"; we know, yet not enough.

The Christian evolutionist is really claiming a sort of pseudo-mystical vision with roots in a sense of kinship with divine Being. He has discovered the secret of God's ways. He knows how God works. Not only is such a claim (as Ronald Gregor Smith reminds us) what Kierkegaard called "pure paganism"; [58] the attitude it encourages may miss both the serenity of the mystic and the joyful assurance of the man of faith. On the other hand, it may produce, by the same token, the very anguish that is a condition of genuine faith.

Standing here at the evolutionary crossroads that man is, how shall I determine which is the right direction for me? What am I to do to become, in the dramatic language of Montanus, a superman? Or, if we prefer other imagery, how shall I keep moving in the orbit that leads to God and not plunge off at the tangent that leads to entropy and destruction? One interpreter will confidently enjoin me to withdraw from the affairs of everyday life and turn contemplatively inward, with strong resolve and with the divine aid at my disposal. So I shall be enabled, like St. Augustine, to discover with my mind's eye "the incommunicable Light" [59] and draw forth from my inmost being all the resources I need to keep me securely within the right orbit. Others will offer me a very different prescription. Insisting, like

[58] R. G. Smith, *Secular Christianity* (New York: Harper & Row, 1966), p. 63.
[59] St. Augustine, *Confessions*, 7, 10, 16: *"intravi et vidi . . . supra mentem meam lucem in- communicabilem."*

Temple, that Christianity must be seen as "the most avowedly materialist of all the great religions," [60] they will urge me to dig deep into matter, so to speak, and enter as fully as possible into the stream of the historical process. Others again will tell me to lose myself in the service of my fellow creatures, like St. Francis of Assisi, who fraternally embraced "Brother Ox" and "Brother Donkey." Yet another will warn me not to give myself up to such picturesque follies but to work always for the consolidation of man, the crossroads of evolution. He will seek to convince me that the lowest and most despicable of men is more worthy of my attention and even of my respect than the best of donkeys and indeed of all the rest of Nature put together. While one objector, deploring religious support of war, will demand that I work at all costs for the peace of mankind, another will remind me that the pacifist ideal is a chimera, since the more the evolutionary struggle enters a spiritualized realm the more terrible the strife. The strife of big fish eating little fish in the ocean is as nothing to the strife mythologically expressed in the battle between Lucifer and the archangel Michael, between St. George and the dragon.

Suppose a group of religiously minded people agree (as not all Christians would) that there is no possible place among them for the aggressive and competitive virtues. They give complete allegiance to Albert Schweitzer's "reverence for life" principle. They believe they can move to whatever stage lies ahead of man by means of that one cardinal principle only. The maxim "Revere life," though it looks attractive, is like saying "Destroy nothing of value." Everyone who has any experience of business administration or even of housekeeping knows how disastrous such a maxim is. We find it is not enough to throw out trash. We must also sometimes throw out good things in order to have room for better ones. As the French proverb has it, the better is the enemy of the good.

In any case, how can I implement indiscriminate reverence for life? Shall I refuse penicillin out of respect for the life of the pneumococcus that has attacked me? Even if I did, my body would still be killing countless bacteria every minute before the pneumococcus killed me. Schweitzer himself, as a medical man, seriously considered that aspect of the question. In India the Jains have gone so far as to use masks to prevent their inadvertently swallowing insects and so sinning against what they take to be the spiritual law of reverence for all forms of life. I may say, however, on the contrary, that I have no need to go out of my way to be so reverential to such low forms of life, or even to dogs or monkeys. My responsibility is to man, now definable, *ex hypothesi,* as the evolutionary crossroads. All *human* life is sacred. That commits me at once to an ethic that would exclude every form of euthanasia in even the most extreme cases as well as, of course, all abortion and no doubt also all artificial forms of birth control, since they do impede the flow of human life which, in the view in question,

[60] William Temple, *Nature, Man and God* (London: Macmillan & Co., 1951), p. 478.

is absolutely inviolable. Suppose that I then revise my claim; I no longer state that all human life is sacred but, rather, that since all men are my brothers and equal before God, I must never prefer one over another. If I happen to be a surgeon I may kill thousands of cats and dogs in medical experiments, yet I dare not give any less time or care to saving a criminal lunatic's life than I give to saving that of the greatest of human benefactors.

If, on the one hand, we deny Savage's dictum that the difference between man and his simian ancestors is "as nothing compared with the wider differences that lie between the lowest men and the Dantes . . . of the race," we may allow ourselves to feel such a loyalty to man that we cannot dare to discriminate between Einstein and the village idiot. If, on the other hand, we admit the dictum, we are asserting an aristocratic principle the implementation of which gives rise to obviously terrifying possibilities. They are terrifying not because of an emotional squeamishness we might feel but, rather, because we know how easily such a principle may be misused—for instance, for genocide on a racial, national, or other arbitrary principle or to excuse the criminal conduct of a group on a similarly arbitrary basis.

Such considerations do not affect, of course, acceptance or rejection of the notion of future evolution. Every spiritual principle is liable to be misunderstood or misused, as indeed was Nietzsche's doctrine of the superman misused by the National Socialists and others. They do point, however, to the dangers attending such a notion. More importantly, they may serve to remind us that though the notion may be attractive and persuasive to sensitive people with a religious turn of mind and may find support in what we already know of our biological past, it remains speculative.

The dangers attending the conduct of scientific experiments that tamper with the human genetic code are very grave, as many scientists recognize. Eric Mascall, a theologian of international repute whose early training was in science, takes the view that the human race today is faced with an even more serious threat in this field of experimentation than is offered by the more visible menaces of nuclear war, overpopulation, and environmental pollution. To recognize that man is in process is one thing. To tamper by scientific experimentation with that process without regard to the grave ethical questions that experiments of this kind pose is a very different thing. Biologists now see the possibility of "an entirely new and potentially much more rapid type of evolution," not dependent on natural selection but "consciously chosen and directed by man himself." Mascall observes that by such means a dictator might insure that the next generation would consist exclusively of children fathered by himself on mothers of his own selection.[61]

The horrors that such possibilities open up for us may be far beyond our present human imagining, and since the changes accomplished might well be irreversible, we ought to think very carefully before condoning

[61] Eric Mascall, "A Theologian's View of Science," *New Scientist and Science Journal,* August 19, 1971. His suggestion is, of course, a *reductio ad absurdum.*

biological experiments of such a kind. The very recognition that man is a creative process rather than a species calls to our attention the need for great caution in the stewardship of modern scientific knowledge in general, but most especially in fields such as genetics and biology. Neither humanists nor Christian theologians have ever claimed that man has some assured status that entitles him to survive. Traditional biblical teaching is, indeed, that since only a remnant may be expected to escape destruction, those who seek to be faithful to God, the Creator of man, have a special responsibility, as Abraham saw when he pled with the Lord to save a remnant of the people and as Lot saw when he fled from Sodom.[62] By any reckoning, man is charged with the custody of his own survival.

QUESTIONS ON CHAPTER VI

1 Why is the nature of man so important a question for the contemporary philosopher of religion?

2 What are the consequences, respectively, of taking man to be (a) a species and (b) a process? Might he be both?

3 There are general biological tendencies toward aggregation and toward individuation. To what extent is man in the same case as all life, and to what extent does he seem to be exceptional?

4 Is the notion of the superman necessarily antireligious? How might a religious form of it differ from an antireligious one?

5 What difficulties do you see in a "reverence for life" principle?

6 In view of the incontestable fact that man is obliged to see everything according to his own measure, how can we ever attain to any knowledge of even our own nature?

7 Critically consider the view that all man's religion is a form of paranoia.

8 In what way does an evolutionary understanding of the universe both clarify the claims of the believer and aggravate his ethical difficulties?

BIBLIOGRAPHICAL SUGGESTIONS

Arendt, Hannah. *The Human Condition.* Chicago: University of Chicago Press, 1958.

Baillie, John. *The Belief in Progress.* New York: Charles Scribner's Sons, 1950.

Chaix-Ruy, Jules. *The Superman from Nietzsche to Teilhard de Chardin.* Translated by M. Smyth-Kok. Notre Dame, Ind.: University of Notre Dame Press, 1968.

62 Genesis 18:16–19:28.

Dobzhansky, T. *The Biology of Ultimate Concern.* New York: New American Library, 1967.

Dobzhansky, T. *Evolution, Genetics and Man.* New York: John Wiley & Sons, 1965.

Dobzhansky, T. *Mankind Evolving.* New Haven, Conn.: Yale University Press, 1962.

Dubos, René. *So Human an Animal.* New York: Charles Scribner's Sons, 1968. An engaging, Pulitzer Prize-winning book by a Franco-American microbiologist with proposals for reversing the dehumanization of man.

Ferkiss, Victor. *Technological Man: The Myth and the Reality.* New York: George Braziller, 1969.

Freud, Sigmund. *The Future of an Illusion.* Translated by Robson-Scott. New York: Doubleday, Anchor Books, 1951.

Freud, Sigmund. *Moses and Monotheism.* Translated by K. Jones. New York: Alfred A. Knopf, 1939.

Freud, Sigmund. *The Psychopathology of Everyday Life.* New York: Macmillan Co., n.d.

Fromm, Erich, and Xirau, Ramón, eds. *The Nature of Man.* New York: Macmillan Co., 1968. An anthology of readings from thinkers from the Upanishads to the present day.

Hart, R. L. *Unfinished Man and the Imagination.* New York: Herder & Herder, 1968.

Haselden, K., and Hefner, P., eds. *Changing Man: The Threat and the Promise.* New York: Doubleday, Anchor Books, 1969. A useful little collection of essays.

Hatt, H. E. *Cybernetics and the Image of Man.* Nashville, Tenn.: Abingdon Press, 1968.

Heschel, Abraham. *Who Is Man?* Stanford, Calif.: Stanford University Press, 1965.

Merleau-Ponty, M. *Phenomenology of Perception.* Translated by Colin Smith. London: Routledge & Kegan Paul, 1962.

Morris, Desmond. *The Naked Ape.* New York: McGraw-Hill, 1967.

Nicholls, William, ed., *Conflicting Images of Man.* New York: Seabury Press, 1966.

Niebuhr, Reinhold. *Man's Nature and His Communities.* New York: Charles Scribner's Sons, 1965. The author's last work.

Niebuhr, Reinhold. *The Nature and Destiny of Man.* 2 vols. New York: Charles Scribner's Sons, 1941 and 1943. The author's Gifford Lectures, very influential on American thought after World War II; see especially vol. 1, "Human Nature."

Noble, E. *Purposive Evolution.* New York: Henry Holt & Co., 1926. Example of a late treatment of the science-religion theme.

Pannenberg, Wolfhart. *What Is Man?* Translated by D. A. Priebe. Philadelphia: Fortress Press, 1970.

Passmore, John. *The Perfectibility of Man.* New York: Charles Scribner's Sons, 1970.

Ricoeur, Paul. *Freedom and Nature: The Voluntary and the Involuntary.* Translated by E. V. Kohak. Evanston, Ill.: Northwestern University Press, 1966. An impressive study of the paradox of the voluntary and the involuntary in relation to fallibility.

Romero, Francisco. *Theory of Man.* Translated by W. F. Cooper. Berkeley, Calif.: University of California Press, 1964.

Scheler, Max. *Man's Place in Nature.* New York: Farrar, Strauss & Co., n. d.

Schillebeeckx, E. *God the Future of Man.* Translated by N. D. Smith. New York: Sheed & Ward, 1968.

Shearman, J. N. *Natural Theology of Evolution.* London: Allen and Unwin, 1915. Charles Gore, in his Gifford Lectures *(The Philosophy of the Good Life.* London: John Murray, 1930) rightly called it (p. 244) "an unduly neglected work."

Simpson, G. G. *The Meaning of Evolution.* New York: Mentor Books, 1957. Argues that since evolution has brought about man, a self-aware being, its future course does not depend on cosmic determinism because, through science, man can conceivably control the future process.

Teilhard de Chardin, Pierre. *The Phenomenon of Man.* Translated by B. Wall. New York: Harper & Row, 1959.

Tournier, Paul. *The Meaning of Persons.* Translated by E. Hudson. New York: Harper & Row, 1957. This book by a French Swiss medical man presents an interesting Christian interpretation of man.

VII

FAITH, DOUBT, AND
EXISTENTIAL ANGUISH

> Doubt must become a constant, creative force; it must
> permeate the whole being to its inmost core.
>> *Léon Chestov (1866–1938),*
>> *Sur les confins de la Vie*

> Atheism is a cruel and long-range affair. I think I've
> carried it through.
>> *Jean-Paul Sartre (1905–), Les Mots*

Anguish as the Prerequisite of Faith

We shall consider faith as having two aspects, "knowing" and "willing."
That is to say, we shall see in it, on the one hand, a cognitive, intellectual
element and, on the other, a conative, moral one. The cognitive element
should enable us to rule out as trivial and irrelevant the notion of a "blind"
faith, "believing steadfastly what you know ain't true." The conative element
should enable us to renounce all intellectualized definitions of faith that
present it simply as belief in and assent to religious proposals (basic or
otherwise) such as we considered in an earlier chapter; for instance, "Jesus
Christ is (or is not) Lord of the universe," and "Mary was (or was not)
conceived without the customary human inheritance of 'original sin.'"

We shall try, then, to show that authentic religious faith is to be understood
both as having an implication of doubt and as entailing what modern
existentialists call *Angst* or "anguish." [1] *Angst* is a profoundly agonizing horror
at nothingness, such as is suggested, though only in a superficially emotional

---

[1] The term used by Kierkegaard was *Angest,* which in its German and modern Danish
form *Angst,* has become universally familiar in the international vocabulary of existentialism. It is not easily translatable. The word "anxiety," for instance, is too meager.
Kierkegaard's English translators, in an attempt to convey the peculiarity of the original
meaning, used the word "dread," but that, too, is misleading and infelicitous. The French
translate it *angoisse* and the Spaniards *agonía.* "Anguish" is probably the best English
rendering.

way, by the experience of standing on the edge of an abyss. It is similarly suggested in our own space-age nightmare of "falling off" or "shooting past" the gravitational pull of earth and into "empty" space. Existentialist writers like Kierkegaard invest it, however, with a deeply inward, personal, and spiritual significance. It is a radical malaise that we suffer in face of the plight of our human condition.

An understanding of that concept of *Angst* is so crucial for our purpose and demands so much knowledge of the background of the modern existentialist movement that before attempting to come to grips with our declared topic we must first consider what we are to understand by an existentialist approach to philosophy. We shall also examine the circumstances in which modern existentialism emerged. To do so will be indispensable for showing *in contemporary terms* why faith plays such a special role in religious life, and what its function is *today* in relation to other religious notions such as death and immortality, pilgrimage and mystical vision. Existentialist philosophy provides us with a means of breaking down the prison of our own narrow intellectualism.

On the streets of Paris, just after the war of 1939–45, when the works of Sartre and Camus were only beginning to be known, and before existentialism was much understood, one could occasionally hear the word *existentialiste* hurled at someone as an abusive epithet, like *cochon* or *salaud*. Philosophers of other schools, from whom perhaps one might have expected some better understanding of existentialist thought, have been, in their own way, hardly less impolite. Idealist and neoidealist philosophers in continental Europe and philosophers in empiricist, analytical circles in the English-speaking world, have denigrated the existentialist movement in both its religious and its antireligious forms and have sometimes even bitterly opposed it. How did the term achieve such sudden street popularity, and what is the nature and value of that revolutionary movement that philosophers of other schools have sought to discredit? How did existentialism come to provide a common vocabulary for the most and the least religious of thinking men? Before attempting to deal with these questions, let us first look at the great existentialist themes. By that means, besides accustoming ourselves to the existentialist vocabulary, we shall see, at the outset, something of its methodology and its stance.

The Great Existentialist Themes

In all forms of existentialism the emphasis on individuality and freedom is so striking that we need not be astonished at finding, as we do, that existentialist writers vary much in the way in which they treat philosophical issues. Nevertheless, there are certain foci or recurring themes that we may consider briefly in turn:

(1) Existence
(2) Individuality
(3) Alienation
(4) Loneliness
(5) Freedom
(6) *Angst*
(7) Despair–Faith

(1) *Existence*. All existentialists take existence as their starting-point. They understand existence, however, in a special way. The significance of their stance must escape us unless we bear in mind that from the time of Plato, the great philosophical traditions had generally recognized, in one way or another, a distinction between existence and essence. Implied in that distinction was the view that there are degrees of being: when I open my eyes and affirm that something exists or shut them like Descartes and am able, through an inspection of my own questionings, to affirm that I exist, I am in both cases talking only of what might be called a superficial "layer" of existence. That is the existence that "meets the eye" of the plain man as he goes about his ordinary business. The philosopher is distinguished by his ability to get beyond that layer to a deeper understanding of what "to be" means. There is this particular chair and that one; there is this particular person I call "me" and that particular person I call "you"; but beyond these lies "the essential being" of all chairs and "the essential being" of all men. You and I are mere exemplars of humanity.

The "essentialist," as we may conveniently call him at this point, is not merely saying that the universal is always better than the particular; he is asserting a view such as the Aristotelian one that since everything is in process nothing has fully realized its potentiality. That is to say, no person or object fully *is*; it has either lost the plenitude of its being or is on the way to attaining it. That which is only becoming is not yet all it is to be or ought to be.

Against that traditionalist, rationalist view, existentialists protested. They were not alone in that antirationalist protest, of course. Empiricists and others had for long protested, too. What distinguished the existentialist protest was that besides its repudiation of the old essentialist philosophies it took the concept of existence very seriously and in a way empiricists as such never did. For to existentialists, existence, whether they consider it to be gracious or nauseating, baffling or mysterious, is always the basic category. They may or may not be inclined, as was Heidegger, to take seriously Leibniz's question "why is there anything at all and not just nothing?" They always, however, accept existence as the philosopher's proper starting-point.

Here I am: who am I? Why am I? What is my relation to the other people who are there and to other things that are standing round me? These are typical existentialist questions. They are not a spectator's questions. They are the questions of one who is personally involved in the questions he is posing. To the existentialist all other types of philosophical questions seem trivial because they are the questions of a mere onlooker.

As essentialists call upon thinking people to look at the essences, so phenomenalists, recognizing a theoretical distinction between the way things may be "in themselves" and the way they appear to us and insisting that the latter are examinable as the former are not, call upon us to give all our attention to the phenomena. Existentialists, however, want us to refer everything to what they see as the ultimate category—existence. Only when we have isolated the notion of existence, have seen it as the ultimate frontier, and have begun to see all things, including ourselves, in relation to it, can we begin to philosophize.

(2) *Individuality.* In the very attainment of that first basic insight about existence, I am confronted by my own individuality. I am an entity among entities such as you and the table. There is no other person exactly like me; there is no other like you; nor is there even any other table exactly like the one we are using, with all its individual scratches and other peculiarities. That awareness of individuality is necessary for my understanding of the way in which entities like you and me and the table stand to each other. Each stands alone. Nevertheless, much as I may cherish our old table and much as I may love you, I stand to my own existence in a unique way, and it is in that way that I am aware of my self. Only I can grasp what it means for *me* to exist. I can know only second-hand what your existence means to you. By the same token only you can grasp what your existence means for you. We cannot show each other more. No matter how much you might love me, you could not be me.

The implications of that seemingly obvious affirmation are incalculable. A doting mother might wish she could suffer her baby son's teething pains in his place, but he must bear them alone. As she seeks to mitigate his pain by tender soothing, so we all try by sympathy to bear the trials and sorrows of our friends, but in the last resort each must bear his own burden. The individual is inextricably and uniquely wedded to his own existence.

Not only so; the particular relation between two people is individual and unique, too. If my wife died there would be no use your trying to console me with the reflection that ours was merely, among millions of others, a splendid exemplar of the conjugal relationship. That would only aggravate my grief, like telling me there are plenty of other women in the world. It would only make me painfully aware that you did not even begin to understand the nature of my sorrow.

Far from being able to say, then, in the old essentialist manner, that the individual, the particular, is to be accounted "less real" than the universal, we must say, rather, that the individual *is* the real. Moreover, individuality, as a positive value, does not come, so to speak, ready-made. It is achieved or won. We might even say that to achieve individuality is to appropriate existence. The more an entity achieves individuality, the more it has realized itself; that is, the more individual it is, the more it is real.

Then would not there seem to be "degrees of being" all over again, varying in reality? No; the existentialist would say, rather, that existence is multidimensional. My cat exists in one dimension of being, a "flat" dimension compared with the one in which I exist. Moreover, if I am aware of myself only as a member of a tribe or as an item constitutive of a crowd, I do not exist as I do if I am able to stand out from the crowd and, in my self-awareness, recognize myself as alone. I am now a *self*.

(3) *Alienation.* That discovery, that awareness of selfhood, is by no means an unmitigated joy. I may delight in it, but at the same time I am dismayed. Not only is the world of external things standing over against and around me; you are standing over against me, making demands of me and judging me. Yet there is no turning back. I cannot really want to escape the self-awareness that characterizes our human condition. I cannot really pretend my cat is more fortunate than I, except in the sense that the table is more fortunate still.

I want to say to you, "Leave me alone"; I want to be "myself"; but there breaks in on me the knowledge that to be myself I must attend in one way or another to you, whether you torture me by making me hate you or torment me by making me love you. At all events I must take you into account. I cannot escape you. Yet I can neither love myself in you nor dissolve you in myself. I may grow or refuse to grow; either way I am forced to recognize that you and I are different. I "come alive" only by loving or hating you; yet the more I love or hate you the more I recognize my "apartness" from you.

I am alienated not only from you, but from the whole of my circumstances. Do not ask whose "fault" it is. The inescapable fact in my self-awareness is that I am alienated from all the non-me around me. When I am able to say that I like you so much that I can feel at home with you and "let my hair down" at your house, I am only saying that I have found a way of achieving a temporary respite, a "let-up" in my sense of alienation.

Of course, everyone has experienced something like that at various points in life. Presumably, we have all experienced it at birth, which may be the most traumatic experience in life, and also on other occasions such as starting school, reaching puberty, leaving school, and so forth. We generally try as far as possible to minimize them. By so doing we are only drugging ourselves to avoid what would otherwise make the aching sense of alienation unbearably sharp. Sometimes, however, in the course of life our attention is called to that alienation in such a way that all the usual means of escape are barred. *Huis clos!* No exit! That is the kind of alienation the existentialists want us to consider. It leads to the next point.

(4) *Loneliness.* My sense of alienation makes me feel utterly alone. No matter how rich or poor I may happen to be, how fortunate or luckless,

how healthy or sick, how solitary or gregarious in my habits, I am suddenly stricken by the sense of being completely and utterly alone. The more I go partying, the more acute my sense of loneliness. I may forget it for a time. I probably use every resource at my disposal to try "to wish away" the loneliness that dismays and frightens me. Still it persists. It hits me when I least expect it—not, perhaps, when I am enjoying a weekend in the country, far from telephones and every other manifestation of human existence, so much as suddenly, in the midst of a noisy party everyone is expected to enjoy. The agony of loneliness has little to do with the physical proximity of people. Everyone knows we can all feel it more acutely in Times Square than on a remote hillside in Montana.

Death, since it lies, strictly speaking, beyond experience, cannot come into our present schema. Nevertheless, dying is presumably the paradigm case of loneliness. We must all die *solo,* with nobody to accompany us in whatever it is we do in dying. Yet in other experiences of life we sense something of that same loneliness that we associate with dying. When, for example, we feel there is no one who can truly understand or care, we experience a kind of dying. When we return to a place where once we had a multitude of friends who loved us and made us feel at the center of everything and we now find them all dead or gone away, the ache of emptiness has the finality of a sort of dying. We say: what was can never be again. We may have a similar sense of our loneliness in the universe when we know that what might have been for us never now can be. Existential loneliness is the loneliness of the individual in his alienation from all the rest of existence.

(5) *Freedom.* If the human predicament went no further than what we have already considered, the proper remedy might well lie in resignation to our fate or, perhaps, in an attunement to the whole universe. If I were simply a self-conscious unit in a wholly self-determined universe, my course would be clear. Feeling myself alienated from other people and from the whole universe, I could do nothing better than try to fit myself to the way things are. My interest would lie in adjusting myself to the reality of the whole of which I would account myself a part. That, indeed, is what certain religions, being nature-pantheisms, enjoin us to do. Indeed, from that standpoint religion could hardly consist of much else.

In the existentialist view, the human predicament is far more poignant. The real sting in the human plight arises from a fundamental polarity that exists in our situation. The world around me is indeed absolutely "given." I can do nothing about it. I cannot change my birthdate or choose my parents. If I become influential enough, I might have the name of my birthplace changed to my better liking, but even if I became the most powerful emperor mankind has ever seen, I could not decide to have been born in Williamsburg or Windsor if I had been born in London or New York. Yet when all that has been said, and the truth of it has burned deep into my consciousness, I discover that not only can I make certain free choices but indeed I am forced to choose. The nature of life forces me to make decisions, as the nature of freeway driving forces me to decide very quickly whether to take the "off" ramp or proceed with the through traffic.

In metaphysical speculations or analytical discussions in a philosophy seminar there is no hurry: we can leave matters where they stand when the bell rings and go on unraveling the problem next week. If we are speculative enough or analytical enough we can go on for the rest of our lives without decisively taking a position. There is no need for us to do so, for the questions are of no personal concern to us. We can pretend to take a position if, for example, we think the professor or other people will like that; but it need never affect our lives. Nevertheless, we can go on building grander and grander systems, perhaps even outdoing Kant and Hegel. In our analytical philosophy we can go on honing our philosophical tools till they are too fine to serve any conceivable purpose. In such ways I can play games with myself. Life, however, is no game. In life I am obliged to make decisions, and in the existentialist view I have genuine freedom of choice to do so.

That freedom is not, of course, limitless. On the contrary, such is the human predicament that on the one hand I am encompassed by circumstances that are absolutely determined for me in advance and about which I can do nothing at all, while on the other hand there are certain choices that I have to make. I have to be a fatalist and at the same time the master of my fate. Life seems to be taunting me with the polarity of freedom and determinism. My freedom seems as burdensome as my non-freedom.[2] It forces me into involvement with the world. Existentialism is a philosophy of involvement. That involvement, which is a key to an understanding of existentialism generally, is also specifically the connecting link between existentialist philosophy and religious faith.

The existentialists, though they give as important a role to freedom as anyone has ever given in the history of philosophy, do not account freedom an achievement—as did Kant, for instance, who considered it the supreme achievement in human life. For the existentialists, freedom is not so much an achievement as a condition of human life, like mortality and hunger. The man whom Sartre admires is the one who accepts "in good faith" (a favorite and perplexing phrase of Sartre's) the responsibilities that his actions involve.[3] The man he despises is the one who, being of "bad faith," is dishonest with himself, hypocritically hiding from himself the realities

[2] Cf. the theme developed by Professor Victor Brombert of Yale in his long article "Esquisse de la prison heureuse," in *Revue d'Histoire Littéraire de la France,* March–April 1971.

[3] On good and bad faith in Sartre, see his *Being and Nothingness,* part 1, chap. 2, section 3. Cf. Mary Warnock, *The Philosophy of Sartre* (New York: Barnes & Noble, 1967), pp. 50 ff., and *Existentialism* (New York: Oxford University Press, Galaxy Books, 1970), pp. 97 ff.

of determinism and freedom. If, on the one hand, he is the sort of man who blames his parents for his own shortcomings, he is a coward. If, on the other hand, he pretends he is driven on to commit various crimes for some imaginary high purpose, he has the viciousness of what is colloquially called "stinker" or "bastard," in the sense of "scoundrel." In both cases he is covering up, pretending to lack a freedom he knows perfectly well he possesses. He is "passing the buck," for example, to his parents or to God. The pseudo-religious man who perpetrates every imaginable kind of wickedness under cover of divine vocation or on the pretext that he is only carrying out the will of Allah is the most vicious abuser of freedom, but the sluggard who is always making deterministic excuses is not in a radically different case. The difference is somewhat like the difference between a sneak-thief and a bank robber.

The individual, having come up against his own existence and facing alone a world from which he feels himself alienated, finds himself, so to speak, "in the middle" of the absurd ambivalence between his absolute freedom and his absolute non-freedom. He is bound to accept his birthplace, even though it may have been a lunatic asylum. Though he may covet a genteel lineage, he must face the fact, if it be a fact, that his father was a felon. He must accept also his medical heredity even though it include congenital bone disease that precludes the fulfillment of his consuming ambition. Yet he not only can but is forced to decide for himself what to do with his life, and even if, like Sartre, he puts his tongue out at it, that, too, is a decision.

Such extreme cases exhibit the absurdity that existentialists stress in the life situation as they see it. Tragedy is present, however, in even the most ordinary sorts of life. Indeed, the very undramatic and unromantic character of most people's lives only accentuates the absurdity of them. You secretly want to be a persuasive orator when in fact you have a stutter so bad that you cannot bear to utter a word. I want to be successful in business while in fact I can hardly make enough to keep out of bankruptcy. The freedom I have is real, but the way things are in life is such as to make it a torture rather than a blessing. I could wish to escape the freedom I have, yet I am not at all willing to give it up. I feel, on the contrary, that I must on no account want to do so.

On the one hand I am trapped like a rabbit in a snare; on the other hand I am so free I literally do not know what to do with my freedom. Once again death provides the paradigm case. I want to do many things in life, but death is always just around the corner. Death is always mocking me, but it mocks me most when I most truly am alive. Not only does death say to me, in effect, "You can't take it with you"; death is saying, "I won't let you finish the job." If you can make believe for a while that life is not absurd, the thought of death, which is as inevitable as its hour is unpredictable, should be enough to bring you face to face again with the absurdity of life. Not for nothing is death depicted as a grinning skeleton. It is the supreme symbol of the absurdity of life. It is even more ridiculous than the proverbial bull in the china shop. And yet while I live I can laugh at death. Such is the antinomy of freedom and determinism, of life and death.

(6) *Angst.* The human plight we have been considering leads to *Angst.* Generally, when we talk of anguish we are talking of anguish about a particular event, a sadness or tragedy about which we are agonizing. By *Angst,* however, the existentialists intend something far more poignant because far more indefinite. It is intransitive, having no object. As Kierkegaard suggests, one cannot be "so anxious about the most horrifying description of the most dreadful something" as one is about an I-don't-know-what.[4] It is a home-sickness,[5] whether we interpret it (as would Christians) as the nostalgia of the pilgrim for his true home with God or (as would nihilists) as the homesickness of an orphan who knows he has no home anywhere.

Heidegger also, acknowledging his debt to Kierkegaard at this point, stressed, in his nihilistic phase, the sense of nothingness-at-the-heart-of-every-thing. *Angst* remains submerged so long as we can cover it up by the routine of the business of daily living, which may include not only what we nowadays call "chores" but also what we call "projects" or even "concerns," many of which may seem very laudable indeed, such as conscientious care for doing a good job or even fidelity in being a good son or a good father. Fine and needful in life as such activities and attitudes may be, they do not touch one's inmost being. *Angst* cannot be forever submerged by even the noblest of the commitments and loyalties of life. Perhaps I have been successful in business and have also acquired a great and deserved respect both for my honesty toward my customers and my thoughtfulness for my employees. I retire from business at an early age, with much fanfare and many presentations. I look forward to a long and pleasant pursuit of my hobbies and greater time to devote to my wife and family. I am not smug about it at all. On the contrary, though life, as people all say, has blessed me and I feel I ought to be the happiest man on earth, I keep whispering to myself, even as I force out the last smile in response to the final flattering presentation or award, "So what?"

So what? The phrase haunts everyone at the most unexpected times in life. A student has tried desperately hard for years to work his way through high school and college. He has done everything from delivering newspapers to working in a copper mine. Now he is ascending the platform on

---

[4] S. Kierkegaard, "The Sickness Unto Death," in *Fear and Trembling and the Sickness Unto Death* (New York: Doubleday, Anchor Books, n.d.), p. 158. (First ed. in English, 1941.)
[5] S. Kierkegaard, *Papirer,* IIA 191, November 6, 1837, in *Søren Kierkegaard's Journals and Papers,* ed. H. V. Hong and E. H. Hong, vol. 1 (Bloomington, Ind.: Indiana University Press, 1967), p. 38.

commencement day, to the plaudits of all his friends. Splendid! They are all proud of him. He has graduated, all obstacles notwithstanding. He is getting a *magna* with Phi Beta Kappa. Everything an ambitious young American could wish for is now at his feet. Yet even as the diploma is put into his hand and before his thoughts turn to the social rejoicing in the hours ahead, perhaps he holds the door of his memory open long enough to see in one flash the absurdity of it all. He is by no means unhappy; yet the gnawing ache is unmistakably there: he cannot feel as happy as he thinks he ought to feel. Something is missing. Perhaps he is wearing the hood of a bachelor of laws, which he has long coveted; yet now he feels for at least one fleeting moment that, like the emperor in Hans Christian Andersen's old fable, he really "has nothing on." He is like a self-made dying multimillionaire: with a huge boxful of bonds at the bank he suddenly sees that he might as well be a pauper. The smell of success may be sweet, but it does not last long on a grave. In moments of grandeur or triumph we are all taunted by that inward voice echoing through our aching emptiness, "So what?" Life looks what Shakespeare calls it—"a tale told by an idiot." [6]

The mood of anguish is quite unlike a sense of apprehension or fear or dread. That is why "dread" is such an unfortunate translation of *Angst.* Fear overtakes us when we are filled with care (*Sorge*) for an *x* that we are afraid may be taken away from us. I fear inflation because it will lower my living standard. I fear the death of my friend because I know I shall miss his friendship. I fear an automobile accident because of the pain and suffering it may bring about. Anguish is not *about* anything because it is unrelated to such cares. It is the breaking in upon me of the import of the facts of existence, notably that nothing is as stable as I like to pretend and could not live without pretending. It is all as if I have become so absorbed in chess that I am literally sweating with anxiety lest I make a wrong move and diligently searching my brain for ways to achieve checkmate before my opponent, to the point where I am saying to myself that I would give everything I own to be able to think up the perfect move and then suddenly I am struck with the silliness of the whole thing. What could it really matter? "It's only a game!" we say; yet we know very well that life is anything other than that. We seem to be full of all sorts of cares and concerns that turn out, however, to be completely meaningless.

That mood is attended by an agonizing sense of freedom. I am immensely free, but free for what? I am like an athlete who cannot understand how people ever find time to do the things they do, since it takes him all his time to keep fit, and who is then suddenly confronted with the question "fit for what?"

Of course, in all the athlete's exertions, in all the student's intellectual strivings, and even in just the simple enjoyment of a pleasant evening at home with a well-cooked dinner, some records, and a few congenial friends,

[6] William Shakespeare, *Macbeth,* act 5, sc. 5, line 26 f.

there is plenty of meaning *of a sort*. But it is a meaning that quickly evaporates. After it is all over, I feel only like a drunk who, having thought himself strong enough to knock out everybody in the bar and witty enough to hold them all spellbound with his brilliance, has at last sobered up to find that the meaning he thought he clearly saw has simply evanesced.

Is there then no residue of meaning? No meaning that *remains*? No, nothing remains. Existence itself turns out, indeed, to be as nothing. The thought is so overwhelming, so unbearable, that I cannot abide it for long. I have to seek refuge, for example, in the company of others who, in effect, are reassuring me as I am reassuring them that there *is* some meaning in life after all. Inwardly I know I am not only lying to them but am encouraging them to lie to me. I like the company of my fellows because we have a sort of common agreement to pull the wool over each other's eyes. We are like incurable cancer patients who console one another by pretending not to notice anything amiss as we make grandiose plans for the future. Now and then, however,.I am suddenly drawn up straight: I *have* no future. That does not mean there will not be tea this afternoon or that I will not be able to watch my favorite television program this evening. It does mean that all the cheery-cheery talk in which we indulge is only whistling in the graveyard. The horrifying reflection is that if only we had the nerve to look straight at ourselves long enough, we should see that intrinsically we are all in exactly the same state as the incurable cancer patient.

Among the most pathetic of the many ruses we employ to avoid *Angst* is that of leaving "memorials" of ourselves for posterity. I know I cannot live forever; yet if I have the money I can arrange for a splendid porphyry tomb, with a fine gilt inscription recounting my deeds and my virtues. Or, more subtly, I can, if I am so gifted, write memoirs that I hope will be admired and read so that even if my grandchildren forget me others will remember. Yet even though I should be successful in making and keeping my name as immortal as Shakespeare's I know it really can make no difference to the fact of my nonexistence. Shakespeare would be no less dead if he had written an even better play than *Hamlet*.

Nor is there any remedy to be found in "choosing to do nothing," for no such choice is available. Even if I were to sit down doggedly and stare steadily at the ocean for the rest of my life, that, too, would be "doing something," and it would lead only to my eventual insanity, which also would have been a choice. I am free; yet I am bound to make choices! No wonder, if I then hear it said that there is a God who so created and arranged existence, that I feel inclined to spit in rage in his face. That is, in fact, precisely what the nihilist does feel, even as he denies that there is a God.

(7) *Despair–Faith*. The *Angst* we have been discussing puts us in the way of despair. Despair (*de-sperare*) is literally hopelessness. How, precisely, I react in my despair is chiefly a matter of temperament. As some people in the face of disaster weep profusely while others go ice-cold, and as some crumple

up like whipped dogs while others rage like angry bulls, so human reaction to *Angst* may vary. We have already seen that the commonest reaction to *Angst* is to try to avoid it, to try to push it below the surface once again in hope that we shall not have to look at it. Most people engage in that covering-up activity almost every moment of their lives and therefore their attitude toward religion is not well described as either negative or positive. They would not like to be labelled religious, yet they would also resent being called atheists.

That is one reason that the term "agnostic" has generally been popular since its invention by T. H. Huxley in the last century, for it carries with it the vague suggestion of suspended judgment, and suspension is exactly what we should all like to be able to achieve in the face of *Angst*. We should all like to suspend further reflection of that horrifying kind and so defer *Angst*-provoking questions *sine die*, as lawyers say—that is, indefinitely shelve them. We want to do with *Angst* what a debtor wants to do with a bill he cannot possibly hope ever to pay.

Though many people have a remarkable capacity for such ostrichlike antics, thoughtful people cannot get away with these all the time, and among them are many who face the consequences of their thoughtfulness. That is why there have always been "committed" atheists, people who definitely repudiate as "phony" all the typically religious stances, which they lump together with the customary crutches and drugs and blinkers that are used to avoid looking directly at the empty meaninglessness of existence. Atheism is by no means a modern phenomenon only. Mersenne, a contemporary and close friend of Descartes, estimated that in their day one Parisian out of six was an atheist.[7] Even allowing for some exaggeration, one may conclude that in that respect the seventeenth century was not very different from our own. So widespread in the eighteenth century was unbelief that one thoughtful observer felt that in fifty years there would not be a priest left in Rome.[8]

No age in which there have been thoughtful people has lacked atheists. Modern atheists who think their atheism makes them in any way original or pioneering can think so only by an ignorance of history.[9]

Simone de Beauvoir, in *Le Sang des autres,* has eloquently expressed a basic existentialist insight that she as a nihilist sees no less than do the religious existentialists. She points out that our reasons for going on living do not fall from the sky: we must create them ourselves. Yet, in her view, knowing that we are creating them ourselves we know we are only fooling ourselves.

---

[7] Marin Mersenne, as quoted with supporting documentation in Erich Frank, *Philosophical Understanding and Religious Truth* (New York: Oxford University Press, 1945), pp. 5 and 19 f.

[8] J. Winckelman in a letter from Rome dated February 26, 1768, as quoted in Frank, *Philosophical Understanding,* p. 5.

[9] "Atheism" is here used in a broad, untechnical sense. The term may be used in a narrower, more specifically seventeenth- and eighteenth-century sense, as a strict antonym of "Theism."

Still, they are the creations of our longing and of our love, and so, as the best props we have, we use them for all they are worth, and they are worth just as much as are our longings and our love.

Here is the nub of existential despair in the face of the absurdity of life. The despair is not a wringing-of-the-hands despair. It is not even the feeling of desperation we experience when hard-pushed and fighting, as we say, with our backs to the wall. It is far worse. We go on willfully allowing ourselves to love, to suffer, to build our whole lives on what we know to be our own inventions. Cheating ourselves in such a way is even more despicable than cheating in a card game. The despicability arises not from a fundamental, still less from a "supernatural" seriousness in the enterprise, but, rather, from the very lack of such seriousness. When life is seen as something flung at you, as a hand at cards is flung down on the table before you, cheating has the peculiar kind of shabbiness that we ascribe to a cardsharp. Sartre's man of good faith is the one who, while he lives his whole life with zest, loving and suffering and building, goes through it with his eyes open to the despair that pervades it at every point. He laughs, but he knows the laugh is hollow. He cries, but he knows the tears are in vain. He builds, but he knows he can be building on nothing but himself, circumscribed as he is by the absurdity of birth and death. Despair as ordinarily understood sounds a cowardly emotion. To despair existentially, however, takes more than mere "guts"; it takes courage *par excellence.*

So far the account is fundamentally the same, whether the existentialist is a nihilist or a religious man. At this point, however, the religious existentialists ask us to go a step further. There is, they insist, yet another step that may be taken, demanding more courage still. It is what Kierkegaard calls "the leap of faith." What Kierkegaard saw as the prime danger in the then fashionable rationalist system of Hegel was the absence of the category of faith. The reason Hegel's system could not accommodate that category was that it is a philosophy of detachment, a spectator philosophy. In contrast, Kierkegaard offered a philosophy of commitment. The act of faith is a leap, but it is not a leap from nowhere. It has a springboard—the one we have been describing. One does not simply awake from a miasmic slumber and decide to take a faith-jump. The conditions of faith are rigorous and severe; nor do they carry any guarantee of success. Despair may be the final outcome. Nevertheless, granted the conditions we have described, the leap of faith is possible.

Perhaps an analogy may be found in the practice of Alcoholics Anonymous, which will not undertake to attempt to do anything for an alcoholic until he is so completely at the end of his rope that he is willing to take the initiative, to call up and to say with all his heart, "I've had it. I'm at rock bottom. Help!" Only then is there hope, for only then can he, so to speak, get enough spring out of the springboard of his anguish to make a leap rather than a fall. The leap of faith likewise takes an extraordinarily profound antecedent probing of the depths of despair. "To believe," writes Kierkegaard, "is like flying, but one flies with the aid of a counteracting gravity. Considerable gravity is necessary for one to become so buoyant that he can fly... And so one may say that the buoyancy of faith is an infinite gravity, and its height is brought about by an infinite compression." [10]

Kierkegaard did not see faith as a descant on doubt. The reason is important: "Faith's conduct with the world is not a battle of thought with doubt, thought with thought." It is "a battle of character." To believe, in that sense, is not to know; it is to will unconditionally.[11] Whatever faith is, it is not what we make do with, *faute de mieux,* when we cannot have the knowledge that is commonly assumed to be preferable to belief. It is not ersatz knowledge. The Greeks assumed that *epistēmē* (knowledge) must always be higher and better than *pistis* (belief). For Kierkegaard the leap is not even, as it is sometimes romantically portrayed in sermons, a leap forward into the darkness. No, it is, rather, a leap backwards into a darkness that is made even worse by a confusing gleam of light: the confusing gleam of light is the fact that the human road signs point the opposite way.[12]

In such very Kierkegaardian images and concepts we begin to see how alien to the concept of knowledge is Kierkegaard's understanding of faith. Faith for him has nothing to do with either "I believe (that is, as far as my meager evidence goes, I am inclined to think) it will rain tomorrow" or even "I know that my Redeemer liveth." On this question more must be said later, when we consider faith in relation to doubt and *Angst.* For the present let us bear in mind that poetic exaggeration plays a large part in Kierkegaard's rhetoric. To try to communicate an idea to which his readers were unaccustomed or resistant he felt he had to carry his imagery to the furthest extremes to which he could possibly take it. He wants to make sure that there is not the faintest shadow of misunderstanding left in us: the essence of faith is an act of the will; it is the supreme act of courage. So, he says in effect, faith is as unlikely to have intellectual elements in it as a soldier facing a bayonet charge is unlikely to be considering his predicament from the standpoint of a physicist or geometrician or even military strategist. Whatever else the soldier is doing, it will not be anything like what any of them does. Stunned with horror as he fixes his own bayonet in reply, he may be praying or cursing or grimacing or howling in terror or roaring with rage; but whatever he is doing it will not be anything contemplative or scientific or intellectual.

Faith, so understood, plainly entails risk. Indeed, it entails a risk no sane man would ever take, a risk for which no actuary could ever conceivably be able to suggest an appropriate insurance premium. As a child I sometimes

---

[10] S. Kierkegaard, *Papirer,* VII'A177, n.d., 1846, in *Søren Kierkegaard's Journals and Papers,* ed. H. V. Hong and E. H. Hong, vol. 2 (Bloomington, Ind.: Indiana University Press, 1970), pp. 9 f.

[11] Ibid., X'A367, 368, pp. 13 f.

[12] Ibid., X'A489, n.d., 1852, p. 22.

fancied what I should do if I suddenly found myself in front of a railroad train. I decided I would leap as high as I could and grab hold of some part of the engine, rather than be run over. Well, we say, perhaps it might just work, but who would ever try it? Certainly I do not propose to stroll in front of an oncoming train to conduct the experiment, but if by some ill chance I did find myself in front of one, who knows—perhaps I just might try. The point is, of course, that no one would ever take the risks involved in faith unless he were truly at his wits' end to know what else to do. Passers-by might yell, "Look! He's crazy, throwing himself at the train! He's trying to kill himself." In fact, my action would be outstandingly antisuicidal. It would be a heroic effort to use the one way left to save my life. At any rate, if you ask what religion is about, the reply must be that it is more like that sort of plight and that sort of spontaneous response than anything in either the standard philosophical texts or the classic theological expositions of doctrine. It is about a man in a bad spot, at his wits' end, not knowing where to turn, who, against both human reason and common sense, hears a call and responds by taking that superabundantly risky leap that faith is. It has nothing to do with "the God of the philosophers and scholars." It has everything to do with "the God of Abraham and Isaac." Abraham, as described by the writers of the Epistle to the Hebrews, is, indeed, a classic biblical exemplar of faith as Kierkegaard understands it.[13]

The Common Ancestry of Existentialism and Process Thought

Existentialism and process philosophy, two of the best known currents in twentieth-century thought, appear at first sight to be entirely unrelated. Sartre and Whitehead are extremely unlike each other, not merely in the way they do their thinking but in what they think about. Teilhard and Kierkegaard have such different concepts of God that one wonders how they both can be, as they are, deeply Christian. Process philosophy is obviously allied to scientific thought. Whitehead was a mathematician and Teilhard a geologist and paleontologist. A common taunt at Teilhard is that he unsuccessfully tries to "marry" his good science with a mystical religion. No one would ever indict Kierkegaard for that. Existentialists are not expected to be scientists. They are often uninterested in and sometimes distrustful of scientific pursuits. Moreover, process thought tends to be optimistic about the future of man while the mood of existentialism is generally pessimistic.

The two currents nevertheless do have some common features that suggest a common root. Most striking among these is their strong focus on man. They have also both been much affected, consciously or unconsciously, by the same evolutionary influences that we found so prominent in late nineteenth-century thought. Nietzsche, for instance, though generally and

[13] Hebrews 11:8.

rightly accounted as much a precursor of modern existentialism in its antireligious aspect as is Kierkegaard on its religious side, is an ancestor of modern process thought, too. That part of his ancestral function has been obscured by widespread inattention to his interest in science. His view that man is unfinished and must be surpassed fits the evolutionary trend in modern scientific thought. We saw in the previous chapter that evolutionary ideas were deeply affecting thoughtful people towards the end of the nineteenth century, not least those with both scientific and religious interests. They intoxicated many great thinkers, among whom Henri Bergson is an interesting example. One of his most influential works, *L'Evolution créatrice,* which appeared in 1907, conspicuously exhibited the same trend, and was of much interest to those religious-minded people who were accustomed to scientific methods and aims. It provoked a spate of books on the place of God in creative evolution as envisaged by Bergson.[14] Bergson was also anti-intellectualist, however, in the sense that he gave intuition and instinct a role that had been generally denied them in traditional philosophical thought. Bergson, like Nietzsche, seems to have had a foot in both doors. They were both precursors of process philosophy, with its scientific orientation, but they both also, though in very different ways, used great intellectual power to decry the deification of intellect, so prefiguring that type of philosophizing that we call existentialist, which—strange and diverse as some of its fruits may be—has roots that lie in the humanistic tradition whose fountainhead is Socrates.

We may say, then, that process philosophy and existentialism are somewhat like cousins who, though they have diverse lineages, share a common ancestor. Both of them see man at the middle of the arena they are inspecting. Process thinkers see him set in the stream of Nature and, surpassing outmoded connotations of that notion, as having made an evolutionary leap and as being now en route to another. He is always, at any rate, en route. Process thinkers, even when they do not happen to be particularly religious in their outlook, are not usually very gloomy about the outcome of the process. If they are religious they are generally conspicuously hopeful about it. Existentialists, on the contrary, as we have seen, regard the human condition as a plight. Circumstances engulf the individual, who finds himself alienated, lonely, auguished, and in despair. Those existentialists who happen to be also religious in their outlook claim a means of escape from that despair, but the twentieth-century existentialist mood is not usually optimistic. Where it claims no special means of overcoming the tragic sense of life, it seeks only to find a way of coping with life's absurdity. Even where it admits of faith it is always about *Angst.* It is vividly expressed in the title of Françoise Sagan's novel *Bonjour Tristesse.*

[14] E.g., J. de Tonquédec, *Dieu dans l'évolution créatrice;* M.T.-L. Penido, *Dieu dans le bergsonisme;* E. Rideau, *Le Dieu de Bergson.*

The Emergence of the Existentialist Mood

Belief in progress was an almost unquestioned dogma in western Europe in the early years of the twentieth century. The quiet optimism of the mood it engendered was so general that it went almost unnoticed. Victorian England took it for granted. Germany, for long an arena of liberal and progressive thought, had participated in the prevailing mood, enjoying an intellectual climate that had permitted humane scholarship, alongside the sciences, to abound and prosper independently of the political ambitions and military aims of her martially minded leaders. Her historians, her philosophers, her scientists, and her critical theologians had all helped to put her in the forefront of international scholarship. Her intellectual energy and economic resources had enabled her to play a role in the world of learning comparable in some ways to the one the United States more recently became accustomed to accept.

The military defeat of Germany in 1918 was therefore naturally attended by a sense of despair that we can perhaps best understand by imagining what we should expect to happen to the cultural and intellectual climate of America in the event of her abject defeat in a future world war. Moreover, there seemed now nowhere to turn for the intellectual zest and cultural vivacity to which Europe had been so long so well accustomed. The toll of the Great War of 1914–1919 is unparalleled in human history. Among the nations of the world the victors were as crippled as the vanquished. France, out of a total force of fewer than 8,500,000 men had had a casualty list of over 6,000,000, including nearly 1,500,000 dead. The British, though their total casualties out of a similar force had been only about half as great, had had nearly a million killed. The Russians, out of 12,000,000, had suffered over 9,000,000 casualties, including 1,750,000 dead. Though the United States had entered the war very late, the Americans had sustained 333,000 casualties out of a force of about 4,500,000, of whom 126,000 were killed. Except perhaps for the United States, which at that time had not attained either economic or military or cultural leadership, the war had not only sapped the victor nations of their economic strength but had stricken their old intellectual optimism and deprived them of their former cultural zest to an extent that we do not easily grasp today. In such circumstances, intellectuals in Germany not only felt cheated of what they had taken for their birthright; as they looked around the world they began to question the very basis of the values that western civilization had taken so much for granted. They had been on the wrong track. Where, then, might they now turn?

Where they did turn depended in part, of course, on their individual interests and concerns, but what generally attracted them intellectually were strains of thought that deviated from rather than conformed to the old scholarly traditions and confident scientific pursuits of pre-1914 Germany and of the whole of the magnificent European civilization the war had so sorely decimated. In the relatively quiet intellectual revolution that took place, there was a tendency among some to look at obscure figures and forgotten byways, as if in hope of finding a straw to which to cling in the wilderness of a now culturally desiccated world.

In that twilight of the old gods, the rediscovery of Søren Aaby Kierkegaard, who by then had been dead for sixty-five years, proved highly provocative. Kierkegaard had been little read outside his native Scandinavia, and but for the propensity of nineteenth-century German scholars for researching obscure authors he might have been hardly known at all—at any rate not till 1879, when a German-Jewish admirer, Georg Moses Cohen Brandes, drew some attention to him in literary circles in Germany. In any case no widespread interest in him developed until, in the early twenties, he found a place among the comparatively little known writers to whom, for one reason or another, the disillusioned German intellectuals were turning in their moral plight and intellectual despair. They found him relevant to their own condition.

The effect of the rediscovery of Kierkegaard was immense. Not only did he much affect thought of such a Spanish Catholic mould as that of Miguel de Unamuno (1864–1936) as well as at least the early thought of Karl Barth, the greatest champion of twentieth-century Protestant theological neo-orthodoxy; his influence on existentialist philosophers such as Martin Heidegger and Karl Jaspers, who are much less specifically religious in outlook, is incalculable.

Franz Brentano (1838–1917) had prepared the way for the postwar revival of existentialist thought by a distinction he had made between two modes of "internal knowledge": (1) that which relates to data (objects) and (2) that which refers to their direction. The idea of direction was to reappear in Edmund Husserl (1859–1938), whose phenomenological method passed easily into existentialism. The work of Max Scheler (1874–1928), who interested himself in what he called "material values," that is, those that excite the "existential content" of the mind, was also very influential.

French existentialism, though indubitably born of the same postwar mood and in part even exhibiting the same influences as post-1918 German thought, manifested from the first a different spirit. That difference is due to the fact that existentialism of the French type has independent roots in a distinctively French philosophical tradition. Though Sartre talks as though his philosophical starting point were a repudiation of Descartes, the greatest luminary in the firmament of French philosophy, his method is not entirely alien from the Cartesian one. Moreover, existentialism, for all its emphasis on freedom, is haunted by a special kind of intellectual doubt, as it is preoccupied with a peculiar sort of moral anguish. Its focus is always, however, on existence. Descartes, though a rationalist *pur sang,* uses a method that begins with doubt and ends with existence: *cogito, ergo sum.* Sartre may have been more influenced by it than he knew or cared to say. He also revealed in his autobiography that he had a much more religious background and outlook in his early life than is generally associated with him. Perhaps, indeed, French Calvinism was to him the spectre that Irish Catholicism was to James Joyce.[15]

Blaise Pascal (1623–1662) and Maine de Biran (1766–1824) are exemplars of a distinctively French way of thinking that is the lineal ancestor of much in modern French existentialist philosophy. In the case of Pascal, one of the greatest geniuses in human history, the ancestry is strikingly plain. Moreover, though Kierkegaard lived two centuries later than Pascal and was also cultural poles apart from him, he knew Pascal's work and noticed the resemblance between it and his own. He quotes both the atheist Feuerbach and the passionately Christian Pascal as seeing no less than himself that suffering is of the essence of the Christian life.[16]

Among existentialists is often included Dostoevski, who could hardly be called a profoundly Christian thinker like Pascal or Kierkegaard, though he happened to be a perfervid Russian nationalist and therefore Orthodox. He hated the Roman Church with the peculiar bitterness that only an Eastern Orthodox could have for it. His passage on the Grand Inquisitor in his novel *The Brothers Karamazov* is well known and makes a fairly good prelude to a study of modern existentialism.[17] Better still for that purpose, however, is his *Notes from Underground,* first published in 1864.[18] Nietzsche, when he read them twenty-three years later, was deeply impressed by them. Nietzsche, an extraordinarily incisive stylist, inveighs mightily in typically existentialist style against hypocrisy and the cruelty of men. Suffering is a characteristic theme in his work. Yet what is most striking in Nietzsche, and is antithetical to the sombre mood of twentieth-century nihilistic existentialism, is his praise of that Dionysian exultation that laughs joyously at everything in a life-affirming shout. It is well expressed in the work of the German poet Rilke.

The existentialist approach to philosophical problems, which the postwar loss of the old intellectual optimism and moral confidence had encouraged, largely displaced the preoccupation with evolutionary ideas that we have seen in so much of the thought of an earlier generation. Though there were still other and more traditionalist voices to be heard in continental Europe in the thirties, the fashion had turned towards a new mode of thought that was to influence men as definitely Catholic as Gabriel Marcel and Louis Lavelle as well as those as specifically antireligious as Jean-Paul Sartre.

[15] Sartre's great-grandfather was a Calvinist pastor and Sartre's mother sent him to a Catholic priest for religious instruction. Albert Schweitzer was his cousin.
[16] E.g., S. Kierkegaard, *Stages on Life's Way,* trans. W. Lowrie (Princeton, N.J.: Princeton University Press, 1940), p. 83.
[17] The passage is reprinted in F. Dostoevski, *The Grand Inquisitor on the Nature of Man,* trans. C. Garnett (Indianapolis: Bobbs-Merrill Co., 1948). *The Brothers Karamazov,* from which it is taken, was first published in 1880.
[18] *Notes from the Underground* (New York: T. Y. Crowell Co., 1969).

Sartre, an Alsatian, was brought up bilingually, and as a young philosophy teacher he made a name for himself as an exponent of German existentialism. In him is to be found not only the most explicit presentation of the mood of twentieth-century nihilistic existentialism; his view that man, through freedom of choice, is his own sole self-creator, accords also with some of the evolutionary thought that existentialism had replaced.

Involvement, Commitment, and Concern

Existentialism, then, is not a theory or school of thought. It cannot be treated as one might treat Hegelianism or Spinozism, or as one might recount a chapter or episode in the history of philosophy, such as British empiricism or Italian neoidealism. It has no strict tenets. It is, rather, a mood or climate. As such it can be defined only in terms of broad tendencies, by saying, for instance, that it is a philosophy of involvement, commitment, and concern.

Characteristic of those who are drawn to existentialism today is an impatience with what they take to be the academic remoteness of traditional philosophy. Their impatience springs from their feeling that traditional philosophy is remote and detached from man's urgent basic concerns. They share the disparagement the eighteenth-century George Berkeley directed at those philosophers who "raise a dust and then complain they cannot see." The existentialists' objection, however, would go further: much academic philosophy is like a lecture on ichthyology to a man who is choking to death on a fishbone.

We have here a clue to the already noted fact that existentialists are generally either distinctly religious or distinctly antireligious, as people commonly judge these attitudes, and are never simply uninterested in religious questions. The reason is that existentialism is nothing if not an insistence on my beginning at the point where I find myself and at which I am involved. It is also nothing if not an ethical stance. Existentialists may reach very diverse conclusions on ethical questions, but they always take off from such questions. Their questions also lie behind all lively religious devotion and commitment. Whether they have faith or not, their philosophical method disposes them to understand what it entails.

Those writers who (not without justification) call Socrates the first great existentialist do so for the same reason that makes others call him a religious philosopher. Socrates was not at all religious in the popular sense in which we call a person religious who loves going to church or synagogue as others love going to theatres or football games. By all accounts Socrates was presumably no great temple-goer. Yet if after reading a few chapters of metaphysical speculation or linguistic analysis, we turn to the *Apology* or the *Crito* we cannot fail to be struck by the focus on the kinds of questions we associate with religious commitments and ethical concerns. Of course, we can detect logical and linguistic questions in the Platonic dialogues. We can also see, in the questions Socrates asks, metaphysical conundrums. Plato did. We may see, too, the transition from an oral to a literary culture. But if the historic Socrates was even slightly like the character depicted in Plato's earlier dialogues, he was a man who was fascinated by questions fundamentally similar to the questions modern existentialists ask: who am I? what should I do with my life? how should I look upon death? Whether we like or dislike the attitude Socrates brings toward his unjust sentence, there can be no doubt that it expresses a stance that is deeply, however unconventionally, religious, and a very definitely ethical commitment. That is why Kierkegaard, who wrote his university dissertation on Socrates, saw in him, an ancient pagan philosopher, a better model for Christian living than was generally furnished by a too cozily established Danish Church. Hegel, who talked endlessly of *Geist* and other notions that sounded "spiritual" enough to be just the sort of thing religious people seemed to like talking about, and whose system many took as a highly suitable ally for Christian thought, was in Kierkegaard's eyes the most irreligious of men.

What made Hegel so odious and Socrates so laudable to Kierkegaard? The former seemed to him a mere spectator while the latter was a participator. Socrates, a pagan Greek, exemplified in his own way the same concerns and commitments for which Abraham, when he "went out not knowing whither he went," was to be commended. The man who, by whatever name he is called, detaches himself from life and "studies" it as a bacteriologist studies a bacillus under a microscope, is no philosopher. He is no more a philosopher than a man who, having gone to watch football games till he knows more about them than any other man alive, is a quarterback.

If such an understanding of "the right way to do" philosophy is religious, then existentialists are all religious. Most people would laugh at the notion of calling Sartre religious, yet it is easy to see that Kierkegaard might well prefer his thought to what he would deem the hypocritical (that is, literally, play-acting) proclivities of the spectator type of philosopher. Nihilistic existentialists like Sartre are religious, however, in the questions they ask rather than in the answers they give. Or, we might say, what is religious about them is their concern rather than their commitment. Both concern and commitment are always found in typical religious existentialists, such as Martin Buber, an observant Jew deeply affected by Hassidic mysticism, and Gabriel Marcel, a practicing French Catholic.

Is Faith a Kind of Knowledge?

Having inspected the character of the ideas that prevail in an existentialist climate and their relation to other modern trends of thought as they affect all contemporary conceptions of faith, we are now better able to consider the nature of faith itself.

Our first task in that undertaking is to try to ascertain how faith is to be understood in relation to knowledge. We have already noticed that Kierkegaard, seeing faith wholly in terms of decision, treats it simply as an act of the will, as if it had no cognitive content at all. He does this, however, because of his intense concern to get over to us, his readers, that aspect of faith that we, especially we who are accustomed to intellectualize everything, are apt to ignore or forget. He succeeds. Nevertheless, the problem of the relation of faith to knowledge remains important. Even if we could deny that there were any cognitive element at all, a problem would remain, if only because such a denial would render the concept of faith incomprehensible.

To say that Abraham "went out not knowing whither he went" is a robust biblical hyperbole of the sort that Kierkegaard echoes in his own writings. No doubt Abraham knew nothing in detail. He had no specific, fully developed plan to settle in a prearranged locale. Perhaps, when he set forth to "the promised land," he did not even know what it would look like or exactly where it was. Nevertheless, he must have known something about it.

Indeed, if we look at the text of the story in Genesis we shall see that he knew more, perhaps much more, than the passage in Hebrews suggests.[19] His father, Terah, when he had left Ur of the Chaldeans, had intended to go to the land of Canaan but had stopped at Haran and settled there.[20] Abraham would probably have learned something about Canaan from his father, and even if he had not, the name itself, which comes from a root that means "low," would tell him that it was (or at least gave the impression of being) lowland rather than mountain country. To know even that much is to know something. Then perhaps Abraham did not know the way? That he had no idea whether to turn north or south, east or west, would hardly be credible. It would be like my saying I had determined to go somewhere yet not only had no idea where but would have to flip a coin several times to decide which among four ways to choose. No doubt Abraham was using a sort of radar of his own, or was, as we say, "following his nose."

The all-important element in his act of faith was the courage to act on meager information. We can understand the importance of this aspect of faith only by asking what difference it would have made if Abraham had *lacked* faith. Abraham, lacking faith, would have done nothing; that is, he would have remained wherever he was, resigned to circumstance, and we may reasonably assume that in such a case we should never have heard much more of him, for there would have been nothing more worth hearing. Practically, the difference would have been the difference between the tragic destruction and the glorious survival of the people of Israel. From the standpoint of both Jews and Christians it is the difference between the fulfillment and the nonfulfillment of God's plan. Still, all that does not affect what has just been noted about the presence of a cognitive element, however meager, in Abraham's faith.

[19] Genesis 12 and 13.
[20] Genesis 11:31.

Though we may take the view that the importance of the cognitive element is minimal in comparison with the conative one that the religious existentialists stress so much, we cannot dismiss the cognitive element as irrelevant for an understanding of the nature of faith; on the contrary, it is an indispensable part of its content. What we can and must do is to consider what sort of knowledge it is that enters into an act of faith.

What Kind of Cognition Could There Be in Faith?

The language that Christians and others use in making their great affirmations is the language of belief. Creeds (from *credere,* to believe) are statements of belief. Indeed, in some accounts, faith has sometimes been mistakenly reduced to nothing but intellectual assent to such religious proposals. Such reductionism is unfortunate on two scores. First, the cognitive element is at most only one constituent of faith and by no means the most important one. Second, belief is commonly contrasted with and held to be inferior to knowledge. The faith of deeply religious people is so strong that in some cases they die for it. Why, then, do not they regularly say "I know" rather than merely "I believe"? If we feel justified in saying we know the boiling point of water is 100° C., why cannot Christians say they *know* there is a God and that he is the Father Almighty and so forth, instead of saying, as in the traditional creeds, that they *believe* in God, the Father Almighty? Surely a Christian, ready to die for his faith, must intend to express much more than the kind of cognition intended in casual statements such as "I believe there is life on Mars" or even "I believe in the Dodgers." Does he boggle at going so far as to say "I know" because he lacks evidence, that is, because the cognitive element in his faith, though strong, is not quite strong enough? Is it not strong enough, for example, to rank with what he is willing to say about the boiling point of water?

"Believing in" and "Believing that"

We must notice a distinction that H. H. Price discussed in his Gifford Lectures.[21] To believe that *p* is true is not the same as believing in *p*.

I may say I believe in a student even though his grades are poor. By that I would claim to see beyond his performance to his promise. He only made a C on the midterm quiz, yet such is my impression of his ability and industry that I feel I can expect him to make a B or even an A on the final examination. I am saying I have hopes for him beyond his present attainment.

[21] H. H. Price, "Belief 'In' and Belief 'That,' " in *Religious Studies* 1 (1965). Reprinted in *Belief* (New York: Humanities Press, 1969), pp. 426–454.

Very different are "believing that" statements. If I told you I had not looked up a student's official transcript but that I believed that his grade was C, I would be expressing neither hope for him nor fear; I would be stating only that I took C to be the fact about his grade. My use of the verb "believe" would, furthermore, indicate that I was not quite sure, for I could have said something such as, "Oh yes, I *know* it's a C: I have just looked it up in the Registrar's office."

The great ancient creeds of the Church proclaim belief *in*: "I believe in God . . . And in Jesus Christ . . . I believe in the Holy Ghost," etc. Nevertheless, creeds often also use "believing that" language. A Greek Orthodox confessional statement, for instance, declares: "We believe a man to be not simply justified through faith alone . . ." [22] A Roman Catholic one requires signatories to say, "I firmly hold that there is a purgatory . . ." [23] A Baptist one begins with the declaration "We believe [that] [24] the Holy Bible was written by men divinely inspired . . ." [25] So it is plain that both "believing in" and "believing that" statements occur in religious discourse. The religious person typically believes *in* God, but he goes on to say, for instance, that he believes *that* the Bible is inspired by God, *that* there is a purgatorial state, *that* bishops are required in the Church, and so forth. He rarely, if ever, says he knows such things, though that is what we might reasonably expect. We might expect it for the same reason that, when I am thoroughly convinced of the gentleness of my best friend's nature and he is convicted of a crime entailing vicious cruelty, you expect me to say roundly, "There must be a mistake. I *know* that John couldn't have done that." Why is the Church, which has been long much blamed for intolerant dogmatism, apparently so reticent in making cognitive claims?

Noteworthy and helpful though the distinction between "believing in" and "believing that" may be, we are still left with the same questions as before we drew it. Why do "the faithful" signify only their belief in what the Bible or the Church teaches instead of affirming their knowledge that these teachings are true? The point, we shall see, is of much importance in understanding the nature of faith, so we may profitably examine more closely the relation between knowing and believing.

Knowing and Believing

Some modern philosophers, including Cook Wilson, have made much of a radical difference they claim to see between knowing and believing. H. A. Prichard, has insisted that knowing is "absolutely different" from believing; that is, they "differ in kind as do desiring and feeling." So "no

[22] Confession of Dositheus, 1672, Decree XIII.
[23] Creed of the Council of Trent, promulgated by Pius IV in 1564 and still exigible.
[24] The word "that" was added twenty years later.
[25] New Hampshire Confession, 1833.

improvement in a belief and no increase in the feeling of conviction which it implies will convert it into knowledge. Nor is their difference that of being two species of a common genus." 26 When we know something we are certain of it; when we only believe it we are uncertain. We may *feel* certain, however, only because we have been thinking without question, "not bothering sufficiently to consider alternatives. People felt certain the earth is flat and they were wrong. If they were indeed only "thinking without question," they could not have *known*, even if they had happened to be right.

One must object: since we can never feel certain that we have sufficiently examined all possible alternatives, can we ever say we really know anything at all, except in respect of analytical propositions such as that the sum of the angles of a triangle must always equal two right angles? In that case we should be left with various degrees of belief, some very shaky and some extremely strong. Suppose, then, that we took three propositions: (1) "John Black's nose is still on his face"; (2) "All dogs can swim"; and (3) "Jesus is Lord." John Black, a Christian, might then say that he had diligently examined all of them to the best of his ability and now felt able to say he had a stronger belief in the truth of (3) than in that of (2) or even of (1).

An objector might well contend, of course, that Black had not examined the alternatives to (3) as well as he had examined the alternatives to (1) and (2). Black might insist that he had done so. The objector might then still properly say, "But in any case your belief that Jesus is Lord is only more forceful than your belief that all dogs can swim; it is still no more than belief, and I happen to have had a dog who drowned, apparently because he could not swim."

Norman Malcolm has argued for a strong and weak sense of "know"; in the strong sense, when I claim to know, I am so certain that "I cannot envisage a possibility that what I say to be true should turn out not to be true." So "it is unintelligible to me (although perhaps not to others) to suppose that anything could prove that it is not so and, therefore, that I do not know it." 27 (That *sounds* like just what the religious person wishes to claim.) Malcolm contends that the fact that in my own case I could not in that strong sense claim to know and at the same time admit that I might turn out to be wrong is a logical, not a psychological, fact. To say (in the strong sense) "I know" *means* to exclude the possibility of error. *You* could see, however, that I was using "know" in the strong sense and yet think that what I claimed to know to be the case might turn out not to be the case.

26 H. A. Prichard, *Knowledge and Perception* (Oxford: Clarendon Press, 1950), p. 87.
27 N. Malcolm, *Knowledge and Certainty* (Englewood Cliffs, N.J.: Prentice-Hall, 1963), as quoted in "Knowing and Believing," in *Knowledge and Belief,* ed. A. P. Griffiths (New York: Oxford University Press, 1967), p. 81.

Alan White, referring to Malcolm's distinction, makes the following observation: "The difference between the use of 'I know' to make a claim and the use of 'He knows' to allow it perhaps provides a clue to why people should have wished to say that knowledge is the limit or highest degree of belief, even while they realized that the criterion of truth is relevant to the former and not to the latter. 'He believes' and 'He knows' are vastly different, but there is much similarity between 'I believe' and 'I know,' between announcing a belief and making a claim to knowledge. As the validity or invalidity of the claim is irrelevant to the reasonableness of making it, so the truth or falsity of the belief is irrelevant to the reasonableness of holding it. The same criteria, namely, good evidence and confidence, operate in judging the reasonableness of each." [28]

When I claim to know that *p* is true I am simply asserting a maximum degree of certainty for my belief that *p* is true. Whether my evidence is adequate or inadequate, good or bad, is beside the point. I think it good and adequate; hence I say "I know" rather than "I believe." You may or may not be persuaded that my claim is grounded on adequate evidence. You are standing outside as a spectator. From one standpoint you can take better stock of the evidence because you are not involved in the knowledge-claim. If a mother says, "I know Johnny is the best-behaved boy in his class," we are likely to feel she has the right to claim only belief, for we suspect her of maternal prejudice in favor of her son. Yet she may have gone into the whole question very carefully and justified her belief from sound evidence, to the point where she "feels entitled," as we say, to call her belief knowledge.

Again, suppose you happen to be so unaccustomed to behavior such as mine that you wonder about my sanity. A friend mentions your suspicions to me. I roar with laughter, saying, "Of course, I am sane. I *know* I am!" You might then say afterwards to someone else, "Why, of course, the poor guy *thinks* he knows; most crazy people do." Who shall judge? Some narrow-minded people would think me crazy if I departed from convention to the extent of, say, wearing funny clothes or taking classical records to the beach to play all by myself in the moonlight. Others would not worry even if I claimed to be a descendant of Julius Caesar. They would say, "Oh, he has a bee in his bonnet about that, but otherwise he's a great guy, as sane a man as you're ever likely to meet." The question of my sanity cannot, however, depend on my own claim, for not only might I be a raving lunatic and protest my sanity; I might have misgivings about it though my mental health were really better than that of many people who never have any doubts about theirs.

When we inspect any case of claims to know and claims to believe, other than the case of analytical propositions, we find that while we can make

[28] Alan R. White, "On Claiming to Know," *Philosophical Review* 66 (1957), as quoted in Griffiths, *Knowledge and Belief*, p. 105. Used by permission of the author.

a formal distinction between knowledge and belief, and that it is practically useful to make it, there is no *radical* distinction that can be drawn. That is not to attempt to affirm a total skepticism about the possibility of knowing anything. Even if such total skepticism were possible, nothing we have found would warrant it. What we have found only undermines the claim that there can ever be knowledge in the sense of an infallible grasp of truth or acquaintance with reality. We can never claim the certainty implied in saying "I know" about anything, so long as doubt is formally possible.

To say, "I know I am in pain" is not an exception, because "I know" adds nothing to "I am in pain": if I did not know I was in pain I could not be in pain, and if I were in pain I could not conceivably fail to know it. You could only believe or disbelieve I was in pain. If you had known me for twenty years and had accounted me extraordinarily stoical in bearing pain you would presumably find no reason now to doubt, when you found me writhing on the floor, that I was indeed in pain, but you would still have to admit I might be acting. If you were an experienced surgeon you could apply various tests, but even then you would have to recognize the possibility that I had done both my dramatic and my medical homework so well that I could fool even you.

The possibility of doubt in such cases might become so minimal that you would very properly say to a persistent objector, "Oh, come off it—we all know perfectly well the man is in pain." And, of course, you would be right. What would emerge, however, is that "knowing" has the status that has just been suggested. It is a prestige word; that is, it means "believing" so strongly as to leave no room for any practical doubt. No one can guarantee anything unconditionally. Neither belief nor knowledge is self authenticating like a formal syllogism or a geometrical theorem.

John Austin has argued similarly in his own way, pointing out that my saying "I know" registers the highest possible cognitive claim in a form that authorizes you to rely on my statement, so that it functions similarly to the way in which "I promise" functions.[29]

Your trust in my promise will depend on your estimate of my reliability. If I have often let you down you will rightly account my promise "not worth a tinker's damn." If you have found me frequently inaccurate in my information or cocksure in my judgments, my claim to know will be correspondingly diminished in value. There will be, as we say, too great a credibility gap for you to accept what I affirm.

There is always, however, some credibility gap, as there is always some reason to doubt my promise. Even though you have every reason to depend on me to go through fire and water to keep it, I cannot guarantee to keep even a promise to meet you as usual for lunch. Not only may there be a traffic jam; I may die on the way. Of course, in such a case you would

[29] John Austin, "Other Minds," *Proceedings of the Aristotelian Society,* supp. to vol. 20 (1946), pp. 170–175.

not hold me to blame. So in the other case you would not blame me for claiming to know, for you would see at once that for all my care and caution I had been naturally mistaken for lack of access to evidence that had later become available.

When I say, "I am certain that *p* is true," I mean, "I know it is certain that *p* is true." In saying "I know" I am also saying that you or any other reasonable person would also know if provided with the evidence available to me. Neither belief nor that special kind of belief we call knowledge is merely subjective. It has an objective aspect. For me to say "I know," not just impetuously or arbitrarily but with judicial caution means not only that I feel sure. As Professor Ayer says, I must also have "the right to be sure." [30]

When we come to consider, however, what constitutes that right, serious difficulties emerge. John Bois, when elected a fellow of St. John's College, Oxford, in 1580, happened to be suffering from smallpox, so friends helped him to get there by carrying him in a blanket.[31] To us it may seem almost inconceivable that any educated person would take a man suffering from smallpox to college, but in terms of the medical knowledge available in 1580 the situation was probably very different. Bois's learned friends, had anyone questioned the wisdom of their action, could possibly have said with judicial caution: "We have considered the suggestion that such an act might be in some way harmful. We have consulted apothecaries of high repute on certain moot points relative to the suggestion, and we are pleased to report that we can now say we know (as we had all along believed) that taking Mr. Bois to college in his present condition is perfectly safe, in the sense that it is not likely to be attended by any serious medical danger to him or to anyone else." In 1580 they might have seemed justified in saying "I know," though no civilized person today would be entitled to say it.

If the distinction between knowledge and a claim to knowledge be invoked for radically separating knowledge from belief, then we end with a useless truism. A claim to know that *p* is true is not knowledge unless *p* is in fact true, but since we can never know for certain whether *p* is true, "knowledge" becomes a name for an ideal situation, one that could not exist in any conceivable circumstances. To say, then, that knowledge is qualitatively different from belief is a truism, like saying that eternity is qualitatively different from time or that duty is qualitatively different from what anybody, however dutiful, ever actually does.

When I say, "I believe it will rain," you see at once that there is doubt, perhaps considerable doubt, in my mind. When I say "I know," I proclaim that doubt is still possible for you, though I am proclaiming to you that I, for my part, have excluded it.

[30] A. J. Ayer, *The Problem of Knowledge* (London: Macmillan & Co., 1956), p. 34.
[31] He was later one of the translators appointed to make the King James Version of the Bible.

The Role of Doubt in Faith

The reason the cognitive element in faith is expressed, as a rule, in terms of belief rather than of knowledge may now be considered. In view of what we have already seen, the rule seems odd. The exceptions serve, indeed, only to draw attention to its oddity.

When I claim to know, I claim to have no doubt. My claim may be judicious or rash. In either case it is only a claim. Doubt is still open to you, who have not made the claim. Religious propositions may sometimes be expressed in terms of knowledge, as when Job cries, "I know that my Redeemer liveth." [32] If you were to say to a deeply convinced Christian, "You don't really believe you are going to enter a fuller life when you die, do you?" your question might goad him into replying, "I don't just believe it; I *know* it." Yet when he is not pushed in such a way he will prefer to say, and his Church will require him only to say, "I believe."

The use of "believe" is closely connected with the profoundly openminded outlook that is characteristic of genuine religion. The deeply religious person claims only to believe, not because he is less sure of what he affirms than he is about some other matters, but because he finds himself forced to doubt *all* claims to knowledge, including his own. His genuinely openminded agnosticism is in sharp contrast to the often disguised (and therefore all the more dangerous) dogmatism of the superficial who are too loudly for or against religion. It has led him to the position that Kierkegaard expressed in his epigrammatic way: "Every truth is . . . truth only to a certain degree; when it goes beyond, the counterpoint appears, and it becomes untruth." [33] On the cognitive side of matters of faith, doubt plays a role that is the counterpart of the role that on the conative side is played by *Angst*. It functions, indeed, as a cognitive element in *Angst*.

We can better understand the nature of credal formulas if we bear in mind that no deeply religious person ever sat down and made up a list of propositions he proposed to believe or to cause others to believe. To the outsider, creeds look like arrogantly dogmatic utterances, but people within the religious community recognize them to be very different. They are reverently agnostic, rather than dogmatic, documents. They express protest against alternative standpoints. It seems natural to believe *p*; nevertheless, we cannot believe *p*; so we are compelled to believe *q*. Though *q* may not be the best possible way of stating the truth we acclaim, we judge it to be better than *p*. The agnostic element in religion is far too great to allow deeply religious people to make strong knowledge claims even about what they strongly believe.

It is that profound agnosticism that enables deeply religious people to see how intolerant irreligion is, whether it sits in the scorner's seat or masquerades as piety. Baron von Hügel reminds us that a seventh-century

[32] Job 19:25.
[33] This remark is characteristic of Kierkegaard's insight.

Christian council anathemized anyone who should deny the incomprehensibility of God.[34] Such an anathema vigorously expresses the profundity of Christian doubt. Such is the epistemological agnosticism of the religious consciousness that even in enunciating doctrines such as, say, the Trinity, one is not so much saying, "You must believe this doctrine" as "You must not be content either with a doctrine that says there are many gods or with a doctrine that says God has only one aspect; instead, you are called upon to believe, rather, this one."

With such a built-in attitude, the believer is also reluctant to say "I know" for a reason similar to that which impelled the early Quakers to decline to take oaths and to insist that they could not improve upon their plain word. The Quaker is no less aware than are other persons, of course, that people tell lies. In calling attention, indeed, to the truism that only liars will commit perjury, he is expressing the opinion that few liars will lie less when required to take an oath to tell "the truth . . . So help me God," than they will tell without such solemnities. The Quaker's insistence that he cannot say more than "yea" or "nay" is a special case of the characteristically agnostic openmindedness that impels "men of faith" everywhere to claim belief rather than knowledge. The Quaker, by declining to take an oath in customary legal form, is by no means diminishing the force of his simple affirmation. On the contrary, he is enhancing it. Quakers have long been noted for the dependability of their word. So "men of faith" everywhere, far from diminishing that "cash value" of "believe," augment it by normally declining to say any more about anything. In the context of their general epistemological agnosticism it is as much as they need to say, and it preserves, moreover, an echo of the doubt with which every genuine believer must wrestle even when he is on the verge of uttering the triumphant "I believe." To say "I know" would be as much a diminishment of the force behind his "I believe" as a Quaker's oath would be of the vigor behind the affirmation he prefers.

Kierkegaard notes that sometimes a policeman, having made a report on oath, is required to "reaffirm" his oath, and he observes that, of course, such a double oath really dissolves the concept of oath-taking. He goes on to write to the effect that what often passes for religious belief is only what an unconvinced preacher does when he brings out one witness after another, supporting the belief attributed to X by the belief attributed to Y, and thereby merely calling attention to his pathetic attempt to disguise his inability to affirm his own belief. And so while "the sweat streams down the preacher's face," he believes only in the sense that he believes "that there have lived people who have believed." [35] Perhaps, indeed, one can

---

[34] F. von Hügel, *The Reality of God* and *Religion and Agnosticism* (London: Dent, 1931), p. 182.

[35] S. Kierkegaard, *Papirer,* XI'A 192. Written shortly before his death.

best grasp the nature of genuine religious belief by looking at such phony substitutes for it.

Tennyson's observation that

> There lives more faith in honest doubt
> Believe me, than in half the creeds[36]

is really an understatement. There lives no faith in any of the creeds except to the extent that they have encompassed that will to doubt that Bertrand Russell claimed he wished to preach in preference to William James's "will to believe." [37] Every genuine affirmation of religious belief contains a hidden qualifier: "*Nevertheless,* I believe . . ." More dramatically, we might say that the cognitive element in authentic religious faith is always a descant on doubt.

It is convenient to notice here a point of which much is often made by those unaccustomed to understanding the inner workings of religious practice. Why allow, let alone encourage, small children, for instance, who have had little opportunity to doubt the religious affirmations with which they are confronted in church or synagogue, to recite the credal affirmations they hear? If what has been said of the role of doubt in the cognitive aspect of faith be true, how can they judge? And if they cannot judge, it seems foolish if not wicked to let them recite such affirmations, which from their lips seem like so much parrot-talk. Of course such formal affirmations by children may be no more than that, as indeed are many adult affirmations, but the fears people commonly express on this subject usually spring from a legalistic understanding of the nature of a creed. There are, indeed, certain occasions when an affirmation of religious belief does have a sort of legalistic solemnity. When, for example, an ordinand for the priesthood signs a credal formula, he attests that in the doubt–faith antinomy, belief has outstripped doubt in such a way as to make possible that solemn attestation that his future role as a priest will require. The liturgical singing or recitation of a creed has a different function: the worshipper joins with the Church in hope that as the doubt–faith antinomy develops he will be among those in whom faith is victorious.

Doubt, as the dark side of the cognitive aspect of faith, is an essential ingredient for faith. The Latin form of the verb *dubito* has two roots, *duo* and *bito*: to be going two ways; that is, to stand at the crossroads, to be of two minds. The crossroads are not crossroads that are passed and forgotten. A lively mind stands in *Angst* at the crossroads daily, and daily makes a choice, making it, as Kierkegaard would say, "in fear and trembling." Theologians, by calling faith a gift, draw attention to its unexpectedness. Faith, while bypassing him who is trying too hard to believe and who therefore

---

[36] Alfred Tennyson, *In Memoriam,* part 96, stanza 3.
[37] Bertrand Russell, *Sceptical Essays* (New York: W. W. Norton & Co., 1928), p. 154.

ends up with a sham, a pretend-belief, overtakes and overwhelms the doubter as he wrestles in his anguish at the crossroads.

Conditions of Faith

In an earlier section of this chapter we considered various characteristic themes of existentialism, and we have paid some special attention to the role of doubt and *Angst*. The primary condition of faith, however, is to be found in neither of these but in the first of the categories we considered—existence. The results we may be willing to see in the man of faith (for example, that through it he seems to enter into a new dimension of life) do not really "clue us in" to the nature of faith. Indeed, such results may give the misleading impression that faith comes about by some sort of divine wand-waving. So to interpret faith is to misunderstand it as much as one would misunderstand the nature of scientific enterprise if one took it to be nothing but a series of leaps from one successful experiment to another. We must distinguish faith from an empty assurance about faith, which is really nothing more than a comforting pat. To understand faith one must understand that antecedent to it is always an existential situation with which the man of faith grapples in doubt and anguish till he is at the brink of despair.

The cognitive element in faith, with its doubt–belief antinomy, provides the springboard. I see what the existential situation is; I wrestle with it in anguish; and I make the leap. That is to say, I choose. But if there is any truth at all in what religious people persistently say about the act of faith, the man of faith finds, in making that leap, that something is given him that was not there before. Piety states the case picturesquely: a hand not my own is stretched out to me to guide my feet in the darkness, and I *re-cognize* the hand as not my own but that of One who compels my trust and whom I *know* I ought to trust. In the robust imagery of the Bible, the sheep know their own shepherd's voice and follow him, but will not follow a stranger, "for they know not his voice." [38] We might also say: in the very moment in which I am stricken speechless, a surge of words breaks in upon me, and I *re-cognize* them to be not my words but the words of One whose words I *know* I ought to make mine. I find myself entering a stream of life that is healthier than my own. I grasp at it as a lost child grasps the hand of his mother as she retrieves him out of the crowd.

Moreover, in the life of faith, these occurrences (which the man of faith might prefer to call transactions) take place not once but over and over again. I am overtaken and driven on by One who makes me aware of how much I ail by sweeping me forward, so to speak, with a health-giving power that I *know*, only too painfully, I lack. Nevertheless, although the man of faith finds all this happening over and over again (the life of faith consists in its happening over and over again), each time it happens is a

[38] John 10:4 f.

break with the past, a "dying to sin," a sudden and a totally new beginning. So the man of faith is not only once turned round ("to be converted" means literally "to be turned round" or "to be turned inside out"); he is turned round over and over again; yet each new turning is a novel turning. As I leap from x to y I know both the wretchedness of being x and the health-giving power that is bestowed on me in y; but I have so far no ability to see the wretchedness of y in the light of the still greater health-giving power of z, which so far has not yet come to me. In other words, the life of faith is a life of growth in faith, but the growth takes place with novelty ensuing upon novelty in such rapid succession that to use the same term "growth" that is used for the slow evolutionary physical and biological processes seems somewhat comical, like calling compulsion at gunpoint "persuasion" or the movement of light at 186,000 miles a second a "journey."

Yet to say that I am overtaken by the health-giving tide is misleading too, because it suggests that though faith does not come as a packaged gift, yet once I have wrestled with the existential situation in the manner described I have nothing more to do: I simply let the tide carry me on. To change the metaphor, I have no more to do than "roll with the punches." That notion is at the root of a great misunderstanding of how faith stands to moral action or, in traditional theological language, the relation of faith to works. A dominant theme in the sixteenth-century Reformation, especially in the mind of Martin Luther, was that a man's salvation is accomplished not through his works but *only* by faith (*allein durch den Glauben*). Luther saw that a man could not be saved by his own efforts, because the condition of these efforts would have been moral arrogance, and the outcome would be despair. As existential anguish is the condition of faith, so faith becomes the condition for all genuine moral striving. That is to say, my faith, instead of dismaying me by the impossibility of lifting myself up by my own bootstraps, encourages me by showing me the possibility of working out my salvation. To strive or not to strive can never be the question because, as we have abundantly seen, it is not a real choice. I am forced to make choices that entail striving. The question is, are my choices to be influenced by an evil, that is, a self-destructive force, or a good, healthy, self-liberating one? Faith-or-works must never be made into a strong disjunction. If a man took the antinomian posture of one who needed to do nothing because he had faith and therefore possessed the admission ticket to heaven safely tucked away in his pocket, he would thereby be proving that he did not have genuine faith at all. To claim to have faith in one's wallet, or framed like a diploma, is a self-contradiction, like boasting that one is the humblest man in the world.

A Skeptical Objection to the Faith-Existence Model

We have been using, in the last two sections, what might be called "the language of believers." Such usage tends to suggest that a certain model is being unquestioningly presupposed and that questions are allowed only upon the details of working it out. An objector might well say, "I can see where you get your model. Experience does suggest it, but you misinterpret experience in such a way as to end up with a gross distortion of what really happens. What has confronted the believer when he takes his 'leap of faith' is really nothing more than his own aspirations and ambitions, which he finds, so to say, 'coming to a head' within him. To talk of his being overtaken by a health-giving power is like talking of my being visited by a great healing power that at last cured me of my influenza when the standard commercial remedies had failed, instead of simply saying that, being a tolerably good patient, I cooperated with the bacteria in my body in driving out the influenza virus and so at last could shout, 'Hooray, I suddenly feel quite well again.' What happens to you when 'faith overtakes you' is just a psychological counterpart of such a physiological occurrence. To give an account of it as if it were a cosmic 'big deal' is very misleading, to say the least, and that is what your faith-existence model does."

That the life of faith can be so interpreted from the outside is obvious. To the man of faith it is impossible so to reduce it. *Ex hypothesi* he is saying that what he has been wrestling with and in the last resort rejecting is precisely that interpretation. The skeptic need not accept the claim, of course, but his skepticism will not affect the believer's certitude; nor should it, except to the extent that it challenges him to go on wrestling.

Suppose you were to tell me you were in love and I doubted it. If you were very inexperienced, my doubt might well be justified, and I might be able to point out to you certain elements in the situation that you had not noticed and that would enable you to see your claim was not so justified as you had supposed. If, however, you were an experienced man or woman, you would not be likely to be affected by any doubts I might voice. You might say, "My dear fellow, don't give me that. I have often thought I was in love when I wasn't, and I have sometimes been so near it that it was really difficult for me to tell. Now that I have 'been around' and know what the spectrum of authenticity and inauthenticity is, I am confident that this is the real McCoy." You still might not convince me, and indeed you would not be likely to be much interested in convincing me. You would have no need to do so, since I could add nothing of real importance to your joy. Nevertheless, you could not blame me even on your golden wedding anniversary if I obstinately persisted, saying, "I still don't think he was ever in love." Nor could you ever force me out of my contention that "love" as understood in such contexts does not occur and is just a way of expressing a particular mode of self-interest.

Now suppose that the objection were more radical. Instead of saying with a tolerant smile, "Oh, I know quite well how you feel when you talk about faith—it's just a misinterpretation of a very ordinary psychological phenomenon," I now say, "Honestly, I haven't the faintest idea what you're talking about." I am now asserting that the claim you are making is unintelligible, since I have *no* experience that corresponds with it, such as might make me feel you are talking about an experience that is familiar to me and that you are traducing by your misinterpretation. In such a case I do not challenge your *use* of a model; I say, rather, that your model is for me no model at all since it relates to nothing that has ever occurred in my experience at all.

You could not refute me logically. Your position would recall the one Bertrand Russell describes in respect to skepticism about knowledge itself. Russell, after specifying various conditions that he took to be required for "knowing" what is "necessary for scientific inference," indicated that he was satisfied that, in the argument he had provided in support of his claim, the conditions had been satisfied. Nevertheless, he went on to say, "If, however, anyone chooses to maintain solipsism of the moment, I shall admit that he cannot be refuted, but [I] shall be profoundly skeptical of his sincerity." [39] To claim total ignorance of what the religious person purports to be talking about when he talks "faith-language" is a claim most people would rightly suspect as a mere intellectual pose. Skepticism about his interpretation, however, is very plausible and may give rise to objections that must be taken very seriously indeed.

QUESTIONS ON CHAPTER VII

1   What are the conditions of faith?

2   What do you see in common between existentialism and process thought and how do they differ?

3   Is faith cognitive? If so, what kind of knowledge is it?

4   What non-cognitive elements do you see in faith?

5   Discuss the difference between "believing in" and "believing that."

6   Consider the difference between knowing and believing, with reference to religious faith.

7   Kierkegaard and Sartre share a common vocabulary and mode of conceptualization. How can their assessment of religious faith differ so radically?

BIBLIOGRAPHICAL SUGGESTIONS
See also under Chapter III.

Barrett, William. *Irrational Man. A Study in Existentialist Philosophy.* Garden City, N.Y.: Doubleday & Co., 1958. A good introduction to the principal existentialist themes.

[39] Bertrand Russell, *Human Knowledge* (London: Allen & Unwin, 1948), p. 515.

Belkind, A., ed. *Jean-Paul Sartre: A Bibliographical Guide.* Kent, Ohio: Kent State University Press, 1970. Indispensable tool for serious studies of Sartre.

Brinton, Crane. *Nietzsche.* Cambridge, Mass.: Harvard University Press, 1941. A brief introductory study of Nietzsche.

Bultmann, Rudolf. *Existence and Faith.* Translated by Schubert Ogden. New York: Meridian Books, Living Age Books, 1960. A useful introduction to Bultmann's writings.

Camus, Albert. *The Fall.* New York: Alfred A. Knopf, 1961.

Camus, Albert. *The Myth of Sisyphus.* New York: Random House, Vintage Books, 1960.

Collins, James. *The Existentialists.* Chicago: Henry Regnery Co., 1952.

Collins, James. *The Mind of Kierkegaard.* Chicago: Henry Regnery Co., 1953. Possibly the best introduction to Kierkegaard.

Diamond, Malcolm. *Martin Buber: Jewish Existentialist.* New York: Oxford University Press, 1960.

Friedman, Maurice. *Martin Buber: The Life of Dialogue.* New York: Harper Torchbooks, 1960.

Frings, M. S., ed. *Heidegger and the Quest for Truth.* Chicago: Quadrangle Books, 1968. Includes a paper by Albert Borgmann, "Heidegger and Symbolic Logic."

Heidegger, Martin. *Existence and Being.* Chicago: Henry Regnery Co., 1949.

Heidegger, Martin. *What Is Called Thinking?* Translated by F. D. Wieck and J. G. Gray. New York: Harper & Row, 1968.

Heinemann, F. H. *Existentialism and the Modern Predicament.* New York: Harper Torchbooks, 1958.

Hong, H. V. and Hong, E. H., eds. *Søren Kierkegaard's Journals and Papers.* 5 vols. Bloomington, Ind.: Indiana University Press, 1967. Kierkegaard, in addition to the twenty-one books he wrote before his death at the age of forty-two, also bequeathed journals and papers which, when printed in Danish, ran to 8,000 pages. These private writings, long unavailable in English, provide in many ways a key to the vast corpus of Kierkegaard's work. This collection, organized according to topic, furnishes almost a Kierkegaard encyclopedia. Indispensable reference work for serious students of Kierkegaard.

Jaspers, Karl. *Nietzsche.* Translated by C. I. Walraff and F. J. Schmitz. Tucson, Ariz.: University of Arizona Press, 1965. An elaborate examination of Nietzsche by a great twentieth-century existentialist.

Jaspers, Karl. *The Perennial Scope of Philosophy.* Translated by R. Manheim. New York: Philosophical Library, 1949.

Jaspers, Karl. *Philosophical Faith and Revelation.* Translated by E. B. Ashton. New York: Harper & Row, 1967.

Jaspers, Karl. *Philosophy of Existence.* Translated by R. F. Grabau. Philadelphia: University of Pennsylvania Press, 1971. Based on lectures given at the Freie Hochstift, Frankfurt.

Kaufmann, W., ed. *Existentialism from Dostoevsky to Sartre.* New York: Meridian Books, 1956. A good collection of writings by existentialists, with a brilliant, though perhaps too "clever," introduction.

Kierkegaard, Sóren. *Attack Upon Christendom.* Translated by W. Lowrie. Princeton, N.J.: Princeton University Press, 1944. Also Beacon Paperback. Kierkegaard's last work. A ferocious satire, to be read after his other works.

Kierkegaard, Sóren. *Christian Discourses.* Translated by W. Lowrie. New York: Oxford University Press, 1940. Also in Galaxy Books paperback. A good starting-place for many students.

Kierkegaard, Sóren. *Fear and Trembling* and *The Sickness Unto Death.* Translated by W. Lowrie. Princeton, N.J.: Princeton University Press, 1941. Also in paperback, Doubleday Anchor Books. A popular starting-place in Kierkegaard's writings.

Kuhn, Helmut. *Encounter with Nothingness: An Essay on Existentialism.* Chicago: Henry Regnery Co., 1949.

Lowrie, W. *Kierkegaard.* New York: Oxford University Press, 1938. Still a very good introduction to Kierkegaard by his translator, a pioneer of Kierkegaard studies in the English-speaking world.

Macquarrie, John. *An Existentialist Theology.* New York: Macmillan Co., 1956. Compares Heidegger and Bultmann.

Marcel, Gabriel. *Being and Having.* Translated by K. Farrer. New York: Harper Torchbooks, 1965. Good introduction to Marcel's unpretentious method of reflection.

Marcel, Gabriel. *Homo Viator.* New York: Harper & Row, 1962.

Marcel, Gabriel. *Man against Mass Society.* Chicago: Henry Regnery Co., 1962.

Marcel, Gabriel. *The Mystery of Being.* 2 vols. Translated by G. S. Fraser. Chicago: Henry Regnery Co., 1950-51.

Marcel, Gabriel. *Philosophy of Existentialism.* New York: Citadel Press, 1961.

Marcel, Gabriel. *Presence and Immortality.* Translated by M. A. Machado. Pittsburgh: Duquesne University Press, 1967. Contains Marcel's "metaphysical journals." 1938-1943.

Molina, F. R. *Existentialism as Philosophy.* Englewood Cliffs, N.J.: Prentice-Hall, 1962.

Molina, F. R., ed. *The Sources of Existentialism as Philosophy.* Englewood Cliffs, N.J.: Prentice-Hall, 1969. Useful anthology of passages from Husserl and various existentialists.

Murdoch, Iris. *Sartre.* New Haven, Conn.: Yale University Press, 1953.

Olson, Robert G. *Introduction to Existentialism.* New York: Dover Publications, 1962.

Patrick, Denzil. *Pascal and Kierkegaard.* London: Lutterworth, 1948. A valuable comparative study by a young scholar whose premature death prevented his becoming well known.

Pieper, Josef. *Belief and Faith.* New York: Pantheon Books, Random House, 1963. Contemporary restatement of Thomist position.

Price, H. H. *Belief.* New York: Humanities Press, 1969.

Richter, Liselotte, *Jean-Paul Sartre.* Translated by F. D. Wieck. New York: Frederick Ungar Publishing Co., 1970.

Roberts, D. E. *Existentialism and Religious Belief.* New York: Oxford University Press, 1957. A useful guide to an understanding of the religious aspects of modern existentialism.

Roeming, R. F., ed. *Camus: A Bibliography.* Madison: University of Wisconsin Press, 1968. Indispensable tool for serious studies of Camus.

Sartre, Jean-Paul. *Existentialism and Human Emotions.* New York: Philosophical Library, 1957.

Schrader, G. A., Jr., ed. *Existential Philosophers: Kierkegaard to Merleau-Ponty.* New York: McGraw-Hill, 1967. An excellent introduction to existentialist philosophy.

Takenchi, Yoshinori. "Buddhism and Existentialism." In W. Leibrecht, ed. *Religion and Culture.* New York: Harper & Brothers, 1959.

Thielicke, Helmut. *Nihilism.* Translated by J. W. Doberstein. New York: Harper & Row, 1961.

Thomte, Reidar. *Kierkegaard's Philosophy of Religion.* Princeton, N.J.: Princeton University Press, 1949. An admirable exposition that many students would find a very helpful introduction to Kierkegaard.

Yanitelli, V. R., S. J. "A Bibliographical Introduction to Existentialism." *The Modern Schoolman* 26 (May 1949).

VIII

MYSTICISM, SACRIFICE,
AND LOVE

Sacrifice is the first element of religion, and resolves itself
in theological language into the love of God.
> *J. A. Froude (1818–1894),*
> *Sea Studies*

Veil after veil will lift—but there must be
Veil upon veil behind
> *Edwin Arnold (1832–1904),*
> *The Light of Asia*

The Nature of the Problem

Mysticism is, as we shall see, a baffling as well as a fascinating topic. The philosophical problems it poses will emerge as we proceed to an examination of various types of mysticism; but we shall do well to inspect briefly at the outset the general considerations we should have in mind as we embark on such a study.

The mystic's claim to grasp that which is admitted to be beyond ordinary intellectual apprehension presents a problem obvious even to those who know little about the diversity of the forms mysticism takes and the relation in which it may stand to other phenomena, religious and otherwise. What sort of evidence could there be for a mystical knowledge? How could one either verify or falsify the mystic's truth-claims?

As soon as we begin to understand something of the variegated character of mystical phenomena, however, we cannot fail to be struck by the fact that mystical experience has been sometimes so much understood in terms of feeling that the question may naturally be raised whether powerful hallucinogens like lysergic acid diethylamide-25 (LSD), which have perception-altering properties, might not produce the same experiences or perhaps even better them. The psychedelic properties of certain drugs was recognized in antiquity, and the possible connection between drug-induced ecstasy and the mystical experience claimed by holy seers and other holy men could not, of course, have gone unnoticed. In modern times, long before the use of drugs was common in civilized occidental societies, Leuba drew attention to the properties of "Mescal, known until recently to Mexican and American Indians only." He quotes an article in the *British Medical Journal* in 1896, in which the author, Dr. Weir Mitchell, relates that at a certain stage of intoxication from the drug "I had a certain sense of the things about me as having a more positive existence than usual. It is not easy to define what I mean." He also has color hallucinations.[1] As with alcoholic and other forms of intoxication, the subject tends to imagine he is cleverer, braver, wittier, and more interesting than he appears to anyone who observes him, often much to the latter's embarrassment or distress. Hasheesh, ether, and nitrous oxide gas also produce psychological phenomena that might suggest experiences similar to those claimed by mystics.[2] Leuba notes that in the ancient world the cult of Dionysius became a pretext for license and debauchery.[3] If the mystic claims to have, through his special experience, an enhancement of life, might not that enhancement be achieved chemically, with a greater degree of efficiency and ease?

When one studies the diversity of forms of mysticism, however, one cannot but conclude that the interpretation of mysticism on which such a question is based would be ridiculously inadequate. It would be as inadequate as would be that of someone who, having noticed that certain Christians engaged in rolling on the floor during worship, assumed that the main purpose of Christianity consists in attaining the enjoyment of a rolling sensation, and proposed therefore that that purpose might be more efficiently achieved, especially in these days of advanced technology, through the use of roller-coasters. That such a suggestion is foolish may easily be shown. The ancient seers, sages, and mystics of India and China, Egypt and Greece, who were by no means wholly ignorant of the properties of drugs, to which they had access without the restrictive legislation that has surrounded them in modern civilized societies, would not have gone to such extreme trouble or engaged in such Herculean feats of mental effort (accompanied sometimes also by physical gymnastics), in the hope of achieving something they could have achieved very much more easily and painlessly by herbal means.

How, then, may we distinguish, say, the kind of mysticism that Leuba takes to be normative, the essential nature of which seems to be the enjoyment of intensity of feeling, from that of those mystics whose whole talk about their quest makes clear one thing at least, namely, that their claim is a cognitive one? These mystics may, indeed, speak of delight or joy or ecstasy that accompanies the fulfillment of their quest, but nothing is plainer than that such joy is a concomitant, no more to be identified with the essence

---

[1] J. H. Leuba, *The Psychology of Religious Mysticism* (New York: Harcourt, Brace & Co., 1925) pp. 23 f.
[2] Ibid., pp. 25 ff.
[3] Ibid., p. 33.

of the mystical experience than is the "hooray" of a mathematician when he solves a problem to be taken to be one of the basic principles of mathematics.

We should pay particular attention, therefore, to what the mystics do seem to be claiming. We shall see, *inter alia,* that mysticism has a striking connection with love, but love may be interpreted, on the one hand, as sexual acts of such crude animality as to lack even the refined eroticism of which civilized human beings are capable and, on the other, as entailing the awesomely sacrificial devotion of a lifetime. Since mystical experience sometimes appears to be the cheapest commodity in religion but at other times the costliest, how are we—even apart from its cognitive claims—to estimate its aesthetic quality as human experience, to say nothing of the value we might decide we ought to attach to it?

When the mystic talks about "knowing," he suggests problems such as are posed by the use of the term "thinking" in reference to, say, (1) what Kant was doing in the *Critique of Pure Reason,* (2) what a modern computer does, and (3) what one is doing when one says, "I think it is going to rain tomorrow" or "I think that's the worst TV commercial I've ever seen." What kind of knowledge can it be? How can it be related to an object, access to which is not at all obtainable in proportion to one's I.Q. but is, on the contrary, wholly unattainable by the ordinary operations of the intellect, though not necessarily held to be altogether divorced from them? How can not only mystics but scholars talk about, say, the Tao, which is by definition that-which-cannot-be-talked-about?

These are mere indications of problems we should have in mind as we look at the phenomenology of mysticism. We may now begin by noticing some of the general characteristics of the great mystical traditions encountered in the history of religion.

The Characteristics of Mysticism

In Theravada Buddhism (a school of Hinayana) and other forms of religion, mysticism, when it occurs at all, can occur without reference to any concept of a creative deity. The mystical experience may not be interpreted as having that context at all. Nevertheless, even in such forms of mysticism the mystics may interpret their experience as disclosing a divine presence that is inwardly operating in them. At any rate, the mystical experience, however interpreted, is always understood to be immediate, intuitive, direct. Wherever mystical experience is set in relation to any sort of conceptualization of God, the mystic always claims that it is, in one way or another, an immediate "contact" with God.

What "immediate contact with God" means will depend, of course, on the way of conceptualizing God. Where, for instance, God is identified with Nature, the mystic may claim the experience of losing his sense of individuality and of being absorbéd into the stream of one-ness. Such a view of mystical experience belongs to a primitive understanding of religion and exposes the subject of the experience to a grave kind of danger, as we shall see. In more developed forms of religion the mystical contact assumes the form of a special claim to knowledge. In contrast to the man who "walks by faith," the mystic "walks by sight." By nondiscursive mental activity, he has access to a direct kind of knowledge often called vision.

Though the kind of knowledge claimed cannot be easily specified, nevertheless there are telling clues. For example, the knowledge is not attained by logical or discursive methods. It is neither deductive nor inductive. It is intuitive, direct. The vision induces ecstasy or rapture. A further clue to its nature is provided by the fact that, of all the analogies the mystics give us in hinting at the nature of their experience, the one they generally most favor is that of human friendship and affection. Indeed, they often candidly associate their experience with sexual love; that is, while insisting that there is, strictly speaking, no analogy at all, they admit that if they were to be pressed for a hint of what mystical experience is like, they would liken it to human love rather than to anything else. Though sexual intercourse is physiologically an act that human beings perform in common with other animals, it has been associated from time immemorial both with love and with knowledge. The terms "love" and "love-making" are widely used for coitus, sometimes as a euphemism, but also because the sexual act is in fact, at least among sensitive and civilized human beings, closely associated with the expression of the most intimate human affection that can exist between a man and a woman. That this particular expression of human love is taken to have a distinctively cognitive element in it is attested by the ancient use of the term "knowledge" as a standard euphemism for sexual intercourse. In the Bible, as in much other literature, a man and woman who have copulated are said "to know" each other. Virgins, such as Jephthah's daughter, "have never known a man." As coitus is considered an act of cognitive love, so the mystic sometimes presents the nature of his experience: conspicuously noncarnal though it be, it is like sexual intercourse in respect of the latter's function as both an act of love and an act of cognition. The cognition is taken to be as intuitive and direct as the love is spontaneous and contactual.

The immediacy of mystical knowledge is expressed at a primitive level by "Crashing Thunder," a member of the Winnebago tribe of American Indians, who relates that as he prayed to "Earthmaker" he was aware not only of his presence but of direct communication with others around him: "This is what I felt and saw. All of us sitting together, we had all together one spirit or soul. I did not speak to them and get an answer to know what has been in their thoughts." [4]

[4] Paul Radin, *Primitive Religion* (New York: Dover Publications, 1957), p. 278. Originally published 1938. "Earthmaker" is God. Cf. (p. 304) Xokera, He-Who-Is-at-the-Root-of-Things.

In the intuitive schools of Mahayana Buddhism, Ch'an, and Zen, the goal is immediate insight such as Gautama himself is supposed to have received under the Bo-tree, that is, the Tree of Enlightenment. The Chinese, in attempting to reproduce the Sanskrit word *dhyāna* (meditation), produced the word Ch'an, which in turn becomes, in Japanese, Zen. *Dhyāna* is the method of salvation, but salvation is actually achieved by *prajnā* (insight, awakening), which is the aim of *dhyāna*. One attains Buddhahood by a direct inspection of one's own nature, not by reading the Buddhist Scriptures or performing ritual or even doing good works, all of which may even prove a hindrance. There is a quaint Mahayana Buddhist story to the effect that the Buddha, as he was about to leave the world, gathered his disciples and gave them a talk. To one disciple, however, he simply passed a flower, smiling as he did so, and that disciple, smiling in return, intuitively understood what the Buddha wished to communicate to him. Interest in that sort of immediate communication is characteristic of mystics of every tradition.

Such considerations help us to understand the etymological origin of the word "mysticism," which comes from the Greek root *mu* in the verb *muein*, to keep silent, to hold one's tongue. The root is onomatopoeic, mimicking the sound made by closing the lips. The expression "keeping mum"—that is, "maintaining a discreet silence"—is etymologically connected with the same root. The mystic maintains silence because he has no choice; what he knows, being intuitively acquired, is discursively incommunicable. Like the lover, he finds words inadequate. Yet no less than the lover he feels impelled to speak, and mystical language, like the language of lovers, is often passionately eloquent. Wittgenstein's much-quoted, aphoristic conclusion to his *Tractatus,* namely, *Wovon man nicht sprechen kann, darüber muss man schweigen* ("What one cannot speak about, on that one must be silent") traduces both the mystical experience and the experience of human love; both lovers and mystics, precisely because of the inexpressibility of their respective experiences, are impelled to pour forth torrents of words. Their words are as logically unanalyzable as the experiences to which they relate are ineffable. Yet for all that they are aware of stammering incoherently, they do not, for they cannot, cease to speak.

Upanishadic Mysticism

Though there is a mystical element of one sort or another in all religion, it is more normative in certain forms than it is in others. The early development of religion in India may be said to consist in a movement that begins with the elaborate ritual sacrifice to which the Vedas, composed about 1500–1000 B.C., served as an accompaniment, and that then branches in two directions. One of these is socio-political and is expressed in the rise of Brahmanism and the caste system; the other is speculative and mystical and is expressed in the Upanishads, which were composed between about the eighth and the fourth centuries B.C. Though what is called in the Occident "Hinduism" embraces such an enormous range of religious phenomena that it seems able to encompass and naturalize almost any religious idea that comes to it, notably including some preupanishadic elements, the influence of the upanishadic spirit permeates all subsequent development of the religion of India, including Buddhism, which was cradled there long before it spread to China and Japan. Indeed, wherever the influence of Indian thought is felt, even indirectly, as in the Hellenic world, some upanishadic influence seems detectable.

The term "Upanishad" means "esoteric teaching." "Esoteric" is contradistinguished from "exoteric" as is "closed" from "open." Esoteric teaching is by definition secret, hidden teaching, not available to all comers but accessible only to those who have been in one way or another initiated into the mysteries. The word "occult," etymologically connected with the Latin verb *celare* (to hide) has the same connotation of hiddenness. The Greek root—whence, as we have already seen, the term "mystic" is derived— expresses a notion closely allied to that of the esoteric and the occult.

The Upanishads originated in oral instructions given to disciples by their teachers. In them are found the wildest flights of poetic fancy and into them may be read many sorts of metaphysical speculation. Underlying the whole literature, certain metaphysical presuppositions, speculative inclinations, and intellectual tendencies, may be detected. For instance, there is a strong monistic tendency that later develops into a fundamental vision and focus; that is, God is seen as a principle of unity. The great upanishadic teachers claim to grasp that fundamental principle, the "real essence of all things," by direct, intuitive insight. Through self-realization one realizes God in one's self. The characteristic function of the Upanishads, however, is to provide disclosures of mystical insight. Their characteristic aim is soteriological.

If you were a disciple applying to be accepted by such a teacher, you might well ask him right away how you are to learn to attain the insight that the teacher has attained. Since the culture would be an oral one, there would be no question of going to libraries. The teacher would talk with you. His primary purpose, however, would not be to impart information to you. It would be, rather, to stimulate you to win for yourself your teacher's secret. Though he cannot impart that secret directly to you, he can put you in the way of discovering it for yourself. The teacher would enter into dialogue with you, and what he said in the course of that dialogue would reflect his metaphysical presuppositions. The purpose of the dialogue, however, would not be to instruct you in metaphysics or even to cause you to do some metaphysical thinking. It would be, rather, to enable you to get directly at the very heart of an "ultimate Reality" which, when you had grasped it, would provide you with the key to all things and save you from the grip of the carnal world in which unspiritual men are trapped.

Two root terms are found in the Upanishads—*ātman* and *brahman*. *Ātman* (like the Hebrew *ruach* and the Greek *pneuma*) originally meant "breath" but came to mean the spirit, self, ultimate essence, or stuff of man. Similarly, *brahman* developed from originally meaning the uncanny power of a primitive magic spell to eventually signifying the "ultimate Reality" at the heart of all things. The term *brahman*, therefore, *can* function, *mutatis mutandis,* as does the term "God" in Judaeo-Christian usage, but, in sharp contrast to the latter, the upanishadic teachers say that *brahman* and *ātman* are one. There is a cosmic self. To call such teaching pantheistic is, however, an anachronism in the sense that at the stage of cultural and intellectual development represented by the upanishadic literature there can be no question of a conscious choosing of pantheism over theism or theism over pantheism. So any attempt to try to show the Upanishads to be one or the other is doomed to failure. There are passages in the Upanishads that suggest, at any rate to a modern western mind, that God transcends all else. According to the *Katha Upanisad, ātman* (spirit) seems to transcend all else, for it "is not born, nor dies. This one has not come from anywhere, has not become anyone. Unborn, constant, eternal primeval . . ." [5] Yet *ātman* permeates everything as does the salt in salt water.[6] Upanishadic mysticism can be shown to be innocent of the kind of distinction that makes the choice between pantheism and theism seem crucial at a later stage in the development of religious thought.

The dominant theme throughout all the upanishadic literature is that the secret of all things is accessible to me when I can learn to grasp the divine Reality (*brahman*) that is available to me in the depths of my spiritual being (*ātman*) because my inmost being and that divine Reality are one. In the mystical experience through which I attain that realization of divine Reality in my deepest self, the distinction between me as the knower and that which is known evaporates, and I enter into union with the Infinite.

From our present-day perspective we are not easily able to appreciate how new and vivid, in those early times, were certain realizations that to us have become familiar and even sacred with age. In very primitive societies the fact that one can speak at all evokes wonder and awe. The bare utterance of words is intoxicating and the exercise of their power opens up boundless, fascinating vistas. Speech is invested with a magical quality. Behind the ritual enunciation of the well-known *aum* syllable[7] no doubt lies such primitive astonishment at the power of speech. A little later, the realization that man, through the exercise of his spirit or mind, can span centuries and fly as on a magic carpet throughout space faster than the flight of the swiftest bird, so transcending both space and time, is an even more awesome discovery.

---

[5] *Katha Upanisad,* 2.18, in R. E. Hume, *The Thirteen Principal Upanisads* (London: Oxford University Press, 1921), p. 349.
[6] *Chāndogya Upanisad,* 6.13, ibid., p. 248.
[7] Sometimes written *om.*

When man finds that he is able to transcend even his biological existence as biological existence once transcended the lifeless matter out of which it emerged, the intoxication of making the discovery exposes him to the danger of failing to see the limitations as well as the powers of mind, which now seem to him even more magically omnipotent than speech had once seemed to be. The kind of preoccupation with *ātman* that is characteristic of mysticism at this stage of human development can lead to a sort of fixation in which spirit, free from the limitations of finite personality, is worshipped. So the worshipper can come to conceptualize as God the limitless *ātman* or spirit to which, in an ineffable meditative experience, he can attach himself and in which he can feel himself lost in awe and wonder.

In view of such considerations, the modern suggestion that *ātman* looks "lower" than a human person shows a misunderstanding of the cultural context of the upanishadic literature. We should attribute to *brahman* neither personality nor impersonality, for the distinction has not yet been made. The distinction that *has* been made is between spirit and nonspirit, to the denigration of the latter and the exaltation of the former. The upanishadic mystic is rejoicing in consciousness, which is very properly called "light," for inseparable from it is intelligence, and "bliss." To discover the seemingly infinite capacity and boundless resources of psychic reality, the life of the spirit, is like entering upon one's first experience of dawn. It is like extrication from a dark prison to the light of day. To borrow a simile of George Meredith's used in a very different context, it is "blissful as a leap to daylight out of a nightmare." There was presumably a long period of semi-darkness in which, perhaps over the course of millions of years, the human spirit was struggling loose from the trammels that were stifling its emergence in the borderland between subhuman and human life. When consciousness dawns, and with it the astonishing powers of mind, the dawn must be indeed more radiant than the sunlit horizon over a green landscape after long years in a gloomy dungeon. We "civilized" people are so accustomed to the possession of consciousness and its powers that at best only with great difficulty can we get back to the wonder of it. To do so demands a spiritual vigor even greater than that required to recover the feeling of our childhood experiences, which is no simple feat.

The prison motif, which, as noted in our last chapter, appears in new and subtler forms in modern European existentialist literature, is expressed in ancient mystical writings such as the Upanishads in a manner closer, no doubt, to the original psychological archetypes. The contemporary Indian mystic Krishnamurti, in his youth a protégé of Annie Besant, the British theosophist and pupil of Madame Blavatsky, echoes yet transmogrifies the mood in a poem in which he tells of a little bird imprisoned in a tree trunk. As the bird tears open the "bars" of his prison he espies a tiny corner of a leaf, which he takes to be "the external world." As he struggles further, he sees the complete leaf; now he is sure he has the whole world just beyond his grasp. In turn he sees part of a branch, then the entire branch, and so on. Finally, with bleeding beak and claws, he is able to escape and fly away, knowing at last with direct, immediate insight and beyond all doubt, that by the power of his wings he is forever free from his prison. That pretty story expresses well the nature of the kind of mysticism that is found at the upanishadic level.

In later times, Indian thinkers, trying to systematize and harmonize the upanishadic teaching, have provided metaphysical interpretations of the literature. These metaphysical interpretations have varied considerably, as one might expect. They are innumerable, but among them are no fewer than six traditionally accepted metaphysical presentations of Indian religious thought. Of these, the one generally accounted the oldest is Sankhya (*sāṁkhya*) which, having preupanishadic roots, is in its developed forms clearly dualistic. Matter (*prakṛiti*) and souls (*puruṣa*) are both eternal and both unequivocally real.

Vedanta, however, one of the other best-known presentations, more consciously purports to reflect the mood of the Upanishads. Vedanta exhibits its teaching in a darshana (world view or, as the Germans say, *Weltanschauung*) that plainly expresses a metaphysical monism. Vedantists treat the external world and human consciousness alike as *māyā*. That is especially noticeable in the thought of Shankara, a Vedanta philosopher who flourished about A.D. 800. *Māyā* is usually translated "illusion," and that is indeed what it came to mean; but two things should be noted for a better understanding of this much misunderstood term. In the first place, the term meant originally "magic power." When, for instance, in the *Śvetāśvatara Upaniṣad*, Nature is called *māyā*, the predicate probably signifies the product of such a power rather than any notion as metaphysically specific as that of nonreality. In the second place, the notion of *māyā* does not appear much in the Upanishads at all, and its first appearance in that literature is a quotation from the Rig-Veda[8] many centuries earlier than the earliest upanishadic literature. In the Rig-Veda, where it often occurs, it indubitably carries the meaning of magical or supernatural power and it has plainly nothing to do with the metaphysical doctrine with which it was later associated by the Vedantists; the Upanishads were probably also innocent of that subsequent intellectualized interpretation.

In trying to recapture the mood of the Upanishads, which may serve as a classic model for all mysticism at a certain level of cultural and intellectual development, we should bear in mind, as was said earlier in the present section, that the aim of the Upanishads is soteriological. As with all mystical communication, the only excuse for attempting to express what is by definition inexpressible is the possibility of helping others to save themselves from whatever forces are taken to be destructive of man's spiritual

[8] Rig-Veda 6.47.18. In this particular case it appears in the plural—*māyin*, magical or supernatural powers.

life. Indeed, not only is the mystical literature of India soteriological in aim; so also is the aim of even the later metaphysical speculation on it. As Professor Eliade reminds us, "In India metaphysical knowledge always has a soteriological purpose." [9]

Mysticism of the upanishadic kind is not separable from either the metaphysical presuppositions that unconsciously lie behind it or the soteriological aims that may consciously motivate it. Nevertheless, it does represent a departure from earlier, purificatory ritual observances. Instead of performing ritual acts through which, with the aid of elders or priests, primitive man hoped to secure salvation by catching on to the coattails of unseen beneficent forces, those so inclined may now not only probe the secrets of the universe, but learn to grasp and appropriate to themselves that power which, as we might say, makes all things "tick." The discovery of such a possibility promises something of the satisfaction we might expect in a shift from alchemy to chemistry, from the slavish following of an ethical code to the intelligent acceptance of an ethical principle. It has no doubt something of the excitement of the transition from law to gospel.

Yet it has an even more fundamentally and genuinely liberating power. We must visualize men and women who have lived in terror of demonic forces beyond human control and who have been worshipping, for example, fertility principles or gods such as the sex-energy that in later Hindu thought is identified with Shiva and is represented in the *linga* and *yoni*, conventional emblems respectively of the male and female genitalia. We must then see some of them as having come to the realization of the power of the mind, with its processes of imagination and thought, at a time in human history nearer the threshold of human consciousness than is our own, and as having seen in that mental realm both the heart of all things and the means of escape from the weary toils of a carnal, birth–death, eating–copulating, existence.

Yoga

Yoga is mentioned in the Upanishads, but it has undergone a long process of development since then. Though presented, like all else, in soteriological terms, it is a mystical technique, a discipline for attaining knowledge. The technique was highly developed by Patañjali, a yogin of the second century A. D. Patañjali had a special devotion to Ishvara, an eternal spirit to whom yogins may look for guidance and help. On this account, Patañjali's doctrine has seemed to some occidental students to be theistic. In trying to understand the nature of yoga we should distinguish carefully between its disciplinary technique, a sort of psychosomatic gymnastic drill, and the purpose of that technique, which is complete release from the limitations of ordinary existence and the entry into a mystical state in which the self, freed from carnal bonds, attains suprarational knowledge.

[9] Mircea Eliade, *Yoga: Immortality and Freedom* (New York: Pantheon Books, 1958), p. 13.

There are traditionally eight steps: (1) *Yama,* consisting of the prospective yogin's undertaking of five vows, the essence of which is as follows: (a) to practice *ahiṁsā,* that is, to abstain from killing any living being; (b) to abstain from deceit; (c) to abstain from theft; (d) to abstain from sexual activity; and (e) to renounce property. The purpose of these vows is to destroy interest in carnal things and prepare the yogin for (2) *Niyama,* the observance of five rules relating to cleanliness, serenity, mortification of the senses, study, and prayer. (3) *Āsana,* posture, such as sitting with the right foot on the left thigh, hands crossed and eyes focused on the point of the nose. (4) *Prāṇayāma,* regulation of the breath: one sits bolt upright with the head, neck, and back as nearly straight as possible, while breathing in and out rhythmically, repeating inwardly the holy Sanskrit syllable *auṁ.* There are various refinements in the breathing technique. (5) *Pratyāhāra,* the exclusion from the mind of all the external world. (6) *Dhāraṇā,* self-emptying of the mind through concentration on a single object or idea. (7) *Dhyāna,* meditation in an all but unconscious mental state. This is the penultimate step in the gradual suspension of consciousness. (8) *Samādhi,* the mystical trance in which the yogin enters into and becomes one with ultimate Reality during the period of the trance. This is accompanied by an ecstatic awareness of the transcending of space and time through liberation from the external world and the attainment of great spiritual power.

While yoga obviously has roots in the primitive identification, already noted, of breath and spirit, it has developed from that stage to a profoundly wise recognition of the mystery in the relationship of mind and body. Parallels are not lacking in the West. Though in the Christian practice of prayer the breathing part of the technique is omitted, Catholic tradition prescribes ritual postures in prayer. For instance, kneeling, joining of the hands, closing or lowering of the eyes, bowing, genuflecting, prostrating, and the like, all have in them an element of recognition of the therapeutic value of such psychosomatic practices. Such psychosomatic therapy is not, however, the aim of either yoga or Christian prayer. The ultimate aim of yoga is the attainment of mystical union with "ultimate Reality."

Bhakti

The word *bhakti* comes from *bhaj,* "to adore," and the principle of Bhakti mysticism, which has played an enormous part in popular Indian piety, is one of adoring love. Through *prapatti,* total self-surrender in love, the soul is led to union with deity. Bhakti is very eclectic, taking many forms. The *Bhāgavata Purāṇa* mentions no fewer than nine, but the dominant theme is love, which overcomes all difficulties. Through the mystical spirit of Bhakti a vast pantheon of Hindu deities could be and was much incorporated into popular devotion. Shiva and Vishnu, Krishna and Rama, and indeed any deity one fancied, could be identified with the Brahman of the Upanishads, yet worshipped individually with passionate love. The upanishadic concept of *saṁsāra*, the chain of reincarnations through which men and women pass according to the inexorable spiritual law of karma that determines the form the reincarnation will take for the appropriate spiritual growth of the individual, who reaps in the next incarnation what he sows in this one, is woven into Bhakti mystical piety and expressed in multifarious cults, all of which have a common core of mystical experience. All bhaktas (practitioners of Bhakti) recognize a special relation between the devotee and his guru or master. The Sikhs, a remarkable body of people adhering to an independent and syncretistic Indian religion founded by Nanak (A.D. 1469–1538), carried the mystical relationship between guru and disciples to the point of regarding the disciple as filled with his guru's spirit, and the whole Sikh body (the Panth) was accounted the embodiment of the guru. Both Nanak and Kabir (mentioned in the first part of this book) were much influenced by Bhakti.

Though many influences besides the general upanishadic background lie behind Bhakti mysticism, the *Bhagavad-gītā*, which took shape several centuries after the Upanishads, must be specially mentioned. In the *Bhagavad-gītā*, which is probably the best known and best loved of all Indian literature, is developed the *avatāra* principle that is essential to Bhakti. The mystical themes of the Upanishads are carried into the Gita, but the upanishadic outlook is warmed and humanized in such a way as to change the character of the mysticism. The infinite, eternal spirit celebrated in the Upanishads now receives human embodiment, by means of a new principle—the *avatāra*. The infinite assumes from time to time and with prodigal diversity human forms through which it expresses itself, proclaiming eternal truths in human language. Krishna, the central figure of the Gita, is such an *avatāra*.

The *avatāra* principle, which is of cardinal importance in the development of Bhakti, looks superficially similar to the orthodox Christian doctrine of the Incarnation, but in fact, for reasons extraneous to our present theme, the *avatāra* principle as it is worked out in the Gita and in Bhakti mysticism is radically different from that extremely complex Christian theological doctrine. That is not to say, however, that they have no common element at all. The *avatāra* provides a means whereby that which would otherwise be ineffable can find human expression within the limits of human thought and propositional discourse. The *Bhagavad-gītā* lays much stress on the distinction between outer and inner—that is, between the life of the body, which is temporal, and the life of the spirit, which is eternal.

The mythology associated with Bhakti is expressed in an enormous variety of guises, but characteristic of all Bhakti is intense personal love and devotion. Metaphysical speculation in Bhakti likewise takes many forms. The object of mystical adoration may be very variously conceived, but the soul of the bhakta always brings to it a warm, intimate feeling of love. The love sometimes seems plainly erotic in quality. As is characteristic of the polytheistic level of religion, the gods themselves engage in erotic activities. Krishna not only fights dragons; he makes love to gopis (milkmaids), and creation itself may be accounted a sort of divine love affair. Such cosmic eroticism is often, however, so allegorized as to give the mystical quest a more restrained and upanishadic flavor. To the followers of Chaitanya, Krishna's love for the gopis is interpreted allegorically as the love that binds God and the soul in mystical union. Krishna is completely identified with Brahman.

With the emphasis on individuality and inwardness that characterizes all mysticism, there is a tendency to look critically not only at caste but at all toilsome religious exercises. All religious institutions, indeed, tend to be de-emphasized. The external trappings of religion come to be accounted unimportant and even a positive hindrance to the love of God that is at the heart of the mystical life. Lacking in Bhakti, however, is any particularly strong ethical concern to sustain such individualist pretensions. The prophetic spirit that appears in Hebrew religion as early as the eighth century B.C., in Amos and Hosea, displaying an intense preoccupation with righteousness and sounding vigorous warnings to those who ignore it, has no counterpart in Bhakti. Not only does Bhakti become in debased forms an excuse for erotic orgies in imitation of the love affairs of the gods; even in its higher forms no particular connection between religion and ethics is seen as essential to the well-being of the mystical enterprise.

The divorce of religion and ethics that Bhakti tends to engender is conspicuous in the Tantric movement, which is, among much else, a revival of the primeval Indian worship of Mother Earth. It exalts the sexual element in human life, exhibiting it in a religious guise. Through Tantric techniques divine powers are believed to be ritually injected into the body, giving it supernatural strength and power, which may then be used for many purposes and by no means necessarily ethical ones. Not only may greater sexual potency or fertility be sought; one may use one's powers for ends such as victory over rivals or calling down rain from the sky. A couple may seek to identify their sexual enjoyment not only with the antics of the gods but with the bliss of the Absolute that is at the heart of all things.

Here we come to an important point for the understanding of mysticism in general. The danger to which all mysticism is exposed is that of trying to attain to union with God while sidetracking duty to man. What happens in degraded forms of Bhakti is that the devotee tries to get union with divine Being on impossibly cheap terms. He indulges himself in fantasies of divine union that are a sort of falling in love with divine love rather than a genuine attempt to come to grips with the demands that such a love must be expected to make. All mysticism, when it so lacks a sense of the divine righteousness and an awareness of the moral demands the Other must be expected to make, easily degenerates into a self-indulgent luxuriating in one's own psyche, a sort of spiritual autoeroticism. The great mystics have always been well aware of this danger.

Even the less degraded forms of mysticism of the Bhakti type tend to dwell on what Kierkegaard called the aesthetic stage of existence, the spectator attitude which, under cover of religion and on the pretext of mystical love of God, is really a retreat from even the possibility of encounter with the Other. Our task in the present chapter must include some consideration of possible criteria for distinguishing such mysticism from mysticism of a more promising kind.

Some Other Mystical Traditions

We may now glance at a few other types of mysticism. A detailed exposition of all types, were it possible, would be not only beyond the limits of our space here but also beyond the scope of our needs. The classic types of Indian mysticism we have briefly examined provide a basis for an understanding of Eastern mysticism in general that is sufficient for our purposes. Though there are, of course, many independent forms of mysticism in Asia, the extent of Indian influence is astonishing.

Buddhism, for instance, which in its Mahayana forms spread to China and Japan, exercising great influence there, is Indian in origin. Zen, one of the best-known mystical Buddhist schools, has, as already noted, Indian roots. Tantric Buddhism has the same essential characteristics that we have seen in Tantric Hinduism. The mystical notion of Bodhisattvas, "little buddhas" who, in order to help mankind, dally longer on earth than they need, probably has roots in common with the *avatāra* notion so prominent in the *Bhagavad-gītā*. *Nirvāna*, a central notion in Buddhist mysticism, is the state of release from the bonds of finitude, which include the categories of human thought and language. Though it does not provide the sense of union with the divine that we find in Hindu mysticism, it is envisaged as an immediate apprehension of Reality, a very Indian theme. Nirvana is, indeed, the ultimate Reality, the quest for which is a characteristic Indian preoccupation. In contrast to Bhakti, however, Buddhism, even in its mystical aspects, tends to be closely connected with the ethical teachings of the religion. To know Nirvana is not only to have superlative knowledge of metaphysical Reality; it is to know the *summum bonum*, the highest good. That, too, however, has Hindu counterparts.

In ancient China both the practice of *tso-wang*, which consisted in sitting with a mind emptied of thought, and the techniques of breath control that were adopted to foster that state, suggest a counterpart to Indian yoga. Out of that ancient Chinese background emerged not only the great Confucius, who may be considered a Chinese counterpart of Socrates, but also the distinctively mystical religion known today as Taoism. The word "Tao," like the Greek word *dikē* used by Plato, means literally "way" or "path." Among Confucians it acquired a function similar to that of *dikē* in Plato: it is "the right way" or "the path of truth." In the mystical teaching of the Taoists it came to have a function similar to Dharmakaya in Mahayana Buddhism which, originally signifying the body of Buddhist doctrine, came to stand for the *buddhatā* or buddha-nature, the suprapersonal Absolute, the supreme Reality underlying and comprising all things. It is the Taoist counterpart of *brahman* in the Upanishads, considered in an earlier section of this chapter. It is the source of all things, transcending time and space.

Much emphasis is placed on the ineffability of the Tao, which is not only beyond words but beyond thought. The word "Tao" is a name for that which is beyond all naming. Chuang-tsu, the first great recorded Taoist teacher, who flourished about 300 B.C., puts the matter thus: "The supreme Tao cannot be talked about, and the supreme argument requires no speaking." Taoists have in fact talked much about the Tao, often as if it were an infinite natural force, perhaps like energy; but others, including, very occasionally, Chuang-tsu himself, have invoked it in personal terms. All attempts to delineate the Tao, however, are bound to be inadequate, since the Tao is by definition beyond the categories of human thought. Nevertheless, metaphysical presuppositions plainly underlie Taoism as, we have seen, they underlie the Upanishads. The Taoist knows, for example, that the Tao supports the universe, shapes and governs its forms, and is older than all things without itself having any age at all. Since the Tao is beyond all human and natural qualities and concepts, the Taoist's task is to empty himself of these so as to be a mirror of the eternal, the Tao. We are reminded of the principle of emptiness or void that is to be found in much Buddhist mystical teaching, for example that of Nāgārjuna, who flourished in India about 200 A.D. and very possibly had a brahmin's spiritual and intellectual training.[10]

Above all, the Taoist knows that through union with the Tao a man is awakened to a higher consciousness of Reality and so can see ordinary experience as by comparison a sort of dream. The Taoist sage, therefore, like the wise man among the Stoics, is not disturbed by human tragedy; he accepts with equanimity riches and poverty, health and sickness, even life and death. So, though such a man is removed from the preoccupations of ordinary society, he affects it for good not only by his example but by breathing into it, so to speak, the inner quiet that he has attained.[11]

Mystical ideas flourished also among the Greeks where, as early as classical times, the mystery religions—notably the Eleusinian and Dionysian mysteries—gave rise to distinctively mystical quests and experiences. Though some writers, for example A. E. Taylor, may have overstressed the mystical

[10] F. J. Streng, *Emptiness: a Study in Religious Meaning* (Nashville, Tenn.: Abingdon Press, 1967), pp. 28 f.

[11] One should note, by the way, that Taoism, as a popular religion, is often very far from preoccupation with the mystical ideas of its great teachers. It can take very debased, superstitious forms in which fortune-telling plays a part. Taoist temples are often much cluttered with idols and the like. For the historical background of Taoist superstition, see Ninian Smart, *The Religious Experience of Mankind* (New York: Charles Scribner's Sons, 1969), pp. 175 ff.

elements in Plato, the possibility of a knowledge of Reality in the World of Forms, by means of an intellectual apprehension wholly transcending all cognitive activities grounded in the senses, entails a view that is characteristic of the great mystical traditions everywhere.

Hellenistic mysticism finds a remarkably vivid expression in the Hermetic literature, a collection of Greek and Latin writings dating from the middle of the first to the end of the third century A.D. and attributed chiefly to Hermes Trismegistus (the triply-great Hermes), a later designation of Troth, an Egyptian deity accounted the father and guardian of all knowledge. These writings contain Pythagorean, Platonic, and Stoic elements, the whole deeply affected by Eastern mystical ideas. The Hermetic writings, containing notions such as the ascent of the soul to God through the seven planetary spheres, are intended to guide men to deification through *gnosis*, the mystical knowledge of God.[12] The characteristic theme of the ineffability of God pervades the Hermetic literature. If we must speak of God, we may dare to call him *nous*, mind, which of all metaphors most fittingly describes him, and *phōs*, light, but in fact no words can describe him and no tongue can utter his name. Silence proclaims him best. Man, in respect of his mind, participates in divinity.

A very striking phenomenon in the early centuries of the Christian era was Gnosticism, a movement of pre-Christian origin having Eastern, probably both Persian and Indian roots. A climate of belief rather than a movement or a school, it took many forms and it affected other religions. It invaded and considerably influenced the Christian Church, especially in the second century A.D. Characteristic teachings included the distinction between the unknowable divine Being and the Demiurge or Creator deity. Mind or spirit is good; matter is evil. The world we know, the handiwork of the Demiurge, is for certain metaphysical reasons antagonistic to the spiritual realities; yet into some men a spark or germ of the divine substance has entered, bringing hope of the possibility of rescue from the evil matter in which the spark had been embedded and imprisoned.

Manichaeism, which was founded by the Persian Mani in the third century A.D. and which became a strong influence throughout the Roman Empire, gaining the allegiance of St. Augustine before his conversion to Christianity, resembled Gnosticism in several respects, conspicuously in the mind–matter dualism. The Albigenses or Cathari, who appeared in the twelfth century in Provence and neighboring regions, threatening to destroy the Christian Church there at that time, had very similar views, and indeed the mystical doctrines of Gnosticism appear in various underground heretical movements in the Middle Ages, affecting to some extent both Christianity and Judaism,

---

[12] See C. H. Dodd, "Hellenistic Judaism and the Hermetica," in *The Bible and the Greeks* (London: Hodder & Stoughton, 1954), vol. 2, pp. 97–248. For the text, see A. D. Nock, ed., *Corpus Hermeticum*, 4 vols. (Paris: Collection Budé, 1945–1954), with French translation by A. J. Festugière, O.P.

long after Gnosticism had ceased to be a possible rival to the former. Modern theosophy, including Rosicrucianism and other occultist movements in our own time, is in many ways reminiscent of Gnosticism, especially in respect of the emphasis on a body of special, esoteric knowledge, a sort of spiritual chemistry, understood by the initiated and capable of being taught to those fortunate enough to be their disciples.

The character of Gnosticism and of the various theosophical and occult types of mysticism that are consciously or unconsciously derived from it is interestingly exhibited in the effect that reading about the Gnostics had on the mind of T. H. Huxley when he first encountered them. He tells us that they seemed to him to profess to know so much about everything that he felt his own intellectual outlook to be so antithetical to theirs that he invented what was at that time, in the nineteenth century, a new word, "agnostic" (that is, "non-gnostic"), to designate his own position. That is how the now very familiar word "agnostic" entered into our language. The Gnostics, in typically mystical fashion, claimed to know the secrets of the spiritual world.

Plotinus, a native of Egypt and a pupil of Ammonius Saccas, a Platonist teacher of the Middle Academy, settled in Rome about the age of forty, where he wrote the *Enneads*. His mystical teachings, which spread throughout the Mediterranean world, gave rise to the development of a new school, commonly called Neo-Platonism, which was so influential that it seemed at one time to be a very serious rival of Christianity, and perhaps it eventually failed to receive popular support only because it may have seemed too intellectualist for simple people to understand. The Neo-Platonists departed considerably from the original teachings of Plotinus in the *Enneads,* but the main purpose of Plotinian teaching was maintained, namely, the attempt to provide a sound intellectual basis for overcoming the gulf between thought and Reality so as to make possible the attainment of mystical knowledge of the One. This mystical knowledge is attained through a method of divesting human experience of all its specifically human elements. When all these have been removed, the way to the One is open. According to Plotinus, the One, who may be considered to be God or the Absolute, has a center everywhere but a circumference nowhere. Only through such mystical procedures can knowledge of God be attained.

Jewish Mysticism

The early experiences of the Hebrews, who had to eke out a living as best they could, trying to maintain their prized independence by working very poor land on the edge of the desert, were such as to develop among them a deep sense of the religious category of faith. This is fundamentally different from, if not, as some maintain, completely opposed to the notion of mystical knowledge as we have seen it in various mystical traditions throughout the

East, from that of Brahman in the Upanishads to that of the Tao of the Chinese. The religion of the Torah and the Prophets is one of righteous concerns in response to the ethical demands of Yahweh, the most righteous God. Yahweh, though he so hides his face that even the great Moses, could he have looked upon it, would have died (and so had to hear and to speak to God through the burning bush), discloses his Word through lawgivers and prophets and above all reveals himself through his acts in history. In that tradition and in these circumstances, the question of attaining mystical knowledge of God hardly arises. God is the-One-who-acts; his people behold his deeds in history. God speaks; his people hearken to the words he puts into the mouth of his prophets. In such religion, mysticism, if to be found at all, is at a minimum; nevertheless, Judaism did develop a very distinctive mystical tradition of its own, which eventually reached full flower in the Jewish Kabbalah of the Middle Ages.

The Hebrew people, after the Exile, were exposed to many foreign ideas. Though they were encouraged by their leaders to resist them, these foreign ideas inevitably exerted their influence, and in Hellenistic Judaism new mystical notions began to come to light. There are mystical elements in the Jewish apocalyptic literature that appeared in the second century B.C. and in the teaching of the Essenes and other Jewish sects. Philo, who lived from about 20 B.C. to about A.D. 50 and belonged to a prosperous priestly family in Alexandria, was an orthodox, observant Jew deeply influenced by Hellenistic mysticism. He called attention to the human capacity for self-transcendence. Once again God is ineffable, the power that is beyond all conceptualization. As in the Hermetic writers, the way to mystical knowledge of God is through procedures such as the renunciation of worldly pleasures and desires, indeed the denigration of all that is mortal, and the quest for that which is beyond all ordinary knowledge and concerns.

By the early medieval period mystical ideas had been so thoroughly acclimated within Jewish thought that elaborate and specifically Jewish forms of mystical speculation developed in great profusion. One of the best known examples is the *Sefer Yetsirah*, the Book of Creation, probably dating between the third and the sixth century A.D., which deals with the constitution as well as the creation of the universe. It is full of a curious mixture of mystical ideas and literalistic fantasies reflecting, for instance, the assumption that the secret of the universe is enshrined in the very form of the letters of the Hebrew alphabet, the very structure of the language of God himself. Such notions played a considerable part in the development of the medieval Jewish Kabbalah and continue to flourish to this day.[13] One must not deduce

---

[13] In Mea She'arim, the orthodox quarter of modern Jerusalem, an elderly Jew stopped me on the street and engaged me in conversation under a blazing sun, giving me a long disquisition on the mystical significance of the letters of the Hebrew alphabet, which he might have continued for hours had not I perceived its probable duration by the time we had reached Daleth, the fourth of the twenty-four letters.

the nature of Kabbalism, of course, from such literalistic superstitions. It is the expression of rich, variegated, distinctively Jewish, and often very beautiful mystical ideas. Alphabet superstition is mentioned only to show how even the most interesting and possibly profitable mystical concepts may be mixed with obviously trivial and misconceived primitivistic fantasies.

In the early Middle Ages, Jewish mysticism had flourished in Palestine, Babylonia, and Egypt. In the ninth century it appeared in Italy, whence it was carried to Germany, where Hasidism, a new movement, greatly affected all German Jewry. The *Ḥasīdīm* ("godly ones") regarded themselves as spiritual descendants of the Hasidim of the second century B.C., who had resisted an earlier tendency to absorb alien forms of mysticism. Characteristic of medieval Hasidism was the cultivation of a mystical piety believed to be conducive to a continual sense of the divine Presence. The aim was to attain, through the love of God, the vision of God. The Hasidim recognized a hierarchy of five invisible worlds, the highest of which was the world of light, identified with the glory of God. The medieval Hasidim were ascetic. They also cultivated the characteristic monastic ideal of indifference to the admiration or disdain of the world. Modern Hasidism, which developed in the Ukraine, where other forms of Jewish mysticism had flourished, may be said to have been founded by Israel Baal Shem, who was born in 1700. Discarding the ascetic and other aspects of medieval Hasidism, the new Hasidim emphasized the immanence of God in the world and the living presence of the divine as the dynamic essence of all things. Seeking mystical ecstasy, they cultivated devotional intensity, consecrating the whole of life to God. Hasidism has developed along various lines, but it has maintained common elements, and its beneficial effects on Jewish life are widely recognized.

Mysticism in Islam

The religion of Muhammad (A.D. 570–632),[14] was deeply indebted to Judaism and Christianity, the only two major religions he had encountered. It envisages in characteristically Semitic fashion a great gulf between the human and the divine. The emphases are on personal surrender and submission through prayer to Allah, whose will is absolutely sovereign. "Islam" means "peace through submission to the will of Allah." Angels, as the intermediaries between Allah and humankind, play a special role. Allah acts in history and speaks through his prophets, who are his earthly mouthpieces. The great religious leaders, including Moses and Jesus, are always seen in the role of prophets, among whom Muhammad is acknowledged as pre-eminent. The Muslim faith is epitomized in the well-known credal statement of Islam: *La ilāha illa Allāh; Muhammad rasūl Allāh:* "There

[14] Muslims date the beginning of their era from A.D. 622. The year consists of twelve lunar months. The Muslim new year 1390 began March 9, 1970.

is no god but Allah, and Muhammad is his prophet." This credal statement, which the muezzin intones from the minaret of the mosque as he calls the faithful to prayer, is the heart of the Muslim faith.

In such a religion, faith, not mystical vision, is likely to be the primary category, and indeed that is, in general, what we do find. Islam does not provide, on the whole, a promising soil for mystical ideas to flourish. In comparison with India, where they seem to grow wild in lush profusion, the Arab world is inhospitable to them. In the history of thought, the Arabs in the Middle Ages were famed for their mathematical and scientific enterprises rather than for mystical preoccupations.

In view of these considerations, the emergence of *Ṣūfī* mysticism within Islam is all the more noteworthy and relevant to the fundamental question of the relation in which mysticism stands to religion. The Sufis appeared within a short time after Muhammad's death. Their name is derived from the word *ṣūf* (wool), from the coarse white wool dress they wore. The dress was not unlike that of Christian monks; the mode of their life somewhat resembled that of such monks; and the mystical ideas they developed bear the unmistakable signs of Neo-Platonic, Stoic, and Christian influence. At the same time not only were the Sufis thoroughly Muslim in their allegiance to Allah and in their acceptance of Islam, but within the Muslim tradition they developed already existing notions that might be said to contain mystical elements in embryonic form. For instance, though Muhammad prescribed certain ritual observances, including hours of prayer, he also recommended that the faithful cultivate a continual remembrance of God. Such a notion, not in itself specifically mystical, since it does not necessarily envisage a direct knowledge of God or a sense of his immediate presence, is susceptible to mystical development. In some of the Prophet's occasional and perhaps atypical utterances may also be seen a possible basis for such a development. For example, his remark that Allah is nearer to man than the jugular vein recalls a Stoic theme echoed in Tennyson's well-known line "Closer is he than breathing, and nearer than hands and feet." Such a notion is provocative of a mystical quest for attaining, through awareness of the divine presence, a direct, intuitive knowledge of God.

Men like Ibrahim ben Adham and women like Rabi'a, both of the eighth century A.D., express a love of God accompanied by a contempt for the world that is reminiscent of the early Christian solitaries. Ibrahim is known to have received from a Christian monk instruction in that cultivation of the inner life that leads to spiritual tranquility and a sense of the presence of God. The Sufis sought to cultivate the inner life and, though they departed more and more in many ways from traditional Islamic teaching and custom, they generally not only venerated the *Qur'ān* with the immense reverence that Muslims bring to the Book but also acknowledged the *Hadīth,* writings that are supposed to contain sayings of the Prophet and stories relating to his life. Some Persian Muslim mystics were, however, more distinctly heretical, and some popular mystical movements tended openly to disdain Muslim orthodoxy. In the Middle Ages, dervishes (holy men, so called from *darwīsh,* mendicant) often manifested eccentric forms of ecstatic behavior, but the orders of dervishes at their best played a role comparable to that of the Franciscans in their early days. Like the Franciscans, the dervishes were popular among the common people, and, also like the Franciscans, they promoted interest in the quest for simplicity of life and a sense of the immediate presence of God.

The dervishes popularized the Sufi mystical tradition, in which direct, intuitive knowledge of God is distinguished from knowledge attained through discursive, intellectual means. As in other forms of mysticism, the Sufi tends to see his life more and more as the life of God himself acting in him. Neither the transcendence nor the absoluteness of God, however, is ever questioned. Even in those forms of Sufism which, in Neo-Platonic fashion, look upon the world as an emanation of God, and conceive of God as the hidden essence of all things immanent in all things, the absoluteness and transcendence of God are held inviolate. Nevertheless, the arbitrariness of the will of Allah that is such a remarkable feature of the religion of the *Qur'ān* tends to vanish with the sense of the gracious goodness of Allah at work in man. Sufism takes many forms and the teaching of the Sufis is very diverse and not always consistent, but for all its resemblance to other forms of mysticism, it is very deeply affected by the peculiar tenets and ethos of the Muslim faith. The significance of that consideration for an understanding of mysticism and of its relation to religion will be treated in a later section of this chapter.

At the same time, all mystics do also tend to transcend their own religious tradition. As John Macquarrie suggests, a thoroughgoing Calvinist with a deep conviction of the absolute sovereignty of God stands closer to Islam than do many of his fellow Christians, while "a Sufi mystic in Islam may find more kinship with Christian mystics than with many of his coreligionists." [15] Again, al-Hallaj, a Persian Sufi who was put to death for blasphemy in A.D. 922 by the Muslim authorities for declaring himself "the True" (*al-Haqq,* by which they understood him to be saying he was Allah, since that is one of the designations of Allah), couches his account of his experiences in terms remarkably like those used by Christian mystics. As a Muslim he does not embrace, of course, the orthodox Christian view of Christ as the Logos incarnate, yet his devotion to Jesus as the model of holiness and the prince of the kingdom of divine grace is very striking. This well-known tendency among mystics to leap over all the bounds of their respective faiths while often remaining more than ordinarily loyal to the faith in which they were nurtured and to which they have given their allegiance, is very noteworthy. We should be careful neither to ignore its immense importance

[15] John Macquarrie, *Principles of Christian Theology* (New York: Charles Scribner's Sons, 1966), p. 148.

nor to deduce from it more than is warranted. The mystic's attitude generally suggests that mysticism, like charity, must begin at home and can never wholly leave it. The great mystical teachers, Buddhist, Muslim, and Christian, all attest the danger attending repudiation of one's spiritual mother and of forgetting the soil from which one has sprung. The mystic has learned better than most people how to grow up, accepting one's origin yet transcending it. "Jerusalem, if I forget thee, may my right hand wither!" [16]

Varieties of Christian Mystical Tradition

In Christianity as in Judaism and Islam there are tendencies toward and against mystical experience. Generally speaking, mysticism is more congenial to the Alexandrian than to the Antiochene tradition and so, since Protestantism adheres more to the latter than to the former, Protestantism would seem more inhospitable to it than are the Roman, Anglican, and Eastern Orthodox traditions. Nevertheless, even in the least mystically inclined of Christian traditions, elements may be detected that would generally be called mystical, while among the traditions most hospitable to mystical ideas we find distinct reservations.

St. Thomas Aquinas, for instance, insists that in this life we cannot "see God's essence"; yet he does not exclude the possibility of a sort of foretaste of the life to come, perhaps (we might say) a preview of the *visio beatifica*.[17] A typical expression of the reservation is to be found in the characteristic advice of Jesuit spiritual directors: one is not to set out with the expectation of mystical experience, but one is to accept it if it should come. That is to say, it is to be accounted a special gift of God—not (as in the Upanishads, for instance) a normal proceeding. These reservations refer to a long history of the Christian Church's encounter with a wide variety of types of mysticism and of its experience of the dangers attending them.

When we look at the New Testament itself, alongside what may be the more characteristic Hebrew emphasis on faith contradistinguished from "vision"—that is, on the sense of absence rather than the sense of the presence of God—we find definitely mystical elements. The story of the Transfiguration, for example, is to be understood in terms of a mystical type of experience already recognized in Judaism.[18] There are echoes in it of the story of Moses, the skin of whose face was radiant when he came down from the mountain where he had been speaking with Yahweh.[19] The notion of a light irradiating the face or the entire body of a man, as if from behind the pores of his skin, making it translucent, or of a light surrounding the head or body of a holy man, is found in Christian and other mystical traditions. The representation of it in Christian iconography in the halo or nimbus is well

---

[16] Psalms 137:5 (Jerusalem Bible); cf. Jeremiah 51:50.
[17] *Summa contra Gentiles,* III, 47.
[18] Matthew 17:2.
[19] Exodus 34:29; cf. Luke 2:9.

known. The light so represented is not, of course, one that is measured in candlepower; it is a spiritual radiance. How can a spiritual radiance be *seen*? It can be "seen" in the way in which intelligence is "seen" when we say, "You can see John's intelligence staring out of his eyes" or "His face is full of intelligence."

St. Paul's report of having been "caught up into" heaven, where he "heard words so secret that human lips may not repeat them," [20] and the notion of being "in Christ" and of "Christ living in me" are all full of mystical tendency, to say the least. So also is the Fourth Gospel, the first chapter of which abounds in mystical themes. John, the author of that Gospel, was accustomed to the thought of two worlds and to moving in both of them—the Hellenistic world, full of mystical preoccupations, and the Judaic world with its traditional emphasis on faith. So, since John is addressing both worlds, we have the twin themes of the presence and the absence of God. To the Jewish world, on the one hand, he is saying that their faith and their hope have been in fact actualized in the Christian community where the mysterious love (*agapē*) of Christ is actually creating a new people in such a way that to share in it is to realize all hopes. To the Hellenistic world, on the other hand, John is saying that eternal life does indeed consist of light and knowledge, which Jesus Christ discloses, but that that knowledge "is not to be confused with intellectual knowledge, mystical speculation or esoteric, secret tradition, such as some of the intelligentsia of the Graeco-Roman world cherished. . . . Knowledge of Christ in this sense, that is, obedience to the prompting of his love—this is the eternal life which the Graeco-Roman world and all other worlds need." [21]

Early Christian writers are often ambivalent regarding the place of mystical experience in the Christian life. The Church's experience with Gnosticism, which in the second century seemed by its extravagances to threaten the very existence of what churchmen took to be the fundamental nature of the apostolic faith, made mystical exploits in principle suspect. There were, as we already have seen, mystical tendencies in the New Testament, however restrained. There was also, however, in New Testament mysticism, resistance to the typical occult ideas fashionable in cultivated society in the Hellenic world. Old pagan mystical ideas continued, nevertheless, to live on, especially in the East.[22]

About the year A.D. 500 a mystical writer now known as Pseudo-Dionysius was writing, probably in Syria, works such as the *Divine Names* and the *Celestial Hierarchy*, which plainly intend to achieve a synthesis between

---

[20] 2 Cor. 12:1–6 (N.E.B.). The words are said to have been *arrēta*, too sacred to utter.
[21] W. D. Davies, *Invitation to the New Testament* (New York: Doubleday & Co., 1965; Anchor Books edition, 1969), p. 516. The whole chapter (pp. 515–518) admirably presents the point in relation to Johannine mysticism.
[22] Pagan ideas persisted long after areas were nominally christianized. Some areas in Europe were not even nominally christianized till a thousand years after the death of Christ. Sweden, for instance, was not christianized till the twelfth century, and the first independent church in Finland was established as late as A.D. 1220.

Christian doctrine (as by then fairly well established in the Church) and Neo-Platonist thought. The basic notion in these Pseudo-Dionysian writings is the union of God and the soul, making possible the deification of man. Pseudo-Dionysius became the great channel through which that special, composite mystical tradition, half Christian, half Neo-Platonic, was mediated within Christianity, where within a mood of orthodox Christian restraint it flourished as a separate tradition, generally tolerated and sometimes encouraged in the Church. It appears in a very restrained form in the Benedictine tradition, which will be considered in a separate section, and then in a more developed form in the later Middle Ages. Ruysbroeck, for instance, the fourteenth-century Flemish mystic, was directly indebted to the Pseudo-Dionysian writings; Eckhart and Boehme are in the same tradition.

In that mystical tradition various ingenious devices were used to reconcile this very Hellenic strain of mysticism with Christian doctrine. For example, the question was raised: since through the Fall man has lost the original powers God gave him, how could his soul respond in such a way as to achieve direct union with God? The mystics answered that though man was indeed as corrupt as official Christian doctrine proclaimed him to be, there remained in him one "cell," one single surviving healthy point of contact, which made possible God's entry into the soul and man's growth in mystical union with divine Being. In that literature occurs also another notion that much affected some kinds of mystical tradition within Christianity. The mind is to be emptied of all intellectual knowledge as well as of all images from the senses, so as to produce a great "darkness" that is an indispensable groundwork for its illumination by God.

The notion of the clearing of the mind of "ordinary" knowledge to make possible its filling with "supernatural" knowledge reappears in later works such as the anonymous fourteenth-century English mystical treatise, *The Cloud of Unknowing*. It appears in the great Renaissance Spanish mystics, a very distinctive Christian tradition. St. John of the Cross (1542–1591), for example, calls for a rejection of images (the Dark Night of Sense) followed by a rejection of the conceptual contents of the mind (the Dark Night of the Soul), in preparation for the mystic union with God. The same observation must be made with respect to both the late medieval German and the Spanish Renaissance mystics—if we are to reject images and thoughts, we must first have images and thoughts to reject. Moreover, the mind that has rejected image x is not the same as the mind that has rejected image y. Then arises the question, are not the metaphysical and theological starting points in some measure at least determinative of the nature of the experience the mystic will have and of the cognition he is to achieve, whatever it be? Such epistemological problems must be considered later.

Among the numerous other mystical traditions to be found in the extraordinarily variegated life of the Christian Church, one more, the Salesian tradition, should be noted here. Developed within the Church in seventeenth-century France, inspired by the life and personality of St. Francis of Sales (1567–1622), and elaborately described by the Abbé Bremond (1865–1933) in his eleven-volume work, *Histoire littéraire du sentiment religieux en France,* the Salesian tradition was very much the child of the humanistic Renaissance. In the Middle Ages the cultivation of the spiritual life had been generally accounted proper only for the cloister or hermitage. It was associated with the austerities of monastic life. Now came a new outlook: the mystic way is open to people living ordinary lives in the world. The mystic, by reason of his having attained friendship with God, will also be a master of human friendship. An Anglican writer has roundly said, "A mystic is one who has fallen in love with God." [23] That is very much in the spirit of the Salesian tradition, which stressed *pur amour*, the pure love of God, at the heart of a Christian humanism (*humanisme dévot*) that issues in a deep human friendship that is inseparable from the mystic's ultimate aim. Through keeping company with God, men and women living ordinary lives in the world acquire a special kind of spiritual charm and capacity for human understanding and affection. To those who had thought of mysticism in terms of hair shirts and severe fastings, the new, humane understanding of the mystic way was immensely attractive and suggested the notion of the beauty, delicacy, and even elegance of the spiritual life. The saint, by virtue of his cultivation of that life, became the perfect gentleman.

Benedictine Contemplation

We must now return to an earlier stage in Christian history to deal with a special mystical tradition. We have already noted that in the Christian Church vigilance to preserve what was commonly accepted as apostolic doctrine acted as a brake on mystical enterprise. In the Latin West there was, however, another restraining force. Rome was indubitably, in philosophy and literature, the inferior of Greece. When the Romans tried to incorporate into their culture the insights of the Greek philosophers and the graces of the Greek poets, they succeeded, by and large, only in mere imitativeness, while bringing into Roman society all the licentiousness of Greek life. Rome's own traditional virtues were administrative and judicial. These, fostering love of order (*ordo*), together with the characteristic Roman Stoic respect for intellectual sobriety and seriousness (*gravitas*), produced in the best type of Roman during the latter days of the Empire a suspicion of the wilder mystical enterprises into which Christianity, because of its inextricable ties with the Hellenic world, was always tempted to engage.

The great founder of monasticism in the West, St. Benedict of Nursia (c.480–550), was typically Roman in temperament and outlook, and the spirit he injected into his monastic community permanently affected even

[23] G. C. Rawlinson, quoted in E. Allison Peers, *Studies of the Spanish Mystics* (London: Sheldon Press, 1927), vol. 1, p. xiii.

the mysticism that grew up in the Benedictine tradition. The peculiarly restrained and austere form of that Benedictine mystical tradition, firmly grounded in a Christian *humanitas* and a *pax christiana*, is exhibited with masterly skill by a twentieth-century English Benedictine abbot, Dom Cuthbert Butler, in a book he advisedly entitled *Western Mysticism* as distinguished from "mysticism in the west." [24]

Dom Butler examines three historical figures whom he takes to be the greatest mystical geniuses in the Latin tradition he has in mind—Augustine, Gregory the Great, and Bernard of Clairvaux. He points out that the term "mysticism" has come to be applied to "many things of many kinds: to theosophy and Christian Science; to spiritualism and clairvoyance; to demonology and witchcraft; to occultism and magic . . . to other-worldliness, or even mere dreaminess and impracticability in the affairs of life; to poetry and painting and music of which the motif is unobvious and vague." [25] It has been identified with all sorts of attitudes, from the deeply sacramental, Franciscan view of nature to a mere distaste for ecclesiastical institutionalism. Noting the influence of Pseudo-Dionysius and the tradition we have considered in the previous section, he goes on to say that, though the work of Pseudo-Dionysius translated into Latin much affected the West, "the old word 'contemplation' held its ground, so that 'mystical' did not become current until the later Middle Ages, and 'mysticism' is quite a modern word." [26]

Augustine's claim is expressed in his well-known words: "My mind in the flash of a trembling glance came to Absolute Being—That Which Is." [27] This claim may be said to be of a conscious, direct, and objective intellectual intuition of "Absolute Being" or, in language more typical of the mystics, as Dom Butler suggests, "the experimental perception of God's Presence and Being." [28] Benedict, in the Prologue to his *Rule*, invites the brethren to open their eyes to "the deifying light." [29]

The attainment of mystical experience of that order does not come cheaply or by accident. It is presumed by all the great Christian mystics to be the fruit of long and arduous training in prayer, perhaps for a great part of an entire lifetime. In the Benedictine tradition, the monk is trained from the first day of his novitiate in strenuous daily exercises in prayer calculated to induce a habit of contemplative activity leading to a sense of the presence

[24] Cuthbert Butler, *Western Mysticism*, 2nd ed. (London: Constable & Co., 1927). It contains, besides an excellent anthology of key passages, the best treatment of Benedictine spirituality available in English and the best introduction both to the appreciation and to the philosophical critique of mysticism.

[25] Ibid., p. 2.

[26] Ibid., pp. 1 and 3. "Contemplation" is not used by Benedict himself. Later Benedictine writers use it to signify a state of mind that arises out of fidelity to the *Rule*.

[27] St. Augustine *Confessions* 7, 23.

[28] Butler, *Western Mysticism*, p. 4.

[29] The *Rule* is the chief source for an understanding of Benedictine spirituality. It is available as a booklet—*St. Benedict's Rule for Monasteries*, trans. L. J. Doyle (Collegeville, Minn.: The Liturgical Press, St. John's Abbey, 1948).

of God. He is taught above all to see Christ in every human being. Experiences such as Augustine describes are always presumed to be unattainable except as the fruit of such long training, yet that long training by no means guarantees any extraordinary degree of contemplative joy.

That the experiences are anything other than wild emotional outbursts is also a typical Benedictine presupposition. They are taken to have, on the contrary, a long and often complex intellectual background. Very Benedictine in spirit is Dom Butler's admiration of Pascal's well-known "Memorial," containing the "barely articulate, incoherent exclamation of Pascal—the intellectual, the philosopher, the master of language and style." Dom Butler says these incoherent exclamations are "for me, beyond all compare the most eloquent and the most realistic" of all attempts to describe mystical experience. Many great minds have found them so.

What is remarkable about the document that Dom Butler so greatly admires? First, its curious precision (Pascal gives the exact date and almost the exact duration of his mystical experience); second, the particularization, the specification (in a very celebrated phrase) of whom he means by "God" (not a metaphysician's Absolute but, rather, Abraham's God); third, and most importantly, the certitude that a *transaction* has occurred. On Pascal's death the document was found, a scrap of parchment, stitched into the doublet he had worn:

In the year of grace 1654 Monday, 23 November,
the day of St. Clement, Pope and Martyr, and others in the Martyrology;
the eve of St. Chrysogonus, Martyr, and others;
from about half-past ten in the evening till about half an hour after midnight

FIRE

God of Abraham, God of Isaac, God of Jacob,
Not of the philosophers and scholars.
Certitude. Joy. Certitude. Emotion. Sight. Joy.
Forgetfulness of the world and of all outside God.
The world has not known Thee, but I have known Thee.
Joy! joy! joy! Tears of joy.
My God, wilt thou leave me?
Let me not be separated from Thee for ever.

For experiences of this order, more is needed than years of disciplined prayer. The mystics see in these experiences divine action. Pascal, though not technically in the Benedictine tradition, has the Benedictine spirit. Augustine Baker, a seventeenth-century English Benedictine, speaks of "fiery trials and purifications." [30] The sixteenth-century French Benedictine Abbot Louis de Blois observes that it is "a great thing, an exceeding great thing, in the time of this exile [that is, in this life] to be joined to God in the divine light by a mystical and denuded union." [31] These contemplatives, like all mystics, tend to use language that superficially sounds pantheistic,

[30] Butler, *Western Mysticism*, p. 14.
[31] Ibid., p. 11.

but which is simply the language of love. In a later tradition, the Spanish mystics sometimes explicitly rule out pantheistic interpretations of the experience by speaking of the cord of love (*hilo de amor*) that binds the soul to God yet by the same token preserves the pantheism-saving distinction between Deity and the mystic. The Benedictines provide similar safeguards by other means.

St. Gregory the Great, the second member of Dom Butler's triad, does it by his insistence on the transience of the act of contemplation.[32] Contemplation is achieved by stealth, in passing, delicately, suddenly. Contemplation is, as Gregory often says, not fixed but snatched—*non solide sed raptim.*[33] The soul is seized by God. The experience lasts for only a fleeting moment; then the soul is exhausted. Exhausted by what? By intense activity. Here is a clue to the nature of contemplation as understood in this tradition. It is anything other than a passive enjoyment. Though it is God who seizes the soul, the soul's response demands such effort that it can take only a moment of the experience before it falls back exhausted. "The mind cannot stand for long above itself." [34] Gregory says that the mind, when in this contemplative ecstasy, is like a dark, empty room through which a chink of light is penetrating the empty darkness.[35] It is only a glimpse of light; yet in so dark a room it seems as though the light is so great the room can hardly hold it. Gregory also stresses the effect such contemplation has in intensifying the subject's self-knowledge, making him humble and even conscience-stricken when he sees himself in the divine perspective.[36]

The twelfth-century St. Bernard of Clairvaux, third in the triad, endeavors similarly to express defining characteristics of the experience. It is paradoxically a sleep that is vigilant.[37] It transports the subject in two ways: in "light" (knowledge) and in "fervor" (love).

What is abundantly clear in this whole tradition is that contemplation is hard work. A phrase associated with the Benedictine tradition says, in allusion to the dignity of labor, "to work is to pray" (*laborare est orare*);[38] but the Benedictine contemplative also finds that that proposition is subject to a simple logical conversion: to pray is to work. The vision the contemplative achieves, whatever it is, is not a luxuriating in ready-made emotions, as indeed notoriously some religious phenomena appear to be. It is, rather, the end-product of a process that entails hard work, usually over a long period of time. It is never interpreted, however, simply as the result of such hard work. It is accounted, as is grace in Christian theology, a special gift of God. Nevertheless, the recipient of a gift must be, or be made to be, capable of receiving it. A man who cannot handle a sailboat is by definition

[32] Ibid., pp. 115 f.
[33] Gregory the Great, *Moralium,* 5.58. Cf. 7.53; 8.49–50; 23.43; 24.11.
[34] Ibid., 5.57.
[35] Gregory, *Hom, in Ezech* 2.5.17.
[36] *Moralium* 5.53; 23.43; 35.3.
[37] St. Bernard *Commentary on the Song of Solomon* 52.3.
[38] The phrase, though late in origin, accords with Benedict's ideals.

unable physically to receive a sailboat as a gift. It certainly does not follow, however, that my having learned to sail will result in my receiving the gift of a boat. The strongly monotheistic presuppositions behind the Benedictine tradition illustrate what has been already suggested in an earlier section of this chapter—namely, that well-developed forms of mysticism are so anchored to underlying metaphysical and theological presuppositions that apart from them they are likely to be grossly misunderstood. It is not enough to ask of a mystic whither he thinks he is going; we ought to ascertain whence, intellectually and theologically, he has come. Nevertheless, to say that is not to take back the observation already made about the relation of mystics to their counterparts in other religions.[39]

Objections to the Logic and Language of Mysticism

Some of the familiar objections to what the mystics say are based upon specially dogmatic philosophical positions, for example, those of so-called logical positivism, materialism, and epistemological phenomenalism. There are, nevertheless, very serious objections that the most philosophically open-minded must consider.

For instance, the upanishadic notion that Brahma is both Being (*sad*) and non-Being (*a-sad*) [40] is paradoxical. We saw much earlier that some paradoxes in religious language are explorable (as, we found, are certain examples taken from Christian theology), while others are intentionally unexplorable, such as the paradoxes of Zen. We might say, then, that the Brahma paradox just mentioned is a way of expressing a metaphysical notion about existence, to the effect that there is an *x* that lies beyond both Being and non-Being. Such a proposal might be unacceptable, of course, for many reasons, but it would not necessarily be unintelligible. The difficulty, however, is that the mystic tends to pour forth paradoxical utterances in such profusion and about such radical metaphysical questions that no method such as we used earlier for exploring paradoxes in Christian theology could be expected to meet the case. For example, God and Nature are identical yet non-identical; that-which-is-(or is-not-) God-and-Nature is both full and empty, both personal and impersonal, both static and dynamic. By what conceivable method could we make sense of such utterances?

Let us propose that "Being" in the upanishadic utterance quoted is used there in a special sense, less comprehensive than what we commonly mean when we set Being (that-which-exists) against non-Being (the non-existent), and that what is really being proposed is a special metaphysical theory such as, say, the essence-existence theory familiar in the Platonic tradition. Then what was being said might conceivably be thus interpreted: what we generally call existence is only a partial, reflective, or participatory existence, not the essential or real, which then may be said to be as much that kind of existence as it is nonexistence; that is, it is neither, in an absolute sense, yet in a participatory sense it is both. A person who, having no words for "inside" and "outside," might perhaps try to describe a bottle as being both convex and concave. So one might call an electric circuit both positive and negative. Again, we might say that evil is real yet nonreal, meaning that it is presented as a reality to me and therefore, though it is not metaphysically an absolute, I have to cope with it as if it were. When the mystic tells us that God and Nature are identical yet nonidentical, we might indeed propose that he is saying that Nature is God in one aspect, yet there is another aspect to God that is not Nature, so that the proposition should be restated: God_1 is nonidentical with Nature, and God_2 is identical with Nature. Such an interpretation, however, does not fit all cases. The great mystics seem to have gone beyond positions susceptible to such comparatively simple interpretations.

We might also propose that such apparent logical contradictions have their origin in pure poetry and that we are reading metaphysics into them. We are accustomed to poets telling us that birds fly with the speed of light yet are motionless in their flight. Such utterances are absurdities to the physicist yet acceptable as lyrical notions, since we can see what the poet is trying to capture. Poets have talked of the sound of plainsong "splashed" across a cathedral clerestory. Moreover, there is no doubt that the mystics do extensively use poetic language. Nevertheless, such a theory would not be at all adequate, because innumerable passages could be cited to show that the mystic is not intending to make *only* a poetic utterance; he is avowedly doing much more.

One might be bold enough to suggest that what is wrong is not the mystics' mysticism but our logic. Our logic, being geared to a fragmented state of affairs such as the world of "ordinary" experience, ceases to work in the realm of mystical experience. Such an objection raises difficult questions about the philosophy of logic that are beyond the scope of our inquiry and of our needs. In the nineteenth century Hegel and other idealists such as Bosanquet proposed special kinds of logic to fit the requirements of particular metaphysical systems or special philosophical positions. More recent philosophers have tended to say that logic is purely analytic and is therefore not designed for telling us anything about the external world but only for analyzing what in fact we say about that world. The laws of logic, such as the law of contradiction, may then be said to be simply linguistic rules. From there we may go on to say that since we are talking about the external world and have certain generally accepted presuppositions about it, we develop certain logical tools to deal with the way we think and talk about the world, as we develop mathematical rules or a grammar of language or of music to show the rationale of the way we talk or sing.

The matter is not so easily disposed of, however, for not only do we have mathematical constructs, such as infinity, of which we have no experience; we can construct grammars of all usable invented languages, such as Esperanto and Volapük, and presumably musicologists could construct a grammar of a kind of music that nobody has ever heard or could hear, being of a range beyond the capacity of the human ear. That is to say, musicologists would know how sounds which, as it happens, we cannot hear, would behave if we could hear them, and perhaps an imaginative composer could write a symphony for dogs, who have a different range of hearing from humans, in hope that they might appreciate it. So, though logic is an analytical tool, it is related to experience somewhat as are, for instance, mathematics and musical grammar. There are sounds that are only theoretically audible and sights that are only theoretically visible, but the rules that apply to our accustomed range would still apply in some way to them, too. So when the mystics talk, as indeed they often do, of a sound that is visible or a sight that is audible, we rightly object that, *prima facie* at least, they are guilty of a category confusion. There is no possible way, in any possible world, in which one could see a sound or hear a sight because *by definition* what we do with a sound is hear it and what we do with a sight is see it. Therefore, whatever the mystic is doing, he is not talking language that is logically explorable *as it stands*. Yet we all know what is meant by "music splashed on a Gothic wall."

Then is it figurative, analogical language? Yes, indeed; but what can the figure, the analogy, be, if the experience relates to a dimension so different from the dimension or dimensions in which we ordinarily move? When poets use figurative language, they are able to assume some knowable basis for the metaphor or analogy they employ. For instance, when the nineteenth-century American poet T. B. Aldrich talks of "weaving our fancies" on "the cunning loom of thought," anybody with even only the most elementary literary education knows exactly what he means because we all have some experience of the process of thinking and some understanding of what one does in weaving cloth. We can even understand what a mystical poet like William Blake is trying to tell us when he writes, somewhat in the manner of Coleridge, of "seeing the world in a grain of sand," for we have all seen a grain of sand and we all have some usable concept of "the world." The difficulty we encounter in the kind of mystical language with which we are now concerned arises when, knowing it is *prima facie* nonsensical, we are nevertheless willing to grant that it is presumably figurative and can see no way in which we could find out what the figure or analogy might be.

When we then ask what the mystic is trying to accomplish when he talks such language, we may be tempted to suppose it is like the Zen paradoxes we considered earlier, which have as their function, not the communication of ideas, but the performance of an action, the inhibition of an action, or the promotion of a state of mind. Such an interpretation, however, will not do at all. Whether we look at Vedanta or the Spanish mystics, it is plain that whatever else the mystics are doing they are attempting not only to induce in us a state of mind but also to communicate to us, implicitly if not explicitly, what we call metaphysical assertions, affirmations about that-which-is-the-case. Part of their difficulty is that they are unable, and know they are unable, to formulate them adequately even to themselves.

Of course, mystical experience *might* be all merely inept attempts at literary expression. The mystics *might* be perhaps so befuddled with emotion as to be unable to express, as skillful poets do, emotions that are almost commonplace among cultivated people and occur even among very ordinary folk. In that view mysticism would be just poor poetry. Perhaps the mystics are only trying to express feelings we all have when we are weighed down by a slightly unusual aggregation of emotions. For instance, there are certain places that so affect us by a variety of associations that, perhaps together with a certain piece of music and a certain frame of mind, they may cause us to feel something that we call "too terrible for words." Sometimes we truthfully tell a friend that "no words can express" the depth of our sorrow at his bereavement. There is now and then something in our hearts that seems to defy expression, let alone description, something that we long to express but cannot. We may be quite willing to admit, however, that it is a combination of quite natural forces.

The possibility that the mystics are indeed misguidedly trying to read a metaphysical truth-claim into their perplexity over such complex human emotions is not to be ignored. If we found such an interpretation really adequate for what the mystics are saying, we should have to accept it; but in fact an inspection of mystical literature as a whole makes abundantly clear that, although of course there is almost certain to be an element of such emotionalism in mystical literature, the principal difficulty in communication with which mystics are grappling is not emotional but logical and artistic. That is, they are unable to conceptualize what they somehow feel ought to be conceptualizable, are unable to express what they feel should be somehow expressible, and are unable to make coherent to their fellow mortals what has seemed superlatively coherent to themselves.

We need not, however, give up either our logic or our language on the one hand or, on the other, the mystics' claims. We have to recognize that the mystics, if their fundamental claim were true (that is, that the experience they have is completely ineffable), would have an impossible task. They might be wrong, however, in their assertion of complete ineffability. We all tend to exaggerate, and mystics are not exempt from that common human tendency.

Perhaps the mystics' experience is not completely ineffable, but only almost so, in which case their task would be not impossible but only extremely difficult and therefore a challenging prospect. In attempting to accept the challenge of communicating their experience they would make mistakes, sometimes ridiculous ones. Like the rest of us when we attempt tasks largely beyond our powers, they would be prone to get things muddled and to talk in a wild or confused way, as, for instance, when we are trying to tell a narrow-minded factory worker who has never been out of his home town what life on a farm is, or a similarly unimaginative farm hand about Fifth Avenue or the Rue Royale. If I told a hypothetical Martian logician about some students who called the University German Circle square, he might well keep on saying, "Come on, now, even on your funny planet *no* circle can be square, *no* square circular. It is a logical impossibility. So don't give me these literary excursions. they couldn't possibly affect the logic." I might at length greet his gibe that the logical acumen of our students was obviously very inferior to the Martians' with a "Dammit, that circle they are talking about *is* square." It is to be assumed that I would not be trying either to plague or to bamboozle him but had simply lost patience. That loss of patience might be reprehensible in a teacher, but then we cannot all have all the virtues all the time. If the claims of the mystics are justified, they must face more occasions for worse exhaustion of their patience.

Well might the mystics lose patience with others, but according to their own testimony their difficulty is not only with others but with themselves. They cannot formulate their experience even to themselves. The intelligent adolescent knows in his heart that his strange "mixed-up" feelings are the result of his psychosomatic maturation. The person who, perplexed by his perhaps overwhelming feelings of joy or despair in connection with certain human situations, also knows that the malaise lies deep in his psyche. The mystics, however, feel certain that their experience is the experience not only of a reality beyond them but of the most important of all realities beyond them, and they feel *Angst* acutely because they cannot express that reality when they feel sure that, in principle, it ought to be expressible. Might it be that their experience is not wholly inexpressible even within the confines of our human language and of the logic we devise as a tool for using it well, though in the state of human knowledge at present and in the foreseeable future there is no way of formulating the mystics' vision?

We may have a clue along such lines in the reflection that if in, say, the eighteenth century a visionary could have seen what scientists now take to be the result of the Einsteinian space–time theory, and had tried to formulate it, that visionary would have inevitably failed to do so not only for others but for himself. In terms of Newtonian physics and in the general state of human knowledge in the Age of Enlightenment, the notion of a nonmechanistic universe and the vision of "curved space" would have seemed indeed ridiculous. Euclidean space is *not* curved, and to have talked of it as curved (whatever be the merits of that particular metaphorical usage today) would have seemed as contrary to logic as talking of a square circle

or of the sound of a sight. Since some scientific thinkers today incline to
the view that much of the intellectual incomprehension of religious ideas
is due to the persistence of outmoded Newtonian models among contemporary professional philosophers, any insight suggested by such a clue ought
to be taken very seriously indeed. The mystics might be seeing in their
own way what no one can possibly express in any human terms because
no conceptual model exists to make possible the formulation of their mystical
vision.

Agapē and *Erōs* in Mysticism

We have seen that mystical phenomena raise a special question to which
we may now address ourselves—the analogy of love. All mystical literature
suggests it, but how could an immense range of phenomena, such as those
to which the designation "mystical" is given, have a single common element
like love?

As we saw in a much earlier chapter, an analogy requires four terms.
The following, for instance, might be proposed:

$$\frac{agap\bar{e}: \text{mysticism}}{er\bar{o}s: \text{love}}$$

Since, however, there may be both erotic and agapistic elements in love
and also in mysticism, that obviously will not do. Let us then propose:

$$\frac{\text{mystic: his mystical experience}}{\text{lover: his experience of love}}$$

If, however, the term "mysticism" is, as Dom Butler has suggested, too vague
to function as a term at all, how can "mystical experience" function as
a term in an analogy?

At one end of the spectrum of mystical experience we have seen (a) a
quest for new feeling-experiences that strongly suggests both an autoerotic
fixation and the attempt, familiar in drug abuse, to enlarge the scope of
such narcissistic preoccupations, and (b) a compulsive tendency to turn back
to old feeling-experiences that similarly remind us of drug addiction. At
the other end of the spectrum is an extremely disciplined engagement that
may include, besides much else, many years of well-organized aesthetic and
conceptual activity. This latter sort of mysticism, contradistinguished from
the other sort, is not anti-intellectual. Though emotion may accompany
it, as indeed it may accompany mathematics and music, it purports to be
by no means essentially emotional but, rather, on the side of reason, that
is, of what Plato would have called *nous*. Yet it is not intellectual in the
sense in which, say, mathematical activity is; nor yet again is it aesthetic
as is, say, musical activity. Such activities may play a role in it, but only
somewhat as science plays a role in the art of medicine. Like medicine it

is therapeutic, and it may be said to be soteriological in aim; nevertheless, while it "saves me" from self-centeredness it always entails the recognition of and moral response to a That-which-is-other, accounted of fundamental importance for its own sake.

What common element could there be in a phenomenon that appears at one end of the spectrum as purely self-seeking and innocent of (when not consciously hostile to, or scornful of) metaphysical enterprises, and at the other end as selfless and as respectful toward these? How can there be a common element in that in which one subject may be a spectator with a lust for novel sensations, while another is a deeply committed participant sensitive to what he takes to be the supreme metaphysical reality confronting him with inescapable moral demands, responsiveness to which constitutes his liveliest and most enduring joy? Not only might love be that common element, but there is no other possible candidate. At first we might be inclined to agree with Dom Butler that the use of the term "mysticism" to cover such a wide range of phenomena is to make the term so unspecific as to deprive it of all useful function. When we reflect, however, that the term "love" is exactly the same case, not only may we begin to see the force of the analogy; it provides us with both a basis for understanding the nature of mysticism and a reason why the spectrum of mystical phenomena must be as wide and as variegated as it is.

Let us examine the parallel between mysticism and love. We all know the sad case of the person who wants to love but who, because of psychological impotence or frigidity, cannot engage in love in a normal way. Such a person may succeed in extricating himself from his pathetic predicament by making the leap from his inverted, futile, self-centered, self-defeating love to a love that is extroverted in the normal way. To do so, however, may be extremely difficult. Everyone experiences some degree of difficulty in turning from a focus inwards to a focus outwards. Those who are unfortunate enough to be permanently "stuck" in their inverted attitude of self-love are unable to come to terms with either themselves or the world. They suffer, therefore, an extreme sense of maladjustment to both. They hate the world for its hostility and themselves for their sterility. Driven by their sad condition into an autoerotic outlook in which perforce they have no alternative but to understand "love" as a pleasurable experience in which the sole value-criterion is the intensity or even simply the "amount" of the pleasure, they become more and more trapped in their own psychic web.

To argue them out of their sorry state is as impossible a task as arguing a suicide out of his self-intended slaughter. To a proposal that in self-giving one "enters into a new dimension of love," or that one "finds one's self by losing it," they will inevitably reply to the effect that these are pseudo-statements, meaningless absurdities. Someone may point out that one cannot love another person without first being able to accept oneself and one cannot accept oneself without first being able to love another person, but how by any kind of linguistic analysis can one ever show what that means in terms of altruistic love to anyone who has not already discovered it for himself in love-making? One may talk of kindness, but the person who has never extricated himself from self-love knows only a *sort* of kindness, is incapable of understanding any other sort, and is no more likely to be taught by any kind of linguistic analysis than a person who has never seen the sea could learn, by such analytical methods, what it is to love a ship, or one who has never been out of Manhattan what it is to love a farm. The difficulty is not that he cannot imagine a ship or a farm; he has seen hundreds of both in pictures, but he has never known the *relationship*, the involvement, the commitment. The plight of the victim of self-love is not merely one of ignorance. On the contrary, he has some knowledge: at least he knows enough to avoid making the leap out of his prison, how to take a stand, how to make a choice against it, and how to adjust to a constricted life as another person adjusts to life in the world beyond the prison of self-love.

What the other sort of mystic does and is can also be seen in terms of the analogy of love. For at the other end of the spectrum from self-love (with all sorts of variations and combinations in between) is a self-giving love that is profoundly sacrificial. The lover will give himself so wholly as to be willing, *in extremis,* to die for the beloved. Not only would he literally give his last cent; if the beloved needed a cornea or a kidney, and a transplant seemed medically promising, the lover would not even hesitate. On the contrary, if he did give his sacrifice so much as a thought it would be to rejoice that he had a kidney or an eye to bestow. That is indeed a very different kind of love, yet it is not wholly detached from the selfish kind.

Nor are we to suppose that it comes out of the clear blue sky. Such love does not come cheap or by instinct. A romantic young couple may *feel* as if the one would sacrifice anything for the other, and that may be a "beautiful" feeling, for through it is prefigured to them a vision of the love they have committed themselves to find; but that love is not found without long and arduous discipline and struggle. The commitment entails hardship and risk. It is a commitment to growth in a relationship and, as in all growth, there is no absolute guarantee of success. The attainment of love and friendship of this order is immensely difficult at best, and without the mysterious germ of desire for it, the quest is as ridiculous as the attainment is impossible. That is why those who have known something of such love and friendship speak of its having been "blessed," for they recognize in it an element (they need not label it "God") that transcends themselves. Engagement in love of this kind is engagement in a process of entry into a new dimension of being.

The best way of trying to grasp the difference between the two extremes of love and the two extremes of mystical experience is by inspecting what lies between, in the intervening frequencies or wavelengths of the spectrum.

Presumably few people, if any, either completely achieve the kind of sacrificial love we have just considered or totally fail ever to emerge from sexual infantilism. Most of us, if not all of us, fall somewhere in between, attaining in varying degrees the maturity that brings self-fulfillment through the conquest of self-love. Such maturity, like sanity, is only a matter of degree; many of us who are eminently sane have mild neuroses of various kinds, and many who are far from being certifiably insane have very severe ones, while many raving lunatics have lucid moments. An important consequence follows from this: few people, if any, are wholly unable to understand what we are talking about when we talk as we have been talking of self-giving and self-love; nevertheless, there are obvious reasons why a person might so habituate himself or herself to a pretense of being unable to see as to become in fact functionally blind, that is, fixed at a point in the spectrum, and unable to move from it.

In mystical experience the case appears to be in such respects precisely the same. Perhaps no one, not even a Pascal or a John of the Cross, has ever fully achieved mystical union with God even in those special moments they so impressively celebrate in literature, and probably no one is totally devoid of any notion of what it means to enter into the dimension of life in which the mystic moves. Many, however, have reached a point where, for psychological reasons, they have shrunk from the challenges and perils attendant upon further progress and have found a *modus vivendi*, a niche, so to speak, where they feel they can hope to settle down and escape further challenge and engagement. When we do that we are saying to ourselves, in effect, what an elderly man or woman might say to a therapist treating an ossifying leg joint: "It's far from what it ought to be, but it will do—*I can live with it.* Leave it alone." Any attempt to disturb spiritual ossification is naturally resisted with similar zest.

Critiques such as Dr. Richard Gale has leveled at the late Walter Stace[41] eloquently exhibit the impossibility of understanding by analytical techniques the most interesting of the problems mysticism raises. Gale's critique seems plausible. Stace, in his *Time and Eternity,* developed a theory of the intersection of the "eternal" and the "natural" orders. That intersection is what the mystic experiences. He lives in both orders and at the moment of his mystical experience the two orders intersect. Gale points out, not without some justification, that Stace, in his answer to the seeming contradiction between the eternal order of being and the temporal one, makes an exclusive disjunction that does not seem to fit his intersection theory. The mystic, during his mystical moment, can see no opposition because then the "natural" has ceased to exist for him, but most of his life is lived in the "natural" order and there he does feel the contradiction. Stace argues

[41] Richard Gale, "Mysticism and Philosophy," reprinted from *The Journal of Philosophy* 57 (1960) in *Philosophy of Religion,* ed. Steven M. Cahn (New York: Harper & Row, 1970), pp. 301–303.

that either we have to take our stance outside the mystical experience, in naturalistic fashion, in which case mystical experiences are purely subjective feelings and emotions, or else we have to take up our stance inside the "eternal," in which case the "natural" order is illusory. In terms of such a strong disjunction there would seem to be no way of taking both these standpoints at the same time. Gale concludes that Stace's intersection theory is incompatible with the disjunction Stace himself makes.

Now of course one could analytically approach the problem of, say, happiness in a very similar way. Let us suppose I am engulfed by poverty, ignorance, and disease and am very unhappy. So accustomed am I to unhappiness that I account it the natural state of affairs, but once in a while I do have a fleeting moment of serenity and joy. During that moment all the misery of my life vanishes. It has ceased, as it were, to exist. Then I return to my "normal" miserable state, in which, being of an analytical turn of mind, I perceive an exclusive logical disjunction. I conclude I must take up one stance or the other; either I must say I was mistaken about that moment of happiness, and admit I did not *know* happiness at all but only had a *feeling* of it when in fact I was not "really" happy, or else I must deny that the misery I generally feel is real, and go on to assert that, on the contrary, I have no reason to commiserate with myself as I do because my feeling of unhappiness is without foundation since logically it can have no basis in reality. It would be very possible for me to go on like that by way of academic exercise, but I would not in fact believe my own logic. I would know I was only playing a game with myself. All the time I would see what had happened. My customary condition was one in which there was an unfair share of human misery; nevertheless, it was not all of a piece, completely flat and invariable. There were slight undulations in it, days or hours when I seemed to get a little the better of my misery and other days when it seemed to get the better of me. By contrast, however, there were those rare moments when I felt so completely victorious over my usual misery that it seemed not to exist, for the excellent reason that in those moments it had in fact ceased to exist.

Analytically, Stace's intersection theory is, of course, incompatible with his exclusive disjunction. Existentially, the suggestion of incompatibility is as trivial as a child's objection that if it be true (as is often said) that I cannot love two people at the same time, then I cannot love myself when I love you. As a matter of fact, that is precisely what a sexually infantile person does say in effect, and every sexually mature person knows why the logic of the reasoning breaks down in the face of the facts.

Very unprofitable indeed are such attempts to deal with the paradoxes of mystical experience, which can be phenomenologically much better understood by an inspection of the paradoxes of human love. Moreover, the whole obvious relation between mysticism and sex is then illuminated.

Mysticism is no more a cheap, neurotic distortion of sex, as Leuba and other such psychologists of the Freudian school have suggested, than is sex a distortion of mysticism, as critics have sometimes forced the unwary protagonists of the mystic into retorting. On the contrary, as there are cheap forms of sex that reflect the infantilism of those who indulge in them, so there are corresponding forms of mysticism. For mysticism is nothing if not the love of God, and that there should be infantile forms of it as well as mature ones is unastonishing. It is also one reason why the statement "God is love" is, even to people who claim to find meaning in the term "God," extremely ambiguous. The ambiguity springs, however, from the nature of love itself. Love, like mysticism (and indeed like religion, as we saw in an early chapter), is not necessarily creative and therefore good; it may be destructive and therefore bad. The love life of a human being reflects the same kinds of failures he may sustain and successes he may achieve in his pursuit of, or response to, the love of God. The question of *agapē* and *erōs* will be taken up again in the last chapter of this book, in a concluding exploration of the concept of cosmic love.

QUESTIONS ON CHAPTER VIII

1   What do you take to be the general characteristics common to all forms of mysticism?

2   Suppose that the description of mystical experience that classical mystical writers give sounds similar to the type of awareness that certain drugs can produce. What would be wrong with going on to assume that the states induced by such drugs are similar to, if not identical with, the states the mystics describe?

3   Consider the relation of yoga to mysticism.

4   Consider the difference between Bhakti mysticism and mysticism in the upanishadic tradition.

5   Is it proper to talk of a "Jewish" or "Islamic" or "Christian" mysticism? Give reasons.

6   Between mysticism and human love a connection is universally recognized. What, precisely, do you take the connection to be?

7   Compare the Benedictine tradition with Gnostic or theosophical types of mysticism. What common elements, if any, do you see, and what radical differences?

8   What is the importance, in relation to mysticism, of the notion of sacrifice?

BIBLIOGRAPHICAL SUGGESTIONS

Bennett, Charles A. A. *A Philosophical Study of Mysticism.* New Haven, Conn.: Yale University Press, 1931.

Bridges, Hal. *American Mysticism: From William James to Zen.* New York: Harper & Row, 1971. Considers a variety of writers such as Abraham Heschel, D. T. Susuki, Rufus Jones, and Thomas Merton, and exhibits the interweaving of American mysticism with pragmatism.

Burnaby, John. *Amor Dei.* London: Hodder & Stoughton, 1938. A study in St. Augustine's theology of love. Useful as contrast to Nygren, *Agape and Eros.*

Butler, Cuthbert, O.S.B. *Western Mysticism.* 2nd ed. London: Constable & Co., 1927. First published in 1922; second edition has "Afterthoughts." The most valuable work in English on the Benedictine tradition; indispensable to students of all Christian mystical traditions.

Cuttat, Jacques-Albert. *The Encounter of Religions.* Translated by P. de Fontnouvelle and E. McGrew. New York: Desclée Company, 1960. A valuable study of Hesychasm.

D'Arcy, M. C., S.J. *The Mind and Heart of Love.* New York: Meridian Books, 1956.

Dasgupta, S. *Hindu Mysticism.* Chicago: Open Court Publishing Co., 1927.

Eliade, Mircea. *Myths, Dreams and Mysteries.* New York: Harper Torchbooks, 1957. Instructive background for the study of mysticism by an eminent contemporary historian of religion.

Graham, Alfred, O.S.B. *The Love of God.* New York: Image Books, 1959 (first published in 1940). An exposition of Benedictine spirituality.

Heiler, F. *Prayer.* Translated by S. McComb. New York: Oxford University Press, Galaxy Books, 1958 (first published in 1932). See especially Chapters 6–8.

Hume, R. E. *The Thirteen Principal Upanishads.* London: Oxford University Press, 1921. Contains a translation of the Sanskrit text, an outline of upanishadic philosophy, and an annotated bibliography.

Inge, W. R. *Christian Mysticism.* London: Methuen & Co., 1899. Though dated and written from a Victorian Christian Neo-Platonist standpoint, still a very useful work by one of the greatest minds of that time.

James, William. *The Varieties of Religious Experience.* New York: Longmans, Green & Co., 1902. A very well-known book, useful for beginners, as an introduction to religious phenomena associated with forms of mysticism.

John of the Cross. *Dark Night of the Soul.* Translated by E. Allison Peers. New York: Doubleday, Image Books, 1959.

Jones, Rufus. *New Studies in Mystical Religion.* New York: Macmillan Co., 1927.

Jones, Rufus. *Studies in Mystical Religion.* London: Macmillan & Co., 1909.

Kirk, Kenneth E. *The Vision of God.* New York: Harper Torchbooks, 1966. A classic study. The author, who was Bishop of Oxford, was much influenced by the Abbé

Bremond, whose *Histoire du sentiment religieux en France,* a monumental work in eleven volumes (1915-32), treats the Salesian tradition in relation to what the author calls *humanisme dévot.*

Knowles, David, O.S.B. *The English Mystical Tradition.* New York: Harper Torchbooks, 1961.

Leuba, James H. *The Psychology of Religious Mysticism.* London: Kegan Paul, Trench, Trubner & Co., 1925. Written from a narrowly Freudian standpoint and very hostile to Christian faith.

McCann, Justin, O.S.B. *Saint Benedict.* New York: Doubleday, Image Books, 1958. A good modern biography.

Newman, L. I. and Spitz, S., eds. *The Hasidic Anthology.* New York: Schocken Books, 1963 (first published in 1934). Useful collection of passages from the Jewish mystical tradition of the hasidim.

Nicholson, R. A. *The Mystics of Islam.* London: G. Bell & Sons, 1914. Useful for Sufism.

Nicholson, R. A. *Studies in Islamic Mysticism.* Cambridge: At the University Press, 1921.

Nygren, A. *Agape and Eros.* Translated by P. S. Watson. Philadelphia: Westminster Press, 1953.

Otto, R. *Mysticism East and West.* Translated by B. L. Bracey and R. C. Payne. New York: Macmillan Co. 1932.

Peers, E. Allison, trans. and ed. *The Life of Teresa of Jesus: The Autobiography of St. Teresa of Avila.* New York: Doubleday, Image Books, 1960.

Peers, E. Allison. *Studies of the Spanish Mystics.* 2 vols. London: Shelden Press, 1927. Contains an extensive and scholarly bibliography.

Poulain, A., S.J. *The Graces of Interior Prayer.* London: Kegan Paul, 1910.

Saher, P. J. *Eastern Wisdom and Western Thought.* New York: Barnes & Noble, 1970. See especially Chapter 2, "Mescalin and LSD: the Problem of Synthetic Sainthood."

Smith, Margaret. *The Sufi Path of Love.* London: Luzac & Co., 1954.

Stace, W. T. *Mysticism and Philosophy.* Philadelphia: J. B. Lippincott Co., 1960. A study which, because of its open-mindedness to both mystical and naturalist stances, provides a useful and attractive introduction to the problems of mysticism.

Stace, W. T., *Time and Eternity.* Princeton, N.J.: Princeton University Press, 1952.

Stiernotte, A. P., ed. *Mysticism and the Modern Mind.* New York: Liberal Arts Press, 1959.

Suzuki, D. T. *Manual of Zen Buddhism.* New York: Grove Press, 1960.

Suzuki, D. T. *Mysticism, Christian and Buddhist.* New York: Harper & Brothers, 1957.

Thurston, H., S.J. *The Physical Phenomena of Mysticism.* Chicago: Henry Regnery Co., 1952.

Underhill, Evelyn. *Mysticism.* London: Methuen & Co., 1911. A standard work on the principal Christian mystical traditions, with an extensive bibliography. Still an indispensable work.

Underhill, Evelyn. *The Mystics of the Church.* New York: Schocken Books, 1964.

Underhill, Evelyn. *Practical Mysticism.* New York: E. P. Dutton & Co., 1915. A small and elementary book.

von Hügel, F. *The Mystical Element of Religion as Studied in St. Catherine of Genoa and her Friends.* 2nd ed. 2 vols. New York: E. P. Dutton & Co., 1923. Very influential in its day and still an important work. Baron von Hügel was a Roman Catholic layman with views that were accounted liberal and advanced in his day.

Watkin, E. I. *The Philosophy of Mysticism.* London: G. Richards, 1920.

Zaehner, R. C. *Mysticism, Sacred and Profane.* Oxford: Clarendon Press, 1957. Includes an interesting chapter entitled "God and Nature" (Proust and Rimbaud) and an account of an experiment at Oxford with mescalin.

IX

DEATH AND FUTURE LIFE

Die, my dear doctor? That's the last thing I shall do.
Henry John Temple, Lord Palmerston (1784–1865),
last words

Even through the hollow eyes of death I spy life peering.
William Shakespeare (1564–1616),
Richard II

The Notion of "Survival After Death"

"To survive" means "to live on," that is, "to go on living." To talk of "surviving death" would seem, then, to be as absurd as speaking of "walking after you have stopped walking." Of course if one could say, "Ah, but you had not *really* stopped walking," then there would be no serious difficulty about saying you went on doing so. So if we could say, "But he did not *really* die," there would be no logical impropriety in our talking of "survival after death."

Some doctrines of immortality do say precisely that. When the self is taken to be a "soul" or "spirit" wholly independent of the body, which is accounted no more than its dress, then death means nothing more than the detachment of the soul's clothes. The "real self" is unaffected. Death has been an incident not fundamentally more important than taking off my pajamas and putting on my shirt. Plato writes as if that were so. Some forms of Oriental religion also envision the self in such a way, and their adherents may even talk of degrees or layers of selfhood. In this view there is an "essential" or "core" self contained within various layers that may be stripped from the self without destroying its identity. Of these layers the body is the most superficial husk.

Such notions are alien not only to contemporary philosophical understanding of the nature of the self but also to the traditional orthodox Christian doctrine of a life beyond death. The notion of a mind or soul operating independently of *any* kind of body seems not only scientifically and philosophically unintelligible in terms of today's structures of thought but also alien to what we know of all dimensions of reality. In any case, it is contrary to Christian orthodoxy. Despite some confusions in early Christian writings, the basic Christian doctrine on afterlife, clearly enunciated by St. Paul,[1] is not one of immortality but of resurrection.[2] Such a view may be beset with philosophical difficulties no less than is the other one, but it is important to see at the outset that if so, they are different difficulties.

Is the Notion of an Afterlife Nonsensical?

As Donald MacKinnon suggests at the beginning of his well-known and perceptive paper on death,[3] many contemporary philosophers tend to regard a claim to survive death as the very paradigm of a nonsense statement, whose syntactical improprieties it is their peculiar business to exhibit. We talk properly, of course, of escaping death, and there are interesting cases of people who, having been legally and medically pronounced dead, "come back to life," so raising interesting technical questions about the definition of the biological event that death is. Death is indubitably a clinical phenomenon and a biological event of paramount importance, attended by speedy decomposition of the corpse, but is there any more to be said about it that might merit philosophical inspection? There might conceivably be examinable evidence for a truth-claim such as those spiritists make who talk about life after death, for they assert that "spirits" produce empirical phenomena (table raps and the like) that can be examined; but how could one possibly examine a truth-claim such as Christians make about resurrection from the dead, for which *ex hypothesi* no such evidence could be available?

Whence, then, comes the conviction that makes the idea of resurrection acceptable to believers? In order to respond affirmatively to St. Paul's call to believe in the power of Christ's resurrection, which, he insists, provides hope for our own resurrection, or else to face the consequence that the whole teaching of the New Testament is "in vain," believers must be able first of all to attach some special and important meaning to the notion of resurrection from the dead. Since *prima facie* there is no way in which we can even go about trying to discover meaning in that which by definition seems beyond all that of which we have any experience at all, the idea of resurrection from the dead seems doomed to unintelligibility unless within some special metaphysical structure that would invest it with meaning.

A doctrine of immortality such as Plato's may look more hopeful. If so, the reason for its greater promise is the one we have already considered:

---

[1] E.g., Romans 6:5 and 1 Corinthians 15:42-58.

[2] See O. Cullmann, *Immortality of the Soul or Resurrection from the Dead?* (New York: Macmillan Co., 1958).

[3] Donald MacKinnon, "Death," in *New Essays in Philosophical Theology*, ed. A. Flew and A. MacIntyre (New York: Macmillan Co., 1955), pp. 261-266.

built into it is a special, metaphysical theory of the nature of the *psyche* as an eternal, indestructible essence, independently operative of the flesh in which it is temporarily embedded during its encampment on earth. Historically, such a metaphysical belief, from patristic times at least, was so woven into Christian doctrine, some resistance notwithstanding, as to seem practically inextricable from it. (Hence the medieval paradox of mortal sin, which "kills" the unkillable, immortal soul.) In the absence of such a metaphysical doctrine, the notion of an afterlife seems singularly unpromising. The basic Christian doctrine of the afterlife is, however, as we have seen, a doctrine of resurrection from the dead. If only the underpinnings of such a doctrine could be exposed, it might become intelligible.

When we then ask whether there is any presupposition that might make feasible an inquiry into the plausibility of a resurrection doctrine, we begin to discover the condition we seek. Being able to invest death with a meaning such as "the beginning of new life" hinges upon the kind of meaning we have already assigned to human existence. Everybody assigns some sort of meaning to it. Even Sartre, for instance, delineates meaning of a sort in the relation of *l'en soi* to *le pour soi,* and especially in the capacity of the individual to make choices, even though making the choice be forced upon him and may consist in putting out his tongue at that which is *jeté là, comme ça.* For all that the nihilists talk about the meaninglessness of life, they do invest it with a kind of meaning. It is not, however, a meaning that could make a resurrection doctrine palatable or desirable, even if it were intelligible. On the contrary, as life is an emetic, resurrection could only be a sort of super-emetic, more nauseating than life itself. Even if the archangel Gabriel were to greet Sartre personally as the latter awakened from the tomb, what could Sartre say other than something like: *"Tiens, encore une fois? Merde alors."* In order to attach meaning to any resurrection doctrine such as the traditional Christian one, we must first be able to discern a particular *kind* of meaning in human life.

Helmut Thielicke is among those who see in the nihilistic existentialists' preoccupation with death a greater valuation of life than they are usually ready to admit. He proposes that their "anxiety about death is actually rooted in a man's consciousness of value, in that his life as a person (the "I") ceases to exist; the unique fades away." [4] He quotes Groethuysen as having arrived at "the entirely correct conclusion that in every instance where 'the last moment' is accorded special significance it receives this significance not by being a farewell to a basically valueless life. On the contrary, death receives its significance from 'the value that is ascribed to life.' " [5]

[4] Helmut Thielicke, *Death and Life,* trans. Edward H. Schroeder (Philadelphia: Fortress Press, 1970), p. 65.

[5] Bernhardt Groethuysen, *Die Entstehung der bürgerlichen Weltanschauung in Frankreich,* vol. 1, *Das Burgertum und die katholische Weltanschauung* (Halle: Max Niemeyer, 1927), p. 83, as quoted by H. Thielecke, loc. cit.

How Believers Invest Death with Meaning

Certainly the believer (as we may usefully dub him here by way of practical shorthand) always sees in human life a nexus of meanings that posit belief that death really is more than the clinical phenomenon and biological event described in medical and legal texts. That is what Kant saw in his own way in his exposition of immortality as one of the three postulates. I act *as if* I were to live on beyond death. While some people are dull-eyed at twenty and radically without hope that human existence encompasses any more than the self-enclosed birth–copulation–death cycle, others at eighty are bright-eyed with relish for whatever may lie ahead. Since what lies ahead cannot be much in terms of life span, so far as gerontologists presently promise, one naturally wonders whether a merciful illusion of endless life may not intrude itself in one's declining years.

That does not seem to be at all the case, however, since typically the octogenarian in question is very acutely aware of the limits of his possible life span and may not be either particularly distressed by it or especially delighted at it. What seems remarkable is that he sometimes takes the trouble to learn new forms of art appreciation, or perhaps a new language, or else makes efforts to keep up with new discoveries in physics, when there are other ways he might conveniently pass away his time in occupations such as chess which keep the mind working without troubling it with last-minute attempts to understand the meaning of life. If at eighty or ninety I were to see death as an absolute end to my existence, I think chess would be one of the most fitting, and a dignified, way of passing much of my time.

The difference between a view such as Sartre's and the alternative suggested in the preceding paragraphs is well illustrated in the remarks of Berdyaev on the subject of the life–death antinomy. Berdyaev, taking notice of the fundamental place of the concept of death in writers like Kierkegaard, Heidegger, and even Freud, and asserting that the question of the immortality of the soul is part of a completely outdated metaphysic, goes on to say: "The fact of death alone gives true depth as to the question of the meaning of life. Life in this world has meaning just because there is death; if there were no death in our world, life would be meaningless. The meaning is bound up with the end. If there were no end, i.e., if life in our world continued forever, there would be no meaning in it." [6] Heidegger rightly remarks, in *Sein und Zeit* that the herd *(das Man)* is insensitive to the anguish of death, feeling only a low fear of it as that which makes life meaningless; but death, besides having this function, has another: it is a sign pointing to a deeper meaning in life. The fact that a life span consisting of an infinite series of time (the *aeviternitas* of the medieval schoolmen) would be meaningless

[6] Nicolas Berdyaev, *The Destiny of Man*, trans. Natalie Duddington (London: Geoffrey Bles, 1937), p. 317.

entails that death *must* occur if life is to have meaning. Of course, such a reflection does nothing to prove that life has this or that meaning. Nevertheless, when life is invested with a meaning such as to suggest resurrection to a life beyond death, death immediately acquires an appropriate meaning. That is no more than to say, however, that if you can first of all walk through life as a pilgrim, you will readily see that life must have an end, for such is the nature of every pilgrimage. An unending pilgrimage is a self-contradiction.

Belief in Afterlife Dependent on Metaphysical Views

If we look at life and death empirically, as we look on biological phenomena in general, we can reach no conclusion more favorable to belief in a life beyond than that which C. D. Broad set forth nearly half a century ago in a careful argument on the subject,[7] namely, that in spite of the absence of evidence of an afterlife and even in the face of some considerations that could be taken as evidence against it, there is no definite evidence against it, though "our ordinary scientific knowledge of the relation of body to mind most strongly suggests epiphenomenalism . . . which is most unfavorable to the hypothesis of human survival." Even an epiphenomenalism, however, provided that it is not the simplistic sort attributed to Simmias,[8] is by no means fatal to belief in a life beyond. (Teilhard's panentheism comprises an epiphenomenalism of a sort.) Yet if we are looking for an independent argument of the classic type we shall look in vain, for there could be no argument for life beyond death (except one based on the alleged occurrence of psychic phenomena, with which we are not concerned here) that was not in one way or another either grounded upon a religious belief in God and in God's having a certain nature, or else a corollary to one or another metaphysical proposition about divine Being or "ultimate Reality." Plato, for instance, in support of his argument for the immortality of the human soul, invoked metaphysical views about the self-motion of the soul and the principle of metempsychosis.

The Cambridge idealist philosopher John McTaggart (1866–1925) provides an illustration of the general contention that immortality doctrines are corollaries of metaphysical views. He conceived of an afterlife without any focus on divine Being in the theistic sense but consisting, rather, in converse among good minds. His pluralistic conception has some affinity with Sankhya doctrine, which we encountered in our last chapter. Sankhya is associated with but antedates the Jains and is one of the accepted forms of Hindu philosophy. McTaggart's conception was likewise dependent on

[7] C. D. Broad, *The Mind and Its Place in Nature* (London: Kegan Paul, Trench, Trubner & Co., 1925), pp. 523–533.
[8] Plato, *Phaedo* 85.

special views, *inter alia* the highly speculative opinion that the occurrence of deep friendships is inexplicable except on the basis of encounter in a previous existence. An argument for a McTaggart heaven cannot be framed without presuppositions such as he invoked.[9]

The "Shape of Death" in the Christian Fathers

The dependence of our understanding of the meaning of death upon our underlying metaphysical presuppositions is dramatically exhibited in the clash between biblical and Greek elements in patristic eschatology. Jaroslav Pelikan has brought the dependence out well in a little treatise on that clash. He considers five early Fathers who represent life as, respectively, arc, circle, triangle, parabola, and spiral.

The proper figure for human life, as presented by Tatian, is an arc, with a sharp beginning and an equally sharp end. In contrast stands Clement of Alexandria who, drawing his ideas from platonized sources, presented immortality as a circle: "The arc of existence does relate human living and dying to God, but it cannot draw the horizontal line of life after death. On the other hand, the circle of immortality successfully draws the line that extends from temporal to eternal existence, but it draws that line so well that the vertical dimension of dying to God and receiving life from him again seems to disappear from perspective. Cyprian seeks to do justice to both the horizontal and the vertical dimension of death. Therefore the most appropriate geometrical image to describe his picture of the shape of death appears to be the triangle. The base of the triangle represents his efforts to include the horizontal dimension, the apex of the triangle symbolizes his stress upon the vertical dimension. Thus Cyprian goes beyond both Tatian and Clement of Alexandria when he includes both the horizontal and the vertical in describing the shape of death as a triangle of mortality." [10] In the horizontal he is able to include, for instance, the classical "consolation literature" that comes from Greek sources and is mediated through Roman Storic writers such as Cicero. There is nothing specifically Christian about it, yet it can be appropriated by Christians. It is when the believer "dies to God, and then lives from God" that the apex of the triangle is seen. "Because trust in God even at the hour of death is more than the expectation of immortality, the Christian picture of the shape of death must have a vertical dimension, even when it uses figures and ideas like immortality or deliverance." [11]

In Origen's concept of eternity, all shapes, including that of death, are presented from a Christian standpoint that is unambiguously espoused to Platonism; yet Origen, in his more cautious moments, as when he is writing

[9] McTaggart's heaven was likened by satirical critics to a perpetual faculty meeting, a prospect which, however it may have looked at Cambridge in those halcyon days, would now be generally accounted an objectionably terrifying description of hell.
[10] Jaroslav Pelikan, *The Shape of Death* (Nashville, Tenn.: Abingdon Press, 1961), pp. 56 f.
[11] Ibid., p. 65.

his celebrated treatise against Celsus, makes clear that a Platonic idealism will not do. The nature of the body is not to be accounted abominable, for it is not involved in evil.[12] The cause of evil lies in mind, not matter. So for all his occasional disparagement of the "arc of existence" he "knows better when he thinks about it." In other words, he is more critical than he sometimes seems of the Platonic tradition that is his heritage. The diversity within historical existence is to be explained with reference to pre-existence of the soul, but what requires it is not the "eternal circle of being" but the act of God. Eternity is not a circle but a parabola.

Pelikan, in referring to Irenaeus, calls his view of the death–life antinomy "the spiral of history." Christ is the new pattern for the spiral, encompassing what was before but enhancing it. Irenaeus, though he has no carefully worked-out theory about the resurrection of Christ, attaches great importance to it in his scheme of salvation. Christ was obedient to the conditions of life, which include death, for to live a genuine human life means to live a life that is formed by the shape of death. "By going through death rather than around death, he transforms the shape of death into the shape of life. As a result of the first curve of the spiral it is necessary to say: 'In the midst of life we are in death.' But as a result of this second curve of the spiral it is possible to say: 'In the midst of death we are in life.' "[13]

What determines the view in every case, represented as it may be by spiral, parabola, triangle, circle, or arc, is the underlying view of the nature of God and of the relation of God to Nature, man, and history. No one could see death as the beginning of new life without a special view of God and these relationships. He who does see death as the beginning of new life will be wise to exercise an *ascesis* of the imagination when it comes to a question of delineating the details of the new life. Questions about the nature of the resurrected body cannot but be conjectural, not to say tiresome, since we have no means of knowing. The New Testament distinguishes *sarx* (flesh) from *soma* (body). The latter, an organizational principle rather than a specific "stuff," is what is said to be "resurrected." We do not know enough even about the functions of the electric impulses in our human brains to warrant conjecture about the composition of a resurrection-*soma*. If *sarx* can be organized well enough to produce a human body and brain, presumably so also could light, electricity, and other similarly less ponderous elements in the cosmos, but for the believer there is at any rate no reason to worry whether God can "do" it. The only question will be whether he does.

The fundamental issue in all these questions is well exhibited by John Baillie when he tells the story of a dying man, a devout Christian, who had asked his doctor if the latter had any conviction about a life after death. The doctor, searching his mind for some words with which to cheer

---

[12] Neither is the body "abominable," of course, to Plato, who sees it as the instrument of the *psyche*. Origen, like his master Clement of Alexandria, was affected by the later Platonism of the Middle Academy.

[13] Pelikan, *The Shape of Death*, p. 114.

his dying patient, heard his own dog scratching at the door of the sick room. "Do you hear that?" he asked. "That is my dog. I left him downstairs, but he grew impatient and has come up and hears my voice. He has no notion what is inside that door, but he knows I am here. You do not know what lies beyond the door, but you know your Master is there." [14] Any belief we may have about death as a beginning of new life must depend in one way or another on a still more fundamental belief about the nature of God and of the relation in which, as individuals, we stand to him. In the same spirit Baillie quotes Whittier's well-known lines

> I know not where His islands lift
> Their fronded palms in air;
> I only know I cannot drift
> Beyond His love and care.[15]

If I can see this life as the gift of God I shall be so thankful for each moment of it that to complain of death would be as churlish as to call a benefactor parsimonious who for fifty years had inexplicably given me an annuity and then as inexplicably let the flow of the cornucopia stop. In the face of such a record of generosity, moreover, I should be inclined to interpret the cessation as, rather, auguring a new and even larger beneficence.

The Nature of Resurrection-Faith

If, then, I am so to see death as the beginning of new life through resurrection, I must first have a twofold foundation of belief: (a) I must be able to see life as a pilgrimage that makes it other than an end-in-itself, and (b) I must see it as under the guidance of One who so cares for me and (as *El Shaddai*) [16] is so able to make his care cosmically effective for me that I may safely rest my future in his hands. The resurrection-disclosure will then readily elicit an affirmative response, for it will become to me the expression of how God will take care of my future in such a way as to fit and enhance my understanding of my pilgrim state and the kind of I–Thou relation in which it is grounded. For Christians, such a belief in resurrection will have as its immediate ground, of course, the belief of the Church from primitive times that Jesus was "raised from the dead." Then questions about the biochemistry of a resurrection-*soma* or the biophysics of a resurrection-*sarx* will become almost as irrelevant, not to say foolish, as questions about the architectural structure of "the heavenly city." In what way Christ "appeared unto Simon," the chemistry of the fish and honey he consumed, and the ecological relation of his body to the closed doors through which he passed, become intellectual improprieties no less than is a category mistake in logic.

[14] John Baillie, *And the Life Everlasting* (New York: Oxford University Press, 1966), pp. 198 f.

[15] Ibid.

[16] An ancient Hebrew term to signify God as "the Almighty" or "the Sufficient One."

I can no more have a means of knowing to what kind of "life" I shall arise than an evolutionary naturalist could have of knowing the next stage in the development of the superman, except that, whatever it be, it will in some way or other fulfill my highest present tendencies and aims.

The Resurrection of What?

As all that a devout Christian need be prepared to say about the nature of the resurrection of Christ is that "he lives," so I need say nothing more than "I shall live." Nevertheless, it is proper and intellectually necessary to inquire what it means to say "I" after death, which seems to "ordinary" empirical observation to be the event whose nature is to remove the possibility of the use of the first person in any tense but more particularly the future. What the resurrection statement affirms is that whatever conditions are required for the enunciation of the first person pronoun shall be provided. They might be provided through reincarnation on this or another planet or galaxy, or else through entry into a new dimension of existence interpenetrating but also transcending the human experience we have. In other words, all that can be said in resurrection-faith is that (a) whatever it means for me just now to say "I" will be included in the "I" that will be the subject of the post-resurrection predicate, and (b) whatever the predicate, it will be a fulfillment of the aims and tendencies I presently call "mine." The rest is veiled.

Why the Death Veil?

Why the veiling? A. E. Taylor suggests a clue in a remark he used to make about the moral implications of a karmic doctrine, contradistinguished from the alternative that has become more traditional in the Occident. Whenever you have the prospect of a few trillion more chances, people will procrastinate. With such a prospect there is no urgency for me to reform and purify my mode of life. Encouraged by karmic doctrine to acquiesce in the circumstances given me, I shall all the more readily postpone decisions I know would improve my karmic lot. The procrastinating propensities of humankind are bad enough even within the confines of our little life span, but when they are bolstered up by assurance of a *saṁsāra* of innumerable future life spans, even the most resourceful preacher would not easily persuade me "to work for the night is flying." He might point out how much more economic and otherwise sensible it would be for me to act now and so save myself much trouble later, but anyone who has tried to impress a teenager with the brevity of human life will see how hard it would be to persuade anyone of the brevity of trillions of years.

In a similar vein, P. T. Forsyth (1848–1921), a celebrated Congregationalist divine, reproached those who he thought were turning the notion of immortality "from an imperative task to a leisurely theme." He presented the challenge: "Do not waste time asking if there is a coming eternity; ask, what must I do to give effect to my present eternity; ask, how shall I be loyal to the eternal responsibility in me and on me?" [17] Preoccupation with the hope of immortality can be unhealthy, because it puts the individual into a spectating role, so luring him from the urgent tasks of his divine calling.

If, instead of walking in faith, we seek Gnostic or theosophical certainties about a life beyond, we emasculate the purpose of this one. If we could see beyond the veils of birth and death, our moral situation in this life would be impoverished. Camus perceives this point in his own way when he argues that mortality infinitely increases the value of human life. The point was made in antiquity. Camus invokes Pindar, who expressed it in his pagan way: "Seek not, my soul, the life of the immortals; but enjoy to the full the resources that are within thy reach." [18] The thrust of Pindar's injunction is one that is relevant to the Christian concept of pilgrimage. We are not to dream away our lives with visions of heaven but to realize to the full the moral possibilities of the here-and-now life we are privileged to enjoy. "Man is perishable," wrote Etienne de Sénancourt (1770-1846). "That may be; but let us perish resisting, and if Nothingness awaits us, let us not act as if that were justice." [19] For a Christian to have an apocalyptic vision of the final triumph of cosmic love and of his individual participation in it is good, but it is good only in so far as it does not bring about the deterioration of the moral value of the present life. Otherwise, the infinite opportunity the pilgrimage affords us is lost. The more we see the present life as a pilgrimage, the less we shall interest ourselves in esoteric guarantees about life beyond. We shall live, indeed, as if there were no life beyond.[20]

Though such moral considerations do not tell for or against the metaphysical truth of karmic theory, they do suggest a reason why the lineaments of the life to come, whatever they may be, must be veiled in secrecy. If people knew they could count on more time for decision, they would not make that decision. Hence the force of the traditional notion of a "particular" judgment for each person after death.

The Concept of Purgatory

Where, as in most of the great religions of the world, there is hope of a fuller life beyond, the question arises, could we expect to grow enough in our few years on earth to be fit to take possession of a quality of life as rich as is envisaged in that eschatological hope? Would not such an expectation be like asking a chimpanzee to enjoy *Parsifal*, or a cat to delight

[17] P. T. Forsyth, *This Life and the Next* (London: Independent Press, 1946), pp. 44–47.
[18] Sir John Sandys, ed. and trans., *The Odes of Pindar* (New York: Loeb Classical Library, Macmillan Co. 1915), pp. 190 f.
[19] E. P. de Sénancourt, *Obermann* (Paris: Bibliotheque-Charpentier, 1901), p. 412.
[20] Cf. the opening section of Chapter X.

in a moonlight minuet at Chenonceaux? Such reflections give rise to the notion of the need for a cleansing or "purgation" preparatory to such envisioned bliss. That notion is expressed, for example, in the doctrine of purgatory which, as a state of "temporary punishment," has played a well-known part in traditional Roman Catholic teaching. Eastern Orthodoxy also provides room for such a purgatorial notion, and though it was repudiated in the Church of England because of widespread disgust at ecclesiastical abuses connected with it at the time of the Reformation, it returned to Anglicanism in a much purified form in the nineteenth century, under Tractarian influence, as a way of providing room for growth and development beyond this life.

In the Reformers' objection to it we can see at work, however, the same kind of consideration that has been applied to the transmigration doctrines in Oriental religion. The heirs of the Reformation instinctively felt that a doctrine of purgatorial preparation removed the sense of the moral urgency the life of faith demands. So they preferred to present the future life in heaven-or-hell terms. One can appreciate the motives behind the propagation of such heaven-or-hell teaching, and admire the sense of urgency it engenders. Nevertheless, the vision of opportunities for growth and development in whatever may lie ahead of us beyond death does make the concept of further life more intelligible. To take a pilgrim view of this life is to see our "home" beyond it, but though such a view entails the notion of clearer vision beyond death (the *visio beatifica* of medieval theology), that very notion is made more intelligible when seen in the light of further pilgrimage beyond death. Of course, where a nonpilgrim view of this life prevails, both clearer vision and further pilgrimage beyond this life must be equally excluded as absurd.

The Pilgrim and the Nonpilgrim View of Life

Apart from a special kind of faith such as we have been considering, a pilgrim view of life is, of course, absurd. How, then, is life to be conceived on a nonpilgrim view? Many answers might be offered in response to the question, "What is, in the nonpilgrim view, the most fitting way to spend life?" To this question the answer cannot easily be other than one to the effect that life is a sack to be filled with "goodies" of one sort or another. The "goodies" need not all be sensuous pleasures, of course. They would include, for instance, intellectual and moral satisfactions. Such an understanding of the life situation is *Angst*-producing if, as is the case, it must be made in the light of the one certainty we have about human life, namely, the uncertainty of its duration. The *Angst* does not arise simply from the notion that we might be overtaken at any moment by death. That would be the case, indeed, even if geriatric researches were eventually so to prolong life as to make it biologically terminable only by accident. The *Angst* arises from both the uncertainty of life and the certainty of death. However long or short my life span may turn out to be, it is of finite duration and it is always and at every moment during its progression an unknown quantity. The sack is of a finite size that is both undetermined and indeterminable.

Human life is bounded by two events: birth and death. As seen from a positivistic standpoint they suggest to us an affront to such dignity as we care to attach to man: we enter life's stage dangling from a placenta and are carried off from it in a wooden box. The absurdity greatly diminishes if I can see my present life as a chapter in, rather than a complete story of, my existence. That does not, of course, make the pilgrim view any more rationally justifiable. On the contrary, except to the eye of faith, it is as absurd as birth and death.

The Concept of Eternal Life Beyond Further Pilgrimage

A pilgrim view of human life not only entails the expectation of afterlife; it suggests that afterlife *also* is a pilgrimage. If I take a pilgrim view of my present life, I cannot well avoid taking a pilgrim view of the life beyond to which it points, if only for the reason that, since death is then seen as the beginning of that new life, it does have beginning and so must be temporal. What may happen in the long run (or whatever one is to call a run that runs no longer) is a very different question. In Christian thought, the distinction is expressed in terms of "purgatory" and "heaven" and is also reflected in the notion of a "particular judgment" and a "general judgment." The latter may be conceived as determinative of a final state that is beyond time.

The concept of eternal order, however baffling, cannot well be ignored, for it plays an important and persistent part not only in Christian eschatology but, in one way or another, in that of most of the great religions of the world. It permeates Hindu and Buddhist thought, reflecting the characteristic Indian denigration of the temporal as belonging to *maya,* the unreality of human circumstance. It also appears in Greek and Persian thought, both of which had influenced Judaism by the time of Christ, and as we have seen earlier in the present chapter, it plays a great part in patristic Christian thought, where it was further complicated by the interweaving of the two very different notions of immortality and resurrection.

The notion is nevertheless fraught with philosophical difficulties. Eternal life is not to be confused with infinite temporal duration, the *aeviternitas* of the medieval schoolmen, for it belongs to a different order, an order *beyond* time. Wittgenstein recognized the importance of the distinction. He opposed the notion of eternal life *(der Ewig)* not only because he could find no warranty for it but because he thought the notion did not accomplish what is commonly expected of it. *Der Ewig* is as much of a riddle as is the temporal life that it is called in to invest with special meaning.[21]

[21] L. Wittgenstein, *Tractatus Logico-Philosophicus* 6.4311, 4312 (New York: Humanities Press, 1961), pp. 146–149.

Wittgenstein is saying that a nontemporal dimension of life is inconceivable. Yet if it be wholly inconceivable, what is it that we conceive when we make the distinction between the "now" and whatever it is that transcends the "now"? To say of a man that he "lives only in the present" means, if taken literally, that he has no memory, no expectation, and therefore no "self" that transcends the "now." To be a "self" *is* to transcend the "now." Even as I encompass more than the "now," I transcend, however minimally, the limitations of temporality. I can stand out from the successive moments of my life, and in so doing I go beyond them. In the very act of integrating past, present, and future, I have some experience of transcending time and of somehow taking possession of a nontemporal dimension. There is something of that also in musical experience. The whole notion of an "inner" or "spiritual" life entails a high degree of such transcendence of time, as does very strikingly the notion of mystical union with divine Being. Even outside the various mystical traditions within Christianity the notion is accommodated — for instance, in such a restrained and "intellectualist" medieval Christian theologian as St. Thomas, who provides for the possibility in the present life, exceptionally, of a foretaste of the *visio beatifica,* the state of "eternal bliss" in which the redeemed enjoy for ever the fullness of the divine presence.

How can we attempt to understand a notion such as is presented to us in the Thomist conception of "heaven," that is, the state of being able to enter into possession of divine Being not "by faith" but directly and in such a manner that time is wholly transcended? The self, as has been suggested, provides only a clue. Such a state of "eternal life" would have to lie at the limit of selfhood, that is, at the point at which all possibilities of selfhood are fulfilled. To Christian understanding, that focus of selfhood is Christ. Through appropriation of what his complete self-giving makes possible for humanity, we may be able in the end to enter into new life "with Christ," and to do that is in some way to receive possession of divine Being and so transcend the temporal dimension. The biblical and patristic notion of our being "raised up to the life of God" is an expression of such an eschatological hope. That, after all, is what is called, in the crisper idiom of the Latin Church, an *assumptio,* a "taking up into" God.

Such an understanding of "eternal life" brings to the here-and-now an intensity greater than it could otherwise have. If that seems paradoxical, the paradox quickly disappears with reflection that through an antinomy (such as the presence–absence antinomy we considered in an earlier chapter), awareness of both elements in the antinomy may be intensified. Schubert Ogden has suggested that if life is, in Heidegger's phrase, "living toward death" *(Sein zum Tode),* each moment of our life is endowed with a "vivacity and intensity" it could not otherwise have.[22] By the same token, when time is seen in antithesis to an eternity that transcends it, it takes on new urgency

[22] Schubert M. Ogden, *The Reality of God* (New York: Harper & Row, 1963), p. 244.

and acquires new meaning. George MacDonald, in his own provocative way, long ago expressed a similar idea: "I came from God and I'm going back to God, and I won't have any gaps of death in the middle of my life." [23] Only when I can see time in all its inexorable movement against me, can I allow no empty spaces in my life, and I can so see time only when I see it against that which is other than itself and transcends it. A so-called "this-worldly" theology, such as was fashionable for a period in the 1960's, lacks such an understanding of transcendence and so ends by diminishing the very here-and-now quality in life that it seeks to exalt. When the present life is seen as a span of time, it becomes once again, as in what we have called the nonpilgrim view of life, a box to be filled that inevitably has large unfilled spaces in it after all.

Why the Double Veil of Birth and Death?

Birth and death, the two frontiers of human life, stand in opposition to each other; yet they also have much in common besides their absurdity.

If, on the one hand, we take the pilgrim view, we may look on them as the two great transitions in human existence in which we venture forth from the familiar to the unknown.[24] In the case both of birth and of death we may be said, in this view, to be more or less reluctantly forced out of an accustomed comfortable but narrow and confined mode of life and propelled into a larger and fuller one.

If, on the other hand, we take the nonpilgrim view, we might well express our skepticism of the alternative one by remarking that, since we cannot even remember anything about our past uterine existence, it seems unlikely, even if there *were* an afterlife, that we should be able to remember anything of the present one. There would be no precedent for such a remembering. What sense, then, is there in talking either of a personal immortality or of a personal resurrection if the person in question suffers periodic total amnesia, being unable to remember as far back as from his present stage to the immediately preceding one? Such a reflection also makes nonsense, moreover, of the notion, traditional in Christian piety, that we may hope to meet our friends in the afterlife and have the joy of knowing and being known of them in a fuller dimension of life. That our birth should be, as Wordsworth calls it, "a sleep and a forgetting," [25] must be, in any case, as perplexing a notion to the believer as it is a nonsensical one to the unbeliever.

Believers may certainly wonder why the periodic oblivion should be so complete, since on the face of it more retentiveness of memory both before and after death might seem a better arrangement for the divine economy.

[23] George MacDonald, *Mary Marston* (New York: G. Munro, 1881), chap. 57.
[24] For this expression of the notion I am indebted to my friend Dr. Edward Roachie Hardy of the University of Cambridge, who attributes it to the late Bishop R. T. Loring of Springfield, Mass.
[25] "Ode: Intimations of Immortality from Recollections of Early Childhood," line 59.

Among Buddhists, who have to deal with the problem in the guise of a traditional Oriental karmic rebirth doctrine, some monks profess to offer specific techniques, such as the practice of reciting Pali texts backwards and trying to recall incidents in reverse order, for strengthening the trans-*saṃsāra* memory. In whatever form the problem emerges, it is one of the most puzzling for those who cherish hope of further life. The pain of parting by death, which can be the most grievous of all human sorrows, is mitigated for believers by the hope of the restoration and enrichment, after death, of the noblest of all human joys, the joy of faithful friendship and enduring love. Of course, one may point out that we mercifully forget much in the present life and that to remember everything would be intolerable. We may well look with thankfulness, therefore, on the oblivion that certainly attends birth and that would seem also, in the absence of special faith to the contrary, to attend death, as either a token of divine mercy (if we take the pilgrim view) or at least (if we take the other) a welcome feature of the cosmic structure.

The hope of resurrection expresses "the biblical idea of God as the Almighty who is free, and who thus is defined by a love which is free." [26] But what, then, becomes of a love imprisoned by such barriers as birth and death? The suggestion that the sense of pilgrimage that faith entails would be diminished were not human life veiled at both ends seems plausible only to the believer. To others the difficulty remains; even granting that there were an afterlife as believers affirm, what could it mean to say that "I" shall live on after death? How could "I" be the same person?

What Is "the Same Person"?

A crucial philosophical difficulty for all types of belief in personal survival, whether "resurrection" or "immortality" doctrines, is expressed in the question, what does it mean to be "the same person"? In both types of doctrine we find the common assumption that "the real me" or "whatever is essential to my identity" is to be preserved. This notion needs to be examined in the light of what has been already discussed.

If I lost a leg, or even both, and even, indeed, if I were to have a combined heart, liver, and lung transplant (an operation that might perhaps be fairly commonly and successfully performed in the future), no one would question that I was still "the same person." Perhaps a man may one day even be able to get a damaged portion of his brain replaced and gradually learn to use it as he had used the part that had become injured, and so seem to be indubitably "the same person" as before, replacements notwithstanding. In all such cases one would say something like, "Poor guy, he's not able to run as he did"; and perhaps even, "You'd hardly recognize him because of the paralysis of his face"; but one would always be able to add something

[26] Wolfhart Pannenberg, *What Is Man?* trans. D. A. Priebe (Philadelphia: Fortress Press, 1962), p. 53.

such as, "But it's still dear old Bob—no mistake about that." Even after a lobotomy, though we may say that the patient's personality has greatly changed, we do not say, "It is a new patient." If, however, I could have a whole brain transplant, would you still point to me and be able to say, "Greatly changed these days, but still the same man"? Surely not. If "I" turned out to be a great musical genius, you would not say my musical talent had been hidden for years and only came out after that operation. Nor, if "I" committed a murder, would you say, "I always knew he had homicidal tendencies. Now, don't you see? I was right." You would say, I hope, something more like, "Don't blame MacGregor. This murderer is really someone else. MacGregor is gone and in justice the crime should not be attached to his name."

In view of that, what could it mean to say my heart has stopped, my brain has ceased to function, and my body has begun to decompose, yet "I live on" or "I shall arise"? Who could the "I" be?

The notion that some parts of me are more expendable than others is clear enough and beyond dispute. We have all shared something of the experience of Teilhard de Chardin who, as a child, was curious about the fact that a lock of his hair, that is, a part of "him," could be cut off and burned away in the fire with no resulting difference to his "self." To say that of my entire body, however, entails a special sort of mind–body dualism. The objection to that is not so much to the notion of an "inner self" as that such a view ignores the fact that the "inner self" seems to be so inextricably connected with the "external self" that its existence wholly apart from the latter seems inconceivable. Has not my whole personality been built up in, with, and through my body? Is saying that the body dies and the soul "lives on" like saying a geranium dies yet lives on? Even that cannot properly be said. We can and do say, of course, "I thought I dug up that geranium, but there must have been some of it left, for here it is growing again." The human being is such a highly developed organism that it is not expected to behave like that.

Just because the human being *is* so highly developed, however, we have no strict guidelines about what we ought to expect. The notion that at such a level of development, the organizing principle that developed my personality in, with, and through my body, *might* reorganize itself in, with, and through a new body (at least in some cases) is not wholly inconceivable.

Questions such as "Where, then, are these 'new' bodies?" and "Why are not their effects detectable in the physically explorable universe?" seem trivial, not least in the light of what we have considered about the necessity of "veiling." There is no shortage of galaxies where all sorts of life could exist, and even on our own planet there is no reason to suppose that beings with "subtle bodies" *(somata)* might not coexist with or without our awareness of them. After all, human beings lived intelligently and perceptively for thousands of years without knowing about electricity, to say nothing of radium.

Peter Geach thinks that if there were such "subtle bodies" they should have forced themselves on the attention of physicists, as X-rays did, by spontaneous interference with physical apparatus. He remarks, "There are supposed to be a lot of 'subtle bodies' around, and physicists have a lot of delicate apparatus; yet physicists not engaged in psychical research are never bothered by the interference of 'subtle bodies.' In the circumstances I think it wholly irrational to believe in 'subtle bodies.' " [27] While no one need suppose that belief in either an immortality or a resurrection doctrine entails belief that such subtle bodies are roaming around in such a way as to make their influence detectable by the "delicate apparatus" of physicists, there is no reason why, if there *were* such subtle bodies in our immediate environment, they should not go undetected. To suppose that the delicate apparatus of physicists *must* be delicate enough to pick them up is surely a remarkably jejune assumption. Yet that is just the sort of assumption that some contemporary philosophers, working with outdated scientific models, are more likely to make than is any imaginative working scientist.

For all that, the notion of the existence of such subtle bodies is of course conjectural, lacking any scientific evidence. As a *suggestion* of how immortality or resurrection might be said to work, however, it is better than any notion of a disembodied self, which is really unintelligible. The fundamental difficulty is not how a personal immortality might conceivably work or a personal resurrection might conceivably occur. The real difficulty is the preservation of the identity of the "me" who is said "to go on living" or "to be raised up." The omission of the body seems to take away all content from the idea of personal identity.[28] If I *were* able to detect my Aunt Matilda under some guise other than the one to which I was accustomed when she used to take tea with me, what could possibly make me say, "That is certainly dear old Aunt Matilda"? Whether she reappeared in the form of a subtle body or as some other person such as Mary Smith or Robert Jones, how could I possibly *identify* her?

The seriousness of the difficulty is not to be underestimated, yet it does seem to be proportionate to the extent of our dependence on external features as means of identification. If my Aunt Matilda had nothing more distinctive than her funny hobbling walk or her rasping voice, then recognizing her without her present body would be no doubt very difficult; but if she were the sort of person whose distinctive presence in a room was unmistakable even when one's eyes were shut or one's attention focused on the six o'clock news, the possibility of identification in an unfamiliar setting would not seem to pose such insuperable difficulties. Some voices are so nondescript that we never learn to recognize them, while another may be so unmistakable

[27] Peter Geach, "Immortality," in *God and the Soul* (London: Routledge & Kegan Paul, 1969), p. 18.
[28] See B. A. O. Williams, "Personal Identity and Individuation," in *Proceedings of the Aristotelian Society* 57 (1956-57): 229–252. When a certain Miss Beauchamp, victim of a dissociated personalities disorder, was nearly cured, she spoke freely of them as differences of mood, adding, "After all, it is always myself."

that even after twenty years we could be in no possible doubt on receiving a telephone call from its owner. A voice on the telephone is a very small part of a person, yet it is often more than enough for recognition. So if Aunt Matilda's presence could be made known to me in any guise, I might well identify it without doubt.

We may then raise the question, how would Aunt Matilda in her new situation recognize *herself* as the person who took tea with me before she died? That question is neither more nor less difficult than the sort of question that is raised about metempsychosis, where I am presumed to have been "incarnate" on earth before, yet cannot definitely remember anything about it. I could be the same person even though I had "lost my memory." The continuity I recognize with my childhood is not diminished by my loss of some of the feeling-tones of childhood; on the contrary, my awareness of the growth I have attained since then enhances my sense of the continuity. Even as I look at my gray hair I still have not the slightest difficulty in identifying with the toddler I was when I stretched my hand up to reach a pitcher on the kitchen table.

While identity without memory might have some relevance to certain theosophical concepts of immortality, it is insufficient for the Christian claim. For there is no doubt that, whatever vision of the future life the New Testament presents to us, it includes the notion of recognizing the friends we have known on this side of death. When Jesus appeared to the disciples they dared not ask who he was because "they knew it was the Lord." [29] The common Christian expectation is not only resurrection to new life but reunion with old friends in a new order of life, which implies recognition. Putting aside for a moment the basic difficulty about how identity can be maintained in a new body, we may well ask how relationships can be continued. When the disciples asked Jesus which of the seven husbands to whom a woman had been married would be her husband in heaven, Jesus replied that men and women, when they are raised up to new life, do not marry but are "like angels in heaven." [30] That is to say, a transformation takes place that transmutes human relationships.

To a young couple in love the prospect of a new relationship between them without sexual intercourse may seem so attenuated as to be unrecognizable as the relationship they know. Yet even in this life the relationship of happily married couples does pass eventually from one in which sexual intercourse seems its essence and chief joy to one in which, much later in life, its importance diminishes, and husband and wife are bound together with closer bonds and in an even deeper and surer love than they could have known in their more tempestuous youth.

All relationships are susceptible to such transformations, and these transformations, far from diminishing our capacity to recognize continuity with the old relationship, make that continuity more clearly recognizable than

[29] John 21:12. (N.E.B.)
[30] Mark 12:25. (N.E.B.)

ever. My friendship with a penniless lad is not changed now that he has become a multimillionaire, nor have I any difficulty in recognizing, in the woman who is now crippled with arthritis, a beautiful girl I knew twenty years ago. Relationships, like individuals, grow, and the growth enhances them. That is the truth that lies behind the commonplace saying that there are no friends like old friends.

The difficulty we see in the notion of our recognizing friends in a resurrected community cannot lie in our fear that the changes in us would prevent recognition. It must lie, rather, in our suspicion that we could not detect the *presence* of our friend at all. No responsible Christian theologian has ever claimed, however, to know anything specific about the nature of the resurrected body, so we must fall back on the principle enunciated in an earlier section of this chapter: as attitudes to death depend on our metaphysical views of the nature of human life, so belief in an afterlife can never be anything other than a corollary to a particular kind of belief in God. If God is what he is affirmed in Christian faith to be, there is no reason why we could not recognize our friends in an afterlife, in which case the customary philosophical objections would all fail. That there *is* any such afterlife must nevertheless always be a matter of faith and not scientifically demonstrable. When faith is removed, the philosophical objections remain very serious indeed.

QUESTIONS ON CHAPTER IX

1   Do statements about survival after death entail a self-contradiction?

2   "I had five heart attacks and on two occasions I died but came back to life." Comment.

3   To what extent is belief in an afterlife dependent upon other, more radical, metaphysical or theological positions?

4   What difference do you see between immortality and resurrection doctrines?

5   Consider the notion of purgatory as further opportunity for spiritual growth.

6   What value, if any, do you see in the ancient doctrine of transmigration or reincarnation and what objections might be raised against it?

7   What difficulties do you see in the notion of disembodied consciousness?

8   Suppose we accept the notion of resurrection to new life in a "glorified" body. What, then, would it mean to assert that my wife and I could recognize each other in that new state?

BIBLIOGRAPHICAL SUGGESTIONS

Baillie, John. *And the Life Everlasting.* New York: Oxford University Press, 1956.

Broad, C. D. *Lectures on Psychical Research.* London: Routledge & Kegan Paul, 1962.

Cullmann, O. *Immortality of the Soul or Resurrection from the Dead?* New York: Macmillan Co., 1958. An important work for the exposition of the difference between immortality and resurrection.

Ducasse, C. J. *The Belief in a Life After Death.* Springfield, Ill.: Charles C Thomas, 1961.

Feifel, H., ed. *The Meaning of Death.* New York: McGraw-Hill, 1959.

Forsyth, P. T. *This Life and the Next.* London: Independent Press, 1946. See especially the chapter "Immortality and Present Judgment."

Frazer, J. G. *The Belief in Immortality.* London: Macmillan & Co., 1913. Gifford Lectures.

Gray, J. Glen. "The Idea of Death in Existentialism." *Journal of Philosophy* 48 (1951): 113–127.

Marcel, Gabriel. *Presence and Immortality.* Pittsburgh: Duquesne University Press, 1967.

Marxen, Willi. *The Resurrection of Jesus of Nazareth.* Philadelphia: Fortress Press, 1970.

Moltmann, J. *Theology of Hope.* New York: Harper & Row, 1965. An influential book for modern eschatological studies.

Myers, F. W. H. *Human Personality and Its Survival of Bodily Death.* New York: University Books, 1961. A classic in psychical research.

Osterley, W. O. E. *Immortality and the Unseen World.* New York: Macmillan Co., 1921.

Pelikan, Jaroslav. *The Shape of Death.* Nashville, Tenn.: Abingdon Press, 1961.

Penelhum, T. *Survival and Disembodied Existence.* London: Routledge & Kegan Paul, 1970.

Phillips, D. Z. *Death and Immortality.* New York: St. Martin's Press, 1970.

Pieper, Josef. *Death and Immortality.* New York: Herder & Herder, 1969. (Original German edition, 1968.)

Price, H. H. "The Problem of Life After Death." *Religious Studies* 3 (1967–1968): 447–459.

Pringle-Pattison, A. Seth. *The Idea of Immortality.* Oxford: Clarendon Press, 1922. Written from a Neo-Hegelian standpoint.

Ramsey, Ian. *Freedom and Immortality.* London: Student Christian Movement Press, 1960.

Shoemaker, Sydney. "Personal Identity and Memory." *Journal of Philosophy* 56 (1959): 868–882.

Taylor, A. E. *The Christian Hope of Immortality.* New York: Macmillan Co., 1947.

Thielicke, Helmut. *Death and Life.* Translated by E. H. Schroeder. Philadelphia: Fortress Press, 1970.

von Hügel, F. *Eternal Life.* Edinburgh: T. & T. Clark, 1912.

West, D. J. *Psychical Research Today.* London: Duckworth, 1954.

Wolfson, H. A. "Immortality and Resurrection in the Philosophy of the Church Fathers." In *Religious Philosophy.* Cambridge, Mass.: Harvard University Press, 1961.

GOD AS KENOTIC BEING

X

THE ANTINOMIES OF RELIGIOUS BELIEF

Understanding is therefore directed by faith, and faith
is developed by understanding.
> *Nicholas of Cusa (1401–1464),*
> *De docta ignorantia*

You explain nothing, O poet; but through you everything becomes explicable.
> *Paul Claudel (1868–1955),*
> *La Ville*

The Function of Antinomies in Religious Belief

"We say that God, who must be at least as high as the highest thoughts He has implanted in the best of men, will withhold His smile from those who have desired but to please Him; and that they only who have done good for the sake of good *and as though He existed not*, they only who have loved virtue more than they loved God Himself, shall be allowed to stand by His side." [1]

These words, which to our contemporary ears sound so conspicuously like an echo of that celebrated twentieth-century German theologian and martyr, Dietrich Bonhoeffer, in one of his most characteristic themes,[2] were actually written by a Belgian poet and essayist in the nineteenth century, before Bonhoeffer was born. Some pages later the same author continues in a similar vein: "I shall be happier than you, and calmer, if my doubt is greater and nobler and more earnest than is your faith; if it has probed more deeply into my soul, traversed wider horizons, if there are more things it has loved." [3]

---

[1] Maurice Maeterlinck, *Wisdom and Destiny,* trans. A. Sutro (New York: Dodd, Mead & Co., 1914), p. 189. The original French edition was published in 1898. Italics mine.
[2] That we should live as if God did not exist (*etsi deus non daretur*).
[3] Maeterlinck, *Wisdom and Destiny,* p. 220.

Such observations provide a clue that can lead to the unraveling of the central mystery that is reflected in the antinomies at the heart of all religious belief. They express an ancient insight into the nature of that belief as it emerges whenever God is seen not merely as an object to be appropriated like air or light but as subject in an intersubjectival relationship. The great religious leaders of every age have all grasped in one way or another the intersubjectival, relational character of the experience of entering into the religious dimension of life, and they have conceptualized the experience accordingly in interpreting it. In so interpreting it they have brought to light the characteristic antinomies of religion: doubt–faith, absence–presence, faith–vision, magic–worship, ritual–sacrament, morality–holiness, skepticism–infallibilism, Babylon–Jerusalem, law–gospel.

The function of these antinomies in our conceptualization of the phenomena of religious experience is complex. Before we can properly grasp it we should examine how religious awareness emerges and develops in human consciousness. Nevertheless, at the outset we may usefully propose that the polarity the antinomies conceptualize is present in the earliest forms of religious awareness. No one really starts out, either by inheritance or conviction, with a purely pantheistic concept of deity in which divine being is absorbed from the external world as water seems to be absorbed by a sponge or ink by blotting paper. Not even in the physical and biological realms is there any process that is in fact as simple as that. Photosynthesis, for example, is not at all simple in that sense. That any sort of religious awareness could occur so simplistically is, then, to say the least, *prima facie,* unlikely. By the same token, no one ever begins with a concept of deity that is completely nonpantheistic. As experience of the absence of God entails experience of the presence of God, so experience of the divine presence entails experience of God's absence.

Nor could there be any individual or society so legalistic as to be devoid of the slightest notion of the gospel that "sums up" the law, any more than there could be anyone so lawless, so antinomian, as to be wholly innocent of the concept of law. The reason is not that it would be difficult; the reason is that it is impossible. Law and gospel are neither antithetical nor complementary; they are aspects of the same reality that emerges with the moral dimension itself. When Jesus declared that he wanted to fulfill or complete the law of Moses as popularly understood, not to destroy it, he was simply enunciating that basic datum of moral awareness. The Sabbath (as a typification of a legalistic observance) is made for man, not man for the Sabbath; nevertheless it *is* "made for man," being the negative pole, as we might say, of that of which the positive pole is the evangelical proclamation that the law set down by Moses has been transcended. It has indeed been transcended; it has been transcended from the beginning, from the moment in which it was first conceptualized, for the conceptualization itself is impossible without the polarization. With the vision of law itself the decalogue (or something like it) is already given; contrariwise, with the enunciation of the decalogue is given the ideal or principle behind the law, which the evangelists proclaim.

Religious ideas do not roll into the mind singly as do marbles into a slot; they emerge as ideational polarizations reflecting the polarization in the experience behind the ideas. Religious awareness entails awareness of the tension in that polarization, as an examination of the emergence of that awareness will show.

Inspecting the Emergence of Religious Awareness

When we ask how religious awareness arises in the human mind, our scientific education disposes us to look for the answer in anthropological research. By observing the customs of contemporary primitive tribesmen and by conducting archaeological investigations into the habits of prehistoric man, we can, indeed, obtain much interesting information. Since by such methods alone we cannot, however, enter into the experiences that lie behind the scientific descriptions, the usefulness of the results the methods offer us is limited to their force in corroborating what we must ascertain by other means. The primary testimony must come from our own experience, however meager that may be. No other method can exhibit to us the real, interior character of the phenomena.

Among typical objections to that procedure, one has obvious weight. To the recollection of all of our experiences, even the earliest that we can remember, we bring the conceptualization of a whole battery of conditioning factors that we had then already built into the experiences we say we "had." These conditioning factors, which include antenatal influences and perhaps also hereditary ones such as Jung has subsumed under his category of the "collective unconscious," so color all our experiences as to deprive them of the elemental quality needed to provide us with genuine enlightenment about the nature of the phenomena that are presented to us in religious awareness. From early childhood we are taught, however unwittingly, to look on things intuitively in certain ways, to invest words with particular meanings and assign to events certain specific interpretations. Even when, a little later, we question our elders' teaching, most of us instinctively accept the underlying conceptual structure that made the ideas and their interpretation intelligible to us in the first place. So the force of our conceptual habits circumscribes our own intellectual protests and sets limits to the scope of even our most vehement youthful rebellion.

While recognizing the force of that objection, we should also notice its limitations. The conditioning factors do indeed affect and may even determine the *form* our interpretation of the phenomena of religious experience shall take. They do not at all necessarily affect the fundamental nature of religious awareness. If, every time you saw a square become a cube, it was a blue square that became a red cube, you might well proceed to the erroneous conclusion that there is some element in three-dimensionality that turns blue things into red. If all my squares were yellow and always became green cubes, I should be liable to fall into a different and equally erroneous opinion. Nevertheless, both of us would have experienced three-dimensionality just as surely as if we had not been confused by the irrelevant concomitants. With the emergence of religious awareness many irrelevancies are indeed introduced, and at least partly on account of them we have that interminable strife that expresses itself in the many foolish squabbles and futile acerbities for which religious controversy is notorious, yet without which religious awareness could not develop. Our present concern, however, is how religious awareness emerges in the first place, and to this question we now turn.

How Religious Awareness Emerges

Consider the following situation.

I am a child. Whether or not I think of myself as "a stranger and afraid in a world I never made," [4] I inevitably find I have to come to terms with that world. It does not obey my will. The extent to which this discovery shocks me will depend on the strength of my willfulness and a variety of other circumstances, but in greater measure or less I am bound to be impressed by the fact that I am up against a world that resists me at every point. I do not wish it so, of course, and my reaction will vary according to my temperament and conditioning, which are, however, among the irrelevant factors we have already touched upon in the previous section. If I happen to be of an irascible or quick-tempered disposition I may stamp my feet in impotent rage; if, instead, I am of a more phlegmatic character, I may sulk. Whatever I do or do not do, I become distinctly aware that my will is being thwarted by an external world.

I may personify that world, as imaginative children and primitive people often do. That is a way of trying to come to terms with the world around me. It is, if you like, a way of trying to do business with that world. I try to make friends with the objects that confront me. I may even talk to them, in Franciscan style, as Sister Tree and Brother Wall. I find some of these "friends" seem to be more kindly disposed to me than others. Shade trees, for instance, have a kindly aspect; brick walls are less easy to make friends with. Yet even brick walls are all right if only you learn to accept their ineluctable resistance to you. Then you may even pat them or stroke them and they will do you no harm. Shade trees, on the other hand, in spite of their seeming benevolence, are just as implacable as brick walls if you try to hit them or walk into them. So far, so good; I can now *handle* trees and brick walls under the pretext of "making friends" with them.

[4] A. E. Housman, *Last Poems* (Chester Springs, Pa.: Dufour Editions, Inc., 1922), p. xii.

Soon, however, I am in for some unpleasant surprises. Partially released from parental protection, I discover that wasps sting. Even objects that are as a rule friendly may turn seemingly hostile: dogs sometimes bite; metals that are normally cool and agreeable to the touch are sometimes unexpectedly very hot, causing me intense pain and shock. The world, I find, cannot be so easily manipulated as at first I may have thought. It is sometimes amenable to my overtures, sometimes seemingly hostile to them. I do not quite know what to make of it. What I cannot avoid recognizing is that the world around me, for all that I try to woo its friendship, seems to be fundamentally unconcerned about me. My rubber playball bounces back at my bidding when I throw it against a wall or on the ground, but when I let it roll away from me, it will no sooner return at my command than if it were a solid lead cube.

What I have discovered is that if I hope to subdue anything in the world around me I must first yield to it in the sense of studying how it works and submitting obediently to the working of its nature. Instead of flinging my ball wildly in play, I learn to bounce it—which, I notice, is much better fun. Still, I have not won a total victory: I have had to yield; I have had to come to terms with the world.

Moreover, I soon find that coming to terms with the world is by no means always so easy. How should I come to terms with the rattlesnake that has killed my brother or the earthquake that so unexpectedly took my uncle's life? However much or little I may be conditioned by parents and friends to fear the world around me or to trust it, I cannot escape its indifference to me. Whether they encourage me, because I happen to be of a timid or fearful disposition, to put more trust in the world around me, or, on account of my naturally warm and loving tendencies, caution me to have a healthy respect for dangers that lurk in seemingly innocuous things, I cannot for long delay concluding to myself that I am in a world that is neither friendly nor hostile to me; rather, it does not care about me in the least, one way or the other.

The trust and the distrust, the friendliness and the hostility, the love and the fear, are all on my side. The other side, though it may appear now as kindly, now as cruel, is really neutral. If, being tenderhearted by nature, I am distressed by cats that eat birds, I learn sooner or later that cats could not possibly have the kind of fine feelings I am expecting of them. Their behavior is instinctive, and their instinct is to kill and eat their prey, which happens to include the birds I happen to love.

Such is the world in which I find myself "a stranger and afraid." My fear is not the fear that birds have of cats, for I am now beginning to learn that through the study of nature I can to a remarkable degree control and subdue it. I learn how to bring my dog to heel and how to ride a pony. As I learn so to come to terms with my environment I lose my fear of it. Even my fear of the dark diminishes as I become better attuned to the world in which I have found myself.

There is, however, another aspect of my environment that has confronted me from earliest childhood. I have had to contend with people. In some respects they are just like everything else around me and are also susceptible to the same kind of study and manipulation by me. From earliest childhood I have begun to learn the elements of practical psychology. I discover, in one way or another, how to wheedle tidbits out of my parents. I try also, so far as I can at that stage, to learn how to cope with the peculiarities of my parents and others who stand in an especially close relation to me. If they dote on me to the point of suffocating me by their affection, I must deal with that; if they neglect me, I must deal with that, too. Parents and other elders and close associates, as a part of nature, are subject, of course, to the same principles as are cats and ponies, hot stoves, and swimming pools. People are a part of the world around me.

Sooner or later, however, I discover that people are *not only* part of the world around me. I find a special factor in them that I do not have to reckon with in anything else but have to reckon with in them. It is true that they react to me in many ways as do other objects in the world I am learning to understand. If I plague them, they become annoyed and retaliate much as bees sting and cats scratch when annoyed. They also tend to purr in their own way when I please or flatter them, much as does my cat when I stroke it. They may be also unaccountably moody and have unexpected and seemingly groundless likes and dislikes that I must learn to take into consideration in dealing with them. In all these matters they are very much indeed a part of the world around me.

Nevertheless, there is another factor that does not fit the general pattern of my world at all. I become aware that not only am I judging them, but they are judging me. Moreover, I have to acknowledge to myself that, in some respects, at least, their judgment carries weight with me. I do not merely have to adapt to the results of it as I have learned to adapt to the lack of resiliency of brick walls and the wetness of water. I do not simply have to deal with it or cope with it; I am challenged by it. That is, I am challenged to change, to reform, to become different from what I am, and I find the challenge is one I cannot with impunity ignore. In old-fashioned language, it touches my conscience; that is, it invades my consciousness in such a way that I account myself *rightly* judged, in the sense that in the challenge of the judgment is disclosed to me a vision of how I can better accept myself.

The force of the challenge lies in its disclosure to me that I have entered into a relationship in which both I and the other person are standing under a common judgment. Between myself and the other person I apprehend the presence of what may be called a "third being," who is present in, or participates in, the relationship in such a way as to be inseparable from it. The inseparability does not make my mother any less a mammal or my little brother any less a chemical compound, but it does mean that people are more than mammalia and chemical compounds. My discernment of the presence of the "third being" may be, and no doubt usually is, at first vague and unclear. An aura of mystery shrouds the whole relationship in which the disclosure occurs. Nevertheless, I am aware of having entered into a dimension lying beyond that of tables and chairs, lakes and lizards, pleasure and pain. In the relationship in which I stand to those who care enough about me to encourage me with their praise and challenge me with their criticism, I discern, however feebly, the presence of the "third being."

Should I happen to hear others speak of "God," it is unlikely, though not impossible, that I shall at first connect that term with my discovery of the "third being," any more than I shall talk, at this stage, of love or sacrifice or worship, all of which belong to the specialized religious vocabulary of adults. Whether I ever identify the "third being" of my experience with the term "God" that I may hear on some adult lips will depend, in the first instance at any rate, on how the term "God" is interpreted to me. If it is explained to me by a religious fanatic I am unlikely to make any identification at all. If it is explained to me by a person of deep religious maturity, the possibility of my making a connection will be much greater. That does not radically affect, however, the reality of the disclosure, any more than, later on, the reality of sexual awareness at puberty will be affected by whether my interpretation of it is guided by a sexually responsible and mature person or a whore. In both cases, the religious and the sexual, the interpretation will develop differently and will eventually modify the nature of the awareness itself; but the awareness will be there within and, in that sense and to that extent, apart from the interpretation.

The intensity of the awareness will depend in large measure on the kind of people I meet, though it will also depend no less, of course, on my willingness to participate in the relationship. If I am fortunate enough to meet someone of lively and mature moral character, perhaps even of the caliber of an Albert Schweitzer, my chances of a vivid awareness and sense of love and awe are greater; but even at the worst I cannot avoid at least some incipient awareness of what it means to enter into moral relationship with other people and to have revealed to me within that relationship the presence that has been here called that of the "third being." The development of my interpretation of that presence is another matter, to which we may now turn.

Do Belief and Unbelief Coalesce?

Belief and unbelief do not come ready-made. They are achieved through the interpretation of experience, which involves the whole being of the individual. The intellect plays an important, but by no means the only part. We should notice that unbelief may take many forms, ranging from a casual tendency to shrink from the attitudes of mind generally associated with religious belief to a carefully worked out atheistic scheme such as has been well presented by the Marxist writer Jaroslav Krejci.[5] Krejci conceives of atheism as the indispensable tool of radical anthropological criticism, safeguarding society from dogmatic or reactionary tendencies in the social system. Atheism, officially established, is seen as the protector of the State from totalitarianism and tyranny and the preventer of the apotheosis of heroes and the glorification of the establishment. It is the best spur to self-criticism, the best sword against stuffy conformity.

These claims are interesting, not least since they are exactly those that protagonists on the other side make for religious belief. The latter have traditionally and characteristically claimed, for instance, that the Church in the Middle Ages saved western Europe from the typically monolithic despotism of the East and that Hitler was able to succeed for a while with his totalitarian rule in Germany only because he was successful in emasculating the Christian Church after earlier destroying German Jewry. That the claims of such atheism should so singularly resemble those of Christianity suggests that atheism may perhaps be most properly regarded as a religion. Let us look more closely, however, at Krejci's exposition.

Atheism, he tells us, discharges an ethically liberating function: it frees conscience from pseudovalues and illusory norms. It destroys fatalism and all injurious forms of passivity by teaching that man is his own legislator and can create all his own values. Krejci's aim is to foster a more virile type of atheism than has existed in the past. Perhaps one of his most interesting observations is his admission that traditional types of atheism have indeed been one-sided and stagnant. He specifies eight "elements and features of stagnation" in the older type of atheism: (1) it had no notion of dialogue and tended to regard opposition as satanic, and it was not sufficiently constructive; (2) it did not struggle against the idols and fetishes of socialism, which are forms of alienation within socialism itself; (3) it did not sufficiently take into account the tragic side of life or the fears of man; (4) it did not do well in proselytizing believers, being unable to provide adequate alternatives to the solutions offered on the believers' side to problems such as death and finitude; (5) by spreading itself too thin it lost intensity; (6) it lacked sociological and psychological support from descriptions of actual group ideology; (7) it lacked an adequate sense of a nonreligious belief; and (8) it failed to seek alliance with believers on what are presumably common enemies, such as militarism and totalitarian government.

A self-critical atheism such as Krejci's draws attention to the curious fact that the more mature and developed religious belief and unbelief become, the more they seem to coalesce. Both belief and unbelief, at this level, are sworn enemies of fanaticism, religious or antireligious. The temper of our age is in one respect radically different from that of the past. As Vahanian has observed, people formerly took religion to offer "a mode of existence

5 Jaroslav Krejci, "A New Model of Scientific Atheism," *Concurrence* 1 (1969): 82–96.

through which the world was *transfigured*," whereas now what is expected of religion is not the transfiguration of worldly things but their subjugation. "Their subjugation is itself the test of a faith that works." [6] Vahanian inclines to share Sartre's view that Christianity must issue, in the long run, in an atheistic humanism.[7] Today, more than ever before, the traditional distinction between belief and unbelief seems to break down. The more both lose their primitive naiveties and acquire a sophisticated maturity, the more strongly believers condemn religious fanaticism and unbelievers the simplistic positivism of a former generation of atheists.

Yet the situation is not to be so easily described, much less explained, by the cultural tendencies of the age in which we happen to live. There remains a radical difference between the believer and the unbeliever in their respective interpretations of the situation that we have called the emergence of religious awareness.

The Conditions of Belief and Unbelief

The unbeliever is indeed confronted, as are we all, with what has been called, for convenience, the "third being" of intersubjectival relationship; but in the dimension thereby disclosed to him he discerns nothing that takes him beyond humanity. Whether he happens to be a village-pump atheist or a Krejci makes no difference at all at that point.

Because the unbeliever discerns nothing in the disclosure situation that takes him beyond humanity, he finds the traditional "God" language, with its vast metaphysical underpinnings, unacceptable and irrelevant to his condition. When we ask why he does not discern what the believer so readily discerns, the answer cannot be simple. For a complete explanation we should no doubt have to attend to a great network of circumstances.

In the first place, however, let us notice the well-known psychological fact that in all ordinary dealings with people our reactions vary enormously. If I like what I see in you, I "warm" to you. In a short time I am opening myself to you spontaneously and even, as we say, "pouring out my heart to you," so that you become to me a "very real person" indeed. I talk much about you, perhaps to the point of causing other people to wonder why you mean so much to me. I tell them it is because you "do something" for me. I find your company good for me. Of course, you might have deceived me by subtle flattery or the like, but if so the friendship will not last. Let us assume that it lasts for many years. We may then ask how I came to detect at the outset that you would be so good for me. The answer will always be something to the effect that "by a right instinct" I saw you could help me to grow, to develop myself along healthy lines. Also, of course, I just liked you for your own sake.

[6] Gabriel Vahanian, *The Death of God* (New York: George Braziller, 1961), pp. 194–195.
[7] Ibid., pp. 226 f.

Suppose, now, that I do not like what I see in you. Then, of course, the opposite occurs. I "go into my shell." I may go on talking politely enough, but I am really not "with" you. I have "written you off." If you do not have a very strong personality or if I do not see you again, I soon forget you and so I truthfully say, when someone asks me a few months later, that I have no recollection of ever having set eyes upon you. For me you do not exist.

Suppose instead, however, that you have an extremely strong personality and that the reason I want to forget you is that I feel you are so much better than I that I resent you and want as far as I possibly can to avoid recognizing your existence. It is not enough for me to belittle you because that is, even to myself, too obviously "sour grapes"—a ruse to disguise my private embarrassment at you. A more skillful way, which either I know by instinct or soon learn from experience, is to objectify you. That is, I recognize you as part of the natural scenery, as, for instance, the assistant accountant at the Ninth Avenue branch of Beacon's Bank, the man who sings tenor in the Newport Glee Club; but whenever anyone talks about you as a real person, a person who is good to know for your own sake, I grow glassy-eyed and may well even pretend not to hear. By the time someone tries, years later, to remind me of you I am able to say truthfully that I cannot remember you at all and have no reason to believe in your existence.

"But you go to the Newport Glee Club," I am reminded, "so surely you remember the tenor?" "Of course, I remember the tenor," I reply. "Every Glee Club has a tenor." "Then I have seen you talking to the teller at the far end of the counter at the bank of which we are both old customers. Surely you must remember him?" "Of course. In fact I am fairly observant and have a good memory: he is tall, dark and I think he has a short moustache. I have never paid any attention to him beyond that. When I go to a bank I go to cash checks and deposit money and so forth. But tellers at the far end of bank counters who are tall and dark and wear short moustaches are very common sights, you know, and to say that the particular one is that friend of yours means nothing to me. I could never see anything in him except a teller at a bank. In any case, it's time for me to get going: I have a tennis date in half an hour."

It is a commonplace of experience that we all do this sort of thing; what should interest us are the conditions under which we do it. We do it at first consciously, because we fear or dislike personal involvement. Then soon we are doing it by habit. When we say tartly, "I do not wish to know that bank teller" (or that Swedish ambassador) socially, we mean we want to objectify him and so regard him as we regard adding machines and embassies, not as we regard a beloved parent or even a cousin or friend. Psychologically, we soon become habituated to ignoring him: we turn him off as we turn off the radio, so that he cannot intrude upon us. If the "third being" were really what believers say, I might well wish to achieve such an objectification.

I can also, however, simply fail to notice that a person is a person. Officials in uniform seem depersonalized, and though reflection would show me they must be persons, I may find it difficult to penetrate the situation and see the man behind the mask. As I am laughing and talking amiably with a congenial companion, a person slips into the room unnoticed. It might even have been someone very important and interesting; yet I was too preoccupied with trivial banter with my friend to notice either the advent or the departure of the other visitor. More probably, I saw out of the corner of my eye someone come and go, but when questioned I was able to say only that I did vaguely notice somebody come in and go out but paid no attention—why should I? The oddity of what happens in a personal relationship can very easily so escape us when we do not fully succeed in recognizing the other person as a subject and treat him instead, at least partially, as an object. So while he sees me as a person, and with me the "third being" that enters into such interpersonal relationships, I may well fail to see him as other than the occupant of a uniform, an object among other objects, and so wholly miss the entry into the situation of the "third being."

Both openness and sensitivity are required of me, then, if I am to grasp an intersubjectival situation and be able to come to terms with the "third being." In any case, probably nobody ever grasps that situation suddenly and clearly as one sees clearly and suddenly one's first banana or one's first kangaroo. The awareness slowly breaks in on me, like a northern dawn, till at last I apprehend the presence of the "third being."

Let us assume, however, that I am neither particularly resistant nor insensitive to the presence I have called the "third being." I may well continue for many years to regard that presence as mysterious and perhaps even fascinating (to use Otto's term for what he calls the "numinous") and not identify it with any theological, metaphysical or religious concept at all. What happens when I am suddenly confronted with such a concept will depend once again on a large variety of circumstances, but unless it strikes me as having some connection with the presence I have actually found in human experience, I am unlikely to have any use for it at all, since it simply will not convey anything to me. The conveyance must take place in intersubjectival relations or not at all. Such a consideration should help us to understand what is meant by those Christians who remark that nobody has ever been converted to the Christian way through reading theology or hearing exposition of doctrine, but, rather, by being *in* the *koinonia*, the Christian community, and "seeing" God at work in it. Even then, of course, there remains a question of interpretation.

One can—and, of course, many do—make no connection at all between the presence of the "third being" and anything in the least like the very metaphysical concepts presented to us in, say, the historic creeds or the prologue to the Fourth Gospel. Such concepts, if we are to interpret them as the believer does, must strike us ineluctably, not merely as apposite, but as somehow "a perfect fit." We must feel inwardly compelled, with the certainty of a man or woman in finding a life's mate, or the assurance a young man sometimes feels when he thinks that the life of a sailor or surgeon or teacher is the only possible life for him.

There is not the slightest reason, however, why I *must* see such connections with such compelling force. Even if the connections were there, they might elude me. Many born teachers are dissuaded from a teaching career for what are bad or trivial reasons. Many people (to their great loss, of course) pass up the opportunity of marrying the "right" person and marry instead for money or other inappropriate reasons, often with disastrous consequences. There is and there could be no logical reason why I should find that a particular poem should "speak to my condition." Indeed, in the course of its communication to me it embarks on a hazardous journey in which the chance of its being "just right" for me usually diminishes all along the line. So great, indeed, are the dangers of its journey that it seems miraculous that it should ever surmount them all and eventually reach its target.

Not at all astonishing, then, is the case in which I simply do not grasp the metaphysical concepts of the Bible and other classic religious literature. The natural reaction in such a case, however, is surely to say something such as, "Sorry, I just don't get it," and leave it at that. That is what we do when, for instance, as occasionally happens among educated people, we find that, say, *Hamlet* or the Parthenon does not "ring a bell." We say, in effect, "Most people seem to see something very splendid in it, but it leaves me cold." Or else, "Maybe I'll rave about it some day, as others do, but meanwhile, since I find it meaningless and therefore boring, may we please talk of something else?" A great many people do say something like that about metaphysical and theological interpretations of religious experience.

More remarkable is the case in which, on the contrary, the meaning of the metaphysical or theological affirmations suddenly breaks in upon me and connects up with my actual experience of interpersonal relationship. That situation is, strictly speaking, unparalleled in human experience; nevertheless, if I had been for years watching a surgeon make examinations and do operations without having any clear idea why he was doing so, and then suddenly caught on to what were his aims, the situation would bear some resemblance to the one the believer sees in his appropriation and acceptance of theological affirmations.

Most remarkable of all, however, is the case of the person who is not at all content to say, "I cannot see anything in these metaphysical and theological concepts, so let's forget them and talk of something else," but insists on laboring over analyses of them in almost full detachment from the phenomena of religious experience. That in such circumstances one should find such exercises worthwhile very strongly suggests a powerful psychological preoccupation with, and abnormal degree of resistance to, relating theological and metaphysical ideas to actual religious experience. In other words, those who profess to find such ideas meaningless yet explore them with almost total disregard for the religious phenomena apart from which they *are* meaningless draw upon themselves the strong suspicion that they are letting a psychological cat out of their own logical bag.

Some writers, incapable of understanding even the most rudimentary elements in the character of religious experience, provide analyses of the believer's interpretative procedure that are wholly irrelevant to the real problems of the interpretation of religion. Professor Paul Edwards provides a luxuriant crop of such analyses of what are nonproblems for both the genuine skeptic and the genuine believer. A random example may be found in a paper in which he is apparently concerned with showing confusions in Tillich's distinction between anthropomorphic and metaphysical conceptions of God.[8] Professor Edwards suggests a momentary reluctance to embark on his project: "It may at first seem pointless for an unbeliever (like myself) to take issue with a philosopher who concedes that 'God does not exist.' But Tillich does make other remarks which unbelievers would or should oppose." Such a frank confession of extreme dogmatism at the outset is strikingly alien to the methodology of any serious inquirer into the phenomenology of religion.

Professor Edwards finds Tillich's theology "compatible with anything whatsoever," but no theology could be anything else unless it were anchored in some actual experience that compels reflection and invites a choice between identification and nonidentification. *All* theology is otherwise bound to sound as absurd as the conversational exchanges of the messenger and the king in *Through the Looking Glass*, which Professor Edwards quotes with an irrelevance that cannot but cause serious students of the phenomena of religion either to gasp or to shrug, if not to do both. For neither the anthropological deity Tillich disapproves nor any metaphysical deity he or any other theologian could ever approve could be intelligibly talked about apart from conditions Professor Edwards totally ignores.

It is, nevertheless, certainly possible to fail to see the connection; that is, it is possible so to interpret the phenomena of religion as to dispense with the theological and metaphysical explanations. Whether doing so is satisfactory is beside the point here. Unbelief of that kind is plainly quite

[8] Paul Edwards, "Professor Tillich's Confusions," *Mind* 74 (April 1965): 192–214.

different from the kind exemplified in writers such as Paul Edwards, whose extraordinary preoccupation with what philosophers of religion could not well avoid calling pseudoproblems is symptomatic of a kind of unbelief rooted in a deep psychological need to disbelieve rather than in a genuine inability to make the interpretative connection that the believer makes.

The Nature–God Antinomy

As I learn, like other organisms, to adapt to my surroundings, I find myself relating to their nature in an ambivalent way, unlike that of nonhuman animals. Dogs and cats, frogs and leopards, do not view nature either with hostility or with affection; they simply and instinctively accept it. Of course, a cat presumably feels hostility to the dog that worries her, as she feels affection for her own kittens; but like other animals she takes up no attitude either of affection for or of hostility to Nature as a whole. I, too, accept Nature as a whole. I have no choice: Nature confronts me, exacting my obedience. I know that to pit myself against the might of Nature would be to make myself ridiculous, as if I were to try to extinguish the sun by throwing a bucket of water at it. Yet besides accepting the ineluctable force of Nature, I also both love her and hate her. On the one hand, I love and admire the flora and fauna of the countryside, and may even wax poetic over the beauty of golden sunsets and pink dawns. On the other hand, I am sometimes angry at Nature. I may call her cruel, as I sometimes call her kind—though, of course, I know she is neither the one nor the other but simply indifferent.

The indifference is, indeed, precisely what I resent. Not only does the sun shine alike on the just and the unjust; submicroscopic beings called viruses hurt and may even kill the noblest and bravest of men as well as miserable oafs and cowards. I perceive that even the tenderness and beauty I sometimes see in Nature are read into her by me no less than what I choose to call her cruelty. I learn, then, to see in Nature neither kindness nor cruelty but what the existentialists call the absurd. Flies feed on the exposed brain of a wounded hero as he lies not quite dead, slain in battle. A man-eating tiger seeks to eat me only because, being old, he has lost his teeth and his youthful agility. Were he a healthy young beast, able to go for antelope, he would not deign to make me his prey. Yet if I feel resentful at this, my resentment should not be directed toward the poor old tiger but at the ways of Nature.

I do come to terms with Nature, but what are these terms? I find I am really only making a truce with her. Perhaps I personify Nature as a goddess, so indicating my respect for her mighty power. Yet my respect is somewhat like that of a conquered people for the conquering army that has subjugated it. Unlike the conquered people, I am in some respects grateful to my conqueror; that is to say, I am glad things are the way they are, and of course I know it would be ridiculous on my part to bear a grudge against Nature such as a subdued people bears against the army of occupation. I like to think of Nature as "good for me" and so I may say, if I please, that she is "good to me;" but I am by no means satisfied with her. I can accept her indifference, which affects me as seemingly indiscriminate benevolence and malevolence. Yet my acceptance is not at all a declaration that I find her satisfactory.

On the contrary, my attitude toward Nature is somewhat like that of an intelligent and adventuresome child toward his parents, or an energetic and enterprising young man toward his home town. He knows very well he has much to be grateful for in the parent who has nurtured him and the people who have borne with his growing pains, but he perceives also their limitations and seeks to transcend them. If he is mature enough to be able to see the whole situation in perspective, he will not flee from his home with a resolve never to set foot in it again, but he will know he must somehow break away from its limitations and go beyond them. For he will have become aware that beyond his home environment lies a realm he must explore, a realm which, though not disconnected with his old environment, has rich and important elements in it that are not to be found in the confines of the home that cradled him.

In my dissatisfaction with Nature that accompanies and grows out of my acceptance of her as she is, I grope for something beyond. Through memory and imagination I find myself in a realm in which I seem to be able to emancipate myself from Nature's confines. In Nature I cannot stop the withering of a rose, yet through memory I can recall a resplendent rose tree and through imagination conjure up a forest of them. In the realm of imagination I do not merely control Nature. That I can do, within limits, through scientific knowledge; but in the realm of imagination I actually transcend Nature by creating a new world of my own. Here I begin to discern an antinomy in what I am apprehending. How am I to interpret it?

Civilized people experience a special difficulty in this interpretative process for the very reason that, unlike primitive people, they have for long taken imagination and memory for granted and are therefore not fascinated by them as are children and people at a more primitive stage of intellectual and cultural development. Civilized people are apt to overlook the peculiar quality of the activities of memory and imagination, explaining them away as merely interesting or odd developments in the physiobiological process. We are also often inclined to belittle them as belonging to a world we pejoratively call subjective and in that sense unreal, a world standing in direct opposition to the world of physics and other sciences. No one, however, who has preserved a vivid memory of the early impact on him of the realm of the imagination can fail to recall with what intensity the reality of that realm imposed itself on him. Its impact, far from seeming less real than that of the physiobiological realm, seemed by comparison with the latter as real as the third dimension of solid geometry is real by comparison with the two dimensions of plane geometry. That I can imagine a magic carpet does not mean there is such an entity available to scientific exploration. It means much more. It means, precisely, that I have performed a feat that has taken me into a realm beyond that of the world that is accessible to scientific investigation.

I live, then, in two worlds. The sense of ambivalence is poignant, except to the extent that I devise dogmas, scientific or metaphysical, to help me to diminish, if not to forget, the poignancy. If I allow the stark ambivalence of the phenomenological reality to confront me, the one supremely worthwhile question that remains is, how am I to interpret the ambivalence I find? What are the viable options and on what grounds is one to be taken as more plausible than another?

An obvious proposal is that what we call "Nature" is the whole of "objective" reality and what we call "God" is what I concoct out of my head, a by-product of my own creative imagination. In other terms, what I call "God" is a symbol of the sum total of my private longings, wishes, and ideals, which are indeed psychologically given to me (that is, given by the internal structure of my own being), while what I call "Nature" is a symbol of the sum total of the reality that confronts me from outside myself. In other terms again, what I call "Nature" is independent of my existence, would have been there even if my parents had not happened to bring me into the world, and will be there long after I have ceased to exist, while what I call "God," however beautiful and noble it may look to me and to others, is as much an offshoot of my existence as is, for instance, my tone of voice or my style of handwriting, and will cease with, and as surely as, my heartbeat.

True, it may well happen to coincide in large measure with your longings, wishes, and ideals, but that is so only because you and I are both human and therefore, broadly speaking, you are a similar sort of being to me, with a general tendency to have the same longings and ideals. In addition, you and I may happen to have had, in general, the same sort of upbringing, so that our longings and ideals tend still further to coincide. Such reflections, however, would not at all affect the interpretation proposed: though you and I each conduct a soliloquy in English, and even if our soliloquy be almost the same, or at any rate along similar lines, the fact remains that you and I are none the less each someone talking to himself.

Nature, God, and Solipsism

What is wrong with such a proposal? It is highly plausible so long as one is content to view what we call "God" as lacking the impact that is exerted upon us, as we have come to acknowledge, by what we call "Nature." It is formally possible to take up the same view with respect to what we call "Nature." Philosophers indeed have considered a view traditionally called solipsism, which proposes that what I take to be an external world, including other human minds, is in fact the creation of my own mind.

No philosopher, however, has for long taken the solipsistic view seriously. Why not? It is theoretically plausible. What is wrong with it is that it fails to do justice to the manner in which the phenomena come to us. As soon as we squarely face facts such as what a brick wall does to us when we run into it and are able to distinguish such facts from a dream experience in a fantasy world, solipsism becomes for us, despite its being a theoretically arguable position, nothing more than an intellectual posture, advocacy of which could be only a learned game, a mildly entertaining byway leading off the path of serious intellectual enterprise.

Why, then, is it possible for us to take up a radically different view with respect to the other pole of experience, the one whose focus is symbolized in what we call "God"? The testimony of religious people is that it comes no less ineluctably and indeed with an even greater impact upon us than the physiobiological world, and certainly as no less independent of our human creativity than is the world whose nature physicists, chemists, and zoologists investigate. Why should it be possible for us to find solipsism an absurdity in respect of the Nature-dimension of our experience and not at all an absurdity in respect of the God-dimension?

We should note, in the first place, at least one factor that makes solipsism so plainly unacceptable in respect of the physiobiological world—our sensitivity to pain. Were we deprived of that sensitivity—as are some paralytics and also, for example, lepers at certain stages of the development of their disease—then presumably we might be able to take solipsism a little more seriously with respect to the world of tables and chairs and brick walls; for they would not so violently or directly hurt us, nor should we so acutely feel their resistance to our will or their demands upon our obedience. A possible explanation, then, of our acceptance of a solipsistic interpretation of what we call "God" (while we so generally repudiate such an interpretation of what we call "Nature") would be that we are at least in some respects insensitive to what we call "God," as are neural lepers in some respects insensitive to what we call "Nature." As we must be physically and biologically healthy to be capable of apprehending the ineluctability and independent reality of the physiobiological world, so we must be spiritually healthy enough to recognize that what we call "God" is an independent reality and to apprehend that reality as such. Only a fully personal being can apprehend a person.

Forms of that proposed explanation are ancient. Ignatius of Antioch, for instance, uses one in an attack on docetism, a doctrine held by some in the primitive Church and accounted heretical. The docetists taught that though God is the creator and source of all things, and might be said to have become man in the person of Jesus Christ, he became so only in appearance (*to dokein*); he did not literally "take human flesh," for that, to people with the basic metaphysical outlook the docetists had inherited, would have been intolerable. Ignatius, in opposing them, attributes their inability to recognize that God was "truly" (*alēthōs*) present in Jesus (that is, present, as some might say, "in reality") to a "lack of reality" in themselves. He charges that the reason the docetists say Jesus suffered only in appearance is that they are themselves only "appearance." [9] Ignatius is saying, in effect, "God comes before your very eyes in the person of the man Jesus, and you take him for a ghost. Why? Because you yourselves are just a bunch of ghosts!"

Of course, what Ignatius says here looks at first sight like a glaring example of the classic *ad hominem* fallacy and sounds like no argument at all. Yet behind his theological shorthand can be constructed an argument which, whether we acknowledge its validity or not, certainly demands serious attention. A liar is generally inclined to suppose all men to be incapable of telling the truth, simply because he is. A thief is apt to doubt the possibility of the existence of an honest man, for no reason except that he is a dishonest one. Hence much of the force of the proverb "Set a thief to catch a thief." The worst effect of deterioration in our character is not that we behave badly; a worse consequence is that we lose the capacity for admitting to ourselves that others might be behaving well. Eventually, indeed, we so obliterate the vision of what it is to be confronted by moral and spiritual health and vitality greater than our own that we lose even the capacity to admit to our consciousness that we understand what such confrontation means. The worst effect of lying, then, is not that the liar gets out of the habit of telling the truth; it is, rather, that he gets out of the habit of recognizing that truth can be told.

What looks at first sight like mere petulance in Ignatius (when he charges that the docetists say Christ suffered only in appearance, "being themselves appearance") may be taken seriously. We may now paraphrase it: unbelievers say there is no independent spiritual reality in what is called "God" because the dimension of spiritual reality in themselves has been diminished to the point where their sensitivity to its compelling force has been lost. As our neural leper, partially desensitized to the world around him, would be better equipped, were he a philosopher, to take solipsism seriously in respect of some aspects of the Nature-dimension in his experience, so he whose sensitivity to the moral and spiritual realm has been gravely diminished is likely to be able to take solipsism seriously in respect of the God-dimension. Therein lies the force of the old notion expressed, sometimes crudely, in traditional Roman Catholic theology, of a kind of sin that is grievous enough to be

[9] Ignatius, *ad Tral.*

called "mortal" because it "kills the soul"; that is, it so stunts our growth that we lose the power to apprehend the compelling quality in the God-dimension as a force external to and independent of ourselves.

Autistic children provide a still more striking case of insensitivity to what we call the "external" or "natural" world. For certain pathological reasons, these unfortunate children are so unresponsive to their surroundings that they do not make even the elementary adjustments to them that normal people all make in early childhood. They remain withdrawn and behave in such a way as to ignore the world around them, the world the rest of us have come to terms with as a barrier that confronts us.

Childhood autism is a condition that has come to be generally recognized since it was first described by Dr. Leo Kanner of The Johns Hopkins University. Its most distinctive symptom is withdrawal: the autistic child is unable to sustain, and often unable to make, emotional relationships with either children or adults, and he may be apparently unaware of his own identity as a person. In specifying a "very interesting common denominator" in the background of all autistic children whom he studied, Kanner makes an observation that underscores the appositeness of autism as a parallel to what we are considering. They all came from highly intelligent parents and, he states, one fact "stands out prominently: the parents and collaterals were for the most part strongly preoccupied with abstractions of a scientific, literary, or artistic nature, and limited in genuine interest in people." [10] Autistic children often show signs of high verbal and other capacity; one committed to heart large portions of the Presbyterian catechism. A report issued in 1970 by the National Society for Autistic Children, under the chairmanship of Dr. G. K. Benson, himself the father of an autistic child, also observes that autistic children are often far more intelligent than, because of their withdrawal, they are taken to be. The etiology, however, remains obscure.[11]

When that point has been made, however, we must also note its limitations. Persuasive though it may be to those of us who recognize through it a distinctive trend in our own experience, we must ask what, more precisely, the point exhibits. It certainly provides no assent-compelling proof that there is a God-dimension confronting us externally, as does the world that scientists study. In the nature of the case, the God-dimension could not do that. At most the believer could use it only to suggest that as a possibility to an unbeliever, or point the way to it. The alternative interpretation—that what we are calling a "God-dimension" is not only an epiphenomenon of Nature but a purely subjective product of the human brain, an element in what the brain secretes as the liver secretes bile—could not be attacked on any logical ground.

[10] *Nervous Child* 2 (1943): 217–250.
[11] See in *British Medical Journal* i (1970): 62–63.

The Doubt-Certitude Antinomy

If we acknowledge that what we have been calling the "God-dimension" does confront us, being at least in some way or other external to, and independent of us, we face another of the several antinomies of religious belief. The believer feels certain he is basically on the right track and is moving in the right general direction, but he is painfully aware of his ignorance of the details. If he happens to be a philosopher, then, of course, he can do much ingenious logical mapwork to show what the relations must be in various structures that would be conceivable. He may even plausibly claim he knows what the structures would have to be, in view of such and such a finding about the manner in which the God-dimension comes to him or, as he may say, "hits" him. He may even more plausibly still claim to do very useful negative mapwork of this kind; that is, he may feel able, simply through logical means, to persuade many people, if not all, that certain structures would be impossible. A glaring example would be "God is the ground of all being, yet he is not."

But as we have seen much earlier, in dealing with paradox and perhaps even more vividly in treating the notion of symbolism in religion, the requirements of logic, however finely developed a logic it may be, do not always help us as much as at first sight one might expect. Not only, as we saw, is every statement about religion peculiarly difficult to analyze, however logically explorable it may be in theory. More importantly still, as we also saw, the realities that come to us through the symbol are "wild," like Nature herself, so that the more apposite the symbols used for them, the more these symbols reflect that wildness that is like the wildness of Nature. We can no more call a theological claim logically impossible than we could dare to say in biology that since wings are for flying through the air, the use of wings for submarine propulsion is logically impossible. Our first sight of a penguin, which uses its wings primarily as flippers for swimming, would show us how wrong we were.

One common temptation is to argue, in effect, that if the realm we have called the God-dimension is external to and independent of us, we ought to be able to inspect it as scientists inspect the Nature-dimension. It might have, of course (and presumably is to be expected to have), a different structure; but it should still be examinable, describable, and classifiable, as is the subject matter of, say, botany or ichthyology. As we have seen, the Gnostics and other exponents of theosophical systems have pretended to provide a "spiritual chemistry," with analyses of the structure of the realm we call the God-dimension.

At first sight such a methodology seems proper. That is to say, if the realm in question is really external to us and confronts us as believers say it does, then not only must believers be forced to come to terms with it as normal children learn to come to terms with chairs and brick walls; believers ought to be able to study and analyze it scientifically as physicists study physics and biochemists biochemistry. That would not mean, of course, that one could talk about it deductively by logical methods any more than one can find out by such means how penguins or giraffes must behave. It would mean, however, that there ought to be a theological science that could tell us how the God-dimension does behave, as zoologists can tell us how kangaroos behave and as pathologists tell us how streptococci behave in various parts of the human body. Such a theological science ought also, then, to be able to help us to predict—at any rate in certain respects and for practical purposes—how the God-dimension may be expected always to behave, no matter what the circumstances.

If I see such methodological procedures as appropriate, I am attesting my sense of the "otherness" of the God-dimension; I am also attesting that this sense of the God-dimension comes to me with a force so compelling that I am able to affirm with certitude its independent reality. It becomes inappropriate only when I then perceive that the nature of the God-dimension precludes the procedure that perfectly fits the Nature-dimension. The reason is, quite simply, that the Nature-dimension is objectifiable. Indeed, once I have overcome my playful childhood attempts at personifying it, it comes to me as already objectified. If I then come to approach the study of it, as we do in scientific pursuits, as an intellectual inquiry, the methodology I use, whatever else it may be, will have to be appropriate to an objectified reality. With the awareness that the God-dimension, though likewise an independent reality, does not come to me as objectified and is not objectifiable (except by an intellectual process that radically traduces its nature), comes a very important discovery. Whatever methodology might be appropriate for trying to understand the God-dimension, those methodologies that have been so successfully employed in the study of the Nature-dimension cannot be right for the other one.

When the believer discovers that aspect of the nature of the God-dimension, the doubt–certitude antinomy, as we may call it, strikingly confronts him. He feels able to affirm with certitude out of his vivid awareness that the reality of the God-dimension is indeed other than himself and comes to him as nonobjectified; yet he has to grope for methods of conceptualizing and otherwise intellectually dealing with the situation, and in the nature of the case these are bound to be extremely difficult to find.

The believer, having seen the otherness of both realms of experience, is apt to feel the methodologies respectively appropriate to them must have on that account something important in common. When he perceives that the difference between the realms, that common element notwithstanding, is so immense as to preclude any common methodology, he is often tempted to grasp at an infallibilist solution. The certitude of his awareness of the God-dimension, together with his perplexity about how to treat it conceptually, leads him to use the psychological device of trying to push away his perplexities and affirm in propositional form a number, sometimes a very large number, of metaphysical positions that he claims to have derived from a revelatory fount such as the Bible, the Church, or some other source whose spiritual authority he feels able to acknowledge. He cuts a half-comical, half-pathetic figure, somewhat like that of a vivacious little boy pretending to be a great lover. Obvious examples include the literalism that is alike characteristic of so-called fundamentalist Protestants and of those who in the anticonciliarist, ultramontane tradition within the Roman Church, so vehemently championed a simplistic doctrine of papal infallibility in the First Vatican Council in 1869–1870.

The key concept in such processes is that of infallibilism. It expresses, on the one hand, the certitude the believer claims to have attained about what is of fundamental importance—namely, the independent reality of the God-dimension. It attempts to disguise, on the other, his embarrassment and malaise in being unable to deal with it as he feels he ought. Not knowing where to turn, he takes refuge in neat propositional utterances that can only lead to a whole network of category confusions and other improprieties. Yet if he resists that temptation, he is liable to be forced into the position of having to say he has no evidence of the independent reality of the God-dimension when in fact he knows perfectly well he has at least as much evidence for it as he has for the independent reality of the Nature-dimension, that is, the world to which scientists give their attention.

What ought the believer to do? He can get no help from the methods of the unbeliever. The latter has a relatively very simple task, for if, *ex hypothesi*, there is no independently real God-dimension at all, the unbeliever's task (to the extent that he is a responsible philosopher) is simply to exhibit logical fallacies in the pronouncements of those who seem to be taking religious utterances seriously. The more seriously the believer does grasp his own intellectual and moral predicament, the more the force of the antinomy is laid upon him. If he does not slip into the infallibilist's trap, he is in danger of falling into that of the skeptic who is still crying out for evidence. The believer, however, if he be a philosopher as well as a believer, knows that the question for him cannot be one of securing evidence that there is an independently real God-dimension; the question for him is much more intricate—namely, how to express in his assertions, with the fidelity to experience that his responsibilities as a philosopher demand, both the element of infallibilism and the element of skepticism.

An example may help to exhibit the intricacy and to clarify the nature of the difficulties. In a discussion that took place at Princeton in 1962, Professor William Alston, working with a remarkably eighteenth-century, deistic concept of God as a being who, if known at all, is known chiefly if not wholly through his operations in Nature, observed that "no human being can have any grounds for expecting an omnipotent Creator to act in one way rather than another." [12] Nevertheless, he went on to say that

---

[12] John Hick, ed., *Faith and the Philosophers* (London: Macmillan & Co., 1964), pp. 83 f.

"in so far as our concept of God has any content," we do "have some reason, on some level of generality, for expecting one thing rather than another; and if the concept has no content then religion evaporates." [13]

Professor Norman Malcolm, in criticizing Alston's paper, surmises that there may be a connection in Alston's thought between the two seemingly incompatible assertions. The connection Malcolm sees is: "Alston is thinking that our concept of God must have some content; and this implies that we shall have some expectations as to how things will be in the world; and the fulfilment or non-fulfilment of those expectations will be evidence for or against the existence of God." [14]

That Malcolm may well be right in his surmise about what Alston is thinking is not particularly relevant here, for it has to do with a question about proof of the existence of God, which nowadays is not a very live question among philosophers of religion. Very relevant to our purposes, however, is this question: does having a concept of God imply having beliefs about God, and if so, what do these beliefs entail? Malcolm thinks it does imply that, and that "some of these beliefs might be called 'expectations.' " [15] Though Malcolm is discussing this question in a subjectivist context alien to our interests here, the question remains highly important. If the external reality of the God-dimension comes to me with compelling assurance, it must have some intelligible content for me. Such a content implies my having some beliefs about it, and (as Malcolm observes) "some of these beliefs might be called 'expectations.' "

We must be careful here not to overlook a crucial point. The beliefs-called-expectations do not come built into the confrontation itself; they are an interpretation of it. In the transition from the confrontation to the interpretation lies much scope, of course, for error. What, then, can be the conceptual content of what I say confronts me? What is it when it comes to me "raw," so to speak, before the interpretative work takes place?

To ask that question is like asking how the Nature-dimension comes to me before I begin to interpret it as mountains and chairs. The answer must include notice of the fact that the work of interpretation begins with the confrontation. I do not receive the impact of the external world, in whatever dimension it may be, and then, having received it, begin to interpret it. It confronts me, rather, in my act of interpreting it. There is no point at which I have the external world without having also my interpretation of it. Nevertheless, I can intellectually distinguish that which confronts me, together with the manner in which it confronts me, from what I read into it. I can properly say, for instance, that the external world in its Nature-dimension comes to me as a frontier, as a limit circumscribing my activities, and also as gracious to me, nourishing my body. At the same time, however,

[13] Ibid., p. 84.
[14] Ibid., p. 109.
[15] Ibid., p. 109.

I have already construed it to be what I call "hot," "cold," "hard," "soft," and so forth. Eventually I may construe it as physicists do. It comes to me as a pattern, rich and variegated, with innumerable interpretative possibilities. So I can be wrong about it; I can misinterpret it. What I am sure I cannot be wrong about is that it is *there* and that it confronts me, however I present to myself the *Gestalt* I find in it.

The same, *mutatis mutandis,* may be said about the God-dimension, though with the great added difficulty that the God-dimension comes to me, not as objectified, but subjectively as another being, as "The Other Being." How does another being come to me? It, too, comes as a barrier, a frontier; it comes also, in however different a way, as gracious and nourishing.

In some respects I can be in no doubt about the character of the person who confronts me, but I also interpret. I do so every time I make a new acquaintance. You come into my office for the first time. I can be in no doubt that you are confronting me, and I get a general impression of you. Let us suppose you have a very marked personality. I cannot but know that you are an extraordinarily warm, vivacious extrovert, or else an unusually cold, flaccid introvert, or whatever the case may be, for that is given with the confrontation. I also, however, make interpretative judgments about you. I may say to myself, "That is a man I could trust with my last dollar," or "I wouldn't trust that man as far as I could throw him." I might even go so far as to say, "On the whole I don't find that man very congenial; but there is something about him I do like, so perhaps in the long run we might be friends. Anyhow, I hope so, for I *want* to like him."

How shall we unravel what I know from what I do not know? Strictly speaking, there seems to be no way of doing so. Still, as time goes on, you disclose more and more of yourself to me in such a way as to convince me, as I might put it, "what sort of person you really are." I do then certainly have expectations about you. I do not absolutize them; that is to say, I shall not commit suicide if you disappoint me, turning out to be a weaker man than I had thought, or a less kindly one. I shall blame it on my interpretation. Moreover, and more importantly, if I have trusted you in the first place, I am not easily seduced into distrusting you. If appearances are against you I shall grieve, but far from jumping to adverse conclusions I shall expect that in the long run my loyalty to you shall be vindicated.

When the God-dimension confronts me, something very similar occurs. I am very much inclined to assume I know far more than I do; nevertheless, I am so inclined only because I do know a great deal.

When I am confronted with the God-dimension, more is given to me than is given when I know you, even if you be the unusually strong personality that has been suggested. So the believer is by no means talking nonsense when he claims to have grounds for his unlimited trust in God. But he may well be exaggerating his knowledge of detail, for he is including what is constructed by means of his interpretation.

For instance, the God-dimension may confront me with such a *kind* of force that I tend to think of it as all-powerful (*pantokrator* or *El Shaddai*). I may then begin to formulate propositions about it, such as the proposition that God can "do anything." These beliefs may or may not be warranted by what actually comes to me in experience. That this is so is unremarkable. People have often made mistakes in interpreting the Nature-dimension, as is well known, and from that, nothing negative can be deduced about the independence of the reality of the external world that confronts us.

Some of the beliefs, however, right or wrong as they may be, not only entail expectations but may be practically indistinguishable from the expectations. If I believe that heat melts ice, that is precisely what I shall expect of it, and indeed in such a matter I have no means of believing it without expecting it. Consequently, when I begin to try to formulate a set of theological propositions about God, I am inclined to develop them on the basis of the expectation I have reached—sometimes, no doubt, with insufficient care to examine what, precisely, I have reached. What is wrong may be neither the theological beliefs nor the logic of the arguments that purport to follow from these beliefs, but the original interpretation that issued as the expectation. Or, of course, in formulating the theological propositions, I may improperly go far beyond the expectations I had genuinely reached.

To be aware of both the dangers and the certainty is to be aware of the doubt–certitude antinomy. As I err in responding to my environment in the Nature-dimension (for instance, in false beliefs that rainbows are solid or in superstitious beliefs that certain stones have magical properties), so I can err in respect of the God-dimension, leading me to false or exaggerated claims about the knowledge of God I possess. As scientists throughout the ages have learned to be critical of claims to knowledge of the external world into which it is their business to inquire, so philosophical theologians have had to wrestle with what is here being called the doubt–certitude antinomy. By that I mean that they have been faced with having to learn how to weigh two elements: (1) the element in the confrontation that gives certitude about the external, independent reality of the God-dimension, and (2) the other element that issues only from our interpretative judgments about what occurs in the confrontation.

To belittle the first is to be skeptical in the pejorative sense of demanding evidence where the need for evidence is not the issue and of artificially forcing oneself into a critical attitude about everything relating to the God-dimension in such a way as to remind us of the behavior of autistic children in respect of the Nature-dimension of the external world. To belittle the second is to fall into the trap of the infallibilist. Both positions are narrow and each in its own way disguises a basic failure to cope with the antinomy under discussion. Success in distinguishing the nature of the certitude from the nature of the doubt, so as to hold them in balance without denigrating the force of either, attests the attainment of a religious maturity that is compatible with neither the dogmatism of the infallibilist nor the intolerance of the autistic skeptic.

The Despair–Faith Antinomy

"The depth of darkness into which you can descend and still live, is an exact measure, I believe, of the height to which you can aspire to reach." [16] This assertion, uttered in the context of the horrors of a situation of war and torture, expresses the despair–faith antinomy that the religious believer has to face.

The lower animals, who are guided through life by instinct alone, are not confronted by the antinomy. They live out their lives till old age or death by accident or the predatory habits of other animals overtakes them. By instinct they are enabled to accept death, and by instinct they are protected to an astonishing degree from accident, often eluding even the wiles of the human hunter. We, on the contrary, though we have preserved a modicum of self-protective instinct, have also attained a capacity for intellectual reflection that prevents us from being able to rest content with instinct as our sole guide. The sudden fall of a shadow will send a bird soaring into the air and a mouse scurrying to its hole. A man, on the other hand, faced with the same situation, wants to know how the shadow is caused so that he may decide whether or not it spells danger and how, by technological or other means, that danger may be avoided.

Man is thus enabled to avoid the almost constant succession of instinctive fears in which other animals live, but the price he pays is high—having escaped from that constant series of little panics, he is faced with one large one. Through rational reflection, he has learned how to cope with his environment so effectively as to make him the undoubted superior of all other animals, because he can easily outwit them. His knowledge, however, brings a new fear and sadness to him of which other animals are innocent. If I learned that my teen-age son were dying of leukemia, my dog would continue to bark affectionately at him, demanding his customary walk, while I would be reduced to mournful silence and inward questionings about the tragedy of life. Though there are times when I am inclined to envy the other animals their greater instinctive power, I could not but know, in such a sad circumstance, that instinct would do nothing more than temporarily hide from me the terrible truth I soon must face. Even the joys of friendship would fade from me and pleasures pall, for in the midst of them I could not forget my overwhelming awareness of tragedy. A sense of the futility of striving and even of the absurdity of living would bear down upon me, leading me into despair.

[16] Letter from Alan McGlashan to Laurens van der Post, quoted by the latter as an exergue for an account of his experience in a Japanese prison camp in World War II, *The Night of the New Moon* (London: Hogarth Press, 1970), p. 33.

To despair is literally to be bereft of hope, to be hopeless. When reason has taken over from instinct, hope is born, for man sees a whole spectrum of possibilities hitherto hid from him; but sooner or later man learns through reason the irrationality of his customary hopes. They come to look more and more like a mere residue of an old instinct, that is, the instinct to go on, even if without thought or purpose, driven by the élan that goads on all that lives. Having become critical of instinct as a guide to life and having seen the enormous advantages of critical reason, I was willing enough to pay the price of the loss of much of the instinctive power I had enjoyed at a more primitive level of existence, but now reason has led me to despair, and instinct can no longer meet my needs. Through reason I feel I have become like a tired and cynical old man who feels he "knows too much for his own good" yet cannot, even if he wished, undo the process that has brought him to his unenviably well-informed state. I have reached a point where the rational dictates to me the appropriateness of despair. At the same time my ancestry of instinct and reason combine to suggest to me that, notwithstanding the appropriateness of despair, I must go on *as if there were no despair.* But how? Certainly not by any rational procedure. Then can I do it by a reversion to instinct? No, for I have irrevocably turned my back on the full and exclusive use of it, so that what is left of my instinct will not function for the purpose of my new need.

At this point one may have recourse to Hume's dictum "Reason is and only ought to be the slave of the passions." That is to say, we may affirm, as Hume does, that reason simply fails to put us into contact with the "simple impressions," the realities that come to us through the empirical world. We must avoid, therefore, falling into the error of supposing that reason can help us to find any principle of connection, any basis for construction, that would yield a structure we could account real. "As the skeptical doubt arises naturally from a profound and intense reflection on these subjects," writes Hume, "it always increases, the farther we carry our reflections, whether in opposition or conformity to it. Carelessness and inattention alone can afford us any remedy. For this reason I entirely rely on them...." [17]

In other words, I may choose to limit reason to its use as a tool of my will, and so confess my inability to make any sense of the world that confronts me, including the occurrence of my son's leukemia, saying in effect: "The basic mistake I can make concerning it is to try to interpret it at all. I can and ought to use reason as an astronomer uses mathematics. But to try to interpret the meaning of the world or make sense of it by means of reason would be like a mathematician's trying to work out the astronomical state of affairs on the basis of mathematical principles."

[17] David Hume, *Treatise on Human Nature*, 4, 2 ("Scepticism with Regard to the Senses"), in *Hume Selections,* ed. C. W. Hendel (New York: Charles Scribner's Sons, 1927), p. 72.

Yet while we must concur with Hume about the limits of human reason, we are left with the puzzlement with which we started. All we have found is that both instinct and reason fail us. Instinct fails us because we have found, through reason, a means of transcending its limitations. Reason fails us because of limitations we now discover to be inherent in it. We must reckon with what we call "the facts" that confront us and these facts will not go away by the use of any logical method or other process of reason, nor can· we find any means of wholly explaining why they are there. Yet I am still none the less tormented by the need to find an explanation for my son's being stricken with a disease that will soon kill him. The reflection that the doctors may find a cure for it in the next decade does not in the least mitigate my personal torment; on the contrary, it may aggravate it. Indeed, my torment would be aggravated worst of all if the medical profession were eventually to announce that it had found a cure the day after he died.

Using reason as a tool, however, I may still inquire whether my failure to make sense of "the way things are" may not arise from my failing to view "the facts" in all the dimensions in which they present themselves. If I have faced the Nature–God antinomy that has been already considered, my son's leukemia will confront me alongside that which has confronted me in what has been called the God-dimension. I am still troubled, still perplexed, but I may see at least a glimmer of hope that there may be a way out of my perplexity.

It is here that the religious believer, having been presented with a disclosure pattern that he can accept and that "speaks to his condition," as the Quaker phrase goes, may make his venture of faith. In face of the shambles of reason, and having only the vestigial remains of the primitive instinct that once guided him, he may find himself able to commit himself to faith in a particular understanding of the structure of the God-dimension. He may at least say, for instance, "I am still able to incline to belief rather than disbelief in God as presented in the Bible, and this inclination of mine makes it possible for me to posit a goodness that lies behind all things, even the tragic fact that my son, whom I love more than anything else in the world, will be dead of leukemia before Christmas."

That is faith. No understanding of it, however, is possible without the reflection that it can no more enter the situation "pure" or "single" than the positive wire can bring you an electric circuit. Faith comes only in the context of some kind of despair, some kind of hopelessness. Despair and faith so walk together, indeed, that faith is dependent on despair for its sustenance, while despair without some measure of faith cannot survive at all. To put the matter dramatically, every man of faith may be regarded as a potential suicide victim spared. Yet the despair–faith antinomy remains. The man of faith is engaged in incessant battle with despair. His belief is that he is on the winning side. The antinomy that is part of the constitution of the earliest stages of his religious awareness is present with him to the end of his life. It is part of what religious awareness is.

The Absence–Presence Antinomy

The religious believer finds himself confronted, as we have seen, with a presence. He finds himself being acted upon by that presence and awakened by it. The presence is both outside him, like the tables-and-chairs world, and inside him, stirring his own being at its core. There is an immense difference in the quality of such experience, on the one hand, and, on the other, that in which we creatively imagine gods, angels, and other spirits.

We now approach a crucial point. Let us call the experiences (a) and (b) respectively. The suggestion has already been made that the difference between (b) and (a) is akin to the difference between imagining a wall and hitting your head against one. Let us say (b) is akin to imagining a paradisiacal island (as in Gaunilo's retort to Anselm's argument) and encountering one. It is akin to it in the sense that if I have the imaginative power to create such an island in my mind, I can do so at all times. The power does not leave me. A child who likes my stories has only to say to me, "I want to hear about that beautiful island again," and off I go into my dream world and conjure it up for him. So long as I have my mental capacity intact I can go on doing it at will. Unless my brain is damaged or I turn senile I can go on twenty years hence doing it just as well as I ever did and at any moment I choose.

Apart from all talk about differences in quality or "feeling tone" between (a) and (b), there is one very striking and decisive difference we must now notice. In contrast to what I find in experience (b), I cannot, in experience (a), turn on the presence at will. On the contrary, very often—in ardent prayer, for instance—I seek it and it does not come to me. In the language of piety, God "hides his face" from me. At any rate, whatever language we talk, I find I want to renew the experience that on former occasions I enjoyed and I also find I cannot do so at will. In experience (a) I can no more induce the experience than I can conjure you up in the flesh when you are not there.

What I experience at such a time is not the presence but the absence of God. Writers who have pointed out that God may be known through his absence as well as (or even better than) through his presence are not merely uttering a description of the nature of religious awareness. They are providing, unwittingly or no, a criterion by means of which, as philosophers, we may distinguish between experiences (a) and (b).[18] There is a striking

[18] I have discussed the absence–presence antinomy in *The Sense of Absence* (Philadelphia: J. B. Lippincott Co., 1968).

analogy in the fact that while I can conjure up vividly before my mind either you, or the Shetland pony on a farm I know, or even my mother who has long since died, there is no way in which I can bring your real presence to me if you choose to absent yourself from me, or see the "real" horse if it is not there, or at my will raise my mother from the dead. The very fact that God is often absent from me and that I have a poignant sense of that absence (as a bereaved person has a poignant sense of the absence of the one he loves) is—together with the experience on other occasions of the divine presence—a striking experiential proof of the existence of God as one who is "standing over against" me and independent of me.

If it were not for the absence of God (that is, if I could conjure up the divine presence at will), I could not be sure of the reality of the encounter. Indeed, I could not but be extremely vulnerable to the obvious philosophical objection that what I take to be (without an ostensive referent in the empirical world) the presence of divine being confronting me may not be what I claim. It not only might be but would be very likely to be no more than the fruit of my fertile imagination.

The absence–presence antinomy also, then, is inseparable from religious awareness. It occurs even in primitive forms of pantheism—for example, in Nature worship or sun worship, when men notice that the sun is sometimes hidden behind clouds or even eclipsed by the moon's shadow, and Nature herself seems to withdraw her beneficent power. Where Mother Earth poured forth her bounty last year, this year's harvest is meager; the rains did not come and the land was scorched dry and fruitless. In the more developed forms of religious awareness, however, the absence–presence antinomy becomes far more strikingly inescapable. It also becomes telling corroboration that, whatever the nature of the encounter that the religious believer describes, it is not self-manufactured.

The sense of the absence of God, familiar to all mature religious believers, is not at all a sense of the loss of one's own powers, as for example, is my feeling of diminished capacity to work effectively when I am tired or of hoarseness when I have been speaking too long or under difficult conditions. In such cases I can detect a correlation between my recuperation from hoarseness or fatigue to the full exercise of my normal powers. Every writer who has sat up late, working too long at a stretch, has had the experience of feeling jaded and unable to muster his ideas and set them down well. A writer, in such a situation, simply goes to bed and, waking up the next morning refreshed, is soon able to cope with the situation that the previous night had so depressed him.

The sense of the absence of God that the religious believer feels is not at all of that order. It is the sense of the taking away of something in a process over which the believer has no control and in which he can see no correlating factors such as the fatigue that brings depression and failure and the refreshment that brings vigor and success. On the one hand, he may be at his liveliest and earnestly on his knees trying to pray, yet he may find only emptiness and heartache such as one feels in bereavement, not least in the midst of the bustle of life and in the face of the invigorating "smell of success." On the other hand, he may be physically and mentally "just ticking over," with his thoughts and feelings far removed from religious concerns, when he is suddenly confronted by the presence of God and filled with the sense of it.

We can now see more clearly why the conviction of believers is so strong. The antinomy that has been considered in this section provides them with a self-authenticating assurance that what they call the presence of God, whatever it is, comes from beyond them and is independent of their own creative imagining. To recognize this is not, of course, to provide any philosophical proof that what believers call "God" is to be properly defined as the term is defined in classical doctrinal formulae.

QUESTIONS ON CHAPTER X

1 The behavioral sciences offer several ways of accounting for the emergence of religious belief. In what way might they fall short as explanations?

2 Critically consider the concept of a "third being" in intersubjectival relationships.

3 If belief and unbelief, as they reach maturity, tend to coalesce, how can a radical difference between believer and unbeliever remain?

4 Discuss the notion of multidimensionality in relation to the God–Nature antinomy.

5 Consider the notion that resistance to the God-dimension might be analogous to autism.

6 With some reference to the Alston-Malcolm discussion, consider what I do when I interpret a confrontation.

7 What limits do you see to human reason and how does your answer affect the use to which you propose to put your reason?

8 What sense does it make to say that God may be better known through his absence than through his presence?

BIBLIOGRAPHICAL SUGGESTIONS

D'Arcy, M. C. *No Absent God.* New York: Harper & Row, 1962.

Koenker, Ernest B. *Great Dialecticians in Modern Christian Thought.* Minneapolis: Augsburg Publishing House, 1971. A sound, readable treatment for students of the tradition, rooted in a pre-Socratic insight that reality is multifaceted.

MacGregor, Geddes. *The Sense of Absence.* Philadelphia: J. B. Lippincott Co., 1968. Brief study of the notion that God is better known through absence than through presence.

MacGregor, Geddes. *Christian Doubt.* London: Longmans, Green and Co., 1951. A study of the role of doubt in faith.

Rümke, H. C. *The Psychology of Unbelief.* New York: Sheed & Ward, 1963.

Sewell, Elizabeth. "The Death of the Imagination." In *The New Orpheus,* edited by Nathan A. Scott, Jr. New York: Sheed & Ward, 1964.

Sheldon, Wilmon H. *God and Polarity.* New Haven, Conn.: Yale University Press, 1954. A profound study of the principle of polarity in all things, without which "no life could live."

Slaatte, Howard A. *The Pertinence of Paradox.* New York: Humanities Press, 1968. A study of the role of paradox in philosophical thought.

Todd, William. *Analytical Solipsism.* The Hague: Martinus Nijhoff, 1968. Sees analytical philosophy as producing "a new sort of solipsist."

Unamuno, Miguel. *Perplexities and Paradoxes.* New York: Philosophical Library, 1945.

Vahanian, George. *The Death of God.* New York: George Braziller, 1961.

Watts, Alan W. *The Two Hands of God.* New York: Macmillan Co., 1969. A study by a popular writer of the myths of polarity.

Wisdom, John. "The Modes of Thought and the Logic of God." In *The Existence of God,* edited by John Hick, pp. 275-298. New York: Macmillan Co., 1964.

XI

EXPERIENCE, REASON,
AND CREATIVE
RELIGIOUS PROTEST

> Faith has no merit where human reason supplies the proof.
>
> *Gregory the Great (c. 540–604),*
> *Homilies*
>
> Experience is the best of schoolmasters, only the school-fees are heavy.
>
> *Thomas Carlyle (1795–1881),*
> *Essays*

What Is Experience?

Before we turn to the important question of how the rational and irrational elements in religion may function in relation to each other, we should first consider a question that has already been importunately demanding attention—what is experience? We have insisted on appealing to experience and have tried to conduct our inquiries with experiential referents. That procedure, however, raises the question now before us. As Professor John E. Smith has remarked:

> Every appeal to individual experience to settle a question carries with it a further appeal, whether implicit or explicit, to some criteria that determine what is to count as an experience or as the content of experience. . . . Without criteria experience becomes so broad that nothing is excluded. It loses its differential meaning, and its effectiveness as a means of bringing general concepts and theories to the test is greatly reduced.[1]

Despite all the difficulties of developing a critical approach to experience, we are forced to develop one in order to avoid vagueness, not to say unintelligibility.

---

[1] John E. Smith, *Reason and God* (New Haven, Conn.: Yale University Press, 1961), p. 173.

On the assumption that we are not content with any account of experience (such as Hume's) that reduces it to one single, identifiable subject matter (sense impressions, according to Hume), we must reckon with its comprising "a great mass of contents resulting from the interplay between the self and the world in which it lives. Experience becomes the great matrix out of which all distinctions arise, but it is itself not wholly identical in nature with any of its contents." [2] If I hope to make experience an intelligible concept, I must not think of it as one-way traffic that is forever flowing in upon me, but as two-way traffic between me and non-me. I do not take in an external world and then adapt it to my needs as I might take a ready-made jacket and have the sleeves lengthened or the lapels widened. The world I take in is always made to measure; that is, I am tailoring it to *my* measure. I am interpreting it in being aware of it as intelligible. Moreover, there is nothing simple or ultimate or primitive about the data of sense. Whatever these are, they are highly specialized (or, as Dewey might say, "reflected") products. So experience is relational, dimensional, and directional. That is why the antinomies, to a consideration of some of which the previous chapter was devoted, play so vital a part in religious awareness. What the believer claims to grasp presupposes that relationality, dimensionality, and directionality, are inherent in experience itself.

I have suggested the example of ready-made and custom-made suits, but, for a reason that is illuminating, that figure will not carry us far. The reason is that a suit merely sits round me, so to speak; it does not really grow into me or I into it. Experience might be better likened to a living skin. In the two-way traffic that experience is, I adapt it to myself and myself to it, as my skin adapts itself both to me and to the external world. My skin, which becomes more sensitive here and more anesthetized there, helps me to adapt myself to the external world. In any case, whatever figure we use (and plainly none could be adequate for so fundamental a category), we should notice that neither do I produce what I call "experience of reality" nor do I simply receive it. Yet when I have that experience I have it whole, with its entire complex of relations, dimensions, and directions. So, while I do tailor my experience, I do not spin the cloth out of nothing. My awareness of the given is always an awareness of distinctions within the given, most notable among which is the distinction between what I can do "on my own steam" (through my extensive powers of imagination) and what I can do only when I have the materials as well as the tools.

We may not be able to isolate precisely what the materials are. If we could, both science and theology might almost go out of business, for we should know both what Nature is and what God is. Yet though we cannot isolate the materials from what we do with them, we are aware that the materials are multidimensional and that the multidimensionality is not our

[2] Ibid., p. 174.

creation but is independent of us. To be aware of that is to be aware of the Nature–God antinomy, as we have seen. We can artificially break experience down into dimensions, and that process springs, of course, from the imaginative and rational character of our minds; but we no more find nondimensionality and then put multidimensionality there than we find a flat world that could be satisfactorily treated by plane geometry and then impose on it a further dimension of our own making for which we have to invent solid geometry. The world comes to us either in all its dimensions or it does not come in any of them.

The central philosophical difficulty for the believer is not that the God-dimension, as we have called it, might be a fabrication of the mind. The difficulty is, rather, that while it confronts us as surely and independently to say the least, as does the tables-and-chairs dimension, it is, as is also that dimension, susceptible to more than one interpretation. Nor is the difficulty that while scientific method provides a good working knowledge of the tables-and-chairs world, there is no generally accepted theological method that does the same for the God-dimension. It is, rather, that no method could do the same for the God-dimension wherever the religious believer makes claims such as he does make when he says, for instance, that God is a personal (or suprapersonal) being and is directly known as such by the believer.

When we examine by what interpretative process the believer who does make such a claim is able to arrive at it, we find that both rational and apparently irrational procedures are used. For instance, Christians sing, in Faber's post-communion hymn:

> Nature cannot hold thee,
> > Heaven is all too strait
> For thine endless glory
> > And thy royal state.
>
> Out beyond the shining
> > Of the farthest star
> Thou art ever stretching
> > Infinitely far.
>
> Yet the hearts of children
> > Hold what words cannot,
> And the God of wonders
> > Loves the lowly spot.
>
> Jesus, gentlest Saviour,
> > Thou art in us now;
> Fill us full of goodness
> > Till our hearts o'erflow.[3]

[3] *The Hymnal* (Greenwich, Conn.: Seabury Press, 1940), no. 348. (Hymn 315 in *The English Hymnal*).

Christians, by means of the doctrine of the Undivided Trinity, also identify the subject of that devotional lyric with Yahweh, the God of Abraham, whom the prophet Elijah found neither in the earthquake nor in the fire but in a still small voice that he discovered by following these phenomena while he was lodging in a cave.[4] Identifying the subject of their experience with the eternal source of all things visible and invisible, learned Christians have provided elaborate metaphysical constructs to show that that eternal fount of all being can be and is the baby Jesus, who is, furthermore, present inside Christians every time they receive the Eucharist. The arguments, valid or invalid as they may be accounted, purport to be rational in the sense that they can be formulated logically in propositional and syllogistic form; yet no Christian would ever claim that anyone could possibly arrive at such a conclusion by rational investigation. In the interpretation of all religious experience, indeed, it would seem that there are both rational and irrational elements. How are these elements to be understood and in what relation do they stand to each other?

The Rational and the Irrational in Religion

Religions, in the early stages of their development, foster no particular awareness of either the rational or the irrational. When an intelligent primitive man performs the rituals that are customary in his tribe, he is not conscious of doing anything like an analysis of thought or of proposing anything such as a reasoned approach to life, and he is certainly not conducting any kind of irrational protest against rationalism. He is simply doing what is customary and familiar. Nevertheless, his religion entails some ethical injunctions and prohibitions, and sooner or later he is going to reflect on these. They may seem to him, as we might say, "good sensible rules," that is, they seem rational compared with those of neighboring tribes. Doubts will eventually arise, however, as contact with other tribes or races will suggest that perhaps his tribe's customs and laws are not so rational after all. In the light of a standard that he can begin to see as common among men, irrespective of race or tribe, the religious beliefs and practices of tribes other than his own, as well as their customs and laws, have much to commend them, once they are seen in context. Moreover, some aspects of the familiar practices of his own tribe will begin to invite his criticism which, though no doubt unvoiced and inward, is none the less troubling to his mind.

What is interesting in such reflections is that to the extent that people think at all, they tend to expect reasonableness in religion. Though religion points to mystery and is, indeed, no religion at all unless it invokes wonder and awe, it is expected to exhibit some sort of intelligible pattern. Among polytheists, for instance, the credibility of the gods decreased as soon as people who were thoughtful as well as imaginative tried to make sense of

[4] 1 Kings 19:9–13.

the accepted pantheon and found they could not do so without intellectual acrobatics designed for conceptual cheating. The Greek poets, ridiculing the gods, taught people to accept them as part of the *mise-en-scène* of the popular imagination, but in such a way as to avoid taking them seriously.

Yet when serious-minded people interest themselves in religious matters they do expect that a religion should hang together at least to the extent of making an intelligible system; they find nonsense unacceptable. As we have seen in other connections, the Christian doctrine of the Trinity, as developed out of early Church councils, is really an attempt to make sense out of what seemed intellectual conflict or confusion. One might even say that the whole corpus of Christian theological literature, from the first-century apologists down to modern times, is—as, indeed, is the literature of all the great religions of the world—an attempt to exhibit some kind of rational structure in what the religion has proposed for acceptance.

More even than that is expected when philosophical rationalism of one sort or another happens to be in vogue. In such times thoughtful people are not content with attempts to beat the oddnesses of religious disclosure into some sort of rational shape, whether of, say, a Platonic or a Spinozistic or Hegelian type or of the sort favored by those who, under the influence of the Enlightenment, talked of a "natural" theology. Proponents of such views, placing reason at the top of the hierarchy of all values, generally attempt to provide a system based wholly on rational inquiry. That is their ideal at any rate, even though they may not feel ready to claim to have attained it. They do not necessarily despise the sense of mystery that is generally and rightly associated with religion, but they prefer wherever possible to be able to put religion on a rational basis, accounting rationality the mark of "true" religion, contradistinguished from vulgar superstition.

Thomas Browne's *Religio Medici,* once a much admired and still a very readable classic, is an example of such an attitude toward the role of reason in religion. John Locke is a celebrated example of a proponent of the view that religion and reason, far from being at loggerheads, are natural allies, being both aspects of the same thrust of the human spirit. Such "natural" theology does not by any means necessarily exclude recognition of the idea of divine revelation; but even where such revelation is acknowledged, it is expected to manifest itself in a way conformable to reason, for God is conceived as pre-eminently rational if not simply identified with the rational principle.

When we ask, however, what the rational principle might be, we find it is always very obviously a construct of the human mind, which by its own nature requires a kind of orderliness for its own efficient working. That reflection suggests that we are looking for a tidy God in order that we may keep a tidy mind, somewhat as we might say we need a tidy desk to produce tidy work. Nevertheless, a natural theology need not be so simplistic. Tennant, for instance, in his *Philosophical Theology,* claimed that his system of natural theology was empirical in the sense that it looked to established facts and inductions, received from the external world; it did not consist of a web of thought apart from that world. Tennant's claim was that his theological system conformed to facts just as much as physics and biology conform to facts which, so to say, are allowed to speak for themselves. Tennant's claim for his system is, indeed, fairly plausible, generally speaking, as are the claims of the authors of other similar systems. Even there, however, the tendency to expect the facts to be manifestations of a principle conformable to our concept of orderliness and rationality is strong.

When we turn back to the nexus of ideas that have their origin in the special insights of Plato, we find (the inadequacies of ancient systems notwithstanding) a vital clue for the discovery of what is amiss in many "rational" approaches to religion. It is true that Plato and his followers expected *to kalon,* the good and the beautiful, to be *kosmion,* orderly; nevertheless, they recognized that there has been somehow or other a diminishment in our capacity to know what rationality and orderliness are. Attempts, often supported by much modern erudition, to present Plato as the classic type of all rationalism traduce him as much as do those who have seen him as a mystic. Plato's genius lay, rather, in detecting, at an early stage in human thought, that people's concept of the things they rightly admire is so blurred and distorted that they are not capable of discerning what their concept may stand for. They are likely, therefore, to have very erroneous ideas about the rationality that they claim to admire. As we might say, "They would not recognize rationality if it walked through the door."

Plato provided a method by means of which he claimed that philosophers, as lovers of wisdom, could learn to grasp what the real world is and therefore of what real orderliness and goodness and beauty consist. The merits and demerits of that method are, of course, beside the point here. What matters to us for our purpose is that Plato saw the innate defectiveness of the human mind, cooped within its own confines ("embedded in flesh," as the old Pythagoreans might have said) and therefore unable to see clearly even what it rightly gropes after.

The importance of Plato's insight lies in its providing us with a built-in self-critical mechanism that makes possible for us the constant subjection to criticism of even our most treasured idealizations of how things ought to be. We are enabled to recognize that our noblest concepts are not noble enough. The reality may be expected to be better than our puny minds are likely to be able to suppose. In any case it is sure to be different. A mathematical prodigy who happened to be blind from birth might construct a concept of a lush countryside from listening to recordings of botanical texts, but if he suddenly acquired his sight he would be surprised by what confronted him and astonished at its being so different from his expectations. Presumably he would be by no means disappointed at what he saw. He might well be disappointed at himself, however, for having had so inadequate a concept of what a lush countryside is.

If forests, meadows, and wild flowers are more beautiful than an intelligent blind man could have imagined and are also far more complex, as physicists have discovered, than a poet's finest dreams, what are we to say of the feeble efforts of even the wisest of men to grasp the spiritual or moral God-dimension that has captured the imagination of all great and good men throughout the ages? All that they have conceptualized, including the concept of rationality itself, is likely to be grievously impoverished when not ridiculously distorted. The concept of rationality in particular is likely to be modeled on the logical processes of the human mind which, for all their usefulness to us, is (like the usefulness of mathematics to an astronomer) only of subordinate value in the discovery of what Being is. Any decently trained engineer could draw a blueprint for a more rational solar system than the one we live in.

The question, then, is, to what extent, if any, should we expect to find in the God-dimension that which we call "rationality"? Are we wrong in expecting to make sense of it? Surely not. We are nevertheless likely to be very wrong indeed in expecting to find out by our ratiocinative methods what the God-dimension is. We should also be very wrong if we expected that the God-dimension, whatever it is, should conform to our rational prescriptions for it. The protest against rationality, which we shall now consider, is concerned with that particular methodological error.

Religious Protest Against Rationality

Theologians, as the spokesmen of religious believers, use ratiocinative discourse in the discussion of their subject matter. That is to say, they develop arguments, take notice of logical implications, and draw forth conclusions, no less than do other men; yet they often call attention, some of them very pointedly, to the limitations of reason. In this, of course, they are not alone. There is a long philosophical tradition that is highly critical of rationalism while using ratiocinative methods for its dethronement, and those whom that tradition has affected (the British empiricists, for instance) have been much disposed to point out the limitations of reason. Hume is a striking exemplar of that tradition, both in his use of ratiocination and in his critique of reason.

Both skeptics and religious believers recognize that reason, with all its implements, has great limitations. The part it plays in the acquisition of knowledge and the attainment of truth is much less than the proponents of the various philosophical rationalisms have expected of it and have tended to claim for it. Skeptics and believers differ more in their interpretation of experiential data than in their attitude toward the role of reason. Nevertheless, when a theologian attacks rationalism in religion, not only is his concern very different from that of the skeptics in their denigration of rationalism, but it may presuppose roles for reason that the skeptics would not allow. An important question, then, is, in what special way does the theologian tend to come into conflict with reason?

Hegel, the pervasive influence of whose philosophy provoked Kierkegaard's eloquent and distinctive protest, affirmed that the real *is* the rational. So, though he could subsume even the irrational within his all-encompassing system, he did so somewhat as existentialists find, in a philosophy of existence, a place for the concept of nothingness. The irrational may have a place in a rational metaphysical system, as has sin in a theologian's soteriological account of the redemptive process, or indeed as discords may have a place in music. Mozart, for instance, uses them in order to resolve them in the totality of the musical composition, though there is, of course, no discordant element in the composition when it is grasped as a whole.

Similarly, the irrational could no more have an ultimate status in the thought of a rationalist such as Hegel or Spinoza than evil could have an ultimate status in the thought of one who accounts it simply the privation of, or absence of, good. For Hegel and other such rationalist philosophers, the irrational comes to be equated with error or failure or defect. Where the human mind fails to do what it should be able to do, it is to be deemed in one way or another irrational; where it succeeds, it is rational. To say that, however, is somewhat like taking note that when I make an arithmetical error in adding up my bank balance I am wrong and when I do not I am right, and then going on to say that my error does not enter, of course, into the arithmetic but arises, rather, from my failure at that point to be arithmetical. So, in a rationalist metaphysic, the human mind is rational when it succeeds in doing what it ought to be doing, because that to which its success or failure relates *is* the rational.

Kierkegaard may be conveniently taken as representative of the protest against all such views of the status of reason. He denies that the real, whatever it is, is to be identified with the rational. He presumably would have been better pleased, for instance, with the category of "gracious being" which Professor John Macquarrie has proposed as the basic one in his christianized interpretation of Heidegger. At any rate, whatever the basic category may be, it is not the rational. To variations upon that theme Kierkegaard devotes much of his voluminous polemic.

Barth, whose early thought owed much to Kierkegaard though he later dissociated himself from that influence, took a similar and sometimes even more uncompromising stand. At one time he even asserted, for example, that the knowledge of God conferred upon the man of faith is so compelling that criteria issuing from that rational judgment play no part in it at all.

And in his famous attack on natural theology, formulated in a reply to Emil Brunner and entitled *Nein,* Barth went so far as to imply that reason is so irrelevant to the revelatory process that God might, if he so chose, reveal himself to a cat.[5]

We must be careful to distinguish two elements in startling theological affirmations of that kind:

1. *On the one hand, they call attention to a datum of religious experience that is often much neglected, misrepresented, or misunderstood in philosophical discussions of religion. The datum these overlook is that the sense of the presence of the God-dimension of experience is so powerful as to cause the believer to feel wholly compelled and possessed by it.*[6] It grips his whole being with such force that logical argumentation about it seems at best trivial and at worst a wicked waste of precious time. The believer does not instinctively engage in the making of judgments about that sense of presence; he is seized by it, and the moral imperatives it brings with it demand his unconditional obedience. All that, which has already been stressed in the present work as a vital part of the phenomenology of religion, is a salutary reminder to those who, being philosophers, are inclined to occupy themselves with questions about the relation of evidence to truth-claims and to discuss religion, therefore, as though such questions were the central field of inquiry for the philosopher of religion. Religious believers characteristically feel no more need to discuss religious questions in that way than most people, whether believers or skeptics, feel they need to discuss questions relating to the existence of the external world. Argumentation about the existence of the God-dimension seems as futile an intellectualist form of escapism as would be a discussion devoted to questions about the existence of the subject matter of chemistry and physics.

2. *On the other hand, philosophers do very rightly find theological affirmations of the type under consideration a challenge, if not an affront, to what all thoughtful people find highest and noblest in mankind—namely, the humble striving of the human spirit after truth.* Theologians as well as scientists discourse in rational terms about their subject matter. What sense, then, can be made of a situation in which there is (a) a claim that God is revealed to man in the Word contained in the Bible and fully and finally revealed to man in the person of Christ, yet at the same time (b) a refusal to admit that "the real believer will be fain to acknowledge that even his consciousness of faith is a human darkness,"[7] and finally (c) an elaborate discussion of the implicates of revelation, including the attributes of God, conducted in the usual way in which philosophers and others accustomed to the use of rational argument commonly seek to clarify their own minds and persuade their readers?

[5] Karl Barth, *Nein,* in E. Brunner and K. Barth, *Natural Theology* (London: Geoffrey Bles, 1946), p. 88.
[6] See John Baillie, *Our Knowledge of God* (New York: Charles Scribner's Sons, 1939).
[7] Karl Barth, *Church Dogmatics,* vol. 1 (Edinburgh: T. and T. Clark, 1936), p. 278. Barth speaks of the form of the Word "amid man's darkness" and of "the presence of Christ in the *tenebrae* of our heart."

We may put the matter more simply. It is one thing to say, as we all say of the subject matter of the sciences, that what confronts us is not discoverable by human reason. It is another to say that because of deficiencies or corruptions in our human reason it is not even recognizable by that means. If the religious critic of human reason goes on to disclaim that his faith is bestowed upon him through words whose meanings are not at all the meanings the words have in ordinary usage (for example, God's goodness is in no way like any human kind of goodness), then we must object that, to say the least, we are being placed in danger of using the intellect expressly to achieve unintelligibility.

To such obvious objections the religious critic of rationalism can reply that, because the kind of verification to be expected in matters of religious belief is different from the kind appropriate to the subject matter of the sciences, the meaning of the words used as the medium of revelation *is* made available to the believer, though hidden from his unbelieving brother. While claims about the subject matter of physics can be verified or disproved publicly, the believer's claims must be verifiable or disprovable only intersubjectively.

An example will help to clarify this point: If I recounted to a schoolmaster of an old-fashioned, authoritarian type that, having been given charge of a large group of juvenile delinquents in a reform school, I rapidly gained their cooperation and respect, he might well ask what forms of discipline and punishment I had used to achieve such successful results. Did I achieve them, for instance, by selecting one or two boys for exemplary punishment, beating them unmercifully in the presence of others so as to show the whole school the dire consequences of misbehavior under my administration? Or had I chosen instead the slower but surer and better way of gradually letting it be known, by fair methods of discipline and the inexorable administration of regular paddling for just cause and with scrupulous avoidance of favoritism or other discriminatory tactics, that I was not to be trifled with, being a man of formidable resolution and strength of purpose? Suppose I replied that I had chosen neither of these methods but instead had gathered the school together and, sitting down informally among them, had told them that in my youth I, too, had been delinquent (having done several things for which, if caught, I could have been sent to a correctional institution), and had then invited them to be my friends, so building up a basis for genuine affection as well as respect.

Few men in the authoritarian tradition (which actually prevailed in many places in the past) would believe me, and many would find my account almost if not quite unintelligible. I could not compel their understanding because, though they might be first-class mathematicians or expert linguists, they would lack the capacity to understand the use of humility and love as instruments for winning the trust of errant young people. Understanding of my story would be confined to those familiar with and experienced in such gentler, friendlier methods of teaching. Among these people, understanding of my story would be universal; yet none would have any means of conveying it to the authoritarian pedagogues. These might well feel able to establish with a good show of reason that either I was lying or I was a little crazy or confused, if indeed I were not both mendacious and insane.

So then, though within the household of faith (as Christians sometimes call the Church) the special meaning of terms such as "love," "humiliation," "grace," and "joy" is directly intelligible, it is not to be expected to be either intelligible by, or communicable to, those standing outside that household. Within that household also, we might expect that a particular, apparent manifestation of the God-dimension may be tested and so verified or disproved—a proceeding suggested by St. Paul and specifically enjoined by the writer of the first Johannine epistle: "Beloved, believe not every spirit, but try the spirits whether they are of God; because many false prophets are gone out into the world." [8] The means of "trying the spirits"—that is, of verification and disproval—cannot be expected to be available to those outside the household of faith.

No tolerant and open-minded philosopher need boggle particularly at what has just been suggested. When we come to ask, however, what these crucially important methods for "testing the spirits" might be we are likely to be disappointed. How shall we know a genuine spirit from a phony one? What are the criteria? Scientific tests such as are used for ascertaining whether an emerald is genuine or not are, of course, out of the question. Indeed, no procedure that could well be called rational is likely to be suitable. Then, are the spirits to be tested by means of a nonrational (not to say irrational) method such as, say, an intuitive one?

Indeed, there might be no radical objection to that proceeding, if only believers were always right in arriving at their judgments. If, within the household of faith, there were a method, however irrational it appeared, by means of which a prophet could be tested for authenticity as surely as by other means we test the authenticity of a fifty-dollar bill or of a dinner plate alleged to be Crown Derby, there would be little need for serious objection. If, even, the household of faith or members of it sometimes made mistakes, admitted them, and could then show clearly where they had gone wrong, so as to move, at least, toward the establishment of a principle of verification and disproval that could be agreed upon as workable within the household itself, only obstinately intolerant unbelievers would need to feel they had grounds for making serious objection.

The difficulty is that believers do have to admit not only to having been sometimes in error in matters of that kind but also to having discovered no principle by means of which they might even hope to be better on their guard against making similar errors in the future. Many sincere and devout believers have been "taken," as they have later discovered, by an impudent scoundrel officiating as a pastor or rabbi or priest. On the other side, perhaps even more tragically, many who have come to be seen as great saints have

[8] 1 John 4:1.

been not only suspected by the faithful but even bitterly persecuted within the household of faith before their sanctity was acknowledged. If believers do not know the sheep from the goats within their own household, what confidence can skeptics place in a claim that believers are ever able to discern anything in the God-dimension at all? How, indeed, can anyone dare to claim any knowledge of the nature of the God-dimension beyond saying, as Locke said of the substratum underlying the physical world, that it is a something-I-know-not-what?

These objections, though very grave, are not entirely unanswerable. First, consider error in our apprehension of the physical world. Optical illusions and the like occur in our apprehension of that world, and our objectification of it makes possible the development of fairly satisfactory explanations of how such illusions occur. Nevertheless, even in that dimension we sometimes make very grave mistakes over a long period, such as our forefathers did in supposing the earth to be flat; but with scientific advance we are able to see in the long run why we were wrong, and we can even intelligently conjecture where we might still be wrong. Generally speaking, however, physical phenomena do not disappoint us as inexplicably as people do. As our body of scientific knowledge grows, the physical world becomes more predictable, but no amount of psychological or other knowledge fundamentally affects the unpredictability of people.

The reason is obvious. In intersubjective relationships there are no rules to which the phenomena can be expected to conform as do physical phenomena. John may seem a young man of the highest promise in every way, yet he may belie all reasonable expectations and turn out a "rotter." David's record, for various reasons, may give most people a very bad impression, yet his friends may discover he has become a saint. As is well known, remarkable impostures have taken place, such as those of professors in highly technical fields who taught with much acceptance for many years at very reputable academic institutions before they were unmasked as highly intelligent and in many ways well-motivated impostors totally lacking any authentic qualifications in their fields. People can both fail to meet our expectations and far outstrip them because, being people, they are free agents with considerable powers of self-determination.

What is peculiar to the religious believer is that, notwithstanding the unreliability of individuals, he maintains his confidence that underlying all of them is a Being who is completely reliable in the sense that the believer can and does trust that, as the Bible assures him, there is in that Being no variableness. The gracious attributes of that Being are accounted completely dependable, so that they cannot be thought of as sometimes there and sometimes not; they must be always there. According to the believer, even when God is hid from us he is outpouring his benevolence. Nothing in God works by fits and starts. Like the sun—which shines, we doubt not, with the same brilliance on overcast days as on clear ones, though we do not see it always shining with equal brightness—God everlastingly sustains his creation, pouring forth his bounty upon it.

What possible grounds could there be for such a belief? The skeptic may well be willing to recognize the God-dimension yet see no reason to make the specific affirmations about it that the believer so confidently makes. In vain would the believer suggest to him the case, say, of an elderly man who, grounding his belief in the knowledge that in forty years of married life his wife has never tolerated departure from a basic minimum standard of cleanliness, rightly refuses to doubt that his house is fundamentally clean even when the furniture is dusty and soiled linen is lying about. He is sure she may be relied upon not to have changed her habits after so long an adherence to them. So he justifiably concludes that any dirt he sees must be only superficial. Just so, the skeptic would point out, of course, that believers seem to attain their confidence with no such lifelong and intimate acquaintance with God, and to maintain it even when (as our discussion of the problem of evil showed) appearances seem to give the lie to such belief. The skeptic could not well resist the conclusion that the believer, having beheld a splendid vision presented in the religious disclosure or revelation, has accepted it as beautiful and then out of obstinacy or fear, adhered to it as true.

That is not, in fact, however, a satisfactory account of the situation. Believers are only incidentally concerned with apocalyptic visions such as are familiar to Christians in the last book of the New Testament. No one ever became seriously committed to Judaism, as was Martin Buber, or to Christianity, as were Wesley and Newman, through any kind of reading. Indeed, no one was ever converted to anything by a set of theological propositions. The religious disclosure that leads to conversion and commitment is mediated through verbal and other symbols, but it is direct in the sense that it comes intersubjectively as a communion of minds.

The believer claims, however, to be confronted by a Being who "comes through" or "shines through" the other minds. The confrontation comes as personal. It not only stands over against the convert; it bears down upon him, surrounds him, and nevertheless also simultaneously grows up within him as a personal power—at first alien to him but insistently working inside his spirit and transforming it as a medicine would work inside the body. In spite of his puzzlement at what is happening, he is convinced that the power that is so radically affecting him, inside and out, is boundless, beneficent, and life-giving. He knows he must both yield to its force within him and at the same time strain to the utmost in actively doing what is unconditionally presented to him as his inescapable duty, which includes independent decision-making.

Because the confrontation is so unlike anything in our experience of the physical and the biological, the believer calls it "personal." By that he means, not that the Being is *a* person, to be added to a list of others such as his friends Edith Jones and Dick Brown, but that it confronts him as persons do and as things do not. Yet it is not a collection or aggregate of persons, such may be supposed to lie behind what may be called the national *Geist,* the college spirit, or the force of public opinion. Indeed, it may be—and often is—as critical of these as it is unconditionally imperative in its demands upon the believer himself. The believer, expressing the uniqueness he finds in what confronts him, calls it "God." For linguistic and cultural reasons, if not as a result of metaphysical speculation, he assigns to God a grammatically masculine gender such as it assigned in the Bible to the God of Abraham and Isaac. The Christian believer identifies God with the one who, in the person of Christ, is proclaimed in the New Testament to be reconciling all things to himself.[9]

Conflict Between Theology and Faith

Collingwood, an English thinker who sought to exonerate religion from the charge of irrationality, and to provide a rapprochement that would bring together what post-Renaissance Europe had fractured, stated uncompromisingly:

> So far from a conflict between faith and reason being inevitable from the nature of things, they are in point of fact necessary each to the other. Faith cannot exist without reason. The infinite is not another thing which is best grasped by sweeping the finite out of the way; the infinite is nothing but the unity, or as we sometimes say, the 'meaning' of finite things in their diversity and their mutual connections. To look for the infinite by throwing away the finite would be very much like making the players stop playing in order to hear the symphony. . . . Reason, conversely, cannot exist without faith. The finite is nothing except as part of a whole.[10]

To appreciate the full significance of these observations, we should bear in mind that Collingwood was a transitional figure in the history of thought in the English-speaking world. In the early days of the analytical movement at Oxford he continued his own individualist line of thought, in the old idealist tradition, being much influenced by Croce and the other Italian neoidealists. Because of these historical circumstances he was long neglected, being considered, in the light of growing philosophical fashions, to be championing an odd survival of a derelict mode of thought. Collingwood was, however, a remarkably perceptive and original thinker who richly deserves the renewed interest he is receiving from some philosophers of religion who can now see him in the light of his own circumstances. In the passage quoted above he perceives, in his own way, a fundamental truth about the inseparability of reason and faith.

[9] For example, Colossians 1:20.
[10] R. G. Collingwood, *Faith and Reason,* ed. L. Rubinoff (Chicago: Quadrangle Books, 1968), pp. 143 f.

Religious protest against rationality cannot be understood apart from the role of the rational in theology, pre-eminently in Christian theology. In contrast to the leaders of many of the great religions, who rely chiefly on the sacred, traditional *mythoi* to express, mythopoeically, what they wish to promulgate as their saving truths, Christian thinkers—from the first-century apologists such as Justin Martyr down to the present day—have been concerned with developing systematic accounts of the implications of Christian faith for human thought and life. There are special reasons for this historical fact. Because Christianity, within a generation of the death of Christ, was spread among Gentiles over a large part of the Mediterranean world, through the missionary efforts of Paul and others, its missionaries were faced at once with the task of making their message meaningful and intelligible in terms of the best rational thought of the day.

The Gentile world, under Greek influence, was pervaded with a profound respect for *logos*, the rational principle. In that climate of thought, nothing was more despised than the formless, the shapeless, the amorphous. Indeed, even in our own times modern Greeks respond instinctively with admiring zest to that which is, or is reputed to be, *morphos*, that is, shapely, having a form that one can somehow grasp, in contrast to the infinite (*to apeiron*), which lacks shape.

At the time of Christian missionary enterprise, the Mediterranean world was ready to listen to almost any new intellectual ideas and systems, but they had to be ideas and systems that had clear, rational form, ideas and systems that conformed to the *logos* or rational principle. Otherwise, people would condemn the systems as inchoate. They would condemn them as we today would condemn certain types of thought as fuzzy. They had very simple and straightforward logical conceptions, and in spite of their great openness to new ideas, they insisted that all modes of thought that were presented to them should conform to these logical conceptions and to the categories of thought that seemed to them clear and intelligible in the way a picture of a dog or a house is intelligible to a child and as, say, a bunch of structureless wavy lines would not be. In meeting the challenge of Gentile thought, Christianity was very decisively married at an early stage to Socratic humanism, and the marriage was indissoluble.[11]

The marriage between Christianity and rational, philosophical humanism was not an accident. Such is the nature of the partners that they would have found each other sooner or later even if historical circumstances had precluded their meeting so early in the development of the Christian Church. Christian ethical teaching, as we find it in the Gospels, was from the first (as might be expected from its Jewish lineage) profoundly concerned with everyday life. Those who followed the Christian way proposed to sanctify and transform all men, and indeed all Nature—which, however, had to

[11] I have developed this theme in *The Hemlock and the Cross*. (Philadelphia and New York: J. B. Lippincott, Co., 1963).

be reckoned with as intelligible apart from Christian teaching. So, as Christian theology developed throughout the ages, requiring increasing preoccupation with classic philosophical problems such as freedom and causality, it did not discuss such problems merely for propaganda purposes, as we might say, or as a concession to the mood of people whom Christians might have hoped to convert.

The nature and concerns of Christianity itself required it to consider such problems. If it had not considered them in terms of Greek philosophy it would have had to consider them in terms of some other kind of rational thought; reason itself, the *logos* principle, is common to the universal activity of the human mind, to which it belongs essentially, however it may be formulated. Christians, had they avoided coming to grips with it, would not only have had to eschew *all* thought; they would have had to renounce their Christian faith, since the duty of involvement in all aspects of human life is a fundamental implicate of that faith.

The involvement must be, of course, honest. The Christian theologian can no more content himself with a mere façade of rationality than he can be satisfied with a mere pretence of marital fidelity. The concern for logic, like a concern for fidelity, must be sincere. Moreover, Christian concern for logic entails an interest in metaphysics, for no matter out of what conceptual or linguistic mold the Christian *kerygma* be squeezed, its message has metaphysical implications. To proclaim the Christian message at all is to present at least an embryonic system of metaphysics.

Here, indeed, is where the protest against rationality inevitably emerges. For as soon as a structure is erected, there is a natural human tendency to try to press everything into it, including the interpretation of the Christian's experience of what he declares to be, as we have seen, the living God, the one who spoke to Moses and dwelt in Christ. It cannot be done. As the animate cannot be squeezed into the mold of the inanimate, so the living and personal cannot be made to conform to the requirements of a cohesive, rational system. Some of the apparent logical contradictions or inconsistencies may be logically explored, as we have seen much earlier in dealing with paradox, but no such explorations could exhibit the full measure of the conflict between systematic accounts of reality (scientific or metaphysical) and the living reality itself as seen by the eyes of faith. When the reality is believed to have at its core (as the Christian faith proclaims) a God who is—to say the least—personal, the conflict becomes acute.

Other Minds, Rationality, and God

Philosophers have for long been interested in the question "How can I claim to know that other minds exist when in fact I have no means of perceiving another's mental states?" For example, while I can perceive that a man has black hair or a birthmark on his forehead, I cannot perceive that he is in pain. Yet I see that he behaves as I do when I am in pain, so I conclude, by analogy, that he is in pain. Professor Plantinga, after considering such analogical methods of arriving at beliefs about other minds and some alternatives to them, together with the question of our knowledge of God, tentatively concludes, "If my belief in other minds is rational, so is my belief in God." [12]

We need not particularly concern ourselves here with the arguments Plantinga advances. Two questions, however, do concern us: (1) Why should theologians suppose that belief in God must be rational? (2) What precisely would be advanced by showing belief in God to be rational, and what would be the limitations of a successful argument to that effect?

We have already to some extent provided in advance an answer to the first question. If God is mediated through our apprehension of *all* human experience and if human experience makes us value the presence of rationality over the lack of rationality, we ought to expect that God will never, so to speak, write off rationality as worthless. This expectation is comparable to the expectation that God should not be less than personal; that is, that he should not diminish the value of the personal that is disclosed to us in human relationships. Indeed, the believer may well insist, so far is God from doing so that he is actually revealed to us in, with and through human relationships; that is, God is disclosed to me through the mediation of my relationship to my friends whom I love. In personal human relationships I may claim to discern the source of all their joys. In other words, I see why I may claim to be right in dearly prizing and highly valuing the personal. I judge that doing so is fundamentally right (not accidentally right) because I claim to discern in all my friends the presence of a common source that is specifically using human personality, in its various intersubjective relationships, as the instrument of its disclosure.

As we have seen earlier, that does not mean that the being who is identified with that source is not more than personal; it means only that personality must be subsumed in the divine Being and manifested in the divine action toward personal beings such as ourselves, so that it could never be said to be a diminishment of the value believed to inhere in God—as would be, say, a moral weakness such as sloth. There could never be anything wrong with being personal any more than there could be anything wrong with being brave, though personality may not be a metaphysical ultimate or bravery the supreme virtue. It is in such a sense that we may properly expect God not to write off rationality as worthless. To do so would be contrary to the divine nature that the believer sees as somehow encompassing it.

To say that rationality is not to be written off as worthless is not at all to say, however, that it is either sufficiently comprehensive or sufficiently definitive to be adequate as a designation of what God is. Far from it, and the inadequacy is, indeed, precisely what the protest against rationality

[12] Alvin Plantinga, *God and Other Minds* (Ithaca, N. Y.: Cornell University Press, 1967), p. 271.

in religion is about. We do not account oaks irrational or oranges illogical because their irregularity inhibits them from conforming to our tidy expectations. So the believer, in his understanding of the relation of rationality to God, can say without affront to logic that there is nothing more irrational about God than there is about a giraffe, a juniper, or the solar system.

We may now come to the second question: suppose we grant that belief in God is rational in the sense that it is not incompatible with reason; what, then, has been achieved? Not only is there nothing irrational in a giraffe, which happens to exist; there would be presumably nothing irrational in a unicorn, which does not. Attempts to show the rationality of belief in God, by the traditional arguments or any other, can do nothing to promote belief or unbelief. The unbeliever is provided with no grounds for belief, and the believer has other grounds already. The ingenious attempts of some contemporary philosophers to rehabilitate or reconstruct a valid form of the ontological argument for the existence of God out of Anselm's turn out to yield conclusions that are practically trivial; that is, they do not add anything novel to people who are already in the condition, which Anselm specifies as indispensable, of *fides quaerens intellectum.*

The whole enterprise of seeking logical proofs, whether by the ontological or any other method, is doomed to failure because it is always possible to propose a rational alternative to the existence of the God of theism. One might even conceivably demonstrate by a series of arguments that belief in the existence of the God of theism is so probable that not to believe it would be difficult for a reasonable man, yet fail to sway the skeptic even slightly. He would recall that at one time, when scientists were only beginning to consider the place of earth in the solar system, proposals that our own little cosmic backwater might be the only planet inhabited by intelligent beings seemed to many imaginative and educated people very unlikely. Such proposals suggested a narrow sort of provincialism, as though an Englishman were to suppose that continental Europe lacked cultural activity or was wholly bereft of moral sense.

Even apart from any facts that might or might not be available to us, we should have seemed to be entitled to dismiss such a parochial view of the universe, against which the odds were so great. Yet now, as we all know, the notion that our planet might be the only one in our solar system to be inhabited by intelligent beings seems not only plausible but probable. Then again, there was a time when the flatness of the earth no doubt seemed *a priori* so probable as to make other hypotheses not much worth considering; now it seems far too improbable to be worth considering at all. There are certainly viable alternatives to the existence of God as conceived by theists, and no kind of logical method or rational argument could do more than show that belief in the God of theism does not entail a fallacy or other logical impropriety.

Religious conviction, then, can never depend on any kind of ratiocinative argument. The outcome of such ratiocination could never proclaim what the believer wants to proclaim. Hence his suspicion of theistic philosophies that purport to be established by deductive, ratiocinative methods. Nevertheless, the compatibility of rationality with belief in God (as with belief in other minds) is important in exhibiting the unity of our apprehension of divine Being as mediated to us both through other minds and through rationality, yet as untrammeled by the bonds of either.

QUESTIONS ON CHAPTER XI

1 The central difficulty of the believer lies in the variety of plausible interpretations of experience. Discuss.

2 Reason might be considered akin to or contrary to God. What other alternatives are there? Discuss them.

3 If there is any point to the antirationalist protest in religion, how can it be discussed rationally?

4 If a religious faith were totally divorced from all rational procedures and philosophical speculations and concerns, would it be intelligible even to the believer himself? Discuss.

5 Consider the difficulties in believing in the existence of other minds.

6 Critically consider Plantinga's proposal "If my belief in other minds is rational, so is my belief in God."

7 What objections might be offered to the proposal that though notions such as "grace" and "humiliation" may seem at best ambiguous and at worst unintelligible to people generally, they are sufficiently intelligible within a specific community such as the Christian Church?

8 In what sense does Tennant claim that his system of natural theology is empirical? Is his claim justifiable? What objections do you see to it?

BIBLIOGRAPHICAL SUGGESTIONS

Baillie, John. *Our Knowledge of God.* New York: Charles Scribner's Sons, 1939. The Scottish Presbyterian theologian, who inclines to a Bonaventurian rather than a Thomist view of our knowledge of God, upholds a "mediated immediacy" position.

Baillie, John. *The Sense of the Presence of God.* Gifford Lectures. New York: Charles Scribner's Sons, 1962.

Gleason, Robert W. *The Search for God.* New York: Sheed & Ward, 1964.

Gotshalk, D. W. *The Structure of Awareness.* Urbana, Ill.: University of Illinois Press, 1969. Considers a situational theory of truth and knowledge.

Kitagawa, J. M. "Chaos, Order, and Freedom in World Religions." In *The Concept of Order,* edited by P. G. Kuntz. Seattle: University of Washington Press, 1968.

Lewis, H. D. *Our Experience of God.* London: Allen and Unwin, 1959.

MacGregor, Geddes. *God Beyond Doubt.* Philadelphia: J. B. Lippincott Co., 1966. Treats the nature and interpretation of religious experience in the light of its multidimensionality.

Macmurray, John. *Freedom in the Modern World.* London: Faber & Faber, 1932. A provocative study by an original contemporary thinker exhibiting self-realization as the moral ideal.

Mansel, H. L. *The Limits of Religious Thought.* London: John Murray, 1859. A classic Victorian study of the limits of religious thought and of the relation of reason to faith.

Novak, Michael. *Belief and Unbelief.* New York: Macmillan Co., 1965. A lively, semi-popular treatment of the search for God.

Pontifex, M., and Trethowan, I. *The Meaning of Existence.* New York: Longmans, 1953.

Smith, John E. *Reason and God.* New Haven, Conn.: Yale University Press, 1961. Especially useful in its examination of what may be understood by the concept "experience."

XII

FREEDOM, RENUNCIATION, AND MIRACLES

By order of the King!
God is forbidden to work miracles in this place.
Satirical notice posted at the church of St.
Médard, Paris, when Louis XV had forbidden
pilgrimages to the tomb of a Jansenist priest
who was credited with the performance of
miracles.

Imaginative Power

When man first begins to emerge from the condition he still shares with other animals, he discovers, as we have seen, that he possesses an extraordinary power—the power to imagine not only what he cannot now see but what he has never seen and even what he thinks he never could see. This power is closely related to memory and intelligence; yet it may be accounted more fundamental than either of these—indeed the very hallmark of humanity—because it stirs in man the first awareness of his spiritual freedom. My recognition that I possess the power of imagination, which fills me with a unique sense of independence, intoxicates me more than ever could the most intoxicating drug or chemical agent. All that and more the power of imagination brings to me. I was bogged down by circumstance, chained like a slave to what I found most thwarting, ground down to what seemed most dreary, not to say soul-destroying, in life. Then, perhaps quite suddenly, I discovered a way out of my prison: I could enter into and take possession of the realm of imagination, the charter of my coming of age, giving me access to a staggeringly rich estate of infinite possibilities.

Many of us, accustomed as we are to the notion of imagination, through a tradition of its abundant use over the course of thousands of years, have almost forgotten the overwhelming force of its liberating power. If none but a recently emancipated slave knows what political freedom means, surely only one who has been chained to the drudgery of a thoroughly carnal, pedestrian, unimaginative existence can know what it means to be vividly aware of what imagination does to free the human spirit from the toils of circumstance and the deadening dullness of the animal cycle of birth, copulation, and death. In the first flush of my new discovery of my imaginative power I "feel like a king." In contrast to my sense of enslavement to the tables-and-chairs world and to the world of other minds, I am now absolute master of a world of my own—a world in which I need brook no interference from anyone and need take nobody into account. I am, indeed, more absolute than the most absolutist monarch, for I can actually *create* my subjects, bringing them to life as I spin them out of my fecund imagination, and then exercising over them—executively, judicially, and administratively—the very power of life and death. Do I now suddenly dislike Harold and Molly whom I have imaginatively created? Then I will destroy them. I do not even have to chop off their heads in the manner of the kings of old. I simply *will* them out of existence.

Of course, in the conduct of these creative and annihilative operations I may encounter some psychological difficulties, but they *are* only psychological difficulties—that is, difficulties internal to my own being; there is nothing outside me with which I have to reckon. Even the English Tudors, even indeed caliphs and sultans, have had counselors to whom they had to hearken, and even the most ruthless dictator must take some account of popular sentiment, but I am unhampered by any external interferences. My will is as absolute as the will of Allah.

There is a good reason for this, for in respect of the realm of my imagination I *am* Allah. I enjoy my power not only for its own sake and for the opportunity of self-expression that it affords, but because of the liberation it has effected. In any area in which I previously felt thwarted or diminished or oppressed I can now superabundantly triumph. If I felt physically feeble I can now astound the creatures of my imagination with my stupendous feats of strength. I make each of them stronger than the strongest man who ever lived, yet I can endow myself with the strength to crush the mightiest of them like an eggshell in the palm of my hand. If I felt sexually inadequate I can now establish a harem of a thousand sensuous houris and by my own fiat endow myself with the potency to impregnate every one of them between midnight and dawn. If I felt intellectually inferior I am now able to assume powers of intelligence so acute and powers of comprehension so vast that I can grasp in a twinkling the subtlest problems in mathematics and logic, express them with unmatched clarity and neatness, and skillfully exhibit their implications in a hundred languages, with occasional trilingual puns in Sanskrit, Hungarian, and Mandarin Chinese thrown in for good measure.

In short, there is nothing I can want to do that I cannot do. True, there are certain internal rules that my imagination must follow, but they are, after all, *my* rules, the rules of *my* psyche. They subject me to no one but myself. Like St. Thomas's God I can do nothing to deny my own nature, but in my own imaginative realm I am none the less God.

The liberating power of the imagination is an ecstasy to every imaginative child, though in our modern technological societies we are discouraged from prolonging the ecstasy. Suppose, however, that we lived in an environment more favorable to the enjoyment of a poetic imagination—for example, an environment such as our cultivated forefathers, who bequeathed to us the great Socratic, humanist heritage, were able to enjoy throughout their lives. Or suppose that, though we do live in a modern technological society, we were nevertheless able to prolong and cultivate an imaginative life, enjoying to the full the realms that the humanist heritage can open up to us, a life in which our imaginations were fired by poets like Coleridge and Wordsworth, by essayists like Montaigne and Lamb, and by storytellers like Stevenson and Poe.

In fact our imaginative life *can* be sustained indefinitely alongside the life we live as we are confronted by an external world of tables and chairs and other minds. We *are* able to live in two realms without becoming either autistic for lack of contact with the external world or oppressed by lack of the freedom the imaginative realm provides. In such a happy condition we can use our imagination to the full, and we can hardly avoid exposure to religious ideas. At that point poetry and religion lie very close together for us. We find we can enjoy religion as we enjoy poetry.

No matter how favorable to the imagination are my circumstances or how successful I may be in living in the two realms, the sense of freedom conferred upon me through the exercise of my imaginative power eventually palls. If I go on luxuriating in it, enjoying religious as well as other ideas as the toys of my lively imagination, I come sooner or later to a point at which imagination, though no less enjoyable, ceases to bring me the refreshing sense of liberation that once it brought. Even in my imaginative revelings I can no longer share Santayana's willingness to pretend that nothing matters but the dreams I dream.[1] Surfeited as I have become by my own imaginative power, what is left for me to do? After so much prodigal self-expansion, where is there for me to go?

Renunciation

The way left is that of self-restriction in the use of my imaginative power. As soon as I exercise such self-discipline I not only pave the way in my mind for an understanding of the difference between poetry and religion, fantasy and faith; I prepare myself, by my self-emptying, for an understand-

[1] George Santayana, "Solipsism," in *Poems of George Santayana*, ed. Robert Hutchinson (New York: Dover Publications, 1970), p. 83.

ing of the self-emptying of God, which is the clue to an unraveling of the most intractable of the mysteries of theistic religion—God's own restraint in the exercise of his omnipotence. Once I can bring myself to the exercise of self-restraint in the use of my imaginative power, I am on my way to an appreciation of God's ways with man.

The kind of self-restraint I must exercise is, however, extremely difficult. In its stead I only too easily substitute mere laziness in the use of my imaginative power, palming off on myself, under pretense of disciplined abstinence, a diminished imaginative vitality that is due to nothing but sloth. Using one's imagination is hard work, and I may well seize on an opportunity to lessen the activity, on the pretext that I am spending too much time in my imaginative realm, to the detriment of my very important relation to the external world. That is not at all, however, what is to be understood by the self-restraint in the use of my imagination that prepares me for an understanding of the self-emptying of God, the mystery that lies at the heart of the Christian faith.

The realm of the imagination provides me with a model of the creative act of God.[2] As in early childhood I learn to avoid the plight of the autistic child by controlling my imagination, first in respect of my sense of space, then in respect of my sense of time, so now by a still more severe restraint of my imaginative power, I may begin to control it with respect to the whole sphere of my existence and all the attendant values I have built into my apprehension of that existence.

What occurs may be dramatized in the following way. Through the attainment of the freedom made available to me in the exercise of my imaginative power, I have divinized myself. In that realm I am, as has been already suggested, not merely king but God. Since I do not only rule my realm but create it, the power conferred on me in the realm of my imagination, which has so exhilarated me by the freedom it has bestowed upon me, is a likeness of what believers see as the creative power of God. It has made me into a deity in my own realm.

Now occurs my opportunity for renunciation. Though my divinity is an imaginary one, confined within my psychic, inner life, the renunciation I may now make transcends that realm. It carries me beyond myself, enabling me to enter into a radically novel dimension of experience. Through self-restraint in the use of my imaginative power, I can now let that power serve rather than stand apart from my relation to the Nature-dimension and the God-dimension that confront me from beyond myself. I am now able to relinquish my place as the focus of the values I create and, without diminishing the vivacity of my imaginative acts, set myself no longer at the center but at the periphery of my value schema. By renouncing the power I possess as creator, I free my creatures (the creatures of my imagina-

---

[2] Austin Farrer held that God gives images directly to the religious consciousness as the matter for later conceptual, theologizing activity. See *The Glass of Vision* (London: Dacre Press, 1948), p. 44.

tion), and so free myself from the dominion that puppet-creatures must otherwise always unwittingly exert over their creator. Using the model provided, I have learned to imitate God who lets his creatures be. I am like a child who, in playing with dolls, learns to renounce the absolute dominion over them that the child knows he could rightly exercise and, instead, simply lets them be, so achieving his own maturity by learning the basic principle of love, which is the principle of sacrifice, the voluntary abdication of power.

Renunciation of Freedom

In the self-emptying of my imagination I do not sacrifice my imaginative ability; I keep that ability and transcend it, as in solid geometry we both keep and transcend linear space. The freedom that the sacrifice of my imagination gives me stands to my imaginative freedom as solid geometry stands to plane geometry. This freedom has, however, a momentous consequence for me; namely, it prepares me for at least finding intelligible the notion of the self-emptying God. In the absence of experience of the freedom that is attained through self-emptying, the theological notion that God the Creator would withdraw himself from his creatures—leaving them to attain to their full spiritual stature and power through combat with "blind" Nature—is not intelligible. It can become so, however, when I know the freedom that comes to me through my own self-emptying.

The only motive that can encourage me to engage in any kind of sacrifice is the motive of love. If I can love my child enough to let him go free, risking his hurt and even his death by natural accident, I thereby relinquish my control of the child, as the child once learned to abdicate power over his teddy bear. Such an experience *can* become to me a symbol of God's self-emptying of his power out of his divine love for me.

The irrelevancy of questions of logical proof in religion manifests itself perhaps more strikingly here than anywhere else. If I have not experienced the creation and enjoyment of new freedom such as emerges in the voluntary abdication of power, you can no more prove to me what it is than you could convince an intelligent but skeptical Eskimo lacking in technological education that a heat wave in Los Angeles could bring about such excessive use of electrical power as to cause people to die of heat stroke during a power cut. By the same token, though the experiential phenomenon of self-emptying could open my mind to the theological proposal that an omnipotent deity declines to use his power because he prefers to let his creatures be, it could no more prove to me that God so acts than my wife could prove she loved me if I resolutely set my heart against believing her.

The presence and intelligibility of a symbol pointing to the activity of an omnipotent and benevolent creator would be nevertheless an enormous advantage to me if indeed the Being to which it pointed did exist and was so acting. For though I might not be in a position to believe today,

I might be in such a position tomorrow, and the availability of the symbol would make possible for me the acceptance of a disclosure or revelation of how that Being does act.

The Importance of Scientific Methodology

In such a view, Nature is not only the creature of God; she stands in a very special relation to him. Nature, in this view, is our fellow creature, but (in infinite contrast to ourselves) there is no freedom in her. She may be said to be specifically deprived of all freedom. That is what makes her explorable by scientific methodologies. That is not to say that Nature is mechanistic in the Newtonian and eighteenth-century sense. It does mean, however, that God does not let Nature be as he lets me be. Nature can be only as God specifies she must be. She has no power of self-determination. God may be said to control Nature with the tightest of all conceivable reins, so much so that Nature may be called, indeed, the "dark side of God," that is, God with all his divine power but without divine love. The divine love cannot be present in any way in Nature for the simple reason that the freedom needed for love—in giving it, in receiving it, and in allowing it—cannot be present in Nature.

Nature, then, is seen as the instrument provided by God both for the emergence of free spirits and for the development of their spiritual freedom. The freedom may exist, no doubt, in minimal, embryonic form even at the lowest levels of life but so scantily as to call almost no attention to its possible presence. In relationships between human beings who have enjoyed the kind of experience we have been discussing in this chapter, the presence and development of the freedom that makes possible renunciation and sacrifice, which is the freedom to love, emerges with unmistakable clarity. In Nature herself there is none. That is, indeed, as has been already said, what makes Nature so susceptible to scientific understanding.

We may now ask the question, what then is the function and place of the natural sciences from the standpoint of a human being who has been awakened to an appreciation of the phenomena we have been considering in this chapter? Because the function of the natural sciences is to study Nature, and Nature is the "dark side of God," the importance from a religious standpoint of the scientific outlook, as of scientific inquiry and scientific knowledge, is incalculable. Science must be to the modern philosopher of religion what philosophy seemed to the medieval schoolmen — the indispensable handmaiden *(ancilla)* in the greatest of all philosophical enterprises. The thinkers of the Middle Ages, in assigning to philosophy the role of *ancilla,* showed their high esteem of it. They did not by any means identify philosophy with dialectic or logic. Still less did they identify it with anything so narrow as the analytical procedures to which twentieth-century philosophy in the English-speaking world has been so largely reduced. When they talked of philosophy they were specifying, in their own Aristotelian way and as far as they could in their time, the attitudes and the fields of exploration that we today call "scientific."

At any rate, in the view of the relation of God and Nature that we are here proposing, we could not easily exaggerate the importance of the sciences, though we could distort it by that narrow scientism that seeks to explain all things by referents in the scientific realm alone. What makes anything scientifically intelligible is the element of necessary connection that emerges in scientific discovery. The fact under investigation no longer appears isolated and unconnected. It fits into a model and thereby becomes intelligible in terms of that model. Yet it is no more than a model. Only those scientists who neglect to observe that the element of necessity is more precisely a property of the model than a property of "wild" Nature herself are likely to subscribe to the narrow scientism that thinks everything can be explained exclusively and completely by what are now called scientific methods. The antireligious dogmas that such scientists may propound are based, not upon Nature as she really confronts them, but upon rationalistic models such as the mechanistic determinism that until comparatively recent times dominated scientific understanding.

In spite of the enormous advances that have been made both in scientific and in ontological and theological methodologies since the days of the medieval schoolmen, no radical change has occurred to affect the fundamental importance of scientific inquiry and the basic place of scientific knowledge in relation to the interests of the inquirer into religious truth. Scientists are never the enemies of religion except to the extent that they engage in forms of reductionism. Our awareness of *wholeness*, which is conspicuous in our understanding of all living beings, precludes such reductionism and greatly diminishes—if it does not altogether destroy—the value of the kind of analytical procedures to which such reductionism leads its practitioners.

A teleological explanation far beyond what analytical procedures can provide cannot be ruled out. A prominent Cambridge philosopher has stressed the futility of resting content with physiochemical explanations of everything and the bigotry of refusing to consider that anything can be an explanation unless it can be so reduced. Though he has certainly no teleological axe to grind, he contends, in a penetrating investigation of scientific method, that not all biological laws are reducible to the physiochemical level and that there is a plasticity of response among living beings that precludes such easy reductionism. Because organisms have more than one sequence of steps by which they may attain their respective goals, the possibility emerges of persisting toward these goals in different ways, according to circumstance, so that a teleological explanation becomes more pertinent than a physiochemical one. "It seems ridiculous," he writes, "to deny the title of explanation to a statement which performs both of the functions characteristic of scientific explanations—of enabling us to appreciate connections and to predict the future." [3]

Whenever Nature is looked at with an imaginative eye rather than in terms of rational models, the wholeness that evades reductionist explanations suggests the need for a kind of teleological explanation that transcends scientific categories and methods. This reflection becomes most of all convincing when we take humanity seriously. Man is part of Nature; yet he also transcends Nature. In self-awareness I am aware of a self-transcendence. As Jaspers says: "Science . . . shows us remarkable and highly surprising things about man, but as it attains greater clarity, the more evident it becomes that man as a whole can never become the object of scientific investigation. Man is always more than he knows about himself. This is true both of man in general and of the individual man." [4]

In short, we can now see in our twentieth-century way what perspicacious thinkers have always seen about the importance and the limitations of the kinds of inquiry and achievement that today we distinguish as scientific. That is to say, we can see, as earlier thinkers saw after their own fashion, that (a) science is an indispensable helper in the pursuit of the ontological and teleological truths disclosed to us through self-awareness—that is, awareness of our inner life—and appropriated conceptually by reflection upon such self-awareness, and (b) science can never by itself provide total explanations. The men of the Middle Ages would have said of our science what they said of their own philosophy, which was its medieval counterpart —that is, that it could never be *domina* (mistress) but is always *ancilla* (helper). Our more recent forefathers tended to read a servility into the term *ancilla* that was never there, as they tended to fear the domination of the *domina* over her partner in the pursuit of knowledge. On the contrary, in the partnership the medieval thinkers had in mind, there could never be either domineering or servility since each partner was, in her own way, engaged in the pursuit of the whole.

So vast and important is the area of modern scientific inquiry and achievement that the mere suggestion of servility becomes ridiculous. Science is concerned with the whole of the impersonal structure that Nature is. That concern envisages the control and prediction, *within certain systematic schemata,* even of man's own psychosomatic structure as well as of the physical universe and of the biological order that emerges out of that universe. The scientist is, so to say, asking questions of Nature and receiving Nature's answers. These answers may perhaps even enable future scientists to produce, for example, living things. For if Nature is, as has been suggested, the dark

---

[3] R. B. Braithwaite, *Scientific Explanation* (Cambridge: At the University Press, 1955), pp. 334 f.
[4] K. Jaspers, *The Perennial Scope of Philosophy* (New York: Philosophical Library, 1949), p. 60.

side of God, the scientist is really studying and learning the ways of God, whether unwittingly or, like Kepler (1571–1630), with a sense of "thinking God's thoughts after him." As in the Middle Ages Duns Scotus (1264–1308), through his appreciation of the notion of creation "out of nothing," understood better than his contemporaries how God stands in relation to Nature, so Kepler saw more clearly than many the creaturely and impersonal character of Nature when he argued against both the Aristotelian and the Ptolemaic cosmology on the ground that they implied that the "planets know mathematics." The planets, of course, know nothing; but we, through mathematics and astronomy, can know what we have to cope with when God is withdrawn from us, letting us be.

A word of caution is needed in speaking of prediction in science. As Professor Torrance remarked,

> It is now clear that prediction is applicable only within certain limited brackets where we are concerned with determinate aspects of nature alone, and that even there prediction is not applied to the relation of events as such but to abstractions from our observations or to our theoretical constructions. . . . Prediction has its place only in argument within a closed system or from fixed premises, physical or conceptual, but the more open a science is the less will be the emphasis laid upon it. It is thus quite wrong-headed to make prediction the hall-mark of all true science, in fact as impossible as it is to reduce inductive processes to transformations in accordance with logical rules.[5]

Torrance also reminds us of Popper's discussion of the logical distinction between routine and conjectural prediction.[6]

The range of the criterion of predictability in science is seen, then, to be as severely limited as must be the criterion of perceptibility when we see how the relativity theory has pushed thought, as Torrance says, "beyond the boundaries of the observable and picturable." [7] That is to say, modern science, with its intricate conceptualizations and abundant use of mathematical formulae, is working, as it ought to work, at a remove from what is given to the imagination. It has also very little to do with the perceptual, tables-and-chairs world of the ordinary man, for it is working and must work with models intellectually proper for the understanding of the impersonal structure that is Nature.

From this, an important consequence follows: religious consciousness need never, and never should, engage in any renunciation of scientific concepts, because these concepts are not and cannot be concerned with the freedom conferred by the God of love. The renunciation that is our special concern in the present chapter must take place at the imaginative level because it is there, in the realm of the imagination, that freedom is born and that

---

[5] T. F. Torrance, *God and Rationality* (London: Oxford University Press, 1971), pp. 7 f.
[6] K. Popper, *Conjectures and Refutations* (London: Routledge and Kegan Paul, 1963), pp. 117 f.
[7] *God and Rationality*, p. 7.

through its renunciation we can gain a clue to the mystery of the incomparable self-emptying love of God, which lets us be to make us free. From the standpoint of religious consciousness, the importance of science lies not least in its showing us how all things work when God withdraws or absents himself from them, leaving only his dark side and showing only Nature—the created battleground for the free spirits he has permitted, through the same Nature, to emerge and learn to enter into that greater dimension of freedom that Benedict called "the deifying light." [8]

In the view proposed, scientific study is not the study of something that is apart from God. If Nature is God's handiwork, there is no "secular" realm standing in opposition to God. The scientist, in constructing the conceptual models that enable him to understand the workings of Nature and in some limited measure to control and predict them, has as his subject matter that which reflects in a special and direct way the same power that the religious believer celebrates—being an aspect of the power of the same God whose almighty benevolence the believer proclaims.

Primitive Concepts of the Miraculous

Among primitive peoples in Australia and Africa, for instance, the notion of the miraculous is comparatively simple. Lacking anything like a scientific methodology for investigating natural occurrences, they take a simplistic, phenomenalistic view of the way things behave. That is to say, they do not inquire much, for they do not have means for much inquiry, into the principles, scientific or metaphysical, that might be held to explain natural occurrences. They observe the phenomena, often very closely indeed, and they detect, no doubt often unreflectively, a general uniformity. They know nothing about a law of gravity, but observation of natural phenomena teaches them to expect apples to fall to the ground. In general they feel no need for an explanation of such behavior. Their attitude in such matters is not fundamentally different from the one taken—much more consciously, of course, and at a much later stage in human development—by those who espouse the view that philosophers call positivism.

Primitive peoples, however, despite the closeness of their contact with Nature, usually have a narrow, limited experience of natural phenomena. Therefore, they often encounter occurrences and events that astonish them. When they do, they are no less inclined than are we to cry, "Wonderful!" Having no means of accounting for phenomena to which they happen to be unaccustomed, they identify the wonder with the manifestation or act of a god or other agency, according to the mode of theological conceptualization that is available to them at a stage at which their religion is as primitive as are their science and their philosophy.

[8] See p. 272.

The early Greeks, for instance, when they encountered such a wonder, cried, *"Theos!"* *Theos* originally meant simply "wonder"—that is, the recognition of the emergence of some natural wonder. Later the word came to be used of any god in the Greek pantheon (or, latinized as *deus,* in the Roman one), such as Mars, the Roman god of war, or Poseidon, the Greek god of the sea. Heroes, being wonderful men, could be similarly acclaimed as godlike, much in the way in which film stars and television personalities have been acclaimed in our time as deities in the popular pantheon of our own day. If the wonder is a lasting one, like the fertility of the earth or the rain in the sky, the god has a permanent status; if it is shortlived, like a hurricane, the god's status is more fleeting, as even today we sometimes speak of a "nine days' wonder," to signify a phenomenon that briefly arouses interest and astonishment and then passes into oblivion. Part of the task of the Greek philosophers was to wean people away from such primitivistic ways of thinking.

Wonders must be distinguished from what is merely a curiosity, as would be the first European an Indian set eyes on or even a parrot to a man who had never before seen one. A parrot, wonderful though it might seem to a man who had seen only sparrows and seagulls, need not more radically astonish him than would an oak a man who had seen only beeches and elms. The parrot would be acceptable because, though novel to the man's experience, it would not contravene his expectations. If, however, he had never seen any kind of living thing that could fly, he might be so astounded at the sight of a bird as to attribute its presence or existence to a divine agency of some sort. Certainly an eclipse of the sun would be likely to have such an effect on one who, having for long watched the heavens, had never seen one and had no idea how to account for the phenomenon. Though primitive man may have no developed cosmology, he does have certain expectations, and he is likely to account miraculous anything that seems unaccountable in terms of his experience, even though it were something that any American high school student could easily explain from an elementary knowledge of modern chemistry or physics.

We must remember to make an often forgotten distinction. The whole of the ancient world, including, of course, the writers of the New Testament, must be classed as primitive with respect to their scientific knowledge. This does not by any means imply, however, that they were stupid or ignorant in other respects; on the contrary—they were in many ways very skilled and subtle. Their understanding of the universe around them was nevertheless, from a modern standpoint, such as to make them vulnerable to the most elementary errors and prone to engage in what seem to us the most absurd fantasies. Experimental science made comparatively little progress till at least late in the Middle Ages, by which time people had become highly sophisticated in the use of philosophical and theological ideas. Those who accepted in principle the notion of miracles tended to interpret them as sensible facts transcending the normal order of things and produced by divine intervention for a special purpose. With the rise of modern science in the seventeenth century, skepticism about the possibility of miracles grew. Pantheists like Spinoza had no need for the concept of the miraculous, since they identified God and Nature. Deists, who separated God and Nature, could find no place for miracles in their systems.

The Humean Tradition

In the eighteenth century, Hume pioneered a trend of thought that accounted the whole concept of miracles nothing but a manifestation of ignorance. Hume treats miracles in the tenth section of the *Essay Concerning Human Understanding*. He defines them as violations of "the laws of nature." They contravene what "a firm and unalterable experience" of Nature has established in the minds of men. As is well known, Hume's repudiation of "necessary causation" did not preclude a high degree of probability in the prediction of events. Experience shows that when we say that every man must die or that the metallic element lead cannot by itself be suspended in the air, we are talking of probabilities so great that for practical purposes we must look on them as though they were certainties until the contrary is shown beyond all doubt. Hume recognized that it is *logically* possible that evidence might be weighty enough to show that a "law of nature" had been violated, but he thinks such a violation very improbable indeed. He claims there is no evidence "in all history" of "any miracle attested by a sufficient number of men, of such unquestioned good sense, education and learning, as to secure us against all delusion in themselves."

Noting the human predilection for what we today might call "yakking about the fantastic," he reminds us that religious people are often so carried away by their fanaticism as to propagate by little lies what they believe to be great truths. "If the spirit of religion join itself to the love of wonder," he says, "there is an end to common sense." Finally, claiming that miraculous stories are to be observed chiefly "among ignorant and barbarous nations," he contends that what he is claiming constitutes "a strong presumption" against their being factual occurrences.

In all the considerations that Hume brings before us, there is really, however, no more than an appeal to common sense and the supposed weakness of historical testimony to warrant belief in miracles. We have noted his admission that the production of evidence for the factuality of an alleged miraculous occurrence is not *logically* impossible. As he goes on, however, it becomes difficult to see what evidence would ever suffice to convince him. He alludes, for instance, to the then recent case of a French Jansenist at whose sepulchre a large number of extraordinary events were popularly believed to have occurred. Many of them were attested "before judges of unquestioned integrity" and "by witnesses of credit and distinction, in a learned age." Nevertheless, Hume dismisses them all without further ado simply on ground of the "absolute impossibility or miraculous nature of the events" recounted. "And this surely," he says, "in the eyes of all reasonable people, will alone be regarded as a sufficient refutation."

Of what, precisely, does Hume's acknowledgment of the logical impossibility of miracles consist? He recognizes that although there is a logical reason why *A* cannot be not-*A*, there could be no *logical* reason that lead balls should not occasionally float in the air; nevertheless, he claims, since experience teaches us that they never do, it would be folly to expect such an occurrence or to believe that anything like it had ever in fact occurred. Moreover, if a lead ball did float in the air, it would call for a review of what we commonly understand of the behavior of lead balls. Again, while it is true that many people love to expatiate on the extraordinary and the marvelous and are prone to credulity about wonder tales, there are also (and in every age there always have been) many people of a skeptical disposition who are just as cautious and incredulous as Hume could claim to be. Nor are they all by any means of an irreligious temper. Deeply religious people are, on the contrary, often the most reluctant to accept miraculous stories that are bruited about by the overcredulous.

Furthermore, it is a matter of historical record that belief in miracles was prevalent among all peoples Hume could have known. His contention that stories about miracles are to be heard chiefly among ignorant and barbarous nations condemns all nations in every age prior to his own, as well as the peoples in his own day whose ancestors had cradled European civilization—for instance, the Greeks and, later, the Italians. It is, moreover, an uninformative contention since he appears to be simply asserting that people who believe in miracles, whoever they are, *must* be ignorant and barbarous.

Hume makes the remarkable affirmation that "in matters of religion, whatever is different is contrary," so that, say, the religions of Turkey and China and Greece could not all be true, and since they all claim miraculous occurrences, any evidence in favor of the Turkish religion is evidence against the Chinese, and so forth. We should note that, as every modern student of eastern religions knows, very little was in fact known by Europeans in Hume's day about Asiatic societies or their religions, and what little information was available was much distorted. Hume and his Scottish contemporaries reveal on many occasions that they had some very distorted ideas about the history of religions in general and of Asiatic ones in particular. What Hume says in this vein may be discounted on that historical consideration alone. He does raise here, however, one question of philosophical importance: might not all or many or at least some of the various religions of the world harbor within them *elements* of truth, so as to make them by no means so mutually exclusive as he accounts them?

Of course, as Hume's modern disciples have easily and abundantly formulated, what Hume is really disposed to say is that when what purports to be a miracle does occur, we have to review the "laws of nature" that we had previously accepted and restate them. For instance, a controlled, scientific experiment was conducted in England some decades ago, to test the genuineness of Indian firewalkers. Slow-motion pictures showed that those who actually walked on a surface heated to an extremely high temperature did so by their having acquired great virtuosity in a special technique, the principle of which seemed to be similar to that which we all use in extinguishing a candle with our fingers. By their use of a highly skilled manner of walking, no part of the foot was in continuous contact with the surface for more than a fraction of a second. No miracle had occurred in the sense of a violation of a law of nature; yet what might have been taken as following from a law of Nature (for instance, that no human being could ever walk barefoot on red hot coals and not be severely burned) would have been shown to be an improper formulation. The principle underlying such philosophical "debunking" of miracles is that so-called laws of Nature are simply formulations of what actually happens.

Now, it is a commonplace of scientific discovery that we do come to notice occurrences that would have seemed miraculous to our forefathers but are explicable to us. An electric shock, for instance, must have seemed both wonderful and very frightening to a people who knew nothing about electricity or its behavior. The removal of certain types of cataract might have been possible long before anything scientific was known about them, and the curing of blindness that would attend such procedures in some cases could not but evoke immense astonishment, wonder, and awe, while today it would result only in acknowledgment of, or admiration for, the ophthalmological surgeon's competence. Contemporary exponents of the Humean tradition tend to assert, as does Patrick Nowell-Smith, that any effective explanation of an allegedly miraculous occurrence, whether couched in "natural" or "supernatural language," will always be in fact a "natural" explanation, so that the very notion of a "supernatural explanation" becomes meaningless.[9] That is an assertion that plainly begs the question. Without begging the question, however, one might well propose that an explanation would always *include* a "natural" explanation, and that would be a very different assertion indeed.

What Is a Miracle?

Philosophers in the Humean tradition generally exhibit a remarkably antiquated and jejune notion of what is to be understood by the concept of miracle. Hume happened to flourish in an age when mechanism was

[9] P. Nowell-Smith, "Miracles," in *New Essays in Philosophical Theology,* ed. A. Flew and A. MacIntyre (London: S.C.M. Press, 1955), p. 253.

in vogue in science and deism in theology. These twin circumstances favored the prevalence of a very special philosophical mood. Since God was deemed to have made the world as a clockmaker makes a clock, the notion of his then tinkering with it to make minor adjustments here and there was ridiculous. It made God look like an incompetent or even senile craftsman. A miracle was conceived to be that sort of divine intervention: God, the grand architect of the universe, having created it according to a certain blueprint of his own design, and having built everything in terms of that blueprint, then returned to the scene and superimposed on his own architectural achievement occasional elements beyond the scope of the original design.

For instance, God, having made the appropriate arrangement for the ebb and flow of oceans, might briefly come back to the scene, stop the tidal processes and introduce an incompatible temporary arrangement to enable the Israelites to flee their Egyptian pursuers. Similarly, having established the laws of planetary motion, he might stop that motion for a day in order to assist the Israelites in their military activities against the Amorites.[10] It is true that in primitive times some people did tend to think along such lines, but they did so without having any special theory such as prevailed in the eighteenth century. Today we are able to advance a view about miracles that not only seems more enlightened but also does much better justice to the claims of religious men. It takes better account of why miracles should ever enter into religious thinking at all.

If, as I have suggested, God creates Nature as the arena for the training and development of free spirits, interference with it is out of the question. God could have no need to interfere with Nature or suspend any of its laws. Even if we admit such a possibility we must recognize that it would be contrary to the divine economy. The essential quality to be expected in all miracles is that they should have a purpose worthy of God. For God to suspend lead balls in the air to demonstrate his power would be both a ludicrous and a purposeless proceeding, making God into a sort of heavenly conjuror bent on entertaining his creatures. To warrant a miracle by any God worth worshipping, there would have to be, by any reckoning, an extraordinarily important and good purpose. Even then, surely one would expect miracles to be performed as economically as possible. There is no need to expect God to be wasteful.

When miracles are portrayed as great productions calculated to demonstrate the powers of God as a theurgist, the obvious objection is not that such performances are too much even for God; the objection is that they are too little. The deeply religious mind does not expect God to act ostentatiously when he could act inconspicuously. For instance, for the Red Sea miracle, there is no need to have had the waters part with a roar as if Niagara had been suddenly transported to the continental divide. The introduction of one or two Israelite intelligence officers among the Egyptians

10 Joshua 10:13.

together with the use of some natural tidal occurrences would have been quite enough for the purpose. The slightest divine suggestion would have been enough to accomplish the rescue of the fleeing Israelites from their pursuers.

Deeply religious people, believing themselves accustomed to see the hand of God frequently in their lives, all attest the almost daily introduction of miraculous elements. By that they mean, not that laws of Nature are ostentatiously or even inconspicuously violated but that a special dimension (what I have called the God-dimension) has intruded upon the "Nature-dimension," thereby enriching it and perfecting it according to the old Thomist principle that "grace does not take away nature but perfects it." [11] So those who say, "If Jesus didn't actually change H_2O into wine but only made people feel as if he had done so, it wasn't a 'real' miracle," are missing the point. To effect violations of the laws of Nature is a proceeding so clumsy that only someone of comparatively low religious development would care to attribute it to God. It would seem a gauche proceeding for God that would hardly even occur to a deeply religious mind. St. Thomas saw this in his own way. He pointed out that an event, to be a miracle, had to be beyond the natural power of any creature to produce;[12] but the event need not disrupt the ordinary course of events at all. Indeed, Bob Smith might be struck dumb at the wonder of a miracle wrought upon him while Jack Brown looked on yawning or grumbling that his coffee was getting cold.

If a miracle is regarded primarily as the intrusion of the God-dimension into the Nature-dimension, the need for showiness disappears; nor would there ever be any point to it anyhow, for if Jack could discern the hand of God as does Bob, no ostentatious, public display of divine power would affect him. "If they do not hear Moses and the prophets, neither will they be convinced if someone should rise from the dead." [13] That is sufficient reason why Jesus often enjoined the beneficiaries of his healing power to "see that no one knows it." [14] However a miracle is to be understood, it need not be presented as the crude, magical performance that in the Humean tradition it is usually given out to be.

For orthodox Christians the paradigm case of miracle will always be, of course, the Incarnation, which for those who account it a miraculous occurrence at all must surely be regarded as a very noiseless one. It was perfectly possible to pass it by and interpret the nativity of Jesus as a very natural occurrence. Only the shepherds heard the angel voices. The Gospel story tells us that a star guided the wise men to Bethlehem but, of course,

[11] *Gratia non tollit naturam sed perficit.*
[12] *Summa contra Gentiles* 3,102.
[13] Luke 16:31 (R.S.V.). I discussed this point at length elsewhere, e. g., in my *Christian Doubt* (London: Longmans, Green, 1951), pp. 42 ff. The same point was made some years later by Karl Barth in the fourth volume of his *Kirchliche Dogmatik.*
[14] Matthew 9:30 (R.S.V.).

that is biblical shorthand. If they were guided, God guided their interpretation of what the star signified. Even if it were true that, as a picturesque legend has it, the oxen kneel every Christmas Eve in honor of the Nativity, nothing could be deduced except that they kneel. Oxen often kneel. No ox violates a law of Nature by doing so. No ox could convince an unbeliever of the doctrine of the Incarnation, and believers would be inclined to suspect any such interpretation of bovine behavior on grounds that for God to go in for such extravagant Christmas showmanship would be out of character, inconsistent with his quiet and inconspicuous methods of self-disclosure. The event that is at the heart of all that Christians account miraculous was in its nature unobtrusive. That is precisely the quality that Phillips Brooks captured in his well-known American hymn:

> How silently, how silently,
> The wondrous gift is given!
> So God imparts to human hearts
> The blessings of his heaven.
> No ear may hear his coming,
> But in this world of sin,
> Where meek souls will receive him, still
> The dear Christ enters in.[15]

Miracles, whatever they are, are always for a special purpose. Scientific explanations are therefore as irrelevant as would be failures to provide them. What is at issue is the purpose believed to be present in the event, not the event as such. The event may indeed be astonishing, but the astonishment is not constitutive of the miracle. Many pedestrian events astonish me, not because I find anything unusual or inexplicable in them as events but because of the timing or the way in which they occur. If I accidentally ran across a Greek friend of mine in Lapland I would account the occurrence remarkable, though, of course, simply a coincidence. If, however, he told me he had been urged in a dream to go to Lapland and had done so, and my meeting him there turned out to be the occasion of my rescue from a terrible disaster that would otherwise certainly have overtaken me, I might be disposed to see in the happening more than mere coincidence. Again, suppose I missed my plane. My having overslept or having been caught in a traffic jam would provide all the explanation I could need. If, however, the plane I missed was a plane that later crashed, I *might* see in my escape an agency beyond the Nature-dimension.

Assertions about miracles always entail interpretation. As primitive peoples do not feel they need what we call a scientific explanation for their understanding of the actual course of events, so a civilized but ungodly person will seek no explanation why the scientifically explicable event occurred in such a way as to save him from catastrophe or death. Only

[15] Hymn 21 in *The Hymnal of the Protestant Episcopal Church in the United States of America* (Greenwich, Conn.: Seabury Press, 1940).

to the extent that one finds the scientific explanation, though perfectly satisfactory in its way, to be nevertheless inadequate will one look for further explanation and, if chance seems too far-fetched to meet the case, there is nowhere to look but to God, who if he creates and controls Nature has surely no need to violate it in order to act in history. Of course, a skeptic could be content with a naturalistic explanation for a thousand astonishing escapes from disaster.

Even our insurance companies seem to know better than the Humeans how God is expected to act, for what they call an "act of God" is, though no doubt usually unexpected, by no means a violation of any law of Nature or of the actual course of events, whatever such a violation could be. An "act of God" is defined as "an operation of uncontrollable natural forces." What distinguishes it from the ordinary operation of natural forces is that it is beyond human control. That uncontrollability is pre-eminently what should be predicated of miracles. What is distinctive in the religious person's attitude is his interpretation. He is always inclined to wonder what is being disclosed to him in the God-dimension. The nonreligious person is not so inclined.

Miracles, Magic, and Science

The magician attempts, in his own way, to control the operations of Nature. The practice of magic has a long and complicated history. That astrology flourished in court circles in the Middle Ages, as did alchemy, alongside what are generally taken to be more intellectually profitable and more genuinely scientific investigations, is well known.[16] Keith Thomas has argued that the quattrocento revival of Neo-Platonism in Ficino, Pico della Mirandola, and other great humanists of the Florentine Renaissance, fostered a new, more intellectual kind of magic. "Since the world was a pulsating mass of vital influences and invisible spirits, it was only necessary that the magician should devise the appropriate technique to capture them. He could then do wonders."[17]

That such pretended wonders were based upon unscientific views of Nature is irrelevant here. What is important is that, like all magicians, the hermetists and alchemists, no less than the village wizard, sought to change or at any rate draw forth novel action from what they took to be Nature. The attempt must have seemed indeed an exciting adventure. Paracelsus hoped to discover a liquid and potable form of gold *(aurum potabile)* that would provide the elixir of long life.[18] Neither the modern technologist nor the tribal witch doctor is any different a case, so far as religious interest in miracles goes. For in so far as anything is taken to be produced by a human technique,

[16] See C. H. Haskins, *Studies in the History of Medieval Science* (Cambridge, Mass.: Harvard University Press, 1924).
[17] Keith Thomas, *Religion and the Decline of Magic* (New York: Charles Scribner's Sons, 1971), p. 224.
[18] Ibid., p. 228.

superstitious or scientific, it could not possibly have any noteworthy religious significance in any age.

There can be little doubt that among the reasons for the repudiation by the early Church of the literature that came to be called the Apocryphal New Testament, a prominent one was the magical flavor of the tales they contained. For instance, there is the story that Joseph, being stupid at his trade, cut some beams too short and that the boy Jesus then pulled them out to the right length.[19] At first sight such a story may look similar to that of the multiplication of loaves and fishes that appears in the canonical Gospels, but there is a profound difference. The story of the lengthening of the beams in Joseph's shop is a tale of pure magic, for by no stretch of the imagination could it purport to exhibit the intrusion of the God-dimension into the Nature-dimension. Not so could God be supposed to act in history, teaching a lesson, manifesting his care, or disclosing his love. The loaves-and-fishes story *can* be interpreted along similarly magical lines, but nineteenth-century biblical scholars such as H. E. G. Paulus (1761–1851), who was among those who were skeptical of popular understanding of miracles, offered alternative explanations. Some scholars about this time began to favor interpreting the feeding of the multitude as the result of Jesus' ability to persuade his audience to produce and to share the food that oriental peasants usually carry with them hidden in their clothes, so that there proved to be plenty for all.

The motivation of such exegetes was generally understood to be rational, anti-supernatural; but as A. D. Ritchie remarks after stressing the scientific improbability of a literalistic, multiplicative interpretation, such an interpretation is "not so much irrational as worthless." To the objection that unless an occurrence is interpreted along such magical lines it cannot count as a miracle at all, Ritchie replies: "To get a miscellaneous crowd of people, even for half an hour, to lay aside fear, suspicion and greed, and really share a common meal with strangers or friends or enemies or anybody is, to my mind, a genuine miracle. To anyone who suggests it is not a miracle at all, the reply is, 'Try if you can do it yourself or anything the least like it.' "[20] Not the least value of Ritchie's and other such observations lies in their bringing to light the notion that the miraculous character of an event is enhanced rather than diminished by depriving it of magical character.

Biblical and Contemporary Conceptions of Miracle

As we have seen, not only has understanding of miracles been vitiated in the popular mind by the confusion of miracle with magic; some contemporary philosophers, even, have been similarly misled by their uncritical

[19] The story occurs in several forms—including, for example, in the Arabic Gospel of the Birth of Mary. See M. R. James, *The Apocryphal New Testament* (Oxford: Clarendon Press, 1924), p. 78.

[20] A. D. Ritchie, *Civilization, Science and Religion* (London: Penguin Books, 1945), pp. 73 f.

acceptance of an understanding of miracle based upon the special, narrow views of science and of theology that prevailed in the eighteenth century. Though modern science attests a certain constancy in Nature, modern scientists are more hesitant than were their Newtonian predecessors in affirming the constancy of action and fixity of principles in Nature.

When we ask, then, what was the religious significance of miracle to the biblical writers, we find there were no comparable concepts of Nature. Such a notion was quite alien to the ancient Hebrews and to their Semitic neighbors in the Near East, neither of whom even had words that could be translated "nature" or "miracle." In biblical Hebrew three words were used for expressing the wonderful: (1) *'ōt,* sign, used of anything that causes astonishment or even attracts attention; (2) *mōpet,* a wonder or portent, often presaging a future event; and (3) *niplā 'ōt,* wonders or marvels. The word *'ôt* is used of the rainbow, as a sign of God's covenant, as well as of the events of the Exodus and the plagues visited upon Egypt. *Mōpet* is used almost as frequently of the plagues of Egypt, but it is also used of the performances of a false prophet,[21] and *niplā 'ôt* is used of all sorts of wonders.

None of these words corresponds to "miracle" as Hume and his followers have interpreted it in more recent times. The early Hebrews were familiar with the idea of the magical, of course, and they recognized the ability of the professional magicians of Egypt, for example; but, they claimed, the power of God (Yahweh) was far greater than any such magical ability.[22] It came to be accounted not only different in degree but different in quality.

Israelite belief never arrived at a conception of Nature such as has come down to us today in our intellectual tradition. The New Testament writers, comparatively little affected by the metaphysical speculations of the Greeks, typically reflect the Hebrew outlook of their authors. So the Greek terms used in the New Testament are: (1) *dynamis,* power, (2) *sēmeion,* sign, and (3) *teras,* an extraordinary occurrence or portent. The first of these Greek terms is a neutral one, referring simply to energies or forces that must be recognized and reckoned with. A *sēmeion* is a sign as in the Hebrew word *'ôt,* and a *teras* may refer to anything wonderful, including any occurrence as in Hebrew might have been called *mōpet.*

The apostles find themselves full of the *dynamis,* the power of Jesus. What we call "miracles" are simply functions of that power. In contrast to the activities of magicians who notoriously use their pretended powers for mischievous as well as beneficent ends, the works of Jesus are always presented in the New Testament as never causing harm to anybody but, on the contrary, generally performed in the course of a ministry of healing. So where Jesus is presented as having some special power over what we should call "Nature" (calming the storm, for instance), it is always in the interest of exhibiting him as pre-eminently able to practice what he preaches about the power of faith in God.

[21] Deuteronomy 13:2 f.
[22] Cf. Exodus 7:20–8:19.

What were the philosophical presuppositions underlying these biblical views of what we call miracles? The early Hebrew writers had little if any tendency toward metaphysical speculation. While it is always misleading if not dangerous to attribute to such writers any definite philosophical presuppositions, we may safely say that the concept of what they acclaimed as wonderful acts of God is more compatible with modern scientific ideas than with the Humean tradition. For these biblical writers, lacking Newtonian and deistic dogmas, and having no doctrinaire view about the laws of Nature, were simply telling what they saw the way they saw it. What they saw was a multidimensional universe—though, of course, they could not possibly have so expressed themselves. That is to say, seeing all creation as the work of God, they simply noted that some of the events they observed had about them a more extraordinary and marvelous character than most. True, every shower of rain was accounted God's act, but when the shower was timely or accomplished an effect that was out of the ordinary, they noted it with special gratitude and awe. So when Jesus, in the course of his ministry, put his teaching into practice by apparently doing the wonders he said were doable, biblical writers acclaimed the wonders he did as signs that he was no ordinary rabbinical teacher but was, to say the least, a very special instrument of God.

When today, in face of what seems the inevitability of a great tragedy, something very unexpected occurs in a most unusual manner and under very extraordinary circumstances so that the tragedy is averted after all, we, too—unless we happen to be conspicuously close-minded—are likely to pause with reverence as well as gratitude for the occurrence. The fact that nothing had happened that a modern physicist or chemist would account at all inexplicable would not in the least diminish our sense of being under providential care. Our response to such a situation would not be, from a philosophical standpoint, radically other than the response of the biblical writers to what they saw going on about them. The philosophical presuppositions in the Humean tradition are, by contrast, quite different from both and are remarkably irrelevant to the contemporary intellectual situation.

Multidimensionality and the Renunciation of Power

Religious people take miracles to be by any reckoning the manifestation of divine energy or power. They see in them an unusualness that calls attention in a special way to the presence of God. Contemporary persons of religious disposition are willing to see the hand of God both in the Exodus and other biblical miracles that are recounted of the lives of primitive peoples in biblical times and also in our own age—for example, in extraordinarily unexpected deliverance from tragic situations. Whatever reliance religious people may place upon stories of the miraculous, however, no mature, deeply religious person ever makes his religious conviction depend upon such unusual manifestations of divine power. On the contrary, to put the matter simply, he is less impressed by unusual manifestations of the divine activity than he is by the much more usual circumstances in which God appears to be in one way or another staying his hand when, from our human point of view, the stretching forth of his hand would seem more apposite.

The religious consciousness tends, indeed, to expect wondrous works of God all the time and interprets the whole created universe as a manifestation of God's wonderful power. Such an expectation does, of course, raise the familiar question, why does God not act more swiftly and plainly in situations of terrible human agony? The multidimensional view of the relation of God and Nature that has been much suggested in the present chapter[23] leads one to expect, not absurdities such as the occasional levitation of Windsor Castle or that carbon dioxide should behave like oxygen on Mondays and Thursdays, but that God, who can presumably handle Nature with unimaginable deftness, would often use it to extricate his creatures from their predicaments if not to prevent them from getting into their plights.

The notoriously grievous pains and sorrows of mankind, to say nothing of the cruelties and miseries of the rest of creation, are witnesses to the absence of any such habitual divine tendency. The suffering which the whole evolutionary process entails constitutes, indeed, a stock objection to the existence of a divine Being like the kind proclaimed in the Bible.

Much as such considerations may at first distress some religiously minded people, even a little experience of living a life of faith soon shows them the indispensability of suffering—for their own spiritual development. In the evolutionary process, not least at the higher levels, suffering ceases, therefore, to astonish them. Human situations in which people of exquisitely refined taste and cultivated upbringing are reduced to abject poverty by sheer misfortune or in which a healthy little boy who is full of life and energy is suddenly and irretrievably crippled, are too well known to need portrayal. Their anguish is as familiar to religious as to nonreligious people. Not less well known to many, however, are the extraordinary and novel sorts of courage that emerge among men and women in coping with such misfortunes.

A notion familiar in most religions, in one guise or another, is that the religious value of suffering depends upon the individual's attitude toward it. Everybody suffers, but if the suffering is no more than the occasion of bitterness, hatred, or despair, it remains nothing but a load to be borne without choice. Suffering, however, can become redemptive when the sufferer not only accepts it but embraces it as an instrument of his spiritual progress. Characteristic of this notion is the traditional Catholic view that my sufferings should be offered up to God, not because they are needed for any great cosmic purpose, which in the Christian view has been fully accomplished by Christ, but rather because the offering of my own sufferings to God is necessary for my appropriation of the redemptive purpose Christ has

[23] I have expounded such a view also in my *God Beyond Doubt* (Philadelphia: J. B. Lippincott Co., 1966), especially in the chapter "Miracles and Multidimensionality," pp. 108–126.

already fulfilled. If the cosmic purpose could be appropriated by me without my offering up my own sufferings to God, the proceeding would be a magical one. It becomes miraculous (that is, it entails the penetration of the Nature-dimension by the God-dimension) through my willingness to accept my suffering to the point of recognizing in it the instrument of my spiritual education, development, and progress, and so, finding in it my richest value, offering that richest value to God as the best sacrifice I have to offer. Of course, such a devotional attitude is attended by psychological dangers of morbid, masochistic wallowing in grief and pain, but there is, after all, no attitude that has not its attendant psychological dangers. The fact that the pursuit of human love and friendship can lead to some very weird and distorted psychological states is no reason for eschewing them as intrinsically unhealthy. At any rate, the universal testimony of holy men and women in all religious traditions is that the royal road to an understanding of God's ways is a willingness to love him, and the test of the authenticity of any kind of love is the degree of willingness to sacrifice.

Through accepting the suffering that is inflicted on me in the course of life and offering it up in sacrifice to God, I learn that it is good for me sometimes to renounce what gives me pleasure and joy in order to achieve a particular purpose that I take to be worthwhile in terms of what Tillich would have called my "ultimate concern." In the language of piety, I engage in self-denial. The value of self-denial is misunderstood by many. It goes far beyond the attainment of negative-sounding virtues such as patience or resignation. Its value stems from the fact that I choose to renounce the use of power that I might well have chosen to exercise. As I have suggested earlier and as we may now more clearly appreciate, this renunciation of power gives me the clue to an understanding of God's nonaction on occasions that seem to the less mature religious believer to be crying out for whatever kind of miracle God ever performs.

We can hardly remind ourselves too often or too emphatically that such reflections do nothing to establish the truth of a theistic view. An atheistic interpretation, which accounts suffering a paradigmatic case of nonvalue, of moral meaninglessness, is still, of course, as intellectually plausible as ever. There can be no logical objection to it. The theistic believer who does experience personal growth through renunciation, however, can begin to see it not only as compatible with the kind of ordering that should be expected in a universe created by the God of love in whom he believes, but also as an indispensable principle running through the whole evolutionary and creative process. He thinks he detects the source and heart of the process in God himself. That is indeed precisely what it means to call God the God of love.

The problem of the miraculous remains. It is, however, transformed. It is no longer expressible in the question, why would God choose frequently to penetrate Nature in a way that religious people recognize as miraculous?

The question is now, if God is distinguishable from Nature, as theists insist, and has created Nature for the development of free spirits, why would he choose ever to penetrate Nature at all? More particularly, why should he enter in a special, allegedly miraculous way into one situation and not into another? The problem expressed in these questions is incomprehensible apart from the concept of divine love. Whether it be soluble even in terms of that concept remains to be investigated. It will be considered in our concluding chapter—after we have attended to the question of the relation to religion of morality, at once its greatest ally and greatest rival.

QUESTIONS ON CHAPTER XII

1 What do you take to be the role of imagination in religion? Consider its limits.

2 Distinguish between fantasy and disciplined imagination. Why might the notion of renunciation be accounted important?

3 What kinship may be seen in methodologies that are appropriate in science and in religion respectively?

4 To what extent is prediction possible in science? What is the importance of the question for the philosophy of religion?

5 What is Hume's position in respect of the miraculous? Consider his presuppositions.

6 What are the biblical terms used for the miraculous and what light does an understanding of the climate of biblical thought cast on the interpretation of miracle?

7 Consider the relation of miracles to magic.

8 Discuss the notion of divine renunciation of power. What is its value for the religious consciousness and what philosophical difficulties do you see in it?

BIBLIOGRAPHICAL SUGGESTIONS
See also under Chapter IV

Aquinas, Thomas. *Summa Theologiae.* In *Basic Writings of Saint Thomas Aquinas,* edited by A. C. Pegis. New York: Random House, 1945.

I, 105, 5–7 (*ed. cit.,* Vol. I, pp. 976–980). Statement of the classic Thomist stance on the possibility of miracle.

Cameron, J. M. "Miracles." *Month,* n.s. 22 (1959): 286–297.

Farmer, H. H. *The World and God.* 2nd edition. London: Nisbet and Co., 1936. In Chapters 7 and 9 is to be found one of the best introductions to the understanding of the concept of miracles.

Farrer, Austin. *The Freedom of the Will*. Gifford Lectures. New York: Charles Scribner's Sons, 1960. A closely argued and much criticized philosophical analysis.

Flew, Antony. *Hume's Philosophy of Belief*. London: Routledge and Kegan Paul, 1961. Chapter 8 contains a discussion of Hume's view of miracle.

Furlong, E. J. *Imagination*. New York: Macmillan Co., 1961. An introduction to contemporary philosophical dialogue on the term "imagination," with special reference to Hume. Useful background for the topic of this chapter.

Hampshire, Stuart. *The Freedom of the Individual*. New York: Harper & Row, 1965. A modern critical defense of the view that the notion of freedom properly enters into the analysis of intentional action. Hampshire seeks to clarify it by a distinction between two kinds of knowledge, one from observation and the other from decision.

Holland, R. F. "The Miraculous." In *Religion and Understanding*, edited by D. B. Phillips. Oxford: Basil Blackwell, 1967.

Hume, David. "Of Miracles." In *An Enquiry Concerning Human Understanding*. In *Hume's Enquiries*, 2nd edition, edited by L. A. Selby-Bigge. Oxford: Clarendon Press, 1902. Classic skeptical attack on the concept of miracles.

Lewis, C. S. *Miracles*. New York: Macmillan Co., 1947.

Mill, John Stuart. *A System of Logic*. New York: Longmans, 1884. See especially III, chap. 25, sec. 2, for a critique of Hume's stance on miracles. Mill, who explored the logic of induction and the scientific method from an empiricist standpoint, set forth in this passage his evaluation of belief in occasional supernatural intervention. The book originally appeared in 1843.

Newman, John Henry. *Two Essays on Biblical and Ecclesiastical Miracles*. New York: Longmans, 1924. An approach by a great nineteenth-century English divine.

Nowell-Smith, P. "Miracles." In *New Essays in Philosophical Theology*, edited by A. Flew and A. MacIntyre. London: S.C.M. Press, 1955. A contemporary essay in the Humean tradition.

Popper, K. *Conjectures and Refutations*. London: Routledge and Kegan Paul, 1963.

Ritchie, A. D. *Civilization, Science and Religion*. London: Penguin Books, 1945.

Schleiermacher, F. *The Christian Faith*. Translated by H. R. Macintosh and J. S. Stewart. Edinburgh: T. and T. Clark, 1928. See especially I, sects. 46–47 for a treatment of the subject of miracle from a classic theological work that interpreted the Protestant tradition in terms of the Romantic movement. The original German edition appeared in 1821.

Slote, M. A. *Reason and Scepticism*. New York: Humanities Press, 1970. See especially chap. 6: "Religion, Science and the Extraordinary."

Smart, Ninian. *Philosophers and Religious Truth*. London: S.C.M. Press, 1964. There is some discussion of Hume's view of miracles in the first chapter.

Tennant, F. R. *Miracle and Its Philosophical Presuppositions*. New York: Macmillan Co., 1926.

Thomas, Keith. *Religion and the Decline of Magic*. New York: Charles Scribner's Sons, 1971. An extensive, scholarly study of the subject with some reference to the concept of miracles.

XIII

ETHICS AND RELIGION

> I . . . think that some very important virtues are more
> likely to be found among those who reject religious
> dogmas than among those who accept them. I think this
> applies especially to the virtue of truthfulness or intellec-
> tual integrity.
>
> *Bertrand Russell (1872–1970),*
> *Why I Am Not a Christian*

> Religion, blushing, veils her sacred fires,
> And unawares Morality expires.
>
> *Alexander Pope (1688–1744),*
> *The Dunciad*

Defining Characteristics

Before embarking on an examination of the relation in which ethics and
religion stand to one another, we must attempt to define, at least in very
broad and general terms, what respectively they are.

Professor de Burgh, in his published Gifford Lectures, relates that in the
discussions following the delivery of those lectures at the University of St.
Andrews, he found that "while some of my critics were inclined to exclude
religion from the sphere of rational activity and to extend the moral life
so as to cover much of what seemed to me to be religion, others stretched
the meaning of religion to include the whole field of moral conduct." [1] He
continues:

> I begin with *Morality,* taking as my text a classic quotation from Butler's
> *Dissertation on Virtue* "The object of the moral faculty is actions, comprehending
> under that name active or practical principles: those principles from which
> men would act if occasions or circumstances gave them power, and which,
> when fixed and habitual in any person, we call his character. It does not
> appear that brutes have the least reflex [*i.e.,* reflective] sense of actions as
> distinguished from events; or that will and design, which constitute the very

[1] de Burgh, W. G., *From Morality to Religion* (London: Macdonald and Evans, 1938),
p. 2, n. 1.

nature of action as such, are at all an object to their perception. But to ours they are: and they are the object, and the only one, of the approving and disapproving faculty. Acting, conduct, behavior, abstracted from all regard to what is, in fact or event, the consequence of it, is itself the natural object of the moral discernment; as speculative truth and falsehood is of speculative reason." [2]

Noting that "Butler assumes as the data of ethics particular acts of will" and that "morality, then, has to do with the acts of individuals," de Burgh goes on to observe that Butler's statement "implies (1) that the moral judgment is passed on the agent's inner intention, and (2) that it is a judgment of practical reason." [3] De Burgh contends that the intention includes the motive. He accounts this point important because "we shall find that the distinction between moral and religious *praxis* turns largely upon the difference of motives." In de Burgh's view, "moral action, strictly interpreted, is limited to the doing of duty for duty's sake." [4] He concludes that "the task of ethics is to transform moral insight into a reasoned system of knowledge." [5]

Though by no means all would accept the duty-for-duty's-sake formula, that formula does point to the notion, on which many lay much stress in contemporary discussions, that ethics has some kind of autonomous domain. That is the point to which we shall attend in this chapter.

Religion, by contrast, "implies worship, and worship in turn implies personal communion with an object transcendent of man and nature." [6] Moreover, though religion is not merely *theoria*, it is, unlike morality, *theoria* rather than *praxis*; but it has its source and its goal, as morality does not, in knowledge. Furthermore, religion, on the practical side, is inspired by a specific motive—namely, the love of God—"so that even moral duties, when performed in the temper of religion, undergo a subtle and significant transformation." [7]

Again, not all will agree with the manner in which de Burgh specifies the respective characteristics of morality and religion. What he says on the subject helps to call attention, however, to something about which most of us will readily agree—that however we choose to define morality and religion, the two are to be accounted very different. Yet they are also closely related. The recognition of the difference, however we choose to specify it, helps to clear the ground for the discussion of the relation to which we must now attend in some detail.

---

[2] Ibid., pp. 2 f.
[3] Ibid., p. 6.
[4] Loc. cit.
[5] Ibid., p. 19.
[6] Ibid., p. 28.
[7] Ibid., p. 33.

The Autonomy of Ethics

"There is no more controversial part of the philosophy of religion today," writes Professor Collins, "than that section concerned with the relation between religion and morality." [8] Most people recognize that ethics and religion have some connection, but what the connection is has become highly controversial. Except for extremists on both sides who either say, on the one hand, that religion is nothing but ethics illustrated by stories and reinforced by liturgical and homiletic arts, or else, on the other, that morality is simply a consequence or outgrowth of a theological position, most scholars who are familiar with the central issues both of theology and of moral philosophy acknowledge that ethics and religion, though connected in one way or another, should each be accorded some measure of autonomy. The question is, what kind of autonomy should it be? Behind that question, moreover, lies another, even more fundamental one—what is the basis for according either or both of them any autonomy at all?

Since the success of the "art for art's sake movement" in the late nineteenth century, most of us have been ready to grant to art a special kind of autonomy. Art, we say, should not be impressed into the service of a particular religious, political, social, or economic view. Flagrantly didactic art, which transgresses that general precept, is almost universally condemned. The principle here is that art never functions well as a slave. Yet neither should it be a master. The artist should be accounted, rather, an innocent child, allowed to express the impressions that come to him as his artistic genius and technical talent suggest.[9] If society does not like these impressions, society should change the situation, so that the artist will have different impressions to express. There is no use blaming the artist for expressing what you happen not to like, for he is only expressing what is there confronting him. It is his métier to do so. If his pictures look disorganized and messy, that is because society is so, and if you dislike such pictures, your remedy is to have society more tidily and neatly organized, whereupon all good artists, being faithful mirrors of the environment in which they live, will produce the tidy, neatly organized pictures you like.

The artist, *qua* artist, can never be moral or immoral, religious or irreligious. Benvenuto Cellini, imprisoned for a time in the Castel Sant' Angelo, with his masterly hand drew in charcoal a crucifix that may still be seen on the wall of the cell from which he plotted an escape. That is the kind of graffito to be expected of such an artist, as from Toulouse Lautrec one would expect something expressive of the more sensuous ambience of his

---

[8] James Collins, *The Emergence of the Philosophy of Religion* (New Haven, Conn.: Yale University Press, 1967), p. 462.

[9] Cf. Heidegger who, while recognizing the danger of the poet's work (he is "exposed to the divine lightning"), calls poetry "the most innocent of all occupations." (*Erläuterungen zu Hölderlins Dichtung* [Frankfurt a. M.: Vittorio Klostermann, 1944], p. 117.)

choice. When writers and artists are told what they must write or paint, the result is inevitably wretched. We say it "lacks soul," by which we mean that artistic autonomy has been violated. If a man is to express himself well as a writer, composer, or painter, he must be free to express without constraint of any kind exactly what he sees.

That kind of autonomy is fairly easy to understand, and most of us find it not difficult to appreciate. Does ethics then present us with a parallel case? No, because moralists always claim to be doing more than merely mirroring what society presents to them. They claim that the ethical system they propose, the code they would enforce, or the situational principle they would commend, have a reference point, not in what is, but in what should be, done. No one takes seriously as an ethical injunction the wearing of the fashionable width of tie. Wearing it would seem to be simply an announcement that the speaker likes conformity to the sartorial fashion of the hour. Some, indeed, would account all ethical statements similarly descriptions of taste ("Thou shalt not steal" means only "I do not like thieves"); but most people attach to ethical statements a value-judgment that goes far beyond personal inclination or taste. When moralists claim an autonomy for ethics, they generally claim, therefore, much more than the aesthetician claims for the field of art.

Rashdall observed long ago: "If the moral judgment is essentially a judgment of value, its sphere must be absolutely all-embracing. . . . People in whom aesthetic interests are stronger than ethical interests frequently attempt to set up a sphere of Art to which Morality is supposed to have no relation whatever. Such persons simply show that they have too narrow a view of what Morality is." [10] Moral value-statements, except where they are taken to be identical with descriptions of taste, seem to be claiming authority over all other value-statements. Otherwise, one might well say: "I am aware of the value-principle contained in the statement 'Thou shalt not steal'; but I find that among my value-judgments is another, conflicting one, namely, 'Emeralds are so beautiful that I value them above all else.' In the case of emeralds, therefore, I make an exception, preferring that value-judgment over the one about not stealing; hence my courageous decision to steal the princess's emerald necklace."

The absurdity in such an assessment of one's hierarchy of values springs from the obvious implication that what is given out as a moral value turns out to be less than what it purported to be. We think so precisely because we think no moral value could ever be supplanted by a nonmoral one. The view, therefore, that ethics, however conceived, is not to be conceived as wholly independent of religion, not as a mere offshoot or application of metaphysical or religious doctrines, is, to say the least, a view that calls for serious consideration.

[10] Hastings Rashdall, *The Theory of Good and Evil* (Oxford: Oxford University Press, 1907), 1: 177–183.

To say that the highway code has nothing specifically to do with religion seems beyond dispute. If I live in Massachusetts I agree tacitly or otherwise to conform to its code. By undertaking to drive a car in Illinois I also assume, even if I do not live there, the responsibility not only of driving on the right but of conforming to all the other rules of the road applicable to the "Land of Lincoln." I could not offer a conscientious objection that, for instance, as a Buddhist I feel religiously forbidden to exceed twenty miles an hour even on the freeway or as an Anglican of British extraction I am religiously bound to drive on the left.

In some matters, however, a religious excuse would be upheld: most people would look with at least some sympathy on the claim of an Orthodox Jew that his religion forbids him to work on the Sabbath and on that of a Quaker that his has always forbidden participation in any form of combatant military service. Generally speaking, however, in consenting to live in a community I consent to accept the moral obligations that that particular community demands of me. In a free society such as the United States, in which, through the exercise of my vote, I have the opportunity to help to put into effect the legislation I want, I may be said to impose laws on myself. I belong to a society that disapproves of murder to such a degree that it imposes this or that punishment on those who commit the crime, and if I commit it I expect, of course, to suffer the same punishment and have no reasonable grounds for complaint if it is inflicted on me.

Laws might be imposed upon me, however, extraneously; that is, I might be coerced into obeying them or into performing certain actions because of a dictator's threats, or because I was too timid to flout ancient custom or tradition, or because priests told me that God had so ordered and that hell awaited those who disobeyed his precepts. Kant called such laws "heteronomous." He includes among them laws that express merely our own desires to which we happen to be enslaved, for he assumes that our rational selves are our real selves. An imperative is genuinely moral, according to Kant, when it is autonomous—that is, when I, as a rational being, impose it on myself.

Fundamentally, that is the kind of autonomy that moral philosophers, whether they happen to be Kantian or not, generally want to claim for ethics. Moralists differ widely, of course, in their view of moral ends. For instance, a utilitarian of the Benthamite type would regard a right act as one that aimed at the maximum of pleasure and the minimum of pain for all those to whose lives the act made any difference. Such a definition would clearly accord a large autonomy to ethics. Mill's utilitarianism, which repudiates the quantitative form of the hedonistic calculus that is commonly associated with Bentham, and seeks to take note of qualitative differences, is in exactly the same case with respect to a claim for the autonomy of ethics. Mill claimed that in the "golden rule" is to be found "the complete spirit of the ethics of utility. To do as one would be done by, and to love one's neighbor as one's self, constitute the ideal perfection of utilitarian morality." [11]

Whether that is an adequate interpretation of the Christian ethic is beside the point. What we have to notice here is that Mill is commending Jesus for specifying the moral law correctly. In such a view, irrespective of what is held to be the "right" ethic, religion is always under its judgment. A religion is good to the extent that it conforms to this or that understanding of the moral law, however this moral law be defined. It is bad to the extent that it departs from it. So one might argue with reservations in favor of Christianity: it well expresses the "right" kind of behavior at such and such a point, though in such and such another point it is weaker than Buddhism or Islam.

All religions come under moral judgment according to a moral principle that is enunciated or assumed, just as all nations and indeed all schools and all golf clubs stand under such a judgment. Orthodox Christians would generally account blasphemous judgments such as "I think Jesus was right about the merciful but a little lacking in moral sensitivity on the subject of the meek." Yet Jesus himself gave his disciples an ethical criterion to enable them to distinguish good from bad prophets: "Ye shall know them by their [moral] fruits." In the first part of this book, we made such an ethical judgment in assuming that Hitlerism was a "bad" religion compared with, say, Methodism or Zen. To make such a moral judgment on religions *is* to sign a declaration of the independence of ethics. It also, however, seems to make religions dependent on ethics.

Is Religion Reducible to Ethics?

A widespread opinion flourished in the eighteenth century, under the influence of the *Aufklärung* (or Enlightenment)—namely, that though religion as traditionally understood was outmoded and would eventually pass into the history of bygone ages, it did contain one element of value. That moral element it contained was, indeed, the essence of religion. The rest, being excrescence, was eminently expendable. If only popular religions could be shorn of the superstitious accretions that encumbered them, they would be found to contain a moral core that was worth preserving.

That view continued to be widely represented in German, American, and English thought during the nineteenth century, alongside Hegel's view of religion as a sort of metaphysic for the kindergarten. Matthew Arnold's once well-known definition of religion ("morality tinged with emotion"), which was mentioned in an early chapter, well expresses a widespread outlook among educated people in Victorian times.[12] A later writer criticized Arnold's

[11] J. S. Mill, "Utilitarianism," in *Utilitarianism, Liberty, and Representative Government* (New York: E. P. Dutton and Co., Everyman's Library, 1910), p. 10.

[12] Matthew Arnold, son of the great English educational reformer, Thomas Arnold of Rugby, was writing partly under the influence of Comte, whose disciple, Littré, he sometimes quoted.

definition as tautological on the ground that by "emotion" could not be meant *any* emotion but only "religious" emotion, thus destroying the definitive quality of the statement.[13] That criticism does not by any means necessarily hold good, however, since one might well hold—as has been widely held under the influence of Freud and others in the psychoanalytical schools—that the emotions religion harbors are very common ones connected with universal human libidinal urges such as the sex drive and the will to power.

If, as we have just seen, a case can be made for the autonomy of ethics, the way is cleared for taking seriously the view that all religion is reducible to ethics. If morality can stand alone, unsupported by any religious sanction or metaphysical or theological doctrine, it seems possible that religion might be nothing but ethics clothed in fables, burdened with hoary superstitions, choked by the dead wood of tradition, and saturated with sultry passion. Then, of course, the purest religion would be the one that was most successful in throwing off its nonethical accretions. One might also expect that the purest religions would be those which had the least amount of nonethical content. Confucianism, for instance, would seem a promising candidate for distinction in religious purity, while Mormons, despite their deservedly high reputation for just dealing and ethical responsibility, would fare badly. Christianity, not least in forms such as Eastern Orthodoxy and the Salvation Army, would no doubt come out very low on the scale. Unitarians and Hicksite Quakers, however, would rate well, perhaps as close runners-up to the Confucians.

There is no doubt that in the minds of many people, the Church has been conceived as an outmoded institution. Nevertheless, many people think its function in promoting "respectable" behavior so far outweighs its doctrinal absurdities that for practical, social reasons, it should be upheld and venerated by the established order—these absurdities notwithstanding. From Professor Braithwaite, from whose penetrating insights into the nature of scientific explanation we quoted in the previous chapter, we have another work which contains such a reductionist view of religion and of its relation to ethics.[14] Braithwaite's position on this relation is far from satisfactory. It differs hardly, if at all, from that popular view that was so much in vogue when Matthew Arnold was offering his definition of religion to his mid-Victorian contemporaries. Braithwaite, in keeping with the more moderate mood that had begun by the middle of the present century to supplant the extravagant claims of the earlier logical empiricists, argued that religious assertions are not as meaningless as these earlier logical empiricists had pretended. True, they are neither tautologies like $2 + 2 = 4$ nor empirically verifiable propositions such as "There are elephants in Tokyo." Religious assertions, though unverifiable, have a use; they have meaning of a kind.

[13] C. C. J. Webb, *Problems in the Relations of God and Man* (London: Nisbet and Co., 1911), pp. 4 f.

[14] See R. B. Braithwaite, *An Empiricist's View of the Nature of Religious Belief,* Eddington Memorial Lecture (Cambridge: At the University Press, 1955). In fairness to Braithwaite one should note, however, that this brief work does not exhaust his position.

Moral assertions, no less unverifiable by the criteria that had been allowed by the early logical empiricists, have a kind of meaning. They express "conative intentions"; that is, they announce the way one proposes to act. So "all restraint of those sickly unfortunates commonly called criminals is discriminatory against them as a class of psychologically disturbed patients, and it is therefore morally wrong" and "violent criminals ought to be flogged at weekly intervals with a rhinoceros whip during the first year of their penal servitude" both state clearly the speakers' respective intentions. The first proposes to vote and otherwise do what he can to see that society does nothing in particular to protect itself from the violent attacks that criminals make upon its more vulnerable members. The second proposes to do whatever he can to toughen the sanctions against criminal violence.

Braithwaite thinks that religious statements are used primarily as moral assertions and therefore function in the same way; that is, they announce a proposed way of behavior or policy of action. Adulterated as they are by the various fables and other paraphernalia that attend them, their character as moral utterances may be obscured; nevertheless, their fundamental nature is ethical. As ethical assertions they may be hidden beneath a smoke screen of incense or smothered under layer upon layer of ancient fables; but in the end the only questions a philosopher can properly ask of religious men are of a nature such as "What kind of conduct is the ritual calculated to discourage?" and "What action is the myth intended to promote?" In this view, religious people for one reason or another associate the moral intent with various myths, liturgies, and ritual acts, but they need by no means assign any meaning to the ritual and myth other than that which is reducible to the ethical assertions they presumptively contain.

Braithwaite takes the religious assertion "God is love" as a prime example of Christian affirmation. He says it expresses the Christian's intention to follow what he calls an agapeistic[15] way of life. Any religious trappings—be they novenas to St. Joseph, parables, or hymns—that may be used as psychological inducements or stimulants to the recommended behavior pattern may surround the ethical assertion, the meaning of which however, always remains that of conative intent; for what matters about such statements is the use to which they are put, and the use of religious assertions, Braithwaite thinks, is always fundamentally the same as that of ethical ones. Braithwaite has no particular difficulty in determining how to assign meaning to "an agapeistic way of life," though that is a question that biblical scholars and theologians have found puzzling, not to say daunting. The reason is that for him the meaning is to be determined solely by the use to which the individual user puts the assertion. Braithwaite says that, if asked for a description of an agapeistic way of life, he personally would "quote most

[15] From *agapē*, the Greek word used in the New Testament in such contexts and translated "love." It is more commonly written "agapistic."

of the Thirteenth Chapter of I Corinthians," but that others might describe it "somewhat differently" and would likewise differently interpret the meaning of various other Christian assertions.[16]

Is Ethics Reducible to Religion?

Before considering the merits and defects of what Braithwaite and others have said about the reducibility of religion to ethics, let us look at the opposite thesis—that all ethical injunctions have their source in a religious truth to which they refer and without the sustenance of which they are worthless.

"Ethical injunctions," as used here, need not exclude purely prudential ethics. The obligation I feel to refrain from driving on the left in New York seems no less absolute than is my obligation to refrain from stealing. True, it depends on a mere convention that exists in most countries of the world and could never be said to be of universal application even if no country happened at a particular time to use a different rule. Even the prohibition on stealing, however, can apply only where some form of the possession of private ownership exists; if property ownership could ever be purely communal, stealing would be presumably impossible and therefore not a subject for ethical injunctions.

The view that morality is reducible to religion entails, if it does not spring from, a profound ethical skepticism. To hold it is to deny that ethical injunctions have that absoluteness attributed to them by those who insist upon the autonomy of ethics we considered in the opening section of the present chapter. Ethical commands and the legalistic ordinances that are used to express and enforce them can have no authority in themselves. Any authority they may have must derive either from the will of the people who make the commands and legislate accordingly or else from God who makes known his will in one way or another—for instance, in the Bible, in the *Qur'ān*, or through the *ex cathedra* utterances of the Pope. In both sets of moral imperatives, that which is ordered can be no better and can therefore have no greater authority than he who orders it. The rules of my college carry whatever moral weight my college carries; my country's laws carry the moral authority inherent in the country itself, whatever that may be. I inwardly recognize the ethical ordinances my father imposes on me only to the extent that I respect him and therefore acknowledge his authority.

The absolute authority I see in ethical injunctions or commandments that express what I take to be God's will resides, not in the ordinances themselves, but in God who so ordains them. So an observant Jew might say to his employer: "I fully acknowledge the rightness of your authority, which requires

[16] *Nature of Religious Belief*, p. 63.

me to work when the business needs me, but One whose moral authority I account greater than yours forbids me to do it today, the Sabbath. In my refusal to obey you there is no insubordination. I in no way lack respect for you. Nevertheless, I account his jurisdiction absolute and yours relative, and I treat accordingly the conflicting orders that issue from you and from him." By the same token one would treat hunting and fishing laws neither more nor less respectfully than one would esteem the proprietor or corporation on whose authority they were issued. That is why property owners tend on the whole to obey such laws, for they tend to respect the kind of people who enact them, while vagrants and other people on the fringes of society, do not, and so are disinclined to obey the laws such proprietors or corporations make.

To those who take the view that ethics is reducible to religion, ethical rules, however rational they may be and however generally accepted by intelligent people, must always seem subordinate to the direct command of the One from whom all rules derive whatever authority they can possess. A governing body may draw up articles of association, a set of rules to be followed; but such a body, having authority to make the rules, has also the authority to make exceptions and to impose additional special obligations in particular cases. So God can presumably overrule any ethical precept. Rules are never made for their own sake; they are always made to serve a purpose. The rational, like the Sabbath, is made to serve man; man is not made to serve the rational.

In *Fear and Trembling* Kierkegaard attacked not only Hegelian but all forms of rationalism, such as Kant's and Aristotle's ethics. Among generally accepted ethical precepts, none seems to commend itself to human reason more than does the one that forbids murder. Yet there is a story in Genesis that Abraham, having been granted a son to his wife when she had been accounted past the age of childbearing, was asked by God to offer up that beloved son, Isaac, as a human sacrifice. Abraham is depicted as having been ready, despite both the personal agony of grief he must have felt and the apparent irrationality of what was being asked of him, to draw his knife in obedience to God's order.

Kant knew that story and had written disapprovingly of Abraham's conduct, accounting it contrary to reason. Kierkegaard not only defended Abraham; he detected in Abraham's choice a course of action that transcended all ethics as generally understood. Abraham, as a "knight of faith," was willing to renounce not only his personal longing to save the life of his beloved son but even also the highest ethical principles he knew, in order to obey what he took to be a direct command from God. For Kierkegaard, Abraham acted as such an exemplar of faith would always act: he obeyed God. Had he been unconfronted by a divine command, he would have obeyed the law, the highest expression of a rational ethic, but faced with a choice between ethical rules and the direct command of

God, he unhesitatingly chose the latter over the former. Kierkegaard leaves us in no doubt why Abraham's choice was right. It was right because it was a decision to choose faith over reason—that is, to put religion above ethics—and in making such a decision the "knight of faith" would no sooner do otherwise than a devoted son would read his mother's letters if he could meet her and listen to her words.

The claim that the highest system of ethics that could ever be devised, even the highest ethical principle that could be formulated, must always be secondary in the eyes of the religious man is understandable. For if a man's religion puts him in any way in touch with God, it must at least occasionally confront him with the necessity of making decisions that are beyond the ethical system and may seem contrary to what the system prescribes. Whence indeed, one might ask, are the highest ethical rules to issue if not from God? Then they are always subject to him, being the mere grammar of his will.

As religion is to be accounted, in this view, the spring of all authentic ethics, so it is the source, too, of all genuine culture, all worthwhile education, all accurate knowledge. For in so far as religious people claim to worship God, the source of all good, they claim to encounter that source, so as to be in some way participating in that on which all human goods depend for their very being. To choose an ethical precept over a religious one would be to imply that God, like all else, stands under an ethical judgment. But if God stands under anything, he is not lord of all, as all monotheistic religions insist. To know his will in any sense and to any extent, however limited, is to be, in that sense and to that extent, above even the ethical rules he prescribes.

Such a position is plainly susceptible to the danger of antinomianism. To account myself above all morality and law would be to set myself up as God. To treat law and morality as of no spiritual importance, being only for those who choose to be so enslaved to them, is not only to ensure social anarchy; it is to court disaster for our own inner life, making us forget our creatureliness and also making us pose as the very confidants of God. That is notoriously, indeed, the danger to which the ethical man sees the religious man to be exposed. Many who start out as Abrahams, obedient soldiers of the Lord, seem to end by fancying themselves, as did Lucifer, equal partners with God, or at the least his closest aides. Among people of all religions, the specter of antinomianism looms large. How many crimes have been committed under cover of "God's will"!

Of course, the religious man will be quick to point out that the dangers of a position are no argument against it, and that genuine acts of faith, far from requiring less moral effort than obedience to ethical precepts or a code of laws, demand far more. Such genuine faith is no more to be confused with blind religious obedience than authentic scientific inquiry, with the bold hypotheses it always requires, is to be confused with reading popular science magazines. The "knight of faith," like the early explorers and pioneers, has to set forth without charts or maps to guide him. Like the pioneer, he must make his own maps as he goes along. He will make mistakes. He may even mistake the Devil for God, but making mistakes is a mark of the exercise of creative human intelligence and will.

Computers, when in good order, do not make mistakes. People do, except when they are behaving like computers. The pioneer—scientist, artist, or saint—is certain to make mistakes and to pay the price of making them. The moral effort attending the creative process in which the "knight of faith" is engaged is not only greater than that of the map reader, however disciplined and diligent; it is of a different order and superior quality. The risk the religious man takes in making the leap into the unknown, seeking the hand of God to guide him, demands moral qualities with which the demands of ethical principles or precepts as presented in Kant or Moore or the Babylonian code of Hammurabi are not even to be compared.

The view that our duty is *defined* by the will of God is an ancient one having eminent modern exponents. "The Good," writes Emil Brunner, a distinguished theologian of our own century, "has its basis and its existence solely in the will of God." [17] Within a Calvinist framework, for example, such a statement may seem satisfactory, but apart from such a special theological context it appears to be tautological, since it provides no basis for distinguishing the Good from the will of God, so that the predicate turns out to be also the subject. Moreover, in the absence of a special theological doctrine, one naturally asks how one is to ascertain the will of God.

Even if one passes over that objection, one confronts another—on what basis am I to decide whether to prefer the God of Muhammad or that of John Wesley, the God of St. Ambrose or that of Zoroaster? Certainly it could not be on an ethical basis, for I cannot have any ethical basis apart from the will of God, which is not always clearly ascertainable. Critics of Islam have claimed, justly or unjustly, that Muslims, on the ground that whatever Allah ordains is right, deny that any ethical objection can ever be raised against anything Muhammad ever did, however contrary it may be to generally accepted ethical principles. Similar charges might be made against Judaism and Christianity, of course, but because of the theology of Islam, in which Allah is so often presented as pure will, the objection from the side of ethics against religion seems, at any rate to those outside Islam, to be particularly forceful.

The exponent of the view that ethics is reducible to religion is interpreting all sense of absolute duty and obligation, all inalienable sense of guilt and of right and wrong, as a sense of being commanded, of being placed under obligation, of being judged, by the only Being who has the right to make absolute demands on anyone. So ethical systems emerging out of special,

[17] E. Brunner, *The Divine Imperative* (New York: Macmillan Co., 1937), p. 53.

purely man-made human situations such as traffic in a harbor or a city are to be seen as precisely that, having the only authority they could derive from being what they are; and for me to treat such laws or precepts as absolute is the way to political totalitarianism and, from a religious stand-point, idolatry.

Russell's Religionless Morality

Despite the historically close connection between religion and ethics and the belief of many that they are inseparable, the view that morality may be achieved without religion deserves special consideration. It certainly looks like a plausible viewpoint. On the one hand are to be found many people who have lived exemplary lives that one might long to have lived, yet who seem to have ignored and even to have been hostile to religion. On the other hand, everyone knows that terrible evils have been perpetrated under religious banners, sometimes even with the applause of the devout. Surely, then, one might well say, a moral life without religion seems not only possible but at least sometimes desirable. Might not religion be even, at least occasionally, an impediment to living such a life?

We must be particularly clear about what precisely is being contrasted here. If, for instance, religion is taken to be the observance of certain ritual acts and conformity to certain institutional requirements, few would question the force behind the suggestion. Morality would fare no better if so formalistically interpreted. If, however, morality is taken to be the whole art of living to the best advantage a life directed toward the fulfillment of the best end one knows, and religion be looked upon as an inner trust that such is the nature of things that in the last reckoning, whatever it be, nothing morally valuable that has been won shall ever be wasted, the need for serious conflict diminishes and may even largely disappear. The call for religionless ethics loses its point.

Let us see, however, what an eminent philosopher noted for his declarations of hostility to religion and much given to moralizing has to say on the question before us. Lord Russell, while still a young man, was already reproaching traditional religion for propagating the notion that in some hidden manner the world of fact is harmonious with the world of ideals. On the contrary, he insisted, we must accept the world as it is and try to love it, however rotten it may turn out to be.[18] So we may pursue our moral values without pretending there is any link between them and the real.

That is not entirely inconsistent, of course, with what, as we have seen, Bonhoeffer was to say and Maurice Maeterlinck had already said, in the previous century, about living "as if there were no God." These writers, however, were pointing, each in his own way, to the nature of religious

18 Bertrand Russell, "The Essence of Religion," *Hibbert Journal* 11 (October 1912): 60.

faith. They were saying, in effect, that faith is not the idiotlike attitude of supine resignation that some think it is, but an attitude requiring to a superlative degree the moral quality of courage. For since God has withdrawn himself from the believer, the believer now feels all alone and must go forth as if without God. He is like the child who, going to school for the first time, suddenly sees he is all alone and must now live as if he had no mother.

Of course, Russell is saying nothing like that at all. He is saying that, however foul Nature may be, she is all there is, and so we humans are a part of her and we had better recognize that as a given fact. Nevertheless, we men and women have human qualities, and Russell thinks we should cherish the values that spring from them and pursue the values to which our nature tends or (dare we say?) ought to tend.

Russell's views, though he modified them in certain particulars over the decades, underwent little substantial change. He always presents religion as unfavorably as possible in contrast to "science." Typical is his satirical account of the canonization of St. Francis Xavier, in the course of which "the Pope officially guaranteed the gift of tongues, and was specially impressed by the fact that Xavier made lamps burn with holy water instead of oil. This was the same Pope who found what Galileo said incredible." [19] Russell seems never to miss an opportunity to denigrate the moral outcome of the rules of institutional religion, carefully noting for ridicule, for instance, that "in the Greek Orthodox Church, two godparents of the same child may not marry." [20]

Why should so great a thinker resort so habitually to polemical devices for showing religion in as unfavorable a light as possible, as at best a superstition of primitive, ignorant, or neurotic people, and at worst a device of crafty rulers and power-hungry and sadistic priests? Nobody who knows anything of the variegated aspects of religion could fail to see ludicrous unfairness in his reporting. What is the quality in religion that makes it so odious in his eyes as to warrant the expenditure of his energy pillorying it with such venomous satire? Russell believed religion to be somehow essentially inhuman, even an enemy of the human race. Far from promoting or assisting moral ends, it is a positive hindrance to their attainment.

Russell's mistrust of religious people is based upon such convictions. But what, more precisely, are the moral values that he most prizes and against which he sees religion to be at enmity? That he was certainly no supporter of conventional morality, either in sexual or in any other matters, is well known. He held up human kindliness as the key virtue, and cruelty, therefore, as the worst vice. For instance, in "What I Believe" he says, "Moral rules ought not to be such as to make instinctive happiness impossible. Yet that

[19] Bertrand Russell, *Religion and Science* (New York: Oxford University Press, Galaxy Books, 1961), p. 85.

[20] "Can Religion Cure Our Troubles?" in *The Basic Writings of Bertrand Russell,* ed. R. E. Egner and L. E. Denonn (New York: Simon and Schuster, Clarion Books, 1967), pp. 598 f.

is an effect of strict monogamy in a community where the numbers of the two sexes are very unequal." [21] In the same work he calls our attention to "the points where superstitious morals inflict preventable suffering," [22] a theme that occurs over and over again in his writings. Religion, he thinks, is strikingly fecund in the production of human suffering.

Nor is he referring only to the superstitious religion of very primitive peoples. On the contrary, he sometimes forgives the cruelties of primitive people and withholds his absolution of us for what he takes to be our own far worse ones. For instance, after noting that the Aztecs "considered it their painful duty to eat human flesh for fear the light of the sun should grow dim," he goes on to say that the fate of the Aztecs' victims, who were quickly killed and eaten, "is a far less degree of suffering than is inflicted upon a child born in miserable surroundings and tainted with venereal disease. Yet it is the greater suffering which is deliberately inflicted by bishops and politicians in the name of morality. If they had even the smallest spark of love or pity for children they could not adhere to a moral code involving this fiendish cruelty." [23]

Russell does not spare Jesus, who comes under condemnation as the author of a vast amount of suffering. For since hell is to be accounted "a doctrine that put cruelty into the world and gave the world generations of cruel torture," and since Jesus, as depicted in the Gospels, taught that doctrine, he "would certainly have to be considered partly responsible for that" lamentable affront to humanity.[24] Russell says he has been told he should not attack religion "because religion makes men virtuous. So I am told; I have not noticed it." He goes on to recount the cruelties perpetrated in the Middle Ages—the burning of witches, the Inquisition, and "every kind of cruelty." [25]

Hardly less remarkable than Russell's attack on religion is the nature of his defense of morality. One might expect him, as a naturalist, to see no reason to defend it at all. There is no morality in the tooth-and-claw behavior of animals, and there is certainly none in natural phenomena generally. Why should there be any in humanity? Moreover, if there be any in humanity, what meaning can be attached to it? And indeed we find that Russell can be sometimes almost as unfriendly to ethical systems as he is to religion. Ethical questions are questions of value and "questions of value . . . cannot be intellectually decided at all, and lie outside the realm of truth and falsehood." [26]

Yet he seems to have neither scruples nor misgivings about defending his particular hedonistic calculus. "It is, in fact, not by ethical theory, but by the cultivation of large and generous desires through intelligence, happi-

[21] Ibid., "What I Believe," p. 380.
[22] Ibid., p. 377.
[23] Ibid., p. 378.
[24] Ibid., "Why I Am Not a Christian," p. 594.
[25] Ibid., p. 595.
[26] *Religion and Science,* p. 243.

ness and freedom from fear, that men can be brought to act more than they do at present in a manner that is consistent with the general happiness of mankind." [27] He makes reference to "the general happiness of mankind" as though such a phrase contained no ambiguities and raised no philosophical problems, though, of course, as one of the most acute minds of the century he could not but see very well how serious such problems are.

Throughout all that Russell wrote on morality and religion runs the general notion that such matters are really matters of taste. His own feeling is that most morality is hardly less vicious than all religion, and what makes both vicious is that at best they lead to unkindness and at worst they perpetrate cruelty. In the perpetration of cruelty, religion is the more efficacious. Cruelty is always the keystone of his negative value-judgments. It is the paradigm of malevolence. More telling still, its opposite turns out to be the sort of love that would be exhibited by a man exclusively engaged in the diminution of cruelty.

Other virtues, of course, may be recognized as ancillary to that one; courage, for instance, is a virtue when it assists the general purpose of the benevolent man, but it is a virtue only as industry would be a virtue to one who accounted thrift the *summum bonum*. Russell's own passionate involvement in social and political causes is well known. He was, for instance, a spirited protagonist of pacifism, and his extreme concern about the dangers of the use of nuclear power, with the attendant possibility of the extermination of the human race through its use in a future war, became an obsession in the last years of his very long life.

No one could say, therefore, that here was a man without ethical concerns. The question would be, rather, on what rational grounds could his naturalistic philosophy lead him to have such concerns? The answer to that question is inescapable: there were no rational grounds except that, since it happens that we are human beings, we have a vested interest in our survival that is even more urgent than our vested interest in "human happiness." It is also no doubt more definable. Since that is so, the conduct of those politicians who risk, if they do not encourage, the possibility of nuclear warfare is both irrational (in the sense in which suicide and gross prodigality are irrational) and wicked. It is in our interest to use our intelligence to see what is going on in high places and to do all that is in our power to stop it. With such a program we may very well agree, but it is surely important to notice that it has little if anything to do with morality in any sense that Socrates or Kant would have recognized as morality, but only with our self-interest as human beings. Russell, like many far inferior minds, often fails to distinguish human rights from human obligations.

That without religion we can have a morality of the kind Russell applauds can hardly even be questioned at all. As soon, however, as we raise any of the very controversial ethical questions that have troubled the minds

[27] Ibid., p. 242.

of moralists throughout the centuries and then look for an ethic standing totally apart from every kind of religious interest, we shall have difficulty finding one.

Russell's moral conceptions, more particularly his understanding of love, seem curiously immature. He speaks vehemently against cruelty, but cruelty is a *symptom* of vice rather than the root of viciousness. He eloquently lauds human tenderness and compassion, but these are only the habiliments of love, not its essence or nature. In all things he was conspicuously a Victorian. The morality and religion he inveighs against are the particular distortions of that period in human history out of which he sprang and which left so indelible a mark upon him.

I would venture the suggestion that Russell is right in supposing, as he seems to do, that only his own kind of morality is really detachable from religion. It echoes the morality of a precocious, sensitive, and brilliant child in love with love, rather than that of a morally mature man or woman who has learned from life the costliness of love. Clothed in a gigantic intellect, as in Russell's case, it may disguise its impotence for a time from those who are dazzled by the splendor of so great a mind. But intellectual acumen alone does nothing in itself to empower a man to experience the sacrificial love apart from which religion is warped and morality emasculated.

Situationism, Contextualism, and the "New Morality"

Before going on to consider the inseparability and distinctness of ethics and religion, we may conveniently look at a movement that has much influenced ethical thought in recent decades. As everyone knows, a revolution in attitudes toward morality has been taking place, with consequences more far reaching than the much-discussed "generation gap." The "new morality" has numbered among its champions not only the naturalists and political revolutionaries who would see Russell as a prophet of the kind of morality they would advocate, but learned Christian divines. Many religious people, nevertheless, have pointed to the "new morality" as providing a dramatic example of what happens to *all* ethical notions when they are used apart from metaphysical or theological tenets to support them. Some, irrespective of the view they take of the "new morality," are inclined to think of even its Christian exponents as making an ethical about-face. In fact, not only has it antecedents and close parallels in the history of ethical ideas, but its proponents are not generally advocating moral anarchy or indiscriminate license.

Nevertheless, in the realm of sexual conduct, proponents of the "new morality" look with incomprehension at the concept of chastity. They view with repugnance the notion of sexual restraint that has been so much idealized and celebrated, not least in Christian literature, and look with disfavor on the ideal behind injunctions to engage in complete sexual abstinence outside marriage. In contrast to traditionalist ethics, proponents of the "new morality" generally tend to account any prolonged continence a nonvalue. The moral revolution is fundamentally, however, the expression of a radical discontent with "established" conceptions of ethics. New knowledge that has come in the wake of scientific and technological progress has brought to light new moral problems with which commonly accepted understandings of morality do not seem fitted to cope.

Christian morals have at various times hardened into legalism, as have the ethical ideals and injunctions of all religions, and a corrective reaction sets in that may suggest parallels with the denunciations Jesus leveled at the legalism that had developed within the religion into which he was born. Such legalism is always a distortion of any religion. Judaism has always had another, very different side, far too little recognized by most Christians, and Christianity has sometimes been rendered odious by the absurdities of ecclesiastical laws and other conventions issued under its banner. Bernard Häring is among those who have sought to combat the legalism in his own Roman Catholic tradition.[28]

The existentialist movement, with its strong emphasis on freedom and the individual, has fostered the notion of decision-making without regard to any universal moral principle or ethical code. In war and in other times of special stress, such isolation in decision-making seems necessary. Few people, if any, however—even if they act without reference to the dictates of their ancestral faith or the ethical expectations of established society—really do act with a total disregard for the moral expectations of their families and friends. The question is, is solitariness in decision-making the stuff out of which the best decisions are made, or is it a departure from a more morally desirable norm?

"Situationism" is a term used to designate ethical theories that may be said to provide a philosophical basis for the moral revolution that has actually occurred. It has been expounded in various forms by modern writers as diverse as Joseph Fletcher and John Robinson. Neither Fletcher nor Robinson, who both happen to be Anglicans, a priest and bishop respectively, would admit to the charge of antinomianism, though both often give the impression, to say the least, that what they are proposing would inevitably issue in such an aberration. Both talk much about love but sometimes without seeming to appreciate either what Dante called its "terrible aspect" or the rarity of the quality of love needed to make situationism work in any society, even in one that might claim to be sensitive to Christian values.

Fletcher argues[29] plausibly enough that what he is saying is what Christians have always recognized—that there are guidelines like the Ten Commandments, but they are *only* guidelines. Behind them, as Jesus taught, is a moral

---

[28] See B. Häring, *The Law of Christ*, trans. G. Kaiser, 3 vols. (Westminster, Md.: Newman Press, 1963–1966).
[29] J. Fletcher, *Situation Ethics: The New Morality* (Philadelphia: Westminster Press, 1966), p. 17.

principle expressible in the simpler commandment to love God and your neighbor. So far so good; but Fletcher's academic treatment of his situationism and his curiously impersonal concept of *agapē* sometimes combine to suggest little understanding of the anguish in human situations and less of the agony in genuine human love.

Robinson is ready to depend on love as having a built-in mechanism, so to speak, that provides it with both the information and the will it needs to accomplish a moral end without reference to moral guidelines or legalistic rules. That is not to say he repudiates the notion that certain kinds of behavior—such as lying and adultery, which are plainly disruptive of any society—are not to be deplored *in general*. Nevertheless, they are, as all ethical rules must be, only broad indications of behavior patterns that generally point to a moral defect.

A medical analogy might illustrate the point. Patients go to the doctor on account of diarrhea. They want it cured, for, as everyone knows, diarrhea is "bad." The doctor, however, while he, too, knows that diarrhea is "bad," sees it as a symptom rather than as an evil in itself. Indeed, without the diarrhea the patient might well have died. Any doctor can easily cure diarrhea, but every conscientious doctor wants to ascertain the cause of the diarrhea and to cure that. There is a whole set of common conditions such as diarrhea that doctors meet every day. Some patients may think of them as diseases to be cured, but no competent physician will. He may sometimes even actually encourage the condition of which the patient complains so as to find means of improving the patient's health at a deeper level. Similarly, there are many moral situations in which it is easy to prescribe standard cures, as an old-fashioned doctor might prescribe rhubarb pills for constipation, but constipation, though generally unhealthy, is not in itself a disease, only a symptom.

Situationism is in some important respects a Protestant phenomenon, a reaction against a rigid and unimaginative ethical code, such as the American frontier ethic. The Catholic tradition—whether in its Roman, Greek, or Anglican form—has for long been accustomed, especially through the use of the confessional, to a more subtle treatment of moral questions. A good confessor, while using traditional commandments as yardsticks, tries to provide special medicines for individual cases.

Contextualism, as presented by Paul Lehmann,[30] is a form of situationism. It differs from the latter chiefly in providing a wider interpretation of what a moral situation is. The contextualist conceives of the situation as somehow encompassing the whole moral situation in the world. Situationism focuses on the immediate situation in which as an individual I find myself.

In order to see how situationism might work and how a contextualist solution might differ from a situationist one, we may usefully reconstruct, out of Sinclair Lewis's *Arrowsmith*, what is by any reckoning a difficult ethical problem. Let us put the situation as follows:

[30] Paul Lehmann, *Ethics in a Christian Context* (New York: Harper & Row, 1963).

Scientists believe they may have discovered a serum that will cure a certain disease, but they lack conclusive scientific evidence. A young doctor, deeply influenced by his teacher who has held up to him the ideal of total dedication to the pursuit of truth by scientific methods, goes to an island where people are stricken with the disease. In accordance with his teacher's training and advice, he decides to test the efficacy of the serum by giving it to Group A (one-half of the victims) and withholding it from the rest, Group B. If the serum turns out to be ineffective, all the victims in both groups will die in agony, as they would have died in any case, but the inefficacy of the serum will have been scientifically proved. If, on the other hand, the serum proves effective—as is expected—only Group B, from whom it has been withheld, will suffer the horrible death, as, of course, would have happened to them in any case. The efficacy of the serum will have been proved sufficiently to satisfy any audience in any scientific academy in the world, and to mankind in general will accrue the incalculable benefit of seeing the disease disappear.

When the people in Group B see that the young doctor has a new, untried cure, they implore him to use it on them also. Their anguish is terrible, for they know that without treatment they will die a horrible death, while in the serum there is at least a ray of hope for them; the serum could not worsen their plight and it might be their salvation. They beg the doctor not to discriminate against them in favor of Group A, as he is arbitrarily doing. The young doctor's human compassion gets the better of his devotion to scientific truth. He succumbs to the pleas, gives the serum to all, and breaks the heart of his old teacher.

A Kantian might argue that since the teacher is proposing to use half of the victims as means, not ends, his proposal is unethical. No one should have been denied the serum unless he so requested. A situationist, asked what he would have done in the young doctor's place, might possibly say that he would have given everyone the serum even if some had offered to forego it. Again, he might have accounted loyalty to the teacher's ideals and injunctions far above a few human lives. In any case, he would point out that no one could ever say what ought to be done in a situation not his own. What a person ought to do always depends on the situation as presented to him at the particular time and in the actual circumstances of its occurrence. An individual cannot even say what he himself might do in other circumstances or at other times. Of course, the person carries with him into the situation various moral guidelines, but like any other guidelines they may be discarded when a better way seems attainable without them. How one determines that a way is good or better is necessarily obscure, because we do not know moral objectives independently of situations. We know only situations that look similar and from whose similarity we construct guidelines.

The contextualist, though he might also be inclined to approve the young doctor's course of action, would call attention to the wider implications of the world scene. The situation of the young doctor, like every situation, has a wider, global context. The basic objection to the contextualist's position is that the individual is put into the position of having to claim to know what the global situation really is, and making such a claim comes close to "playing God."

Situationism and contextualism turn out, indeed, to be two different understandings of situationism, and the very difference between them exposes the problem at the root of situational ethics—namely, what is a situation? Faced with an ethical problem, people are generally tempted to persuade themselves that it could have no consequences beyond a certain radius that they think they can delineate. Notoriously, what are taken to be neatly fenced-off situations have a way of spilling over with a frightening array of hitherto unimagined repercussions and sometimes into an area of previously unsuspected vastness. The unexpected repercussions of what had been taken to be harmless, private deviations from accepted ethical standards form a large part of the stock-in-trade of novelists. For example, a simple-minded alcoholic steals a pencil drawing from a friend, pawning it for a few dollars to buy himself a fifth of scotch whisky. The drawing turns out to be one of Leonardo's rough sketches. A chain of consequences takes place that the alcoholic and indeed perhaps no one could have foreseen. Cloak-and-dagger scenes occur in all the leading capitals of the world. People are killed. The wife of one of the assassins drowns herself. The daughter of one of the assassins' victims throws herself off a cliff. One of the orphaned children takes to dope. In short, out of a trivial theft comes forth a seemingly endless chain of evil.

A bizarre example may serve to exhibit further the situational issue. A man and his wife, with their six children, are riding by horse-and-buggy to Minsk. Only the man can drive, and they do not know how far they have still to go. Finding themselves overtaken by a pack of savage, hungry wolves, the parents see that the whole family will be devoured. In hope of fending off the pack long enough to get out of danger, they decide, with heavy hearts and much weeping, to throw the youngest child to the wolves, which do in fact stay behind to attend to their meal. Were the parents justified in that particular situation in such an act, even though otherwise all eight persons would have been devoured?

The macabre story (which, by the way, I heard as a little boy—decades before anybody heard of situationism) does not end there. Situation$_1$ gives way to situation$_2$. That is, the wolves, their appetites whetted, again overtake the travelers; the next youngest child is thrown to them; and so on till at last the man and his wife, having thrown all six children to the wolves, are driving in sorrowful silence, when once again the wolves return, whereupon the man says: "My dear, we have followed a sound ethical principle so far. I will not desert it now." So saying, he throws his wife to the wolves and shortly thereafter arrives in Minsk alone.

In situation$_1$ there seems much to be said, on rationalist principles, for the action that was taken. In situation$_2$ it may seem not much less plausible, but by the time we come to situation$_6$ it has come to seem outrageous, while in situation$_7$ it is ridiculously so. Yet is there really any radical difference among the seven situations? Has not the problem arisen from the use of situational ethics in situation$_1$?

Adultery is a more commonplace example. Men and women, under the stress of passion, are often ludicrously blind to even the most probable consequences of their acts. They easily talk themselves into taking their conduct to be an entirely private affair that is nobody else's business. It could hurt nobody, for nobody else need know of it. So they think; yet almost any friend could have foretold unlimited sorrow for many as the outcome. Not only is the situation likely to be far larger than the situationist sees, but as one perceptive contemporary writer has observed:

> The interests of society and of future generations will almost always deserve extremely serious consideration, and the wisdom of society and of past generations will almost always deserve more attention than the individual in his enthusiasm is liable to offer at once. . . . Such deeper considerations will not necessarily restore old patterns of ethical behaviour; new situations may indeed call for new decisions. But they will deepen the debate . . . by reminding optimists of the depth and breadth of sinful selfishness.[31]

There lies the heart of the problem that deeply religious people have seen not only in situationism but in all ethics. Situationism is not as novel as some have supposed. The principle of situationism appeared long ago—for example, in some of the post-Kantian literature, wherever radical, individualist interpretations of Kant's categorical imperative were proposed.

Kant tells me I must always treat persons as ends, never as means to an end, and I must do no act that I would not wish to have universalized. For instance, making a promise with no intention of keeping it could not be made into a universal law. To want to see such an act universalized would be to want to see promises worthless, and that would entail a contradiction. I must always ask myself whether the course of action I propose is the sort a rational being would wish everyone to pursue, and then I must act as though the maxim of my action were by my will to become a universal law of Nature.[32]

If I am a morally sensitive and conscientious person I shall be doubtless very tough on myself in interpreting that ethical principle. But if I am,

[31] D. L. Edwards, *Religion and Change* (New York: Harper & Row, 1969), pp. 314 f. The author, fellow and dean of King's College, Cambridge, edited *The Honest to God Debate* (Philadelphia: Westminster, 1963).
[32] I. Kant, *Critique of Practical Reason,* ed. and trans. L. W. Beck (Chicago: University of Chicago Press, 1949), p. 80.

as are most people, very ready to blind myself to the claims of others and to exaggerate the just extent of my own, I may proceed very differently. Suppose I plan to commit adultery with my best friend's wife, who thoroughly approves of the idea. We agree with Kant that one should never treat people as means but only as ends. Since we are both willing partners to the proposed act, that well-known principle is not to be violated. We also agree with Kant's rule that one must do no act that one would not wish to have universalized. Now there is no doubt in our minds that we do not wish adultery universalized. Not only does my friend's wife trust in her husband's fidelity; not only do I wish my own wife to refrain from adultery; I recognize that, if adultery became general, marriage would be destroyed and promiscuity would become the sexual norm. Neither my partner in the proposed adultery nor I wish to see such results.

In our situation, however, there are some very unusual elements. As we consider them, we say to ourselves: if there were another case *exactly* like ours, with all the special elements in it that our situation contains, we should have no objection to the persons doing what we propose to do. We are not about to commit adultery in general but adultery in a special situation. There could be no question of universalizing our special conduct, since there are so few instances, perhaps indeed only our own. In other words, the maxim we acknowledge is not "Never commit adultery" but "Never commit adultery unless in situations *a, b, c,* . . . and our situation is one of these."

Kant himself was a bachelor and had no children, and his critics have naturally pointed out that if childlessness were universalized there would be no one left to practice the moral law. Such a result would be incompatible with his principle. Presumably Kant made a personal reservation, then, such as "Have children unless you cannot or will not," which reduces the principle to situationism.

There is a further and very profound problem to be considered here. Even apart from the unforeseeable effects my actions have on society at large, they have an effect on me. They may even be said to constitute me. Not only must I ask, "What is a situation?"; I must also ask, "Who am I?" And I find that out of my acts I build up the self I call "me." I function in many ways—perhaps as a member of a rock-and-roll band, as a vestryman in my church, as an angler, as a father, as a son, and as a user of the public library. In each of my functions I enter into special functional situations.

The situationist considers each of these situations apart from all others, but in each one of the situations he is building up his character as a self. The model we should set before us when we think of the history of the self is not that of a series of short stories or little songs, each independent of the other, but of a single epic or symphony. Though there may be a multiplicity of cantos or movements, one work is being built that will be a failure unless there is a principle of unity in it. In building my moral character, my personal selfhood, I cannot with impunity try to cut off and isolate pieces of it—a few bricks here, a mantel there, and here and there a window or a door. I must recognize that when I build anything I am building all. Whatever I do with and to myself in this or that function of my life I do to all of myself. Even if I were a Robinson Crusoe, set apart from society as a hermit on an otherwise uninhabited island, what I did, the care I took of my body, the use I made of my time, the diligence with which I sought means of preserving my sanity and strengthening my capacity for resolve—these would all count in the self I was creating. In such extraordinary circumstances, ethical problems would change, of course; yet they would not vanish. At the least I would still have duties "to myself."

Ethics and Religion Inseparable Yet Distinct

The fact that autonomy can be rightly claimed for ethics is not incompatible with the view that all ethical reflection has a religious root. Nor is the claim of some religious people that religion is the ultimate source of all morality necessarily injurious to the autonomy moralists claim for ethics. If, as seems the case, the two are inseparable, how exactly are they related?

First of all, let us note the obvious objection that religions, at certain stages of human development, have very little—if any—ethical content. More telling still, many religious people seem strikingly insensitive to ethical considerations, while, on the contrary, some people who have no stomach at all for religion in any recognizable form—institutional or mystical—are conspicuously full of ethical concern. Not only do they live a life that is by any reckoning morally exemplary; they struggle hard to bring about what they account moral progress in society. That religious observers may think, justly or otherwise, that such "righteous unbelievers" have a blind spot is beside the point. The point is, rather, that men and women such as Leslie Stephen (Virginia Woolf's father), George Eliot, and many others who could not easily be called religious even in the loosest sense and certainly not in any conventional sense, have exhibited a seriousness of purpose and a concern for probity of conduct that could well serve as a model for many thousands of very dubious characters who make a noisy parade of their highly· questionable religious pretensions. Even if we set aside primitive religions in which ethics plays almost no noticeable part at all, we cannot conclude that the practice of religion provides the highest moral guide for society.

Of course, many great moral reforms may be promoted and effected through the zeal and perseverance of certain religious men and women. We might even go further, pointing out that the kind of moral activity that the most profoundly religious people promote and make effective is of a higher—that is, more creative—quality than are any of the kinds

attainable through following ethical precepts or recognizing ethical principles. We might even go so far as to acknowledge the typical Christian claim
that though honesty among nonreligious people may be just as good an
honesty as any religion can produce, there are nevertheless certain specifically
Christian virtues (for example, Christian humility and Christian compassion)
that are of a special quality and are found only as Christian products. Yet
when all that is said, few people—even among those who as stalwart supporters
of religious claims would consider, say, the clergy in the United States today
to be by and large a very fine and dedicated body of men—would go so
far as to identify them as a body with the moral leadership of the nation.

Some religious writers use very strong language in defending religion as
the indispensable motivating power behind every kind of worthwhile morality. When we ask, "What is a worthwhile morality?" we may be told it
is one that in one way or another entails a sense of absolute obligation,
contradistinguished from mere political or social decencies, such as the
requirements of protocol in certain circles in Washington.

Professor W. G. Maclagan, in recognizing that morality (in the sense of
such "decencies") is possible without religion, notes that the possibility of
such religionless morality "is conceded readily enough even by one so critical
of 'mere morality' as is Oman; but it is conceded in the significant words
'Never . . . can morality without religion penetrate from good form to
goodness, from manners to morals.' " [33] Maclagan thinks that a nonreligious
morality is "very precarious." Either it breaks up under the pressures to
which it is vulnerable or else it will transform itself into "a more genuine
morality, no longer uncritically accepting but reflectively approving its code
and drawing strength from a personal recognition of absolute obligation."
He admits that such a genuine morality can exist independently of religion,
if by religion is understood "something other than and, as it were, extraneously supporting the attitude of moral commitment. On the other hand
there is good sense in saying that genuine moral commitment is itself religious
in quality whether or not a man so describes it in his own case." [34]

Finally, Maclagan admits that he can even agree with those who put
the matter as extremely as does Oman, saying that "morality is *not* possible
without religion." But he points out that he is then accepting it "as an
analytic truth"; that is, the term "religion" is being used to *mean*, "in Professor
Paton's words, 'the most supreme development of the moral will' and not
'the foundation upon which morality is built.' " Maclagan contends, however,
as would many others, that "religion" is much richer than what is expressed
in "the most supreme development of the moral will." [35]

---

[33] W. G. Maclagan, *The Theological Frontier of Ethics* (New York: Macmillan Co., 1961),
p. 182, quoting John Oman, *Grace and Personality* (New York: Association Press, Giant
Reflection Book, 1961), p. 61.
[34] Maclagan, *The Theological Frontier of Ethics,* p. 183.
[35] Ibid., pp. 183 f. Here Maclagan is quoting H. J. Paton, *The Good Will,* p. 440.

The disjunction Paton suggests here is important for our purpose. As we have already seen, there are some who, after the eighteenth-century manner, would strip religion of everything but what they take to be its moral "core" and, claiming there to find "true" religion, acknowledge its claims to be absolute. By this reckoning, Kant no less than Socrates would certainly be accounted pre-eminently a religious man. The ethical element in religion is so strong, by any account, that affirmations of that kind can be very persuasive.

The ancient Stoic and other writers who celebrated in literature the grandeur and nobility of a moral life, as well as many of the men and women who exercised the finest influence in the life and thought of the nineteenth century, are all, each in his own way, deeply religious. In this sense, Cicero (though no one would ever bracket him with Muhammad or St. Paul), Kant (though none would count him with Kierkegaard or St. Francis), and Thomas Jefferson (though none would link him with John Wesley or Dwight Lyman Moody) all seem strikingly religious when compared with, say, Ovid or Mark Twain. What distinguishes the group that includes Kant from the other that includes Mark Twain certainly cannot be any noteworthy attachment to, or interest in, places of worship or acts of prayer, for in that respect there would be, on the whole, little difference between these two groups. What makes Cicero and Kant and Jefferson seem religious by contrast with the other group is their incontestable interest in, and concern about, a kind of morality that by any reckoning lies very close to the heart of all the highly developed religions of the world. Buddhists and Muslims as well as Christians and Jews would all see such an element in these men and respect them accordingly for it.

Yet that element, inseparable from religion as it is, cannot be identified with it. What was most distinctive about, say, William Booth, the founder of the Salvation Army, was not his vigorous championship of righteousness in an age of many social wrongs; nor was it even his indefatigable struggle to ameliorate the lives of the very poor and outcast in Victorian England. It was, rather, his passionate (some might say fanatical) preaching of the Gospel, his evangelical zeal for converting men and women to Christ. His book, *In Darkest England and the Way Out*, published in 1890, exposed social evils and proposed remedies such as rescue homes and farm colonies. That side of his work, which was encouraged by King Edward VII, has been enormously influential throughout the world, not least in the United States. Behind it, however, was a religious leader, the fierceness of whose evangelistic style of preaching had brought him into conflict with the Methodist Church to which he originally belonged—even though that Church had itself emerged a century earlier with a similar motivation and a comparable religious flavor and effect, as a protest against the Church of England. So William Booth, no less than John Wesley, is easily classed—despite vast differences in manner and in mood, in tradition and in taste—with Kierkegaard and Luther, with

St. Vincent de Paul and Pope John XXIII, but not at all with Cicero or Jefferson or Kant.

With respect to the quality of the ethical concern of all these people, perhaps no difference could be clearly shown—though some theologians, after the fashion of Karl Barth, might insist otherwise. Be that as it may, there is at any rate a great difference of another sort. In one group we find a lively faith in, and love for, a personal Being, with a sense of the urgency of the need to celebrate that love by praising and worshiping him. Members of this group, generally speaking, would be suspicious of any attempt to separate religion and ethics. They would say, in effect, that God is the good and the good is God; that acting rightly is acting in accordance with the will of God; and that anyone who is acting rightly is a child of God. They would say, nevertheless, that it is crucially important to know the source of all that we call good, and they would insist that the praise and worship of God is not only our "bounden duty," as the priest says at the Preface of the Mass, but our first duty. So the motto "God first" would be one to which all would unhesitatingly subscribe, in whatever theological idiom they would express it. In one way or another they would see the sovereignty of God that Calvin so much stressed as demanding, even before other "absolute" moral commitments, the "praise and glory" that all religious people love to render to their creator.

Kant, Cicero, and others in their camp would not conceptualize in that way, much less so express themselves. To do so would be generally repugnant to them because they would already have established in their own minds a metaphysical presupposition that the pivot of the moral life, whatever it is, is not what these other men (such as Booth and Pope John) say it is but, rather, a principle that is built into the universe, a spiritual law like the Indian karma, somehow corresponding to what are loosely called "physical laws."

A basic difference, then, has emerged between ethics and religion. Though all mature, developed religion has profound ethical concerns and is inseparable from ethical commitments of one sort or another, the religious man would account idolatrous any attempt to put an ethical concern or principle or ideal at the summit of his experience or the center of his life. He would insist that even ethical conduct, vital though it indubitably is for the life of religion, must never take the place of God. By "God" he would mean in this context a Being, at least personal, on whom, as the creator of all things, including finite spirits such as ourselves, every good action, like everything else, depends. No duty, therefore, could ever come before that of "giving glory to God."

That does not mean, however, that the religious view encourages a man to neglect his moral obligations on the pretext of staying in church to sing hymns. It means, rather, that God should always be the focus of his thoughts and actions, so that the most lowly of tasks is ennobled when he who performs it is doing it as to God. The Benedictine emphasis on the dignity of labor, on which we touched in a previous chapter, would be unintelligible apart from that concept, which makes a nobleman out of the laborer who cleans the latrines to the glory of God and a serf out of the prince who, in the rule of his kingdom, has in mind only his people or, as we might say, "doing a good job" as an executive.

The calculus of holiness can never be either the number of hours spent in church or the quality of the good works performed, but always the direction of a man's whole being toward God. The religious man is a man in love with God, and a man's love for God is no more measurable than is his love for a woman. After all, a man's love for his wife is measured neither by the number of times he kisses her good morning, nor by the costly gifts he buys her, nor even by his readiness in helping her to clear the table or to fill the dishwasher, but simply by the genuineness of his love. Without loving her he might do all these things from a sense that he ought to do them or the belief that they constituted the kind of behavior expected in his social milieu of the good husband he wanted to be. By the same token he might love her deeply yet through forgetfulness or sloth neglect to do any of these things. In the latter case she could forgive him; in the former she would have been better off not to have married him.

Religion Without God

Some would distinguish religion from ethics, however, on a different basis, without reference to the particular metaphysical and theological presuppositions that lie behind the concept of God we have been considering. For instance, we touched earlier on the possibility of Robinson Crusoe's having ethical obligations, even if only to himself. Some would contend that ethical obligations always entail relationship with society, or at least with another person, so that Crusoe, at any rate before the appearance of Friday, could have had no ethical life at all.

He could have had a religious life, however, and in point of fact Defoe depicts him not only as a religious man but as having a very traditionalist cast of religion. Remembering Whitehead's definition of religion as "what a man does with his solitariness," we might expect Crusoe to be in a favorable position for being religious but in no position at all to be moral. Self-respect, for instance, would be a religious rather than a moral quality in a man, for a man's private attitude toward himself and toward whatever he inwardly accounted of ultimate importance would be his "personal religion," whatever his metaphysical presuppositions, hidden or declared, might be.

Professor Bartley well brings out the nature of this understanding of the distinction, rightly observing that it has "a venerable heritage in British philosophy." [36] Lord Keynes, recounting the influence G. E. Moore had exerted over him and other undergraduates at Cambridge who were later

[36] W. E. Bartley, III, *Morality and Religion* (New York: St. Martin's Press, 1971), p. 53.

to become members of the Bloomsbury Group, wrote, "We accepted Moore's religion . . . and discarded his morals . . . meaning by 'religion' one's attitude towards oneself and the ultimate and by 'morals' one's attitude towards the outside world and the intermediate." [37] As Bartley suggests, the protest of Leonard Woolf that Keynes's recollection was wrong and that "Moore and their companions at Cambridge were all quite concerned about practical politics and public morality," serves to reinforce the distinction.

The distinction had been similarly drawn in Mill's charge that Bentham had left something out of his account of human nature. What Mill thought Bentham had left out had been the very things that Keynes was now calling "religious"—"such as the love of beauty, and the development of inward consciousness, of which Moore was to write so powerfully in the famous last chapter of *Principia Ethica.*" Bartley also quotes J. W. N. Watkins (a disciple of Popper), whose words echo the distinction Keynes made: "Morality should be understood in an extraverted way as concerned with our behaviour towards others. I draw a sharp distinction between a man's morality and his personal religion and private ideals." [38] Watkins concludes that quests for personal salvation (what the Jungians see as integration) are inner quests, and that without them "any so-called morality that may crop up in our external, *outer* behaviour is usually either conventional, coincidental or accidental." [39]

The Emergence and Maturation of Morality and Religion

Whether one thinks the bare possession of a sense of having an inner life, of being what the French call *un homme intérieur*, is enough to justify accounting a man religious is beside the point. The point is that the religious consciousness does, at any rate, find its *beginnings* (as we have abundantly seen) in the inner, private life of man, while the moral life has its beginnings in his relation to other people. When we go on to observe, however, the way in which the religious life *develops*, we see at once that it depends for its development on those very relationships that provide the beginnings of ethical conduct. That is what is recognized by those who say, in the sometimes misleading language of religious people, that God is more easily found "in the face of my brother" than on our altars or in the metaphysical concepts we use in the formulation of our creeds.

From the standpoint of ethics a similar distinction might be made between emergency and maturation. The moral life may have its beginnings in—and may persist after a fashion for a long time with—convention, contract, and

[37] Ibid.

[38] J. W. N. Watkins, "Negative Utilitarianism," *Proceedings of the Aristotelian Society,* supp. vol. (1963), pp. 96 ff.

[39] Ibid., pp. 52 ff. He refers to the discussion of this question between R. W. Hepburn and Iris Murdoch in Strawson's essay; see I. T. Ramsey, ed., *Christian Ethics and Contemporary Philosophy* (London: S. C. M. Press, 1966).

even mere expediency and unimaginative imitation. Such conventional and mimetic morality, however, being uncreative, must have support in the interior life of the man who hopes to develop a moral vigor of his own. What passes for morality is generally mere observance of a code or adherence to a principle, but that is as much a primitive ethic as an amoral religion is a primitive religion. A creative ethic requires an inner life, the tending of one's own soul, as Socrates liked to say, much as an authentic religion needs people to respect and love and a world to serve and transform.

That every young man ought to long to put the world right and that he can do it only by first putting himself right, has become a trite remark. Yet it is an expression of the very point at issue here. Religion does begin with putting oneself right though it involves putting the world right, while morality begins with putting the world right but cannot proceed without putting oneself right. So for very general purposes we may account the tending of one's soul as the specification of the religious endeavor and concern, and we may contrast it with the moral actions with which, sooner or later, it will be inextricably bound up. In such a way we preserve and insist upon the autonomy of both ethics and religion while recognizing both their inextricability and their mutual dependence. In this view their respective autonomies are, of course, diminished. They are no longer absolute. Yet they are not wholly destroyed by seeing them as the warp and woof of the same spiritual fabric.

Such an understanding of religion plainly makes Socrates and Pico della Mirandola religious men, which indeed they were. That is not to say that their religion was all it might have been. Nor is it to say that the best of religions is to be condemned for the evildoing of its exponents—any more than ethics is to be denigrated because, as more than one librarian has assured me, more books on ethics are stolen than are stolen in any other field.

QUESTIONS ON CHAPTER XIII

1 What may be said for and against the view (a) that ethics is wholly dependent on religion, and (b) that religion derives all the value it has from its ethical content?

2 Critically consider views such as Russell's that religion is a positive hindrance to the attainment of human values.

3 What defects do you see in Braithwaite's understanding of religion? What, if anything, is to be said for it?

4 Since there is no connection between morality and art, why need there be any connection at all between morality and religion? Might not they be better kept entirely distinct?

5 Critically consider Abraham's conduct as Kierkegaard presents the situation.

6 If religion contains a nonmoral element, how can a moral judgment be made on it? In particular, consider the following statements: (a) "Hitler's religion was a very bad one" and (b) "Most Baptists I know are kinder and more humane than most Methodists I know; therefore the religion of the former, so far as my experience goes, is better than that of the latter."

7 Distinguish between situational and contextual ethics. What issues do they raise for the philosopher of religion?

8 What ambiguities do you see in the concept of religion as "vision"? How would you resolve them?

BIBLIOGRAPHICAL SUGGESTIONS

Bambrough, Renford. *Reason, Truth and God.* London: Methuen, 1969.

Bartley, W. W., III. *Morality and Religion.* New York: St. Martin's Press, 1971. A brilliantly incisive, brief treatment of the subject.

Beach, W., and Niebuhr, H. R., eds. *Christian Ethics.* New York: Ronald Press, 1955.

Beauvoir, Simone de. *The Ethics of Ambiguity.* New York: Philosophical Library, 1948.

Bonhoeffer, Dietrich. *The Cost of Discipleship.* New York: Macmillan Co., 1960.

Bonhoeffer, Dietrich. *Ethics.* New York: Macmillan Co., 1965.

Bonhoeffer, Dietrich. *Letters and Papers from Prison.* New York: Macmillan Co., 1962.

Camus, Albert. *The Rebel.* Translated by A. Bower. New York: Random House, 1956.

Cranston, M. *What Are Human Rights?* New York: Basic Books, 1962.

Curran, C. E. *Christian Morality Today.* Notre Dame, Ind.: Fides Publishers, 1966.

DeWolf, L. Harold. *Responsible Freedom.* New York: Harper & Row, 1971.

Ewing, A. C. *The Morality of Punishment.* London: Routledge and Kegan Paul, 1919.

Fletcher, Joseph. *Situation Ethics.* Philadelphia: Westminster Press, 1966.

Furfey, P. H. *The Morality Gap.* New York: Macmillan Co., 1969.

Gustavson, J. M. "Context Versus Principles." In *New Theology,* edited by M. E. Marty and D. G. Peerman. New York: Macmillan Co., 1966.

Hare, R. M. *The Language of Morals.* London: Oxford University Press, 1952.

Hare, R. M. "Religion and Morals." In *Faith and Logic,* edited by Basil Mitchell. London: Allen and Unwin, 1957.

Krook, Dorothea. *Three Traditions of Moral Thought.* Cambridge: At the University Press, 1959. Three traditions are distinguished—a religious one stemming from Plato and Christianity, a secular one stemming from Aristotle, and a modern humanist one that includes, for instance, D. H. Lawrence.

Lehmann, Paul L. *Ethics in a Christian Context.* New York: Harper & Row, 1963.

Lewis, H. D. *Morals and the New Theology.* London: Gollanz, 1947. Discusses attempts by theologians to exaggerate the gulf between ethics and religion.

MacKinnon, D. M. *A Study in Ethical Theory.* New York: Collier Books, 1962.

Maclagan, W. G. *The Theological Frontier of Ethics.* New York: Macmillan Co., 1961.

Macmurray, John. *The Self as Agent.* London: Faber & Faber, 1957.

Macquarrie, John. *Three Issues in Ethics.* New York: Harper & Row, 1970.

Macquarrie, John, ed. *A Dictionary of Christian Ethics.* Philadelphia: Westminster Press, 1967.

Messner, Johannes. *Social Ethics: Natural Law in the Western World.* Translated by J. J. Doherty. Rev. ed. St. Louis: B. Herder Book Co. 1965.

Muelder, Walter G. *Moral Law and Christian Social Ethics.* Richmond, Va.: John Knox Press, 1966.

Niebuhr, H. Richard. *Christ and Culture.* New York: Harper & Row, 1951.

Niebuhr, H. Richard. *Radical Monotheism and Western Culture.* New York: Harper & Row, 1960.

Niebuhr, Reinhold. *An Interpretation of Christian Ethics.* New York: Meridian Books, Living Age Books, 1956.

Nielsen, Kai. "Some Remarks on the Independence of Morality from Religion." In *Mind* 70 (1961): 175–186.

Nowell-Smith, Patrick. *Ethics.* London: Penguin Books, 1954.

Oman, John. *Grace and Personality.* New York: Association Press, Giant Reflection Book, 1961.

Osborne, Ronald E. *Humanism and Moral Theory.* London: Allen and Unwin, 1959. A study of ethical theory from a standpoint that ignores religion but uses the referents of psychology and psychoanalysis.

Paton, H. J. *The Modern Predicament.* London: Allen and Unwin, 1955. A sympathetic exposition of the moral *a priori* along Kantian lines.

Ramsey, Ian, ed. *Christian Ethics and Contemporary Philosophy.* London: S.C.M. Press, 1966.

Ramsey, Paul. *Deeds and Rules in Christian Ethics.* New York: Charles Scribner's Sons, 1967.

Ramsey, Paul. *Nine Modern Moralists.* Englewood Cliffs, N. J.: Prentice-Hall, 1962.

Rauschenbusch, W. *Christianity and the Social Crisis.* New York: Macmillan Co., 1907.

Robinson, John A. *Christian Morals Today.* Philadelphia: Westminster Press, 1964.

Ross, David. *The Right and the Good.* Oxford: Clarendon Press, 1930.

Russell, Bertrand. *Why I Am Not a Christian.* New York: Simon and Schuster, Clarion Books, 1957.

Warnock, Mary. *Existentialist Ethics.* New York: St. Martin's Press, 1967.

Wilson, John. *Reason and Morals.* Cambridge: At the University Press, 1961.

XIV

CONCEPTUAL MODELS
AND COSMIC AGAPĒ

Other [birds] (the heavier and slower, like the crow)
make a great hullabaloo when they start to fly: they
let go with one foot, then grab it again, so that they
don't take off; then they work with their wings while
still continuing to hold tight with their feet. . . .
Søren Kierkegaard (1813–1855),
Journal

An eclipse of the sun is something that occurs between
the sun and our eyes, not in the sun itself.
Martin Buber (1878–1965),
The Eclipse of God

Restatement of the Central Issue

In Part 1 of our study we attended to problems accounted crucial in the
contemporary philosophical study of religion. In Part 2 we have reexamined
basic aspects of the phenomenological structure of religious experience. We
should therefore be better equipped to restate, as we must now do, the
central issue in the philosophy of religion and to reconsider it in the light
of all we have learned and may be willing to discern.

As we look back on the contours of our study, we see that one feature
strikingly dominates all of them. Whatever the conceptual models we
construct to exhibit the truth of a religious assertion, we always fail to exhibit
a necessary connection between the conceptual model and the ontological
reality it is intended to disclose. We have explored characteristic antinomies
in religious experience, to which the opening chapter of Part 2 was devoted.
In exhibiting these polarities we have suggested connectors between the poles,
showing that the phenomena of religion are very much more complex and
their study therefore much more delicate and subtle than at first might
have been supposed. Behind all the antinomies, polarities, and ambivalences
that so abound in any thoroughgoing attempt to examine the subject matter
of religious discourse is a basic one that leaves us with a fundamental skeptical

objection. It is not, however, an objection that applies only to the subject matter of religious discourse. As we shall presently consider, it confronts scientists, for example, as well as theologians.

The difficulty lies in bridging the gulf between thought and reality, specifically what old-fashioned metaphysicians unashamedly called "ultimate reality." At an early stage we recognized that there is no way in which the existence of God as an ontological reality entirely independent of human experience could be logically established. As Heidegger neatly says, "Faith has no room in thinking." [1]

God could never be discovered by logic, but neither could radium. As we have abundantly seen, logic (like mathematics) is only a tool in the pursuit of truth. It is, indeed, an indispensable tool. Yet not only is it a mere tool; it is a tool that can get in the way of the user. The fact that it is indispensable does not diminish the consequences of the fact that it is also obstructive. A house painter's ladder can get in his way, though without it he could not paint the house at all. The house painter's ladder, however, is a nuisance only now and then, and on the other hand he might conceivably dispense with it, while logic is obstructive all the time yet never dispensable.

Thought is the only instrument with which any understanding of life can be attempted at all, and it functions also as a constant impediment to the understanding we seek and must obtain concerning the reality that seems to some to be reaching out and inviting our understanding. Not for nothing is a person with a good sharp mind said to have "a mind like a steel trap." The sharper the mind, the more efficiently it closes in upon its epistemological prey, and in doing so it traps itself in its own snare. Inside, there is not light enough to see clearly what has been trapped, though the light is eminently suitable for cutting the prey in pieces.

The case of morality, which we considered in the preceding chapter, exhibits the point in a special way. Since moral conduct, unlike thought, runs close to the stream of life, one might expect that, as indeed some have supposed, it should coalesce with religion. Yet while moral conduct has been seen to be generally religion's friend, it has been seen to be its rival too. What brings the two into conflict is the presence of a rational element in all morality that is not, so to speak, "soluble in religion." For all morality, whether hedonistic or oriented to a concept of duty or obligation, always has a calculus, and that calculus has a rational structure. Morality is always in one way or another informed by reason and intellect, however it may seem to transcend its rational and intellectual informants.

Ethical reflection is indispensable to human society; nevertheless, I may be an exemplary citizen without knowing it. For instance, in the city of Podunk there may be a local traffic ordinance number 1729, which forbids unnecessary use of the horn. You may remark, "Oh, I should have told

[1] Martin Heidegger, *Holzwege* (Frankfurt a. M.: Vittorio Klostermann, 1950), p. 343.

you about 1729. How did you know to abstain as you did from honking?" I might reply that I knew nothing about the ordinance but that I never honk unnecessarily, wherever I am. As a generally considerate driver I do not need to be told of ordinance 1729 in Podunk. Perhaps I had led such a sheltered life that it had not even occurred to me that anyone would be so inconsiderate as to use the horn otherwise than in a serious emergency, to avoid an accident.

Indeed, once you ask me how I do the right thing without reflection on the rules, you are likely to prove annoying. And if you keep on asking me how I manage to avoid spilling my coffee on my shirt, you may have me doing just that before the "coffee break" is over. For you shall have started me on a train of rational reflection with results like that produced on the centipede who was happily wending his way till he was asked which of his legs followed which. He became so puzzled that he lay paralyzed in the ditch trying to work out the answer. In cross-examining, counsel in court sometimes use questions along the same lines for the express purpose of bamboozling the witness by making him try to explain what has never occurred to him as in need of explanation, such as why he always takes (or even why he sometimes does not take) the pepper before the salt.

Not only can analytical procedures have such debilitating effects; they can hinder the imaginative activity. Indeed, all forms of reasoning tend to diminish our openness to the nature of Being, in whatever guise it confronts us, scientific or theological. Yet there is no way in which we can do without analysis or dispense with reasoning. The question is, rather, can we overcome the barrier to the apprehension of reality that thought, in the course of its indispensable role in apprehending it, creates? All quantitative concepts and mathematical procedures impoverish and may even kill the creative spiritual vitality that religious people value. Measurement reduces the loveliest garden and the holiest church on earth to nothing. If you want to make certain of missing whatever is worth seeing in the genius of Churchill or Newman or Lincoln, weigh and measure the subject of your inquiry.

All conceptual models, as we shall see, have a deceptive, misleading, constrictive element in them (though some may have it more than others), and the poignancy of our situation in the pursuit of truth lies in our knowing that we must construct them, and in knowing also that the abstractions of thought do separate us from the concreteness of reality. Some may be tempted to throw away the models and rely on instinct or intuition, but that is like throwing away the only map you have because it does not tell you all you want to know or because it sometimes misleads you. The opposite temptation, however, is more likely among people accustomed to the use of conceptual tools. Just because we can grasp the conceptual model and find it satisfying, we are much tempted to idolize it—that is, to say it is the nearest we can get to the reality and so we had better not pretend to go beyond it. We shrink from venturing beyond the known in the direction of the unknown; yet that is precisely what models are for. They are intended to be at least occasions of disclosure of truths about ontological and metaphysical realities.

The Logic of Theological Models

Before going further, let us discuss conceptual models in general and, more specifically, what a theological model is and what may be expected of it. Professor Max Black distinguishes what he calls "scale models" from what he calls "analogue models." By the first he means, for example, the kind of model a salesman provides when he wants to show his customer how a new house or car or dress will look.[2] By the second he means a model that "is guided by the more abstract aim of reproducing the *structure* of the original. . . . Thus the dominating principle of the analogue model is what mathematicians call 'isomorphism.' "[3]

The Bishop of Durham (Ian Ramsey) proposes to call Black's scale models "picture models," noting that they have been used both in science and in theology. Lord Kelvin, for example, used the image of "waves in an ethereal sea" to depict the way in which light is propagated, and religious writers have similarly called on their readers to picture God as a king or shepherd or father, and have pictured the end of history in terms of a model containing fire, clouds, blood, smoke, and so forth. Both the scientist and the theologian find such picture models useful, but, of course, they both require of their readers a willingness to see that not only are the models only pictures; they depict only special features. As the scientist hopes no one will think that light is really behaving just as the waves in the Atlantic behave, so the theologian hopes his readers will not think God really carries a shepherd's crook as in the *Pastor Bonus* iconography.

The reason for Ramsey's terminological preference in the second case is even more significant. For in the second case the models *are supposed to have* a closer connection with what they stand for. Their similarity to it is not merely a pictorial similarity; it is a structural similarity. The model does not merely sketch or paint that of which it is a model; it mimics it in such a way as to come closer to the orginal than can the picture model. It calls attention to both the presumed similarity with, and the difference from, the original. As Ramsey says, "It is precisely such similar-ity-with-a-difference that generates insight, that leads to disclosures when (as we say) 'the light dawns.' To give a rough example: it is two pictures rather similar but in some points significantly different, that in a 3-D viewer lead to an apprehension of 'depth.' "[4]

[2] Max Black, *Models and Metaphors: Studies in Language and Philosophy* (Ithaca, N. Y.: Cornell University Press, 1962), p. 221, as quoted by Ian Ramsey, *Models and Mystery* (London: Oxford University Press, 1964), p. 2.
[3] Max Black, ibid., p. 222, in Ian Ramsey, ibid., pp. 9 f.
[4] Ramsey, ibid., p. 10.

These isomorphic models, then, are intended, no less than picture models, to disclose something that is not actually present in the structure. Dramatic art presents us with a striking example of the use of such a model. When a great actor portrays, say, John Fitzgerald Kennedy or Charles de Gaulle, he is not content to mimic his speech or the style of his walk. He so mimics the whole structure of the man, the whole unity of his body and soul, that perhaps I say, "Why, it's Kennedy to the life—it's his 'spitting image'!" or even, "He *is* de Gaulle." Now, of course, I know it could not possibly be Kennedy or de Gaulle that I see now, since they are both dead. Since I happen to have seen them both in the flesh, I might well say, "It's uncanny—you'd really think they were there on the stage"; but, of course, I have the advantage of being able to say both, "It is a magnificent piece of acting," and, "I know it is *only* acting."

Very different is the case when the actor is supposed to be portraying, say, Moses. Not only have I never seen Moses, but some biblical scholars question whether he ever existed at all in the way in which his story is chronicled in Exodus. How, then, could I ever say, "It's Moses to the life"? Moses, if he did exist, might have been seven feet tall or a dwarfish hunchback, for all I know. Still, I am quite likely to say something like, "What a great Moses he does" or else, "It's not a very good Moses." What can I possibly mean? I can only mean that the actor has or has not succeeded in portraying the most convincing Moses I can construct out of all the constructions of him in my head. The question of portraying the "real" Moses (if there ever was one) simply cannot arise.

To take a subtler case, I might say I liked Peter O'Toole's portrayal of King John. Let us assume that, though I am not an expert, I do know a good deal about the period. The day after seeing the performance I remark to you what a splendid King John he did. I am overheard by a professional historian, an expert in the period, who raises a supercilious eyebrow and says: "Haven't you heard? A manuscript containing some well-authenticated descriptive material turned up and was put in the British Museum last week. I went to London personally to examine it, of course, and it shows, incidentally, that, with many others, you have a very wrong notion of King John's appearance and demeanor. In the light of our new knowledge, that whole performance was a travesty." Though the information might shake me considerably, I might still persevere, saying: "Well, some of the details may have been inexact, but from all that I know it did capture his *spirit*. What does it matter, after all, whether the hair is black or blond? What matters is that you get the feel of the man, and that is what Peter O'Toole has done for us."

Suppose, however, that later still the expert came to me with conclusive historical proof that the whole of English history of that period had been deliberately falsified. No such king ever existed. The whole story of a King John is a fabrication, an oft-repeated, hoary legend, no more. Then the best I could say would be something like, "Anyhow, it's still a marvelous portrayal of King John *as I always imagined him.* Many other people liked it, too, so we must all have imagined the same thing—how's that for a coincidence?" The coincidence could be, of course, very easily explained. Peter O'Toole would be no less splendid an actor than he was before, but the ontological status of what he was portraying would have suffered fatally. Now, when I said I still thought his King John was good I could mean only what I meant in saying I thought John Gielgud did a splendid Hamlet though I did not think Hamlet's father's ghost was convincing.

In terms of dramatic criticism I might well be right all the way through. The point is that the structure of the model has never really led me outside my own mind. How, then, could even such an isomorphic model, to say nothing of a picture one, serve well in either theology or science, where the model is expected to lead me to cosmic disclosures, to an understanding of a state of affairs that exists independently of my mind?

At this point we may usefully look for a few moments at the tests that a penetrating American theologian—Professor Robert P. Scharlemann of the State University of Iowa—proposes for theological models.[5] Dr. Scharlemann, who is much influenced by Tillich's thought, departs from Ramsey's schema of models and qualifiers,[6] as he does also from another one proposed in a paper by Professor Ferré.[7] Scharlemann proposes to operate

> with the *basic structure of domains* as providing part of the material for a theological model and with *connectives* as providing the other part. As I shall be using the term, a model is distinguished on the one hand from observational or analytical *description* and on the other hand from a *symbol.* It differs from a description because the content of a model is not intended to be the report of an observation of how an object appears or really is. Yet at the same time, it does mean to provide a way of cognitively dealing with that object; even if the model contains no description of the object it refers to, it does allow one to come to terms with the object.

Models, according to Scharlemann, are testable constructs. When we come to the four tests he proposes, however, we find that we fare no better than before. The tests are admirable for their purpose, but they do not test all that might properly be expected of them.

First, Scharlemann tells us, a model must not break down in view of actual experience. When this happens it may be replaced by another. He takes Job's as an example. The model Job is using tells him that God punishes wrongdoers, but Job finds that, on the contrary, God seems to reward them and punish the righteous. So the model must be replaced. Similarly, the

---

[5] In a paper presented at the Iowa Theological Conference at Cedar Falls, Iowa, 13 March 1971. Quoted by permission.
[6] As presented in his *Religious Language* (New York: Macmillan Co., 1957) and *Christian Discourse* (New York: Oxford University Press, 1965).
[7] F. Ferré, "Mapping the Logic of Models in Science and Theology," in *New Essays on Religious Language,* ed. Dallas High (New York: Oxford University Press, 1969), pp. 54–96.

model "God is freedom and destiny" is testable. Scharlemann specifies: "If there is a case in which the conditioning of destiny amounts to a loss of freedom, then the model . . . breaks down."

The second test is whether the model uses a connective that is "significant"; "a significant connective is a connective that does indeed quiet the question about intelligibility." That is, the connective must be significant *to the user*; the connective "God chooses" might be all right for Tom but not for Jack. Thirdly, the significant connective must be "universal in the sense that it holds good for those who find it significant as well as for those who do not." Scharlemann cites Tillich's use of the cross as an example of such a universal connective: the fact that it will be rejected by some proves that its meaning has been to that extent understood. The fourth test is "whether a model that claims to be final really is final."

What is tested is, however, the intelligibility and logical adequacy of the structure of the model and of its relation to a state of affairs and the willingness of the user to interpret that state of affairs as intended. For instance, the test whether "God is freedom and destiny" tells us only that if the model passes the test, freedom and destiny, are not what we may have thought them to be and that the name proposed for the transcendence of destiny by freedom is "God." "Fate" would do as well except that it has been pre-empted for use in a model where there is no possibility of freedom. In brief, Scharlemann through his tests can analyze the structure of the model, but he then must say, in effect, no less than must Ramsey, "Now, do you see?" In both cases the penny still must drop. The penny may indeed drop, but the penny that drops may turn out to be after all only a penny in the mind. In terms of the religious truth-claim, that penny is counterfeit money. We shall have more to say of that later.

The Positivistic Objection

When we look at radical objections to the acceptance of any of the most fundamental truth-claims, metaphysical or religious, we find that while they may take many forms they are all in the long run reducible to one basic contention. That basic contention is that the apprehension of religious ideas occurs in the mind of the religious man and no way of sustaining these claims as independent of him could be generally acceptable. This contention, though it is often expressed in psychological forms such as Feuerbach's well-worn one that the gods are nothing but man's *Wünschwesen* (wish-beings), is basically positivistic.

The objection is just as relevant to proposals about the cosmos that are put forward in scientific terms as it is to theological assertions. We shall see that the verificational procedures on which positivistic philosophers have laid so much stress allow for no discrimination in the long run against one or the other. As Max Planck noticed long ago, the positivistic theory "is that physical science has no other foundation than the measurements on which its structure is erected, and that a proposition in physics makes any sense only in so far as it can be supported by measurements. But since every measurement presupposes an observer, from the positivistic viewpoint the real substance of a law of physics can never be detached from the observer, and it loses its meaning as soon as one attempts mentally to eliminate the observer and to see something more, something real, behind him and his measurement." [8] Not only does Planck's remark apply to the positivistic kinds of scientist who influenced the early twentieth-century logical positivists; it applies also to Hume himself. All who think like Hume in these matters are phenomenalists; that is, they refuse to allow any discussion of anything other than the phenomena as they are presented to and found in the observer. To talk of "the reality" that might or might not lie behind these phenomena, which philosophers had traditionally accounted the philosopher's special business—at any rate in his metaphysical role—is, according to such positivistic theorists, to talk *un*philosophically.

Whatever we may think of the narrowness of the positivist's view of the philosopher's business, we must not fail to notice that his skepticism can be as much a skepticism about science as it is a skepticism about religion. As Planck pointed out in the paper just quoted, positivists—however much they may take themselves to be "proceeding without presuppositions"—are committed, if they are "not to degenerate into an unintelligible solipsism," to the premise "that every physical measurement can be reproduced, so that its outcome depends neither on the personality of the individual performing the experiment, nor on the place and time of the measurement, nor on any other attendant circumstance. But this simply means that the factor which is decisive for the result of the measurement lies beyond the observer, and that one is therefore necessarily led to questions concerning real causal connections operating independently of the observer." [9] Planck went on to remind his audience how, "up to quite recently, positivists of all hues" had put up the strongest resistance to the introduction of atomic hypotheses," acceptance of which entailed the acceptance of universal constants.[10] Noting, toward his conclusion, the profoundly religious disposition of the greatest of scientists (for instance, Kepler, Newton, Leibniz), he remarked, "Religion and natural science do not exclude each other, as many contemporaries of ours would believe or fear; they mutually supplement and condition each other." [11]

The basic difficulty, however, remains, though religion and science share the burden of it.

[8] Max Planck, "Religion and Natural Science," in *Scientific Autobiography and Other Papers,* trans. F. Gaynor (New York: Philosophical Library, 1949), pp. 170 f. The paper in the original German, *Religion und Wissenschaft,* consists of a lecture originally delivered in 1937.
[9] Ibid., p. 171.
[10] Ibid., p. 173.
[11] Ibid., p. 186.

How a Bad Penny Drops

Though the verificational procedures and criteria of the positivist raise special questions about the meaning of religious assertions on which philosophers in the early days of logical empiricism laid much stress, the fundamental objection, as we have seen in the last section, applies to theological assertions as it applies to scientific ones. The reason lies in the positivist's phenomenalism, which operates as much in the one realm as in the other.

The positivist's objection need not prevent his investing religious assertions with meaning. He may agree, if he happens to be so inclined, that religious symbols and theological models do indeed refer to realities. He may even recognize these realities as important, but they are psychological realities—realities that inhere in the human psyche. They are not the realities about which the religious man wishes to make his proposals, which purport to be about realities independent not only of humanity but of Nature herself.

The objector may begin by pointing out that he has no use for certain notions and may claim they are unintelligible *in the form in which the believer insists on formulating them.* For instance, he would not accept for discussion, since to do so would contravene his basic negative assumptions, notions such as that there is a Being at the heart of the universe who has certain attributes, creates all that is not-he, acts in world history, and discloses himself in certain ways to human beings. Nor would the objector accept, say, a "law of Karma" as a Buddhist might formulate it. Nevertheless, he might very well be ready to admit that these affirmations are not unintelligible when formulated according to his requirements. They could refer to very important psychological realities.

Let us suppose a special but by no means unusual case of an objector endowed with much psychological insight. He testifies that there have been times when he has been plagued, through timidity and fearfulness, with the sense of being utterly alone, and he has then experienced a pleasant awareness of having emerged from the great community of the human race. He rejoices in that awareness with a vigor commensurate with the pleasure of his discovery. His pleasant awareness is indeed a reality. He may even say: "May it never leave me! I love it! I want to bask forever in it, feeling one with Dante and Shakespeare and Muhammad and Heraclitus. I shudder at the prospect of finding myself once again in that state of isolation and loneliness." If he should lose the sense he prizes, he will long for its return. He will enter into situations that he thinks may induce its return. For instance, he may perhaps try reading history or making pilgrimages to India, Greece, and other great foci of the development of the human spirit. Endowed as he is with penetrating psychological insight, he may perceive the therapeutic efficacy of prayer and so may even go so far as to couch his longings in that form.

So eager may he be to recapture the warm presence that, as he remembers, brings so much pleasure and prevents so much malaise, that he may even

go further. He may attend churches or synagogues or mosques, trying out
the ritual and the prayers. These he may well address to God—taking care,
of course, to note (for the sake of his intellectual integrity) that by this
term "God" he means the reality that he so much enjoyed in his psyche
and wishes to enjoy again. Eventually the psychic reality he seeks may
present itself to him again. In the course of time he may become so accustomed
to its periodic loss and gain that, having, of course, the high degree of
perspicacity without which he could never have gone so far as he has, he
may think he sees very well what religious believers mean by notions such
as the absence and presence of God. He may also think he sees what they
mean by gratitude to God and kindred notions. When the warm glow of
his sense of togetherness with Homer and Voltaire, Lincoln and Longfellow,
Socrates and Goethe, once again supervenes, he feels as grateful as a victim
of periodic neuralgia feels when the pain goes away and he is once again
at ease.

If he happens to be also scientifically minded he may extend his sense
of oneness beyond humanity and into that Nature out of which humanity
emerged. Now the thought of the simians, the jellyfish, the algae, and even
the dust of the earth, as that thought surrounds his mind, provides him
with an even richer glow. He feels at peace with all the phenomena he
has ever studied. At the same time, in the very act of carefully preserving
his basically positivistic principles, he has added to his enrichment a sense
of intellectual accomplishment: he feels he now understands what religious
people are saying when they talk about God and grace and the whole panoply
of theological doctrine. By this time he may very well be a prominent member
of the local community church and a generous benefactor to its favored
objectives.

To many he will look and sound as much a religious believer as anyone
could be, besides being far less rude than was Kierkegaard about the smug
sacerdotal triumphalism and other ills of the institutional Church. Yet in
fact he has never moved a step beyond the positivism with which he started.
He has only refined it. He is still saying, like his scientific counterpart so
well described by Planck, that to go further than that would be to talk
unphilosophically, since it would be to talk of alleged entities, alleged realities,
that one could not possibly know about. Ever mindful of Wittgenstein's
concluding observation ("Where we cannot speak we must shut up"), he
has never once sought to flout it; yet at the same time he has found a
means of eloquently and persuasively discoursing, if not on the forbidden
subject, at least with the vocabulary of the transgressors.

We must all feel some measure of sympathy with the positivist's mood,
for it is one few, if any of us, have wholly escaped. Yet concealed in it
are a dogmatism and a narrowness that at first do not show themselves.
The objector thinks he is "proceeding without presuppositions," but in fact
he is making a gigantic one—namely, that he *ought* to have no openness

to ontological or metaphysical speculation. The results of that stance are comparable to those Planck describes when the view is taken "that a problem in physics merits examination only if it is established in advance that a definite answer to it can be obtained. If physicists had always been guided by this principle, the famous experiment of Michelson and Morley undertaken to measure the so-called absolute velocity of the earth, would never have taken place, and the theory of relativity might still be non-existent." [12]

Openness the Condition of Discovery

If we look at the history of recent scientific discovery we find one fact so striking that its consequences deserve to be well pondered in any consideration of the central issue that now confronts us in the philosophy of religion. From the time of Newton (1642–1727) till the year 1900 the developments in physics had turned up no fundamentally new principles. That was the year Max Planck introduced the quantum theory, which might be said to involve a much more radical departure from Newtonian physics than even Albert Einstein (1879–1955) was to make with his relativity theory.

Quantum theory, in contrast to relativity theory, is principally concerned with the microcosmic, the smallest things—namely, atoms. Planck's introduction of the quantum h was a revolutionary novelty, affecting the whole understanding of the structure and behavior of atoms. In the course of the scientific revolution that took place in the early decades of the present century, scientists such as Rutherford, Bohr, de Broglie, Born, Heisenberg, and Schrodinger all contributed special insights, notably the two last, to whom must be chiefly attributed the later and more radical form of the quantum theory, which dates from 1925. By the use of an abstract mathematical theory of groups, the quantum and the relativity theories put forward by Planck and Einstein respectively were combined in such a way as to revolutionize our understanding of the nature of the universe.

What is especially significant here, however, is that the mathematical structures had been already independently established by pure mathematicians before the twentieth-century scientific revolution took place. The empirical facts, moreover, were already observable. Only creative imaginative insight was needed to go beyond, to grasp and take possession of the new discoveries. Scientists are much more likely to fail through what Whitehead called "the fallacy of misplaced concreteness," [13] mistaking the abstract for the concrete, than on account of mathematical error. The mistake is the same kind of mistake that primitive man makes when he identifies his models (for instance, the universe as living and breathing, like a gargantuan animal) with the reality beyond them.

[12] Ibid., pp. 139 f.
[13] A. N. Whitehead, *Science and the Modern World* (Cambridge: At the University Press, 1932), pp. 72 f.

In modern science the positivist is, indeed, much worse off. For his failure arises, not from a methodological error, but from a methodological dogma forbidding the very kind of speculation without which we could not possibly have advanced beyond Newton, nor indeed could Newton have advanced beyond his predecessors. The positivist, by the terms of his rules, inhibits all discovery. That is what Planck saw so clearly in making the observations quoted earlier. The modern quantum theory could never have been developed but for a theory invented by Rutherford and Bohr. That highly imaginative theory about the atom has now been displaced. Their presentation of the structure of the atom has become only a sort of pictorial vision, useful for some broad generalizations, but too simple. Yet without that theory, in all its shortcomings, the later developments in quantum theory could never have taken place.

The example is a dramatic one, but the same principle holds good even in what appear to be the most trivial scientific hypotheses. Positivists are always ready to resist speculative inquiry, whether in science or in philosophy, when the result of the hypothesis might damage the narrow metaphysical dogmas that lie behind their methodological proscriptions. Much contemporary philosophy is still far too closed in. For example, philosophers are often, if unwittingly, far too much under the influence of outworn Newtonian models.

The need for openness in the pursuit of ontological, metaphysical, or religious truth is obvious. The question is, how it is to be attained? We must first ask, however, of what such openness consists. It is plainly comparable in some respects to the kind of openness we have seen to be so necessary to scientific discovery. The methodological difference between scientific and theological pursuits is reflected in differences in the way in which the openness is apprehended in science and in religion; but if, as the later Heidegger contends, truth (*alētheia*) is to be conceived as the "disclosedness" of what is, there can be in the long run no dichotomy between the openness Planck commends to the scientists and the openness Heidegger enjoins upon his disciples. We may say, at any rate, that to attain a genuinely religious temper the narrownesses that produce the literalisms and dogmatisms of both the intolerant atheist and the intolerant theist must be overcome. They constitute a fundamental obstruction to the religious temper. More than that negative requirement, however, is needed for religious openness.

We may look for a clue in what Heidegger has to say about openness of being. Heidegger does not identify being with God; yet, as Macquarrie suggests:

> It would be true to say that in his thought, Being has taken the place of God; for Being undoubtedly is furnished with most of the attributes that have been traditionally assigned to God, and Being seems to perform most of the functions that have belonged to God. Being is the incomprehensible that cannot be counted as an *ens creatum* [created being] and yet has more

reality; Being both transcends the world and is immanent in it; Being is the author of revelation and grace.[14]

Though by no means everyone would go so far in christianizing Heidegger's thought as does Macquarrie, the point he makes is well taken.

Heidegger admits the ambiguity of the term: " 'the Open' . . . is, as a metaphysical term, ambiguous." [15] He is much influenced by two German poets: the first is the romantic Neo-Hellenist Johann Christian Friedrich Hölderlin (1770–1843); the second is Heidegger's nearer contemporary Rainer Maria Rilke (1875–1926).[16] Rilke uses the term *Urgrund*, which is translated "Nature," but Heidegger warns us that we are to understand it "in the broad and essential sense in which Leibniz uses the word *Natura* capitalized. It means the Being of beings. . . . What Rilke calls Nature is not contrasted with history. Above all, it is not intended as the subject matter of natural science. Nor is Nature opposed to art. It is the ground for history and art and nature in the narrower sense." [17]

Heidegger, who seeks intellectual roots in early thought (the Upanishads as well as the Pre-Socratics), does not forget that for the early Greeks *physis* had a dynamic, living quality. It was not set in antithesis to the spiritual, as physics might be said to be antithetical to ethics, the *Naturwissenschaften* to the *Geisteswissenschaften*. Heidegger sees far more in early Greek thought than primitive gropings in the direction of modern science. Only because of the ineptitude of our age for ontological and metaphysical pursuits have 'the Greeks become for many today "just a better class of Hottentots, and our modern science infinitely more advanced in comparison with theirs." [18] That is precisely where, in Heidegger's view, so many contemporary scholars not only undervalue our Greek heritage but completely miss the point of what the Greeks were saying about *physis*. The term carried within it no differentiation between the animate and the inanimate. Rilke likewise makes none. *Nature* is to be understood, in Rilke, as designating "Being in the sense of beings as a whole." Heidegger quotes Nietzsche: "Being—we have no idea of it other than 'living'—How can anything dead 'be'?" [19]

Nature, then, "ventures" living beings and "grants none special cover." Moreover, "venture includes flinging into danger. To dare is to risk the game. . . . If that which has been flung were to remain out of danger, it would not have been ventured." [20] Nevertheless, the beings that are ventured

[14] J. Macquarrie, *Martin Heidegger* (Richmond, Va.: John Knox Press, 1968), p. 57.
[15] Martin Heidegger, *Poetry, Language and Thought*, trans. A. Hofstadter (New York: Harper & Row, 1971), p. 107.
[16] See W. H. Werkmeister, "Heidegger and the Poets," *The Personalist* 52 (Winter 1971): 5–22.
[17] Heidegger, *Poetry, Language and Thought*, pp. 100 f.
[18] Martin Heidegger, *Einführung in die Metaphysik* (Tübingen: Max Niemeyer Verlag, 1953), p. 12. The translation is mine.
[19] Ibid. My translation.
[20] Heidegger, *Poetry, Language and Thought*, p. 102.

are "not abandoned. If they were they would be just as little ventured as if they were protected. Surrendered only to annihilation, they would no longer hang in the balance. . . . Being, which holds all things in the balance, thus always draws particular beings toward itself—toward itself as the center." [21] Rilke compares the venture (*Wagen*) of being to the force of gravity; he calls it "the unheard-of center." [22] We may think of every existent in that which is being risked (*als Gewagtes*) as placed on a scale (*Wage*). As Professor Werkmeister reminds us, the English terms do not convey the interrelatedness of the German ones.[23] These suggest the image of a cosmic "pull." So Heidegger can say that the ventured beings are pulled within a cosmic draft. Heidegger goes on then to tell us: "Rilke likes to use the term 'the Open' to designate the whole draft to which all beings, as ventured beings, are given over. . . . In Rilke's language, 'open' means something that does not block off. It does not block off because it does not set bounds. It does not set bounds because it is in itself without all bounds. The Open is the great whole of all that is unbounded." [24]

Heidegger finds Rilke congenial as illustrating, if in a somewhat Nietzschean way, what Heidegger wants to say about his own development from his intellectual beginnings as a nihilistic existentialist. He can use Rilke as a prophet of the admixture of his own thought. The later Heidegger's thought is highly susceptible to a religious (if theologically ambiguous) interpretation. Though some interpreters may go too far in so understanding him, there can be no doubt that his personalistic concerns, his concept of Being as *physis* actively unfolding or disclosing itself, and existentialist *motifs* such as "Being-toward-death" all have deeply religious applicability. Heidegger does not use the term "God," which he thinks has been degraded in theological usage, but what he predicates of Being is often very like what classical theologians have predicated of God. At any rate, his religious applicability makes his concept of openness suggestive for our purpose.

We spend a large part of our lives blocking ourselves off from what I have called the God-dimension. Not only our petty concerns, but the nature of mental activity itself, ensures this. Both imagination and conceptualization have this effect. Imagination does it by imposing forms upon us. Conceptualization, however, besides imposing forms, also locks us up within abstractions. We must note, moreover, a paradoxical difference between the effect of imagination and the effect of conceptualization.

On the one hand, the more we conceptualize and the better the instruments we devise for conceptualization, the likelier we are to trap ourselves inside the intellectual trap we set. The pure mathematician, for instance—unless he is fortunate enough to have other qualities, as not infrequently happens—is

[21] Ibid., pp. 103 f.
[22] *Sonnets to Orpheus* II, 28, as quoted in Heidegger, *Poetry, Language and Thought.*
[23] "Heidegger and the Poets," p. 22, n. 3.
[24] *Poetry, Language and Thought,* p. 106.

notoriously prone to shut himself off from an appreciation of even the most obvious and most widely acclaimed values in human life. The most abstract thought, which might be accounted the purest kind of thought, is generally acknowledged to be the most useful instrument we have; yet it can be the most detrimental to openness.

On the other hand, the more I use my imagination, the less its forms imprison me. A person of dull imagination is much more likely to be tied down, bounded by forms, than a vivaciously imaginative one, who is accustomed to flitting incessantly from one form to another. The imaginative person faces another danger, however, which we noted in an earlier chapter. Though the forms he uses are too numerous and variegated to permit of his being captured by any one of them, he may be held prisoner, for all his agility, by the process of imagination itself. The imaginative person has nevertheless one great advantage, the one that, as we have already noted, Heidegger sees in the past: he is "innocent." His innocence does make him liable to danger, but it also protects him. Like a little bird among savage bears, he is too small to be noticed and too swift to be caught. His greatest advantage, however, is that his wings enable him to see beyond the prisons of the mind.

Logic, which Heidegger calls deontologized thinking, is unauthentic. It has divorced itself from Being. All thought must do this unless it can somehow hold itself in tension so as not to close in upon itself and lose openness to Being. Heidegger, using again his technical but suggestive terminology, speaks of "ek-sisting," by which he means standing out in the open of Being so as to let Being have its say. Philosophy, instead of revealing truth, has tended to veil it; that is, by analyzing the truth instead of looking at it, it not only distorts the truth but hides it. This hiding is a necessary part of disclosure of truth, but it is not and could not be the whole of the disclosure.

What Heidegger commends to us certainly sounds very like what is typically urged, as we have seen, by the great mystics of the Church. This is not merely a passive waiting for God as we wait for a bus. It is a creative response to what confronts us in our openness to God. That openness to God calls for listening rather than speaking, but another requirement is living in such a way as to be always on the *qui vive* for divine disclosure. That sense of the distanced presence of God as lurking in the shadows of life, as the sun hides behind a cloud, ever ready to emerge in disclosure of himself, is what our ordinary (especially our technological) outlook particularly obscures from us to our great detriment.

A Methodology of Openness

Whatever we may think of Heidegger's concept of openness, we can hardly escape the force of the suggestion—already glimpsed by Plato and prefigured in the Neo-Platonic tradition—that our thought shuts us off from that to which we need to be open. As we have seen, thought—our indispensable truth-grabbing instrument—shuts us inside with the truth it traps, leaving us imprisoned with our meager epistemological prey. Well we may ask, by what means, then, can we hope to achieve the openness that is commended?

The term "love," though no less ambiguous than the term "God," points the way to a possibility for our purpose. The term is used of what engages the whole being in communion with boundlessness. Love is by its nature a breaker of bonds. The term is also a root metaphor in all religious discourse. Used to render key words in the writings of Sufis and Sikhs, Hebrews and Hindus, Buddhists and Confucians, besides being in the forefront of the language of all Christian mystical traditions, it may be taken to stand for a notion that is central to, and universal in, all religious literature. For these reasons it merits special exploration as a possible key term for a methodology of openness.

Writers have used the term with a whole spectrum of meanings. Every student of elementary New Testament Greek is taught to distinguish the word *agapē* (which the King James translators rendered "charity" and most modern translators "love") from two other Greek terms, *philia* (friendship) and *erōs* (desire). Even the latter of these two terms, however, is ambiguous, since contemporary attitudes have brought about diminishments of its original connotation, which included an element of debonair joy alien from the ruttishness of most contemporary understanding of the erotic. Before we consider in what way the term *agapē* might provide a clue to what we need for a methodology of openness that would take us into a dimension beyond the enclosures of our customary and indispensable modes of thought, we must examine the linguistic roots of the notion we propose to offer.

The Term *Love* in Religious Discourse

The Hebrew word *'āhab*, is employed in a variety of contexts in much the same way as the English word "love" that is used to translate it. It can be used of riches or of places, for instance, but it most often refers to sexual attraction between men and women. It can also be used, however, of every kind of friendship and to express every quality of attachment, ranging from that of sexual excitement to that of a deep, lasting, spiritualized affection. When it is eventually applied to the relation between God (Yahweh) and his people, the analogy is apparently that, as in a lasting marriage a man loves his wife with great fidelity and his wife responds with loving faithfulness, so Yahweh may be said to love his people. Love is the response he expects from them. There is no evidence of the use of this analogy before the eighth century B.C., when Hosea introduced it.

According to one picturesque reconstruction of the story of Hosea's life, over which there is much technical controversy among biblical scholars, Hosea's own wife Gomer was unfaithful to him. She sank very low, but such was the prophet's love for her that he forgave her and took her back, perhaps even bought her back out of slavery, in hope that they might take up their love again in the desert where it began. The prophet's message, then, is: the love of God for his people Israel is like Hosea's love for Gomer. He will forgive Israel, but Israel on her part must be willing to make a fresh start by forsaking foreign idols and the allurements of the cultures that go along with them and return to the simplicity of the conditions when Yahweh first sought out and chose his people Israel as a man seeks out and chooses his wife.

Hosea's allegory provides a clue to how, even at primitive levels of human development, a connection was perceived, however dimly, between human love and the moving force at the heart of the universe—the force that Dante in his medieval Italian way was to call, in the last line of the *Commedia*, "the love that moves the sun and all the stars." In the fifth century B.C., the Chinese sage Mo-tzu (or Motse) taught that "Heaven loves men dearly" and "loves the whole world universally. Everything is prepared for the good of man." [25] In the eighth century A.D., a Sufi mystical writer distinguishes between "two loves, love of my happiness, and perfect love, to love Thee as is thy due." [26]

The same notion of a contrast between an imperfect, still self-centered, loving response to God and a purer, more fully self-giving one is reflected in the distinction made in medieval Latin Catholicism. Traditionally, *attritio*, a penitent's sorrow for his sins on account of the infinite misery they will bring him, is contrasted with *contritio*, sorrow for them because they displease God whom he so dearly loves. In many religions, then, appears the notion that the relationship to be developed between God and his people (later also God and the individual) is one to which the relationship of human love is analogous. We have seen, in an earlier chapter, how deeply that notion is entrenched in mystical literature.

Behind what is expressed in the analogy of love, however, is a metaphysical assertion about God. At the heart of the universe, Being outpours itself in such a way that human acts of love provide our best analogy. Yet the analogy holds in some degree even in the least spiritualized forms of love. The Greeks saw that even in erotic love, the kind of love they called *erōs*, were elements that provided ground for such an analogy—notably the elements of longing wonderment and what has been already called, earlier in this section, debonair joy. That insight is much impoverished in our own day, when a revolution in sexual attitudes has been accompanied by a general tendency toward obsessive attitudes about sex—including, for instance, emphases on techniques and unrealistic expectations—which smother and even destroy the elements that make erotic love a reflection of that which is at the heart of all things.

[25] Yi-pao Mei, *Motse, the Neglected Rival of Confucius* (London: Probsthain, 1929), p. 145.
[26] Cited by H. A. R. Gibb, *Mohammedanism* (New York: Mentor Books, 1955), p. 103; attributed to R. A. Nicholson, *Literary History of the Arabs*, 2nd ed. (Cambridge: At the University Press, 1969), p. 234.

The term *erōs* does not occur in the New Testament, which uses *philia* for the love that is found between two friends, and *agapē* (which occurs infrequently in profane Greek literature) to designate the Christian concept of love. Jesus presents *agapē* as the love we are enjoined to have for our neighbor as well as for God. Our neighbor includes our enemy, and the reason for this is peculiarly important. Though the two kinds of love (of God and of neighbor) are presented equally when they appear under the guise of duties (the guise proper to the Law, the Torah, from which Jesus is quoting),[27] our love of neighbor depends wholly on our love of God and therefore must be wholly independent of our neighbor's conduct. We are reminded that the sun rises on the evil as well as on the good; the rain falls on both the unjust and the just.[28]

To see that God provides the whole course of Nature irrespective of our conduct is to see that we are not to discriminate in our *agapē* between those whom we account our enemies and those whom we call our friends, for by doing so we should be acting as though the source of *agapē* were in humanity. If the source were to be found in humanity—where indeed, of course, modern exponents of so-called scientific humanism locate it—the distinction between friends and enemies would make sense, since we could claim to find in our friends a focus for *agapē* that we cannot find in our enemies. If, however, the source is in God, the distinction makes no sense at all. It would be like discriminating between the sun as shining on the river and the sun as gilding the muddy pool. Love of friends by itself is insufficient, not merely because it does not go far enough, but because it has failed to identify the source of love. "Even the publicans" love those who love them,[29] but that love is not enough because they mistakenly identify those who love them with the source of the love. Jesus required his disciples to see the *agapē* that appears in human relationships as issuing primordially from God.

There is, however, another pitfall, a recognition of which also provides us with a clue to the nature of the metaphysical assertion that is being made about divine love. Having recognized that the source of the love we find in our friends and must learn to discern in our enemies lies beyond both our enemies and our friends, we might well be tempted to ignore both and never to seek anything but the highest, the *summum bonum*, which is God. As a Cambridge scientist notes:

> The injunction to love the highest, while fundamental, is a bleak, bare and in its way partial, statement of what the Christian religion is about. Adhering to this alone can easily lead, in those who are but little aware of the hidden motives and complexities of their own nature, to a self-centered and priggish

[27] Matthew 22:34–40; Mark 12:28–34; Luke 10:25–28, Cf. Deut. 6:5; Lev. 19:18.
[28] Matthew 5:45. Cf. Seneca, *De Beneficiis,* bk. 3, sec. 25: The sun shines even on the wicked.
[29] Matthew 5:47.

care for one's own soul, a belief in the desirability of "nurturing one's spiritual resources" (to quote a horrible phrase recently much in use in certain religious quarters), which is stultifying to one's spiritual growth and alienating to one's fellows.[30]

By contrast (here he paraphrases H. A. Williams), "the process of growing up into self-awareness, recognizing our fears and guilt over what is buried within us for what it is, results in a maturity from which flow all the highest achievements of human life; of which the greatest is the capacity to give oneself away in love. And self-effacing love, risking the loss of our all, so it sometimes seems of our very soul, is the very core of the teaching of Christ." [31]

That is well said, and in so specifically Christian an understanding of the working of the love of God, the author's detection of "an awareness, often subconscious, which is the power behind the scientific conscience and scientific unselfishness," [32] suggests the close connection we have noted earlier between the scientific quest for truth and the deeply religious man's love of God.

As the scientist, even while holding up the ideal of scientific truth, pursues it not in an idle, passive admiration of Nature but through the industrious exploration of scientific phenomena, so the genuinely religious man sees God through the diligent exploration of the workings of God's love in human situations. That is only to say, however, that one no more tries to look directly at God to understand the manifold power of his creative love than one would look directly at the sun instead of at the sunlit dunghills and muddy pools and shining rivers to grasp the nature of sunlight.

If we ask, however, for the psychological ancestry of any kind of love that has surpassed the erotic stage, we find the immediate ancestor is gratitude of one kind or another. Jesus perceived this psychological truth in teaching, as he did, that the love of God is attained through gratitude for "the forgiveness of sins." Such is his message in, for example, the story of the harlot who anointed his feet with precious ointment: what a great sense of forgiveness she must have had in order to love as she did! [33] The self-righteousness he deplored in some of his hearers is a barrier to love because it has already diminished, if it has not killed, the spirit of thankfulness out of which only can love spring. The condition of *agapē* is absent to the extent that gratitude for life itself is impoverished.

[30] W. H. Thorpe, *Science, Man and Morals* (Ithaca, N. Y.: Cornell University Press, 1966), p. 139.
[31] Ibid.
[32] Ibid., pp. 139 f.
[33] Luke 7:47. Traditional renderings of the text tend to obscure the original intent of the Greek, which in context suggests what has been said above—that the woman's extraordinary exhibition of love shows her sense of a great forgiveness. Paul Tillich brings this point out well in *The New Being* (Charles Scribner's Sons, 1955), pp. 3–14.

Agapē and Openness to Being

When we ask why *agapē* is commended to us as superior to every other kind of love, conventional explanations tend to misguide us. Preachers sometimes say, for instance, that the difference between *erōs* and *agapē* may be understood through the distinction we make when we say, for instance, "I can't abide red-haired people, so I cannot say I like John Smith, who has a flaming red head and beard. But I can still love him as I love all human beings, and that is surely more important than merely liking him." Such a distinction suggests that the superiority of *agapē* lies in its being more universalized and objective, less personal and subjective. That cannot be the way to draw the distinction, for if it were, the more impersonal and detached the love, the better it would be—which would ill accord with what the great religions teach and would be conspicuously antithetical to every Christian tradition and destructive of all Christian life.

There is nothing more rarefied or more elevated about *agapē* than about *philia* or *erōs*. On the contrary, *agapē* expresses itself in situations that are as earthy as any other. According to Christian orthodoxy, the paradigmatic case is the Incarnation, which entailed the earthiness of a lowly human birth and the agony and shame of a criminal's death. Whatever the distinction between *agapē* and other concepts of love, we must look for it elsewhere.

What St. Paul acclaims in his paean in praise of *agapē* provides a hint.[34] Faith and hope are great marks of the Christian life; yet *agapē* is so much better that without it faith and hope would be nothing. *Agapē* is infinitely generous, so it manifests itself in great patience. It keeps no scores, harbors no grudges, never gloats; but above all it *never measures itself.* Limits or boundaries are utterly alien to it; it does not know what they are. To say, as St. Paul does, that *agapē* never fails, or never comes to an end, is to say it knows no limits. It always faces everything. As we might say colloquially today, it never "cops out." In all these predications we have pointers to the power of *agapē* in attaining openness.

No definition of love in terms of union is adequate. It is too egocentric even for authentic human love, which always transcends mere union. The partners are not merely united in a two-togetherness. The authenticity of human love may be tested, indeed, by the extent to which it surpasses such two-togetherness and opens up into a disclosure of Being. Writers on human love with viewpoints as diverse as those of Dietrich Bonhoeffer, Karl Jaspers, Gabriel Marcel, Erich Fromm, Abraham Maslow, and Alan Watts all attest, each in his own way, that human love to be genuine must have such an element in it. Otherwise the two partners are still separate, isolated in their respective egocentricities. The attempt to unite the other person to oneself or oneself to the other person cannot issue in agapistic love. As we saw earlier when discussing the notion of the "third being" in human I–Thou

---

[34] 1 Corinthians 13.

relationships, there is in human love neither merely a one-way nor even merely a two-way traffic but always an opening out beyond the two partners. Any love that lacks this element is only a pact to engage together in self-love.

Whatever may be thought of the official Roman Catholic stance on birth control and kindred issues in sexual ethics and however vulnerable to criticism that stance may be for the legalism, arbitrariness, and other shortcomings frequently alleged against it, it does express a recognition, distorted as many take it to be, of the nature of authentic human love. As soon as love is reduced to nothing more than a performance under a contract, long or short, for mutual enjoyment, the path to authentic love is closed. What conservative opinion in the Roman Catholic Church sees, obscurely or no, is the great truth that genuine love always opens itself to and seeks to engage the whole of Being. Such human love is very closely allied to the love of God, while self-love is the enemy of both. The enmity, far from being diminished by the cooperation of a partner, is thereby reinforced. Agapistic love, however, conjugal or amical, opens out the whole person to God in such a way as is expressed in liturgical sacrifice when the worshippers seek to be united with all other beings—including their beloved on both sides of the veil of death and even such higher orders of being as may exist (in the antique language of the liturgy, "angels and archangels and all the company of heaven")—in openness to God.

The Cognitive Element in *Agapē*

The writer to the Philippians prays that his readers' *agapē* may grow richer in "knowledge and insight." [35] The association of love with knowledge is very ancient and widespread. In the Bible and elsewhere in ancient literature, copulation is often called "knowing." [36] So we read that Jephthah's daughter "had never known a man," [37] which means simply that she was a virgin. The use of the term was not necessarily euphemistic like our "making love." Classical Hebrew had no word corresponding to our "mind" or "intellect." To us who are accustomed to distinguishing the knowledge that $3^3 = 27$ from the intellectual belief that it is raining in Valparaiso, the biblical use of "know" seems imprecise. For the biblical writers, "knowing" is primarily experiencing, feeling, entering into possession of an object. The same verb is used for knowing an art or a craft. The same root, moreover, is used in the affirmation that "out of the mouth of the Lord comes knowledge and understanding." [38]

I use "knowing" in that more general biblical sense if I say, "I *know* England." My claim would not be refuted by your discovering that I did

[35] Philippians 1:9–10 (N.E.B.). The King James Version has "knowledge and judgment." The Greek is *en epignōsei kai pasē aisthēsei.*
[36] E.g., Genesis 4:1, 4:17, 4:25; Numbers 31:18, 31:35; and Judges 21:12.
[37] Judges 11:39.
[38] Proverbs 2:6.

not know where Clitheroe is, a village in Lancashire. I could know England better than any other man alive and still not know Clitheroe. I might know England far better than most people even if I were not quite sure precisely where Manchester lies or what exactly is the course of the Severn. "Knowing England" in the sense intended has only an incidental connection with a particular knowledge of geographical details. If I say that I know England I mean that I have so much experience of living in England that I understand English ways, English institutions, and English prejudices so intimately that I can feel immediately at home and would be an infinitely better guide to visitors there than any geographer or political scientist as such.

Such knowledge is inseparable from my love of England. Yet my loving England does not mean that I might not feel at times inclined to punch an Englishman in the nose or even to blow up Darlington. It does mean that I am so attuned to England that my love for that country is not a mere subjective emotion such as I might have for Mallorca or Corfu; nor is it a nostalgia such as I might have for my home town; nor yet again is it a mere happy acceptance such as I may have for my place of work.

It would be nearer to what Heidegger calls *Befindlichkeit*, an ontological dis-position.[39] It means I am attuned to England in such a way as to point to the primordial mood by which I can so love all things as "to let them be." In loving England I accept the whole course of England's nature, "warts and all." Such a love is inseparable from ethical responsibility and makes me a far more dependable inhabitant of the country than could any pledge of allegiance or declaration of loyal citizenship, however sincere. It is also inseparable from the special kind of knowledge we have just been considering, in which I am ready to embrace Being.

All acts of knowing presuppose the breakdown of an obstacle to knowledge. My ignorance of the fact that a letter has been placed on my desk was till now an obstacle to the knowledge I now have of it. We properly speak of having a psychological "block" to German or mathematics. I can know what a too rapid speaker is saying only as soon as I overcome the obstacle of my inability to follow his delivery. If the obstacle to my knowledge of God is the self-closing-ness of thought that we have already treated (the most formidable of all obstacles), *agapē* is the only means of overcoming it.

The act of cognition that *agapē* provides has prototypes in comparatively commonplace experiences. If Freud's account of the emergence of infantile consciousness is at all near the mark, we might find a prototype of *agapē* in the "dual unity" of the mother-child relationship in infantile experience before emancipation from the mother closes the child within its separatist thought. Not only is that early mode of consciousness all but completely forgotten; even if some dim memory of it be carried on in our subconscious

[39] Martin Heidegger, *What Is Philosophy?*, trans. W. Kluback and J. T. Wilde (New York: Twayne, 1958), p. 77.

mind, we are likely to be instinctively inclined to denigrate it because of the extremely limited scope of the only experience we then had of such a mode of consciousness as compared with the vigor and efficiency of our later mental life. If that were the case it would help to explain why we so strongly tend to set love and knowledge in opposition to each other. Be that as it may, agapistic love as it operates in Christian life is an unintelligible concept apart from its cognitive aspect. It confers an extraordinary, unique grasp of Being. The girl who gives a kidney to save her sister's life and even the astonished and heartbroken father who walks out in the middle of the night to bail his son out of jail are not simply performing benevolent or compassionate acts. What they have done is not just a moral happening. Through their love they have uniquely grasped Being. They have entered into a knowledge of God, by reason of which they will never be the same again. To dramatize the situation we might say they opened up to the knowledge of God as rosebuds bloom, open up, and become roses.

Breaking the Barriers to Being

We began this study with questions about the nature of religion. We found religion very multifaceted indeed, having social, institutional, metaphysical, mystical, and ethical elements in it. We may now ask the question all over again: in what does the religious attitude fundamentally consist? We might now answer simply: openness to Being.

Throughout the course of our explorations I have insisted that there is a cognitive element in religion; that is, when religion lacks that element it lacks what gives it life. Lively religion always purports, explicitly or otherwise, to put us in the way of "knowing God." We have found, however, that "knowledge of God" is a highly ambiguous concept. Nothing is more characteristic of the religious consciousness than agnosticism of an especially profound kind—that is, the agnosticism that accompanies recognition of the force of Tersteegen's remark that a comprehended God is no God at all. The religious consciousness does not expect to understand God; nevertheless, no less characteristically it claims to know God. Whatever the knowledge is, it is not analytic. So the quest for logical proofs is mistaken, not to say jejune. The knowledge of God is more like the knowledge we have of the empirical world through observation and scientific inquiry; yet is it not that kind of knowlege either.

We can best grasp what knowledge of God is by asking what stands in the way of it. We have found that thought, which is an indispensable cognitive tool, is also an obstacle, blocking us off from Being. As common experience shows us, to the extent that in our relation to other people we are deprived of reason, we are given over to passion and prejudice, even to the point of our refusal to admit that a certain person exists. From the remark "For me he does not exist" to the assertion "He does not exist" is a short step. Yet we can also obscure from us even our own dearest friends. I may be "standing in my own light," so that when I look at my friend I am obscuring from myself what he really is. I am preventing his disclosure of himself from getting across to me.

The religious consciousness is nothing if not an awareness of letting in, yet shutting out, the light that discloses Being. Even as I insist on making religious truth-claims, I am conscious that in the very act of making them I am blocking off the divine disclosure. That is, I am aware that while I must make these truth-claims, my attitude ceases to be characteristically religious when I make them. No attitude is so characteristically religious as is openness to Being. If there be any injunctions in religion that more clearly than any other express what religion is, apart from ethical or institutional or social or mystical elements in it, they are such as "Hear the Word of the Lord" and "Let all the earth keep silence before Him."

In the intellectual exercises that people must perform in "working at" their religion, they are in danger of "overkill." To tend the soil effectively we must learn something about agriculture and we must also engage in backbreaking work, but the more we see the benefits that accrue to such efforts, and so diligently cultivate the soil, the more we are prone to forget to let Nature act. Nature, when she acts, reveals to us precisely that which complements and fulfills our own efforts to understand her. The gardener who has a "green thumb" is the one who, while he does not for a moment neglect his work, has learned the most difficult of all agricultural lessons—how to get out of the way and let Nature take over. God likewise discloses himself to us freely, as we can discover as soon as we get out of the way.

Norman Malcolm relates that one of Wittgenstein's favorite English phrases, which he delivered "with a most emphatic intonation and mock solemnity of expression" was "Leave the bloody thing alone." [40] For instance, after he had been helping Malcolm to repair a toilet and the repair had been completed, Malcolm's proposal to make one further adjustment elicited from Wittgenstein the use of that phrase.[41] The profound truth underlying the use of a seemingly vulgar colloquialism is not merely that things work better when we do not tinker unnecessarily with them; it is that we learn more about their nature when we let them be. If this be true of anything so purely mechanical as a toilet, it is likely to be much more vividly true of human beings themselves. In a superlative degree, then, it is true of Being, which is ever disclosing its nature to us, whether we get in the way of the disclosure or not.

We have seen, moreover, that *agapē* is presented as an instrument of openness, breaking down the barriers erected against it. *Agapē* has the function of letting us escape from the prison of our thoughts without diminishing

[40] Norman Malcolm, *Ludwig Wittgenstein: A Memoir.* (London: Oxford University Press, 1958), pp. 85 f.
[41] Ibid., p. 86.

their cognitive power. It quiets the noise of the uncreative, static discharge we set up between ourselves and the disclosure of Being. Because *agapē* is characteristically self-emptying, self-renouncing, abstemious in the use of even its own life-giving power, the exercise of it accustoms us to be unastonished at, if not to expect, asceticism on a cosmic scale. If *agapē* proves to be such a cognitive instrument, it does so by virtue of its leading us to whatever there may be in Being that is knowable. Only in such a sense could the concept of "knowledge of God" become intelligible.

We must be careful to notice that such agapistic knowledge, whatever it may be, is not by any means necessarily or even typically mystical. Mystical experience, as we have seen, comes in many guises, but it always presupposes some kind of union between the mystic and God. The knowledge that comes from openness to Being by no means implies any such mystical union. To admit the possibility of such mystical experience is to admit that agapistic love can issue in such mystical union, but we need not bring mystical experience into question at all. If to the knowledge that comes from openness to Being we were to affix a theological label, the one to attach would be from the Christian doctrine of the Third Person of the Trinity.

According to that doctrine as traditionally developed, the infusion of the Holy Spirit on the Church at Pentecost brought *wisdom* to the apostles, and eventually to all believers. It does not unite them to God in mystical union. They still walk in faith, but the curtain against knowledge of God is drawn aside. The only unforgivable sin is the sin against the Holy Spirit, and it is unforgivable only because it blocks out the *agapē* that brings forgiveness. The believer, living "in the Spirit" (a favorite phrase of Paul's) is no longer insulated from God. No longer diabolically lured into preoccupation with the trivia that deflect him from openness to God, he is so filled with the life-giving power of the Spirit that he can experientially grasp the Being of God as he could never do by any kind of reasoning or thought. From the earliest times, however, the danger of mistaking demonic operations for those of the Holy Spirit was well recognized. Emotionalism bereft of thought has always been for this very reason suspect. *Agapē* needs thought as its ground. What transcends thought, making possible openness to Being, is the polarity between *agapē* and thought.

What does it mean to talk of agapistic knowledge? By what operation of the mind does it work? What are the criteria of meaning, of verification and falsification? In trying to answer these questions we may best begin by looking first at the operations that lead to other kinds of knowledge. Mathematical knowledge, for instance, is attained through elaborate processes of abstraction and deduction. Empirical knowledge, such as it is, and though it may be better accounted belief, could never be attained in that way. It is attained only through observation, and that is plainly a kind of openness to what has been called in our study the Nature-dimension. The attainment of scientific knowledge requires, besides that openness, both inductive and deductive procedures. But for scientific discovery, as we have seen, openness is the decisive factor, the factor that makes the difference between nondiscovery and discovery. Successful scientific discovery requires to an extraordinary degree the absence of intellectual prejudice.

One naturally asks how one attains that extremely rare condition. What talent or gift does a scientist need to become a discoverer? There is, however, no possible answer, for it is really a nonquestion, like asking, "How do I become an Einstein or a Planck?" The condition is not the possession of a rare quality or gift but, rather, the divesting oneself of a vast number of intellectual possessions. It is an ascesis of the mind.

From such reflections we may go on to say that our difficulty in attaining agapistic knowledge comes from our intellectual possessions that cause us to stand in our own light. There is no further quality or possession that will lead us to agapistic knowledge. What is needed is, rather, the self-emptying of the intellectual possessions that stand in our way, *without losing* the intellectual gifts, talents, and possessions that are indispensable to the cognitive act. Openness to Being, then, consists in divesting ourselves of intellectual *impediments*. It is a mental humbling, bearing an analogy to the Humbling of God that is theologically expressed in the traditional doctrine of the Incarnation, which Christians proclaim as the central verity of their faith.

The experience of men of faith, notably but by no means only those of the Christian Way, is that all the exercises their religion enjoins them to perform and all the theologizing that their minds lead them to engage in are useless except to the extent that these performances enable them to disenable themselves, so filling them with power that empowers them to renounce their power. In the unconscious magnanimity that is a concomitant of such renunciation, the mind is at last put in the position of "seeing" the Spirit at work. Looking at a community that is in search of that experience while standing in its own light provides, by comparison, the best way of seeing what the action of the Spirit is, and of showing that, whatever it is, it does not issue from humanity. It comes, rather, from the outpouring of Being itself, whose *agapē* would outpour itself on all creation even if humanity had destroyed itself to the last victim of its technological suicide.

Creative Self-Limiting Ascesis

"Already before the Passion," writes Simone Weil in her characteristic style, "already by the Creation, God empties himself of his divinity, abases himself, takes the form of a slave." [42] In that proposal lies the clue we need for answering the age-old *unde malum* question in such a way as to provide, through a new perspective on an ancient theological insight, a more credible doctrine of God and a better understanding of the nature of religion.

[42] Simone Weil, "New York Notebook," in *First and Last Notebooks*, trans. R. Rees (New York: Oxford University Press, 1970), p. 70.

All the great religions of the world teach, in one way or another, ascesis. The term, as traditionally understood, is ambiguous. It comes from the Greek, *askēsis*, exercise, and *askeō*, I strive, in the sense of working hard as an athlete works to win a trophy. This verb occurs only once in the New Testament,[43] where the Christian life is compared to the games, in preparation for which every athlete who competes is "temperate in all things." As we would say, he keeps himself "in training." The notion of ascesis was already present in Jewish antiquity, especially in the Wisdom literature of the Septuagint. In the Christian tradition the key text on the subject has generally been taken to be the one in which Jesus says that anyone who wants to be his disciple must take up his cross and follow him.[44] In this warning Christians traditionally have seen a positive side, enjoining hard work (striving) and a negative one (self-denial).

The distinction, by introducing a negative conception of self-denial, has had the unfortunate effect of causing widespread misunderstanding. In the religions of the Orient, not least Hinduism and Buddhism, ascetic practices have often taken very extreme forms. The Christian Fathers took over from the Stoics the idea of ascesis as a way of purifying the soul from its passions and so preparing it for the contemplative love of God. Monasticism, both in the East and in the West, encouraged the use of ascetic exercises to bring about the mortification of the senses. So fastings, abstinences from meat, barefoot pilgrimages, hairshirts, and even whips and other austerities were accounted suitable weapons for the war against the flesh.

Even when the spiritual combat was seen less in terms of a mind–matter dualism, self-denial was commonly presented only as a rooting out of unwanted elements in the soul (such as human affections and human pride), the cleansing of the soul to ready it for better things. In Protestantism, the Puritans, as is well known, produced their own form of asceticism, banning almost all recreational pursuits as ministering to the carnal side of man. In Catholic practice theologians have often pointed out that ascetic exercises are instrumental only and should not be taken as ends in themselves. Nevertheless, the basis of asceticism has too often been seen in a misleadingly negative guise, echoing an old Gnostic mind–matter dualism.

What has been obscured in the ascetic tradition and is further obscured in the inevitably violent reactions against so negative and life-destroying an interpretation of ascesis, is a central datum of creative experience. By obscuring that datum the nature of divine Being itself is obscured. Ascesis is more—not less—important than it appears in popular misrepresentation.

It is also infinitely more life-giving and creative. Self-denial, self-abnegation, self-emptying, and self-restraint do not consist merely in the crushing and subduing of refractory elements in human nature in hope of raising it to a higher order of being in which such restraints will no longer have

[43] 1 Corinthians 9:25.
[44] Mark 8:34.

any place. If self-restraint has a place at all (and I believe its place is central in all authentic religion), it has it precisely because *in the exercise of it* we enter into the activity of a higher order of being. That is, the raison d'être of self-limitation is not that something is taken away from us so that we may be better fitted to approach God unencumbered by our natural propensities; it is, rather, that in our ascetic life we are mimicking or reflecting or participating more closely in divine Being, whose very nature is to create through self-limitation of his infinite power.

Through the removal of the concept of self-limitation from the concept of Being, the positive significance of the tradition of ascesis has been obscured and sometimes all but lost. Self-denial then appears as a denial of life, and self-restraint as a masochistic diminishment of the full splendor of human personality. Humility appears as fit only for a Uriah Heep, and chastity is ridiculed as at best a neurotic perversion and at worst an outrage and an affront against human rights. On the contrary, humility, chastity, and other forms of self-limitation and self-restraint belong to the creativity of Being itself. Without them we are stunted and doomed to extinction, because to exert our powers to the utmost, to squeeze as much as possible out of them and out of life, is to destroy our being, not to fulfill it. Human chastity and humility can be at most but analogues, of course, of the chastity and humility of divine Being. But in them alone can we have any notion at all of what divine Being is and is not.

The widespread contemporary concern over ecology exhibits only a partial understanding of what is at issue here. To see the destructiveness inherent in the prodigal waste of our material resources and the possibility of the physical annihilation of the human race through disregard for our planetary or space environment is to see only a peripheral effect of a more deep-seated prodigality. This more deep-seated prodigality arises from the wanton exercise of our *personal*, individual powers. At this fundamental level we squander not material resources like air and vegetation but the very principle of our existence, our participation in Being itself.

Professor Lynn White glimpses the underlying issue here when, in presenting Francis of Assisi as a sort of patron saint of ecology, he remarks that the "key to an understanding of Francis is his belief in the virtue of humility—not merely for the individual but for man as a species. . . . His view of nature and of man rested on a unique sort of pan-psychism of all things animate and inanimate, designed for the glorification of their transcendent Creator, who, in the ultimate gesture of cosmic humility, assumed flesh, lay helpless in a manger, and hung dying on a scaffold." [45] The "Poor Man of Assisi" does indeed present the issue in a dramatically winsome fashion, but the greatest sages and prophets of all the major religions of the world have seen it, each in his own way, and have expressed it in

[45] Lynn White in *The Environmental Handbook*, ed. Garret DeBell (New York: Ballantine, 1970), p. 24.

their universal condemnation of pride, lasciviousness, and greed. The ascetic tradition present in all creative religion, though it sometimes degenerates into ritualistic legalism, reflects a vision of the same basic principle of the self-limitation (*kenosis*) of Being.

In the two following concluding sections I shall present a possible interpretation of the way in which we might in some measure understand better than we can in traditional conceptualizations, the workings of the divine economy. There are, of course, many alternatives. I claim only that the interpretation I shall offer has advantages for those who, having been in any degree persuaded by the considerations advanced in this book, are disposed to take seriously the kind of openness of mind which, more especially in Part 2, I have commended to my readers. I hope, therefore, that all will find the following kenotic proposal worthy of philosophical critique and that some may find in it an illuminating disclosure of what lies at the heart of the phenomena of religion.[46]

Ascesis, Cosmos, and *Agapē*

Ascesis, when more fully apprehended, is seen to exhibit the nature of love. As soon as ascesis ceases to be taken as a burden, a goad, or a chastisement for refractory children and comes to be viewed as having affinity with the kenotic principle of Being itself, the meaning of the "God-is-love" assertion can be clarified. For then we are enabled to see that love, far from being an emotional departure from, or protest against, the orderly and the rational, is the kenotic principle behind them. *Cosmos* and *logos* derive their meaning from *agapē*. When love degenerates into enjoyment it becomes eventually an instrument of destruction, dethroning at the same time order and reason which, being aspects of love, are quickly devitalized without it. That is why thought without openness to Being is self-ensnaring. Yet though our intellect can trap and close us off from Being, the exercise of our will in wantonly spending all the powers at our command is fraught with even more deadly consequences—namely, that we go on expending ourselves uncreatively till we are entirely dissipated, ontologically bankrupt.

Such spiritual extravagance is what people who use the language of Christian theology call sin. The classical sixteenth-century Reformers, both Lutheran and Calvinist, accounted concupiscence, which may be identified with the inordinate desire for aggrandisement, possession, and self-expansion, fundamentally sinful. The Jansenists took a similar view. The notion that concupiscence is the root of all evil, is, of course, far more ancient than

---

[46] In a paper on the Kenosis in Christian theology (*Anglican Theological Review* 45 [January 1963]: 73–83), I have already tentatively suggested that *all* divine self-revelation would have to be kenotic: "No communication or intimation of God to man is possible without divine self-humiliation of some sort" (p. 81).

the Reformers. Under the guise of the love of money, it was deplored in the fourth century B.C. by Diogenes[47] and is specified in the New Testament as the root of all evil[48]—an assertion echoed by many, including Chaucer.[49]

Nevertheless, in Catholic theology concupiscence has generally been accounted a consequence of Original Sin rather than sin itself. Pride, the first of the seven "capital" or "deadly" sins enumerated in the Middle Ages, has been traditionally identified with the sin of Lucifer, which has been taken to be the archetype of all sin. According to the ancient myth, Lucifer, the highest of the angels, rebelled against God, was hurled from heaven, and became the leader of the forces of destruction, being identified with Apollyon, the Destroyer.[50] Lucifer is depicted, in contrast to God, as the hate-filled self-expansionist *par excellence*. By his aggressive strategy and tactics he hopes to outdo God, but according to the biblical view he cannot succeed. Traditionally, the reason he cannot succeed is not specified, except in general terms to the effect that, as both St. Paul and Vergil knew, love conquers all things.[51] The reason it conquers all things is inextricably bound up with what lies behind Dante's discernment that it is "terrible in aspect."

The reason is that creative Being, in contradistinction to the self-aggrandizing, self-expansionist proclivities of the forces of destruction, is creative *because* it is infinitely self-emptying. The cosmic ascesis in the divine economy is the principle of creative Being itself. We participate in its creative success to the extent that we practice self-restraint in the expenditure of our personal powers, a practice that might almost be called spiritual thriftiness. By the same token, to the extent that we try to grab existence as an object, squeezing life to its dregs, we participate in Apollyon's inevitable and eternal failure. Ascesis so understood is inseparable from *agapē*.

Ascetic theology and mystical theology are traditionally distinguished: the first has been accounted the study of the spiritual life in so far as that life is accessible to human effort assisted by divine grace; the second has been understood as the study of the spiritual life in so far as that life is dependent on the operation of divine grace. A theological dispute on the relation between them may throw light on the matter now before us. The ascetic life has been usually understood as having three stages or degrees—the purgative, illuminative, and unitive stages. Some have understood the highest—that is, the unitive stage—to belong more properly to mystical theology. These regard mystical union as the normal, even though not necessarily the most frequent, outcome of the ascetic life. Others, wishing to make a rigorous separation of the ascetic life and the mystical life, have insisted on keeping the unitive stage as part of the subject matter of ascetic theology.

[47] See Diogenes Laertius, *Diogenes*, bk. 6, sec. 50.
[48] 1 Timothy 6:10.
[49] Chaucer, *The Pardoner's Tale* (Prologue).
[50] Rev. 9:11. *Apollyon* comes from the Greek verb *olluō*, I destroy.
[51] Cf. 1 Corinthians 13 and Vergil, *Eclogues* 2, line 68: "omnia vincit amor."

The dispute is, I believe, artificial, arising out of the tendency to see the ascetic life in a negative way, and a failure to recognize that ascesis is at the heart of creative Being, whence only, of course, issues the possibility of the mystical union with which mystical theology is concerned. When ascesis is seen, not as a feeble human attempt at spirituality, but as descriptive of Being itself, the traditional distinction between two kinds of theology, though it does not disappear, greatly diminishes in significance, becoming, rather, a question of difference of methodology in the conduct of the interior life. For no longer is the ascetic life to be seen as human effort contradistinguished from the outpouring of divine love that the mystical life is traditionally taken to be. *Both* may now be so identified, because while every such ascesis must be seen as a participation in the action of divine *agapē*, all *agapē* (*par excellence* that of divine Being, its source) must be seen as ascesis.

Agapē, when so understood, loses much of the vagueness commonly associated with it. It is the principle of creativity in Being itself, and that principle is ascetic, in the sense that it is eternally kenotic, self-limiting. Being limits itself through the *cosmos* and *logos* that flow from its kenotic, self-emptying activity. Being limits itself also through its omnibenevolent and omnigenerous will to bestow freedom on all that it creates. Such is the divine ascesis that there are no strings, no hooks, no conditions to the freedom it bestows. It reserves nothing to itself.

An implication of this view is that creation *must* be evolutionary in the sense that everything that Being creates must struggle to enter into the fullness of its potentialities, presumably over the course of trillions of years as measured in our temporal reckoning. It means also that our development cannot be achieved without our participating in the Kenosis, the self-emptying of God, for that is the principle of Being itself. To be able so to participate is what it means to be free; that is, we are free to the extent that we learn to participate in the divine Kenosis, the self-emptying. It does not mean, of course, that we create ourselves, for without the divine self-limiting that lies behind us and upon which we wholly depend, we could not be at all.

Our freedom gives us, however, at every moment a choice—either to expend all we are by exerting our powers, whatever they are, to the utmost, which is Apollyon's way, the way of annihilation; or, by the practice of ascesis, to continue to foster the creative process. If we choose the way of prodigality, we do so without hindrance, for Being as here conceived is so creative that any such program of hindrance would be contrary to the divine economy. To the extent, however, that we choose the kenotic way, the way of self-limitation, of self-restraint, we are assured of abundant succor for our enterprise, for in our act of ascesis we are "doing," in our own finite mode, the *agapē* on which all our "doing" depends.

The order we discover in Nature may be regarded, then, as the dark side of God, the side that is shrunken, so to speak, through the creative withdrawal of the outpouring of the divine *agapē*. Yet Nature, being *kosmia*, orderly, patterned, exhibits vestiges of her origin in divine Being. That is why she is partly explorable and partly inscrutable. She might even be considered in relation to God as is a still to a moving picture, since for all her process and flux she is, in contrast to the outflowing movement of the divine *agapē*, agapistically static. "The heavens tell out the glory of God" only as a still tells out the motion picture. Such a view precludes pantheism, of course. It also makes panentheism unnecessary: all creatures are in Nature; they are not and never could be "in God." Yet to the extent that, through the exercise of their freedom in the appropriation of *agapē*, they triumphed over their *agapē*-denuded environment, they might be taken up into the divine orbit. Such a prospect, however conceptualized, would come close to the traditional Christian eschatology, except, of course, that it provides no room for a traditional concept of hell. Instead, those who failed would be victims of a principle of entropy and so be extinguished. Extinction would be the inevitable consequence of their unrestrained use of their freedom and the resultant ontological bankruptcy.

Providence and Freedom

The concept of divine providence is viewed with suspicion by many, who see it as introducing an arbitrary element in the divine will, favoring some at the expense of others. The objection is particularly strong when the very difficult concept of election and the still more perplexing topic of predestination are discussed. Predestination should be seen as a special development, presented as a metaphysical corollary of the concept of providence. It plays a particularly important part in certain traditions of religious thought. Islam, for example, makes much of it. Indeed, if Muslim theology could be shorn of this concept, the whole character of the religion of Muhammad would be radically changed.

In the Christian tradition many people associate the notion with Calvin, whose particular version of it is indeed striking; but it is as inseparable from the Catholic tradition as it is from the thought of the Reformers. Thomas Aquinas teaches it no less definitely and unreservedly than does Calvin. One reason that many people have associated it less with St. Thomas is that he introduced it on a metaphysical level in the course of his treatment of the doctrine of God, so that it was kept in the background of Thomist thought and has played little part in popular Catholic preaching. Calvin, by contrast, when he introduced it, treated it as a practical, soteriological question, affecting the whole concept of salvation, so that it was inevitably brought to the forefront of popular preaching in the Reformed tradition. The concept of providence, however, is consonant with all religious thought and is inseparable from that of the Judaeo-Christian heritage.

If Being, having sent forth created beings, left them entirely to their own resources, to make or to mar themselves, to win through or to perish, the arbitrariness of the result would be even more startling. Humanity, left to cope unaided with Nature as she is splendidly depicted, for example, by Paul Elmer More,[52] would survive only temporarily and then only by good chance. More, after describing the beauty of the Severn valley in the heart of England's picturesque countryside, turns his mind back to "the incalculable years" through which the land had passed before it had been rendered fit for its present lush cultivation. Fiery convulsions had tossed up the mountains; water had relentlessly scooped out the river bed and had then retreated, leaving "a fertile champaign."

Under the serene masque, however, was "an army of countless individuals, each driven on by an instinctive lust of life as if engaged in a vast internecine warfare—each blade of grass fighting for its place under the sun and obtaining it by the suppression of some other plant, each animal preying for sustenance upon some other form of life." The peaceful harmony that More now saw in the Severn valley could never have been attained by "the common principle of life," which operated under a system of ruthless, tooth-and-claw, "callous selfishness" that brings about the development not only of an instinct to take every possible advantage of weakness but of a disposition to gloat at the agony of the tortured victim of the hunter. How, out of the astounding cruelty of Nature could the idyllic peace of the Severn valley arise? [53]

How precarious, we may add, is the magnificent civilization that makes possible its tranquillity! Not only is it threatened by fire, flood, famine, tempest, and earthquake, as is all else that is noblest in humanity; its survival is dependent upon a very thin layer of human kindliness and compassion, of human rationality and constructiveness, of human courage and hope. With what mercurial speed these dispositions can evanesce is only too well known to those who have seen, for instance, how the offspring of a generation of gentle, cultured, honest, and humane people in Germany, seemingly fine young men and women, were perverted after a comparatively brief training by the *Schutzstaffel* into monsters of cruelty and deceit. The more we learn to love our fellow men, the frailer we find human virtue and the less ready we are to rely upon it. Though Pope exaggerated when he affirmed that no other animals are as predatory on their own kind as is man, there is no reason to suppose that man exhibits any general tendency to improvement over "tiger fell" and "cruel bear."

[52] More (1864–1937), a prominent man of letters and progenitor of the New Humanism, a critical movement in the twenties and thirties, and twice considered for the Nobel Prize, is still too little known today outside specialist circles. See A. H. Dakin, *Paul Elmer More* (Princeton, N.J.: Princeton University Press, 1960). Also F. X. Duggan, *Paul Elmer More* (New Haven, Conn.: Twayne, 1966).
[53] P. E. More, *The Sceptical Approach to Religion* (Princeton, N.J.: Princeton University Press, 1934), pp. 78 ff.

Men of faith have all been much impressed by such considerations about the natural environment with which they have had to struggle. They have always also discerned, however, another element, which arises in what has been called in this book the God-dimension. The presence of that other element has confronted them in terms of a guiding hand. God acts in history.

A characteristic expression of this discernment is as follows:

Though God sets humankind within a natural environment which, propitious as it may be for the maintenance and propagation of life, is fundamentally indifferent to man, he nevertheless keeps a watchful eye on his children. While Nature is indifferent to my welfare, God is not. The very hairs of my head are all numbered.[54] That providential concern presupposes God's omniscience: not a sparrow falls to the ground without his will.[55] Not one sparrow is forgotten by God.[56] God, though he orders Nature, is never constrained by Nature, which always affords plenty of room, so to speak, for his providential hand. The man of faith, looking back at the history of his life, recognizes that nothing happened in it that could not be explained in naturalistic terms; nevertheless, in the way his life situation has developed, in the turn events have taken at moments crucial for him, he finds a quality that seems to him too striking to be explained away as accident or coincidence.

Many Jews, after the Babylonian exile, which at the time seemed a grievous chastisement, recognized that had there been no exile, the Hebrew people would have become too smug to learn. In the Hebrew Scriptures are several strands of thought on God's providential care at the personal level. There is a basic belief that no individual survives except through the special sustaining power of God. Primitive peoples like the Hebrews were more impressed by the bare fact of personal survival in the hostile environment in which they were set than the average person today in a highly developed society is likely to be—the threat of nuclear destruction notwithstanding. Each invididual was more ready to acknowledge astonishment that he had survived at all. There was also, however, a recognition that the capacities and powers of certain individuals could blossom forth in exceptional ways. The sense of deliverance from the forces of Nature, including the cruelties of angry men, was very strong. "If Yahweh had not been on our side . . . they would have swallowed us alive and burnt us to death in their rage." [57] Above all, God was believed to be at work in the spirits of men.

Christians are deeply affected by a sense of God's guidance. Luther, perhaps in an overdramatic way, spoke of God's having led him "like an old blind horse." The medieval cathedral builders are said to have "built better than they knew," and no mature Christian is without some experience of looking

---

54 Matthew 10:30; Luke 12:7.
55 Matthew 10:29. Cf. *Hamlet*, act 5, sc. 2.
56 Luke 12:6.
57 Psalms 124:1 (Jerusalem Bible).

back at the decisions he has felt obliged to make in life and seeing that these decisions seem to have been really better for him than he knew, or could possibly have known, at the time. The Christian often feels the sense of guidance more conspicuously in unanswered than in answered prayers. He had asked for a special favor. He had felt that if only that favor might be granted to him opportunities would be opened up for him that would change his whole life for the better. Now in retrospect he sees that had his prayer been answered the result would have been calamitous. So he sees God's guiding hand at work in having graciously withheld an answer to his prayer.

Such a man of faith is interpreting everything, of course, in terms of divine providential care. His life is basically happy, and his sense of the assurance of God's care precludes for him the destruction of his assurance by anything that has happened in his own life. The man of faith is fundamentally convinced that his life is more than a "charmed life"; it is directly under the surveillance of God whose watchful eye and guiding hand are ready to save him from any situations that could be *radically* hurtful to him. That there *are* such situations, however, he is in no doubt. He knows what could happen if he were left in the hands of Nature, unaided by God.

A whole Christian philosophy of history has been developed that presupposes providential care on a cosmic scale as well as on an individual level. According to all orthodox Christian understanding of the Incarnation, its whole purpose was the fulfillment of God's providential concern to make possible the salvation of humanity. Indeed, when modern theologians discuss the traditional doctrine of the Virgin Birth, some arguments against it center upon the notion that since God has plenty of room in Nature to exercise his providential activity, the traditional understanding is contrary to what is otherwise known of the divine economy. What is never in question is that God acts in human history.

In this view, God never acts providentially in such a way as to involve the suspension or diminishment of Nature. Neither, however, does God ever in any way undermine the freedom of the individual. From the standpoint of the man of faith, that is why prayer, even the prayer that is mercifully left unanswered, plays so vital a part in the relation between God and man. God does not coerce or cajole or contrive. He does not so load the dice of fortune that the individual cannot lose, but he does "stand at the door and knock," ever ready to come to the aid of those who beseech him in their distress. That some are unmoved to call upon him either in pleasant circumstances or in unpleasant ones is to the man of faith an attestation that God is as honest and patient as he is uncoercive. He does not load the dice, but, rather, "as tenderly as a father treats his children, so Yahweh treats those who fear him." [58]

[58] Psalms 103:13.

God, in the pastoral imagery of the Gospels, is likened to a shepherd who, having a hundred sheep, loses one and goes out into the mountains to search for it till he finds it.[59] The parable, like all parables, is geared to bring out a particular characterization. It brings out the notion that what is unimportant in the Nature-dimension may be infinitely important in the God-dimension. The parable does not attend at all to the problem of freedom and responsibility. Human beings, if their freedom and responsibility were as limited as those of sheep, could not possibly achieve anything like the destiny proposed for them in the New Testament. If the parable were to be taken as attending to the whole situation, we should be left with the notion that man's freedom is limited to an ability to stray slightly from a groove preassigned to him by God.

In contemporary technological terms, a machine could be devised to correct such minuscule aberrancy. For such a function, a providential, caring God would be *de trop*. If God is to be conceived as exercising providential care (and that is at the heart of biblical teaching), he must be conceived as having a much mightier and more delicate task than steering back lost sheep from the wilderness to the fold. Every wise parent or teacher performs more difficult tasks in developing a human personality when, to prevent its destruction, the teacher seeks to avoid, on the one hand, suffocating it and on the other, letting it run to seed.

If we are to envisage God in anything like theistic terms, we must recognize what the eighteenth-century deists so clearly saw—that God must be presumed to leave his creatures, including human beings, to the mercy of an inexorable and indifferent Nature. Yet the postulate of a God-dimension's acting only as, according to a popular ancient cosmology, Atlas supported the earth,. will not do. The universal testimony of the religious consciousness is that into the freedom we enjoy and the responsibility for our self-development it imposes, is introduced an element of divine providence. The man of faith walks in darkness, yet with a light shining ahead of him. He is on his own; yet he is not alone. He is tossed about on a rough sea; yet he knows he can reach his haven if he will. He has every reason to strive; yet he need not fret.

The paradigmatic case of divine providential care, confirming for the believer the assurance he finds as the God-dimension is unfolded in his experience, is the central teaching about the Incarnation—according to which God, by opening up a possibility hitherto closed, makes available a redemptive path. That path, like every path providentially disclosed to created beings, does not interfere with the freedom of the individual. On the contrary, it increases its scope by introducing a new possibility of choice. For where before a path was closed, affording at that point no room for choice, now a path is open and with it a new choice emerges.

[59] Matthew 18:10–14; Luke 15:3–7.

So with every providential engagement of Being. Kenotic Being, in the limitless activity of its self-limiting, ceaselessly pursues created beings with an infinity of agapistic ruses, cosmic and acosmic. The man of faith does not pretend to know, nor could he need to know, whether there is so much entropy in the redemptive process that the number of the victorious is as low as the writer of the Apocalypse suggests,[60] or, as Origen thought, the divine Kenosis continues in pursuit of created beings till even the Devil shall be saved. The man of faith knows only that Being, far from violating the freedom of man's will, graciously encourages its enhancement at every turn. His freedom grows, indeed, with each exercise of his own agapistic ascesis, through which alone he can joyfully appropriate the superabundant power made available to him in the outpouring of the infinite *agapē* of Being.

QUESTIONS ON CHAPTER XIV

1 What do you take to be the central problem in religion? Give reasons.

2 Discuss the principle of isomorphism.

3 Distinguish between scale (picture) models and analogue models.

4 What constitutes a good theological model? To what extent and in what ways are all theological models (a) illuminating and (b) misleading?

5 Discuss the concept of openness with reference to (a) scientific discovery and (b) religious disclosure.

6 Consider *agapē* in relation to (a) cognition, (b) openness to Being, and (c) creativity.

7 Why does openness to Being demand a special methodology and what might be the principles of such a methodology?

8 Critically examine the kenotic proposal presented in the concluding section. (a) In view of all that has been taken into consideration in the course of the book, what services might the proposal perform? (b) What philosophical problems does it raise?

BIBLIOGRAPHICAL SUGGESTIONS

Craik, K. J. W. *The Nature of Explanation.* Cambridge: At the University Press, 1943. Suggests a continuity between the workings of the external world and our perceptual and thinking operations.

[60] Revelation 14:3.

Elsasser, W. M. *Atom and Organism.* Princeton, N.J.: Princeton University Press, 1966. Shows how insusceptible are living structures to conceptualization by our logic of homogeneous classes.

Erickson, S. A. *Language and Being: An Analytic Phenomenology.* New Haven, Conn.: Yale University Press, 1970.

Fichte, J. G. *Science of Knowledge.* Edited by Peter Heath and John Lachs. New York: Appleton-Century-Crofts, 1970. Relevant to the notion of self-limitation. Fichte expounds his concept of the self as immediately self-limiting.

Gorodetzky, Nadejda. *The Humiliated Christ in Modern Russian Thought.* New York: Macmillan Co., 1938. A useful study of the role of the kenotic principle in Orthodox, especially Russian, theology.

Heidegger, Martin. *Poetry, Language and Thought.* Translated by A. Hofstadter. New York: Harper & Row, 1971.

Jones, O. R. *The Concept of Holiness.* London: Allen and Unwin, 1961. Includes a discussion of the relation of holiness and personality.

Langford, Thomas A. "Michael Polanyi and the Task of Theology." *Journal of Religion* 46, 1, 1 (January 1966): 45–55.

Macsey, R., and Donato, E., eds. *The Language of Criticism and the Sciences of Man.* Baltimore, Md.: Johns Hopkins Press, 1970. Papers on the structuralist controversy.

Mascall, Eric. *The Openness of Being.* Gifford Lectures. London: Darton, Longman and Todd, 1971.

McIntyre, John. *On the Love of God.* London: Collins, 1962.

Piaget, Jean. *Insights and Illusions of Philosophy.* Translated by W. Mays. New York: World Publishing Co., 1971. Attacks the notion of a superscientific knowledge.

Piaget, Jean. *Structuralism.* Translated by C. Maschler. New York: Basic Books, 1970.

Polanyi, Michael. *Knowing and Being.* Edited by M. Greene. Chicago: University of Chicago Press, 1967.

Polanyi, Michael. *The Logic of Liberty.* Chicago: University of Chicago Press, 1951.

Soloviev, Vladimir. *The Meaning of Love.* London: Geoffrey Bles, 1945.

Torrance, T. F. *God and Rationality.* London: Oxford University Press, 1971. A contemporary theologian's critique of the detachment of much modern theology from both experience and contemporary scientific inquiry. Takes the view that it is vitiated by mechanistic concepts that are holdovers from outmoded Newtonian science.

Vick, George. "Heidegger's Linguistic Rehabilitation of Parmenides' 'Being.' " *American Philosophical Quarterly* 8 (April 1971): 139–150.

Vycinas, Vincent. *Earth and Gods.* The Hague: Martinus Nijhoff, 1969. An admirable study of the thought of the later Heidegger.

Weil, Simone. *First and Last Notebooks.* Translated by R. Rees. New York: Oxford University Press, 1970. These desultory scraps from the pen of a twentieth-century religious genius provide extraordinary insights.

GLOSSARY

Even fairly advanced students, while they may be familiar with a certain group of terms (such as might comprise, for instance, *mana* and *saṃsāra*) may be unfamiliar with other terms, such as *equivocity* and *Averroism*. This glossary is provided partly for their convenience in quickly obtaining at least a working, if sometimes rough-and-ready, aid. It is provided primarily, however, for beginners and others who may find it a convenient means of checking technical and other terms used in the text. It is in no case to be expected to provide detailed expositions of the subtle problems and intricate controversies that will sometimes immediately suggest themselves to specialists. The historical development of certain terms—for example, *nous* and *nirvāna*—is far too complex to permit their being treated to the satisfaction of scholars and also remain within the scope of a beginners' practical tool.

Academy.   The grove of olive trees near Athens, in which Plato taught, was called the Academy (*akadēmeia*). The work of the Academy (later known as the Old Academy) was continued under various leaders. In the third century B.C. Arcesilas of Pitanē, who introduced the skeptical doctrines traditionally called Pyrrhonism and engaged in controversy with the Stoics, was the founder of what is known as the Second or Middle Academy. The skeptical attitude was further developed and a reconciliation with the Stoic school was effected in the first century B.C. Antiochus of Ascalon, the leader of the conciliatory movement, claimed to have restored the Old Academy.

Aeviternity.   The medieval schoolmen distinguished time from *aeternitas* and *aeviternitas*. *Aeviternitas* is an infinite temporal series—unending time; *aeternitas* is a nontemporal order transcending all temporal sequence—that is, eternity.

Ahimsā.   Nonviolence. An ethical doctrine according to which all injury to any living being is accounted wrong. Generally accepted in both Hinduism and Buddhism and carried to extremes by the Jains (q.v.).

Alexandrian Tradition.   The theology of the early Church at Alexandria tended to be Platonic and mystical. Origen (c. 185–c. 254) greatly influenced the Alexandrian school. The tradition finds expression later in the allegorizing methods of biblical interpretation in the Middle Ages, and to this day there are contrasting and complementary tendencies in Christian theology that may be called Antiochene (q.v.) and Alexandrian respectively.

Analogy. A method of predication whereby a concept derived from an object that is relatively well known is applied to one that is relatively unknown. The use of analogy in discourse about God presupposes that God, though largely inaccessible to us, is not wholly unknowable. While in human language nothing can be predicated of God univocally (that is, on the assumption that there is an unqualified likeness between God and man), we need not say the predication must be completely equivocal (that is, on the assumption that there can be no similarity at all). For example, the kindness$_2$ predicated of God cannot be by any means the same as the kindness$_1$ predicated of human beings; nevertheless, it need not be so totally dissimilar as to make kindness$_2$ wholly meaningless in human discourse. The basis of analogy lies in relationships; that is, 4:6 as 26:39. The *analogia entis* ("analogy of being") in medieval theology is based on the notion of such a relationship: we may say that (God: his being) as (Man: his being).

Analytic/Synthetic. If the truth-value of a proposition depends only upon the cognitive meaning of the terms it contains (e.g., "No bulls are pregnant" and "2 + 2 = 4"), the proposition is said to be analytic. If it depends also on factual referents beyond itself (e.g., "Some cats have no tails," "Some clover is quatre-foiled," and "The velocity of light is 186,000 miles per second"), it is synthetic. Kant laid the basis for the distinction. For him an analytic judgment is one in which the predicate concept is included within the subject concept, and so, since its sole criterion is the law of contradiction, it requires no verification by experience. A synthetic judgment, having a predicate concept not included within the subject, depends on ground beyond itself.

Anchorite. From the Greek *anachōreō*, "I withdraw." A hermit; used especially of a recluse who lives in strictly confined quarters. In the Middle Ages, the life of the anchorite was recognized as part of the religious life of the Church, and sometimes a parish church had an anchorite's cell attached to it.

Ancilla. See *Domina.*

Anglicanism. The system of doctrine and practice upheld by those Christians who are in ecclesiastical communion with the ancient see of Canterbury. Anglicans are distinguished from Protestants by their claim to be in the apostolic succession of bishops as required for Catholic order, and from Roman Catholics by their claim to be also heirs of the Reformation. Many Anglicans see themselves today as having special affinities with Eastern Orthodoxy. The Anglican Communion comprises, besides the Church of England, various autonomous churches of which the Episcopal Church of the United States is an example. All recognize the spiritual leadership of the Archbishop of Canterbury. The traditional Anglican ethos encourages not only learning and piety but a deep reverence for Scripture and the early Christian councils and a high regard for Catholic tradition in general. Anglicans attach much importance to the Book of Common Prayer as an authoritative expression of doctrinal orthodoxy as well as a liturgical focus.

Angst. Kierkegaard used the term *Angest* (older Danish spelling) to express an agonizing premonition prompted by a sense of dread at being on the edge of an abyss of nothingness. The German equivalent is *Angst*, widely used in existentialist philosophy. Usually translated *angoisse* in French, *agonía* in Spanish, it has no completely satisfactory English rendering.

Antinomianism. The view that Christians, because of the grace they receive, are dispensed from the need to observe any ethical precept. The term, by extension, may be applied to the view of anyone who claims to be exempt from all law. Many Gnostic sects taught there is such a sharp cleavage between matter and spirit that nothing done in the corporeal realm could make any difference in the spiritual one. The Nicolaitans, for instance, mentioned in Rev. 2:6 and 2:14 f. and traditionally accounted an actual sect existing in New Testament times, are presented as urging a return to pagan practice in sexual and other matters that they supposed could affect only the body, not the spirit. Some extremists at the Reformation, such as Johann Agricola (c. 1494–1566) and some groups of Anabaptists, vigorously opposed by Luther, taught antinomian doctrines, claiming that these followed from Luther's doctrine of justification by faith. Antinomian views are said to have been widespread in Oliver Cromwell's England, and sects advocating abundant sin in order to obtain correspondingly great forgiveness have existed in Russia and elsewhere.

Antiochene Tradition. The theology of the early Christian Church at Antioch tended to be historical and Aristotelian, in contrast to the Platonic tendencies of the Alexandrian tradition (q.v.). The Antiochenes also tended to emphasize the humanity of Christ.

Apocalpytic. A literature that purports, through an unveiling of the meaning of present events, to exhibit the future. Apocalypse (Greek, *apokalypsis*) means "unveiling" or "revelation." Jewish apocalpytic literature, which dates from the beginning of the second century B.C. to the end of the first century A.D., has its origin in the growing conviction that the attainment of Jewish national aims was hopeless except through the intervention of God who, the apocalpytic writers believed, would destroy Israel's enemies and establish the messianic kingdom of God on the earth. Early Christian writers inherited the apocalpytic spirit, which appears in various places but notably in the book called the Revelation (or Apocalypse) of St. John the Divine.

Apocrypha. The Greek term *ta apokrypha* means literally "the hidden things." Its technical use is attended by various ambiguities too complex to be fully treated here. Briefly, the term is used in two different senses: (a) Traditionally it is used of certain books (e.g., Wisdom, Tobit, Ecclesiasticus) not included in the text of the Hebrew Bible that was recognized at the Jewish Synod of Jamnia (c. A.D. 100) but nevertheless held in high esteem among both Jews and Christians, almost all of them being included in the Septuagint (q.v.). (b) Modern biblical scholars also use the term "apocryphal New Testament" to denote an early Christian literature which, though it may perhaps in some cases embody some elements of an authentic, trustworthy oral tradition, was excluded from the New Testament as received by the early Church. Such works were excluded because, for instance, they contain Gnostic or other interpretations deemed heretical or because the stories they recount of the life of Jesus are trivial and fanciful, having been obviously devised to meet a growing demand for details not provided in the accepted Gospel narratives.

A Priori/A Posteriori. Kant used the term *a priori* to designate all principles and judgments whose validity is not dependent in any way on sense impressions. Space, for instance, cannot be apprehended through the senses and, being a necessary condition of experience, it must be *a priori*. The opposite is *a posteriori*, a term applied in logic to inductive reasoning (see *Induction*) and in philosophy generally to the data of the mind that originate in the external world and are accepted as coming through the senses.

Ascesis. The term, from the Greek *askēsis*, which means literally "exercise" or "work" is used to signify the rigorous self-discipline and self-restraint that constitute an element in the practice of most, if not all, the great religions of the world. The verb *askein* (whence *askēsis*) is used by St. Paul (1 Cor. 9:25) in a passage in which he compared the Christian's striving to that of an athlete in the games. Asceticism was a familiar notion among the Stoics and other ancient philosophical schools, being used to denote a set of practices believed to promote virtue and to curb vice. Buddhism has an elaborate set of ascetic rules for monks and others who wish to strive for perfection. In Christian thought, Origen and Clement of Alexandria developed the notion of ascetic discipline as a way of purging the soul of its earthly passions and attachments and preparing it for the pure contemplation of God. The ascetic ideal, already present in the Wisdom literature (e.g., Proverbs and Ecclesiastes) and characteristic of much New Testament teaching, was highly developed in the patristic and medieval periods, finding expression in the eremitical and monastic ways of life, which demand both external disciplines such as fasts and abstinences and great interior self-restraint. The ascetic way was chosen and stressed by those who, in later medieval times, wished to use it as a protest against the worldliness of many of the clergy. After the Reformation it reappeared in the Puritan movement, for example. Asceticism however, was only one of three great influences in the medieval Christian outlook. There were two other important influences, one humanistic, the other mystical. These three elements have counterparts in most of the great religions of the world.

Athonites. See *Athos*.

Athos. The chief place of pilgrimage for Eastern Orthodox Christians and focus of the spirituality of that tradition. Founded a thousand years ago or more, and known as *Athōs* or *ho hagios oros* ("the holy mountain"), it consists of some twenty independent monasteries and many smaller houses organized as a religious republic under the protection of Greece and situated on the northernmost of three peninsulae that project into the Aegean Sea from the coast of Macedonia. The monasteries, which contain many valuable manuscripts and ikons, observe (except for Vatopedi) the old Julian calendar, which runs thirteen days behind the Gregorian calendar of the West. The Athonite rule has from early times prohibited not only women but even female animals. Contrary to popular belief, the reason appears to have been not so much misogynic as to discourage the monks from diverting their attention from their spiritual exercises and into pursuits such as breeding animals for food or profit.

Ātman. In the Vedas, the absolute or universal Self, the ultimate as discovered in oneself. *Brahman-ātman* is the unity of self with ultimate Reality, in which the distinction between self and nonself is broken down.

Aufklärung. Enlightenment. A German term applied primarily to an eighteenth-century rationalistic and optimistic movement, intellectual and cultural, whose general aim was emancipation from intolerance, prejudice, and adherence to outmoded convention. The Enlightenment is often understood as including similar tendencies about the same time in England and France, expressed by thinkers such as Locke, Newton, Diderot, and Voltaire.

Aum. A syllable used repetitiously in some forms of Hindu religious practice and believed to exercise mystical power over those who use and meditate upon it. It is held to symbolize the fundamental reality of the universe.

Avatāra. Avatar, the incarnation or manifestation of a god in earthly form, human or animal. In the cult of *Viṣṇu* (Vishnu, q.v.) there are traditionally ten avatars, of which Rama and Krishna are the most popular. Avatars of deity are, however, innumerable. Not only have Orthodox Hindus come to regard Buddha as an *avatāra* of deity; the ordinary man in India has a tendency to acclaim any conspicuously holy or very great person as an *avatāra.*

Averroism. The philosophical doctrines taught by Averroes (Ibn Rushd, 1126–98), the descendant of a Muslim family at Córdova, Spain. His theories came to be known in the thirteenth century and much affected thought at the University of Paris. He followed Aristotle—then little known in the Latin world—but he interpreted Aristotle with the aid of Neo-Platonic notions. His teachings, which could be squared with Muslim orthodoxy only by his doctrine of "two truths" (one theological, one philosophic or scientific), were seen to be plainly incompatible with Christian faith. Thomas Aquinas, especially in his insistence that truth must be one (that is, it is the same whether it appears in one guise or another), addressed himself to the philosophical problems of his day with Averroes much in mind.

Benedictine Order. The order of monks founded by St. Benedict of Nursia (c. 480–c. 550), generally accounted the patriarch of monasticism in the Latin West, where, though some orders of monks follow other rules, the Rule of St. Benedict became normative for most monastic communities.

Bhagavad-Gītā. A long episode interpolated about the first century A.D. into the Mahābhārata, a vast Indian epic poem. It is an eclectic work which, providing support for *bhakti* (q.v.) is probably the most beloved single document in all the literature of India.

Bhāgavata-Purāṇa. The *Purāṇas* ("ancient stories") constitute a very popular treasury of Hindu folklore. Of these the *Bhāgavata-Purāṇa* is one of the most important. It is concerned with the early life of Krishna, the story of which attained great importance in devotion to Vishnu, one of the triad of deities the *Purāṇas* honor. See *Shiva.*

Bhakti. A popular form of Hinduism in which the worshipper engages in warm, loving devotion to a particular deity as a means of approaching, through feeling, the highest reality. A practitioner is called a *bhakta.*

Blik. A term used by R. M. Hare—presumably invented by him—to designate a life-stance, an attitude toward the universe or interpretation of the way things are. A *blik* does not have the logical function of an assertion, nor could it function as does an assertion or even a system of assertions. Hare contends, however, that because a *blik* expresses a fundamental attitude, having the right one is very important indeed; hence theological utterances that are *bliks* (e.g., "The souls of the righteous are in the hand of God") behave logically as do statements such as "The solar system will continue in its regular course tomorrow as it did yesterday." No facts or number of facts could "disprove" a category of thought so ultimate as is a *blik.*

Brahma.   See *Shiva.*

Brahman.   In the Vedas, "ultimate Reality," Being-in-itself. See *Ātman.*

Brahmanism.   Hinduism in its institutional aspect, especially in respect of its traditional caste system, in which the priestly caste (the *brahmins*) is the highest.

Camaldoli   (sometimes anglicized *Camaldolese*). An ancient order of quasi-hermits founded by St. Romuald about the year 1012 at Campus Maldoli, near Arezzo, Italy. The habit is white. An American hermitage of the order has been established in modern times near Big Sur, California.

Cartesianism.   The philosophical system of René Descartes (1596–1650), the father of modern philosophy. The Latin form of his name is Cartesius, whence the adjectival form, Cartesian.

Carthusians.   An ancient Catholic order of strictly contemplative, semieremitical monks founded by St. Bruno in 1084 at the Grande Chartreuse in the Hautes Alpes, France. The extremely severe rule has been little modified since the beginning, and the order, because of its conservatism, retains some distinctive and interesting medieval practices. The habit is white. A Carthusian monastery is called a charterhouse, after the mother-house in France.

Ch'an.   A Chinese School of Buddhism. See *Zen.*

Chasīdīm.   See *Hasīdīm* (for which it is sometimes used as an alternative transliteration of the Hebrew). Also written *Hasideans* and *Hasidaeans.*

Chiliasts.   Adherents of a view, encouraged by Jewish and Christian apocalyptic, that Christ will return to earth to reign for a thousand years (from the Greek *chilioi,* "a thousand"), as suggested in Revelation 20:1–5. Also called Millenarians. Millenarianism (Chiliasm) is a Christian adaptation of the Jewish conception of a messianic kingdom, fostered by apocalyptic such as is found in the books of Daniel, 2 Esdras, and Enoch.

Chün-tzu.   In Chinese literature, the superior, noble, magnanimous man who embodies in himself all the Confucian virtues in their proper proportion.

Connaturality.   The notion, in Thomist philosophy, of sharing the same nature. For example, earthly goods such as bread and wine, trees and rivers, are connatural to man.

Contextualism.   A modified form of situationism (q.v.). The term is applied especially to the form proposed by Paul Lehmann, in which the context of the situation is taken into account and interpreted in terms more or less vaguely Christian—for example, "What God is doing in the world," which seems to be always "making and keeping life human."

Cosmological Argument.   One of the traditional arguments for the existence of God. It is based on the principle of causality. Aristotle provided the groundwork for it. It was attacked by Hume.

Cosmology. The term (from the Greek *kosmos,* meaning "order" or "the world") denotes that discipline, recognized by philosophers of the *Aufklärung* (q.v.) as a branch of metaphysics that treats the world considered as a totality in time and space. Kant, who also used the term, did not account its conclusions warranted. The term was used by Christian Wolff (1679–1754) in the sense in which such investigations were envisioned in antiquity and by the Schoolmen (q.v.). This definition included what would nowadays be the domain of physics and other "natural" sciences.

Darshana. A term used in Hinduism for any system of philosophical thought. A way or point of view.

Dead Sea Scrolls. See *Qumran;* also *Essenes.*

Decalogue. From the Greek *deka* ("ten") and *logos* ("word"). The Ten Commandments attributed to Moses and traditionally received as divinely revealed to him on Mount Sinai and engraven on two tables of stone. Many modern biblical scholars assign to the Decalogue, in the form in which we know it today, a much later date, probably the seventh century B.C.

Deduction/Induction. Deduction is logical inference in which a conclusion necessarily follows from given premises; for example, if we grant that Abraham Lincoln was a man and that no men have tails, we must also grant by deductive inference (i.e., we deduce) that Abraham Lincoln was tailless. Induction proceeds very differently, moving from the observation of particular cases to general conclusions. For instance, from experiment with various metals we observe that metals behave differently and each behaves invariably in respect of its conductivity of electricity, and that copper, in all cases tested, always conducts it; by inductive inference we conclude that copper conducts electricity. John Stuart Mill provided five "canons" or rules of induction; but the methods of inductive inference have never been formulated in a completely satisfactory way. When formulated, the conclusions they yield, however readily we accept them, can never be (strictly speaking) more than highly probable at the most. Nevertheless, while deductive inference only exhibits what is already implied in given premises, inductive inference belongs to a process of discovery.

Deism. Originally used like "theism"—that is, in opposition to "atheism"—but now restricted to the special view advanced in the seventeenth century and classically expounded by John Toland (1670–1722). Deism, so understood, repudiates as superstitious all supernatural elements in Christianity. It rejects the need for revelation but adheres to belief in God as the One Supreme Being, creator of the world. The earlier deists admitted concepts of providence; but as deism developed it emphasized its antisupernatural aspects and particularly its repudiation of all divine intervention. John Locke, though he disavowed deism, exerted considerable influence in a deistic direction—not least upon the founding fathers of the United States, whose theological opinions were predominantly deistic.

Determinism/Indeterminism. Determinism may be understood as (a) the philosophical doctrine that all the facts in the universe, and therefore also in human history, are absolutely dependent upon and conditioned by principles, causes, or laws, and (b) the psychological doctrine that human action is determined wholly by physical and psychological conditions and that all concepts of human freedom are therefore illusory. Indeterminism is the view that volitional decisions are at least in some cases and in some degree independent of such physical and psychological conditioning.

Deus sive Natura. See *Pantheism.*

Dharma. A Sanskrit term from the word *dha*, "to sustain." The Pali equivalent is *dhamma*. It signifies primarily the cosmic moral law, the order that sustains the world. It might be translated "religious duty," being used in Hinduism to signify age-old custom and ritual covering the whole spectrum of life. In Buddhism it has acquired a variety of meanings that include (1) the notion of the truth about the nature of observable facts and events and (2) the conduct that is morally right in view of the Truth so revealed. The Code of Manu is a classic example of a manual for teaching the way of *dharma.*

Dharmakaya. In Mahayana Buddhist schools of thought is developed the metaphysical notion that the universe comprises a triple body (*Trikaya*)—a tripartite reality in which the Dharmakaya, or "body of Essence and Being," is the eternal reality that is the ground and source of the phenomena that compose the universe as known by the senses. In contrast to Vedantist thought, in which Brahman-Atman is the inconceivable Absolute, the Dharmakaya of Mahayana Buddhist thought envisages an activity that suggests a counterpart to the Christian notion of divine *agapē.*

Dialectic. As the art of debate by question and answer, the beginning of dialectic is usually associated with Socrates in the Platonic dialogues. Plato accounted it the science of first principles and the capstone of all sciences because it provides, he believed, the clearest kind of knowledge. Aristotle distinguished dialectical reasoning, which proceeds by syllogism (q.v.) from opinions generally accepted, from demonstrative reasoning, which begins with primary and true premises. Kant uses the term as the name of that portion of his *Critique of Pure Reason* that deals with special difficulties that arise when an attempt is made to apply the categories of the understanding to a realm where they cannot be applied—that is, beyond the phenomena. Hegel treats dialectic as the distinguishing feature of speculative thought. It is exhibited in the construction of thesis, antithesis, and the synthesis that resolves them.

Ding-an-sich. A Kantian term (German, "thing in itself"), used of that which lies beyond and is independent of human experience and observation.

Dionysian Mysteries. In the mystery religions of ancient Greece the candidates underwent a preparatory purification, often in the sea, followed by instruction; then came the enactment of a myth through dramatic representation of cultic divinities, with the laureation of the candidates to mark their full initiation. The oldest and most restrained of these mystery religions was the Eleusinian, the central figures of which were Demeter and her daughter, the Korē. By contrast, the Dionysiac cult, which made ritual use of wine, was much wilder and more violent. See *Dionysus.*

Dionysus. In Greek mythology, the son of Zeus and Semelē and probably by origin a Thracian deity. Often represented as a youth with luxuriant hair and a wine cup or grapes in his hand. In the later cult of Dionysus are ecstatic and mystical elements. "Dionysian" and "Dionysiac" are adjectival forms.

Dionysius, Pseudo-. A mystical writer who flourished about A.D. 500. The adjectival form is "Pseudo-Dionysian." See *Neo-Platonism*.

Docetism. A tendency among some in the early Christian Church to consider Jesus Christ a *dokēma*—that is, a "vision" or "appearance"—rather than a tangible reality, and therefore to account the humanity, including the passion, of Christ apparent rather than real. It was strong in the second century, when Gnostic mind–matter dualism was at its zenith. The view was vigorously attacked by Ignatius of Antioch and has been traditionally denounced as heretical.

Dom. A title given to monks of the Benedictine order. It is a contraction of *Dominus*.

Domina. Latin term, the female counterpart of *dominus,* "lord" or "master." Used also of the lady of the house as opposed to her *ancilla,* "handmaid." In medieval scholastic thought, philosophy was seen as standing to theology as the *ancilla* stands to her *domina*.

Dominicans. A Catholic order of friars founded in the thirteenth century. St. Thomas Aquinas is its most celebrated son. The official name is *Ordo Praedicatorum,* Order of Preachers. They wear a white woolen habit under a black mantle. Because of the reputation they developed as watchdogs of orthodoxy they were sometimes called, by way of a medieval pun, *Domini canes,* the Lord's dogs.

Doulia. See *Latria*.

Election. See *Predestination*.

Eleusinian Mysteries. See *Dionysian Mysteries*.

Empiricism. This term, though it covers a wide spectrum of philosophical views, may be applied to any philosophy that insists on referring everything to observation and experience as the ground of all philosophical inquiry. Francis Bacon (1561–1626), in his call for the repudiation of theoretical preconceptions and prejudices and his insistence on the observation of Nature, typifies the dawning of the empiricist spirit. With such an approach to the basic problems of philosophy, difficulties quickly emerge; for instance, what is allowed to count as experience becomes highly controversial. William James (1842-1910), who held that the relations between things are as much matters of direct particular experience as are the things themselves, called his own position "radical empiricism," a designation sometimes also applied to the view of David Hume (1711-1776) that all ideas are derived from and reducible to sensations. Modern phenomenology (q.v.) takes a very different view, however, of the nature of experience.

Empiricism, Logical. See *Logical Positivism*.

Epiphenomenalism. The view that consciousness is a by-product of matter, so that the brain might be said to secrete thought as the liver secretes bile.

Epistemology. From the Greek *epistēmē,* "knowledge." The philosophical investigation of the origins and structure of knowledge and of the validity of truth-claims. Some Kantians used the German equivalent *Erkenntnistheorie* ("theory of knowledge") before the end of the eighteenth century; but it was not generally used in German till Eduard Zeller adopted it in 1862 in the title of a book. The English term was presumably first used by the Scottish philosopher James Frederick Ferrier in 1854.

Equiprobabilism. See *Probabilism.*

Equivocity. See *Analogy.*

Eschatology. From the Greek *eschatos,* "last," and *logos,* "discourse." "Discussion of last things"; more specifically, that part of theology that deals with the destiny of humanity and of the individual.

Esoteric. A term used of occult, secret doctrine or anything that belongs to an inner circle of initiates—for example, the Pythagorean brotherhood. The antonym is "exoteric."

Essenes. A Jewish sect mentioned in early writers such as Philo and Josephus. The Essenes probably originated in the second century B.C. and came to an end about the second century A.D. They would have numbered, at the time of Christ, about four thousand. There is no mention of them in the Bible or Talmud. Their life was simple, severe, and communistic, and they took vows of obedience and secrecy. See *Qumran.*

Eucharist. The term, from the Greek *eucharistia,* "thanksgiving," is used for the central act of Christian worship commonly called the Mass and sometimes, among heirs of the Reformation, Holy Communion. The latter term, however, more properly refers to the sacrament that is administered in the course of the celebration of the Eucharist or Mass.

Ex Cathedra. The Greek term *kathedra* means "throne" and is used (as is its Latin counterpart, *cathedra*) of the chair or throne designated for a bishop's use. The church in which it is located is called a cathedral. The phrase *ex cathedra* is used specifically of pronouncements made officially by the Pope, which the first Vatican Council declared to be infallible when they relate to matters of faith or morals. No means exists, however, of determining precisely which statements satisfy all the conditions necessary for accounting papal pronouncements *ex cathedra* utterances, and the whole notion of papal infallibility is attended by many historical ambiguities as well as difficulties perplexing even to those Roman Catholic theologians who are in principle sympathetic to it.

Existentialism. Fundamentally, a philosophical protest against the view that behind existence lies a "more fully real" order of being, an "essential" order. Existentialism gives rise to a way of philosophizing which, like that of the phenomenologists, covers a wide spectrum of twentieth-century thought. With roots in both Kierkegaard (1813-1855) and Nietzsche (1844-1900), it developed into a vigorous philosophical movement after World War I, especially in continental Europe. In general, it exalts the role of the will and denigrates that of reason; hence its emphasis on the theme of freedom and on the notion that man is continually creating himself. In contrast to the characteristic methods of the natural sciences, which stress detachment from the object of their studies, existentialists call for involvement and commitment. While some, like Jean-Paul Sartre, are strongly nihilistic and atheistic, and others, like Gabriel Marcel, are deeply religious, all oppose determinism (q.v.) and stress individual decision.

Fall. In traditional Christian theology, humankind was originally by nature wholly good. Man was also wholly free and he freely chose sin, so effecting a radical deterioration in his nature. The change in the human condition is attributed to what theologians call the Fall of Man. See *Sin, Original.*

Fatalism. The doctrine that all things happen strictly according to a prearranged fate or necessity. Though akin to determinism (q.v.), it is not to be taken as synonymous with it, since some forms of determinism allow that there may be an element of freedom in some human actions. Fatalism has no place for any individual initiative, nor need it even recognize any rational sequence of events. The Stoics taught a kind of fatalism in which everything is subject to rational law, while the Epicureans interpreted fate as simply blind chance.

Fathers. See *Patristics.*

Feeling Tone. The term is used in various ways to denote a pervasive quality in any effective state, a particular quality in one's awareness measured in terms of pleasantness and unpleasantness. It is used by aestheticians to denote the quality of a work of art that embodies or is calculated to convey emotion.

Fides Quaerens Intellectum. "Faith seeking understanding." Phrase used by St. Anselm (c. 1033–1109) as the title of the treatise that eventually became the *Proslogion,* in which he expounds the ontological argument for the existence of God.

Fons et Origo. The phrase (Latin, meaning literally "fountain and source") is traditionally applied to what is accounted the cause of anything. So Cicero called Cilicia (a region in Asia Minor) the *fons et origo* of war. Theists account God the *fons et origo* of all that is non-God.

Franciscans. A Catholic order of friars (Order of Friars Minor) founded by St. Francis of Assisi in 1209, whose members, interpreting the vow of poverty literally, undertook a very simple life. Because they originally wore a grey habit they were popularly called the Greyfriars—in contrast to the Blackfriars, the Dominicans. The Franciscans now wear brown. Beginning with an anti-intellectual tendency they very quickly became, with the Dominicans, the leading intellectuals of the Church, counting among them, for instance, Grosseteste, Roger Bacon, and John Duns Scotus.

Geist. The German term used to denote the spiritual contradistinguished from the natural. It is not readily translatable into English, since "mind" is too intellectual and "spirit" either too religious or too "spooky" a rendering. Similar difficulties arise in translating the French *esprit,* since *un homme d'esprit* is a man of wit and sharpness of mind and *un homme spirituel* is a man whose attitude and interests pertain to the interior life of man rather than to externals; these interests, however, might be musical or literary and need by no means be religious. *Geist* has been used of nations—to express, for instance, the whole drive of the German national consciousness. Much used in Hegel and the German idealists, *Geist* is etymologically connected with the English word "ghost," as in "Holy Ghost" and "ghostly father," the latter an archaic term used for a confessor or spiritual counselor.

Gestalt. German term, meaning "shape" or "form." Used in psychology and also in philosophy to express, in opposition to analytical notions, the view that the parts do not exist prior to the whole but derive their character from the structure of the whole. *Gestalt* psychology is sometimes called Configurationism.

Gnosticism. From the Greek *gnōsis*, "knowledge." The term is used by modern scholars to designate a climate of philosophical and religious thought that was widespread in the ancient Graeco-Roman world. Most characteristic of it were two basic presuppositions: (1) spirit and matter are at enmity with each other, and (2) the secrets of the spiritual world may be taught to initiates as a sort of spiritual chemistry. In the form in which it confronted the Christian Church it reached its zenith in the second century. A characteristic doctrine was the distinction between the Demiurge or Creator God and the inaccessible and unknowable Divine Being.

Grace. The term comes from the Greek *charisma* (whence "charismatic"), rendered *gratia* in Latin. In Christian thought it is the supernatural aid (classically conceived as divine energy working in the soul) bestowed by God on a human being for his or her spiritual development. The reality of grace has never been in dispute; but the manner of its working has been a highly controversial question.

Hadīth. The name of a compilation of the life and teachings of Muhammad which, with the *Qur'ān* (q.v.), constitutes the supreme authority on Muslim religion and law.

Hagiography. The study of the lives of the saints.

Hammurabi, Laws of. Hammurabi was the sixth king of the first (Amorite) dynasty of Babylon (c. 1728–1686 B.C.). The laws were found in fragmentary form, engraved on a diorite stele (now in the Louvre), at Susa in Elam, a territory to the east and northeast of the valley of the Tigris and the Euphrates in the Zagros mountains. They contain 282 articles and provide the single most important source of information about the customs, economy, and social structure of Mesopotamian society in the second millenium B.C. and attest, together with other materials, that a common body of customary law existed in Mesopotamia as far back as the third millenium B.C. Certain passages in the Torah (Pentateuch), the first five books of the Hebrew Bible, show interesting parallels with the Laws of Hammurabi.

Hasīdīm *h* pronounced *approximately* as *ch* in German *ach*. Literally, "pious ones." The singular is *hāsīd*. The word is used in two senses: (1) to designate those conservative Jews who, in the second century B.C., resisted prevalent Hellenistic influences, sought to maintain the scribal interpretations of the Hebrew Law, and were probably the immediate ancestors of the Pharisees (literally, "separated ones"), who flourished as a Jewish party in the time of Christ; and (2) as a title for Jewish mystics who stand in the tradition of a Jewish sect founded in the eighteenth century and whose teachings and practices have received support from the twentieth century Jewish existentialist thinker Martin Buber (1878–1965). The founder, Israel Baal Shem Tov (c. 1700–1760), taught that worship can occur at any time or place in a pure and contrite heart. The *hasīdīm* stressed the joyful aspects of Jewish life and the accessibility of God in everyday living.

Hedonistic Calculus. See *Utilitarianism.*

Hesychasts.   Adherents of a system of mysticism called hesychasm (from the Greek *hēsychos*, "quiet") propagated in the Greek Orthodox Church by monks on Mount Athos in the fourteenth century. They taught that by an elaborate system of ascetic exercises, with special emphasis on perfect quiet of mind and body, man could arrive at the mystical vision of the Divine Light. These exercises later became more mechanical, yogalike breathing exercises, accompanying the ejaculatory prayer "Lord Jesus Christ, Son of God, have mercy on me." Hesychasm eventually became a focus of controversy between the Eastern and Western Churches.

Hinayana.   Literally, "the Lesser Vehicle." In contrast to Mahayana (q.v.), it is the kind of Buddhism that repudiated liberal developments and assimilation in other oriental religions and claimed to be more faithful to the Buddha's original teaching. See *Theravada*.

Hyperdoulia.   See *Latria*.

Hypostasis (plural: *hypostaseis*).   Greek term ambiguously used, sometimes almost synonymously with *ousia*, "essence" or "substance," but also to signify "individual reality." In the course of the Christological controversies of the fourth century that led to the formulation of the doctrine of the Trinity, the term was used to speak of what are now called the three "Persons" of the Godhead. The formula "three *hypostaseis* in one *ousia*" came to be acknowledged as the core of Christian orthodoxy on the subject. The Latin West came to call the *hypostaseis* "persons"— from the term used for the masks (*personae*) worn by Roman actors in performing their roles.

Idealism.   Any metaphysical system that uses the ideas of mind as the basic clue to an understanding of reality. It has taken many forms in the history of thought. Characteristic of much Indian thought, it was accommodated by Plato to that of the West. Christian thought, because of the strongly Neo-Platonic influence that entered into it, has been much affected by idealist views. The work of Berkeley, an eighteenth-century philosopher and Christian bishop, provides an interesting example of a thoroughgoing idealism in the form of an immaterialist philosophy in which everything is referable to mind. Many, however, would account such a thoroughgoing idealism to be incompatible with the data of Christian revelation, which includes Creation as well as the Incarnation and Resurrection. The thought both of Kant and of Hegel is in the idealist tradition. Those who, in the late nineteenth century and afterwards, sought to rehabilitate and reexpress idealist principles are commonly called neo-idealists. Among these would be included Bradley, Bosanquet, Croce, Dilthey, and Royce.

Immanence.   See *Transcendence*.

Indeterminism.   See *Determinism/Indeterminism*.

Induction.   See *Deduction/Induction*.

Jains.   Followers of Mahavira, who flourished in India in the sixth century B.C. Jain monks take five vows, the first of which is an extremely comprehensive reverence for life and renunciation of all violence. They also renounce all sexual enjoyment and all attachment to earthly things.

JHWH.   See *Tetragrammaton*.

Kabbalism. A Jewish system of theosophy (q.v.) using an esoteric method of interpreting the Hebrew Bible. It acquired some influence in the late Middle Ages and in the Renaissance, showing tendencies akin to Gnosticism (q.v.).

Karma. Sanskrit term; Pali equivalent is *kamma*. The moral or spiritual law of action and its inevitable consequence. It is a fundamental concept among Hindus, Buddhists, Jains, and Sikhs. See also *Saṁsāra*.

Kenosis (Adjectival form: *kenotic*). The term comes from the Greek verb *kenoō*, which may be translated (cf. Phil. 2:7) "I empty myself." Traditional Christian teaching has always recognized a self-emptying of God in the acceptance of union with a physically limited humanity in Jesus. In an attempt to answer questions such as "If God was fully in Christ, was Jesus omniscient and omnipotent when he was an apparently helpless baby at his mother's knee?" some Lutheran theologians in the nineteenth century, however, went much further. They proposed that the divine attributes were abandoned in order for God to become man. English theologians of the period, such as Charles Gore (1853–1932), inclined to the view that God emptied himself only to the extent of permitting the existence in Jesus of the limitations of a human self-consciousness.

Kerygma. Greek term meaning "preaching"; used by modern scholars of the element of proclamation (contradistinguished from teaching) that is found in the Christian Gospel.

Koan. From the Chinese, *kung-an*, which originally referred to a document concerning an official transaction. As adopted in the practice of the Rinzai school of Zen (see *Zen*), it meant simply "an item on the agenda." A *koan* is set by the Zen master as a mental exercise of such a nature that it violates basic logical rules; for instance, the master might tell the student to hear a smell or design a basement above the attic. The purpose of the *koan* is to jolt the student (see *Satori*) into enlightenment. The enlightenment is not, however, an intellectual enlightenment. The purpose of the *koan* might be described as forcing the student to escape from the prison of his intellect by growing "wings" (as we might say) that lead him into new life. Zen teachers sometimes express this as follows: How does a primitive form of life first learn to see? Having no eye, it gropes after seeing, though it cannot even know what seeing is. By sheer effort of the will it develops a sensitive spot on the skin, which it eventually develops into and organizes as the extremely complex organ of sight. So the mind, though baffled by the *koan*, does not give up. In the long run, the student grows beyond the prison of his own logic.

Krishna (anglicized form of the Sanskrit *Kṛṣṇa*.) The hero of the *Mahābharata* and divine charioteer of the *Bhagavad-gītā*. He is practically, though not theoretically, accounted the *avatāra* (q.v.) of Vishnu (see *Shiva*).

Latria. In Roman Catholic theology, three kinds of worship are recognized, all designated by Greek terms. *Doulia* is the kind proper to saints and other creatures whose sanctity merits admiration and devotion. To Mary, as pre-eminent among all creatures, is given *hyperdoulia*—an outstanding degree of *doulia*. *Latria*, however, being the worship proper to the Creator, must be reserved for God alone.

Lingam. Phallic symbol, prominent in the worship of Shiva (q.v.).

Liturgy. From the Greek, *leōs* ("people") and *ergon* ("work"), *leitourgia*, "the work of the people." In the ancient world the term was used of any public duty, but before the time of Christ it had become well established as a term applied to the services of the Temple at Jerusalem. In Christianity it is traditionally used, especially in the Eastern Churches, as the title of the Eucharist (q.v.). In English it is also used in a broader sense to include, for instance, the canonical hours of prayer such as matins, vespers, and compline, and indeed all public worship (as contradistinguished from private devotion).

Logical Empiricism. See *Logical Positivism.*

Logical Positivism. The Vienna Circle of philosophers, founded by Moritz Schlick in 1924 and including Rudolf Carnap among its members, encouraged a trend in twentieth-century philosophical thought, one of whose earliest manifestations was a school of philosophy whose members emphasized the unity of science and the use by philosophers of the attitudes of mind supposed to be characteristic of those who pursued the natural sciences. Characteristic of this school was an interest in questions of meaning and an insistence on the application to all philosophical questions of the methods of verification and falsification used in the natural sciences. Its members were generally called "logical positivists"; later, some disciples of the movement preferred to be known as "logical empiricists." The movement had older roots, however, in the history of thought—especially in the radical empiricism of David Hume (1711–1776) and also in the rise of symbolic logic from its foundation by the English mathematician George Boole (1815–1864) through its later development by others, notably Gottlob Frege (1848–1925). The logical analysis of language by Frege, Whitehead, Russell, and Wittgenstein constituted a parallel movement, which Russell combined with similar trends. Some of the earlier exponents of logical positivism had presented the tenets of the school too uncritically, not to say crudely, and much modification of the earlier expositions later took place. The whole approach of all such movements in philosophy, however, is open to radical criticism for its basic presuppositions, and some think its highly dogmatic tendencies express a mood that is not only often bitterly antireligious (as is obvious) but also radically antithetical to the traditional openness of the philosophical spirit to which an older generation had been accustomed to see as fostering authentic philosophical inquiry by providing not only room for dialogue between skeptics and religious men but a climate of thought hospitable to many different ways of philosophizing.

Mahayana. Literally, "the Great Vehicle." In contrast to Hinayana (q.v.), it comprises the kinds of Buddhism that developed with the missionary spread of Buddhist teaching in China, Japan, and elsewhere beyond the Indian subcontinent.

Mandala. In Tantrism—Hindu or Buddhist—magical significance is attached to formulae (tantras), to sacred words (mantras), and to diagrams or pictures (mandalas). Buddhist mandalas typically consist of a circular lotus (which is the eternal birthplace of the gods), containing a square sacred edifice with four gates which indicate the four cardinal points and also the seasons of the year. In the center is a Buddha or other sacred figure. Its circularity expresses wholeness or perfection while its quaternity or squareness contains much symbolism, earthy and psychic. The whole mandala expresses completeness and integration. Jung thought he saw in the medieval rose window in which sits Christ the Victor (often supported by the four evangelists) a western counterpart to the mandala.

Mana. In primitive religions certain places or objects are believed to be invested with a mysterious, impersonal force. The force is neither good nor bad in itself; but it can be put to good use by those (for example, magicians) who know how to handle it, and it is very dangerous to those who do not. To touch or even approach such a place or object is taboo, being strictly forbidden by tribal custom.

Manichaeism. Manes or Mani (c. A.D. 215–275), of Persian origin, was the founder of an eclectic system whose most conspicuous characteristic was a sharp mind–matter dualism. He called for severe mortification of the flesh. His sect was established in Egypt in the third century and at Rome in the fourth and was flourishing in Africa soon afterward. Augustine, before his conversion to Christianity, was a Manichee, and Manichaean influence has been traditionally attributed to later medieval sects such as the Albigenses and the Bogomiles, though the extent of that influence is a matter of scholarly dispute.

Maya. A Sanskrit term, used in Hinduism and among the Sikhs to express the notion of the illusory character of the phenomenal world compared with Brahma (q.v.).

Metempsychosis. The doctrine, traditional in Hinduism and Buddhism, that the human soul migrates from one body to another till at last, being completely purified, it overcomes the karmic cycle (see *karma* and *saṁsāra*) within which human action brings about rebirth. The notion is also found in many modern spiritualistic, theosophical, occult, and neo-Gnostic movements that have their roots in ancient Indian modes of conceptualization. In such forms it implies metaphysical presuppositions, for example, that the human soul, being eternal, dons and discards human flesh as one does clothes. In the light of such a view, all human existence is generally seen in negative terms, as purgation if not as punishment, so that the end of the metempsychotic process is seen as release from the burden of existence. Pythagoras and Plato both accepted a form of metempsychosis, which was also widely presupposed in the climate of thought from which primitive Christianity emerged. It is found, too, in Jewish Kabbalism (q.v.). Augustine expressly repudiated it. Some Christian writers, notably Origen, find a place for a form of it; but in Christian tradition it has generally been accounted heterodox, since it has seemed to be incompatible with the Christian doctrine of resurrection, contradistinguished from immortality. Whether all forms of it, for instance Origen's, are to be so accounted is nevertheless open to question.

Millenarianism. See *Chiliasts.*

Monism. The metaphysical view that all reality is fundamentally of one "substance" or character.

Montanism. In Phrygia, in the second half of the second century A.D., Montanus led an apocalyptic movement, proclaiming that the Heavenly Jerusalem would soon descend at a place near Pepuza, Phrygia. The Montanists, adherents of this movement, lived in expectation of the speedy outpouring of the Holy Spirit and exhibited the characteristic mood of opponents of institutionalism. They soon developed, especially in Roman Africa, extremely ascetic tendencies, with rigorous fasts and special disciplines, and regarded as carnal those who observed only the standard Roman discipline. Their most distinguished representative was Tertullian (c. 160–c. 220), who, besides being the first Christian theologian to write in Latin, by his legally trained mind greatly affected the thought of the Latin Church.

Myth. From the Greek *mythos,* "story"; the presentation in symbolic form of fundamental insights, obscurely glimpsed, about the nature of reality. Often misleadingly used (for example, in the nineteenth century, by D. F. Strauss) in a pejorative sense signifying the fictitious. It is with such a signification of the term in mind that the twentieth-century Protestant theologian Rudolf Bultmann has called for a program of demythologization of the New Testament writings.

Naturalism. The view that the universe is self-existent, self-explanatory, and self-directing. Naturalists generally see the world process deterministically (see *Determinism*) and man as only its incidental product.

Natural Philosophy. The term "philosophy" (literally "the love of wisdom") formerly included all knowledge (*scientia*) that could be attained through the use of human reason. What is now called psychology, for instance, was till comparatively recent times included as one of the philosophical disciplines, like ethics and logic. Physics, chemistry, and other such sciences were called "natural" philosophy—that is, the philosophy of Nature contradistinguished from the philosophy of Being or Mind or God.

Natural Theology. Medieval theologians held that though some truths about God—for example, the Incarnation and the Trinity—could be known only through divine revelation, other truths—such as the existence of God—were accessible to and could be worked out exclusively by human reason (cf. Rom. 1:18 ff.). The body of knowledge about God that could be attained through the latter means alone came to be called "natural theology" (contradistinguished from "*revealed* theology). Natural theology may be regarded, therefore, as a philosophical rather than as a theological discipline and so as an antecedent of what is now called the philosophy of religion. Though the Reformers generally rejected the concept of natural theology, the use of the term was revived—especially by those who, like the English deists (see *Deism*), stressed the role of reason in religion.

Neo-Platonism. The philosophical system of Plotinus (c. 205–269 A.D.), which was a mystical and religious development of Platonic doctrines. It flourished in Alexandria, whence it spread to Rome and the rest of the Empire, including Athens. The dualism between reality and thought is overcome in the One which is God and may be attained by mystical experience. Christianity, though accounted by Neo-Platonists a rival and even a foe, drew many Neo-Platonic elements and influences to itself, especially in the West, through St. Augustine. Pseudo-Dionysius (fl. c. 500), who attempted a synthesis of Neo-Platonic and Christian teachings, greatly influenced various Christian mystical traditions in the Middle Ages. His influence was enhanced by his having been confused at that period with Dionysius the Areopagite, mentioned in Acts 17:34.

Nirvāna (Pali, *nibbana*). According to the early Buddhists, the "I" is a mere appearance: salvation consists in its disappearance or "blowing out" (the literal meaning of *nirvāna*) of ignorant craving. Nirvanic bliss is the state of emancipation from such finite limitation and of release from all the restrictions of existence in the phenomenal world.

Noumenon. See *Phenomenalism.*

Nous. Greek term, usually translated "mind." Anaxagoras (c. 500–428 B.C.) used it in contradistinction to matter to designate what he took to be the rational principle that provides matter with order. Plato and Aristotle used the term in their respective systems, and in Plotinus it appears as the first of the emanations from "the One" and therefore the emanation most nearly resembling "the One." As thought or universal intelligence, it signifies the rationality which, according to Plotinus, undergirds the world. In some of the Gnostic systems (see *Gnosticism*), *nous* took on a function analogous to that of the Holy Spirit in Christian thought and life.

Numinous. A term coined by Rudolf Otto (1869–1937) to denote what he took to be the essential element, amoral and nonrational, in religious experience which includes the sense of awe and self-abasement in face of a fascinating mystery. It is unanalyzable *(unentwickelbar).* Its object is the holy *(das Heilige).*

Occultism. A term (from the Latin *occulere,* "to cover up," akin to *celare,* "to hide") used to designate any theory or practice involving a belief in hidden, esoteric (q.v.) powers and the possibility of subjecting them to human control. Associated with magic rather than worship. Modern forms of occult religion usually represent revivals and modifications of the outworn Gnosticism (q.v.) that flourished in the ancient world and reached its height about the second century of the Christian era.

Om. See *Aum.*

Ontological Argument. One of the traditional arguments for the existence of God. It purports to show that the existence of the idea of God necessarily entails the independent existence of God. Anselm (c. 1033–1109) and Descartes (1596–1650) provided separate forms of it. The argument in its Anselmic form was repudiated by Thomas Aquinas (c. 1225–1274) and in its Cartesian form by Kant (1724–1804). Nevertheless it continues to attract philosophical interest.

Ontology. The philosophical discipline, a branch of metaphysics (from the Greek, *to on,* meaning "that which is") that treats Being. Those who acknowledge a reality independent of the mind contrast ontological realities with, for example, psychological realities.

Ousia. See *Hypostasis.*

Panentheism. The term, meaning literally "everything in God," was coined by K. C. F. Krause (1781–1832) and is used to designate the belief that the Being of God includes and penetrates the entire universe in such a way that though all is not to be identified with him, all exists in him.

Pantheism. The term, coined by John Toland (1670–1722), means literally "everything God." It is used of those systems in which God and Nature (or God and the universe) are identified. The most remarkable and thoroughgoing of these is that of Baruch Spinoza (1632–1677), who speaks of *Deus sive Natura,* God or Nature. Mysticism has a generally pantheistic tendency, and though pantheism is incompatible with Christian doctrine, writers in some Christian mystical traditions have exhibited such tendencies. It is characteristic of much Indian thought and has widely affected Asia—for example, in Mahayana Buddhism. Pantheism may be either religious or irreligous; that is, it may be interpreted in one way or the other. It is diametrically opposed, however, to traditional Jewish, Christian, and Muslim teaching; and among those who particularly stress—as did Martin Buber (1878–1965)–the transcendental character of God, pantheism is accounted fundamentally irreligious.

Pantokratōr. Almighty; literally, "ruler of all things," from the Greek verb *krateō,* "I rule," and the root *pan,* "all." Used in the Septuagint (Greek version of the Bible; compiled no earlier than the third century B.C.) and translated in English versions as "Lord of Hosts." It was rendered in Latin *omnipotens*—whence our English word "omnipotent," which misleadingly suggests "able to do anything."

Paradox. The term, from the Greek *paradoxon,* meaning "contrary to expectation" (*para,* "beside"; *dokein,* "to think"), has several meanings in common usage today; but fundamentally it is used of a statement that appears to be either self-contradictory or at least contrary to common sense—for example, "a well-known secret agent." Logical paradoxes were known to the ancients (e.g., "I am lying" is false if true and true if false), but interest in mathematical paradoxes was much stirred in modern times by the publication in 1897 by Burali-Forti of the paradox of the greatest ordinal number, followed by Russell's publication in 1903 of the paradox of the greatest cardinal number. Mathematical and logical paradoxes are generally offered as a challenge to find their solution; that is, however puzzling they may seem, they are presumed to be soluble. The immense importance that paradox has assumed in the philosophical study of religion today is due in part to its role in the thought of Pascal and Kierkegaard and its very different function in Zen, but also to the peculiar interest that religious utterances can evoke in the light of the attention contemporary philosophers pay to the analysis of language.

Patristics. In Christian theology, the study of the early Fathers—that is, the important Christian teachers who wrote between the beginning of the second and the end of the eighth century A.D. "The patristic age" is generally taken to comprise approximately that period.

Persona. See *Hypostasis.*

Phenomenalism. The philosophical view that knowledge is limited to the phenomena, contradistinguished from whatever may be held to lie behind them as "noumenal realities." The Greek word *phenomenon* (plural, *phenomena*) means "appearance" and is opposed to *noumenon,* which Kant used as a term to designate the unknowable reality behind the phenomenal world. See *Ding-an-sich.*

Phenomenology. The term, though used in various senses since the mid-eighteenth century, is now most commonly understood as a designation for a philosophical outlook developed by Edmund Husserl (1859–1938) and others. While modern phenomenological schools vary considerably both in their understanding of the task confronting them and in their methods of pursuing it, the phenomenological approach is characterized by a preoccupation with the fundamental character of subjective processes. Intentionality, for instance, plays an important part in it. Phenomenologists interest themselves, therefore, in the characteristic themes of psychology, and their work has also some broad affinities with that of existentialism (q.v.).

Phenomenon. See *Phenomenalism.*

Pneuma. Greek; "breath" or "spirit," corresponding to the Hebrew *ruach* (q.v.).

Prajnā. Sanskrit term used to express the notion of the realization of, or insight into, the true and abiding nature of the self.

Prakṛiti. In Samkhya (q.v.), matter, which is accounted one of the two basic elements of the universe. See Puruṣa.

Predestination/Election. Predestination is a traditional doctrine of Christian theology based partly on the ancient Hebrew conception of an elect or chosen people. It is affirmed by Augustine, Thomas Aquinas, Bellarmine, Luther, and Calvin. Predestination is held to occur in eternity, election in time. Though frequently caricatured as a peculiarly terrifying and enervating form of determinism, it has been developed alongside a vigorous assertion of human freedom and responsibility to exhibit the limitations of the creature and the gulf that lies between him and his Creator. Far from terrifying, the doctrine has been a source of profound consolation and assurance to those who have taken it into the ambit of their devotional and personal, contradistinguished from their intellectual, life. Far from enervating, it has made some of those who have held it in strong forms—for example, Calvinists—excessively activist. The reason for both the assurance and the stimulus to action is that those who believe themselves to be saved, as did Augustine, "between the bridge and the river" or, as William Camden (1551–1623) put it in an epitaph, "betwixt the stirrup and the ground," feel a deep urge to serve God loyally since they feel sure that he who so rescued them shall never forsake them and therefore, however unaccountably, must have chosen them for himself. Nevertheless, the question of predestination and election has been the source of long, bitter, and (in the view of many contemporary religious thinkers) exceedingly unprofitable theological controversy.

Premise. See *Syllogism.*

Probabiliorism. See *Probabilism.*

Probabilism. A system of moral theology based on the general notion that where the morality of an action is doubtful, an opinion that may be accounted probably defensible may be adopted even against an opinion that may be accounted more probably defensible. Probabilist principles, having been discussed much earlier, were promoted by the Dominicans at Salamanca in the sixteenth century. Both Dominicans and Jesuits developed the doctrine. The celebrated Spanish Jesuit, Francisco de Suarez, taught that where there is doubt about a law, human freedom should be allowed to prevail. In 1656, however, a general chapter of the Dominican order opposed probabilism, promoting instead the system that came to be known as probabiliorism, according to which, in case of doubt, one may claim liberty only when it can be held to be more probably defensible than the opinion that favors the law. Probabilism was severely pilloried about the same time by Blaise Pascal, whose Jansenist sympathies made it abhorrent to him. The Jansenists favored the system called rigorism or tutiorism, according to which one must follow, in case of doubt, the "safer opinion" *(opinio tutior)*—that is, the one requiring adherence to the law—unless there could be shown to be moral certitude against it. Tutiorism was condemned by Pope Alexander VIII in 1690. Probabiliorism was much favored by many, notably in France under the influential leadership of Bossuet; but eventually probabilism prevailed, especially as modified in Alfonso Liguori's doctrine of equiprobabilism, according to which the stricter course is to be followed if the doubt is as to the cessation of the law, while the laxer course may be followed if the doubt is as to the law's having ever existed. See *Situationism.*

Purāṇas.   See *Bhāgavata-Purāṇa.*

Puruṣa.   In Sānkhya, the nonmaterial element of the universe, spirit, soul, or mind. See *Prakṛiti.*

Pythagoreanism.   A philosophic brotherhood founded in the sixth century B.C. by Pythagoras, who greatly advanced mathematical science. Influenced by Orphism, the Pythagoreans believed in transmigration of the soul. Plato was influenced by the thought of this school.

Quakers.   The followers of George Fox (1624–1691) were organized in 1688 as a distinctive group called simply the Friends. Much persecuted in England for their nonconformity, they represented a radical movement in Protestantism, rejecting many basic tenents of the Reformers in favor of an extreme emphasis on the doctrine of the Inner Light as authoritatively superior to both Bible and Church. The Friends also rejected the sacraments and made much of certain external observances such as the use of "plain speech" (for instance, "thou" and "thee" were used as the regular mode of address to each other instead of the "you" that by then had come to be customary in polite conversation), plain, unornamented dress, and the repudiation of all forms of art, including music, as foolishly secular. The use of the term "Quaker" dates from 1650, by Justice Bennet, whom George Fox had bidden to quake at the Word of the Lord. Some of the Friends, however, attributed its use to the experience of trembling or quaking that occurred among some of them at meetings. Their intransigent pacifism has generally brought them into conflict with the State, but their devotion to great social causes and to education has attracted widespread admiration, while their enviable reputation for strict honesty has won them almost universal respect. Under Elias Hicks (1748–1830), an American Quaker, a group severed themselves from the main body. Their followers are sometimes called Hicksites.

Qumran.   Between 1947 and 1956 were discovered in caves near Qumran, at the northwestern end of the Dead Sea, the remains of a large collection of Hebrew and Aramaic manuscripts, mostly in fragmentary condition. Most of the biblical books are represented, as well as several works relating to and shedding much light on a Jewish community or sect that flourished at Qumran about the time of Christ. The manuscripts date from between 20 B.C. and A.D. 70 and are very important both paleographically and for the study of the background of Christianity, as well as for the light they shed (mostly corroborative) on our knowledge of the text of the Hebrew Bible. See *Essenes.*

Qur'ān (popularly anglicized *Koran*).   The Islamic Scriptures. Muslims traditionally treat the Qur'ān with literalistic reverence. Some believe the Arabic text is a copy of a celestial original.

Rama. The hero of the Ramayana, an epic poem that is an important source of popular devotion in Hinduism. Rama is the seventh *avatāra* (q.v.) of Vishnu (see *Shiva*).

Rationalism. This term, though used in various senses in reference to very diverse stages in the development of human thought, may be applied to any philosophical system that looks to human intellect and reason to provide the starting point of philosophical inquiry and its criterion of truth. Rationalists, instead of claiming to begin with awareness of observed aspects of Nature, as do those who profess empiricism (q.v.), take as their point of departure some insights that they account fundamental and the implications of which they follow out by careful deductive analysis. The certainty Descartes felt about having a clear and distinct idea of perfection exemplifies such a reliance, as does his confidence in mathematics as the methodological key to an understanding of reality.

Reincarnation. See *Metempsychosis*.

Rigorism. See *Probabilism*.

Rosicrucianism. An esoteric movement whose devotees venerated emblems of the rose and the cross as twin symbols of the Resurrection of Christ and redemption. It goes back to two anonymous early seventeenth-century works, now assigned to the Lutheran J. V. Andreae (1586–1654), having medieval alchemist features. The movement spread extensively in the eighteenth century and has been closely associated with freemasonry.

Ruach. Hebrew, breath or spirit. See *Pneuma*.

Sacramentum. From the Latin, "oath," a misleading rendering of the Greek *mysterion*, "mystery." A sacrament is defined by St. Thomas as "the sign of a sacred thing in so far as it sanctifies men" and in the English Book of Common Prayer as "an outward and visible sign of an inward and spiritual grace...." The Eucharist (q.v.) is the Christian sacrament *par excellence* and constitutes the day-to-day sacramental life of the Church. Baptism, as a sacrament, has a unique place, since it is the means of initiation into the Church as the Body of Christ. Other rites, however, including marriage and ordination, are recognized as having a sacramental character. In Catholic theology certain accessories used in the sacramental life of the Church (such as vestments, altar lights, holy water, ashes, and oil) and pious practices (such as grace at meals) are sometimes called "sacramentals."

Sacred Heart. Catholic devotion to the Sacred Heart of Jesus can be traced as far back as St. Bernard in the twelfth century; but it was for long restricted to a special circle of mystics. Later, in the sixteenth century, it was fostered by the Carthusians (q.v.) as a more general devotion. In France, both the Jesuits (founded in 1540 by Ignatius Loyola) and the Visitandines (an order of contemplative nuns founded in 1610 by Francis of Sales) fostered the devotion, for which Jean Eudes tried to provide a theological foundation. The visions of Margaret Mary Alacoque, a Visitandine, immensely popularized the devotion throughout the Roman Catholic Church, in which it came to be permitted by Pope Clement XIII in 1765. In 1856 in honor of it Pope Pius IX proclaimed a special feast of the whole Church.

Salesian Tradition.   A method of Catholic devotion, similar to, but much less formal than, that of the Jesuits. Developed in France in the seventeenth century, it owed its inspiration to the teaching of St. Francis of Sales (1567–1622), Bishop of Geneva. The Salesian movement was characterized by an emphasis on the notion that the mystical life is not restricted to special classes like monks and nuns, as had been commonly supposed, but is accessible to ordinary people living in the world.

Samkhya.   (Sanskrit, *sāṅkhya*.) In Hinduism, the dualistic philosophy or darshana (q.v.) that emphasizes the attainment of salvation through distinguishing between *prakṛiti* and *puruṣa* (q.v.).

Saṁsāra.   Reincarnation, metempsychosis, transmigration of the soul through successive rebirths. *Karma-saṁsāra* constitutes a cycle in which human deeds perpetually result in further incarnations. See *Karma.*

Sannyāsi.   One who practices *sannyāsa*, the life of ascesis (q.v.). The *sannyāsi* is a "holy man," often mendicant, sometimes silent and half-naked.

Satori.   In Zen, the enlightenment (Chinese, *tun wu*), which on account of its suddenness is likened to the way a mirror instantaneously reflects whatever is held up to it. The Rinzai school of Zen used the *koan* to achieve the *satori*. The Sōtō school objects to such methods on the ground that since all methods of striving are self-destructive, the *satori* should be attained spontaneously. See *Zen* and *Koan.*

Scholasticism.   See *Schoolmen.*

Schoolmen.   Name given to the teachers of philosophy and theology in the medieval universities or schools such as Paris and Oxford. Thomas Aquinas and John Duns Scotus are eminent examples.

Septuagint.   The most influential of the Greek versions of the Hebrew Bible. Modern scholars generally take it to be the work of several Alexandrian Jewish translators over a lengthy period of time, being probably completed some time in the second century B.C. It includes various writings that circulated among Greek-speaking Jews and that are now designated in the English Bible as the Apocrypha—for example, books such as Wisdom and Ecclesiasticus. Commonly designated by scholars as LXX, it is of immense importance in biblical study, not least since it was the version generally accepted by the early Christian Fathers as the standard form of the Old Testament. The New Testament writers themselves quoted from it.

Shiva.   Vedic deity who, with Brahma and Vishnu, constitute the great triad in the pantheon. They are sometimes regarded as the universe in its triple role of creator (Brahma), destroyer (Shiva), and preserver (Vishnu).

Sikh.   A Punjabi term, from the Sanskrit *cisya*, meaning simply "a disciple" or "student"; more specifically used of a follower of Nanak, who attempted to combine elements in the religion of both Hindus and Moslems. The Sikh religion was developed in India in the sixteenth and seventeenth centuries. The Sikhs have a reputation as militant warriors. Those who belong to the Khalsa, a group founded by Gobind Singh, bear the name "Singh," which means "lion." The Sikhs ignore caste distinction, eat meat, encourage ascetic practices, and renounce liquor and tobacco. They reverence the *Granth*, the Sikh Scriptures.

Sin, Original. In traditional Christian theology, the state into which humankind has deteriorated as a result of the Fall (q.v.). Because the deterioration has radically enslaved humankind—and made it prone to sin—human freedom, though not destroyed, has been much injured. Theological controversy on technical details of the doctrine has abounded since patristic times. For general purposes original sin may be usefully understood in simple terms as an inherited spiritual disease by reason of which we human beings, crippled and blinded, are so inclined to go the wrong way that we need divine help to enable us to go the right way.

Sins, The Seven Deadly. The seven "deadly" or "capital" sins—that is, those at the root of all evil human acts—are, based on a list found in Gregory the Great (c. 540–604) and traditional throughout the Middle Ages: (1) pride, (2) covetousness, (3) lust, (4) envy, (5) gluttony, (6) anger, and (7) sloth.

Situationism. A view of ethics which, in its radical form, insists on an ethical decision tailor-made to the uniqueness of each individual in each particular ethical situation. Forms of situationist ethic have been expounded in the English-speaking world by professedly Christian writers such as the American J. B. Fletcher and the English John A. T. Robinson, but the notion has its roots in continental European existentialists—e.g., Ortega, Sartre, and Karl Jaspers—and was developed extensively by others such as Ludger Jaspers, Cesare Luporini, Renato Lazzarini, Antonino Poppi, O.F.M., and Angelo Parego, in a literature that goes back to at least the decade preceding World War II. The notion, like that of contextualism (q.v.), was adumbrated even before World War I in some of the writings of John Dewey (1859–1952)—for example, in his *Studies in Logical Theory* (1903)—and further developed in his *Logic, Theory of Inquiry* (1938). See *Probabilism.*

Societas Fidelium. In the Middle Ages, in the Latin West, the term "Church" (*ecclesia*) became ambiguous. As controversies developed between the papalist and conciliarist parties, some appealed to a theological principle implicit from earliest times—namely, that in the last resort the Christian Church consists not in bishops or councils but the whole company of Christ's faithful people, the *societas* or *congregatio fidelium*. St. Augustine had already spoken of a Christian *respublica*, borrowing a term that the Romans had used neutrally of Rome under any form of government, being applicable, for instance, to the Roman Empire at all stages.

Solipsism. From the Latin *solus* "alone" and *ipse* "oneself." The philosophical position that the individual self is the only one existent, so that other selves are illusory. The notion is a formal one since probably no one has ever seriously held that view. Many philosophers, however, have been methodological solipsists, holding that the self is the only real object of knowledge or else (as in much philosophy since Descartes) that it is the only profitable starting point for inquiry.

Sophists. Wandering teachers who, in the fifth century B.C., came from foreign cities to Athens, where they sought to popularize learning. In showing young men how to achieve success—for example, in political life—they tended to subordinate the pursuit of truth to the use of knowledge for practical ends. Rhetoric, for instance, became more popular than the study of the cosmic panorama that had been the preoccupation of learned circles. The new concern for persuasion in argument led many to a relativism in which truth was accounted subjective (man is the measure of all things); nevertheless, that very concern raised the question whether, among the various opinions the Sophists canvassed, there might be a core of truth that was independent of the individual inquirer. Socrates, a Sophist himself, criticized sophistic relativism but fostered the quest for the universal to which it led (e.g., the concept of bravery rather than instances of brave men or deeds) and in doing so provided mankind with the basis for a new conceptual vocabulary.

Stoics. Graeco-Roman philosophers whose school was founded by Zeno of Citium. They were so called from the porch (Greek, *stoa*) in which they originally foregathered in Athens. In contrast to Plato they taught a monistic pantheism: God is the all-pervasive energy that creates and sustains the world. God is identified also with the principle of reason, the *Logos*.

Sufis. Members of a mystical Muslim sect that first appeared in the eighth century and was influenced both by Gnostic ideas and by the practices of Christian monks. They have varied considerably in their teachings, sometimes moving very far from Muslim orthodoxy. The name comes from *ṣūf*, meaning "wool," a reference to the coarse woolen robe they adopted.

Surd. In mathematics, an irreducible radical; an irrational number whose square is an integer. Applied by some writers to those elements in the universe that appear not to be conformable to any rational pattern.

Syllogism. In traditional formal logic, an argument in which a conclusion is reached from two premises so interrelated that each provides part of the conclusion. The premise that contains the predicate is called the major, and the one that contains the subject is called the minor premise. The simplest kind of syllogism is the categorical, of which an example is: all sophomores are undergraduates; some sophomores wear spectacles; therefore some undergraduates wear spectacles. An example of a pure hypothetical syllogism is: if the ground is wet we do not eat outside; if it has rained the ground is wet; therefore if we eat outside it has not rained. The dependence of the argument on two premises, neither of which could by itself yield the conclusion is illustrated in the French story of an elderly *abbé* whose hostess, to make conversation, had suggested that hearing confessions must be dull since they must nearly always be about the same old human weaknesses. To this the *abbé* agreed but added that, nevertheless, in his case, it happened that the first confession he had heard long ago as a young priest had been one of murder. Shortly thereafter the next guest appeared who, when about to be introduced to the priest, remarked, "No need for that—the *abbé* and I have known each other all our lives. In fact, I was his first penitent." Neither piece of information by itself could have yielded the obvious and dramatic conclusion; together they did, and the logical structure of their doing so could be formulated in a syllogism.

Symbol. In a large sense, anything that is presented to the mind as standing for something other than itself. In this sense, all thought is symbolic. Words are symbols as well as are the symbols of logic, algebra, chemistry, theology, and other fields. The symbols and signs of logic and mathematics are generally speaking arbitrary; there is no reason, for instance, other than convention, why the $+$ should not be used for $-$ and $-$ for $+$, or why the $\sim$ logicians use for negation should not be replaced by, say, $\#$. Some symbols used in religion do no more than remind us of something—such as the crescent and the cross (for Islam and Christianity respectively)—while others, such as light, might possibly lead us directly to some understanding of that which they symbolize.

Synthetic. See *Analytic/Synthetic.*

Tabu (Taboo). See *Mana.*

Talmud. A collection of Jewish literature ancillary to the Hebrew Bible and accounted authoritative as a spiritual guide for observant Jews. It consists basically of the Mishnah (Hebrew, meaning "instruction"), which is a collection of the Jewish Oral Law. The compilation is traditionally attributed to Rabbi Judah ha-Nasi (A.D. 135 – c. 220) and also embodies the Gemara, a rabbinic commentary on the first part of the Mishnah. The Talmud appears in two recensions—the now incomplete Jerusalem or Palestinian Talmud and the much larger Babylonian Talmud, which Jews account more important.

Tantrism. An esoteric movement in Hinduism and Buddhism. It makes much use of magical formulae and erotic practices as devotional aids.

Taoism. Literally, *tao* means "the way," being a Chinese counterpart to the Greek *dikē.* Derivatively, it was used, somewhat as Plato used *dikē,* to signify the "right" way—that is, the cosmic way, the way of the universe, the principle of its structure. To follow the Tao is to live in harmony with the structure of the cosmos. Taoist thought in China is very ancient and represents a naturalistic philosophy. The Taoist religion, which appears in popular and debased forms, appeals to the ancient thought of the Taoist school of philosophy, from which, however, it should be sharply distinguished.

Teleological Argument. One of the traditional arguments for the existence of God. It has its roots in Plato and Aristotle but was classically formulated in more recent times by William Paley (1743–1805), according to whom every biological species may be seen as designed to serve its own needs. From this premise he argues to an intelligent and purposeful Creator. Though it is no longer tenable in precisely that form, it is still used by those who see the survival of life in conflict and strife as evidence of a divine purpose.

Teleology. The term (from the Greek, *telos,* "end") probably originated with Christian Wolff (1679–1754) and denotes the science of final causes or ends. It refers especially to any system that interprets the universe as having purpose or design.

Tetragrammaton. Literally "four-lettered word." Term used by scholars for the Hebrew word JHWH (one of the proper names of God), which Jews held to be too sacred to utter. When reading the Scriptures they substituted the word "Adonai." For the reader's convenience they inserted the vowel points of "Adonai" into the unutterable word "JHWH," so yielding in some English renderings since the sixteenth century the erroneous and mixed form "Jehovah." Modern scholars generally think that "Yahweh" represents the original pronunciation before the substitution of "Adonai."

Theism. Generally used to denote any philosophical system that accepts a transcendent and personal God who preserves and rules the world he has created. The term, probably invented by Richard Cudworth in 1678, was originally used as the antonym of atheism but later acquired a more restricted and distinctive meaning in contradistinction to pantheism and deism (q.v.).

Theosophy. From the Greek, *theos* "God" and *sophia* "wisdom." In a general sense, any philosophico-religious system, having esoteric and usually pantheistic features, that purports to provide knowledge of divine Being apart from faith. Much akin to Gnosticism (q.v.). In a narrower sense, the movement promoted by Madame H. P. Blavatsky, who founded the Theosophical Society in New York in 1875.

Theravada. A conservative type of Buddhism, which emphasizes the Pali canon of the Buddhist Scriptures.

Totem. In primitive religion, an object—often an animal—with which the tribe associates itself and from which it may take itself to be descended.

Tractarianism. In the nineteenth century a very influential movement occurred, the aim of which was to restore to the Church of England an awareness of her Catholic heritage. This aim was expounded in a series of *Tracts for the Times*, begun by John Henry Newman in 1833. Though Newman defected to Rome in 1845, other Tractarians, notably E. B. Pusey and John Keble, continued the movement, which gained an extremely influential following. Tractarianism, attacked by a theologically liberal wing of the English Church and widely suspect by many, restored and revitalized not only English Church life but that of all Anglicanism (q.v.). It was associated with, but should be distinguished from, another movement of the same period that was liturgical and ritualistic rather than doctrinal and theological. The Tractarians, in fostering a profound sense of the historic continuity of the Catholic tradition in its Anglican form, greatly stimulated English theological scholarship, especially patristics. It also helped to put the Reformation into perspective so that Anglicans could see themselves as heirs both of the Reformation and also, more importantly, of historic Catholic tradition, ethos, and life.

Transcendence/Immanence. The term comes from the Latin verb, *trans scandere*, "to climb across" or "to go beyond." In its broadest sense the term refers to anything that surpasses something else; for instance, the third dimension of solid geometry transcends the two dimensions of plane geometry. One might even say that Hungarian transcends one's linguistic ability. Those philosophers who admit a concept such as the Absolute (sometimes identified with God) say it transcends all other metaphysical categories. Epistemologists who postulate realities beyond the observable phenomena say these realities transcend the phenomena. Immanence, from the Latin *immanere*, "to remain in," may be accounted the opposite of transcendence. Kant treats that which is experienced as immanent in contradistinction to that which, being beyond experience, is transcendent and therefore unknowable. Pantheists take God to be entirely immanent in the universe, while Orthodox Jews and Muslims regard him as essentially transcending it. Christian orthodoxy makes much of the doctrine that God both transcends the universe and, taking human flesh in Christ, is also immanent in it.

Transmigration. See *Metempsychosis.*

Truth-Claim. The claim that a proposition is sufficiently supported by evidence that warrants its acceptance as true. Though it need not be in propositional form, it should be able to be expressed in one. For a truth-claim to be meaningful certain conditions are required, for instance, that the proposition can be given a self-consistent formulation that permits the formulation of a self-consistent alternative. The logical subject of the proposition must be one that permits reference to it (not, for instance, an artificial term such as Bamwunk), and the predicate must be one that can be significantly assigned to the subject: the predicate "is pregnant" could be applied to a woman or a mare but not to a stallion or a man or a table. Nevertheless, when, precisely, the conditions are satisfied is in some cases very disputable.

Tso Wang. An ancient Chinese meditative technique in which the distinction between self and others is forgotten. The aim is to become one with the infinite.

Tutiorism. See *Probabilism*.

Unde Malum? Literally, "whence evil?"—the question posed by a consideration of the presence of evil in a universe created by a God who is said to be omnipotent and benevolent.

Univocity. See *Analogy*.

Upanishads. An important collection of Sanskrit literature, later than the Vedas and revered in all schools of Hindu and Buddhist thought. The central concept of the Upanishads is that of Brahman (q.v.). The most important oral compositions that constitute the Upanishads were developed between about 800 and 500 B.C., especially in the sixth century, contemporaneous with the period in which Pythagoras, Confucius, Zoroaster, and Buddha flourished. There are traditionally 108 Upanishads, but of these 13 are pre-eminent and are the ones generally discussed. The Upanishads may be regarded as a continuation of the Vedic tradition.

Utilitarianism. In a general sense, any system of moral philosophy in which utility is the supreme value, so that the proposition "x is valuable" $=$ "x is useful." More narrowly the term is used of a British school of moralists, whose leading exponents were Jeremy Bentham (1748–1832), John Stuart Mill (1806–1873), and Henry Sidgwick (1838–1900) and whose positions, though they differed significantly, had a common basis. Bentham, supposing that pleasures and pains can be treated on a purely quantitative basis, thought he could develop a "hedonistic" or "felicific" calculus of values; that is, a means of calculating the amount of happiness (which utilitarians have closely associated, and some have almost identified, with pleasure) so as to achieve "the greatest happiness for the greatest number."

Vedanta. Literally, "the end of the Veda." The most influential *darshana* (q.v.) of Hinduism. It follows closely the upanishadic tradition and generally speaking expresses a monistic and idealist type of thought.

Vedas. The most ancient writings in the literature of India.

Vishnu. See *Shiva*.

Weltanschauung (plural, *Weltanschauungen*). German term, meaning "world view." Used to express a panoramic view of the way things are, such as exhibits fundamental metaphysical presuppositions.

Wu-Wei. The principle whereby one achieves one's goal without aggressive or meddlesome action. The Taoist sage, knowing that he is one with all things, does not resist but yields to Nature. So, in consciousness of his power, he is able to produce without possessing, to act without pushing himself forward. As a ruler he will govern without dominating. The term also appears in some forms of Mahayana Buddhism and is associated with *satori* (q.v.): when the *satori* comes, there is no action in it. An illustration of the principle frequently offered is that of the boughs of a healthy tree which, when laden with snow, bend with it and so remain lively and resilient instead of breaking, and therefore dying, under the burden.

Yahweh. See *Tetragrammaton.*

Yoga. A technique for attaining salvation through the practice of certain exercises in posture and breathing, which result in inner self-discipline. The practitioner is a *yogi* or *yogin.*

Yoni. An Indian and Tibetan symbol of the female genitalia.

Zen. This Japanese term comes through the Chinese *ch'an* from the Sanskrit *dhyāna*, deep meditation, which the Upanishads tell us is "assuredly more than thought." Zen, a Japanese school of Mahayana Buddhism, appeared in several forms between the twelfth and seventeenth centuries and has considerably affected Japanese life and culture, not least in engendering restraint as a hallmark of good taste in social manners, design, architecture, and the celebrated Japanese art of flower arrangement. Zen is primarily an effort to actualize in oneself the unitary character of all things. In the *satori* (q.v.), a flash of insight, one breaks down the duality of the *I* and the *not-I*. The two chief Zen schools today are: *Rinzai* (Chinese, *Lin-Chi*) and Sōtō (Chinese, *Ts'ao-tung*).

Zoroastrianism. Zarathustra (Greek form, *Zoroaster*) was born in Persia. The traditional date of his birth is 660 B.C., which most modern scholars consider fairly accurate, though some argue for a somewhat later and others for a much earlier date. In Zoroastrianism, which was the religion of the great Persian Empire for more than a thousand years before the coming of Islam, are found both monotheistic and dualistic elements, the relation between which is a matter of scholarly dispute. Manichaeism (q.v.) was a Zoroastrian heresy. The modern Parsees, who are to be found mostly in the region of Bombay, constitute, along with a few thousand Iranians, the contemporary representatives of the ancient Zoroastrian religion.

INDEX